Guide

Pubs & Bars

timeout.com/london

ABSOLUT
Country of Sweden
VODKA
This superb vodka
was distilled from grain grown
in accordance with more t
400 years of Swedish tradition
40% VOL.
700 ML.
IMPORTED
PRODUCED AND BOTTLED IN ÅHUS, SWEDEN
BY THE ABSOLUT COMPANY
A DIVISION OF V&S VIN&SPRIT AB.
ABSOLUT SECURITY.
TBWA
ABSOLUT COUNTRY OF SWEDEN VODKA & LOGO, ABSOLUT, ABSOLUT BOTTLE DESIGN AND ABSOLUT CALLIGRAPHY ARE TRADEMARKS OWNED BY V & S VIN & SPRIT AB. © 1986 V & S VIN & SPRIT AB. WWW.ABSOLUT.COM

Contents

Central

City

West

South

East

North

Published by
Time Out Guides Ltd
Universal House
251 Tottenham Court Road
London W1T 7AB

Tel + 44 (0)20 7813 3000
Fax + 44 (0)20 7813 6001
e-mail guides@timeout.com

www.timeout.com

Editorial

Editor Andrew Humphreys
Assistant Editor Claire Fogg
Consultant Editor Jim Driver
Reviewers Catherine Arbuthnot, Ismay Atkins, Yves Baigneres (also *Heath haze*), Frank Broughton, Rhonda Carrier (*Watery pints*), Vicky Cohen, Joanna Connelly, Peterjon Cresswell, Sally Davies, Guy Dimond, Jim Driver (also *EastEndings, London pride, Office drinks*), Richard Ehrlich, Peter Fiennes, Claire Fogg, Danny Fryer, Janice Fuscoe, Will Fulford-Jones, Charlie Godfrey-Faussett, Will Hodgkinson, Andrew Humphreys, Dean Irvine, Sarah Jacobs, Ruth Jarvis, Phil Jones, Jenny Knight, Richard Lines (also *Cocktail cruise*), Alex McFadyen, Patrick Marmion (also *Stars in bars*), Chris Moore, John O'Donovan (also *Shots on location*), Nick Rider.
Researchers Cathy Limb, Val Reid
Proofreader Rachel Sawyer
Indexer Jackie Brind

Editorial Director Peter Fiennes
Series Editor Sarah Guy
Guides Co-ordinator Jenny Noden

Design

Art Director John Oakey
Art Editor Mandy Martin
Senior Designer Scott Moore
Designers Benjamin de Lotz, Lucy Grant
Picture Editor Kerri Miles
Deputy Picture Editor Olivia Duncan-Jones
Scanning/Imaging Dan Conway
Ad Make-up Glen Impey

Advertising

Group Commercial Director Lesley Gill
Sales Director & Sponsorship Mark Phillips
Sales Manager Alison Gray
Advertisement Sales James Coulbault, Terina Rickit, Jason Trotman
Copy Controller Angie Davis
Advertising Assistant Catherine Shepherd

Administration

Publisher Tony Elliott
Managing Director Mike Hardwick
Group Financial Director Kevin Ellis
Group General Manager Nichola Coulthard
Circulation Director Jim Heinemann
Production Manager Mark Lamond
Production Controller Samantha Furniss
Marketing Director Christine Cort
Marketing Manager Mandy Martinez
Marketing Executives Sandie Tozer, Sammie Squire
Marketing Secretary Claire Hojem
Accountant Sarah Bostock

Photography Matt Carr, Sol Abajo, Alys Tomlinson, Dominic Dibbs, Tony Gibson.
Cover photography Jonathan Knowles/Telegraph Colour Library.
Illustrations Matt Johnson.

Maps JS Graphics 17, Beadles Lane, Old Oxted, Surrey RH8 9JG.
Street maps based on material supplied by Alan Collinson and Julie Snook through Copyright Exchange.

The editors would like to thank: Christi Daugherty, Guy Dimond, Gadi Farfour, Noam Friedlander, Terina Rickit, Andrew White.

Repro by Precise Litho, 34-35 Great Sutton Street, London EC1.
Printed and bound by Southernprint, Factory Road, Upton Industrial Estate, Poole, Dorset BH16 5SN.

Distributed by Seymour Ltd (020 7396 8000)

Time Out

Free glass of wine or bottle of beer for every reader

This year we have linked up with some of the top style bars in the capital to offer readers a drink on us.

Cut out the vouchers on the card at the back of this guide, take them with you when you go to any of the bars listed below and enjoy a bottle of beer or glass of house wine free of charge.*

Cargo, Kingsland Viaduct, 83 Rivington Street, EC2 (see p127 for review)

Living Room, 443 Coldharbour Lane, SW9 (see p165 for review)

Match, 45-47 Clerkenwell Road, EC1 (see p109 for review)

Match Bar, 37-38 Margaret Street, W1 (see p42 for review)

Medicine Bar, 181 Upper Street, N1 (see p222 for review)

Red Star, 319 Camberwell Road, SE5 (see p167 for review)

Sosho, 2 Tabernacle Street, EC2 (see p132 for review)

Offer valid until 31 March, 2002

* See vouchers for full terms and conditions.

CARGO

LIVING ROOM

MATCH

MATCHBAR

MEDICINE BAR

REDSTAR

SOSHO

LIVINGROOM

About the Guide

The Guide is arranged by area because we reckon that's how most people drink. If you're after something more specific than a good pub or a groovy bar in your area, then turn to page 234 for **Where to go**: a rundown on different types of drinking establishments by theme, from those with great gardens to the ones with killer cocktails. Some of the best are highlighted in our **Critics' choice** boxes, scattered throughout the guide and indexed on page 234.

Opening times

We only list the opening times of the bar or pub. We do not list the opening times of any attached restaurant, brasserie or shop (although these may be the same). Note that opening times and food-serving times in particular may change. It is also worth noting that most City pubs and bars are closed at the weekend.

Food served

As above, we only list the times that food is served in the bar or pub, not in any attached restaurant or brasserie. 'Food served' can mean anything from cheese rolls to a three-course meal. When the opening times and food-served times are run together (Open/food served), it means that food is served until shortly before closing time. We haven't included any establishment that requires you to eat in order to be allowed to drink.

Admission

In some cases, particularly in central London, pubs and bars charge admission after a certain hour. Where there is a regular pattern to this, we have listed the details. Note that more and more venues are becoming members-only after a certain hour, although the rules are often blurred. We don't include in this guide places that are strictly members only, so no reviews here for the likes of the Groucho or Soho House.

Credit cards

The following abbreviations are used: **AmEx** American Express; **DC** Diners Club; **MC** MasterCard; **V** Visa.

Babies and children admitted

Under 14s are only allowed into the gardens, separate family rooms and the restaurant areas of pubs and wine bars, unless the premises has a special 'children's certificate'. If the establishment has a certificate, children can go in as long as they're with an adult. Those aged 14-17 can go into a bar, but only for soft drinks. It's an offence for a licensee to serve alcohol in a bar to anyone under 18. Unless drinkers can prove they're at least 18, the licensee can refuse to serve them and can ask them to leave the premises. In our listings look out for *Babies and children admitted* as a guide to whether your children are welcome or not.

Disabled: toilet

If a pub claims to have a toilet for the disabled, we have said so; this also implies that it's possible for a disabled person to gain access to the venue. However, we cannot guarantee this, and no matter how good the arrangements appear, we recommend phoning in advance to check feasibility.

Function room

Means the pub or bar has a separate room that can be hired for meetings or parties; some do not charge for this.

Late licence

We have listed any pub or bar that is open until midnight or later as having a late licence. Our **Late-night drinking** feature (*see p22*) brings together all those places where it's possible to get a drink *after* midnight.

Music

Unless otherwise stated, bands play in the evening. The same goes for any other form of entertainment listed. For a round-up of our favourite **DJ bars** see page 129.

No-smoking room/area

Very few pubs or bars have a no-smoking room or area (the JD Wetherspoon chain is an exception to this rule); we've listed the ones that do. But note that a separate no-smoking area is not necessarily much protection from the usual smoky pub or bar.

Vegetarian dishes

Be warned that this may mean no more than a cheese sandwich or a plate of chips, although some pubs (particularly gastropubs) and bars do make more of an effort.

The reviews in this Guide are based on the experiences of the *Time Out* reviewers. Bars and pubs are visited anonymously, and *Time Out* pays the bill. No payment of any kind has secured or influenced a review.

Sponsors and advertisers

We would like to thank our sponsor Perrier for their involvement in this Guide. We would also like to thank the advertisers. However, we would like to stress that they have no control over editorial content. No bar or pub has been included because its owner has advertised in the Guide; an advertiser may receive a bad review or no review at all.

the elbow room

 WESTBOURNE GROVE

"A pool hall like no other in the capital... relaxed and stylish."
Time Out

"The coolest place to play pool" - Elle

"Devotees wonder how they ever did without this designer
pool hall" - The Guardian

 ISLINGTON

"I must have died and gone to heaven... The Elbow Room is like
New York only better" - The Independent

"A wonderful pool hall/bar/restaurant,.. your cue for a seriously
good night out" - Time Out

"An ingenious combination of pool hall and nightclub" - GQ

 SWISS COTTAGE

Opening May 2001

Info: Rosie Parkyn
Tel: 020 7278 3244
e-mail: rosie@elbow-room.co.uk

The chain gang

Unless you believe in striking coincidences and the ineffectiveness of name patenting, you will have noticed that there are several pub/bar chains that have spread their tentacles across London. Having bought up old pubs, banks and shop premises, these corporate giants have found a recipe for success: often following the formula of spacious, pine-drenched premises, a few beers on tap and still more by the bottle, safe 'n' sound music and a menu on which everything is usually served with rocket and fries. In short, if you've seen one, you've pretty much seen them all – although you might not be sure which one. And you probably had an OK time, much as you would with the right people and a bottle of booze in an airport lounge.

Of course, the formula varies from chain to chain, as does the size – **Davys** has 40 London outlets, **Café Med** only six – and there are undoubted reasons for their popularity. Some – such as the City-centred **Corney & Barrow** wine bar chain – have a fine reputation for their wine and food; others, such as **All Bar One**, **Slug & Lettuce** and **Pitcher & Piano** have become the natural meeting – and picking-up – points for young Londoners. **O'Neill's**, another success story, has recently expanded, converting many former **Firkins'** premises with its Irish-style theming. And, yes, they

are popular – no doubt because of their reliability, efficiency and, above all, predictability. You know the decor, ambience, food and drink before you've even stepped through the door.

All this is by way of explaining this guide's policy towards these chains. We have not reviewed every outlet, but we offer, instead, reviews of the best, and have listed the rest in the **Also in the area...** postscript for each region. Call it tokenism if you like. We prefer to call it positive discrimination.

Here is where to find the reviews:

All Bar One (*branches, at time of writing – 39; see p151 for review*)
Stripped pine, cream walls, big tables, tasty food, tolerable beers and enticing racks of decent – if pricey – wine. Popular with young conservatives.

Babushka (*4; see p99*)
Hip, many-flavoured vodka-bar chain with ambient sounds midweek and noisy DJ nights come the weekend.

Balls Brothers (*10; see p113, p117*)
Deeply trad wine bars (with a hefty list majoring in French wines), particularly big in the City.

Bar 38 (*2; no review*)
Scottish & Newcastle's brash bar concept, aiming at those who think they're too hip for All Bar One but aren't confident enough for Denim.

Belgo & Bierodrome (*8; see p68, p169*)
Famous for ze potent Belgian beer and ze mussels, but these days maybe a leetle too corporate for ze image.

Café Flo (9; see p54)
The chain that likes to think it's not a chain. Each branch presents itself as a classy one-off, but really it's the same brasserie food, with a few tables set aside for drinkers.

Café Med (6; see p68)
Good-time venues still stuck in the zeitgeist of the '90s. Pleasant enough (yep, Mediterranean) food.

Café Rouge (32; see p48)
Safe and affordable brasserie staples in French-flavoured cafés. Reliable for a light lunch.

Corney & Barrow (12; see p54, p119)
Lavish wine cellars, smart interiors, smooth service. Boozer of choice for City wine snobs.

Davys (40; see p54, p191)
Sawdust on the floor, barrels of ale, and some fine wines by the glass.

Dôme (11; see p55)
The original brasserie chain – the French food is fair enough, but service can be lacklustre. Fortunately you can drink too.

Edward's (5; no review)
Shiny seating matches the shiny shirts in this bright and hateful piped-muzak pulling den. Lairy verging on hairy at weekends.

Eerie (3; no review)
Soulless spook-themed pubs that wouldn't raise the hackles even on Scooby Doo. Frightful nonetheless.

Fine Line (8; see p44)
Fuller's take on the style bar, with added breakfast opeing at certain branches, DJ evenings at others. All Bar One with a dash more class.

Firkins (11; see p183)
Some stunning buildings, average ales, and excruciating wit. But now the in-house breweries have gone is there any point?

Hogshead (7; see p63, p119, p177, p186)
Boozy venues par excellence, typically in converted characterful premises, flogging real ales and international beers at knock-down (fall down?) prices.

It's A Scream (7; no review)
Take any old pub, stick up colourful signs, standardise the drinks for student consumption, and crank up the volume. Hey, It's A Scream!

Jamies (15; see p42, p123)
Attentive service in a place that majors in wines, yet where punters display a bewildering allegiance to bottled beers.

JD Wetherspoon (49; see p91, p118, p198, p200, p213)
Either the rescuer of the pub, bringer of no-smoking areas and a saviour of real ale or the bringer of soulless city centre barn boozers – it all depends on your point of view.

O'Neill's (17; see p225)
The persistent 'Oirish' pub chain, aimed at those pining for Guinness, Irish stew and big screen sport. Not usually frequented by the Irish.

Pitcher & Piano (17; see p83)
Noisy, large, unpretentious, up-for-it. Well-spaced light-wood furniture and the occasional sofa – you could call it ageing Habitat.

Rat & Parrot (14; no review)
Bargain-basement boozers where the party never stops, provided you're up for standard drinks and loud music.

Ruby in the Dust (5; see p223)
Thumping music and the chance to be transported back to the feel of sweaty school discos. This time with bottled lager and basic but decent food.

Slug & Lettuce (19; see p190)
The original and possibly still the best. Bright and breezy, pine-with-everything, but with slightly upmarket ambitions, appealing to a suited crowd.

Tup (10; see p150, p184)
Part-smart, part-traditional pubs with an airy wine bar feel. But why the ram theme?

Walkabout Inn (3; no review)
Regent Inns' Australian theme bars. Condemned as clichéd, but packed with southern hemisphere drinkers, so they must be doing it right.

Central

Bayswater & Paddington

Archery Tavern

4 Bathurst Street, W2 (020 7402 4916). Lancaster Gate tube. **Open** 11am-11pm Mon-Sat; noon-10.30pm Sun. **Food served** noon-3pm, 6-9.30pm daily. **Credit** AmEx, DC, MC, V.

Given that the few pubs around Lancaster Gate tend to be filled with tourists, the Archery is a good little place to know about. The genteel front room sticks to the most traditional of pub formulae – plates on the walls, bunches of dried hops and regulars who commandeer their favourite seat and ask the staff (by name) to turn the music down. There's a less fussy back room with a bare-board floor, a TV, games machine and its own service hatch to keep the mixing of nobs and proles to a minimum. Real ales are well represented with Badger Best, Tanglefoot and Sussex, and draught lager is the very tasty Hoffbräu; a Cask Marque by the door attests to how well it's all kept.

Babies and children admitted. Games (board games, darts, fruit machine). Quiz (9pm Sun; £1 to play). Satellite TV. Tables outdoors (pavement). Vegetarian dishes.

Fountains Abbey

109 Praed Street, W2 (020 7723 2364). Edgware Road tube/Paddington tube/rail. **Open** 11am-11pm Mon-Sat; noon-10.30pm Sun. **Food served** 11am-10pm Mon-Sat; noon-10pm Sun. **Credit** AmEx, DC, MC, V.

A generic, cavernous T&J Bernard pub that profits from a location 200m east of Paddington station. There are few surprises but it does the job: a good choice of beers (including Theakston's, Courage and regular guest ales), a reasonable wine list and basic stodgy pub grub (filled Yorkshire puds, burgers, pies, sandwiches and wraps). Lunchtime it's a popular pie, pint and a read of the paper sort of place; evenings it gets rowdy with commuters having a swift one or two before the 19.15 home to Hanborough. It's big enough to comfortably absorb crowds.

Babies and children admitted (until 6pm). Function room. Games (fruit machines, golf machine). Tables outdoors (pavement). Vegetarian dishes.

Leinster

57 Ossington Street, W2 (020 7243 9541). Bayswater or Queensway tube. **Open** noon-11pm Mon-Sat; noon-10.30pm Sun. **Food served** noon-3pm, 5-9pm daily. **Credit** MC, V.

Ever since the demise of the Moscow, one of London's finest punky pubs, some ten years ago (reincarnated first as the Ashes, now as the truly appalling Aussie-themed Bar Oz), all the fun of boozing has gone out of Bayswater. The Leinster is about the best of a decidedly average to awful bunch of locals. It dates from the same period as the surrounding wonderful Victorian mansion blocks, but has been made over as a modern-style pub. Thankfully, it works. Big and airy with large windows, it also has a curious mezzanine level reached by a wrought iron spiral staircase, which is where the table football and TV screens are hidden so that they don't interfere with the drinking downstairs. Sadly the beers are decidedly poor, but the forecourt area is pleasant and we went a bundle on the bar girl with the Louise Brooks haircut who really knows how to hold a cigarette.

Babies and children admitted (separate area). Function room. Games (board games, chess, fruit machine, golf machine, quiz machine, table football). Satellite TV (big screen). Tables outdoors (patio). Vegetarian dishes.

Leinster Arms

17 Leinster Terrace, W2 (020 7402 4670). Lancaster Gate or Queensway tube. **Open** 11am-11pm Mon-Sat; noon-10.30pm Sun. **Food served** 11am-8pm Mon-Sat; noon-8pm Sun. **Credit** MC, V.

Bayswater is bed and breakfast land – home to budget travellers, business trippers and all manner of transients. Pub patrons are only ever local for a few nights and then they're gone. Take our last visit to the Leinster Arms: four suited blokes with broad northern accents at the bar; a couple seated off to the side discussing real-life experiences and *The Beach*, and two girls on the comfy benches consulting a Lonely Planet. No matter how pleasant a pub is – and the Leinster Arms is reasonably pleasant, though with an exterior that promises more than the interior delivers – the lack of regulars makes for a notably soulless drinking experience. The place used to be famed for its real ales, but they're largely gone save for Tetley's and London Pride.

Babies and children admitted (until 8pm). Games (backgammon, darts, fruit machine, quiz machine). Jukebox. Satellite TV (big screen). Tables outdoors (pavement). Vegetarian dishes.

Mitre

24 Craven Terrace, W2 (020 7262 5240). Lancaster Gate tube/Paddington tube/rail. **Open** 11am-11pm Mon-Sat; noon-10.30pm Sun. **Food served** noon-9.30pm daily. **Credit** MC, V.

Enormous, corner-sited, traditional old pile just behind Lancaster Gate. The beautifully tiled entrance hall offers three etched-glass doors to choose from: Ladies Only, Saloon & Billiards Bar and Private Bar. Unfortunately, the rooms they once designated are largely gone, partitions removed to form one vast L-shaped bar. However, heaps of dark wood fittings, a deep-red patterned carpet and more etched glass maintain that resolutely old-fashioned feel. A line up of quiz nights, karaoke, live football, drinks offers and food (gammon steaks, scampi, filled Yorkshire puds, all around £6) attempts to cater to all tastes. Similarly, drinks run from real ales (Greene King Abbot, Marston's Pedigree) to flavoured vodkas. We especially like the seated raised pavement area with its cobbled mews setting, and there's a massive cave-complex of a basement (with resident ghost) well suited to parties.

Babies and children admitted (separate room). Function room. Games (darts, fruit machines, pool table). No-smoking area. Quiz (8pm Sun; free to play). Satellite TVs. Tables outdoors (patio, pavement). Vegetarian dishes.

Royal Exchange

26 Sale Place, W2 (020 7723 3781). Edgware Road tube. **Open/food served** 11am-11pm Mon-Fri; noon-4pm, 7-11pm Sat; noon-4pm, 7-10.30pm Sun. **Credit** MC, V.

Unprepossessing from the outside, the Royal Exchange is actually a bit of a gem. In an area largely made up of hotels, shops, offices (not to mention the enormous Paddington Basin building site, flyovers and some grim, grim architecture), it's a pub with heart. It's very much a family-run affair, reflected in the slightly chintzy but very homely interior adorned with flowers and nick-nacks. It draws a regular and slightly boisterous crowd; in this guide last year we mentioned the singing and sure enough, on our most recent visit, the rabble of elderly gents at the end of the bar broke into an improvised 'The pubs are alive with the sound of boozers' – and this was a Monday lunchtime. Pints of Brakspear and double spirits are just over the £2 mark, and the hostess knocks up a fine steak sandwich for well under a fiver.

Jukebox. Satellite TV. Tables outdoors (pavement). Vegetarian dishes.

AKA. *See page 18.*

Swan

66 Bayswater Road, W2 (020 7262 5204). Lancaster Gate tube. **Open/food served** 10am-11pm Mon-Sat; 10am-10.30pm Sun. **Credit** AmEx, DC, MC, V.

As far as we're aware, this is the only pub with outdoor seating looking on to Hyde Park. For this reason, and this reason alone, can the Swan be popular. Even on a wintery February evening, the forecourt seating was busy with scarf-swaddled visitors clasping pints in two gloved hands. Braving the elements makes sense here because the interior of the pub is a disaster: modern, ugly and dominated by a large food counter peddling the kind of grub you'd only resort to stranded for hours at Terminal 2 (Bucharest). The night we visited a Brylcreemed pianist was trying to whip up interest for a sing-a-long in the back room, importuning chip-eating Germans, an American in a stetson (truthfully) and a swell of Scandinavian girls. The beer is acceptable (real ales included Theakston's and Courage Best), so take a seat outside and if there's no waitress service shout your order from the door.

Babies and children admitted (high chairs). Games (fruit machine). Jukebox. Music (trad pianist 7.30pm Mon-Sat; free). Satellite TV. Tables outdoors (forecourt). Vegetarian dishes.

Victoria

10A Strathern Place, W2 (020 7724 1191). Lancaster Gate or Marble Arch tube. **Open** 11am-11pm Mon-Fri; noon-11pm Sat; noon-10.30pm Sun. **Food served** noon-2.30pm, 6-9.45pm Mon-Sat; noon-4pm, 6-9pm Sun. **Credit** MC, V.

Shame, shame, shame. Occupying a wedge-shaped site on the south side of Georgian Gloucester Square, the Victoria is remarkably ornate with subtly painted wood panelling, exquisitely patterned mirrors, and a parade of globe lamps along the bar (and being Fuller's the beers aren't bad either). It's a gorgeous little period piece. But tragically the effect is destroyed by the 'drink your way around the world' displays of flags and bottles, world posters and other backpackerish tack that are more suited to a pub in the Walkabout chain. And frankly we could have done without the brassy antipodean attitude behind the bar too. It had us wondering who on earth the punters are that drink here; posh residential square, pub with its sights set firmly downmarket. Our recent Saturday night visit offered no clues because we were about the only people in. Is there a message there to Fuller's?

Babies and children admitted (until 4pm). Function room. Satellite TV (big screen). Tables outdoors (pavement). Vegetarian dishes.

Also in the area...

Café Rouge Unit 209, Whiteleys, Queensway, W2 (020 7221 1509).
Fettler & Firkin 15 Chilworth Street, W2 (020 7723 5918).
Gyngleboy (Davys) 27 Spring Street, W2 (020 7723 5482).
Rat & Parrot 99 Queensway, W2 (020 7727 0259).
Slug & Lettuce 47 Hereford Road, W2 (020 7229 1503).
Tyburn (JD Wetherspoon) 20 Edgware Road, W2 (020 7723 4731).

Belgravia

Antelope

*22-24 Eaton Terrace, SW1 (020 7824 8512). Sloane
Square tube.* **Open** 11.30am-11pm Mon-Sat. **Food
served** 11.30am-3pm Mon-Sat. **Credit** AmEx, MC, V.
Despite a recent refit aimed at making this more of a
gastropub, the Antelope retains some of the unpretentious
atmosphere of the original inter-war boozer. This successful
marriage of traditional and contemporary seems popular with
the inhabitants of Sloaneland; pin-striped types talk hard
business in the soft seats at the rear, while Barbour-wearing
'farmers in the city' avoid the smoke and head for the dimly
lit dining area. This leaves an occasionally raucous crowd of
Eatonites and American businessmen to jockey for position
at the elegant and original central bar.
*Babies and children admitted (Sat lunchtime only). Function
room. Games (fruit machine, quiz machine). No piped music or
jukebox. Specialities: real ales. TV. Vegetarian dishes.*

Grenadier

*18 Wilton Row, SW1 (020 7235 3074). Hyde Park
Corner tube.* **Open** noon-11pm Mon-Sat; noon-10.30pm
Sun. **Food served** noon-3pm, 6-9.30pm Mon-Sat; noon-
9pm Sun. **Credit** AmEx, DC, MC, V.
Barely lit by orange light, the interior of the Grenadier with
its stripped floor, candy striped wallpaper and the inevitable
military memorabilia is as worn and comforting as a pair of
retired general's slippers. Comfort doesn't preclude glamour,
and it was to the Grenadier that Madonna repaired after her
recent Brixton Academy show, hosting a private party in the

pub after closing time. It's not just that this was her local
when she rented a house in the same tiny mews last summer,
the pub has always been associated with cash and celebrity.
It is, apparently, Chris Evans' favourite place and a long-time
haunt of the young and titled. But it has its good points too.
In the small front room most drinkers stand or perch on stools
at the large square bar, and with no music the eavesdropping
opportunities are excellent and rewarding; we had a couple
of foreign businessmen trying out their English on the

Critics' choice
views

Founder's Arms (p161)
Ugly pub but knockout view of St Paul's.

Phoenix (p227)
Capital view from north London's highest point.

Tenth Bar (p50)
High Street Ken rooftop bar.

Vertigo (p124)
Killer cocktails and London from 42 floors up.

Windows (p67)
Mayfair from on high at the Hilton's 28th floor.

---

friendly cockney barmaid and 'a couple of Sloanettes discussing racy reads. Add good beer (Courage, Marston's and Theakston's), fine traditional British cooking, and who needs Madonna?
Babies and children admitted. No piped music or jukebox. Restaurant. Specialities: real ales. Vegetarian dishes.

Grouse & Claret
14-15 Little Chester Street, SW1 (020 7235 3438). Hyde Park Corner tube/Victoria tube/rail. **Open** 11am-11pm Mon-Fri. **Food served** noon-2.30pm Mon-Fri. **Credit** AmEx, DC, MC, V.
It's not often that we say such a thing, but this is a pub that would benefit from a refit. It's a post-war effort and there's more boxy teak veneer here than you'd find in a G-Plan furniture factory. Not old enough to be venerable, it's just plain dated and more than a little oppressive. Still, the place has always looked immaculate whenever we've dropped in, often smelling of polish. Smart uniformed staff are both efficient and friendly and the Badger Ales are well kept. Large parties of after-work drinkers squeeze themselves into the nooks and crannies of the lounge, leaving the public bar to quieter, board-game playing locals.
Babies and children admitted (lunchtimes, dining area only). Function rooms. Games (board games). Specialities: real ales. TV. Vegetarian dishes.

Library
Lanesborough Hotel, Hyde Park Corner, SW1 (020 7259 5599/www.lanesborough.com). Hyde Park Corner tube. **Open/food served** 11am-11pm Mon-Sat; noon-10.30pm Sun. **Credit** AmEx, DC, MC, V.
Not a library at all, we're afraid; the books lining the wall are fake – a design detail that exemplifies the Library's none-too-subtle decorative take on the gentleman's club. The bar is nonetheless elegant, with heavy dark-wood panelling, deep wing-backed leather armchairs, five-foot-high flower arrangements and French Empire-style chandeliers. Italian staff are also surprisingly charming and service is excellent. Naturally, drinks don't come cheap, but they are exceptional. Vodka Martinis (£9.50) are the thing here, arriving in chilled crystal glasses, and having a delicious bite. We reckon they could well be the best we've had. Further value is added by a piano player with an imaginative take on standards. If you can handle the prices, it all makes for a very special treat.
Babies and children admitted (drawing room only). Disabled: toilet. Function rooms. Music (pianist 6.30-11pm Mon-Sat; 6.30-10.30pm Sun). Specialities: cigars, vintage armagnacs and cognacs. Vegetarian dishes.

Nag's Head
53 Kinnerton Street, SW1 (020 7235 1135). Hyde Park Corner or Knightsbridge tube. **Open** 11am-11pm Mon-Sat; noon-9.30pm Sun. **Food served** noon-9.30pm Mon-Sat; 12.30-2.30pm Sun. **No credit cards.**
Whether the floor of the pint-sized saloon bar has been raised, or the area behind the counter is sunken, the net result is that bar staff address your navel. Which is odd. But everything else about this place is decidedly comfortable: the blazing real fire, '40s big band music and a loquacious landlord have a word for everyone. Walls are crammed with World War II memorabilia, interspersed with photos of some of the great war horses of 20th-century English letters. Museum-piece slot machines on the walls add to the eccentricity. Down mouse-size steps there's a tiny snug where hot food, salads and sandwiches are served at lunchtime. In the recent past this establishment has been frequented by the type of nouveau pissheads that make the gossip columns, but thankfully old-school drunks with their trilby hats and fruity voices seem to

be back in the ascendancy, ensuring that once again the Nag's Head is among the most civilised watering holes in SW1.
Vegetarian dishes.

Plumbers Arms
14 Lower Belgrave Street, SW1 (020 7730 4067). Victoria tube/rail. **Open/food served** 11am-11pm Mon-Fri; noon-3pm Sat. **Credit** AmEx, DC, MC, V.
Behind a majestic frontage this is a cosy, medium-sized single-bar pub with a fine mahogany serving area and a gentrified Edwardian air. Although doll-sized models of bathroom porcelain decorate the place, real plumbers would probably find themselves excluded by the prominent 'no soiled clothing' notices. Instead, when we visited midweek the place was full of suited professional types having a swift Courage Best before heading on to commute home from nearby Victoria station. Faded, framed newspaper articles document the Plumbers main claim to fame, which came in 1974 when a distraught Lady Lucan stumbled in to raise the alarm after discovering her murdered nanny and being attacked herself at the Lucan family home across the street.
Function room. Games (darts, fruit machine). Satellite TV. Tables outdoors (pavement). Vegetarian dishes.

Star Tavern
6 Belgrave Mews West, SW1 (020 7235 3019). Knightsbridge or Sloane Square tube. **Open** 11.30am-11pm Mon-Fri; 11.30am-3pm, 6.30-11pm Sat; noon-3pm, 7-10.30pm Sun. **Food served** noon-2.30pm, 6-9pm Mon-Fri; 6.30-9pm Sat; noon-2.30pm, 7-9pm Sun. **Credit** AmEx, DC, MC, V.
If everyone has the requisite map reading skills then this is a good pub for groups to meet. It may be situated in a pretty mews, but in contrast to most nearby places it is large and brightly lit, usually bustling with noise emanating from sizeable knots of good-natured drinkers. Other than some fine stained glass, the interior is unremarkable – but on winter evenings the open fires keep things cosy, while in summer it's pleasant outside beneath the hanging lobelia. It's a Fuller's house, so the beer is good, and the standard pub grub is at least very reasonably priced. Like so many pubs in this part of town, there's a bit of colour attached – in this case, the Great Train Robbers are supposed to have planned their heist in the upstairs bar, also the venue for Christine Keeler's tryst with John Profumo.
Babies and children admitted. Function room. No piped music or jukebox. Vegetarian dishes.

Also in the area...
Rat & Parrot 4 Elizabeth Street, SW1 (020 7730 3957).

Bloomsbury & St Giles

AKA
18 West Central Street, WC1 (020 7836 0110/ www.akalondon.com). Holborn tube. **Open** 6pm-midnight Mon; 6pm-1am Tue; 6pm-3am Wed-Fri; 7pm-3am Sat. **Food served** 6pm-midnight Mon (snacks only), Tue; 6pm-1am Wed-Fri. **Credit** AmEx, DC, MC, V.
The last time we popped into this minimal chic sister bar and restaurant to the ground-breaking End nightclub, changes were afoot. The mezzanine restaurant was about to undergo a major overhaul. By the time you read this it should already have happened. The downstairs bar remains warehouse-sized, lightly scattered with tables and chairs, with a gleaming metal serving area and various industrial-style

fittings adorning the walls. Incongruously, the big screen TV at the far end was showing *The Weakest Link* as we arrived and Anne Robinson's bile was at odds with the friendly and helpful service we encountered at the door and at the bar. Bottled beers (nothing on tap) include Stella, Hoegaarden and Rolling Rock, with around 30 listed cocktails and approaching 40 wines. Our Spanish '94 Alicante Marius Reserve at £14 a bottle was excellent.
Disabled: toilet. Film screenings (7pm Mon; free). Music (DJs 6pm Thur-Sat; admission £5 after 10.30pm Fri, £15 after 9pm Sat). Restaurant. Satellite TV (big screen). Vegetarian dishes. **Map 1/L6**

Angel
61 St Giles High Street, WC2 (020 7240 2876). Tottenham Court Road tube. **Open** 11am-11pm Mon-Sat; noon-10.30pm Sun. **Food served** noon-3pm, 5.30-9pm Mon-Sat; noon-3pm Sun. **Credit** MC, V.
Around the end of 1999, Yorkshire brewers Samuel Smith took over the Angel and gave it a makeover. Keeping the Victorian essentials, they cut the public bar off from the lounge, created a Lilliputian saloon bar (room enough for six) and a sparkling new gents downstairs. They scrapped the Theakston's Best (hurrah!) and replaced it with Old Brewery Bitter, plus the likes of Ayingerbräu lager and Sam Smith's Stout. Giant Yorkshire puds arrived, stuffed with a farmyard for less than a fiver and sirloin steaks were, and still are, £6.75. The wallpaper in the lounge is now an almost tasteful gold flock; there are opulent red and gold drapes over original windows; and there's even a posh carpet that doesn't squelch as you walk to the bar. The public bar is pretty unchanged, except that it's now become a meeting place for clubbers.
Babies and children admitted (weekend afternoons only). Games (darts, fruit machine). No piped music or jukebox. Tables outdoors (garden). Vegetarian dishes. **Map 7/K6**

Duke (of York)
7 Roger Street, WC1 (020 7242 7230). Russell Square tube. **Open** noon-11pm Mon-Fri; 6-11pm Sat. **Food served** noon-3pm, 6-10pm Mon-Sat. **Credit** MC, V.
Looking not unlike a pastiche of a 1950s bar – all two-tone yellow paintwork, red-formica topped tables and a scuffed linoleum floor – the Duke has become one of the area's trendier hang-outs. A decade ago you'd have been sitting next to printers from the *Guardian* and local posties, these days it's much more likely to be Justin from Wang-Key Films or Tara from *Tip-Top* magazine. The beer's up to scratch, especially the real ales we tried, and a couple of legal secretaries on the next table were on their second bottle of house red, so it can't be too dreadful. Food is pricey but good and tends towards Modern European with a nod to traditional British. Those in the know head for the quieter room at the rear.
Function room. Restaurant. Tables outdoors (pavement). Vegetarian dishes. **Map 3/M4**

Enterprise
38 Red Lion Street, WC1 (020 7269 5901). Holborn tube. **Open** noon-11pm Mon-Fri. **Food served** noon-3pm Mon-Fri. **Credit** AmEx, MC, V.
Pub fitters are responsible for the depletion of acres of forest and those responsible for this smart Edwardian boozer have much to answer for. The floor and walls are constructed from solid timber, as is the long framed serving area that occupies almost one wall of the extensive bar. Running opposite is a row of rather grand engraved mirrors framed by nifty cream and green ceramic wall tiles, and at the rear there's an ample wooden box which doubles as a comfortable seating area. Beers include draught Bass and London Pride (both rather

tasty when last sampled) and there's a short but pleasingly varied wine list.
Games (quiz machine). No-smoking area. Tables outdoors (garden). Vegetarian dishes. **Map 3/M5**

First Out
52 St Giles High Street, WC2 (020 7240 8042). Tottenham Court Road tube. **Open/food served** 10am-11pm Mon-Sat; 11am-10.30pm Sun. **No credit cards**.
London's only gay vegetarian café has a basement bar that's stylishly decked out with a shiny wood floor (natch), blue and cream walls and that stick-type furniture you only seem to find in gay bars. Every Friday is 'Girl Friday', a women-only event, but aside from that the crowd is pretty mixed, with maybe the propensity of lesbian students tipping the balance. It's a friendly place with strong community spirit, as exemplified by the much-used noticeboard. Drinks are generally cheaper than at neighbouring 'straight' bars, and spirits and mixers are often sold at bargain prices. Bottled beers include Freedom and Sol. Food is good and you can stuff yourself with salad (or cake) and suchlike for under a fiver.
Babies and children admitted. No-smoking area (upstairs). Vegetarian dishes. **Map 7/K6**

Glass Bar & Solution
Marlborough Hotel, Bloomsbury Street, WC1 (020 7636 5601/www.radissonedwardian.com). Tottenham Court Road tube. **Open** *Solution* 8am-11pm Mon-Sat; 11am-6pm Sun. *Glass Bar* 11am-11pm daily. **Food served** *Solution* 11am-10pm Mon-Sat; 11am-6pm Sun. *Glass Bar* 11am-10.30pm daily. **Credit** AmEx, DC, MC, V.
The Marlborough Hotel's glass frontage reveals two very different drinking areas on either side of its well-lit entrance hall. Solution is an open plan bar/restaurant with clean lines and the sort of square armchairs you only get in hotel lobbies – which is essentially what this is. Across the lobby lies the cosier Glass Bar, with its grey drapes, olive green walls, brown leather armchairs and a back-lit corner serving area from where friendly but formal staff dispense cocktails and bottled beer. You can get a pint of draught Grolsch if you really want, but you do get the feeling they'd rather you had a half. Prices are about normal for a hotel bar, which means around 50% more than in the pub – the price you pay for mixing with well-heeled tourists from Maine and Milan.
Babies and children admitted. Disabled: toilet. Vegetarian dishes. **Map 1/K5**

Grape Street Wine Bar
224A Shaftesbury Avenue, WC2 (020 7240 0686). Holborn or Tottenham Court Road tube. **Open** 11am-11pm Mon-Fri. **Food served** noon-10pm Mon-Fri. **Credit** AmEx, MC, V.
Tucked away at the quiet northern end of Shaftesbury Avenue, the Grape Street Wine Bar is simply but pleasingly decorated in cream and green, and run by cheerful, welcoming staff. Perhaps inevitably for a small basement bar, the atmosphere tends to be close and crowded on busy nights, though there are a few quiet nooks and crannies. You can tell the house drink is champagne from clues left in the small, pale green entrance hall. It lies at the top of steps that lead down to this subterranean wine bar and the main decoration is upturned champagne bottles in light fittings. A blackboard over the stairs announces the food specials – it was leek and potato soup, wild boar terrine, lamb cutlets when we last popped in. Downstairs the same green is set off by a darker version and the walls are peppered with framed prints. The regulars are a jolly lot of all ages with the men mostly in suits, the women quite demure. The atmosphere is helped along by copious consumption of wine, from a list offering a wide

range, with many available by the glass. A small bookcase offers 'The Grape Street Library – feel free to browse and borrow', which is nice.
Babies and children admitted. TV. Vegetarian dishes.
Map 1/L6

King's Bar
Hotel Russell, Russell Square, WC1 (020 7837 6470/ www.principalhotels.co.uk). Russell Square tube. **Open** 11am-11pm Mon-Sat; 11am-10.30pm Sun. **Food served** noon-9pm daily. **Credit** AmEx, DC, MC, V.
The Hotel Russell was designed by Charles Fitzroy Doll in 1898 and opened on Derby Day, 1900. Its style is described as 'François-premier château' and the recently renovated hallway and King's Bar are reminders of a past that saw it as one of the most exclusive hotels in Europe. These days you're more likely to find a party from Okinawa than encounter the crown heads of Europe back from the races, but the setting remains impressive. The bar's ceiling is high and decorative, with crystal chandeliers you wouldn't let the Trotters near, and seating is luxurious leather-bound sofas and armchairs around chunky low-slung tables. A huge fireplace glows in winter with a roaring (albeit gas-powered) blaze. Drinks are unremarkable – much as you'd expect in a tourist hotel bar – though prices aren't as frightening as feared.
Babies and children admitted (until 6pm). Function room. No piped music or jukebox. Vegetarian dishes. **Map 1/L4**

Lamb
94 Lamb's Conduit Street, WC1 (020 7405 0713). Russell Square tube. **Open** 11am-11pm Mon-Sat; noon-4pm, 7-10.30pm Sun. **Food served** noon-2.30pm, 6-9pm Mon-Sat; noon-2.30pm Sun. **Credit** MC, V.
The Lamb's clientele is a cross section of Holborn humanity that stretches from besuited lawyers downing a pint before swearing-in, to telecom engineers who swear before, during and after. The decor is tarted-up Victorian, with an original mahogany bar edged with etched-glass snob screens and matching windows and mirrors. The panelled walls sprout pictures of thespians and other forgotten Victorians, and the ceiling boards are painted angry red gloss. The polyphon by the door still works in return for a small charity donation. Behind the serving area there's a tiny no-smoking bar and beyond that more seats, with a puny patio outside. The beer's Young's and good, the wine's well up to scratch and the food is above average for the area's pubs.
Babies and children admitted. Function room. No piped music or jukebox. No-smoking area. Tables outdoors (patio). Vegetarian dishes. **Map 3/M4**

Museum Tavern
49 Great Russell Street, WC1 (020 7242 8987). Holborn or Tottenham Court Road tube. **Open** 11am-11pm Mon-Sat; noon-10.30pm Sun. **Food served** 11am-10pm Mon-Sat; noon-10pm Sun. **Credit** AmEx, DC, MC, V.
Rebuilt in 1855 with four entrances to five bars, the once opulent British Museum Tavern is reduced to a single long bar dominated by a wooden serving area backed with original mirrors and plenty of carved Victorian woodwork. Once the likes of Orwell and Marx used to pop in for their 'brain tonic', but nowadays it gets by on the tourist trade. Being a thin room, it can get pretty hard to move about when relatively few people sit in the wrong seats and bar stools – which they invariably will. Four real ales (including Adnam's if you're lucky), and food tends to be the usual pub serving of pies, fish and chips, with pasta bake for oddball veggies.
Babies and children admitted (over-14's only). Tables outdoors. Vegetarian dishes. **Map 1/L5**

mybar
11-13 Bayley Street, WC1 (020 7667 6000/ www.myhotels.co.uk). Goodge Street or Tottenham Court Road tube. **Open/food served** 11am-11pm daily. **Credit** AmEx, DC, MC, V.
mybar is as much a café as a bar and thanks to a tie-in with Yo! Sushi, offers raw fish until 11pm. As you'd expect from a hotel where single rooms start at £150, it tends to attract the more well-heeled clientele, which in the evening includes the likes of local designers and sometimes even staff journalists from an essential magazine with offices nearby. The minimalist style of the room includes the serving area, all glass and light, from which eager young staff dish up cocktails, wine and bottled beers, while we (the punter) sit almost on top of them and scrutinise their every movement. Meanwhile, passers by, who can't believe that all those beautiful young people are concentrated in one place, stare at us through the large picture window. The built-in fish tank in the wall is obviously symbolic.
Babies and children admitted (until 6pm). Disabled: toilet. Function rooms. Vegetarian dishes. **Map 1/K5**

Old Crown
33 New Oxford Street, WC1 (020 7836 9121/ www.old-crown.co.uk). Holborn or Tottenham Court Road tube. **Open** 11am-11pm Mon-Sat. **Food served** noon-3pm, 5.30-9.30pm Mon-Sat. **Credit** AmEx, MC, V.
From the cream and green frontage you can tell that this tarted up boozer isn't your typical Bloomsbury pub. Inside the small ground floor bar, the walls are marbled yellow, and two enormous metal crowns hang from the ceiling sprouting long, squiggly branches that end in lights. A wooden serving area takes up most of one wall, and large picture windows provide views of New Oxford Street. Upstairs an even tinier room stacked with easy chairs is christened the Staropramen Lounge, where twinkling fairy lights and fantasy wall paintings give an impression of what a Prague bar-room would look like if conceived by Mervyn Peake. There's no bar upstairs, so head downstairs, to be greeted by staff who are invariably female, tall, European and statuesquely good looking. This is where you order your Staropramen – or draught Bass, or even a cocktail with a daft name. Food is bistro style with the inclusion of some tourist favourites.
Function rooms. Music (live band 6.30pm Tue; free). Specialities: 100 shooters. Tables outdoors (pavement). TV. Vegetarian dishes. **Map 1/L5**

Plough
27 Museum Street, WC1 (020 7636 7964). Tottenham Court Road tube. **Open** 11am-11pm Mon-Sat; noon-10.30pm Sun. **Food served** noon-7pm, snack menu 7-10pm daily. **Credit** AmEx, MC, V.
Although overshadowed by the **Museum Tavern** (*see above*) at the other end of the road, there's a lot to be said for the Plough: the three draught bitters on offer (Pedigree, Burton and Adnam's when we last visited) are more appealing to the real ale freak than those up the road, and the bar staff certainly appear friendlier and less harassed. There's also more comfortable seating, with nests of tables, chairs and banquettes in the front bar and a line of stools against a shelf in the back. Food is available and they can also rustle up a cappuccino or latté, if that's your cup of tea. Not as historic as the Museum, but the large mirrors, nicotine-orange ceiling and walls, and wood panelling give it the antique feel.
Babies and children admitted (separate room). Function room. Games (fruit machine). No-smoking area. Quiz (first Mon of month; 50p to play). Satellite TVs. Tables outdoors (pavement). Vegetarian dishes. **Map 1/L5**

Late-night drinking

L ondon may be a thriving cosmopolitan city, but it often falls short of that sought-after ideal of 24-hour convenience. Go for a pint at your typical London boozer and chances are you'll be booted out at 11pm or so, cutting short what would otherwise have been a merrily prolonged drinking sesh. Current licensing laws (unlikely to be relaxed until at least 2003) can easily end up putting an unwelcome curfew on your evening. Few new bars are being granted late-night licences now that councils such as Westminster (responsible for Soho where many late-night haunts are clustered), Camden and Kensington & Chelsea are rallying behind local residents and clamping down on places that might increase night-time activity. The good news, however, is that late licences – although in too-short supply – are still held by around 350 London venues. Door policies vary: some charge admission, while others prefer to keep things free and easy. We've gathered together a list (organised by area – Central, City, West, South, East and North) of those London bars where you can get a drink even after the clock strikes twelve.

Central

10 Room (*p53*) Piccadilly Circus.
Open 5.30pm-3am Mon-Fri; 8pm-3am Sat.
10 Tokyo Joe's (*p53*) Piccadilly.
Open 8pm-4am Wed-Sat; 8pm-12.30am Sun.
79CXR (*p53*) Leicester Square.
Open 1pm-2am Mon; 1pm-3am Tue-Sat.
190 Queensgate (*p86*) South Kensington.
Open 11am-1am Mon-Sat; 11am-midnight Sun.
AKA (*p18*) Bloomsbury.
Open 6pm-midnight Mon; 6pm-1am Tue; 6pm-3am Wed-Fri; 7pm-3am Sat.
Amber (*p73*) Soho.
Open noon-1am Mon-Fri; 4pm-1am Sat.
Atlantic Bar & Grill (*p54*) Piccadilly Circus.
Open noon-3am Mon-Fri; 5pm-3am Sat.
The Backpacker (*p50*) King's Cross.
Open 7pm-2am Fri, Sat; 3.30pm-midnight Sun.
Bar Code (*p73*) Soho.
Open 1pm-1am Mon-Sat.
Bar Madrid (*p40*) Fitzrovia.
Open 4.30pm-3am Mon-Sat.
Bar Soho (*p75*) Soho.
Open 4pm-1am Mon-Thur; 4pm-3am Fri, Sat.

Bar Sol Ona (*p75*) Soho.
Open 5pm-3am Mon-Sat.
Blues Bistro & Bar (*p75*) Soho.
Open noon-midnight Mon-Thur; noon-1am Fri, Sat; noon-midnight Sun.
Boisdale (*p93*) Victoria.
Open noon-1am Mon-Fri; 7pm-1am Sat.
Café Bohème (*p75*) Soho.
Open 8am-3am Mon-Thur; 24 hours Fri, Sat; 8am-midnight Sun.
Cafe Lazeez (*p76*) Soho.
Open 11am-1am Mon-Sat; noon-10.30pm Sun.
Candy Bar (*p76*) Soho.
Open 5pm-1am Mon, Tue; 5pm-3am Wed-Fri; 4pm-3am Sat; 5pm-midnight Sun.
Château Bar (*p62*) Mayfair.
Open noon-2am Mon-Fri, Sun; 3pm-2am Sat.
Cheers London Piccadilly Circus (*p54*).
Open noon-3am Mon-Sat.
Circus Restaurant & Bar (*p76*) Soho.
Open noon-1.30am Mon-Fri, 6pm-1.30am Sat.
Columbia Bar (*p90*) Temple.
Open 11am-1am Fri.
Corney & Barrow (*p54*) Leicester Square.
Open noon-midnight Mon-Wed; noon-2am Thur-Sat.
Corts (*p44*) Holborn.
Open 11.30am-11pm Mon-Wed; 11.30am-2am Thur, Fri.
Cuba (*p49*) Kensington.
Open noon-2am Mon-Sat; 2-10.30pm Sun.
Denim (*p55*) Leicester Square.
Open 5pm-1.30am Mon-Sat; 2pm-midnight Sun.
Down Mexico Way (*p55*) Piccadilly Circus.
Open noon-3am Mon-Sat.
The Edge (*p79*) Soho.
Open noon-1am Mon-Sat.
Freedom (*p79*) Soho.
Open 11am-3am Mon-Sat; noon-midnight Sun.
Garlic & Shots (*p80*) Soho.
Open 5pm-midnight Mon-Wed; 6pm-1am Thur-Sat.
Havana (*p63*) Mayfair.
Open noon-3am Mon-Wed; noon-3am Thur-Sat; 5pm-1am Sun.
The Langley (*p32*) Covent Garden.
Open 4.30pm-1am Mon-Sat.
Mandarin Bar (*p51*) Knightsbridge.
Open 11am-2am Mon-Sat (licensed until 10.30pm).
Mash (*p42*) Fitzrovia.
Open 7.30am-2am Mon-Fri; 11am-2am Sat.
Mondo (*p81*) Soho.
Open 6pm-3am Mon-Sat.
O Bar (*p81*) Soho.
Open 3pm-3am Mon-Sat.
L'Odéon Bar & Restaurant (*p55*) Piccadilly Circus.
Open noon-1am Mon-Sat.
Office (*p43*) Fitzrovia.
Open noon-3am Mon-Fri; 9.30pm-4am Sat.
OnAnon (*p55*) Piccadilly Circus.
Open 5pm-3am Mon-Sat.
Opium (*p81*) Soho.
Open noon-3am Mon-Fri; 7pm-3.30am Sat.
Oxygen Bar (*p56*) Leicester Square.
Open 3pm-2am Mon-Wed; 3pm-3am Thur-Sat.
Pharmacy (*p71*) Notting Hill.
Open noon-3pm, 5.30pm-1am Mon-Thur; noon-3pm, 5.30pm-2am Fri; noon-2am Sat.
Phoenix Artist Club (*p81*). Soho.
Open 5pm-2.30am Mon-Wed; 1pm-3.30am Thur, Fri; 1pm-3.30am Sat.
Point 101 (*p24*) Bloomsbury.
Open 10am-2am Mon-Sat; noon-midnight Sun.

Pop (*p83*) Soho.
Open 5pm-3.30am Mon-Thur; 5pm-4am Fri; 8pm-5am Sat.
Popstarz Liquid Lounge (*p50*) King's Cross.
Open 5.30pm-2am Mon-Thur; 5.30pm-1am Fri, Sun; 5.30pm-3am Sat.
Prince of Wales (*p48*) Holland Park.
Open noon-1am Thur.
Queen Mary (*p91*) Trafalgar Square.
Open noon-1am Thur; noon-2am Fri, Sat (summer); noon-2am Fri, Sat (winter).
Roadhouse (*p38*) Covent Garden.
Open 5.30pm-3am Mon-Sat; 4pm-1am last Sun of the month.
Saint (*p56*) Leicester Square.
Open 5pm-2am Mon-Thur; 5pm-3am Fri; 7.30pm-3am Sat.
Sak (*p83*) Soho.
Open 5.30pm-2am Mon, Tue; 5.30pm-3am Wed-Sat.
Salsa! (*p83*) Soho.
Open 5.30pm-2am Mon-Sat.
Six Degrees (*p85*) Soho.
Open noon-1am Mon-Sat.
Soho Spice (*p85*) Soho.
Open 11.30am-midnight Mon-Thur; 11.30am-3.30am Fri, Sat.
Sound (*p56*) Leicester Square.
Open noon-1am Mon-Thur; noon-4am Fri, Sat; noon-midnight Sun.
Sports Café (*p56*) Piccadilly Circus.
Open noon-2am Mon-Thur; noon-3am Fri-Sat.
The Spot (*p56*) Covent Garden.
Open noon-1am Mon-Sat; 6pm-1am Sun.
Two Thirty Club (*p86*) Soho.
Open 5.30pm-1am Mon-Sat.
Village Soho (*p86*) Soho.
Open 4pm-1am Mon-Sat.
West Central (*p57*) Leicester Square.
Open basement bar 10.30pm-3am Fri, Sat; 10.30pm-2am Mon-Thur.
Windows (*p67*) Mayfair.
Open 5.30pm-2am Mon-Fri; 5.30pm-2am Sat.
Woody's (*p72*) Notting Hill. *Open* 7pm-2am Mon-Sat.
Yo! Below (*p86*) Soho.
Open noon-midnight Mon, Tue; noon-1am Wed-Sat; 5-10.30pm Sun.
Zeta (*p67*) Mayfair.
Open noon-3am Mon-Sat.

City

Al's Bar Café (*p104*) Barbican.
Open 8am-midnight Mon; 8am-1am Tue; 8am-2am Wed-Fri; 10am-2am Sat.
Charlie Wright's (*p127*) Shoreditch & Hoxton.
Open noon-1am Mon-Wed; noon-2am Thur-Sun.
Dust (*p107*) Barbican.
Open 11am-1am Thur; 11am-2am Fri; 7.30pm-2am Sat.
Fluid (*p107*) Barbican.
Open noon-midnight Tue, Wed; noon-2am Thur, Fri; 7pm-2am Sat.
Herbal (*p128*) Shoreditch & Hoxton.
Open 11am-2am Tue-Sun.
Lime (*p131*) Shoreditch & Hoxton.
Open 11am-1am Thur, Fri.
The Reliance (*p132*) Shoreditch & Hoxton.
Open noon-11pm Mon-Thur; noon-2am Fri; 6pm-2am Sat.
Shoreditch Electricity Showrooms (*p132*) Shoreditch & Hoxton.
Open noon-midnight Thur; noon-1am Fri, Sat.
Vibe Bar (*p200*) Whitechapel.
Open 11am-1am Fri, Sat.

The White House (*p172*) Clapham.
Open 5pm-midnight Mon-Tue; 5pm-1am
Wed; 5pm-2am Thur, Fri; noon-2am Sat;
noon-midnight Sun.

East

291 (*p193*) Hackney.
Open 5pm-midnight Mon-Wed; 5pm-2am
Thur, Fri; 11am-2am Sat.
Cock & Comfort (*p188*) Bethnal Green.
Open 2pm-2am Fri; 1pm-2am Sat; noon-
midnight Sun.
New Globe (*p189*) Bow.
Open noon-midnight Mon-Wed; noon-2am
Thur-Sat.
Royal Oak (*p188*) Bethnal Green.
Open 1pm-2am Mon-Sat.

North

Bar Gansa (*p202*) Camden.
Open 10am-midnight Mon, Tue; 10am-1am
Wed-Sat.
Bar Latino (*p216*) Islington.
Open 8pm-2am Mon-Thur; 6pm-2am
Fri, Sat.
Bar Lorca (*p229*) Stoke Newington.
Open noon-1am Mon-Thur; noon-2am Fri, Sat;
noon-midnight Sun.
Bartok (*p202*) Camden.
Open 5pm-midnight Mon-Thur; 5pm-1am Fri;
noon-1am Sat; noon-midnight Sun.
Café Corfu (*p203*) Camden.
Open noon-12.30am Mon-Sat; noon-10.30pm
Sun.
Chapel (*p217*) Islington.
Open noon-midnight Thur; noon-1am Fri, Sat.
Cuba Libre (*p219*) Islington.
Open 11am-2am Fri, Sat.
Embassy Bar (*p221*) Islington.
Open 5pm-1am Fri, Sat.
King's Head (*p222*) Crouch End.
Open cellar bar/comedy club noon-midnight
Mon-Thur; noon-1am Fri, Sat.
Hope & Anchor (*p222*) Islington.
Open basement 8.30pm-1am Mon-Sat;
7pm-midnight Sun.
Kings Head (*p222*) Islington.
Open 11am-midnight Mon; 11am-1am
Tue-Thur; 11am-2am Fri, Sat; noon-1am Sun.
Matt & Matt Bar (*p222*) Islington.
Open 6pm-midnight Tue-Thur; 6pm-2am Fri;
7pm-2am Sat.
Medicine Bar (*p222*) Islington.
Open 5pm-midnight Mon-Thur; 5pm-2am Fri;
noon-2am Sat; noon-10.30pm Sun.
Monarch (*p208*) Camden.
Open 8pm-midnight Mon-Thur; 8pm-2am
Fri, Sat.
Quinns (*p208*) Camden.
Open 11am-midnight Mon-Thur; 11am-1am
Fri, Sat.
Ruby in the Dust (*p223*) Islington.
Open 8pm-2am Mon-Sat.
Salmon & Compass (*p223*) Islington.
Open 5pm-midnight Mon-Wed; 5pm-2am
Thur; 4pm-2am Fri, Sat; 4pm-10.30pm Sun.
Shillibeer's (*p216*) Holloway.
Open noon-midnight Mon-Thur; noon-2am Fri;
6pm-2am Sat.
WKD (*p209*) Camden.
Open noon-2am Mon-Thur; noon-3am Fri, Sat;
noon-1am Sun.
World's End (*p213*) Finsbury Park.
Open noon-midnight Mon-Thur; noon-12.30am
Fri, Sat.
Zd Bar (*p225*) Kilburn.
Open 5pm-1am Mon-Thur; 5pm-2am
Fri, Sat.

West

Bardo (*p136*) Fulham.
Open 5pm-midnight Mon-Thur; 5pm-1am Fri;
noon-1am Sat.
Havana (*p138*) Fulham.
Open 5pm-2am Mon-Thur; noon-2am Fri, Sat.
Shoeless Joe's (*p140*) Fulham.
Open noon-midnight Mon-Wed; noon-1am
Thur-Sat.

South

2 Brewers (*p168*) Clapham.
Open 4pm-2am Mon-Thur; 4pm-3am Fri; 2pm-
3am Sat; noon-midnight Sun.
Bar Lorca (*p162*) Brixton.
Open 5pm-2am Mon-Thur; noon-3am Fri, Sat;
noon-midnight Sun.
Bedford (*p150*) Balham.
Open 11am-11pm Mon-Wed; 11am-midnight
Thur; 11am-2am Fri, Sat.
Bierodrome (*p169*) Clapham.
Open noon-midnight Mon-Wed; noon-1am
Thur; noon-2am Fri, Sat.
Brixtonian Havana Club (*p162*) Brixton.
Open noon-1am Tue, Wed; noon-2am Thur-Sat.
Bug Bar (*p164*) Brixton.
Open 7pm-1am Wed, Thur; 7pm-3am Fri, Sat;
7pm-2am Sun.
Cave Austin (*p159*) Blackheath.
Open 11am-midnight Mon-Wed, Fri, Sat;
11am-2am Thur.

Cynthia's Robotic Bar & Restaurant (*p161*)
Borough.
Open noon-1am Mon-Wed, noon-3am Thur-
Sat, noon-midnight Sun.
Dogstar (*p164*) Brixton.
Open noon-2.30am Mon-Thur; noon-4am
Fri, Sat; noon-2am Sun.
Duke of Devonshire (*p150*) Balham.
Open 11am-midnight Mon-Thur; 11am-2am
Fri, Sat; noon-midnight Sun.
Fridge Bar (*p164*) Brixton.
Open (main bar) 9pm-2am Mon-Wed;
7pm-2am Thur; 7pm-4am Fri; 8pm-4am
Sat; 8pm-3am Sun; *(chill-out bar)* 6am-noon
Sat, Sun.
Junction (*p164*) Brixton.
Open 4pm-midnight Mon; 4pm-2am Thur, Fri;
noon-2am Sat; noon-midnight Sun.
The Plug (*p181*) Stockwell.
Open noon-midnight Mon, Sun; noon-
2am Thur; noon-3am Fri, Sat.
Sand (*p172*) Clapham.
Open 5pm-2am Mon-Sat; 5pm-1am Sun.
Satay Bar (*p165*) Brixton.
Open noon-2am Fri, Sat.
SW9 (*p165*) Brixton.
Open 9am-1am Fri; 10.30am-1am Sat.
Swan (*p182*) Stockwell.
Open 5pm-2am Mon-Thur; 5pm-3am Fri; 7pm-3am
Sat; 7pm-2am Sun.
Tea Rooms des Artistes (*p156*) Battersea.
Open 5.30pm-1am Fri-Sun.

Point 101

101 New Oxford Street, WC1 (020 7379 3112/
www.meanfiddler.com). Tottenham Court Road tube.
Open/food served 10am-2am Mon-Sat; noon-midnight
Sun. **Credit** AmEx, MC, V.
The Mean Fiddler Group's flagship central London bar
suffers from a grim bunker-like setting, occupying two
sizeable floors beneath Centrepoint. Consequently it's not
their most stylish outlet, but the local clubbers and younger
tourists who flock here obviously appreciate the minimalist
'canteen-style' set-up. On the ground floor are metal stools
and chairs, large oval light wood tables and a long bar
stretching down one side. Upstairs is a function room, toilets
and another room with intimate booths. Draught beer is
strictly keg with the likes of Guinness (naturally) and
Carlsberg and more adventurous bottles, including
Staropramen and Asahi. The wine list isn't bad but tourists
tend to concentrate on standard cocktails. Food is of the soup
and pasta variety.
Babies and children admitted (until 5pm). Function room.
Music (DJs 9pm Mon-Sat; free). Tables outdoors.
Vegetarian dishes. **Map 7/K6**

Queen's Larder

1 Queen Square, WC1 (020 7837 5627). Holborn or
Russell Square tube. **Open** 11am-11pm Mon-Sat; noon-
10.30pm Sun. **Food served** noon-3pm, 6-9.30pm daily.
Credit MC, V.
When it comes to tiny, cosy pubs, this has to be one of the
tiniest and the cosiest in town. Horseshoe-shaped around a
small bar serving the likes of Marston's Pedigree and
Wadworth 6X, the style is traditional and, as befits the name,
the walls are decorated with portraits of various royals.
Comfortable banquettes and precarious stools (room only for
a dozen or so sitting) house a wide range of locals, ranging
from gangs of office types to workmen playing the jukebox
and fruit machine. Upstairs is a small room that doubles as
restaurant at lunchtimes. The name comes from the days
when George III was being looked after by Dr Willis in a
house opposite and his loyal wife, Queen Charlotte, hired the
cellar to store his goodies.
Babies and children admitted (until 9pm). Games (fruit
machine). Jukebox. Restaurant (no-smoking area). Tables
outdoors (pavement). TV. Vegetarian dishes. **Map 1/L5**

Truckles of Pied Bull Yard

Off Bury Place, WC1 (020 7404 5338/www.davy.co.uk).
Holborn or Tottenham Court Road tube. **Open/food**
served 11.30am-10pm Mon-Fri; 11.30am-3pm Sat.
Credit AmEx, DC, MC, V.
A stylish member of the Davy's wine bar chain, despite the
name and setting – in a cloistered yard just off Bloomsbury
Way – Truckles is not in the least bit olde worlde. It's bright,
uncluttered and very yellow, with comfortable modern sofas
and chairs around low tables. A downstairs area offers a
darker and more intimate experience, or – as one wag has it
– 'Aleister Crowley meets Ann Widdecombe'. In warmer
months the courtyard's a good place to sit outside and order
from the compact wine list of mainly Davy's own, most of
which are available by the glass. Beer fans should be kept
happy by the bottled Bishop's Finger. There's an obligatory
open-view kitchen, and the food's not bad; starters like dill
marinated Scottish herring fillets, cold main courses of the
order of 'plate of finest ham' and hot dishes like bangers and
mash and grilled salmon supreme.
Babies and children admitted. Function rooms.
No-smoking area. Restaurant. Tables outdoors
(courtyard). Vegetarian dishes. **Map 1/L5**

Vats Wine Bar & Restaurant

51 Lamb's Conduit Street, WC1 (020 7242 8963).
Holborn or Russell Square tube. **Open** noon-11pm Mon-
Fri. **Food served** noon-2.30pm, 6-9.30pm Mon-Fri.
Credit AmEx, DC, MC, V.
A cosy wine bar of the old school with a sturdy wood floor
and walls of light wood laminate hung with grotesque
cartoons and prints. At the rear – behind the cloakroom area
– is another room dominated by trompe l'oeil murals. But it's
the front bar where the regulars hang out, a mix of characters
and would-be characters who seem to range from pencil-thin
chain-smoking young women who would have been called
'debs' in bygone times to mouthy middle-aged men in loud
check suits. Sit-com writers would love Vats: the one-liners
we overheard would have kept *Absolutely Fabulous* in
business indefinitely. Wines are well chosen and kick off at
around £3 a glass, with the good stuff coming in between £15
and £20. Pasta and grilled salmon are well under a tenner.
Babies and children admitted. Function room. Tables
outdoors (pavement). Vegetarian dishes. **Map 3/M4**

Vespa Lounge

Under Centre Point House, St Giles High Street, WC2
(020 7836 8956). Tottenham Court Road tube. **Open**
6-11pm daily. **No credit cards.**
A 'lesbian bar with gay men as guests', Vespa is a laid-back
first floor bar with plenty going on. It's bigger than the
Candy Bar (*see p76*), and comes with less attitude. Aside
from the red-topped pool table, expect entertainment such as
the 'Bevy of Birds and Beer' student night on Tuesdays (with
special deals on bottled beers) and the 'Laughing Cows'
comedy night on the last Sunday of each month (for which
there's an admission charge). The place has recently been
made over, with a blue hue and new spindly furniture.
Draught Stella, bottled beers and cocktails are served from a
tiny corner bar. Customers tend to come in three broad
categories: tattooed dykes, hard-faced E-heads, but with your
average lesbian casual miss in the majority.
Comedy night (8pm last Sun of month; admission £5/£4
in advance). Games (pool table). Satellite TV (big screen).
Map 7/K6

Also in the area...

All Bar One 108 New Oxford Street, WC1
(020 7307 7980).

Chelsea

Anglesea Arms

15 Selwood Terrace, SW7 (020 7373 7960). Gloucester
Road or South Kensington tube. **Open** 11am-11pm Mon-
Sat; noon-10.30pm Sun. **Food served** 6.30-9.30pm Mon-
Sat; 6.30-9pm Sun. **Credit** MC, V.
The Anglesea has been around since 1835; Dickens drank
here when he lodged a few doors down at No.11. It's changed
considerably since then, and is now a large airy, single-room
bar with a restaurant at the back, but it does retain Victorian
character courtesy of etched-glass snob screens, requisite
William Morris-type wallpaper and dark wood furnishings.
There's a TV, but the place remains free of games machines
or a jukebox. It's where the haute bourgeoisie slip into their
rugby shirts and sup a good selection of beers (including
Adnam's and Brakspear's). The forecourt is extremely
popular in summer. Don't let the braying boozers put you off.
Babies and children admitted (before 6pm). No piped
music or jukebox. Satellite TV. Specialities: real ales.
Tables outdoors (terrace). Vegetarian dishes.

Lamb. *See page 20.*

Bluebird

*350 King's Road, SW3 (020 7559 1000/
www.conran.com). Sloane Square tube, then 19, 22 bus/
49 bus.* **Open** noon-11pm Mon-Fri; 11am-11pm Sat;
11am-10.30pm Sun. **Credit** AmEx, DC, MC, V.
Part of the Conran empire, Bluebird is housed in a converted
1930s garage and comprises a restaurant, café, food hall,
kitchen shop and the Bluebird bar. Small, chic and classically
Conranesque (pine, aluminium and strong bright colours) it's
the perfect spot for watching Chelsea stroll by – a pastime
happily indulged in by its well turned out, largely female
clientele. Cocktails, beers and a good list of wines from
around the world are served at prices every bit as costly as
you might imagine. On warmer days many of the customers
spill out into the courtyard (be warned: outside tables are
reserved for diners at certain times). A pleasant place for a
quick aperitif but not somewhere to stay for a session,
however well cashed-up you are.
*Babies and children admitted (in restaurant). Disabled:
toilet. Function room. Music (pianist weekend lunchtimes).
Restaurant. Tables outdoors (forecourt). Vegetarian
dishes.*

Builder's Arms

*13 Britten Street, SW3 (020 7349 9040). Sloane Square
or South Kensington tube.* **Open** 11am-11pm Mon-Sat;
11am-10.30pm Sun. **Food served** noon-2.30pm, 7-10pm
Mon-Sat; noon-3pm, 7-9.30pm Sun. **Credit** MC, V.
Whoever designed the smart interior of the Builder's Arms
knows a thing or two about Chelsea. Ottomans, still-life
pictures, leather sofas and a very handsome corner fireplace
suggest an everlasting sense of conservatism, but
interspersed with slightly dissident artistic touches, like the
large painting of Salvador Dali staring piercingly at the
drinkers. So successful is it at marrying the borough's
contrasting elements that it appeals to the whole age
spectrum, from the red-cheeked innocents on the run from
public school, to the red-nosed buffers on the run from life.
The choice of drinks is similarly all-embracing; a good range
of beers is on tap (including Adnam's and London Pride), 30-
odd wines (ten of those by the glass), and about a dozen malt
whiskies. Among the dishes on the interesting (and popular)
menu are tasty mains like pigeon and green bean salad with
soy dressing (£5.95), and duck breast with lentils, truffle oil
and cabbage (£10.95).
*Babies and children admitted. Disabled: toilet. Satellite TV.
Specialities: wines. Tables outdoors (patio). Vegetarian
dishes.*

Cadogan Arms

*298 King's Road, SW3 (020 7352 1645). Sloane Square
tube, then 11, 19, 22 bus.* **Open/food served** 11am-
11pm Mon-Sat; noon-10.30pm Sun. **Credit** AmEx, MC, V.
A dark, creaky old pub on the King's Road? We continue to
be amazed every time we visit, but the old-codgers-only
exterior successfully keeps the emissaries of change at bay.
Inside, a low-beamed ceiling (not original) and classic Tudor-
style bar help to create the feel of a ship's galley, with plenty
of little nooks and crannies for you to hide away in. Draught
ales include Theakston's XB, Courage Best and Courage
Directors, and there's unspectacular but good-value grub of
the chicken kiev, fish and chips sort. Ultimately though, the
best selling point of this pub is that it offers some much-
needed sanctuary from screeching Sloanes and their Tim
Nice-But-Dim hubbies.
*Babies and children admitted (until 8pm). Games (fruit
machines, pool tables, quiz machine). Jukebox. Satellite TV
(big screen). Vegetarian dishes.*

Chelsea Potter

*119 King's Road, SW3 (020 7352 9479). Sloane Square
tube.* **Open** 11am-11pm Mon-Sat; noon-10.30pm Sun.
Food served noon-6pm daily. **Credit** AmEx, DC, MC, V.
The Chelsea Potter had a bit of cash spent on it a couple of
years back, but really it hasn't changed much since the days
when the King's Road punks gathered here to be snapped by
tourists. It's pretty gloomy inside – the light gets soaked up
by the dark patterned carpet and heavy furnishings – but the
pavement benches are a perfect spot to people watch. It's a
cheerful and unpretentious place; the food's not up to much,
nor is the wine, and they only serve a couple of ales (Courage
Best and Directors) but nobody seems to mind. Shoppers pop
in for a break during the day, while at night the place is
packed with pre-clubbers eyeing each other up and drinking
for England. On our last visit, a man next to us was dancing
with his trousers round his ankles and it wasn't even eight.
*Babies and children admitted (until 5pm). Games (fruit
machines). Jukebox. Tables outdoors (pavement). TV.
Vegetarian dishes.*

Chelsea Ram

*32 Burnaby Street, SW10 (020 7351 4008). Sloane
Square or Fulham Broadway tube, then 22 bus/C1, 11, 31
bus.* **Open** 11am-11pm Mon-Sat; noon-10.30pm Sun.
Food served noon-3pm, 7-10pm Mon-Sat; noon-2.30pm,
7-9.30pm Sun. **Credit** AmEx, MC, V.
This bright corner gastropub still looks as welcoming as ever,
decked out in summer shades of green and yellow, with bare
floorboards at the front and sea grass for the diners at the
back. The menu isn't as cutting edge as some (chicken breast
with creamed leeks and mushrooms in puff pastry £9.95;
spiced lamb burger £8.45) but the food is well prepared and
beautifully presented. The wine list is divided into Old and
New World and runs to about 30 choices, about 15 of which
are available by the glass, and with a smattering of pudding
wines and ports. During the day the older regulars prop up
the bar, while at night – especially Friday and Saturday –
crowds of young white professionals compete to be heard.
*Babies and children admitted (dining area only). Function
room. No piped music or jukebox. Tables outdoors
(pavement). TV. Vegetarian dishes.*

Cooper's Arms

*87 Flood Street, SW3 (020 7376 3120). Sloane Square
or South Kensington tube.* **Open** 11am-11pm Mon-Sat;
noon-10.30pm Sun. **Food served** 12.30-3pm, 6-10pm
Mon-Sat; 12.30-3pm Sun. **Credit** AmEx, MC, V.
A Young's house, the Cooper's Arms is traditional but
definitely not fusty: it has plenty of pine furniture, a
smattering of cushions, vintage ocean liner posters, a huge
chalked-up wine list and community noticeboard. A superior
bar menu offers the likes of lamb chops with parsnip mash
and mint jus, or escalope of pork with field mushroom, rocket
and prune armagnac sauce, all at sound prices. Chelsea
Registry Office is just round the corner so the upstairs
function room with its grand 5m table rescued from a Jarrow
shipyard is often booked up with wedding parties. Physically
and aesthetically comfortable, the Cooper's Arms strikes
exactly the right note for the area.
*Babies and children admitted (until 8pm). Function room.
No piped music or jukebox. TV. Vegetarian dishes.*

Cross Keys

*1 Lawrence Street, SW3 (020 7349 9111). Sloane
Square tube.* **Open** noon-11pm Mon-Sat; noon-10.30pm
Sun. **Food served** noon-3pm, 7-11pm Mon-Fri; noon-4pm,
7-11pm Sat; noon-9.30pm Sun. **Credit** AmEx, MC, V.

But for the sculpture over the fire of a fat friar lifting his habit to warm himself, the inside of the Cross Keys is a delight. The friar would be at home on a saucy seaside postcard, but he doesn't fit with the rest of the modern gothic decorations (which come courtesy of the creators of **Beach Blanket Babylon**, *see p99*). There's a large tondo of St George slaying the dragon, plenty of decorative mirrors, stained glass, and a cross-looking Aslan wearing a gaudy crown (which looks exactly like one of those air-fresheners you get on the back shelves of mini-cabs). The bar seems more spacious because most of the ceiling has been cut away to let a large spidery chandelier hang down from the room above (which is available for hire). Through the back is a glass-roofed restaurant decorated in an artfully bucolic theme; tasteful wicker panels, whitewashed garden implements and rustic benches. The inventive menu includes foie gras and wild mushroom terrine and toasted brioche (£5.95) and roast breast of duck with sweet potato rosti (£12.95). The affluent and youngish customers enjoy Courage Directors, Theakston Best and an extensive range of wines.
Babies and children admitted (high chairs). Function rooms. Restaurant. Vegetarian dishes.

Fox & Hounds

29 Passmore Street, SW1 (020 7730 6367). Sloane Square tube. **Open** noon-3pm, 5.30-11pm Mon-Fri; noon-3pm, 6-11pm Sat; noon-3pm, 6.30-10.30pm Sun. **Food served** noon-2.30pm, 5.30-8.30pm Mon-Fri. **Credit** MC, V.
Tucked away behind Sloane Square station, prior to August 1999, this was London's last 'beer-only' pub, serving pints and wine only, no spirits. But after being sold to Young's the Wandsworth brewer introduced whiskies, gin, rum and vodka, and a fancy menu, and gave the place a makeover. Nowadays, despite a history going back to the early 19th century it's looking quite modern – bright and airy despite its diminutive size, full of pale wood, pews and bookshelves. That's not to say it's a bad place; far from it, it's very pleasant on a quiet weeknight, and both beer and food are good, although it suffers from a serious table shortage, and there's little room at the bar. For these reasons it's best avoided at weekends.
Babies and children admitted. No piped music or jukebox. Vegetarian dishes.

Front Page

35 Old Church Street, SW3 (020 7352 2908/ www.frontpagepubs.com). Sloane Square tube. **Open** 11am-11pm Mon-Sat; noon-10.30pm Sun. **Food served** noon-3pm, 6-10pm Mon-Fri; noon-10pm Sat; noon-6pm Sun. **Credit** AmEx, MC, V.
This self-consciously civilised place is perfectly suited to the genteel backstreets of Chelsea. Whereas the proles are given flashing slot machines and laminated menus offering fried food, the toffs prefer clubby wooden panelling, mucky (but discreet) prints of a chambermaid having a bath, and nursery scoff (along with things like half a dozen oysters). It's a fine place to retreat after a day's tiring shopping or to have an intimate chat over a bottle of wine by the fire at the back. The sparkling bar serves Brakspear's, Theakston XB and Bombardier as well as about 30 wines (eight of which by the glass). It livens up considerably on Friday nights and when they pull down the big-screen TV for rugby internationals, but overall, it's quiet, clean and conservative – just like the regulars.
Babies and children admitted (until 5pm). Function room. No piped music or jukebox. Satellite TV (big screen). Vegetarian dishes.

Lomo

222 Fulham Road, SW10 (020 7349 8848). Fulham Broadway, South Kensington or Earl's Court tube. **Open/food served** 5pm-midnight Mon-Fri; noon-midnight Sat; noon-11.30pm Sun. **Credit** AmEx, MC, V.
A style-tapas bar with a slick, hip approach befitting its locale. Decor is sleek: mostly metal and terracotta-red, with an undulating bar and tall, round drinking and talking tables. Blackboard specials supplement a varied menu of small raciones (£5-£6), but it seems that it's the cocktail list that really pulls the punters in (£4-£6.50), especially during happy hours (5-7pm). For more serious drinkers the wine list offers some fine labels: Spanish, French and New World. There's also a rather disappointing range of bottled beer. Staff are warm and welcoming, and our only real gripe is the slidey orange plastic stools – but don't worry, the Chelsea and Westminster Hospital is just opposite if you take a tumble.
Babies and children admitted. Restaurant. Vegetarian dishes.

Moore Arms

61-63 Cadogan Street, SW3 (020 7589 7848). Sloane Square tube. **Open** noon-11pm Mon-Sat; noon-10.30pm Sun. **Food served** noon-3pm, 6-9pm Mon-Thur; noon-3pm Fri-Sun. **Credit** AmEx, DC, MC, V.
A large town pub among the even larger town houses of Cadogan Gardens, the Moore Arms is a dark, ornate and slightly shabby establishment that attracts a mixed crowd of younger anti-King's Road drinkers and gruffer older types (here for real ales Abbot's and Friary Mew on our last visit). Despite the generous proportions of the interior, the place is cosy enough, with an assortment of areas in which to take a seat – including a sitting-room bit with a log fire and a pool room. Most locals head straight for favourite spots at the acres of bar. It's certainly seen better days, but the Moore Arms is still a good bet for a snug seat on a cold winter's night.
Babies and children admitted (until 7pm). Games (pool table, quiz machine). Satellite TV. Tables outdoors (pavement). Vegetarian dishes.

Orange Brewery

37 Pimlico Road, SW1 (020 7730 5984). Sloane Square tube. **Open/food served** 11am-9pm Mon-Sat; noon-9pm Sun. **Credit** AmEx, DC, MC, V.
Three years of Scottish & Newcastle ownership are beginning to take their toll at this former favourite. Some outstanding beers are still brewed on the premises (SW1, SW2, Pimlico Porter and seasonal ales), but sadly the tasteless decor makes it difficult to enjoy the brewer's art. It's fast becoming a self-theming pastiche with plastic Orange Brewery take-out bottles decorating the cheap-looking bar, along with bits of hessian claiming to be sacks full of hops, olde worlde beer crocks and Victorian brewing memorabilia (S&N take note: nobody falls for this kind of tat). Tacky painted blackboards advertise uninspired food and the choice of wines is execrable. Not as popular as it used to be and it's not difficult to see why.
Games (fruit machines, golf machine). Jukebox. Specialities: own brewed ales. Tables outdoors (pavement). TV. Vegetarian dishes.

Phene Arms

9 Phene Street, SW3 (020 7352 3294). Sloane Square or South Kensington tube. **Open** 11am-11pm Mon-Sat; noon-10.30pm Sun. **Food served** noon-3pm, 6-10.30pm Mon-Fri; noon-4pm, 6-10.30pm Sat, Sun. **Credit** AmEx, DC, MC, V.
Governments fall, fashions wax and wane, but the dependable Phene stands firm as the most convivial pub in Chelsea. If a

Crown & Anchor. *See page 31.*

marketing man were in charge, he'd certainly rip out the large central bar (complete with wrought iron fittings and cheesy red lanterns) and the faded pub carpet, but with these would go its heart and its charm. The regulars at the Phene – and thankfully there are still a fair few of them – are part of the old Chelsea; they've no interest in discussing City bonuses or astronomical house prices, but they come here for the good beer (including Old Speckled Hen, Courage Directors and Adnam's), good company and decent pub grub. The garden is lively practically year round, thanks to its heaters, although a run-in with the difficult neighbours a few years back means that it has to be vacated 20 minutes before last orders. Otherwise, near perfect.
Babies and children admitted. Function room. No piped music or jukebox. Restaurant. Specialities: real ales. TV. Tables outdoors (garden, roof terrace). Vegetarian dishes.

PJ's Bar & Grill
52 Fulham Road, SW3 (020 7581 0025). South Kensington tube. **Open/food served** noon-midnight daily. **Credit** AmEx, DC, MC, V.
A smart bar-cum-restaurant at the South Ken end of Chelsea with decor that suggests something between an American gentleman's club and a planter's retreat. The 'PJ' stands for Polo Joe's and photos celebrating the sport, as well as huge rusty old mirrors, adorn the wood panelled walls. The old America ambience is further increased by the mahogany central bar and, if you're lucky enough to acquire a table, waitress service – even if you're only drinking. The extensive wine list (kicking off at under £4 a glass, £11.50 a bottle) is better than the selection of bottled beer.
Babies and children admitted (high chairs). Satellite TV. Tables outdoors (pavement). Vegetarian dishes.

Sporting Page
6 Camera Place, SW10 (020 7376 3694/ www.frontpagepubs.com). Bus 11, 14, 19, 22, 328. **Open** 11am-11pm Mon-Sat; noon-10.30pm Sun. **Food served** noon-3pm, 6-10pm Mon-Fri; noon-6pm Sat, Sun. **Credit** AmEx, MC, V.
Apparently one of the country's biggest sellers of champagne, the Sporting Page (sibling to the **Front Page**, *see p27*) fills its windows with trophies of empty Bolly bottles. Inside, walls are covered in tableaux of various jolly sporting scenes, while the black-and-white floor gives something of the feel of a Parisian brasserie. Old soaks with their secretaries sit separately from crowds of post-rugby match lads, who drink more than is reasonably considered possible and shout things like 'You want the truth? You can't handle the truth,' and bellow with laughter. You may find the very decent wine list a saving grace. Then again, maybe not.
Babies and children admitted. No piped music or jukebox. Satellite TV (big screen). Specialities: Bollinger. Tables outdoors (pavement). Vegetarian dishes.

Surprise
6 Christchurch Terrace, off Flood Street, SW3 (020 7349 1821). Sloane Square tube. **Open** noon-11pm Mon-Sat; noon-10.30pm Sun. **Food served** noon-10pm Mon-Sat; 1-10pm Sun. **Credit** MC, V.
Hidden in a warren of residential mewsy back streets, the Surprise is a classy, refurbed pub with plenty of dark polished wood and stained glass windows. Seating is at a central bar or courtesy of the odd shabby sofa. A tiny lounge area offers non-regulars respite from the stares of the residents, but no protection from the 'you're not from round here, are you?' attitude of the bar staff. Food was off when we visited (the menu was under revision) but it used to be good and ales include Bass, London Pride and Robinson Best Bitter. Don't

look like you've just stepped off the King's Road (as we did, and indeed, had) and you might be OK.
Games (darts, fruit machine, shove ha'penny, shut the box). No piped music or jukebox. Satellite TV. Tables outdoors (pavement). Vegetarian dishes.

Also in the area...
All Bar One 152 Gloucester Road, SW7 (020 7244 5861).
Dôme 354 King's Road, SW3 (020 7352 2828).
Pitcher & Piano 214 Fulham Road, SW10 (020 7352 9234); 316-318 King's Road, SW3 (020 7352 0025).

Covent Garden & the Strand
Africa Bar
The Africa Centre, 38 King Street, WC2 (020 7836 1976). Covent Garden tube. **Open** 5.30-11pm Mon-Sat. **Food served** 12.30-3pm, 6-10pm Mon-Sat. **Credit** AmEx, DC, MC, V.
This cosy subterranean bar gets very busy at weekends when African bands are playing upstairs in the ground-floor hall. Otherwise it's a sleepy affair, with a smattering of ex-pats and old Africa hands sitting around the bar sucking on bottles of South African Castle lager and resolutely ignoring the no-smoking sign perched on top of the Grolsch pump. It's a small room with a balding, sticky red carpet, red banquettes and little in the way of decoration other than a handful of old tourist posters flogging Kenya and Zimbabwe. Loud Jit and Township Jive music tumbles from a large speaker and there's invariably a happy atmosphere. The African food in the adjacent Calabash restaurant is to be avoided.
Babies and children admitted (in restaurant). Function room. Music (live bands Fri, Sat). Restaurant. Satellite TV (certain sporting or Africa related events only). Vegetarian dishes. Map 2/L7

American Bar
Savoy Hotel, Strand, WC2 (020 7836 4343/ www.savoygroup.co.uk). Charing Cross tube/rail. **Open** 11am-11pm Mon-Sat. **Food served** 11am-2.30pm Mon-Sat. **Credit** AmEx, DC, MC, V.
You need to be smartly dressed to be welcomed at this cocktail bar a few steps up from the Savoy's main lobby. Head barman of 25 years Peter Dorelli runs a tight ship. Uniformed waiters

Critics' choice
gastropubs
Anglesea Arms (p148)
Well-kept ales and superb value-for-money food.
Crown (p188)
E3 pub that takes its food very seriously.
Duke (of York) (p19)
International and supremely sensible menu.
Salt House (p228)
The best reason to visit St John's Wood.
Lord Stanley (p207)
Ramshackle decor, great vibe, fine food.

hover and offer impeccable service to those who pass muster. It's said that the first ever Martini cocktail in Britain was served here, and the vodka Martini, served in a frosted glass, is still heavenly. Malt whisky is another speciality, with 69 on offer, including a Strathisla 1955 (£32.55/50cl). Adventurous tipplers take note: this bar is also reputed to mix the finest absinthe cocktails in town. Most cocktails are a tenner or more, and you won't get much change from a fiver for bottled beer (Carlsberg Elephant, London Pride, etc). Surroundings are suitably opulent, if a little dated. Despite the Hollywood prints on the wall the clientele are more Discreet Old Money than International Jet Set, though you might still spot the occasional celebrity. The only off-note is the pesky pianist.
Dress code. Function rooms. Music (pianist 7-11pm Mon-Sat). No-smoking area. Vegetarian dishes. **Map 2/L7**

Bank

1 Kingsway, Aldwych, WC2 (020 7379 9797/ www.bankrestaurant.co.uk). Covent Garden or Holborn tube. **Open** 11am-11pm Mon-Sat; 11.30am-10pm Sun. **Food served** noon-3pm, 5.30-11.30pm Mon-Fri; 11.30am-3.30pm, 5.30-11.30pm Sat; 11.30am-3.30pm, 5.30-10pm Sun. **Credit** AmEx, DC, MC, V.
A mega restaurant with a bar attached, Bank is big and brash but seldom less than busy. The bar area to the left of the entrance is visible through large picture windows and decorated with colourful giant seaside scenes painted onto the terracotta-coloured walls. A giant (everything's big here) glass light-affair hangs threateningly over the circular bar, but the thrusting young executives who make up the majority of customers don't appear to notice or care. Most seem to be drinking out of cocktail glasses, though bottled beer has its followers. Cigars are popular (the bigger the better) and the thing here is to make an impression and be seen. Food is upmarket and showy – centred around the likes of langoustines, caviar and fish. Serving staff are efficient and polite, but stop a little way short of being friendly.
Babies and children admitted (children's menu, high chairs, restaurant only). Disabled: toilet. Restaurant. Vegetarian dishes. **Map 4/M6**

Bar des Amis

11-14 Hanover Place, WC2 (020 7379 3444/ www.cafedesamis.co.uk). Covent Garden tube. **Open/food served** 11.30am-11pm Mon-Sat. **Credit** AmEx, DC, MC, V.
A little bit of Continental chic opposite a great British building site, this small basement wine bar beneath the stylish Café des Amis offers a relaxing atmosphere, around 80 French wines and brandies, plus a bar menu centred around simple Gallic cuisine. Expect the likes of shellfish bisque, fluffy omelettes and a cheese plate of three or five perfectly kept French cheeses – one of which could probably be smelled in Brittany. The decor includes the customary light wood floor, with blue and pink upholstered square stools and hidden lighting. The serving area is an island in the centre of the room and we've never encountered anything other than helpful and informed service. Customers tend to be upmarket, sleek and well heeled. Think *Paris Match.*
Babies and children admitted. Tables outdoors (terrace). Vegetarian dishes. **Map 2/L6**

Bar Aquda

13-14 Maiden Lane, WC2 (020 7557 9891). Covent Garden tube/Charing Cross tube/rail. **Open** noon-11pm Mon-Sat; noon-10.30pm Sun. **Food served** noon-5pm daily. **Credit** MC, V.
Lively gay bar: colourful, noisy and totally extrovert. Walls are blue and cream, furniture is minimalist and modern, and

the overall theme is the sea – barracuda, geddit? Customers are typically male, thirtysomething or over, with a fair number of lone sharks surveying the shoal. Dress is smart casual or else after-work suits. It has to be said that with the whole of Covent Garden to choose from, no one would come here for the drink alone, it being a standard mix of lagers and nitro-kegs at prices that are a good 20% above the area's norm. But then somebody has to pay for flamboyant bar staff and loud club music.
Disabled: toilet. Vegetarian dishes. **Map 2/L7**

Box

32-34 Monmouth Street, WC2 (020 7240 5828). Covent Garden or Leicester Square tube. **Open** 11am-11pm Mon-Sat; noon-10.30pm Sun. **Food served** 11am-5pm daily. **Credit** AmEx, MC, V.
Laid-back, young and gay café-style bar that's less cruisey than most. Eschews the kitsch and glitter for a clean-cut look of wooden floor, bright light walls and unfussy small square tables. The crowd is similarly polished, sleek and cool – first-timers could be forgiven for thinking they'd walked into a Rupert Everett casting session. Basement toilets are unisex à la *Ally McBeal* and so plush that you might do as we did and mistake them for part of the bar. Draught beers include Leffe Blonde and Stella Artois and there's a good supply of bottles, slammers and cocktails. Were we dreaming or was that a photograph of Eric Sykes on the wall? And does Hattie Jacques know?
Babies and children admitted (daytime only). Tables outdoors (pavement). Vegetarian dishes. **Map 2/L6**

Brasserie Max

Covent Garden Hotel, 10 Monmouth Street, WC2 (020 7806 1000/www.firmdale.com). Covent Garden tube. **Open/food served** 11am-11pm Mon-Sat; 11am-10.30pm Sun. **Credit** AmEx, MC, V.
Despite its obvious class, this upmarket bar at the Covent Garden Hotel is one of London's less intimidating five-star bars. The young staff are friendly and unlikely to look down their noses at the punters, provided (of course) the punters play the game and don't turn up in overalls or T-shirt and shorts. It's decidedly a cocktail bar and the single unbranded draught lager and bottles in the fridge tend to lose out to Martini cocktails and Manhattans. Prices are far from outrageous. The decor is low key and cool with light grey walls, chunky wood furniture and chrome fittings. Bar food (from just over £5 to around £15) includes stuff like seafood chowder, organic tofu in miso soup and pan-seared salmon.
Babies and children admitted. Function rooms. Restaurant. Tables outdoors (pavement). Vegetarian dishes. **Map 1/L6**

Café Baroque

33 Southampton Street, WC2 (020 7379 7585/ www.cafebaroque.co.uk). Covent Garden tube/Charing Cross tube/rail. **Open/food served** noon-midnight Mon-Sat. **Credit** AmEx, DC, MC, V.
At the classier end of Covent Garden's drinking dens is this very civilised ground-floor wine bar, appended to a more ambitious restaurant upstairs. The walls are cream and dotted with mirrors, the lampshades are tassled and the tablecloths are the whitest, crispest linen. As long as you look respectable the welcome is friendly and the service spot on. The wines are predominantly French and well chosen, beers are the usual bottled variety and food is a sort of British 'tapas' – char-grilled asparagus salad, sweet potato and parsnip chips and such – mostly vegetarian, costing between £1.50 and £5.50. Customers tend to be the type who read more than a book a year, with a preponderance of opera buffs.

There's a special 'opera club' upstairs on the last Tuesday evening of each month.
Babies and children admitted. Games (backgammon, chess). Tables outdoors (pavement). Restaurant. Vegetarian dishes. **Map 2/L7**

Coach & Horses
42 Wellington Street, WC2 (020 7240 0553). Covent Garden tube. **Open** 11am-11pm Mon-Sat; noon-10.30pm Sun. **Food served** noon-2.30pm daily. **Credit** MC, V.
Aside from the proliferating foliage outside and the occasional lick of paint, nothing seems to change at this tiny Irish-run local near the eastern edge of Covent Garden Piazza. The small single bar is traditionally decorated with a red patterned carpet, stools along one side and a wood-surrounded serving area opposite. One of the main attractions is the Dublin-brewed, non-pasteurised Guinness at roughly the same price everyone else normally charges for the standard Park Royal stuff. Real ales include Courage Directors. Then there are the giant lunchtime baps, which come heaped with fillings such as hot salt beef, roast lamb or ham for £4 and worth every penny. This is where staff from other pubs come on their time off, otherwise it's stuffed with theatrical types, Irish ex-pats and anyone who happens to be passing and appreciates a good pub.
Specialities: 80 whiskies. Vegetarian dishes. **Map 2/L6**

Coal Hole
91 Strand, WC2 (020 7379 9883). Embankment tube/ Charing Cross tube/rail. **Open** 11am-11pm Mon-Sat; noon-8pm Sun. **Food served** noon-5pm daily. **Credit** MC, V.
Back in pre-Victorian times, coalheavers were a big enough consumer group to be reckoned with and this baroque curiosity is named in their honour. And it's still something wonderful to behold. The intricate plasterwork, hanging banners, stained glass, marble reliefs, and (fake) period beams hark back to a heraldic past that may never have existed. The theatrical links are strong and the Wolf Room is named after the Wolf Club, a society for inhibited husbands founded by actor Edmund Kean. The cellar houses a dingy wine bar, but the real drinkers happily quaff their real ales (the Marston's Pedigree is particularly good here) and lagers on the usually packed ground floor. If you're male, wear a suit and work in the neighbourhood, chances are you'll already be a regular.
Babies and children admitted (until 6pm). Function room. Games (fruit machine). Tables outdoors (pavement). Vegetarian dishes. **Map 2/L7**

Cross Keys
31 Endell Street, WC2 (020 7836 5185). Covent Garden tube. **Open** 11am-11pm Mon-Sat; noon-10.30pm Sun. **Food served** noon-2.30pm daily. **Credit** MC, V.
A friendly traditional pub with wood panelling and a hardware shop's worth of copper and brass kettles, and kitchen utensils hanging from the ceiling. At odds with this is the pop memorabilia decorating the bar canopy, which includes signed pictures by The Beatles, Elvis and other less hardy perennial '60s popsters. Seating is comfortable and arranged in semi-booths, with another room upstairs that doubles as 'function suite' and lunchtime dining space. Customers are a complete cross-section of local life, with young pre-clubbers rubbing elbows with old codgers who have been coming here since it was a fruit and veg hangout. We even spotted a famous TV comedian mulling over a pint of real ale and *The Times* one lunchtime not too long ago.
Function room. Games (fruit machine). Tables outdoors (pavement). Vegetarian dishes. **Map 2/L6**

Crown & Anchor
22 Neal Street, WC2 (020 7836 5649). Covent Garden tube. **Open** 11am-11pm Mon-Sat; noon-10.30pm Sun. **Food served** noon-6.30pm daily. **Credit** AmEx, MC, V.
Identity crisis ahoy. Not too long ago this was one of Covent Garden's last remaining unmodernised boozers. Then the renovators came along and the ground floor was transformed into the look of the moment, light and pristine with violet painted pillars, minimal seating (a scattering of high stools) and a fashionably multicoloured backlit serving area. Which is fine, but you just know they're going to have to do it all over again in another couple of years. The real ales when we called in were Courage Best, Directors and John Smith's Cask, not an inspiring set, but they'll do. Upstairs is a room similarly decorated with its own bar (real ales here, too) set out with small tables for dining. Food includes home-made soup of the day, spicy chicken salad and Thai green chicken curry. There's a small but adequate wine list of 12, kicking off at just under a tenner a bottle. Customers on the early Friday evening we stopped by were a mix of tourist couples and after-hours office workers.
Babies and children admitted (restaurant). Function rooms. Restaurant (available for hire). Satellite TV. Vegetarian dishes. **Map 2/L6**

Detroit
35 Earlham Street, WC2 (020 7240 2662/ www.detroit-bar.com). Covent Garden tube. **Open** 5pm-midnight Mon-Sat. **Food served** 6-11pm Mon-Sat. **Credit** AmEx, MC, V.
A low-ceilinged, cave-like basement bar – with mud-brown walls and a warren of intimate spaces – may not appeal to the claustrophobic, but this funk-soundtracked journey into the bowels of Covent Garden is clearly a hit with Detroit's groovy young punters. Cheerful staff make cocktails comprising all the classics plus some overproofs. If you've an iron constitution try a Cherryade: absinthe, cherry vodka, sloe gin, lemon juice and Perrier (£10). There's a small wine selection (eight each of whites and reds, five champagnes), ranging from £12.75 a bottle to a ton for Krug Grand Cuvee, and bottled beers (Stella, Mash, Sagres) come in at around £3. Food's good (there's a restaurant attached) and a snack of deep fried calamari or chorizo is under a fiver.
Function rooms. Music (DJs 7.30pm Wed-Sat; free). Restaurant. Vegetarian dishes. **Map 2/L6**

Footlights Bar
Le Meridien Waldorf, Aldwych, WC2 (020 7836 2400/www.fortehotels.co.uk). Covent Garden or Temple tube. **Open/food served** 11am-11pm Mon-Sat. **Credit** AmEx, DC, MC, V.
It's unusual to find a West End hotel bar selling real ale, and although the prices are around 50% higher than in nearby pubs (keeps out the riff-raff), it's almost worth it to sip London Pride and Bass in such hallowed surroundings. Perhaps more appropriate would be to order from the rather fine range of whiskies, champagnes or cognacs. Not that the Footlights Bar is particularly opulent: the mirrors ringed with bulbs behind the bar bring to mind a star's dressing room (Danny La Rue, perhaps?), a feeling added to by the red banquettes and thick shag carpet. Customers tend to be groups of business people concluding a deal over a cocktail ('Any chance of a shag, Miss Brahms?') and American couples in checked trews convinced they've stumbled across a real London pub.
Disabled: toilet. Function rooms. Vegetarian dishes. **Map 4/M6**

Freedom Brewing Company
*41 Earlham Street, WC2 (020 7240 0606/
www.freedombrew.com). Covent Garden tube.* **Open**
11am-11pm Mon-Sat; noon-10.30pm Sun. **Food** noon-3pm,
6-10pm Mon-Sat; noon-6pm Sun. **Credit** AmEx, MC, V.
A spacious underground brew-bar, minimalist in style with
exposed brick vaulting and air ducts, a long metal serving
area running down one side and bench tables opposite. The
steel brewing vessels and pipework are exposed as a feature.
It's stark and slightly futuristic – Ikea meets Metropolis. Only
their own-brewed beers are sold: outstanding Pilsner, wheat
beer, pale ale, fruity Soho Red and the new Freedom Organic.
Expect to pay around £3 a pint or bottle. The wine list
features just six whites and six reds at roughly the same per
glass. There's also a screened-off restaurant space where
sterling but unexciting food such as Thai spiced mussels or
lamb steaks is served for prices under a tenner.
Restaurant. Vegetarian dishes. **Map 2/L6**

Freud
*198 Shaftesbury Avenue, WC2 (020 7240 9933). Covent
Garden or Tottenham Court Road tube.* **Open** 11am-
11pm Mon-Sat; noon-10.30pm Sun. **Food served** 11am-
4.30pm Mon-Sat; noon-4.30pm Sun. **Credit** MC, V.
A mercifully unspoilt old stager among West End style bars,
Freud is a tiny basement venue with granite walls and slate
table tops that help it retain an air of faintly Gothic romantic
gloom. By day there's a cool, languorous air to the place; in
the evening the bar heats up, playing host to a mixed,
youthful and vaguely arty set. It serves bottled beers (Budvar
and Beck's), 32 cocktails (starting around a fiver), and simple
bar food of the salad, sandwiches and cake variety. There's
also an impressive choice of around 30 decently priced coffees,
around half of which feature liqueurs. Ace toilets.
*Babies and children admitted. No-smoking tables (11am-
4.30pm). Vegetarian dishes.* **Map 1/L6**

Kudos
*10 Adelaide Street, WC2 (020 7379 4573/
www.kudosgroup.com). Embankment tube/Charing Cross
tube/rail.* **Open** 11am-11pm Mon-Sat; noon-10.30pm Sun.
Happy hour *downstairs* 4-6pm Mon-Fri; 6-8pm Sat, Sun
(both floors). **Food served** noon-6pm daily.
Credit AmEx, MC, V.
Regularly voted by the gay press as the best gay bar in
London, Kudos is a smart, busy boyz' venue for a pretty
party crowd. Upstairs, half the L-shaped room is given over
to tables and chairs, and there's a changing menu with
'campservice.' Downstairs is a video bar with two big screens
where booty-shaking is practically compulsory. Music is
predominantly pop trash and retro. Every Thursday is
CrushBar night; every time the featured artist is up on the
screen, bottles of Carling and Carlsberg and vodkas and
mixer are two for one. Other nights have similar good time
gimmicks. The crowd here is very cosmopolitan – if you had
a wall map and some tacks, you'd soon have most of the
globe covered.
*Music (music videos nightly; DJs 8pm Wed, Sat; free).
Vegetarian dishes.* **Map 2/L7**

Lamb & Flag
*33 Rose Street, WC2 (020 7497 9504). Covent Garden
or Leicester Square tube.* **Open** 11am-11pm Mon-Thur;
11am-10.45pm Fri, Sat; noon-10.30pm Sun. **Food served**
11am-3pm daily. **No credit cards.**
Formerly known as the Bucket of Blood (can't think why they
changed the name) because of an association with prize
fighters, the Lamb & Flag was built in 1623 and is practically
the last remaining wooden-framed building in London. The
fussy interior, all plaster and wood, dates from Georgian
times and the artefacts – including the 'Coutts is in/out' slider
sign, framed *London Evening Post* from 1744 and 'English
Cheese Pub Award 1983' – were added at various times since.
They're big on real ales, so look for up to four examples,
including Young's ordinary and Bombardier, as well as a
worthy selection of malt and specialist whiskies. Upstairs is
the John Dryden room (he was duffed up outside in 1679)
where you can get hearty British-style grub during the day
and early evening, but once the offices come out there's barely
room to lift your pint, let alone order and eat. The whole place
quietens down after about 9pm and reverts to being one of
the most charming pubs in the West End.
*Babies and children admitted (upstairs bar only). Music
(live jazz band Sun eve). No piped music or jukebox.
Satellite TV. Vegetarian dishes.* **Map 2/L7**

The Langley
*5 Langley Street, WC2 (020 7836 5005). Covent Garden
tube.* **Open** 4.30pm-1am Mon-Sat. **Food served** 6pm-
midnight daily. **Happy hour** 5-7pm Mon-Sat. **Credit**
AmEx, MC, V.
The Langley's discreet 'blink and you'll miss it' entrance may
suggest exclusivity; what you get is a huge, low-ceilinged
basement retro-bar with lots of exposed brick and breeze
blocks. Furniture is '70s retro and the grey walls are enlivened
with stripy, swirly designs that make you think Austin
Powers (although the intention was possibly Bridget Riley).
It's popular with a young casual crowd who are slightly too
hip for All Bar One but appreciate a good time. The drinks
menu has its fun too, with 'then cocktails' like Snowball,
Moscow Mule and Pina Colada, and 'now' drinks such as
Yeah Baby, Honey Krusher and Mint Julep (eh?!?). Oddly
enough they both cost the same. There's also wine, beer,
spirits and even Babycham. Appealingly, the bar food menu
includes mug of soup with soldiers, chicken and mushroom
pie, scampi and chips in a basket and fishfinger sandwich.
During happy hour (5-7pm) they are all £3.
*Disabled: toilet. Function room. Restaurant. Vegetarian
dishes.* **Map 2/L6**

Lobby Bar
*One Aldwych Hotel, 1 Aldwych, WC2 (020 7300 1000/
www.onealdwych.com). Covent Garden tube/Charing Cross
tube/rail.* **Open** 9am-11pm Mon-Sat; 10am-10.30pm Sun.
Credit AmEx, DC, MC, V.
One of London's better hotel bars, the Lobby is imaginatively
decorated with vast, ceiling-high arched windows and
ostentatious objets d'art. The chairs are enormous high-
backed affairs that make the sitters look like toddlers, but are
surprisingly comfortable. Staff are smartly dressed, efficient
and surprisingly friendly, customers are a mix of hotel guests,
City boys and theatre-goers. Cocktails – there are 18 Martinis
alone to choose from – and spirit-mixes are the thing to drink,
although wine and bottled beers are available. Prices are
slightly above the norm but about what you expect for an
over-styled five-star hotel bar. No food is served but then
many of the customers here are en route to one of the hotel's
two restaurants, Indigo and Axis.
*Babies and children admitted. Disabled: toilet. Function
rooms. Restaurants. Vegetarian dishes.* **Map 4/M7**

Lyceum Tavern
*354 Strand, WC2 (020 7836 7155). Covent Garden,
Embankment or Temple tube/Charing Cross tube/rail.*
Open 11.30am-11pm Mon-Sat; noon-10.30pm Sun. **Food
served** noon-4pm, 5-9pm Mon-Sat; noon-6pm Sun.
Credit MC, V.

Porterhouse. *See page 36.*

Great reasons to visit your local J D Wetherspoon

- Great food - served till 10pm
- Award winning wines
- Real ales & guest beers
- Amazing prices

BARKING
BARNET
BEXLEY
BRENT
BROMLEY
CAMDEN
CITY OF LONDON
CROYDON
DAGENHAM
EALING
ENFIELD
FULHAM
GREENWICH
HACKNEY
HAMMERSMITH
HAVERING
HARINGEY
HARROW
HILLINGDON
HOUNSLOW
ISLINGTON
LAMBERTH
LEWISHAM
MERTON
NEWHAM
REDBRIDGE
SOUTHWARK
SUTTON
TOWER HAMLETS
WALTHAM FOREST
WANDSWORTH
WESTMINSTER

With over 480 freehouses across the UK check out your nearest local @
www.jdwetherspoon.co.uk

A popular Sam Smith's pub at the Aldwych end of the Strand, slightly overshadowed by the neighbouring Wellington. It has two distinct parts: downstairs is the pub proper, with a useful row of wooden cubicles running down one side, a long raised bar opposite and a small games area (with dartboard, TV and tables) at the rear. Here you'll find a cosmopolitan mix of office and blue-collar workers, younger tourists and after-work couples. Middle-aged tourists and senior office workers tend to head upstairs to the first-floor bar and 'restaurant' with its beige and cream patterned paper, leather-bound armchairs and sofas arranged casually around low tables. Food tends to be tourist-orientated pub food and (bearing in mind its limits) has been declared pretty good. *Babies and children admitted. Games (darts). Tables outdoors (pavement). Vegetarian dishes.* **Map 2/L7**

Maple Leaf

41 Maiden Lane, WC2 (020 7240 2843). Covent Garden tube. **Open** 11am-11pm Mon-Sat; noon-10.30pm Sun. **Food served** noon-9.30pm daily. **Credit** AmEx, DC, MC, V.

Offering a theme of Canada and all things Canadian, the Maple Leaf attracts a mishmash of local office workers in suits and guys and gals 'on the razzle up west', with a smattering of Canadian ex-pats. The decor borders on pastiche, with Native American totems, a menacing carved 'Red Indian', a framed Mountie's uniform and a moose head. The beers are the usual Scottish & Newcastle standards with 'real' Directors and Theakston Best, and the added Canadian-ness of Molson on tap and in bottle. The multi-screen TVs play sport endlessly and it's more likely than not to be ice hockey. Just don't expect any *South Park*. *Babies and children (until 5pm, restaurant only). Games (fruit machine, quiz machine). Restaurant. Satellite TVs. Vegetarian dishes.* **Map 2/L7**

Marquess of Anglesey

39 Bow Street, WC2 (020 7240 3216). Covent Garden tube. **Open** 11am-11pm Mon-Sat; noon-10.30pm Sun. **Food served** noon-10pm Mon-Sat; noon-9pm Sun. **Credit** AmEx, MC, V.

A big cream-coloured corner pub opposite the Royal Opera House, the Marquis of Anglesey appeals to two distinct groups. The ground floor with its square pillars, mirrors and pictures of Covent Garden's theatrical past is where the after-work drinkers and tourists congregate, downing decent pints of Young's ordinary and Pilsner or sipping from the extensive and very comprehensive wine list Young's has introduced to all their pubs. Then there's the upstairs, which is principally a quite decent pub-restaurant serving a mix of freshly cooked specials and fish and chip type stand-bys, plus a small but comfortable seated area at the front with the odd potted palm tree and a view towards the Piazza. Seating is at a premium, especially during the 9pm rush that occurs each evening when the orchestra from one of the neighbouring theatres piles in for an interval drink. *Babies and children admitted (restaurant only). Function room. Games (fruit machines). No-smoking area (restaurant). Restaurant. Vegetarian dishes.* **Map 2/L6**

Marquis of Granby

51 Chandos Place, WC2 (020 7836 7657). Covent Garden tube/Charing Cross tube/rail. **Open** noon-11pm Mon-Sat; noon-10.30pm Sun. **Food served** noon-5pm daily. **Credit** MC, V.

Considering its proximity to the commuter stampeding grounds around Charing Cross, the Marquis of Granby is a pretty decent boozer. A wedge-shaped pub situated between Charing Cross nick and the post office, it boasts carved wooden partitions, glorious glasswork, and two of the biggest and brashest Victorian gas heaters this side of *Gormenghast*. Unlikely as it may sound, the clientele tends towards the arty. On a recent visit we spotted a couple of booksellers, a comic novelist and a brace of stage-hands from the Coliseum, next door. You can usually expect at least one stand-out beer among the four on hand-pump and while a companion found his Grolsch 'very well kept, offering up all those complex lager flavours'. Quite. The Timothy Taylor Landlord was better. The bargain-priced Sunday roast is said to be the bee's-knees. *Babies and children admitted (upstairs, until 6pm). Function room. Restaurant. Vegetarian dishes.* **Map 2/L7**

Navajo Joe's

34 King Street, WC2 (020 7240 4008). Covent Garden tube. **Open/food served** noon-11pm Mon-Sat; noon-10.30pm Sun. **Happy hour** 5.30-8.30pm Mon-Sat. **Credit** AmEx, DC, MC, V.

There's some sort of concocted story about a noble American Indian who's been robbed of his land by the white man and forced to open a bar in Covent Garden, but we don't believe a word of it. Although not under Native American ownership, Joe's is still a classy joint. A metal balcony runs the length of one wall, overlooking a steel-fronted serving area with a copper-topped bar, standing in front of a back-lit, ceiling-high (and the ceiling is certainly high) display of bottles. Further decoration includes three video art screens, a bizarre metal cow's head sculpture and oil paintings depicting a couple of Native Americans. They claim the largest selection of mescals and tequilas outside Mexico (getting on for 300), and their rums are rising. Otherwise it's bottled American-style beers, wines and cocktails. The food menu carries on the South-western theme with the likes of quesadillas, tortillas and burgers. The staff are young and suitably eager and, on the whole, pretty helpful. Customers tend to be well heeled, young and pretty loud. *Babies and children admitted. Function room. Restaurant. Vegetarian dishes.* **Map 2/L7**

Opera Tavern

23 Catherine Street, WC2 (020 7379 9832). Covent Garden tube. **Open** noon-11pm Mon-Sat; noon-10.30pm Sun. **Food served** noon-3pm, 5-8pm Mon-Sat. **Credit** AmEx, MC, V.

This small friendly pub was built in 1879 and offers a fire in winter and wall-to-wall opera memorabilia all year round. The floor has recently been restored to its, er, Victorian glory and the carpet whipped out, but the seats – particularly in the tiny raised area at the back – are comfortable and the beige painted walls and red upholstery help create a warm atmosphere. There are usually three real ales on offer (Bass, Adnam's Best and Greene King IPA when we last passed through), as well as the usual lagers and suchlike, and the small but wide-ranging wine list suits all but the most picky tastes. Fairly decent pub grub is served during peak hours. *Games (darts, fruit machine, pool table, quiz machine). Satellite TV. Vegetarian dishes.* **Map 2/L6**

PJ's Grill

30 Wellington Street, WC2 (020 7240 7529). Covent Garden tube. **Open/food served** noon-midnight Mon-Sat; 11.30am-4pm Sun. **Credit** AmEx, DC, MC, V.

As the name implies this is actually a restaurant but there's a busy bar at the front that non-diners are encouraged to use. The look of the place – mahogany panelling, dark wood floor, rows of large mirrors and sporting paraphernalia on the walls – brings to mind a Boston gentleman's club, and service is suitably on the ball. The house champagne is something of a

bargain at under £20 a bottle and quite palatable, so no wonder it sounded like Gunfight at the OK Corral time on the early evening we visited. Bar snacks are available (own-made soups, salads, etc) or you can head down into the restaurant for an upmarket grill. The atmosphere is good, especially when the bar is buzzing after work, and it's a great place to star spot; just remember that it's rude to stare.
Babies and children admitted. Restaurant. Tables outdoors (pavement). Vegetarian dishes. Map 2/L7

La Perla
28 Maiden Lane, WC2 (020 7240 7400/ www.pacifico-laperla.com). Covent Garden tube/Charing Cross tube/rail. **Open** noon-11pm Mon-Sat; noon-10.30pm Sun. **Food served** noon-midnight Mon-Sat; noon-10.30pm Sun. **Happy hour** 4-7pm daily. **Credit** AmEx, MC, V.
A bright and busy 'cantina' that aims to recreate Mexico in Maiden Lane – only without the flies. The colour scheme utilises the old standby of beige and sand, and there's enough bare wood around the place to build a ranch. Lured no doubt by the promise of multifarious tequila and mescal (almost 50 different types), reasonably priced cocktails and Latino music, the customers tend to be young, casual and pretty well heeled. Those who know about these things rate their selection of whiskies and bourbons, and drinkers who relish bottled beers chilled to within a millimetre of their lives are in for a treat. Food is Tex-Mex and grilled fish.
Babies and children admitted (restaurant only). Restaurant. Specialities: Mexican beers, 70 tequilas. Vegetarian dishes. Map 2/L7

Porterhouse
21-22 Maiden Lane, WC2 (020 7836 9931/ www.porterhousebrewco.com). Covent Garden tube/ Charing Cross tube/rail. **Open** 11am-11pm Mon-Sat; noon-10.30pm Sun. **Food served** noon-3pm, 5-9pm Mon-Fri; noon-9pm Sat; noon-5pm Sun. **Credit** DC, MC, V.
Oliver Hughes and his partners spent £7.5 million turning a nondescript Covent Garden office building into a multi-zoned bar you'd not be ashamed to bring your priest and his girlfriend to. Dark wood and copper fittings give it the feel of an upmarket Irish hotel bar, but quirky touches like an open-gutted mechanical clock, iron staircases and an abundance of nooks and crannies, add some class. The chief selling point is their range of nine own-brewed beers imported from Dublin. Although not 'cask-conditioned' (the Irish aren't good on 'real ale'), the beers are at least unpasteurised and the best knock the spots off most of what London's other brew bars are offering. Stand-outs are the slightly salty Oyster Stout (made with real molluscs), the hoppy Temple Brau and flavour-packed, high alcohol An Brainblasta (seven per cent abv). Bottled beers include British and Belgian specialities. Although it's a bar not a restaurant, the food's good. Expect steaks, raw oysters, own-made vegetable soup and pasta. Just don't expect the staff to know anything about the beers, especially those from Belgium.
Disabled: lift; toilet. Function room. Music (live bands 8pm Wed-Sat, Irish band 3-7pm Sun; free). Satellite TV (Irish sports, large screen). Tables outdoors (pavement). Vegetarian dishes. Map 2/L7

Porters Bar
16 Henrietta Street, WC2 (020 7836 6466). Covent Garden tube. **Open** noon-11pm Mon-Sat; noon-10.30pm Sun. **Food served** noon-10pm daily. **Credit** AmEx, DC, MC, V.
A separate entity from Porters restaurant next door, this is a dark red, cream and lilac painted space appealing to those looking for something more upmarket than a pub but not as

flash as a style bar. In the year between visits we've noticed a narrowing of real ale choice to Boddington's (never really number one for purists) and the ubiquitous London Pride. Most of the noisy young drinkers who packed the place on the Tuesday evening we called in were drinking wine and cocktails with a healthy number of besuited men quaffing bottled lager and Hoegaarden. There's a quieter basement dining and drinking space with large refectory-like tables but it suffers from a constant procession of people traipsing through on their way to the toilets.
Restaurant. Tables outdoors (pavement). TV. Vegetarian dishes. Map 2/L7

Punch & Judy
40 The Market, WC2 (020 7379 0923). Covent Garden tube. **Open** 11am-11pm Mon-Sat; noon-10.30pm Sun. **Food served** 11am-7pm Mon-Sat; noon-5pm Sun. **Credit** AmEx, DC, MC, V.
One of London's busiest boozers, it doesn't help that the pub's two bars are separated by a long staircase. Downstairs is a stone-flagged cellar bar with a long thin serving area taking up almost half of the room. Upstairs the square bar is Regency-style, with a balcony looking out over Covent Garden Piazza towards St Paul's church. It's a fine view but spoilt by perpetual overcrowding. International backpackers have taken over from office suits as the core clientele and if you're interested in sharing stories of loose bowels in Lagos and dope smoking in Dahab, then here's your chance. Drinks are the usual mix of lagers and bitters. Gourmets of pre-prepared pub grub will appreciate the likes of cottage pie and vegetable curry.
Babies and children admitted (designated area, until 8pm). Jukebox. No-smoking area (downstairs). Tables outdoors (courtyard, terrace). TV. Vegetarian dishes. Map 2/L7

Retox Bar
The Piazza, Russell Street, WC2 (020 7240 5330 /www.retoxbar.com). Covent Garden tube. **Open** 5-11pm Mon-Wed; 5pm-1am Thur; 5pm-3am Fri, Sat. **Food served** 5-11pm Mon-Sat. **Admission** £5 after 9.30pm Fri, Sat. **Credit** AmEx, MC, V.
This newly opened basement bar is a classy, good-looking joint at the eastern end of Covent Garden Piazza. There's liquid art on the stone walls, the floor's stone, and the sweet soul music was too loud for the barman to hear what we were ordering. It was also too loud for us to hear him say what turned out to be 'Sorry I missed that, can you try again?' We're told it's owned by the people behind Tiger Lil's, the DIY diners, and with characteristic panache, they started out by offering six 'bespoke individual drinking programmes'. The idea is that you get the ingredients on a tray and you mix your own cocktails. Whether this idea survives remains to be seen. Ready-made cocktails are also available, as are standard beers, with Hoegaarden and Leffe Blonde on tap. Customers tend to be young, casually dressed and loud. Well, they'd have to be, wouldn't they?
Music (DJs Tue-Sat). Vegetarian dishes. Map 2/L6

Retro Bar
2 George Court, off the Strand, WC2 (020 7321 2811). Charing Cross tube/rail. **Open** noon-11pm Mon-Fri; 5-11pm Sat; 5-10.30pm Sun. **Credit** MC, V.
Tucked away in an alleyway just off the Strand, this former backstreet boozer is the very antithesis to the stereotypical idea of a gay bar. It's an offshoot of the **Popstarz** (*see p50*) empire, and consequently is full of people who are gay but obviously feel different – not from straight people, but from the majority of other gay people. The theme as well as the clientele is indie-chic, with punks, Gallagher-types and

Retox Bar

glitterites mixing with the odd after-work suit and young tweedie. The main ground-floor bar is decorated with portraits of Boy George, Spandau Ballet and ABBA on sand-coloured walls, with a tiny stage (room enough for one Jarvis Cocker-thin performer only), wood laminate flooring and a mishmash of pub furniture. Upstairs is a smaller room where loud up-to-date alternative music attracts an even younger crowd. Drinks are the gay bar norm (though no emphasis on cocktails here) and in our experience the staff are about the friendliest in town.

Eurovision and cabaret night monthly. Games (fruit machine, quiz machine). Jukebox. Music (DJs most nights; karaoke 9pm Wed; free). Quiz (9pm Tue; £1 to play). **Map 2/L7**

Roadhouse

The Piazza, Covent Garden WC2 (020 7240 6001/ www.roadhouse.co.uk). Covent Garden tube. **Open** 5.30pm-3am Mon-Sat; 4pm-1am last Sun of month. **Food served** 5.30pm-1am Mon-Sat; 5.30-10pm Sun. **Happy hour** 5.30-10.30pm Mon-Wed; 5.30-8.30pm Thur, Sat; 5.30-7.30pm Fri. **Credit** AmEx, MC, V.
Love it or loathe it, Roadhouse is a phenomenon: a dedicated party venue, the atmosphere's loud and frenzied, and it's inevitably packed (queues run literally around the block at weekends). Live acts appear every night: mostly covers bands, but also original artists. House DJs are augmented by radio names and play a non-stop mix of dance music from the '60s to the present day. The room itself is decorated with flash lighting effects and original 1950s USA signs and logos. A couple of Harley Davidson motorbikes hang above two bars and there's even a midget helicopter 'flying' over the stage. It can get a little cheesy, but hey! isn't that the way with parties? An American railroad diner car serves burgers, fajitas and the like, while the three bars serve mainly bottled beers and cocktails at prices that are pretty keen during happy hours, but standard CG the rest of the time.

Disabled: toilet, wheelchair assistance to basement. Games (pinball machines). Music (bands 11pm nightly; admission £4 after 9pm Mon-Wed (ladies free); £6 after 9pm Thur; £10 after 9pm Fri; £7 7.30-9pm, £10 after 9pm Sat). Vegetarian dishes. **Map 2/L7**

Round House

1 Garrick Street, WC2 (020 7836 9838). Covent Garden or Leicester Square tube. **Open** 11am-11pm Mon-Sat; noon-10.30pm Sun. **Food served** 11am-10pm Mon-Sat; noon-9.30pm Sun. **Credit** AmEx, MC, V.
Not so much round as crescent shaped, this TJ Bernard ale house has something of the feel of a goldfish bowl about it, with customers exposed to the gaze of passers-by through large windows. Conversely, it's also a great place for people watching. In summer the large screen doors fold back and the pub spills out with drinkers and public getting in each other's way. An impressive selection of real ales (mostly Scottish-Courage staples like Directors and Theakston, but the occasional goodie, too), wheat beers, bottled Belgian specialities, Czech lagers and suchlike, is wasted as everybody seems intent on guzzling bog-standard lagers. Food is the usual chain pub ale and beef pie stuff. You're probably better off nipping over to Tesco Metro opposite.

Babies and children admitted (until 7pm). Games (fruit machine). Vegetarian dishes. **Map 2/L7**

The Spot

29-30 Maiden Lane, WC2 (020 7379 5900). Covent Garden tube/Charing Cross tube/rail. **Open** noon-1am Mon-Sat; 6pm-1am Sun. **Admission** £5 after 9pm Fri,

Sat; £5 after 8pm Sun. **Happy hour** noon-7pm Mon-Sat. **Food served** noon-8pm Mon-Sat. **Credit** AmEx, MC, V.
Divided up into four spaces, the Spot has recently been done-up and the larger bars now have a strange neo-classical look about them – all nymphs and what-have-you. That and the extravagant chandelier in the oddly rectangular Oval Room brings to mind an English 18th-century country house. The loud popular-club music that permeates the place does its best to dispel visions of Capability Brown, as do the thrusting young things who move along to it. Our favourite bar is to the right of the front entrance, with its simple white-washed stone walls and a cream tiled floor. Because it gets so busy in here, seating is kept to a minimum, so grab a stool or expect to stand. Draught beers are pub standards – Caffreys, Guinness, etc – but cocktails and bottled beers seem to be what everyone's drinking and prices are at the bottom end of the Covent Garden scale.

Babies and children admitted (in restaurant). Function room. Music (DJs 7pm Thur-Sun, live music 9.30pm Sun; admission charges as above). Restaurant. Satellite TV (big screen). Vegetarian dishes. **Map 2/L7**

La Tartine

14 Garrick Street, WC2 (020 7379 1531). Covent Garden or Leicester Square tube. **Open** noon-11pm Mon-Fri. **Food served** noon-10.45pm Mon-Fri. **Credit** AmEx, MC, V.
An upmarket wine bar in the cellar of the L'Estaminet restaurant that is something of a Rugby Union stronghold – match action photographs line the tangerine-painted walls. The average customer is in his thirties or early forties, male, dressed in a handmade suit, and is probably accompanied by a stylish woman wearing the latest Bond Street fashion. In all the times we've called in, we've never had anybody give way to us on the stairs, which either says a lot about the self-confidence of La Tartine regulars or the low self-esteem of our reviewers. The wine list is quite extensive and surprisingly reasonably priced, with bottled Kronenbourg 1664 available for yobbos. Food, as you would expect, is good, French-flavoured and decent value for money.

Babies and children admitted (restaurant only). Function room. No-smoking area (restaurant). Restaurant. Vegetarian dishes. **Map 2/L7**

Also in the area...

All Bar One 19 Henrietta Street, WC2 (020 7557 7941).
Belgo Centraal 50 Earlham Street, WC2 (020 7813 2233).
Café Rouge 34 Wellington Street, WC2 (020 7836 0998).
Champagne Charlie's (Davys) 17 The Arches, Villiers Street, WC2 (020 7930 7737).
Dôme 32-33 Long Acre, WC2 (020 7379 8650).
Faun & Firkin 18 Bear Street, WC2 (020 7321 0355).
O'Neill's 40 Great Queen Street, WC2 (020 7269 5911); 14 New Row, WC2 (020 7557 9831); 166-170 Shaftesbury Avenue, WC2 (020 7379 3735).
Rat & Parrot 63-66 St Martin's Lane, WC2 (020 7836 2990).
Savoy Tup 2 Savoy Street, WC2 (020 7836 9738).
Tappit Hen (Davys) 5 William IV Street, WC2 (020 7836 9839).
Walkabout Inn 11 Henrietta Street and 33 Maiden Lane, WC2 (020 7379 5555).

Earl's Court

Blackbird

209 Earl's Court Road, SW5 (020 7835 1855). Earl's Court tube. **Open** 11am-11pm Mon-Sat; noon-10.30pm Sun. **Food served** noon-8.45pm daily. **Credit** MC, V.
Short on soul but big on buzz, this is primarily a pub of convenience, benefiting from a location right opposite Earl's Court tube station. It's certainly handy but it can get a little noisy as the din at the bar never quite drowns out the thunderous rumble of traffic outside. It's a locals' local favoured by Earl's Court residents rather than the area's more famously transient population. Chances are they're more appreciative of the selection of real ales, which includes Fuller's London Pride and Chiswick Bitter. Huge windows and dark wood fittings mean the place is handsome enough: solid partitions even provide a degree of privacy (albeit even at the expense of clear access to the bar), while the low-hanging lights are elegant but leave you feeling slightly exposed. The pub's one concession to modernity is the bar stools – an unusual design, triangular like a bicycle seat but without the same requirement of balance.
Games (fruit machines). TV. Vegetarian dishes.

King's Head

17 Hogarth Place, SW5 (020 7244 5931). Earl's Court tube. **Open** noon-11pm Mon-Sat; noon-10.30pm Sun. **Food served** noon-3pm, 5-8pm Mon-Wed; noon-6pm Thur-Sun. **Credit** DC, MC, V.
Hogarth Place is tucked mid-way along a quiet residential side street, a world away from the bustle of Earl's Court. You almost wonder where did everybody go? Push open the door of the King's Head and you've got your answer. Vibrant and an obvious local favourite, it's a pleasingly down-to-earth local. There's no decorative tack, just unreconstructed pub with a minimum of fuss to lend the ideal measure of reassurance for workers keen to unwind with a pint of Guinness or London Pride. Food is sturdy pub grub at its most basic: burgers, pies and baguettes, little else. Evenings can be male-dominated and loud, but the atmosphere is convivial enough. Arrive early and nab one of two low-lying leather sofas (prized alcove spots close to the gas fire), else resign yourself to leaning at the freestanding wooden bar – a thoughtful addition for when seats run out.
Babies and children admitted (until 5pm). Games (fruit machines, video game). Satellite TV (big screen). Vegetarian dishes.

Prince of Teck

161 Earl's Court Road, SW5 (020 7373 3107). Earl's Court tube. **Open** 11am-11pm Mon-Sat; noon-10.30pm Sun. **Food served** 11am-3pm, 6-9pm Mon-Sat; noon-3pm Sun. **Credit** MC, V.
'G'day. Welcome to Oz,' reads the lobby notice, hanging just above a vending stand crammed with copies of *New Zealand News UK*. Inside, it's accessorised with a stuffed, flea-bitten 'roo atop the bar, dunnie doors labelled 'Sheilas' and 'Bruces', and wall-to-wall posters of Oz scrawled with thick black marker-pen: 'Aussie, Aussie, Aussie, Oi! Oi! Oi!', 'Surfers Go', and suchlike. Do we detect a theme here? But young, raucous, stuffy and carpetless, this is above all a rough-hewn drinking den. Most punters are out to get lashed and there's no food to slow the consumption of draught Fosters and bottled Toohey's or VB (there is Young's for those who prefer their beers with taste). Take a detour upstairs, though, and the Princess lounge bar seems to have been transplanted from another pub. Mellow, fusty, ever so

quiet and absolutely English, right down to the giant snaps of Prince Charles and the Queen Mum pulling pints. *EastEnders* upstairs or *Home And Away* down, take your pick, but either way the Teck is thoroughly deserving of its alternative appellation, the 'Prince of Tack'.
Babies and children admitted (upstairs bar). Games (fruit machine). Jukebox. Restaurant. Satellite TV (big screen). Vegetarian dishes.

Troubadour

265 Old Brompton Road, SW5 (020 7370 1434). Earl's Court tube. **Open** 9am-midnight daily. **Admission** free-£5 (depending on performance). **Food served** 9am-11.30pm daily. **No credit cards.**
A bit of a survivor, the Troubadour is an odd arty/intellectual café-bar that's been around since the '50s. A dark and slightly brooding exterior disguises an interior of dishevelled charm and enforced intimacy, tiny and narrow with a muddle of mismatched tables. Helpful staff are quick to hand out menus, although you're not obliged to eat. Many do though, enticed by the delicate pastries heaped on the counter and a menu of satisfying hot dishes from home-made soup and burger and chips to much lighter Mediterranean fare. Wine is available by glass or carafe and there's bottled beer (including Budvar). Over the years the Troubadour has nurtured some famous creative talents: Bob Dylan once gave an impromptu rendition of 'Blowin' in the Wind', while Charlie Watts used to be resident drummer. We can't imagine where there was space for a band, but Troubadour's current expansion into a full club will change all that. Effortlessly atmospheric.
Babies and children admitted. Comedy (Tue). Function room. Games (board games). Music (jazz Thur, folk and blues Fri). No-smoking area (in restaurant). Poetry (Mon). Restaurant. Tables outdoors (garden, pavement). Vegetarian dishes.

Warwick Arms

160 Warwick Road, W14 (020 7603 3560). Earl's Court or High Street Kensington tube. **Open** noon-11pm Mon-Sat; 10am-10.30pm Sun. **Food served** noon-3pm, 6-9pm Mon-Fri; 10am-4pm Sun. **Credit** AmEx, MC, V.
Despite boasting London's answer to the Monte Carlo Rally most of the day, the brief frenetic length of Warwick Road that links Kensington High Street and Cromwell Road can boast three above-average boozers. Of these, for us the Warwick just has the edge. Built in 1823, it's been sympathetically renovated – lots of exposed brick and woodwork – and retains many of the original features, including an alcove now dedicated to WB Yeats that's perfect for clandestine meetings (if you can bear the judgmental gaze from a picture of the poet). Another plus is that it's a Fuller's pub with its full range of ales. There's freshly cooked pub grub (fish and chips, pies, baked potatoes) but if you're really hungry we'd recommend nipping into the excellent Iranian restaurant next door.
Games (fruit machine). No-smoking area. Restaurant. Tables outdoors (courtyard, pavement). TV. Vegetarian dishes.

Also in the area...

Dôme 194-196 Earl's Court Road, SW5 (020 7835 2200).
O'Neill's 326 Earl's Court Road, SW5 (020 7244 5921).
Rat & Parrot 123 Earl's Court Road, SW5 (020 7370 2760).
Richmond (It's A Scream) 180-184 Earl's Court Road, SW5 (020 7244 5941).

Fitzrovia

Bar Madrid

4 Winsley Street, W1 (020 7436 4649/
www.latenightlondon.co.uk). Oxford Circus tube. **Open**
4.30pm-3am Mon-Sat. **Food served** 7pm-3am Mon-Sat.
Happy hour 4.30-9pm Mon-Sat. **Credit** AmEx, MC, V.
You've got to work for your drink at Bar Madrid. The cavernous,
but light and bright, curving basement room doubles as a
makeshift dance studio with a Brazilian carnival every Monday,
salsa classes Wednesday, free lessons for beginners Thursday,
and anything goes Friday and Saturday. There are two bars,
where a lack of seating keeps patrons on their feet. Party spirit
cocktails go for £2.80 during an extended happy hour, plus there
are bottled beers – although a disappointing absence of Spanish/
Latin American brands. A tapas area was quiet when we visited,
but then the food didn't look that appealing. The mixed crowd
is intent on having a good time without being overly rowdy. A
great singles venue, albeit not one for the inhibited.
Function room. Music (DJs nightly, live Mon). Restaurant.
Satellite TV. Specialities: cocktails. Vegetarian dishes.
Map 1/J6

Bradley's Spanish Bar

42-44 Hanway Street, W1 (020 7636 0359). Tottenham
Court Road tube. **Open** 11am-11pm Mon-Sat; 2-10.30pm
Sun. **Credit** MC, V.
It's only several paces off Oxford Street, but the apparent
muggers' paradise that is Hanway Street presumably scares
off casual trade leaving Bradley's to a band of happy regulars
delighting in their well kept little secret. A Fitzrovian
institution, its tiny, flock-wallpapered ground-floor bar is
crammed with bullfight memorabilia, Barcelona FC pennants
and a busted-up flamenco guitar. Hurrah! Because the real
musical deal is found in the basement, which as far as we
know has the last vinyl jukebox in London. An altar of
musical bliss, it holds a mix of forgotten classics and feel-
good booze anthems, all of which conspire to affect a sense of
timelessness in the windowless, cavern-like environment.
Beer-wise the accent is on the Spanish stuff, including the
standards (Sol, Dos Equis, San Miguel) as well as Cruzcampo,
and when we visited sangria was on tap at £2 a half.
Jukebox. TV. **Map 7/K6**

Bricklayer's Arms

31 Gresse Street, W1 (020 7636 5593). Tottenham Court
Road tube. **Open** 11am-11pm Mon-Sat; noon-10.30pm Sun.
Food served noon-2.30pm, 5.30-8.30pm Mon-Thur.
Credit MC, V.
A strange one, this. Tucked into a seeming dead-end nook
between Oxford Street and Tottenham Court Road, on first
appearances it appears to be a poky little smoky old man's
pub. But beyond the cramped and dowdy front room, there's
a more boisterous back room where a group of local types
were enjoying a game of darts on our most recent visit.
Investigate further and upstairs is a spacious lounge bar with
a big fireplace and young 'uns reclining on sofas. This is more
like it. It's a Samuel Smith's pub, so the beer isn't to everyone's
taste, but the decent food is a visible draw – spinach wraps,
Thai lemon chicken, mushroom stroganoff, all £5 to £7.
Games (darts, fruit machine). Vegetarian dishes.
Map 1/K5

Champion

12-13 Wells Street, W1 (020 7323 1228). Oxford Circus
tube. **Open** 11.30am-11pm Mon-Sat; noon-10.30pm Sun.
Food served noon-2.30pm, 5.30-8.30pm Mon-Fri; noon-
3pm Sat, Sun. **Credit** MC, V.
How good are you at identifying Victorian heroes and
heroines? Florence Nightingale. Lamp lady. WG Grace?
Cricketer. Captain Webb? First man to swim the Channel (we
just looked that one up). Earl of Mayo? Uh, give up. Alright,
it's not the most engrossing of pub pastimes but the large
stained-glass panels depicting these characters are beautiful
to look at. Add a solid central horseshoe bar and Tiffany-
esque hanging lamps, comfortable seats, some around a
blazing fire, and the ground-floor saloon is traditionalist pub
perfection. Pity about the over-loud music and games
machines though. Mercifully free of office crowds it's
pleasantly quiet at lunchtime, possibly because the very basic
grub is less than enticing. No matter, their loss. And we just
looked up the Earl of Mayo – a viceroy of India, fatally
stabbed by a convict. So there you go.
Function room. Games (darts, fruit machine, quiz
machine). No-smoking area. Restaurant. Tables outdoors
(pavement). Vegetarian dishes. **Map 1/J5**

Cock Tavern

27 Great Portland Street, W1 (020 7631 5002). Oxford
Circus tube. **Open** 11.30am-11pm Mon-Sat; noon-10.30pm
Sun. **Food served** noon-2.30pm, 6-8.30pm Mon-Thur;
noon-2.30pm Fri; noon-6pm Sat, Sun. **Credit** MC, V.
Edwardian makeovers are two-a-penny these days, but with
its cloister-like serving area, attractively tiled floor and Gothic
fireplace, the Cock's more convincing than most. Both floors
of what's a pretty large pub were absolutely heaving with
under-thirties on our midweek visit, possibly due to its
proximity to Oxford Street. Bearing this in mind, ladies might
want to take advantage of the 'Chelsea clips' under every table
to keep their handbags safe. How typically considerate of
Samuel Smith's. Prices for food and drink (Sam Smith's ales
and Ayingerbräu lager) are reasonable, particularly for the
area. Ignore the dour upstairs bar with its unappealing Happy
Eater-type fare (sausages and chips, breaded cod), and order
the ploughmans at the downstairs bar; it's advertised as
'probably the best in the world', which it isn't, but it is good
with no less than ten cheeses to choose from.
Games (fruit machines). Tables outdoors (pavement). TV.
Vegetarian dishes. **Map 1/J5**

Crown & Sceptre

86 Great Titchfield Street, W1 (020 7307 9971).
Oxford Circus tube. **Open** 11am-11pm Mon-Fri; noon-
11pm Sat; noon-10.30pm Sun. **Food served** noon-3pm
Mon-Fri; noon-4pm Sat, Sun. **Credit** AmEx, MC, V.
A corner-site pub with a high ceiling and huge glass windows
overlooking the densely restauranted junction of Great
Titchfield and Foley. It's uncluttered, airy and light, with an
elegant old wooden central serving area, simple wooden
furniture and the odd leather couch. We like it. Lunchtimes
it's packed with local workers, most dining off what is a rather
limited menu (burgers, sausage and mash, fish and chips). In
the evenings the crowd gets younger and the volume goes up,
with a backtrack of blasted dance music. Major sporting
events are shown on the big screen. A range of wines are
served by the glass, and standard nitrokegs are supplemented
by a couple of real ales (Bass and London Pride).
Games (video games). Satellite TV. Vegetarian dishes.
Map 1/J5

Fitzroy Tavern

16 Charlotte Street, W1 (020 7580 3714). Goodge
Street tube. **Open** 11am-11pm Mon-Sat; noon-10.30pm
Sun. **Food served** noon-2.30pm, 6.30-9.30pm Mon-Thur,
Sat, Sun; noon-2.30pm Fri. **Credit** AmEx, MC, V.
The Fitzroy trades heavily on its glory days as London's
leading bohemian hangout from the 1920s to the '50s.

London crawling: Cocktail cruise

If you thought hotel bars were the exclusive domain of tourists and besuited corporate parties, think again: London's 'boutique' hotels provide some of the hippest hangouts around. At the same time, a few old favourites continue to supply a more refined night out than any beer-and-crisps boozer could ever hope to offer. So if you've tired of tobacco-stained locals, or of cramped, noisy DJ bars, put your glad-rags on and sample the louche life of the lobbyist.

Start at the Sanderson hotel, Ian Schrager's latest bit of London chic-ery. Any brave enough to face down the male model doormen can be wowed at the magnificent **Long Bar**, where tall bar stools return stares with Dali-esque eyes stencilled on their backs. Cocktails are magnificent, but if you need to ask the prices you can't afford them; this is, after all, a bar belonging to a hotel where the penthouse suite goes for £2,500 a night.

A block distant, **Oscar** is the light, airy lobby bar of the Charlotte Street Hotel. It's dominated by a zinc-topped serving counter from behind which a bust of Edward VII (husband of Queen Charlotte, after whom the street's named) keeps a watchful eye. The atmosphere is one of unostentatious luxury with plushly upholstered armchairs and refreshments in the shape of an extensive cocktail list (starting at £8.50), afternoon teas and bottled continental beers.

Exit Oscar, head down Percy Street, cross Tottenham Court Road and you'll find **mybar**, the feng-shui-ed bar belonging to the Conran-designed myhotel. Pass through the narrow front room and lounge in the back where sculptural sofas grouped around the fireplace resemble a Conran Shop window display. Early evenings, the place fills with style-conscious local workers soothing away end-of-day tensions with tipples from the heady cocktail menu: try a Brain Shooter (Baileys, Frangelico and Southern Comfort, £5).

A brief, head-clearing walk south to Monmouth Street brings you to **Brasserie Max**, accessed through the stately lobby of the Covent Garden Hotel. A sister establishment to Oscar, this large bar has an identical metal-topped bar, but dark wood panelling, upholstered chairs and tricorn hat-shaped lampshades create a country house look. Customers here are as likely to be sipping glasses of draught lager (£2.70) as the more expensive cocktails (£8 and up).

Continue south along Monmouth Street to St Martin's Lane and the impossibly trendy hotel of the same name. Walk purposefully through the sweeping white lobby to the **Light Bar**. Priority is given to residents but if you arrive early, are dressed the part (Armani is preferable) and it's not too packed, then the clipboard on the door may let you in. It's a long, narrow, corridor of a bar with distinctive decor by Philippe Starck. The space is dominated by four 'light wells' decorated with giant images of grinning schoolboys, a slightly surreal addition to an otherwise understatedly stylish venue. Service is taken care of by stick-thin waitresses in strapless black dresses.

If you fail at the door at the Light Bar, you could do much worse than to head down to the Strand and the reliable **American Bar** at the Savoy. No cocktail crawl is complete without a visit to the bar that introduced the science of 'mixology' to London (American barman Harry Craddock take a bow). For suitably retro refreshment, try Craddock's own invention, the White Lady (gin, lemon juice and Cointreau, £8.90).

Last stop, One Aldwych, a hotel in a restored Edwardian building at the eastern end of the Strand, and home to the capacious **Lobby Bar**. This high-ceilinged, triangular space is scattered liberally with monumental modern sculpture. Residents compete for armchair seating with a jolly after-work crowd. Sample from the list of 19 Martinis (£8), including the inky, liquorice flavoured Gotham.
Richard Lines

American Bar (*p29*) Savoy Hotel, Strand WC3 (020 7836 434).
Brasserie Max (*p30*) Covent Garden Hotel, 10 Monmouth Street, WC2 (020 7806 1000).
Light Bar (*no review*) St Martin's Hotel, 45 St Martin's Lane Hotel, WC2 (020 7300 5500).
Lobby Bar (*p32*) One Aldwych Hotel, 1 Aldwych, WC2 (020 7300 1000).
Long Bar (*no review*) Sanderson, 50 Berners Street, Fitzrovia, W1 (020 7300 1400).
mybar (*p19*) myhotel, 11-13 Bayley Street, WC1 (020 7667 6000).
Oscar (*no review*) Charlotte Street Hotel, 15 Charlotte Street, Fitzrovia (020 7806 2000).

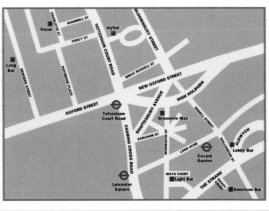

Orwell drank here, as did Dylan Thomas (thrown out more than once for ankle-biting unsuspecting ladies) and Albert Pierrepoint, the last chief hangman. But although old black and white photographs of former patrons adorn the walls, the present plasticky seats and ugly games machines don't do much to help the atmosphere. Come instead for a busy, after-work boozer that keeps free spirits flying high with giant four-pint pitchers of Samuel Smith's brews. Quieter corners can be found in the Writers and Artists' Bar downstairs, but it was exuberance and high jinks that characterised the place on our recent visit – so much better, we think, to stay up with the crowds. History hounds should just settle for the book *The Fitzroy: Autobiography of a London Tavern*, available at the bar.
Function room. Games (fruit machine, quiz machine). Satellite TV. Tables outdoors (pavement). Vegetarian dishes. **Map 1/K5**

Hope

15 Tottenham Street, W1 (020 7637 0896). Goodge Street tube. **Open** 11am-11pm Mon-Sat; noon-10.30pm Sun. **Food served** noon-2.30pm Mon-Fri; noon-3.30pm Sat. **Credit** MC, V.
Next time you're trawling down the Tottenham Court Road and fancy a bite, forgo the Burger King, the Pizza Hut, the splattering of dubious kebab joints and take a well advised detour down Tottenham Street to the Hope. The interior is decidedly unremarkable, but never mind that because its reputation rests squarely on its sturdy food and wide range of beverages. The Hope boasts a Sausage Emporium, with some 13 bounteous bangers (including three vegetarian options) from £3.50, all served with plenty of mash and baked beans. As if that wasn't fine enough, the pub keeps 40 rotating guest ales and four regulars including Flowers and Old Speckled Hen, plus Leffe in bottles. Top all that off with old-fashioned puds like spotted dick or treacle pud with custard, if you dare. Heaven for the portly of figure and spirit.
Comedy (Tue). Function room. Games (fruit machine). Jukebox. Satellite TV (big screen). Specialities: real ales. Tables outdoors (pavement). Vegetarian dishes.
Map 1/J5

Jamies

74 Charlotte Street, W1 (020 7636 7556). Goodge Street tube. **Open** 11am-11pm Mon-Fri. **Food served** noon-2.45pm, 6-9.15pm Mon-Fri. **Credit** AmEx, DC, MC, V.
With its long, curved wooden bar and bold blocks of sunshine-yellow, reds and purples on the walls, Jamie's feels like a laid-back gastropub that just happens to major in wines. The acres of floor space with functional wooden tables make it more suitable for groups than couples, and come early evening it's stampeded by media herds. Bottled beers are bewilderingly popular given that the wine list offers such a perfectly selection drawn from all the major wine-producing countries of the world. There's a good choice of champagne, with Taittinger non-vintage and Brut Prestige rosé both served by the glass. A surprisingly unpretentious menu includes a Mediterranean meze platter and a well-laden oriental plate, both ideal for sharing, as well as several mains. If you prefer a bit of elbow room while dining, you can always head downstairs to the mezzanine restaurant. The friendly staff, who frequently came to our table unbidden, get Brownie points for attentiveness.
Function rooms. Restaurant. Satellite TV. Specialities: wines. Tables outdoors (patio). Vegetarian dishes.
Map 1/J5

Jerusalem

33-34 Rathbone Place, W1 (020 7255 1120). Tottenham Court Road tube. **Open/food served** noon-11pm Mon-Fri; 7-11pm Sat. **Credit** AmEx, MC, V.
By day, Jerusalem is surprisingly light and airy, by night the thick red velvet curtains are drawn across the basement windows and this spacious dive becomes a dark, groovy club space. In addition to the heavy drapes, vast refectory tables that seem to have been constructed from the timbers of the Ark, wrought-iron candle holders and gilt mirrors add to the Gothic effect. A long, stone bar, which dominates one wall, is spectacularly well stocked with huge arrays of bottled beers, wines and spirits, and draught Beck's, Hoegaarden and Leffe Blonde. Bar snacks are available or restaurant fare is served in a separate raised seating area. Dishes are pricey but interesting (jerk chicken with plantain and coconut lime broth, pumpkin, ricotta and artichoke lasagne). Punters range from clubbers to office blokes, with a few foreign language students blown in off the street. It may not be the Holy Land but it's well worth a pilgrimage, especially if plans to extend its licence till 3am receive the go ahead.
Music (DJs Mon-Sat). Restaurant. Vegetarian dishes.
Map 1/K5

King & Queen

1 Foley Street, W1 (020 7636 5619). Goodge Street tube. **Open** 11am-11pm Mon-Fri; 11am-3pm, 7-11pm Sat; noon-3pm, 7-10.30pm Sun. **Food served** noon-2.30pm Mon-Fri. **Credit** MC, V.
This young slip of a reviewer felt a mite uncomfortable walking into this fairly hot, stuffy pub populated chiefly by smoking men. Maybe they were sitting too close to the open fire, or perhaps a tobacconists' convention had come to town. More likely, they were drawn here by the 'Adnam's Ales and Beers' sign hanging outside at this uneventful end of Foley Street. That and the fact that the King and Queen is one of those increasingly rare beasts: a central London pub that looks as if it has never been – nor, indeed, ever will be – made over for modern times. According to staff, it's also a pub with a history. The upstairs function room once hosted Chartist meetings, Karl Marx drank here, and Dylan played here when it was a popular folk music venue in the early '60s. It still holds a monthly folk evening. And they probably still mutter darkly about the day Bob went electric.
Babies and children admitted (daytimes). Function room. Games (fruit machine). Jukebox. Music (folk club, monthly). TV. Vegetarian dishes. **Map 1/J5**

Mash

19-21 Great Portland Street, W1 (020 7637 5555). Oxford Circus tube. **Open** 7.30am-2am Mon-Fri; 11am-2am Sat; 11am-10.30pm Sun. **Food served** 7.30am-11pm Mon-Fri; noon-11pm Sat; noon-10.30pm Sun. **Credit** AmEx, DC, MC, V.
Still going strong two years on, Mash continues to combine novelty and idiosyncratic flair with chain-bar corporate efficiency. We still love its space-age retro look of sleek lines and brightly lit curves – all reminiscent of the sort of bar Buck Rogers and friends would let their hair down at. Furnishings are sparse, although there's a cosy sunken lounge area with massively enlarged, backlit (and sneakily subverted) 1970s travel brochure pics on the walls. Its 'home brew' beers – mash, wheat, strawberry cream and peach from the gleaming on-site micro-brewery – are an acquired taste; order a four-glass sampler to see if you'll get it. Fans can pick up a Mash eight-pint mini-keg to take away (£12.50). Cocktails are far more sophisticated than those knocked up in your average

bar, but a good deal pricier too. Decent grub is also available (fancy pizzas for just under a tenner).
Babies and children admitted (until 8pm). Disabled: toilet. Function room. Music (DJs Thur, Sat). Restaurant. Specialities: own-brewed beers. Vegetarian dishes.
Map 1/J6

Match
37-38 Margaret Street, W1 (020 7499 3443/ www.matchbar.com). Oxford Circus tube. **Open** 11am-midnight Mon-Sat. **Food served** 11am-11pm Mon-Sat. **Credit** AmEx, MC, V.
Part bar, part club (there's a DJ booth bang in the middle of the drinking area), this is a Hoxton-style venue come to the West End. A soothing coffee and chocolate colour scheme, warm lighting, low leather sofas and obliging bar staff draw a crowd who have probably travelled here especially rather than just casually dropped in while passing. Patrons tend to be less glacially hip than their N1 counterparts. Nothing on draught, but there are unusual bottled beers (Anchorsteam, Pilsner Urquett, EB, Union), wines and a large selection of cocktails, including in-house creations (Match originals £5.75) and a range named after *The Magnificent Seven*. The bar food has a Far Eastern/Latino feel; it's competent, but unlikely to satisfy more demanding taste buds. We'd skip it and go for another Yul Brynner instead.
Babies and children admitted (daytimes). Disabled: toilet. Function room. Music (DJs, Wed-Sat). Specialities: cocktails. Vegetarian dishes.

Newman Arms
23 Rathbone Street, W1 (020 7636 1127). Goodge Street tube. **Open** 11.30am-11pm Mon-Fri. **Food served** noon-3pm, 6-9pm Mon-Thur; noon-3pm Fri. **Credit** MC, V.
The near Dickensian location – under an archway in a well-worn flagstone alley – and darkened, leaded windows suggest a truly outstanding pub. It isn't. But it is a comfortable little den that serves the best pint of Bass we've had in central London for a long time. The friendly over-tartaned downstairs bar is schooner-like, with a low-slung ceiling and shelves of fake books. Upstairs is a sedate, panelled function room where Egon Ronay award-winning pies are served (£6.95 with potatoes and veg). Very good they are too, but get here early if you hope to get a table. Otherwise, let the wait staff know you want to eat then wait downstairs with a pint. Movie junkies and London cultists know the pub for its associations with the Michael Powell film *Peeping Tom*.
Function room. Restaurant. Vegetarian dishes. **Map 1/J5**

Office
3-5 Rathbone Place, W1 (020 7636 1598). Tottenham Court Road tube. **Open/food served** noon-3am Mon-Fri; 9.30pm-4am Sat. **Admission** £5 after 8.30pm Fri; £7 Sat. **Happy hour** 5-7.30pm Mon-Fri; 9.30-10.30pm Sat. **Credit** AmEx, MC, V.
Originally named for the benefit of after-work boozers who could quite truthfully ring their spouses at 8pm to inform them 'I'm at the Office', the crowd these days is largely young and single. Suited types tend to dismiss it in favour of the many wine bars in the area, so despite a prime location mere seconds from Oxford Street it can take a while to fill up. In terms of look, the place is a bit of a jazzed-up function hall with a patched together floor and multicoloured neon lighting. Not our choice of venue for an early evening drink – although on our last visit a *Hollyoaks* heart throb was imbibing cheerfully – but things start to hot up later on when the DJs get busy. Bottled beers include Beck's, Budweiser and Molson, while among the lurid-sounding cocktails are Bubblegum, Woo-Woo and Sloe Comfortable Screw (£3.95 a

glass, £11.95 a pitcher); shooters include a Quick Phuck. Check *Time Out* magazine's clubbing section for guest DJs and club nights.
Babies and children admitted (until 6pm). Music (DJs Wed-Sat). TV. Vegetarian dishes. **Map 1/K5**

Rising Sun
46 Tottenham Court Road, W1 (020 7636 6530). Goodge Street or Tottenham Court Road tube. **Open** 11am-11pm Mon-Sat; noon-10.30pm Sun. **Food served** 11am-10.30pm Mon-Sat; noon-10.30pm Sun. **Credit** AmEx, DC, MC, V.
You wouldn't believe it, these days the Rising Sun is as traditional as pubdom gets, but we still remember when this was Presley's, an Elvis theme bar. Now it's a T&J Bernard pub, with an unquiffed clientele of local office types, University of London students, and shoppers taking time out. They're well served by an impressive selection of bottled beers (including Leffe Blonde, St Peter's and Schneide Weisse), which goes some way to compensating for the unexciting line-up on draught. A food menu offers a huge choice of dishes (sandwiches, pies, platters, filled Yorkshire puds, wraps), which are all reasonably priced, if unremarkable. If you drop by 'off peak' you may even be able to relax in a seat by the fire with one of the papers provided. Sure, it's a pub-by-numbers alright, but as the management would surely tell you, if it ain't broke, don't fix it. Unless it's a pub called Presley's.
Specialities: real ales. Tables outdoors (pavement). TV. Vegetarian dishes. **Map 1/K5**

Sevilla Mía
22 Hanway Street, W1 (020 7637 3756). Tottenham Court Road tube. **Open/food served** 7pm-1am Mon-Sat; 7pm-midnight Sun. **Credit** AmEx, DC, MC, V.
Seedy entrances like the one leading to Sevilla Mia more usually have signs Sellotaped to the walls reading 'Busty Model Upstairs'. (In fact, upstairs is members-only drinking dive The Troy Club.) Arrive too early and this tatty little basement Spanish bar is hardly any more appealing than the entrance would suggest. But as the night wears on and it begins to fill up the place becomes almost homely. Heartfelt Spanish pop serenades some lonesome Spaniards and a crowd seeking refuge from current killjoy licensing laws. It gets loud and smoky and the toilets become even more grim, but if the choice is between this and an N8 night bus ride home, then personally we'll stick with the place that serves sangria.
Vegetarian dishes. **Map 1/K5**

The Social
5 Little Portland Street, W1 (020 7636 4992/ www.thesocial.com). Oxford Circus tube. **Open/food served** noon-midnight Mon-Sat. **Credit** MC, V.
Born out of the record label Heavenly Social, this rather over-hyped tiny industrial-style space attracts a loyal crowd who can't get enough of it. On the ground floor there's a narrow galley bar (where movement is impossible when it's busy) decked out with pine panelling and tables fixed diner-style along the wall. We like it for the wonderfully eclectic jukebox. Downstairs there's another darker, slightly less cramped bar where the decor gets more industrial and the DJ-driven sounds that bit harder and louder. The choice of beer is small (draught Kronenburg and Red Stripe only, but bottled Hoegaarden), while the cocktail list is limited and safe. Grub is bedsit fare – baked beans on toast, eggy bread and fishfingers. The whole place screams student but maybe they're just being ironic?
Jukebox. Music (DJs Mon-Sat, live music £3 Wed). Specialities: Social cocktail. Vegetarian dishes. **Map 1/J5**

Also in the area...

Ha! Ha! Bar & Canteen 43-51 Great Titchfield Street, W1 (020 7580 7252).
Lees Bag (Davys) 4 Great Portland Street, W1 (020 7636 5287).

Holborn

Cittie of Yorke

22 High Holborn, WC1 (020 7242 7670). Chancery Lane or Holborn tube. **Open** 11.30am-11pm Mon-Sat. **Food served** noon-9pm Mon-Sat. **Credit** AmEx, DC, MC, V.
Originally built in 1430, this gothic masterpiece had to be rebuilt in 1923 when the old structure crumbled. From the end of the 19th century to 1979 it was part of the Henekey's wine bar chain and the bar in the back room – said to be the longest in Britain – was known as 'Henekey's Long Bar'. The booths opposite were built around 1901 to enable lawyers (who still form the main part of the clientele) to speak privately with clients, and the giant vats lining the gallery are original wine and spirit butts. The high vaulted ceiling led to the nickname the 'Cathedral Pub'. These days there's another, smaller bar at the front decorated with paintings of local notables through the ages and a vaulted wine bar downstairs. Being a Sam Smith's pub means that the likes of Old Brewery Bitter, Extra Stout and Ayingerbräu Pils and Prinz are served at bargain prices.
Babies and children admitted (downstairs). Function rooms. Games (darts, fruit machine). No-smoking area. Restaurant. Tables outdoors (pavement). Vegetarian dishes. **Map 3/M5**

Corts

78 High Holborn, WC1 (020 7242 4292). Holborn tube. **Open** 11.30am-11pm Mon-Wed; 11.30am-2am Thur, Fri. **Food served** 11.30am-7.30pm Mon-Fri. **Credit** AmEx, MC, V.
Taking over what used to be a nerdy computer shop and turning it into a good-looking bar has certainly brightened up this end of High Holborn. The main drinking area can be glimpsed through the picture window, with its dark green and blue walls, glass bricks and an unusual upturned-looking serving area. Scattered around seemingly willy-nilly are the odd sofa, comfortable modern chairs and simple round tables. Beyond all this there's another smaller room that serves as a lunchtime restaurant and down below a basement area called Absolutions – do we detect a whiff of sponsorship? Stella Artois and Hoegaarden are the two draught beers, there's an extensive wine list, cocktails for around a fiver, and decent food of the seared tuna variety.
Babies and children admitted (daytimes). Digital TV. Disabled: toilet. Function rooms. Games (arcade machine). Music (DJ, Fri). Restaurant. Salsa class (7pm Mon). Vegetarian dishes. **Map 4/M5**

Fine Line

77 Kingsway, WC2 (020 7405 5004). Holborn tube. **Open** 9am-11pm Mon-Fri. **Food served** 9am-10pm Mon-Wed; 9am-9pm Thur, Fri. **Credit** AmEx, DC, MC, V.
Although the Fine Line chain of café-bars is owned by Fuller's brewery, they seem remarkably shy about plugging their own fine beers (only London Pride is available on hand-pump). Instead, the light wood bar is dominated by lager pumps and a cappuccino machine, while most of the blackboards go on

Princess Louise. See page 47.

about the wines on offer. Typically for the chain, the bar is one large single room with huge picture windows. Walls are painted beige and stone, and sofas complement more standard seating. Food kicks off with breakfast and runs through to dinner with good value deals such as char-grilled Scotch rib-eye steak for a tenner.

Babies and children admitted (noon-3pm). Bar available for hire. Disabled: toilet. Music (disco night Thur). Restaurant. Specialities: cocktails. Vegetarian dishes. **Map 4/M6**

High Holborn
95-96 High Holborn, WC1 (020 7404 3338). Holborn tube. **Open** *bar* 5-11pm Mon-Fri. **Food served** *restaurant* noon-2.30pm, 6.30-10.30pm Mon-Fri. **Credit** AmEx, MC, V.
The first big plus is that so few other people seem to know about this excellent bijou basement cocktail bar buried beneath the cavernous restaurant of the same name. The interior is well designed, a tasteful mixture of modern '70s retro and classic '20s deco, with good lighting and must-have leather armchairs, their design inspired apparently by the classic Aston Martin sports car. The cocktail list is fabulous, free of silly names and clearly composed by someone who's in the mix; the drinks made for us were expertly done. They're a bit pricey (all classic cocktails £7, champagne cocktails £8), but absolutely worth it. There's even a couple of beers on tap and decent wines by the glass. It's the ideal boy-meets-girl venue but limited space means get there early or you'll have to meet elsewhere.
Bar and restaurant available for hire. Disabled: toilet. Restaurant. Vegetarian dishes. **Map 4/M5**

King's Arms
11A Northington Street, WC1 (020 7405 9107). Chancery Lane or Russell Square tube. **Open** 11.30am-11pm Mon-Fri. **Food served** noon-2.30pm Mon-Fri. **Credit** AmEx, DC, MC, V.
Considering that it's a traditional-style pub proud of its real ales (Greene King IPA and Marston's Pedigree were both in fine fettle when we last visited), the King's Arms attracts a predominantly twentysomething crowd. Red curtains and upholstery, nicotine-coloured walls and a blazing fire in winter make for a cosy atmosphere. There are a couple of rooms upstairs available for letting or just to cover the over-spill, and the lunchtime food, as one regular confided over a couple of lagers, is good solid British pub grub, but the 'cook wouldn't give Gary Rhodes any nightmares'.
Babies and children admitted (separate room). Function rooms. Games (darts). No-smoking area. Satellite TV. Specialities: real ales. Tables outdoors (pavement). Vegetarian dishes. **Map 3/M4**

Na Zdrowie
11 Little Turnstile, WC1 (020 7831 9679). Holborn tube. **Open** noon-11pm Mon-Fri; 6-11pm Sat. **Food served** noon-9pm Mon-Fri; 6-9pm Sat. **Credit** MC, V.
Tucked away down the rat run that connects High Holborn with Kingsway, this small grey and gold vodka bar and café is popular with local office workers as it is with Polish ex-pats. A local independent film company based around the corner uses the place as its canteen; hearty Polish grub such as pierogi (dumplings) and bigos (hunter's stew) can be had for under a fiver. When it comes to vodka, you'll be hard pressed to find a better selection

than the 30 or so found in here. We always go for the Sliwowica (dry plum spirit) or Luksusowa (potato vodka). It's worth knowing that kosher vodkas are available for passing rabbis, and we know an art director who swears by tea rum (drunk with tea). Pick of the half dozen Polish beers is EB. Incidentally, the name isn't Polish at all, it's an anagram of David Bowie.
Specialities: vodkas. Tables outdoors (pavement). Vegetarian dishes. **Map 4/M5**

Princess Louise
208 High Holborn, WC1 (020 7405 8816). Holborn tube. **Open** 11am-11pm Mon-Fri; noon-11pm Sat. **Food served** noon-9pm Mon-Sat. **Credit** AmEx, DC, MC, V.
Named after Queen Victoria's fourth daughter, the Princess Louise was built in 1872 and is now a Grade II listed building. Pride of place goes to an intricately carved, horseshoe-shaped, wooden central bar that incorporates a period clock and mirrors – it is one of the best and last remaining examples of the work of WH Lascelles and Co, who were to Victorian pub joinery what Uriah Heep was to obsequiousness. The walls are covered with superb stained glass and huge etched mirrors, and the ceiling is the original moulded plaster, finished off in dark red and gold. Although it used to be a free house, Sam Smith's of Tadcaster now runs the place and so expect the likes of Museum Bitter (drawn from oak barrels in the cellar) and Ayingerbräu lager at bargain prices. Food is typical pub grub but specials are reputedly worth a go.
Babies and children admitted (daytime). Function room. Games (fruit machines). No piped music or jukebox. Vegetarian dishes. **Map 1/L5**

Three Cups
21-22 Sandland Street, WC1 (020 7831 4302). Chancery Lane or Holborn tube. **Open** noon-11pm Mon-Fri. **Food served** noon-2.30pm Mon-Fri. **Credit** AmEx, MC, V.
It's good to know that there are still small, comfortable, unspoilt local pubs in the centre of town, and this one-bar Young's house hidden away in a side street between High Holborn and Theobalds Road is one of the best. Outside, lush baskets cascading with flowers hang over the pavement, whilst within the decor is 'cosy Victorian' with dark red and cream paintwork and plenty of dark wood fittings. Being Young's, you know that the beer is going to be good, and the high proportion of customers downing pints of 'ordinary' and Special speaks for itself. It's best to avoid the 5-6.30pm rush, when office workers descend on the place like locusts and babble about torts and disbursements. Otherwise customers tend to be real ale buffs, students and local workers. The simple lunchtime food (ham, egg and chips, three cheese pizza, Cumberland sausage and mash, etc) is well worth a punt.
Function room. Games (fruit machines, quiz machines). Specialities: real ales. Tables outdoors (pavement). TV. Vegetarian dishes. **Map 3/M5**

Yorkshire Grey
2 Theobalds Road, WC1 (020 7405 2519). Chancery Lane or Holborn tube. **Open/food served** 11am-11pm Mon-Fri. **Credit** AmEx, MC, V.
One of London's very few brew-pubs has relaunched its cellar operation in the capable hands of Heriot Watt brewing graduate Ramsay Bothwick, who takes regular trips up to Yorkshire to acquire the correct yeasts from a 'well known brewery'. The names of the beers reflect the strong legal base of the clientele with Barristers Best Bitter and the stronger QC leading the prosecution, plus special brews of porters, winter warmers, milds and wheat beers appearing in suitable

seasons. The boozer itself is a bastion of wood and glasswork with the customary wood board flooring, sturdy furniture and partitioned drinking areas.
Function room. Games (fruit machines). Specialities: own-brewed real ale. Tables outdoors (pavement). TV. Vegetarian dishes. **Map 3/M5**

Also in the area...
All Bar One 58 Kingsway, WC2 (020 7269 5171).
Bierodrome 67 Kingsway, WC2 (020 7242 7469).
Bung Hole (Davys) Hand Court, 57 High Holborn, WC1 (020 7831 8365).
Jamies 50-54 Kingsway, WC2 (020 7405 9749).
Knights Templar (JD Wetherspoon) 95 Chancery Lane, WC2 (020 7831 2660).
Penderel's Oak (JD Wetherspoon) 283-288 High Holborn, WC1 (020 7242 5669).
Pitcher & Piano 42 Kingsway, WC2 (020 7404 8510).
Shakespeare's Head (JD Wetherspoon) 64-68 Kingsway, WC2 (020 7404 8846).

Holland Park

Academy
57 Princedale Road, W11 (020 7221 0248). Holland Park tube. **Open** noon-11pm Mon-Sat; noon-10.30pm Sun. **Food served** noon-3.30pm, 6-10.30pm Mon-Fri; noon-10pm Sat, Sun. **Credit** MC, V.
Academy is probably so named because it is a little school of pub excellence. It's always top of the form for friendly, unobsequious service, a good range of wine and beer and thoughtfully created pub cuisine. Food is probably the major attraction with a variety of Franco-Greek starters for around £4 and enticing mains for £8 or so, including an excellent wild boar sausage with leek and bacon mash. A short but alluring wine list is similarly priced to lead into temptation with the good French country house wine at just £8 a bottle. Decor is unfussy: whitewashed with a dash of purple behind the bar, simple wood furnishings throughout and abstract line drawings and thick colourful paintings on the walls. All of which makes it highly attractive to a sophisticated thirty- to fortysomething clientele. Being Holland Park, the shadow of Gucci and Chanel always looms, but you shouldn't let that put you off.
Babies and children admitted (until 9pm). Function room. Specialities: cocktails. Tables outdoors (garden, pavement). Vegetarian dishes.

Castle
100 Holland Park Avenue, W11 (020 7313 9301). Holland Park tube. **Open** 11am-11pm Mon-Sat; noon-10.30pm Sun. **Food served** noon-3pm, 6.30-10pm Mon-Fri; noon-10pm Sat, Sun. **Credit** MC, V.
Sitting on one of the city's more impersonal thoroughfares (Holland Park Avenue), the Castle offers an equally impersonal vibe. That's not to say it's not popular: on a Friday night condensed sweat runs in rivers down the windows as a young cattle market crowd revels in loud DJ music and intoxicants. At other times, the air is clearer and it is possible to pull up one of the big heavy seats and enjoy what feels like an old-fashioned '30s railway station waiting room. Ordinary gastropub food is available, but this is not the sort of place to linger over a meal.
Babies and children admitted (restaurant, daytime). Music (DJs Thur-Sun). Restaurant. Tables outdoors (pavement). Vegetarian dishes.

Julie's Wine Bar

137 Portland Road, W11 (020 7727 7985). Holland Park tube. **Open** 9am-11.30pm Mon-Sat; 10am-10.30pm Sun. **Food served** 12.30-2.45pm, 7.30-10.30pm Mon-Sat; 12.30-3.30pm, 7.30-10pm Sun. **Credit** AmEx, MC, V.

Perfect for those who don't like populous or popular pubs, Julie's is a quiet retreat for ladies who lunch or lotharios who court. It's also the ideal venue for extra-marital dalliances, being a labyrinthine affair, with small rooms sub-divided further by oriental screens and crammed with ornate artefacts and hanging baskets of ivy that obscure sightlines. The overall effect of the decor could be described as posh hippy. The sensibly sized wine list is a good balance of Old World and New World, carefully selected for quality. In addition there's a decent selection of cocktails and a few bottled beers. Bar food consists of the likes of olive mash and smoked salmon, or there's an à la carte menu served in the restaurant next door.

Babies and children admitted (crèche 1-4pm Sun, £9.50 including food). Function rooms. Restaurant. Specialities: wines. Tables outdoors (pavement). Vegetarian dishes.

Ladbroke Arms

54 Ladbroke Road, W11 (020 7727 6648). Holland Park tube. **Open** *summer* 11am-11pm Mon-Sat; noon-10.30pm Sun; *winter* 11am-3pm, 5.30-11pm Mon-Fri; 11am-11pm Sat; 11am-10.30pm Sun. **Food served** noon-2.30pm, 7-9.45pm Mon-Sat; noon-3pm, 7-9.45pm Sun. **Credit** MC, V.

The Ladbroke Arms doesn't set out to affect airs and graces, but well heeled locals make it seem that way. There is a distinctly Chiantishire quality to the decoration confirmed by the copy of *Country Life* in a wicker magazine wall rack. By contrast, the tartan carpet is a bit of a design faux pas, not a little reminiscent of Scotrail (First Class, natch). But if you can endure the shawl and brogue community together with the artificially rural ambience, forbearance will be richly rewarded. The real ales (Directors, Broadside, Tiger and Abbot's) here are always well kept, the wines up to the high standard demanded by discriminating types everywhere and the pub cuisine abreast of culinary fashion. The staff are always delightfully well mannered and there is a security bonus – this is the after-work local for the Notting Hill cop shop over the road.

Babies and children admitted. Specialities: real ales. Tables outdoors (terrace). Vegetarian dishes.

Prince of Wales

14 Princedale Road, W11 (020 7313 9321). Holland Park tube. **Open** noon-11pm Mon-Wed, Fri, Sat; noon-1am Thur; noon-10.30pm Sun. **Food served** 6-9.30pm Mon-Sat; noon-3pm Sun. **Credit** MC, V.

You don't expect to find a good ordinary local in an area like Holland Park, but here it is. In actual fact there is a significant population of non-millionaires hereabouts and they're well served in this down-to-earth, friendly establishment. The swirly carpet and garish chain pub Victoriana may offend but there's relief in the beer garden to the rear. Back inside, the bar divides into sturdy wooden alcoves with televised sport tending to dominate and a good-sized pool table in one room. Punters are a mix of old and young, and some evenings it's all a bit Queen Vic, but there's nothing wrong in that. Don't expect anything fancy on the menu or behind the bar: this is very much a local pub for local people.

Babies and children admitted. Disabled: toilet. Games (fruit machines, table football, pool table). Jukebox. Satellite TV (big screen). Tables outdoors (garden). Vegetarian dishes.

Kensington High Street

Abingdon

54 Abingdon Road, W8 (020 7937 3339). High Street Kensington tube. **Open** noon-11pm Mon-Sat; 12.30-10.30pm Sun. **Food served** 12.30-2.30pm, 6.30-11.30pm Mon-Sat; 12.30-3pm, 6.30-10.30pm Sun. **Credit** AmEx, MC, V.

From the outside, the frosted glass windows and austere grey painted walls of the Abingdon give the impression of an exclusive eaterie. Don't be put off: this is an establishment which takes drinking seriously and has a bar staff who are enthusiastic verging on the gushing. The cool minimalist decoration of the bar area (grey wall panelling, slatted wood bar) is softened by candlelight and a couple of over-stuffed sofas. The minimalist ethic extends to the bottled beer list, but only because the emphasis is instead on wine, with over 30 served by the glass. Most of the clientele are a slightly upmarket take on the usual wine bar suspects – fur mufflers appeared to be de rigueur with the ladies – but the presence of a couple of elderly tweedy intellectuals, who seemed to be regulars, indicates that the Abingdon may have wider appeal.

Babies and children admitted (high chairs). Restaurant. Specialities: wines. Tables outdoors (pavement). Vegetarian dishes.

Britannia

1 Allen Street, W8 (no phone). High Street Kensington tube. **Open** 11am-11pm Mon-Sat; noon-10.30pm Sun. **Food served** noon-2.30pm, 6-9.30pm Mon-Sat. **Credit** AmEx, DC, MC, V.

With fine oil paintings of sailing ships above the two open fireplaces and a display of china running the length of the walls, the Britannia has the relaxed upmarket feel of a country house hotel. At the weekend most of Kensington's residents are in the sticks enjoying the genuine article, so if you like your pubs with atmosphere, come during the week when the place has a bit of custom. The combination of Young's beer and a cellarman with exacting standards means that the Britannia serves arguably the best pint in the area. This inevitably leads to the serving area being dominated by middle-aged men, but there are plenty of tables in the large extension for couples or groups of women and there's a conservatory for families.

Babies and children admitted (conservatory). Function room. Games (darts, fruit machine). No piped music or jukebox. No-smoking conservatory (lunch only). TV. Vegetarian dishes.

Café Rouge

2 Lancer Square, Kensington Church Street, W8 (020 7938 4200/www.caferouge.co.uk). High Street Kensington tube. **Open/food served** 10am-11pm Mon-Sat; 10am-10.30pm Sun. **Credit** AmEx, MC, V.

The interior of Café Rouge Kensington is a welcome twist on the usual stripped-down bistro look common to most branches of this 35-strong 'franglais' chain. A central spiral motif makes for plenty of curved edges and circular features, with a nod to art nouveau in the design of the furniture. An abundance of hard surfaces (blond wood, stainless steel, tiled floor) means that sounds are amplified but once a particularly noisesome child fell silent our waiter's French accent and a mellow jazz soundtrack were sufficiently soothing that we could happily finish the sports pages. Continental lagers dominate the beer selection – naturally – and there's a rather more extensive wine list, priced from £2.50 a glass, £9.45 a bottle. The menu (and most people are

here to eat) leans towards brasserie staples, and service is attentive, polite and unpushy.
Babies and children admitted. Function room. No-smoking area. Tables outdoors (terrace). Vegetarian dishes.

Churchill Arms
119 Kensington Church Street, W8 (020 7727 4242). High Street Kensington or Notting Hill Gate tube. **Open** 11am-11pm Mon-Sat; noon-10.30pm Sun. **Food served** noon-2.30pm, 6-9.30pm Mon-Sat; noon-2.30pm Sun. **Credit** DC, MC, V.
With every inch of wall and ceiling covered (butterflies, brass jugs, wicker baskets, chamber pots, photos of historic US presidents, Churchilliana) the otherwise unremarkable interior of this large pre-war pub has been transformed into a fascinating junk shop jungle. Add to this trappings such as mullioned windows and a roaring fire, not to mention lovingly tended ales (Fuller's) and model service, and you have what is arguably Kensington's finest boozer. Very decent Thai food is also served up by Asian ladies in the conservatory. As a result, the place is invariably packed with locals and better-informed tourists (the Churchill is a guidebook staple). However many bodies at the bar though, the staff have an uncanny ability of always knowing who's next.
Babies and children admitted. Games (fruit machine). No piped music or jukebox. Restaurant. Satellite TV.

Cuba
11-13 Kensington High Street, W8 (020 7938 4137). High Street Kensington tube. **Open/food served** noon-2am Mon-Sat; 2-10.30pm Sun. **Happy hour** noon-8.30pm Mon-Sat; 2-8.30pm Sun. **Credit** AmEx, DC, MC, V.
London has a surfeit of Cuban theme bars (Cuba in Waterloo, Cuba Libre in Islington, Havana Square in Mayfair, Havana in Fulham) and, to be honest, we haven't got much good to say about most of them. The sooner we get this whole Buena Vista thing out of our systems and move on, the better. This particular take on Cuba is no worse than most, although the murals of colonial colonnades are particularly hideous and more reminiscent of a motorway services food court than the communist Caribbean paradise. But the Latino film posters are graphic classics and the *son* soundtrack was exuberant without becoming grating. We also enjoyed our cocktails: plenty of Havana rum mixed with mint, brown sugar and limes. Beers are at least Spanish, and with salsa classes, a late licence and a happy hour lasting a third of a day, Cuba is certainly worth a visit.
Dance class (salsa Mon-Wed, Fri, Sat; samba Thur). Music (Latin nightly). Restaurant. Specialities: cocktails. Vegetarian dishes.

Devonshire Arms
37 Marloes Road, W8 (020 7937 0710). Gloucester Road or High Street Kensington tube. **Open** noon-11pm Mon-Sat; noon-10.30pm Sun. **Food served** noon-2.45pm, 6-8.45pm daily. **Credit** MC, V.
Despite a clientele that's more likely to hail from Kansas than Kensington, the Devonshire retains the atmosphere of a true local. In fact, it's only in high summer, when the pretty front garden comes into its own, that permanent residents of the royal borough frequent the place in numbers. The rest of the time it's down to gaggles of corn-fed American teens, who gravitate to the pool room at the back. A black-and-white colour scheme, piped music and gratuitous blackboard art are a nod to the knowing that this pub is part of the Nicholson chain, but there are a few more personal touches, such as an elaborate display of Britvic orange bottles. Now whether you'd travel to a pub to see a display of Britvic bottles is another matter, but if you happen to be in the neighbourhood

and thirsty then it's a decent enough no frills boozer.
Games (fruit machine, pool table, video game). Satellite TVs. Tables outdoors (garden). Vegetarian dishes.

Goolies
21 Abingdon Road, W8 (020 7938 1122/ www.goolies-bar.com). High Street Kensington tube. **Open** 12.30-3pm, 6-11pm daily. **Food served** 12.30-3pm, 6-10.30pm daily. **Credit** AmEx, DC, MC, V.
So the owners are Antipodean, but still, it's like when Clive James does his spot on unfortunate product names abroad: the Portuguese soft drink called Pis and all that. What possessed them to christen a discrete, upmarket wine bar with such a dumb name? Still, it doesn't seem to adversely affect trade; when we last visited a number of diners were tucking into adventurous modern British-Pacific Rim cuisine in the back restaurant, while a smart group at the bar quaffed from a wine list mainly culled from the New World, with plenty of choice for under £20. An elliptical skylight provides plenty of illumination during the day, but at night the bar switches to soft lighting, with a soft adult rock soundtrack barely audible above the murmur of voices. The barman has a shaven head and goes by the name of Dragon, but rather than the Bond villain he seems cut out to be, he has all the charm of 007 combined with the efficiency of Miss Moneypenny.
Babies and children admitted. Restaurant (available for hire). Specialities: wines. Vegetarian dishes.

Hillgate
24 Hillgate Street, W8 (020 7727 8543). Notting Hill Gate tube. **Open/food served** 11am-11pm Mon-Sat; noon-10.30pm Sun. **Credit** MC, V.
First impressions that this is a pretty unexceptional boozer are quickly revised if you chance it with a seat at the bar. This is one of those great 'real' pubs, used and abused by every section of the local community, from pinstriped elderly eccentrics to groups of glammed-up girls getting hammered on their way up to the West End. It's the sort of place where one pint quite easily becomes a session, and it's got a rotating selection of real ales (IPA and Abbot's when we last were in residence) so that the drinking is a pleasure. Simple pub grub ensures you don't have to give up your seat to hunger.
Babies and children admitted. Disabled: toilet. Satellite TV (big screen). Specialities: real ales. Tables outdoors (pavement). Vegetarian dishes.

Scarsdale
23A Edward Square, W8 (020 7937 1811). High Street Kensington tube. **Open** noon-11pm Mon-Sat; noon-10.30pm Sun. **Food served** noon-3pm, 6-9.45pm daily. **Credit** AmEx, DC, MC, V.
Someone should tell the locals that the Scarsdale is now a gastropub. On the Saturday we visited, drinkers were crammed into the main bar in such numbers that diners were in danger of getting fag ash in their salsa verde. Their fault for not taking advantage of the separate dining area, patrolled by polite but firm staff and offering a fairly adventurous menu at steeper than average prices. Back in the bar, gilt-framed mirrors and oil paintings around a coal-effect fire, along with modest bits of statuary and fake topiary create a kind of England-en-Provence feel, and there's a handsome serving area illuminated by broad, cut-glass windows overlooking a pretty, gas-heated terrace. A decent worldwide wine selection complements Courage ales on tap. The sheer liveliness of the place is a welcome change from the slightly moribund weekend atmosphere of other Kensington drinking holes.
Babies and children admitted (in restaurant). Restaurant. Specialities: real ales. Tables outdoors (garden). Vegetarian dishes.

Tenth Bar

Royal Garden Hotel, 2-24 Kensington High Street, W8
(020 7937 8000/www.royalgardenhotel.co.uk). High Street
Kensington tube. **Open** noon-2.30pm, 5.30-11pm Mon-Fri;
5.30-11pm Sat. **Credit** AmEx, DC, MC, V.
All you need to know about the Tenth Bar is that the name
refers to the floor it's on and that the view – from the Albert
Hall in the foreground to Canary Wharf in the distance – is
superb. Anything else is incidental. So, the fact that the
selection of drink is less than wonderful: so what. That the
pianist's renditions of show tunes are insipid: so what. That
the gaudily coloured canapés are so naff they belonged in a
Ferrero Rocher ad: so what. Just don't come on a day with
poor visibility or you'll be royally pissed off.
Disabled: toilet. Music (live jazz 8pm Sat, restaurant).
No-smoking area (restaurant). Restaurant. Specialities:
cocktails. Vegetarian dishes.

Windsor Castle

114 Campden Hill Road, W8 (020 7243 9551). High
Street Kensington or Notting Hill Gate tube.
Open noon-11pm Mon-Sat; noon-10.30pm Sun.
Food served noon-10.30pm Mon-Sat; noon-10pm Sun.
Credit AmEx, MC, V.
A once-great pub, but many of its finer features have been
eroded by time and redevelopment. Inside, at least the
fabulous 1930s oak panelling connecting the three snug bars
remains. Subdued lighting and cosy coal-effect fires are a
plus. Best spot is at the bar with a pint of Bass or London
Pride and a bowl of chips, but this doesn't deter large groups
from cramming into small nooks to eat high piles of
Lyonnaise sausages from white plates too big to go into a
domestic dishwasher. Meanwhile, even if making room for a
bigger kitchen has shorn the pub garden of much of its
character, it still remains one of the largest and prettiest in
Zone One.
No piped music or jukebox. No-smoking area (lunchtime).
Tables outdoors (garden). Vegetarian dishes.

Also in the area...

Café Flo, 127-129 Kensington Church Street, W8
(020 7727 8142).
Dôme 35A & B Kensington Court, Kensington High
Street, W8 (020 7937 6655).
Rat & Parrot 206 Kensington Church Street, W8
(020 7229 8421).

King's Cross & Euston

The Backpacker

126 York Way, N1 (020 7278 8318/www.thebackpacker.
co.uk). King's Cross tube/rail. **Open** 7pm-2am Fri, Sat;
3.30pm-midnight Sun. **Happy hour** 8-10pm Fri, Sat (£5
all you can drink). **No credit cards.**
Don't let the makeover fool you; the walls may be bright,
there may be a spanking new neon 'thumbs up' sign outside
but, for antipodean bolt-hole Backpacker, it's boozy business
as usual. The on-the-door security still cares, asking if
you've been before and know what to expect. And the
answer is 'Yes. Mayhem'. Every night there's a drunken
party-cum-riot in full salubrious, celebratory swing. There's
a shooters chair to inebriate the drunken crowd further still,
already rendered senseless on an infamous mix known as
Green Death (contents a close-kept secret, £3.50) and, on the
night we were visiting, a band that kicked off with Men At
Work's 'Down Under'. Sawdust, dancing, drinking and

spillage: the Backpacker is so specific in its image of fun, it
could almost be a fetish.
Music (DJs 10pm Fri-Sun, free; live band 5pm Sun,
admission £3). Tables outdoors (courtyard). TVs.

Head of Steam

1 Eversholt Street, NW1 (020 7383 3359/
www.theheadofsteam.com). Euston tube/rail. **Open** 11am-
11pm Mon-Sat; noon-10.30pm Sun. **Food served** noon-
2.30pm, 5-8pm Mon-Fri; noon-3pm Sat; noon-4pm Sun.
Credit MC, V.
A haven for foiled commuters, the Steam is a small, traditional
pub just outside Euston station that – come the summer – has
a lovely view of Euston Square. It smells of warm bodies and
spilt beer and what little carpet there is will stick to your feet
but the commuters are joined by a tight crush of locals, office
workers and even the odd tourist, attracted by the pub's
devotion to real ales (nine are rotated on tap, including
regulars like Summer Lightning or Holts, and at least one
mild). Small it may be, but the Steam still manages to fit in a
no-smoking area and a bar billiards table. The decor, as you'd
expect, takes the form of railway memorabilia, including
station signs, lamps, uniforms and signals.
Babies and children admitted (separate area, until 9pm).
Games (bar billiards, fruit machine). No-smoking area.
Satellite TV. Vegetarian dishes.

Popstarz Liquid Lounge

275 Pentonville Road, N1 (020 7833 3022). King's Cross
tube/rail. **Open** 5.30pm-2am Mon-Thur; 5.30pm-1am Fri,
Sun; 5.30pm-3am Sat. **No credit cards.**
Indie boyz and indie girlz come out to play at this bright and
breezy pub-club off-shoot of the gay alternative club night of
the same name, next door at the Scala. The venue has recently
undergone a makeover: *out* are the separate bars and garish
multi-coloured decor (though the plush purple sofas, dance
floor and mirror balls remain); *in* are yellow walls and purple
ceiling, a '70s-style glass-tile bar, raised platform seating
areas at either end and a more private, seated balcony above.
They've even found space downstairs for a small chill-out
room, complete with cushions, low tables and even lower
lighting. Some things though are just too precious to change
and we're pleased to note that Madonna still rules the decks.
Games (football table, pool). Music (DJs nightly).

Ruby Lounge

33 Caledonian Road, N1 (020 7837 9558/www.ruby-
lounge.co.uk). King's Cross tube/rail. **Open** 4-11pm Mon-
Thur; 3-11pm Fri, Sat; 4-10.30pm Sun. **Credit** MC, V.
It may be ruby – all red of walls, ceiling and furniture – but
lounge it is not. Unless thumping trax, a trendy graphic-
design brigade crowd, a hugely ornate lampshade looming
large over the central bar and nary a space to call your own
is your idea of laid-back. Funky chunky sofa aside, there's
very little by way of seating, so stand and get wobbly with
the likes of Hoegaarden and Staropramen or by working your
way through an extensive range of cocktails, including the
Absolut Passion for £4.50. DJs at weekends add to and
increase the mix.
Music (DJs 6pm Fri, 8pm Sat, all day Sun; free). Tables
outdoors (pavement).

Smithy's Wine Bar

Leeke Street, WC1 (020 7278 5949). King's Cross
tube/rail. **Open** 11am-11pm Mon-Fri; private functions
only Sat, Sun. **Food served** noon-3pm, 6-10pm Mon-Fri.
Credit AmEx, MC, V.
Undergoing major refurbishment at the moment, but
Smithy's is always open to all who can find it (tucked down

a cobbled side street off King's Cross Road). Its own cobblestone floor remains intact and it's still the last word in dark, candlelit intimacy. So relax and slosh your way through a selection of over 200 wines, about 120 of which are available by the glass. Good food is available from an ever-changing modern European menu. Due to renovations usual entertainments such as comedy, jazz and tarot readers are off until the summertime, when the owners will reassess their options. In the meantime, Smithy's sticks to what it does best: creating a laid-back space in which to relax. The only things likely to intrude upon the ambience are the builders' signs, apologising for the inconvenience. Not a problem.
Babies and children admitted (until 6pm). Function rooms (after refurbishment). Restaurant. Tables outdoors (pavement). Vegetarian dishes.

Waterside Inn
82 York Way, N1 (020 7713 8613). King's Cross tube/rail. **Open** 11am-11pm Mon-Fri; noon-11pm Sat; noon-10.30pm Sun. **Food served** 11am-9.30pm Mon-Fri; noon-9.30pm Sat; noon-8pm Sun. **Credit** MC, V.
The Waterside has the dubious distinction of having a Pizza Hut on the premises, which at least saves you all the bother of staggering home drunk to order one. All council-house red brick styling on the outside, and Walthamstow mock-Tudor within – leaded windows, fake wooden beams, brass nick-nacks – it's not the most appealing of places, but it goes a long way towards being redeemed by a cheering open fire for winter nights and a summer beer garden that overlooks a sedate stretch of the Regent's Canal. Beers include regular guest ales and there's even a plump selection of takeaway booze including, for £14.99, a five litre Budweiser keg. Perfect if you're planning to pop off to a party after.
Babies and children admitted (until 7pm). Games (pool table, table football). Jukebox. No-smoking area. Restaurant. Satellite TV (big screen). Tables outdoors (canalside terrace). Vegetarian dishes.

Also in the area...
O'Neill's 73-77 Euston Road, NW1 (020 7255 9861).

Knightsbridge

Australian
29 Milner Street, SW3 (020 7589 6027). Sloane Square tube. **Open** 11am-11pm Mon-Sat; noon-10.30pm Sun. **Food served** noon-3pm, 6-9pm Mon-Thur; noon-3pm Fri-Sun. **Credit** AmEx, DC, MC, V.
You don't expect folks who've paid two-and-a-half million quid for their gaff to frequent a local boozer with bottled lagers, overflowing ashtrays and sticky carpets. Well they don't; they go to the Australian, which is to the average boozer what a Bentley is to a Mondeo. Buffed and polished to perfection, it's a handsome traditional-style place full of dark wood, with a smattering of tasteful cricketing memorabilia. A row of pumps at the bar delivers real ales (Adnam's, Greene King IPA, Tetley's and Pedigree), while shelves behind hold a lovingly arranged array of wines and champagnes. Clientele are well groomed, wearers of tweedy suits, cashmere coats, and soft leather trousers – not so much an 'after-work' as a 'don't need to work' crowd. Underdressed as we were, we nevertheless felt completely comfortable in our corner, sipping the 'wine of the week' and cursing our parents for bringing us up to expect nothing better than Wetherspoons.
Babies and children admitted (until 6pm). Games (darts). No piped music or jukebox. Satellite TV. Tables outdoors (pavement). Vegetarian dishes.

Bunch of Grapes
207 Brompton Road, SW3 (020 7589 4944). Knightsbridge or South Kensington tube. **Open/food served** 11am-9.45pm Mon-Sat; noon-8.45pm Sun. **Credit** AmEx, DC, MC, V.
The 'local' for Harrods is a fine 18th-century old pile with the most perfect of Victorian interiors added slightly later – a working set of etched-glass snob screens, a cast-iron balcony and plenty of beautiful mahogany, including a hand-carved vine with grapes. Best of all is a bow window at the front, which is actually a separate semi-circular booth, and an excellent vantage point for watching Knightsbridge shoppers. Beers are disappointing, with Courage the only real ale and nothing bottled better than Beck's and Budweiser. There's a restaurant upstairs with stalwart English pub food.
Babies and children admitted (restaurant only). Games (fruit machines). Restaurant (available for hire). Vegetarian dishes.

Fifth Floor Bar
Harvey Nichols, 109-125 Knightsbridge, SW1 (020 7235 5000). Knightsbridge tube. **Open** 11am-11pm Mon-Sat; noon-6pm Sun. **Food served** noon-4pm, 5-11pm Mon-Sat; noon-4pm Sun. **Credit** AmEx, DC, MC, V.
It surprised us to find that a bar housed in the capital's most 'dahling' department store isn't really a good place for a woman to sit on her own. You'll either be suspected of trying to pick people up or people will try to pick you up. If you don't fancy the attention, turn up with a friend or two. The lack of square feet around the large central bar ensures that the place is nearly always heaving. If you can snag one of the well upholstered bar stools, though, you can order bottled beers (Beck's, Budvar, Stella); or, raise the stakes to a fresh fruit Daiquiri or a Cosmopolitan (both £7.50). Better still, go for a Fifth Floor Smash, a posh-totty confection of champagne, strawberries, Cointreau and wild strawberry liqueur (£8).
Disabled: toilet. Restaurant. Vegetarian dishes.

Mandarin Bar
Mandarin Oriental Hyde Park, 66 Knightsbridge, SW1 (020 7235 2000). Knightsbridge tube. **Open/food served** 11am-2am Mon-Sat; 11am-10.30pm Sun. **Credit** AmEx, DC, MC, V.
If there's anyone you've ever wanted to impress, here's where to bring them. The Mandarin Oriental (opposite Harvey Nichols) is one of London's most dazzling grand old dames, recently spruced up with a multi-million pound makeover. But while the hotel is all marble and burgundy red trad, the Mandarin bar is minimalist catwalk chic. Handsome cocktail magicians work their tricks at a sleek horseshoe bar, with all the bottles and tricks of the trade hidden behind smoked glass screens. The choice of tipple is staggering and best tackled via samplers: a 'Cold Step' is three different vodka shots served in dramatic glassware for a very reasonable £8.50. Alternatively, they claim to have 5,500 wines from which to choose, and a vast collection of Cuban cigars. Sheer luxury, but affordable.
Disabled: toilet. Music (live 9pm-1am Mon-Sat; 6.30-10.30pm Sun). Specialities: cigars, cocktails. Vegetarian dishes.

Le Metro
L'Hôtel, 28 Basil Street, SW3 (020 7591 1213). Knightsbridge tube. **Open** 7.30am-midnight Mon-Sat; 8am-noon Sun. **Food served** 7.30-11.30am, noon-3pm, 6-10.30pm Mon-Sat; 8-11am Sun. **Credit** AmEx, DC, MC, V.
Le Metro, which is in fact the basement bar of L'Hôtel just behind Harrods, should win an award for its clever use of

Shiraz. *See page 56.*

limited underground space. It's a chic place that was chilling to the trancey beats of Morcheeba when we called in for an afternoon sharpener. Settling back in the grey banquette seating we sipped a suitably chilled, gooseberry-infused Trinity Hills sauvignon blanc from New Zealand (£15.80), admired the bucket of pink fuschias on top of the bar and hoped the staff were smirking with us, not at us. The mainly French wine list is a manageable size, with one page for whites and one for reds. Virtually all the wines are served by the glass (starting at under £3). Food is European, well made but not very imaginative, and a tad pricey (sausage and mash, £8.50).
Babies and children admitted. Specialities: wines. Vegetarian dishes.

Osteria d'Isola

145 Knightsbridge, SW1 (020 7838 1044). Knightsbridge tube. **Open/food served** noon-10.30pm Mon-Sat; noon-9.30pm Sun. **Credit** AmEx, DC, MC, V.
If you enjoy posing amid chrome and leather and enjoy Italian wines, then chances are you'll love Osteria d'Isola, the ever-so-slightly relaxed basement area of Oliver Peyton's award-winning Isola restaurant. It sells only Italian wines, and we counted 64 available by the glass (excluding sparklers). The drawback is that they're damned expensive. We figured out that the average price per glass at this place is a whopping £9.79 (cheapest is Vigna Palazzi Falerio dei Colli Ascolani 1998 at £4.50). Instead you might try one of the taster options, such as Native Italian Varieties (£13.50), comprising five 7.5cl shots. There's also a great, typically Peyton range of cocktails.
Babies and children welcome; high chairs. Disabled: toilet. Dress: smart casual.

Paxton's Head

153 Knightsbridge, SW1 (020 7589 6627). Knightsbridge tube. **Open** 11am-11pm Mon-Sat; 11am-10.30pm Sun. **Food served** noon-11pm Mon-Sat; noon-10.30pm Sun. **Credit** AmEx, MC, V.
A sparkling example of an Edwardian boozer: polished mahogany bar with colonnade, brilliantly decorated mirrors and loads of curlicues and what-nots. It's immaculate and almost worthy of a museum. Except the ambience in the pub is more AKA than V&A: grooving club music, low lighting, young black-clad serving staff, and a downstairs chill-out lounge with comfy seating, Pac Man and a membership scheme with discounts on cocktails and shooters. In a similarly schizo fashion, drinks range from real ales (Wadworth 6X, Tetley's, Speckled Hen) to Breezers and flavoured vodkas, and the clientele is two-parts suited (upstairs) to one-part shaggy haired and casual (downstairs). Food is mostly pan-Asian (pad Thai £5.55, nasi goreng £5.65), but you can also get scampi and chips (£6.55).
Babies and children admitted (until 6pm). Function room. Games (fruit machines, games machine, quiz machine). Satellite TV. Specialities: cocktails. Vegetarian dishes.

Swag & Tails

10-11 Fairholt Street, SW7 (020 7584 6926). Knightsbridge or South Kensington tube. **Open** 11am-11pm Mon-Fri. **Food served** noon-3pm, 6-10pm Mon-Fri. **Credit** AmEx, MC, V.
Deep in a warren of pretty mews, fronted by a horticultural display fit for the Chelsea Flower Show, this is an upmarket pub that would rather be a restaurant. On the night we visited it was completely full, and we were the only people not eating. Even the blokes at the bar had plates in front of them. Food is chalked up on a board, and choices on our visit included the likes of char-grilled swordfish (£11.25) and roast boneless quails (£11.50). For a place that still feels resolutely pubby –

big bar area, lots of stripped pine, pub-type seating – albeit a little flouncy, prices are high. While the uniformed staff left us to enjoy pints of hand-pumped Bombardier (£2.40), we couldn't help but feel guilty that we weren't eating or hadn't partaken of the studied ranks of Bollinger standing guard over the bar.
Babies and children admitted (separate area). Bar available for hire (weekends). Restaurant. Tables outdoors (conservatory). Vegetarian dishes.

Also in the area...

Café Rouge 27-31 Basil Street, SW3 (020 7584 2345).

Leicester Square & Piccadilly Circus

10 Room

10 Air Street, W1 (020 7734 9990/www.10-room.co.uk). Piccadilly Circus tube. **Open/food served** 5.30pm-3am Mon-Fri; 8pm-3am Sat. **Credit** AmEx, MC, V.
If your name's not down, you're not getting in. Even if your name is down, you're probably still not getting in. Whine, plead, wheedle or just plain front it out. Alternatively, turn up in a limo to slightly improve your chances. The effort may or may not seem worthwhile, depending on your tastes. If, however, your tastes run to purple palatial splendour (deep purple walls, lilac drapes, matching ceilings, with contrasting red and blue chaise longues and sofas) then this should be right up your street. Drinks are… Well, who cares? Drinks are hardly the point; they could serve tap water here and punters would still order it double. Sadly the staff err on the wrong side of aloof and the toilets are lacking. We do, though, love the armchairs, which are enormous and much coveted for their comfort. Shame the coat hasn't been made yet that could conceal them on the way out.
Function room. Games (backgammon). Music (DJs 9pm nightly, live band 9pm Mon-Wed, 6pm Thur; free). Vegetarian dishes. **Map 2/J7**

10 Tokyo Joe's

85 Piccadilly, W1 (020 7495 2595/www.10-tokyojoes.co.uk). Green Park tube. **Open/food served** 8pm-4am Wed-Sat; 8pm-12.30am Sun. **Credit** AmEx, MC, V.
It's been open a little over a year now and – considering the folk responsible for the 10 Room were also behind this offering – approaching with caution would seem warranted but, thankfully unnecessary. In terms of attitude, the two are poles apart. Friendly doormen and even friendlier staff are on hand to meet, greet and welcome you to this chic, sleek and celestial basement bar. Descend the Clarges Street stairs and into God's waiting room: large, minimalist and, initially, whiter-than-white. Pod-like organic clusters of seating spread across the floor, while private booths dominate the far end. Ambient lighting shimmers through soothing shades of gold and green, sapphires and soft, soft reds, and the music blasts out through wafer-thin speakers. When in the private booths, both lighting and music can be altered at whim. Impressive.
Vegetarian dishes.

79CXR

79 Charing Cross Road, WC2 (020 7734 0769). Leicester Square tube. **Open/food served** 1pm-2am Mon; 1pm-3am Tue-Sat; 1-10.30pm Sun. **Happy hour** 8-10pm daily. **No credit cards.**
It could be tatty, it could be immaculate throughout – but in this shotgun shack of a gay bar it's just too darn dark to tell.

It's a boozy-cruisey affair, with late nights and cheap drink promos aplenty. A few tables and chairs adorn the raised dais to the rear and there are a few more on the extra-cruisey mezzanine area above. The decor, the staircase and balcony give this bar a wild-west edge that's really quite apt as, on any given night, there's more than a few lone, itchy-fingered gunmen on the prowl. Twin ceiling fans stir-up the heady atmosphere and, as the guys get squiffy on house doubles for as little as £2 a go (including mixer), the jukebox steadily cranks things up by degree.

Games (fruit machines, pinball, quiz machine). Jukebox. Music (DJs 10pm Thur-Sat; admission £3 after 10.30pm Mon-Thur; £4 after 10.30pm Fri, Sat). Tables outdoors (pavement). **Map 7/K6**

Atlantic Bar & Grill

20 Glasshouse Street, W1 (020 7734 4888). Piccadilly Circus tube. **Open** noon-3am Mon-Fri; 5pm-3am Sat; 6-10.30pm Sun. **Food served** noon-2.30am Mon-Fri; 6-11.30pm Sat; 7-10.30pm Sun. **Credit** AmEx, DC, MC, V.
The days of the Atlantic Bar popping up in the tabloids with chain-smoking regularity have gone. Now you're more likely to bump into jobbing PRs than Madonna. But, if the glory has faded, the grandeur certainly hasn't: from the sweeping staircase and ornate chandelier by the entrance, to the fake leopardskin and wood panelling in Dick's Bar and the marble-columned glory of the main bar and restaurant – the Atlantic remains the last word in polished panache. It's a tremendous setting for a wide range of wines, champagnes and imported beers whilst making believe that you're in the last days of the Empire, obsequious staff and venison-oriented food included.
Function room. Music (DJs 10pm Mon-Sat; free). Restaurant. Vegetarian dishes. **Map 2/J7**

Café Flo

11 Haymarket, SW1 (020 7976 1313). Piccadilly Circus tube. **Open/food served** 10am-11pm daily. **Credit** AmEx, MC, V.
If the knowledge that, as you sip your Cabernet Sauvignon, people and up down the country are enjoying theirs in an identical setting doesn't worry you too much, then you might enjoy the calculatingly Gallic ambience of Café Flo. To its credit, branches of the chain stock a wide range of beers and reasonably priced wines (£9.85-£21.30 a bottle), plus a decent selection of delectable little somethings. The staff, who could never be accused of overt fawning, are polite and refreshingly well informed about their food and beverages. Pity that the food is so bland. Fine for a glass of wine and quick snack, but we wouldn't go beyond that. Expect to share your air with the provincial jet set, up for a day's shopping and museum going in the Big Smoke.
Babies and children admitted (until noon, back room). Function room. No-smoking area. Restaurant. Tables outdoors (pavement). Vegetarian food. **Map 2/K7**

Cheers

72 Regent Street, W1 (020 7494 3322). Piccadilly Circus tube. **Open** noon-3am Mon-Sat; noon-10.30pm Sun. **Food served** noon-3am Mon-Sat; noon-10.30pm Sun. **Happy hour** 3-7pm Mon-Thur. **Credit** AmEx, MC, V.
Even the reruns have now ceased but here, in this tribute bar at least, the memory lives on. It's a barn-sized place with plenty of built-in TV screens showing either past episodes of the old Bostonian comedy, sports or *The Simpsons*. Character bon mots and photographs line the walls. Food comes with names such as Norm's Big Burgers and Sammy's Sandwiches and – should you feel you haven't really spent enough – a small souvenir stand lurks just within the doorway. Velvet ropes and security staff outside bestow a lofty status the place does not deserve. Packed every night of the week, you may wonder, was *Cheers* really that hugely popular? Fact is, the punters rammed inside couldn't give a damn if anybody remembers their names or not, just so long as the place serves after pub hours.
Babies and children admitted (until 7pm; high chairs). Disabled: toilet. Music (DJs 10pm Mon-Sat; admission £5 after 10pm, £8 after 11pm). No-smoking area. Restaurant. Satellite TVs (big screen). Vegetarian dishes. **Map 2/J7**

Cork & Bottle

44-46 Cranbourn Street, WC2 (020 7734 7807). Leicester Square tube. **Open/food served** 11am-11.30pm Mon-Sat; noon-10.30pm Sun. **Credit** AmEx, DC, MC, V.
Wedged in between a sex shop and a theatre ticket outlet, this is an oasis of cultured calm amid Leicester Square's hectic neon-lit tomfoolery. A subterranean time capsule (sunk in the 1970s), patrons descend a spiral staircase to reach an enchanting grotto-like huddle of small rooms and alcoves filled with candlelit tables. It's been going for over 29 years now and remains a great place to enjoy wine (no beer or spirits here). An enormous, idiosyncratic list (over 200 wines) fizzes with owner Don Hewitson's enthusiasm and knowledge. Although the range rises to Vintage Krug at £150, for the most part affordability is high on the list of priorities. Food is surprisingly adventurous for self-styled bistro fare and also reasonably priced. Hewitson also owns the **Hanover Square Wine Bar** (*see p63*) and **Shiraz** (*see p56*).
Babies and children admitted. No-smoking area (daytime). Satellite TV. Vegetarian dishes. **Map 2/K7**

Corney & Barrow

116 St Martin's Lane, WC2 (020 7655 9800/ www.corney-barrow.co.uk). Leicester Square tube/Charing Cross tube/rail. **Open/food served** noon-midnight Mon-Wed; noon-2am Thur-Sat. **Credit** AmEx, DC, MC, V.
Sandwiched between an upstairs restaurant and basement champagne bar, Corney & Barrow's flagship West End wine bar has an impossibly prime location on the edge of theatreland facing St Martins-in-the-Fields. Predictably, it does extremely well from the pre- and post-show crowds, selecting from some 38 wines available by the glass and presented under grape variety headings. C&B also majors in champagnes (house champagne, £6.25 for a large glass), both straight and flavoured, and in champagne cocktails (all £7.95). Wine bar fare includes the likes of ciabatta with grilled vegetables and goats cheese. Cuban cigars complete the picture.
Disabled: toilet. Function room. No-smoking area (restaurant). Restaurant. Vegetarian dishes. **Map 2/K7**

De Hems

11 Macclesfield Street, W1 (020 7437 2494). Leicester Square tube. **Open/food served** noon-midnight Mon-Sat; noon-10.30pm Sun. **Credit** AmEx, MC, V.
The world is, indeed, a great big melting pot and so it is that you find London's only Dutch pub off the main drag in Chinatown. Although we have it on good authority that De Hems does indeed resemble an 18th-century Netherlands ale house, it isn't immediately different from your average traditional London pub. Except that the service is faster. And more polite. Also, the beer is better (Oranjeboom and Leffe Blanc among the extensive choice) and comes in those giant goblet-style glasses. There are linguistic lessons to be learnt here too, as the signs and much of the menu is in Dutch. Thus, 'veg uitsmijter' is Dutch cheese, pesto and fried eggs on bread, while 'naar' is the toilet.
Comedy (Wed). Dutch night (6pm first and third Thur of month; free). Function room. Games (fruit machine). Vegetarian dishes. **Map 7/K6**

Denim

4A Upper St Martin's Lane, WC2 (020 7497 0376).
Leicester Square tube. **Open/food served** 5pm-1.30am
Mon-Sat; 2pm-midnight Sun. **Credit** AmEx, DC, MC, V.
As we went to press, Denim was due to close for a refit. That's
the trouble being cock o' the hoop: all too soon you're the last,
stringy chicken on the butcher's rack. For what it's worth, we
did like the loud and lurid in-your-face pink decor; what we
didn't like was how the place seemed to be going to seed –
rusty sinks in the toilets, for instance. We look forward to the
relaunch and future tussles with the doormen.
Dress code (Sat). Function rooms. Music (DJs Wed-Sat;
admission £5-£10 after 9pm Fri, Sat). Restaurant. Tables
outdoors (pavement). Vegetarian dishes. **Map 2/L6**

Dive Bar

48 Gerrard Street, W1 (no phone). Leicester Square
tube. **Open** 5.30-11pm Mon-Sat; 6-10.30pm Sun.
No credit cards.
Little changes in this scruffy basement bar, located beneath
Chinatown's King's Head pub; since our last visit there's a little
more graffiti on the toilet doors, the single drinking room seems
a little more shabby – if that's at all possible – and the floor is
that much more adhesive. But there's still the womb-like tunnels
with their rows of tables and benches, just large enough to
accommodate shouted conversation, beer spillage and murky
fumbles. Small it may be, but that doesn't stop the management
whacking in a DJ when they feel the occasion merits it. One big
difference: there's now a bloody great brass padlock on the door
to the gents and the key resides with the bar staff.
Music (DJs Fri, Sat). **Map 7/K6**

Dôme

8-10 Charing Cross Road, WC2 (020 7240 5556).
Leicester Square tube. **Open/food served** 10am-11.30pm
Mon-Sat; 10am-11pm Sun. **Credit** AmEx, MC, V.
Dômes have been around since 1983 when Courage brewery
joined forces with Karen Jones and Roger Myers to transform
the Bird in Hand in Hampstead from a fairly grotty north
London boozer into a faux French café with knobs on. Coming
up for 20 years later, after a few tweaks of style, the decor is
familiar but effective: beige paintwork, light wood serving
area and flooring, topped off with fancy chandeliers and
French Impressionist prints. You get the feeling that they'd
rather you ate – and the food is exactly as you'd expect from
a café modelled on something posh in Paris, all fancy
baguettes and steak frites – but it's not compulsory. Drinks
include coffees, wines (French, of course), light beers
(European, including Beck's) and unambitious cocktails.
Expect to encounter groups of sensible women, middle
management and upmarket tourists.
Babies and children admitted (high chairs). No-smoking
area. Restaurant. Vegetarian dishes. **Map 2/K7**

Down Mexico Way

25 Swallow Street, W1 (020 7437 9895/
www.downmexway.com). Piccadilly Circus tube. **Open**
noon-3am Mon-Sat; noon-10.30pm Sun. **Food served**
noon-midnight Mon-Sat; noon-10pm Sun. **Credit** AmEx,
DC, MC, V.
Theme bars are inherently tacky but this Latin-inspired bar-
restaurant feels a little less plasticky than most – stylish even.
Its downstairs bar –́ done out in tasteful shades of blue, edged
with ornate Spanish-style tiling and embellished by little
wrought-iron what-nots – is topped by a gorgeous blue glass
ceiling. At the bar there are over ten different tequilas on offer
and the beer range includes Sol, Tecate, Dos Equis and San
Miguel. There's a small dance area and DJ booth where, for

a £7 cover charge weekends, you can get all hot and sweaty
to those sexy Latin sounds. Ariba!
Babies and children admitted (restaurant only). Function
room. Music (DJs 9pm Wed-Sat; admission £7 after
8.30pm Thur-Sat). Restaurant. Salsa lessons (6-8pm
Thur, Fri; free). Salsa and samba dancers (Fri, Sat
evenings; restaurant). Vegetarian dishes. **Map 2/J7**

Imperial

5 Leicester Street, WC2 (020 7437 6573). Leicester
Square or Piccadilly Circus tube. **Open/food served**
11am-11pm Mon-Sat; noon-10.30pm Sun. **Credit** AmEx,
DC, MC, V.
Given its location just off the top of Leicester Square, the fact
that the Imperial has managed to remain a rather down-to-
earth, no-nonsense boozer is something of a marvel (the
nearby crusty old Falcon succumbed to the epidemic of Irish
theming just last year). Its lack of polish and adherence to
traditional pub browns and large antique mirrors is to be
applauded. Just a pity about the poor showing of beers (only
Courage Best on tap for those that prefer their beer with taste).
Gents, watch yourselves on the perilously steep stairs down
to the toilets.
Games (fruit machine, video golf game). Tables outdoors
(pavement). Vegetarian dishes. **Map 2/K7**

Ku Bar

75 Charing Cross Road, WC2 (020 7437 4303/
www.ku-bar.co.uk). Leicester Square tube. **Open** 1-11pm
Mon-Sat; 1-10.30pm Sun. **Happy hour** 1-9pm daily
(cocktails). **No credit cards.**
This pleasant, unpretentious gay bar is just a couple of doors
down from **79CXR** (*see p53*); it too has blacked-out windows,
but there the similarity ends. The decor is modern and
comfortable, with pale yellow walls adorned with wrought-iron
candelabra and pop pics (Boy George, Kylie, Spice Girls). It's a
two-floor affair, with milling around the bar and minimal
seating downstairs contrasting with the intimate, candlelit
tables and comfy chairs above. It draws a young, fashionable
and sceney crowd fuelled on alcopops and bottled beer, and
one which regularly spills out on to the streets because of or
– more usually – even despite the weather.
Specialities: bottled beers, cocktails. **Map 7/K6**

L'Odéon Bar & Restaurant

65 Regent Street, W1 (020 7287 1400). Piccadilly Circus
tube. **Open** 11am-1am Mon-Sat. **Food served** noon-
2.30pm, 5.30-11pm Mon-Sat. **Credit** AmEx, DC, MC, V.
Regent Street's paean to sophistication and comfy chairs
maintains its crown as the only bar in London where you can
truly get away from it all on a Saturday night without having
to drink four pints of snakebite first. Popular during the week
as a client-greeting hot spot, come the weekend the only
concern you'll face is from the bar staff ensuring your table's
thoroughly clean before you sit down. This doesn't come
cheap (champagne cocktails £7; mint julep £6) but drinks do
provide value for money and there's an excellent wine list.
Plus there's that wonderful view down Regent Street. If you're
looking to impress someone, this is the place to take them.
Babies and children admitted. Disabled: toilet. Function
room. No-smoking area (lunchtimes only). Restaurant.
Vegetarian dishes. **Map 2/J7**

OnAnon

1 Shaftesbury Avenue, W1 (020 7287 8008). Piccadilly
Circus tube. **Open/food served** 5pm-3am Mon-Sat; 5.30-
11.30pm Sun. **Happy hour** 5-7.30pm daily. **Admission**
(over 25's only) £3 after 11pm Mon-Wed; £5 after 11pm
Thur; £10 after 10pm Fri, Sat. **Credit** Am Ex, MC, V.

A recent addition to the Piccadilly scene, and you've got to hand it to them – the name may sound like a load of wank, but OnAnon is a huge and impressive-looking collection of eight bars under one roof, right next to Piccadilly Circus. Each bar has distinct decor, from a Chesterfield lounge leading through to a sleek bar, to a kitschily fake hunting lodge like something out of *Twin Peaks*. It's much more convincing as a theme-led night out than its trashily downmarket branch Tiger Tiger. All the bars share a menu of deep-fried snacks and a limited drinks list of bottled beers, a few wines and poorly made cocktails. Still, the fact that it's big and open until 3am has already endeared the place to weekend ravers. *Babies and children admitted (café only, daytime). Disabled: toilet. Dress code. Function rooms. Music (DJs, 11pm Mon-Thur, 10pm Fri, Sat; admission charges as above).* **Map 2/K7**

Oxygen
17-18 Irving Street, WC2 (020 7930 0907). Leicester Square tube. **Open** 3pm-2am Mon-Wed; 3pm-3am Thur-Sat; 3-10.30pm Sun. **Happy hour** 3pm-2am Mon, 5-8pm Tue-Sun. **Credit** AmEx, MC, V.

The Leicester Square setting is a turn-off to many, but Oxygen isn't bad at all. At ground level it's dark, brooding and heavy on the metal – tables, chairs, the bar top, you name it. Industrial gothic they call it. The bar area is spotlit but elsewhere there are only candles to lighten the gloom. Upstairs is similar but the mood changes slightly with the addition of wood and wrought iron features. Candles are legion and there are two working open fireplaces. Domestic gothic. Beer is bottled (San Miguel, Beck's, Red Stripe, all £2.90) and there's a menu of cocktail standards (£4.25 each, or £10.95 for a two-pint jug). Given the location it's remarkably idiot-free and lacking in door-policy pretension. *Function rooms. Music (DJs 8pm Thur-Sat; admission £5 after 10pm Fri; £7 after 10pm Sat). Satellite TV. Tables outdoors (pavement).* **Map 2/K7**

Saint
8 Great Newport Street, WC2 (020 7240 1551). Leicester Square tube. **Open/food served** 5pm-2am Mon-Thur; 5pm-3am Fri; 7.30pm-3am Sat. **Admission** £5 after 9pm Thur; £7 Fri, Sat. **Credit** AmEx, DC, MC, V.

A cheesy, dramatic entrance – you descend down a wide staircase bathed in purple neon – sets the tone for this brash, voluptuously sculpted hangout for wannabe glamorous, monied youth. There's more perma-tans, sparkly jewellery, blonde highlights and Gucci gear than you can shake a stick at. Early (Essex) birds will get the curvacious sofas lining one wall, otherwise it's mainly standing room only. Choice of beers is limited, but there's compensation in the array of vodkas and cocktails (which are really what this place is about). Specials between 5.55pm and 9pm as part of their 'five after five' promotion mean that it needn't be expensive to drink here during the week, with five beers for £5 or five cocktails for £10. The Saint is heaving at weekends, when it becomes a quasi-club; even during the week the management operates a guest list. Come here for preening, posing and 'avin' a larf. If you feel old or fancy a chat, give it a miss. *Disabled: toilet. Dress code (Fri, Sat). Music (DJs 8pm Tue-Sat). Restaurant. Vegetarian dishes.* **Map 7/K6**

Salisbury
90 St Martin's Lane, WC2 (020 7836 5863). Leicester Square tube. **Open/food served** 11am-11pm Mon-Sat; noon-10.30pm Sun. **Credit** AmEx, DC, MC, V.

It's a grand old pub, is the Salisbury, with a grand old history to match. The wooden plaque outside says so. Built in 1892 as a restaurant (on the site of an earlier pub), it was transformed into the greatest of Victorian London gin palaces six years later and crammed with a grand mahogany bar, fantastic acid-etched glasswork and art nouveau bronze statuettes. Much of this ornamentation survives, and is looking pristine thanks to a refurb of a year or so back. Sadly, the thesps who formerly frequented the place were long ago driven out by tourists and the clientele no longer matches up to the setting (for a look at the pub of old, see the 1961 film *Victim*). Avoid the back room, which is rather grim, but do try for a seat in the snug, round behind the bar (with a door off St Martin's Court), a cosy little space warmed by a fire in winter. *Babies and children admitted (in separate area). Function room. Games (fruit machine). Tables outdoors (pavement). Vegetarian dishes.* **Map 2/L7**

Shiraz
12 Upper St Martin's Lane, WC2 (020 7379 7811/ www.donhewitsonlondonwinebars.com). Leicester Square tube. **Open/food served** 11am-11pm Mon-Fri; 5-11pm Sat. **Credit** AmEx, DC, MC, V.

It's hard to believe that the contemporary Shiraz with its clean lines and restful blues and lilacs, is owned by the same proprietor as the cluttered **Cork & Bottle** (*see p54*). Maybe they are the yin and yang of wine bar philosophy. The wine list at Shiraz lingers on the shiraz/syrah grape variety, but it's extensive and varied enough to cater for all palates. In addition to sampling the wine, people seem to come to Shiraz to talk, while mellow jazz tinkles away in the background. The bar area leads through to the dining area at the back where choices include the likes of seared kangaroo loin. *Babies and children admitted. No-smoking area (restaurant). Restaurant. Tables outdoors (pavement). Vegetarian dishes.* **Map 2/L6**

Sound
Swiss Centre, Leicester Square, W1 (020 7287 1010/ www.soundlondon.com). Leicester Square or Piccadilly Circus tube. **Open/food served** noon-1am Mon-Thur; noon-4am Fri, Sat; noon-midnight Sun. **Admission** (non-diners) £5 after 9pm Mon-Thur; £10 after 10pm Fri, Sat. **Happy hour** 5-8pm daily. **Credit** AmEx, MC, V.

As a home to Channel 5's *Pepsi Chart* every second Tuesday what were you expecting, cricketing prints and horse brasses? What you get is a bar that strives nightly to recreate the manic energy of a hyped-up studio, with pseudo-glam decor, a plethora of TV and video screens, and DJs. Add happy hours that get you three bottles of Miller for £5, staff who veer from false sincerity to rock star stroppiness and a sizeable dance floor, and you and your mates can be S Club 7 for a night. *Disabled: toilet. Dress code. Function room. Music (DJs 5pm nightly; admission charges as above). Restaurant. Satellite TVs (big screen). Tables outdoors (terrace – café only). Vegetarian dishes.* **Map 2/K7**

Sports Café
80 Haymarket, SW1 (020 7839 8300). Piccadilly Circus tube. **Open/food served** noon-2am Mon-Thur; noon-3am Fri-Sat; noon-10.30pm Sun. **Happy hour** 3-7pm Mon-Thur. **Admission** £3 Mon-Thur after 11pm; £5 after 11pm Fri, Sat. **Credit** AmEx, DC, MC, V.

Outside of a Tottenham Court Road shop window, we can't remember ever having seen so many TV screens all in one place; they're everywhere in this American-style theme joint, behind the bar, above the bar, hanging off the walls, dangling from ceilings, built into dining booths, even above the urinals. And all are tuned to sport in all its many forms. What few surfaces don't have a screen attached are bedecked with sports paraphernalia, including dirt bikes and an F1 racing

car. Participatory urges are catered for with table football, pool, video games and even a small basketball cage. Meanwhile, staff cavort in cheerleader garb as they dispense the beer (lager, of course) and tex-mex grub. Neither food nor drink is anything to shout about, but given the usual accompaniment to a game is a hotdog or burger that's presumably not an issue.
Babies and children admitted (until 6pm, children's menu, play areas). Disabled: toilet. Dress code. Function room. Games (PlayStations, basketball court, pool tables, table football, video games). Music (DJs 10pm Mon-Thur; 9pm Fri, Sat). Restaurant. Satellite TVs (big screens). Vegetarian dishes. Map 2/K7

Studio Lounge
Waterstone's, 203-206 Piccadilly, W1 (020 7851 2400). Piccadilly Circus tube. **Open** 11am-11pm Mon-Sat; noon-6pm Sun. **Food served** noon-4pm, 6-8pm Mon-Sat; noon-4pm Sun. **Credit** AmEx, MC, V.
Boozy bookworms can browse potential purchases from the fifth-floor bar at Waterstone's leviathan Piccadilly bookstore. It may be a noisy contrast to the more hushed tones of the shop proper, but here you can recline in minimalist surroundings – plain white walls, tiled floor – and read, gossip, pick through the evening meal menu and take in a fine panorama that includes Big Ben, the Houses of Parliament and the London Eye. Waiter service removes the inconvenience of actually have to order at the bar. Wines start at £2.95 a glass, champagnes at £6.25 and bottled beers include the likes of Budvar, Ichiban and Tsingtao, at £3-£3.95, and St Peter's Golden Ale at £3.95 for 50cl. Indulge too much, however, and you run the risk of waking up next to a book, the title of which you cannot remember.
Babies and children admitted (until 5pm). Function rooms. Restaurant. Tables outdoors (balcony). Vegetarian dishes. Map 2/J7

Titanic
81 Brewer Street, W1 (020 7437 1912). Piccadilly Circus tube. **Open** 5.30pm-3am Tue-Sat. **Food served** 5.30-11.30pm. **Credit** AmEx, MC, V.
Despite the infamous name, and some recent less than glowing reviews concerning the food, Titanic steams on. Modelled very approximately on the White Star Line's luxuriant liner, it still looks impressive, with a spacious bar with plenty of elbow room for diners and seating for barflies. All maroon deco, the one major drawback remains its nine enormous mirrored spinning balls, which can induce headaches, if not epilepsy. Drinks served at the sumptuous oval bar include cocktails from £7.50, Martinis from £6.50, a modest selection of wines and champagnes and bottled beers by the likes of Kirin, Budvar and Hoegaarden. And while it may have been largely absent from the news and gossip columns for the past 12 months, it remains bloody difficult to get in.
Disabled: toilet. Music (DJs 11pm Thur-Sat). Restaurant. Vegetarian dishes. Map 2/J7

West Central
29-30 Lisle Street, WC2 (020 7479 7980). Leicester Square tube. **Open** *main bar* 3-11pm Mon-Sat; 3-10.30pm Sun; *theatre bar* 5-11pm Mon-Sat; 5-10.30pm Sun; *basement bar* 10.30pm-3am Fri, Sat; 10.30pm-2am Mon-Thur. **Admission** (basement only) from £3; depending on promoter. **Credit** MC, V.
West Central? Party Central, more like – a permanently packed-to-the-hilt gay pub-cum-club with hugely popular theme nights. The ground floor is a bar that gets more disco as the evening goes on. Refuge can be taken in the upstairs, living-room sized Theatre Bar, all red velvet and gold cherubim. Alternatively, step up the pace in the small and clubby basement bar with dancefloor. Drinks are basic pub prices.
Function room. Music (DJs 8pm nightly). Quiz (8pm fortnightly Tue; £1 to play). Map 2/K7

Zinc Bar & Grill
21 Heddon Street, W1 (020 7255 8899/ www.conran.com). Oxford Circus or Piccadilly Circus tube. **Open/food served** noon-11pm Mon-Sat. **Credit** AmEx, DC, MC, V.
It's a case of same-old, same-old at this small, but nonetheless popular Conran effort that, crowd aside, is thankfully thin on pretension. But, why not? If it ain't broke... Most of the area is taken up by the restaurant, although the bar area itself – gun-metal grey with pop rivets – is sizeable and usually pretty busy. Even if you don't intend eating, it's pleasurable to observe the chefs going about their business in the open-plan kitchen. Cocktails (from £6) dominate, and there's a fine selection of champagnes, ranging from £32.50 to £120 a bottle. Beers include Freedom, Peroni, Budvar and Sapporo (all £2.75). A small selection of post-prandial cigars is also available.
Babies and children admitted (restaurant only). Disabled: toilet. Function room. Restaurant. Tables outdoors (terrace). Vegetarian dishes. Map 2/J7

Also in the area...
All Bar One 84 Cambridge Circus, WC2 (020 7379 8311); 48 Leicester Square, WC2 (020 7747 9921); 289-293 Regent Street, W1 (020 7467 9901).
Café Flo 50-51 St Martin's Lane, WC2 (020 7836 8289).
Champagne Charlie's (Davys) 17 The Arches, Villiers Street, WC1 (020 7930 7523).
Moon Under Water (JD Wetherspoon) 28 Leicester Square, WC2 (020 7839 2837).
Slug & Lettuce 14 Upper St Martin's Lane, WC2 (020 7379 4880).

Critics' choice
pub quizzes

Approach Tavern (p188)
Sample question: Tae kwondo is now an Olympic sport. In which country did it originate?

Bricklayer's Arms (p127)
Name the famous pop star who came third in the Brickie's Tuesday night quiz.

Dog & Bell (p173)
Which country has the most sheep?

King William IV (p215)
According to the Vatican, how many bishops were there in February 1997?

Rosemary Branch (p223)
Which Chislehurst takeaway inspired a Banshee's song?

Marylebone

Barley Mow
8 Dorset Street, W1 (020 7935 7318). Baker Street tube.
Open 11am-11pm Mon-Sat; noon-5pm Sun. **Food served**
11.30am-3pm Mon-Sat. **Credit** AmEx, DC, MC, V.
It may be one of the oldest pubs in Marylebone (built 1871)
and original in almost every detail, but on our cold January
visit we were deeply thankful for the addition of gleaming
white radiators. Many years ago this site was in the midst of
cornfields, and the pub signboard still portrays the old rural
tradition of celebrating harvest with a toast across a sheaf of
barley. For another colourful bit of living history, plough your
way through the punters downing cheapish brews (Tetley's
£2.15, Greene King IPA £2.30, Marston's Pedigree £2.30) to
the narrow passage left of the bar where you'll find two tiny,
fully enclosed pawnbroking booths, each with a pair of facing
benches and its own stretch of bar. What goes on now behind
their tall wood partitions and latched doors? Arrive early and
you might be able to claim one and find out.
Games (fruit machine, quiz machine). Satellite TV.
Specialities: real ales. Tables outdoors (pavement).
Vegetarian dishes.

Beehive
*7 Homer Street, W1 (020 7262 6581). Edgware Road
tube.* **Open** 11am-3.30pm, 5.30-11.30pm Mon-Thur;
11am-11pm Fri, Sat; noon-10.30pm Sun. **Food served**
noon-2.30pm Mon-Fri. **Credit** MC, V.
Londoners are reputed to cherish their anonymity, but anyone
would have a hard time keeping to themselves here. It's partly
that the pub is so small – conversational intimacies are
impossible – and partly that the good-natured regulars seem
to relish newcomers. As soon as we'd been fixed up with a
pint (Young's), we were solicited for our opinions on the West
Ham game of the night before. Then we were treated to a
builder's eye-view of London area by area (Maida Vale is tops,
Fulham gets the thumbs down). All the while, the silver-
haired barman swung his hips to Diana Ross. If you've a few
opinions of your own, this would be the place to share them.
Babies and children admitted. Tables outdoors (pavement).
TV. Vegetarian dishes.

Carpe Diem
*28 Paddington Street, W1 (020 7935 0556). Baker
Street tube.* **Open/food served** 10.30am-10pm Mon-Fri;
noon-10pm Sat; noon-5pm Sun. **Credit** AmEx, MC, V.
A laid-back sort of place which, the evening we visited, had a
fair number of after-workers winding down with a pint and the
crossword – so, not so much 'seize the day' as release it. We
lazed about with a Stella and flipped through the papers and
comics thoughtfully provided. Hunger pangs are countered
with a hugely varied café-style menu offering brunch, lunch or
supper. Select from basic spuds and sarnies, giant plates of
sociable snacks to share (nachos £7.45, vegetable dim sum £7)
or full-on mains like a hefty 8oz rump steak (£8.50). Service is
cheerily informal – the waitress leans in and calls you 'darling'
– and little cards are placed on each table that read simply
'Thank you and everything'. Isn't that sweet?
*Babies and children admitted (high chairs). Bar available for
hire (Sat, Sun). Games (quiz machine). No-smoking area.*
Restaurant. Tables outdoors (pavement). Vegetarian dishes.

Chapel
*48 Chapel Street, NW1 (020 7402 9220). Edgware
Road tube.* **Open** noon-11pm Mon-Sat; noon-4pm,
7-10.30pm Sun. **Food served** noon-2.30pm, 7-10pm daily.
Credit AmEx, DC, MC, V.

A gastropub by numbers, this has all the key elements (plate
glass windows, stripped wood, open kitchen, laboriously
described dishes with the prerequisite goat's cheese, rocket
and parmesan shavings well in evidence) but is severely
lacking when it comes to details like warmth or personality.
Beers are adequate (Carling, Grolsch, Caffrey's, Stella, IPA or
London Pride). Fortunately for Chapel the food is very good,
and considerably more flavourful than the bland surroundings
would suggest. Goat's cheese salad (£5) and roasted courgette,
mascarpone and almonds (£8) were both delicious. The beer
we'd sunk called for starch, but unfortunately our request for
chips was met with 'No side orders. Just what's on the board'.
See what we mean about the lack of a human touch?
*Babies and children admitted. Function room. Tables
outdoors (pavement, garden). Vegetarian dishes.*

Churchill Bar & Cigar Divan
*Churchill Intercontinental, Portman Square, W1
(020 7486 5800). Marble Arch tube.* **Open/food served**
11am-11pm Mon-Sat; 5-10.30pm Sun. **Credit** AmEx, DC,
MC, V.
Overwhelmed by the aura of well bred nonchalance, we were
nearly convinced that this was a private gentleman's club,
instead of the upmarket hotel bar that it is. A pianist was
playing to smart middle-aged men amid warm mahogany
panelling and humidors; the whole place accented not only
by rich fabrics but also by thick, curling wreaths of sweet
cigar smoke (from Punch Margarita, £7, to Cohiba
Esplendido, £25). Attentive waiters bring free and copious
bar nibbles and can also advise on the selection of 70 malts
(£7, or vintage £16) and luxury liqueurs (top notch is
armagnac ch. De Laubade 1908 at £95). Although available,
few buy beers (Michelob £4, Grolsch £4.60). It's just a shame
that the same care and attention has not been lavished on the
menu. 'Light snacks from the Far East' presents an Anglicised
mess that includes Middle Eastern spicy lamb kofters [sic]
with houmous £6.75, while prices for more substantial scoff
(cod and chips £14.95) are startling.
*Babies and children admitted (until 7pm). Disabled: toilet.
Function rooms. Music (pianist 5.30-11.30pm Mon-Fri).
Restaurant. Satellite TV. Specialities: cigars, whiskies.
Vegetarian dishes.*

Dover Castle
*43 Weymouth Mews, W1 (020 7580 4412). Regent's
Park tube.* **Open** 11.30am-11pm Mon-Fri; noon-11pm Sat.
Food served noon-2.30pm, 6-9pm Mon-Fri; noon-2.30pm
Sat. **Credit** MC, V.
Tired of over-priced London? A quick pint down the Dover
Castle might help. Sitting pretty right in the middle of a tiny
and exclusive-looking West End mews, it is incredibly cheap.
Our generous benefactor? The redoubtable Sam Smith. Old
Brewery Bitter is £1.64 a pint, Extra Stout is £2, Organic
Lager and Pure Brewed Lager are £2.36 a bottle.
Consequently the place is always busy with the well informed,
sunk in old-fashioned leather chairs and sofas. Private do's
and more formal society meetings often happen in the
adjacent rooms beyond the small L-shaped main bar.
*Babies and children admitted (daytime). Function room.
Games (quiz machine). TV. Vegetarian dishes.*

Feathers
*43 Linhope Street, NW1 (020 7402 1327). Marylebone
tube/rail.* **Open** noon-11pm Mon-Thur, Sat; 11am-11pm
Fri; noon-10.30pm Sun. **Food served** noon-3pm Mon-Fri.
Credit MC, V.
The Feathers is so small that when we arrived we peered
about its drab interior looking for the door to the main bar.
But no, the poky entrance room is all there is. A dozen people

makes a crowd here – splendid if you're agoraphobic, uncomfortably cramped otherwise. Drinks are unexciting, with just a couple of real ales (Flowers Original, London Pride). Food is also old school – though we were caught by surprise at the mention of bobotti (a South African curried mince dish), which the barmaid claimed was a customer favourite. The shabbiness appears beloved by locals and may even, it seems, be a recipe for longevity – plenty of the regulars looked to be 80 plus.
Babies and children admitted. Jukebox. Tables outdoors (garden, pavement). TV. Vegetarian dishes.

Henry Holland
39 Duke Street, W1 (020 7629 4426). Bond Street tube. **Open** 11am-11pm Mon-Sat; noon-8pm Sun. **Food served** 11am-3pm Mon-Sat. **Credit** MC, V.
Henry Holland (1745-1806) was an English architect. He did the Drury Lane Theatre (later burnt down), the first designs for the Brighton Pavillion and remodelled Woburn Abbey. He was not responsible for this pub, which dates back only as far as 1956, but chances are he would have approved. Swing through magnificent double doors inset with delicate panes of pale blue frosted glass, to an interior set with elongated mirrors and hung with scalloped art deco chandeliers. Art nouveau posters add colour and there are meticulously detailed prints of old buildings. The range of beers is pleasing (Flowers Original, London Pride, Wadworth 6X, Hoegaarden). Unsurprisingly given the location down a side street beside Selfridges, trade is made up largely of pit-stop shoppers.
Function room. Games (fruit machines). Jukebox. Satellite TV. Specialities: real ales. Tables outdoors (pavement). Vegetarian dishes.

O Bar
21A Devonshire Street, W1 (020 7935 6121). Baker Street or Regent's Park tube. **Open/food served** noon-11pm Mon-Fri; 5-11pm Sat. **Happy hour** 5-7pm Mon-Sat. **Credit** AmEx, MC, V.
'Girls Just Wanna Have Fun' should be the soundtrack of this newly opened branch of the O Bar (*see p81*), which has cheekily kept the outdated Devonshire Arms' *Time Out* recommendation sticker in its window. On the Thursday we visited every table bar one was crowded with single-sex groups of the female kind. Why that should be, we don't know. Maybe it's the flamboyant decor of yellow patterned tiles, ornate mirrors in dark-green frames, and the whole shebang doused in blue from tinted uplights. Or perhaps it's down to the champagne cocktails (£5) and cheap Thai menu (mains around a fiver). Whatever it is, we're sure the management doesn't miss the blokes, not the way these ladies were knocking back the booze.
Babies and children admitted (until 5pm). Function room. Vegetarian dishes.

O'Conor Don
88 Marylebone Lane, W1 (020 7935 9311). Bond Street tube. **Open** 11am-11pm Mon-Fri. **Food served** noon-10pm Mon-Fri. **Credit** AmEx, MC, V.
An antidote to the blight of the Irish kit-pub, this ambitious free house feels like the genuine article. The secret? Simple. It's run by an Irish family (the O'Callaghans) who've smoothly blended the best of Irish-style drinking and dining across three good-sized floors. Ground level is where most people congregate. Speedy floor service is a helpful crowd pleaser and the Guinness (including Draught Bitter and Extra Cold Regular) is predictably plentiful (as is the accompanying paraphernalia – everything from mirrors to floor tiles to a toy toucan). Venture downstairs and you'll find Moy Mell, an

air-conditioned haven of natural brick and wood that offers UDV malts. Upstairs, meanwhile, is country house-style dining room Ard-Ri, where hearty Irish stew or beef in Guinness casserole can be followed by a quick Irish Coffee pick-me-up.
Babies and children admitted (daytime). Bar available for hire. Restaurant. Specialities: Guinness. Vegetarian dishes.

Tsar Bar
Langham Hilton, 1C Portland Place, W1 (020 7636 1000). Oxford Circus tube. **Open** noon-11pm Mon-Fri; 6-11pm Sat. **Food served** noon-3pm, 6-10.30pm Mon-Fri; 6-10.30pm Sat. **Credit** AmEx, DC, MC, V.
Oil paintings of Russian life adorn tiled walls, a humidor houses the 'Tsar's Cigar Collection' (Hamlet miniatures to Cohiba Siglo 5) and bow-tied waiters flit between tables, trailing red 'Russian' sashes from the waist. The initial hilarity of the theme wanes quickly (dry-roasted peanuts served in the bottom half of a matrushka doll, anyone?), but the drinks are an entirely more serious business altogether. This is, after all, a place where vodka is lovingly served in two-part glasses, the lower section containing crushed ice. Choose from 101 varieties, many at £5.50 per 50ml glass but be prepared to dig deeper for the raw sensation of 79.9% Pure Spirit 140 (£8.50), vodka combinations (£9.90-£13.90) and absurdly named vodka cocktails (£8.50-£11.50). The food menu includes Slavonic faves such as borscht, but caviar sold by the gram (£2) is more like it.
Babies and children admitted (high chairs). Disabled: toilet. Function rooms. Restaurant. Vegetarian dishes.

William Wallace
33 Aybrook Street, W1 (020 7487 4937). Baker Street or Bond Street tube. **Open** 11am-11pm Mon-Sat; noon-10.30pm Sun. **Food served** noon-3pm, 6-9pm Mon-Fri; noon-8pm Sat, Sun. **Credit** AmEx, DC, MC, V.
Don't let the big shiny Coke machine outside this recently relocated pub fool you: the William Wallace is vigorously Scottish. Beer? It's Scottish: Calders, the 'official beers of Scottish rugby'. Spirits? Sixteen malts, from Glen-this to Glen-that (£2.50 each). Lunch? Try a Nessie's Monster (£4.95), a sandwich crammed with pork sausage and onion relish. For dinner there's haggis, neeps and tatties (£6.25). Staff and customers are entirely welcoming to those of us who don't qualify for a kilt, but beware: when it comes to sporting events such as the Six Nations Cup they just might be serious about the sign 'Parking for Scots only. All others will be towed.'
Babies and children admitted (upstairs). Function room. Games (fruit machine, pinball machines, pool table, quiz machine). Jukebox. Music (live Scottish, Sat). Satellite TV. Specialities: malt whiskies, Scottish real ales. Tables outdoors (pavement). Vegetarian dishes.

Windsor Castle
29 Crawford Place, W1 (020 7723 4371). Edgware Road tube. **Open** 11am-11pm Mon-Sat; noon-10.30pm Sun. **Food served** 11am-3pm, 6-11pm Mon-Fri; 6-11pm Sat. **Credit** DC, MC, V.
While we stood outside the Windsor Castle, pondering whether the shelves of royal memorabilia were part of a cherished personal collection or up for sale, we overheard a heavily French-accented passer-by. 'I thought it is just something to buy,' she announced disparagingly. So we weren't alone in thinking the Windsor Castle looked like a tourist shop, a rather quaint idealised vision of ye olde souvenir shop, but a shop nonetheless. Inside, as if to maximise store turnover, no space has been left free from nick-nacks and clutter. As you sup your Bass, Hancock's HB or Guinness, wall-to-wall photos and brightly lit display cabinets vie for your attention – celebrating everything that

O'Conor Don

has made England what she is today: Churchill, Dame Vera Lynn, the royals (of course) and actress Wendy Richards (well she did open the place in 1990). All of which makes the Thai food pretty incongruous.

Babies and children admitted. Restaurant (available for hire). Tables outdoors (pavement). Vegetarian dishes.

Also in the area...

All Bar One 7-9 Paddington Street, W1 (020 7487 0071); 5-6 Picton Street, W1 (020 7487 0161).
Café Rouge 46-48 James Street, W1 (020 7487 4847).
Basement 92 (Davys) 92 Wigmore Street, W1 (020 7224 0169).
Dock Blida (Davys) 50-54 Blandford Street, W1 (020 7486 3590).
Lees Bag Wine Bar (Davys) 4 Great Portland Street, W1 (020 7636 5358).
Marylebone Tup 93 Marylebone High Street, W1 (020 7935 4373).
The Metropolitan Bar (JD Wetherspoon) 7 Station Approach, Marylebone Road, NW1 (020 7486 3489).

Mayfair

American Bar

Connaught Hotel, 16 Carlos Place, W1 (020 7499 7070/ www.savoygroup.com). Bond Street or Green Park tube. **Open/food served** 11.30am-3pm, 5.30-11pm Mon-Sat; 5.30-11pm Sun. **Credit** AmEx, DC, MC, V.

Quite what is so American about the Connaught's famed bar – save for the other drinkers on the night we visited – is a mystery to us. The decor here is nothing if not English stately home, albeit the kind of aristo-chic that you'll find in exclusive upper-class New England country clubs (oak panelling, comfy floral seating, stags' heads mounted on the wall). Almost before we'd had a chance to sit down, the solicitous barman had begun to apologise for the lack of a cocktail menu (it had gone missing earlier in the evening), but then made up for it by mixing an impeccable Vodka Martini and a joyously naughty Brandy Alexander. Beware of the 'optional service' that'll be added onto your bill: ours pushed the £19 tab up to £21.43 and, had we not spotted it, would have sneakily enticed us into tipping twice.

Disabled: toilet. Dress code (after 6pm). Function rooms. Vegetarian dishes.

The Audley

41-43 Mount Street, W1 (020 7499 1843). Green Park tube. **Open** 11am-11pm Mon-Sat; noon-10.30pm Sun. **Food served** 11am-9.30pm Mon-Sat; noon-9pm Sun. **Credit** AmEx, DC, MC, V.

In terms of fixtures and fittings, the Audley has it made. A grand corner pub with high ceilings, it's all delicious original Victoriana: high-backed red leather benches, smart tables and a gloriously incongruous (it's a pub, after all) chandelier. Punters, though, are the standard Mayfair mix of the rich and the richer, with local office staff filling the place at lunchtimes and after work. What's more, and in true London fashion, no one appears to notice the grandiose nature of the building in which they're drinking. A fine range of wines makes up for unremarkable beer, while the unmistakable smell of money prevalent throughout the area here took the form of a couple of old buffers puffing on a pair of temptingly pungent cigars.

Babies and children admitted (daytime). Function room. Tables outdoors (pavement). Vegetarian dishes.

Château Bar

Mayfair Intercontinental Hotel, Stratton Street, W1 (020 7629 7777/www.interconti.com). Green Park tube. **Open/food served** noon-2am Mon-Fri, Sun; 3pm-2am Sat. **Credit** AmEx, DC, MC, V.

The Château is at the more characterful end of chain hotel bars but that is unmistakably what it is, from the over-patterned carpets to the over-refined piano music and the lack of a distinct clientele. Or much clientele at all, on the night we visited. It's comfortable, with lots of club chairs and wooden-panelled walls, though too large to be entirely cosy, and signed 'celeb' pics on the wall are never a good sign. Prices were a little high, too, with most cocktails from a predictable list £9 and Martinis, more interesting (among them a Bitch on Wheels with crème de menthe) at £12. There's a good list of whiskies. Staff were friendly and nibbles free and copious but the food menu was expensive (£10 for focaccia with mozzarella, tomato and tapenade). Not a place you'd go out of your way to visit.

Disabled: toilet. Function rooms. Music (pianist 6pm-midnight Mon-Sat). Restaurant. Vegetarian dishes.

Claridge's Bar

Claridge's Hotel, 49 Brook Street, W1 (020 7629 8860/ www.savoygroup.com). Bond Street tube. **Open/food served** 11am-10.45pm Mon-Sat; 4-10.30pm Sun. **Credit** AmEx, DC, MC, V.

When Claridge's revamped its bar a couple of years ago, it was a bold move for so traditional an institution. But one that paid off – not only has it become fashionable, nay chic even, it consistently pulls in the crowds, and not just any old riff-raff, either. It's worked because all of its keynote characteristics – impeccable standards of drinks, service and decor, and just a modicum of snootiness (we were treated to a raised eyebrow here and there from the impeccably besuited staff) – have survived unmolested. It's a low-lit den of restrained deco classicism with a longish bar opening into a wider area at one end that can be reserved for private parties. Sitting at the bar gives you an object lesson in the art of cocktail making. Martinis (£8.50), served in crystal, are immaculate; Daiquiris and other fruit drinks – including what might be a possibly ill-conceived strawberry Caiprihina – use punnet-fresh ingredients. It's a select list but we wouldn't bet on stumping the bar staff with any ad hoc request. Top-end wines and champagnes (six by the glass) are also available, along with a snack list of luxury foods – probably good if the premises-baked (and free) bar snacks are anything to go by.

Disabled: toilet. Function rooms. Restaurant. Vegetarian dishes.

Coach & Horses

5 Bruton Street, W1 (020 7629 4123). Bond Street or Green Park tube. **Open** 11am-11pm Mon-Fri; 11am-8pm Sat. **Food served** 11am-9.30pm Mon-Fri; 11.30am-6pm Sat. **Credit** AmEx, DC, MC, V.

Another cosy little pub offering solace to Mayfair non-cocktail types. Not the sort of place you expect to find just off Berkeley Square (no nightingales to report), it's housed in a small timber-framed building on a street packed with offices and other potential pub custom. Come 5.30pm they cram into this place – far more of them than can comfortably fit. Commendably professional bar staff are adept at multi-tasking and despite the lack of elbow space the atmosphere remains orderly. Still, better to come later.

Babies and children admitted (in restaurant). Function room. Games (fruit machines). Restaurant. TV. Vegetarian dishes.

Dorchester Bar

Dorchester Hotel, 53 Park Lane, W1 (020 7629 8888/
www.dorchesterhotel.com). Hyde Park Corner tube. **Open**
11am-11pm Mon-Sat; noon-10.30pm Sun. **Food served**
noon-11.45pm Mon-Sat; noon-10.30pm Sun. **Credit** AmEx,
DC, MC, V.
The Dorchester is known as one of the most desirable
temporary addresses in London, but even so, nothing can
really prepare the first-time visitor for the extraordinary
opulence that awaits in the sunken bar. There's a mirror
theme throughout: even the piano – played nightly – is
covered in tiny pieces of reflective glass. Glitz and glamour
are complemented by plush comfort, though the deep yellow
armchairs aren't particularly well suited to the kind of cosy-
up romantic intimacy that a trip here might stir up. Our fault
for not snagging a comfy banquette booth. Our Cosmopolitan
and Caipirinha, from a long list of cocktails, were both mixed
to perfection and incredibly moreish. It's pricey, mind (two
drinks totalled £18), but what did you expect? Other huge
pluses came with the impeccable waitress and maitre d'
service, the complimentary nibbles and the menu that clearly
states service is included with the drinks. A more or less
unique touch in a deliciously unique bar.
Disabled: toilet. Dress code. Function rooms. Music
(pianist Sun-Tue; jazz band Wed-Sat. Restaurant.
Specialities: cocktails. Vegetarian dishes.

Guinea

30 Bruton Place, W1 (020 7409 1728). Bond Street or
Green Park tube. **Open** 11am-11pm Mon-Fri; 6.30-11pm
Sat. **Food served** noon-2.30pm Mon-Fri; 6.30-11pm Sat.
Credit AmEx, DC, MC, V.
On a recent visit we clocked a poster on the wall for ski
holidays offering any Guinea drinkers a free bottle of
champagne with every booking made – which gives you a
few clues as to the kind of drinkers who frequent this place.
It's a tiny little boozer serving largely as a waiting room for
those wishing to dine in the award-winning (it's won gongs
for its pies) but pricey Guinea Grill to the rear; indeed, the
only other drinkers present when we visited had the gall to
ask the barman if there were any 'full-size pubs' in the area.
But non-diners are welcome and, being Young's, the beer is
good. The decor is pleasantly olde worlde and the barman
was one of the warmest and friendliest we've ever come
across in London.
Function room. No piped music or jukebox. Restaurant.
Tables outdoors (pavement). Vegetarian dishes.

Hanover Square Wine Bar

25 Hanover Square, W1 (020 7408 0935). Oxford
Circus tube. **Open** 11am-11pm Mon-Fri. **Food served**
11am-10.30pm Mon-Fri. **Credit** AmEx, DC, MC, V.
Those familiar with the wonderful **Cork & Bottle** (*see p54*)
just off Leicester Square will appreciate this sprawling yet
cosily romantic wine bar tucked away at the south side of
Hanover Square. Like the Cork & Bottle, the Hanover Square
Wine Bar & Grill is located in a basement; like the Cork &
Bottle, it offers an inventive list of wines at reasonable
prices; and like the Cork & Bottle, its decor and ambience
succeeds in evoking the halcyon days of the wine bar – the
1970s – better than most, despite only having opened in
1993. Oh, and like the Cork & Bottle, the Hanover Square
Wine Bar is owned by Don Hewitson – which explains a
whole lot. The food is bistro-style fare and the clientele less
snooty than you might expect at a Mayfair wine bar. All in
all, a winning enterprise.
Babies and children admitted. No-smoking area.
Restaurant. Specialities: wines. TV. Vegetarian dishes.

Havana

17 Hanover Square, W1 (020 7629 2552). Oxford Circus
tube. **Open/food served** 5pm-2am Mon-Thur; 5pm-3am
Fri-Sat; 5pm-1am Sun (membership only Sun).
Admission £3 after 10pm Mon, Tue; £5 after 9pm Wed,
Thur; £5 8-9pm, £10 after 9pm Fri, Sat. **Happy hour**
5-7.30pm Mon-Fri. **Credit** AmEx, DC, MC, V.
If this is a glamorous, exciting representation of modern Cuba,
then can we have our money back, please? The huge
popularity of this Hanover Square hangout is, frankly, a little
mystifying. The decor is easily the best thing about it: all eye-
catching colours and startlingly upholstered seating.
Everything else, though, sucks, from the tapas to the diet
Latin music being pumped out for the benefit of a clientele
that's more Harlow than Havana. Cocktails are fairly cheap
as London cocktails go, but you can taste why. Our Margarita
only contained a meagre measure and a half of spirits (two
parts tequila to one part triple sec), and was weakened further
by an excessive amount of lemon/lime mix; the Mojito was
little better. And the sale of 24-bottle crates of lager at a
startling £59.95-£64.95 so that delusional, desperate punters
can take the party home with them (as the menu advises)
smacks of exploitation. Avoid.
Dress code. Music (DJs 9pm nightly, Brazilian
band 8pm Sun, salsa band 9pm Thur). Restaurant.
Vegetarian dishes.

Hogshead in St James's

11-16 Dering Street, W1 (020 7629 0531/
www.hogshead.co.uk). Bond Street or Oxford Circus tube.
Open 11am-11pm Mon-Sat. **Food served** noon-9pm
Mon-Thur; noon-8pm Fri, Sat. **Credit** AmEx, DC, MC, V.
The name is geographically inexplicable: after all, the area
known as St James's sits to the south of Piccadilly, while this
boozer lies at the very opposite (northern) edge of Mayfair.
Still, that aside, the Dering Street Hogshead does well to
maintain the fine reputation its chain has garnered, even
among those for whom chain bars are anathema. It does so
almost entirely by dint of its fine drinks ranges: a dozen nicely
chosen wines by the glass (and more by the bottle) and an
above-average rotating selection of bitters that come with a
money-back, drinks-replaced guarantee. While the decor is
functional and unmemorable, the layout of the pub is a bonus:
three floors and some nicely hidden alcoves mean that
escaping from the braying Essex office boys during the early
evening is pleasingly straightforward. Add in a good pub
grub menu (our burger was well priced and splendid) and you
have a fine watering hole.
Disabled: toilet. Function rooms. Games (fruit machines,
games machine). No-smoking area. Vegetarian dishes.

The Loop

19 Dering Street, W1 (020 7493 1003/
www.theloopbar.co.uk). Oxford Circus tube. **Open/food**
served noon-1am Mon-Sat (over 25's only). **Admission**
£5 after 10pm Mon-Sat. **Happy hour** 5-7pm Mon-Sat.
Credit AmEx, MC, V.
The plate-glass windows that guard the entrance of this year-
old hangout just off Oxford Street reveal a small but well-
stocked bar; nothing too interesting, nothing too unpleasant.
However, what they don't reveal is what lies beneath. From
these modish but fairly humble origins, the Loop stretches
way underground, expanding out over two labyrinthine
underground floors to encompass bars, a restaurant (most
mains are around £10-£11) and even a club. Friday nights
doubtless see the place jam-packed with Essex boys and girls;
the wet Wednesday we dropped by saw the place largely
empty, but those that were present had clearly been enjoying

Zeta. *See page 67.*

cocktails and beers at the bar for the majority of the evening. The pulsing commercial dance music is probably best appreciated when in such a state, but the clever layout means escape to a quieter corner is easy enough. Something, as they say, for the weekend.
Dress code. Music (DJs Thur-Sat). Restaurant. Specialities: cocktails. Vegetarian dishes.

Mash Mayfair

26B Albemarle Street, W1 (020 7495 5999). Green Park tube. **Open/food served** 11am-11pm Mon-Sat. **Credit** AmEx, DC, MC, V.
Opened in late 2000 (replacing the much-missed Coast restaurant), this is a sibling of the long-established **Mash** on Great Portland Street (*see p42*). Expect interesting micro-brewed beers (in this case brewed off premises), plus Mediterranean brasserie food. Unfortunately, on our last visit the dishes weren't up to scratch, especially for the prices charged. Pop in for an excellent pint, and to admire the orange spaghetti dangling from the ceiling, but don't bother lingering over a meal.
Babies and children admitted (restaurant only). Function room. Restaurant. Specialities: cocktails, own-brewed beer. Vegetarian dishes.

The Met Bar

Metropolitan Hotel, 19 Old Park Lane, W1 (020 7447 1000/www.metropolitan.co.uk). Hyde Park Corner tube. **Open/food served** 11am-6pm daily (members only from 6pm). **Credit** AmEx, DC, MC, V.
Non-members and residents are only allowed into the Met's much-touted celebrity bar before 6pm and consequently see it at its worst: empty, lacking atmosphere and looking like a club before all the guests have arrived. Which effectively is what it is. The decor, loosely Manhattan themed with a dodgy mural, DJ booth, black floor and lots of maroon leather booths, best suited to post- rather the pre-dinner drinking, doesn't help. But boy do the staff know what to do with a cocktail, and they're nice about it, too, even bringing snifters of strange liqueurs for taste-testing. The list is long and inventive without being silly, with a page of Martinis such as the Cosmo made with your choice of fresh fruit (£7), fashionable/retro long drinks such as the Caribbean cocktail, a gingery twist on a sea breeze, some absinthes and some interesting Daiquiris – including a fine vanilla version for £7. Execution is faultless, though at these prices some nibbles would have been nice.
Disabled: toilet. Music (DJs 11pm Mon-Sat). Specialities: cocktails. Vegetarian dishes.

Mulligans of Mayfair

13-14 Cork Street, W1 (020 7409 1370). Green Park or Piccadilly Circus tube. **Open** 11am-11pm Mon-Sat. **Food served** noon-3pm, 6-10pm Mon-Sat. **Credit** AmEx, DC, MC, V.
To call Mulligans an Irish theme bar is, perhaps, to do it down by association with the vile, bicycle-in-window Oirish O'chain that takes up so much valuable real estate in central London. But – even if it is considerably posher than that particular high-street staple and considerably more restrained in its Irishness – an Irish theme bar it is. The only draft beer served in its dark wood-lined main bar is Guinness, though lager-lovers will be appeased by the bottled presence of Beck's, Budvar and Stella Artois and whiskey-lovers will find plenty of obscure Irish brands with which to further pickle themselves. Food, served in the basement, comes courtesy of chef Leon Papworth, and is highlighted by the justly famed, freshly imported oysters.
Babies and children admitted (daytimes). Restaurant. Specialities: Irish whiskies. TV. Vegetarian dishes.

Polo Bar

Westbury Hotel, New Bond Street, W1 (020 7629 7755). Green Park or Oxford Circus tube. **Open/food served** 11am-11pm daily. **Credit** AmEx, DC, MC, V.
The Polo Bar has nothing to do with Ralph Lauren beyond the fact that a few of the wealthy punters probably own walk-in wardrobes full of it. Rather, the main bar at the Westbury Hotel is a tribute to the sublime Rowntree's mint with a hole in it. Just kidding – it's polo the toffs' sport, the hotel and the sport having been intertwined since 1927, when polo player Michael Phipps built and opened the New York Westbury. The decor is predictably polo memorabilia and trinketry (including mallet-shaped door handles) enlivening a posh but frankly naff trad English scheme including some hideous tartan chairs. Happily, the cocktails are in far better taste, at least if our cockle-warming Black Russian and tangy Whiskey Sour were anything to go by. Nibbles were conspicuous by their absence, but service was otherwise efficient.
Babies and children admitted (restaurant). Function room. Music (pianist 5-9pm Mon-Fri). Restaurant. Specialities: cocktails, whiskies. TV. Vegetarian dishes.

Punch Bowl

41 Farm Street, W1 (020 7493 6841). Green Park tube. **Open** 11am-11pm Mon-Fri; noon-6pm Sat. **Food served** 11am-7pm Mon-Fri; noon-5pm Sat. **Credit** DC, MC, V.
Proof that working-class people are permitted in Mayfair can be garnered at this earthy, slightly scruffy but rather loveable hide-out in the heart of London's most moneyed locale. There's precious little special about the Punch Bowl, and in any other area its forgettable decor and unremarkable mix of drinkers (labourers, a few tie-loosened office staff) wouldn't pass comment, but here plain ordinariness becomes a rare treat. A warm welcome is guaranteed, as is a decent beer (well kept Old Speckled Hen, on our visit) and a seat at a table. The piped music came courtesy of Kiss FM, and non-conversational entertainment includes a fruit machine plus, upstairs, a dartboard. The pub grub is serviceable enough.
Function room. Games (darts, fruit machine). Jukebox. TV. Vegetarian dishes.

Red Bar

Grosvenor Hotel, Park Lane, W1 (020 7499 6363). Marble Arch tube. **Open** noon-11pm Mon-Sat; 7-11pm Sun. **Credit** AmEx, DC, MC, V.
No prizes for guessing the colour scheme at the Grosvenor's main bar. Scarlet dominates, which sounds as if it ought to be either very trendy or dangerously decadent, but in fact it's neither. While it's comfortable enough, and while the service was above average, the bar is seriously lacking in intimacy and is about as racy as an executive lounge at an international airport. On the plus side, our cocktails – it's a cocktail kind of place – were both good, with the perfect Manhattan outstanding, but at £8.50 each (excluding service), so they should be. A word of warning, though: the hotel's popularity with awards ceremonies may mean – as it did for us – that an evening visit here is further spoilt by the presence of pockets of freeloaders and expense-accounters who've been drinking since their gongs were given out at lunchtime.
Babies and children admitted. Disabled: toilet. Dress code. Satellite TV. Specialities: cocktails.

Red Lion

1 Waverton Street, W1 (020 7499 1307). Green Park tube. **Open** 11.30am-11pm Mon-Fri; 6-11pm Sat; noon-3pm, 6-10.30pm Sun. **Food served** noon-2.30pm, 6-9.30pm Mon-Fri, Sun; 6-9.30pm Sat. **Credit** AmEx, DC, MC, V.

Hidden away in the wilds of Mayfair, a few doors down from one of central London's smallest petrol stations, this Scottish & Newcastle boozer is a lovely little find. It's also, apparently, not to say surprisingly, a discovery that few drinkers make because we had no problems getting a table by the fire here on a night when other nearby pubs were completely packed. It's a cosy pub that pulls off the rare trick of appearing smaller than it actually is, thanks to some judiciously placed wood panelling and pleasing snugs and nooks. Service was fine, even if the Greene King IPA wasn't in great shape, and the atmosphere one of genteel but unsnooty civility. Don't bank on eating here, mind: the bar food looked tired and unappetising, while the prices in the restaurant at the back were sky-high even by local standards; fish and chips for £14.50 anyone?
Babies and children admitted (children's menu). No piped music or jukebox. Restaurant. Tables outdoors (pavement). Vegetarian dishes.

Running Footman

5 Charles Street, W1 (020 7499 2988). Green Park tube. **Open** 11.30am-11pm Mon-Fri; 11.30am-3pm, 7-11pm Sat; noon-3pm, 7-10.30pm Sun. **Food served** 11.30am-10pm Mon-Fri; 11.30am-2.30pm, 7-10pm Sat; noon-2.30pm, 7-9.30pm Sun. **Credit** AmEx, DC, MC, V.
Named in honour of and once frequented by the manservants who used to scurry along in front of their aristocrat employers' carriages warning people of the 'danger' fast approaching, the Running Footman these days draws a mix of office workers in search of after-work sustenance and tourists in search of a slice of traditional Londonalia. The former, one feels, will probably go away happier than the latter, for this is an entirely pleasant if totally unremarkable Scottish & Newcastle boozer with little to distinguish it from the pack save its inexplicable ban on stools at the bar. The Directors was decent enough, though it was the sole ale on offer when we visited. Food ranges from the reasonably priced (beef and ale pie £4.95) to the inexplicably expensive (chicken carbonara £7.25). The barmen, meanwhile, should learn not to clear people's drinks before they've finished them.
Babies and children admitted. Function room. Games (fruit machine, quiz machine). Jukebox. Tables outdoors (pavement). TV. Vegetarian dishes.

Scotts

20 Mount Street, W1 (020 7629 5248). Bond Street or Green Park tube. **Open** noon-11pm Mon-Fri; 5-11pm Sat. **Food served** (restaurant) noon-3pm, 6-11pm Mon-Sat; noon-3pm, 6-10pm Sun . **Happy hour** 5.30-7pm Mon-Sat. **Credit** AmEx, DC, MC, V.
This modern bar feels somewhat like an afterthought underneath a popular seafood restaurant, which is a shame, because it is a rather nice place. You descend down a spiral staircase that winds around a glass-enclosed bubbling fountain. Below, a pianist plays tasteful jazz, but the bar itself is often empty. The staff – doorman included – are welcoming and friendly, and the bartender mixes a mean cocktail; try the eponymous Scotts No. 1 (gin, Cointreau and orange juice, £6.50). But, despite all the positives, this place still feels like a glorified waiting room.
Function rooms. Music (jazz 7.30-11pm Sat, pianist 7-11pm Mon-Fri). No-smoking area (restaurant). Restaurant. Specialities: cocktails. Tables outdoors (pavement). Vegetarian dishes.

Shelley's

10 Stafford Street, W1 (020 7493 0337). Green Park tube. **Open** 11am-11pm Mon-Sat; noon-5.30pm Sun. **Food served** 11am-5pm Mon-Sat; noon-5pm Sun. **Credit** AmEx, MC, V.

A large corner pub on three floors, this Nicholson's establishment is nothing special, but has a loyal after-work following. The cream and dark red colour scheme falls squarely between two stools: neither a light and airy bar nor a dark and mysterious pub. Upstairs in the Sports Bar there are at least distractions like the pool tables and quiz machines. Downstairs there's a restaurant with a simple menu. Decentish beers, like Tetley, Pedigree and London Pride, and lagers (Stella, Carlsberg) are consumed in fairly large quantities.
Babies and children admitted (daytimes). Function room. Games (fruit machine, pool tables, quiz machine, table football, video game). Music (DJ Fri). Restaurant. Satellite TV. Vegetarian dishes.

Shepherd's Tavern

50 Hertford Street, W1 (020 7499 3017). Green Park or Hyde Park Corner tube. **Open** 11am-11pm Mon-Sat; noon-10.30pm Sun. **Food served** 11am-10pm Mon-Sat; noon-9.30pm Sun. **Credit** AmEx, DC, MC, V.
Named, like nearby Shepherd Market and Shepherd Street – indeed, it sits on the corner of Hertford and Shepherd Streets – after architect Edward Shepherd, who built much of the area in the 18th century. The Tavern is less visually notable than its near-neighbour **Ye Grapes** (*see p67*), but it's also usually a lot quieter, and getting a seat in its dimly lit, dark-wood confines is usually a likely prospect. The drinkers here seem to be long-term locals – the barmen called many by their first names – and the relaxed atmosphere are a million miles away from the bustle on Piccadilly, just a short walk distant. Some of its country-pub charm is challenged by the blinking fruit machine in the corner of the room, but overall, this is a nice enough place. Food is pricey – shepherd's pie (but *of course*) clocks in at £7.25 – but it is served pleasingly late.
Babies and children admitted (dining area only). Games (fruit machines). Jukebox. Restaurant available for hire. Satellite TV. Specialities: real ales. Vegetarian dishes.

Trader Vic's

London Hilton, 22 Park Lane, W1 (020 7493 8000). Hyde Park Corner tube. **Open** 5pm-1.30am Mon-Sat; 5-10.30pm Sun. **Food served** 6pm-12.30am Mon-Sat; 6-9.45pm Sun. **Credit** AmEx, DC, MC, V.
As an exercise in kitschy chic, it's hard to imagine anywhere in London tops this joyous, incongruous bar at the Hilton, even if some of the resident drinkers don't appear to appreciate the absurdity of locating a Hawaiian-themed hangout in the basement of a Park Lane tower block. Costumed waitresses and live hula music – played by a bonkers Lenny Kravitz lookalike – add to an ambience already pushed over the edge by the wild decor, which never fails to raise a smile. The lengthy list of over-the-top cocktails runs to more than 100, but doesn't include Pina Coladas; still, we asked, the waitress didn't bat an eyelid, and the drink (£6.50), when it arrived, was lovely. The Mai Tai (£7), too, was delicious, and it was easy to understand why it's the most popular cocktail on the menu. Less easy to understand is how on earth this bar came to be built in the first place, but drinkers in London should raise a glass to whichever Hilton lackey thought up such a hair-brained idea and revel in one of the capital's most wonderfully insane watering holes.
Babies and children admitted (in restaurant). Disabled: toilet. Function room. Music (live Latin music 10.30pm Mon-Sat). Restaurant. Vegetarian dishes.

Windows

Hilton Hotel, Park Lane, W1 (020 7493 8000). Green Park or Hyde Park Corner tube. **Open/food served** noon-3pm, 5.30pm-2am Mon-Fri; 5.30pm-2am Sat; noon-3pm Sun. **Credit** AmEx, DC, MC, V.

We visited Windows, the Hilton's 28th-floor bar, directly after the Met Bar: from one end of the cocktail continuum (exclusive, windowless, fashionable) to the other (inclusive, panoramic, the naff side of classic) in barely a hundred yards. Walking in, there were two shocks: the first that our jeans-wearing companion was allowed to enter without comment (though generally the clientele were resplendently dressed); the second was the floor-to-ceiling view on two sides, which literally stopped us in our tracks. The rest of the decor is nice enough: low-lit hotel luxury, slightly but pleasantly retro, with a notable sit-at grand piano and a slightly sunken bar, but you barely look at it given the competition. The drinks too were almost irrelevant, though there was nothing at all wrong with them bar a disappointing Margarita, and the prices were kind given the setting: £7.95 for the classics and after-dinner drinks, £8.95-£9.95 for the alcohol-loaded and interesting house specials. The perfect place to take out-of-towners and jaded city folk.
Babies and children admitted (in restaurant).
Disabled: toilet. Dress code. Function rooms. Music (pianist 6.30pm-2am Mon-Sat). Restaurant. Specialities: cocktails. Vegetarian dishes.

Windmill
6-8 Mill Street, W1 (020 7491 8050). Oxford Circus tube. **Open** 11am-11pm Mon-Fri; noon-4pm Sat. **Food served** noon-3pm, 6-9.30pm Mon-Fri; 12.30-3pm Sat. **Credit** AmEx, DC, MC, V
The heavens had opened on the night we stopped by the Windmill. So, unfortunately, had the ceiling of the pub, thanks – the jovial Australian landlord told us, without batting an eyelid – to an overflowing toilet upstairs. Not the best time to be reviewing the place, perhaps. Still, we didn't mind, since we already knew this splendid, quiet Young's hide-out, located just a stone's throw from Regent's Street, very well indeed. It doesn't change much, either: award-winning pies (it's kind of twinned with the **Guinea**, *see p63*), the usual well-kept array of Young's beers, loads of spare seats, no piped music and a friendly vibe throughout. Our only complaint – a common one with Young's pubs – is the garishness of the lighting. Otherwise, leaky ceiling or not, this remains a fine pub in which to lose track of an evening.
Function room. Games (fruit machine). No-smoking area (lower bar). No piped music or jukebox. Restaurant. Vegetarian dishes.

Woodstock
11 Woodstock Street, W1 (020 7408 2008). Bond Street tube. **Open/food served** 11am-11pm Mon-Sat; noon-10.30pm Sun. **Credit** AmEx, DC, MC, V.
Given its location – a shopping-bag's toss from Oxford Street – it's a pleasant surprise that the Woodstock isn't perpetually packed with weary weighed-down shoppers. Situated, logically enough, on Woodstock Street (opposite another surprisingly calm pub, the Spread Eagle), this T&J Bernard boozer doesn't do a great deal to stand out from the pack but we like it because we've never had trouble grabbing a table at lunchtime, while at 8pm one recent Wednesday winter night, there were only a dozen drinkers spread over two tables. Quite why the music needed to be cranked up so loud, then, was a mystery, but the good selection of ales (Abbot, Courage Best and Wychwood Romeo on our most recent visit) helped ease our throbbing heads. Well worth remembering if you're on forced duty in or around Oxford Street.
Babies and children admitted (daytimes). Games (fruit machine, quiz machine). Jukebox. Specialities: real ales. Tables outdoors (pavement). Vegetarian dishes.

Ye Grapes
16 Shepherd Market, W1 (no telephone). Green Park or Hyde Park Corner tube. **Open** 11am-11pm Mon-Sat; noon-10.30pm Sun. **Food served** 12.30-2.30pm daily. **Credit** MC, V.
One of London's more unique little corners – almost traffic-free, it's frequented by a terrific mix of Mayfair poshies, lost tourists, diners looking for Sofra, and shuffling gents on their way to enjoy the small community of prostitutes tucked away in side alleys – Shepherd Market gets the boozer it deserves in Ye Grapes. A handsome corner pub with an exterior drenched in attractive greenery, it's all done out in red velour, similarly seedy lighting and nasty flock wallpaper, with stuffed animals in glass cabinets providing eccentric visual distractions. However, thanks to this – and to an atmosphere noticeably livelier than at most Mayfair pubs – Ye Grapes is incredibly busy of an evening, and finding a seat is tricky. With bitter ranging in price from £2.50 to £2.60 and lager starting at £2.60 (Stella clocks in at £2.80), it's also incredibly pricey for a pub, but few seem to mind either that or the fact that it recently stopped serving its decent pub food.
Babies and children admitted (until 2.30pm, dining only). Function room. Games (fruit machine). No-smoking area (dining). Vegetarian dishes.

Zeta
35 Hertford Street, W1 (020 7208 4067/ www.zeta-bar.com). Green Park or Marble Arch tube. **Open** 11am-1am Mon, Tue; 11am-3am Wed-Fri; 5pm-3am Sat; 5-10.30pm Sun. **Admission** £5 after 11pm Mon-Sat. **Food served** 11am-1am Mon-Fri; 5pm-1am Sat; 5-10pm Sun. **Credit** AmEx, DC, MC, V.
Next door to the super-kitsch tiki bar **Trader Vic's** (*see p66*), the Hilton has built a second bar in the basement as its alternative to the palm-fronded beach bar look. It's all a bit Los Angeles: the design makes oblique references to oriental minimalism, while the staff are dressed like hip priests. The cocktail list is divided into two separate parts: the 'old testament' being fairly traditional, while the 'new testament' is a more novel mix of fresh juices and healthy additives with less healthy liqueurs (the ludicrous suggestion being that you can get smashed while doing yourself good). What's certain is that the cocktails are excellent and the prices OK for a very good hotel bar (Champagne cocktails £7.50, Cosmopolitans or Martinis at £6.50, for example). Two brands of absinthe are sold at £9 a shot (Sebor at 55 per cent abv, and Hill's at 70 per cent abv) and 'sharing' bar bites like Canadian crab or Russian fillet of salmon (around £9) are also available.
Bar area available for hire. Music (DJs nightly, live Mon). Specialities: cocktails. Vegetarian dishes.

Also in the area...
All Bar One 3-4 Hanover Street, W1 (020 7518 9931).
Balls Brothers 34 Brook Street, W1 (020 7499 4567).
Chopper Lump (Davys) 10C Hanover Square, W1 (020 7409 3201).
Marlborough Head (Eerie) 24 North Audley Street, W1 (020 7629 5981).
O'Neill's 7 Shepherd Street, W1 (020 7408 9281).
Pitcher & Piano 1 Dover Street, W1 (020 7495 8704); 10 Pollen Street, W1 (020 7629 9581).
Slug & Lettuce 19-20 Hanover Street, W1 (020 7499 0077).

Notting Hill & Ladbroke Grove

192

192 Kensington Park Road, W11 (020 7229 0482).
Ladbroke Grove or Notting Hill Gate tube.
Open 12.30-11.30pm Mon-Sat; 12.30-11pm Sun. **Food**
served 12.30-3pm, 6.30-11.30pm Mon-Fri; 12.30-3.30pm,
6.30-11.30pm Sat; 12.30-3.30pm, 7-11pm Sun. **Credit**
AmEx, DC, MC, V.
The old joke about 192 is that it's where you go for telephone
numbers – influential ones that is, not just your nearest
plumber. But despite a preening media culture of mutton and
lamb trying to look like they've just walked off the pages of
Hello, there is much to recommend this most narcissistic of
watering holes. The wine list runs to over 80 classic varieties
from around the globe, and the house wine is always good
and temptingly priced. Cocktail lovers are also well served
but beer drinkers must settle for an exiguous range of bottled
lagers. Besides, 192 is principally a café-restaurant serving
good, but inconsistent modern European cuisine. Unless you
want to sit upright at a dining table in what is a small, often
crowded venue, this is not the place for a prolonged drinking
session – however attractive seats on the street and their
toned-up occupants may seem.
Babies and children admitted. Restaurant. Tables outdoors
(pavement). Vegetarian dishes.

Beat Bar

265 Portobello Road, W11 (020 7792 2043). Ladbroke
Grove tube. **Open** 11.30am-11pm daily. **No credit cards**.
There is a good warm vibe about the Beat Bar, but its youth-
club atmosphere is best enjoyed by grungy, studenty types
warming up for a night's clubbing. It's a concrete mausoleum
relieved with IKEA furniture and a few strong colours with
smelly, graffitied toilets beyond. Classic cocktails are served
by the jug, placing an unwholesome emphasis on quantity
not quality (£10 small jug, £12 large jug). Draught beer
choices are limited to Grolsch or Guinness. By day the music
and atmosphere is funky, friendly and ambient, by night it's
more techno, happening and hardcore.
Babies and children admitted (until 6pm).

Bed

310 Portobello Road, W11 (020 8969 4500). Ladbroke
Grove tube. **Open** noon-11pm Mon-Sat; noon-10.30pm
Sun. **Food served** noon-3pm, 6-9.30pm Mon-Thur;
noon-9.30pm Fri-Sun. **Credit** AmEx, MC, V.
Presumably named so people could make jokes about going
to Bed together or spending the day in Bed. Equally likely it's
short for Bedouin because this formerly down-at-heel boozer
(previously the Caernarvon Castle) now has a decidedly North
African feel; terracotta tones, velvet cushions, bare wood,
fretted light shades and even the whiff of a camel's armpit.
The odour recedes into the smoke on a busy night as laid-back
locals lounge to the sounds of Natacha Atlas and assorted
tabla beats. Bed successfully recaptures the louche Notting
Hill of before the estate agents moved in. Unfortunately, the
bar's not up to much and it's best, therefore, to stick to pints
of lager rather than risk disappointment with the cocktails.
Music (DJs 7-11pm Wed-Sun). Tables outdoors (terrace).
Vegetarian dishes.

Belgo Zuid

124 Ladbroke Grove, W10 (020 8982 8400/
www.belgo-restaurants.co.uk). Ladbroke Grove tube.
Open/food served noon-3pm, 6-11pm Mon-Fri;
noon-11pm Sat; noon-10.30pm Sun. **Credit** AmEx,
DC, MC, V.

Belgo Zuid may sound a lot like Belgo pseud but there's
nothing pretentious about this small balcony bar overlooking
the huge mussels and chips Belgian dining room. It's a
slightly cramped and even gloomy space that best serves as
a meeting point for aperitifs before rucking in the restaurant
below or exploring further afield. But make no mistake, the
range of beers – which in theory at least runs to 100 (blond,
amber, dark, fruit and even 'wine beers') mostly for around
£1.90-£3.50 a bottle – plus Trappist ales and some weird beer
cocktails, is enough to keep lovers of ale detained indefinitely.
There's also a dangerous selection of schnapps and, as you'd
expect from a country sharing a border with France, there is
a good mix of wines too. Bar snacks follow the restaurant's
seafood and fries specialities.
Babies and children admitted (children's menus, high
chairs). Disabled: toilet. Restaurant. Vegetarian dishes.

Café Med

184A-186 Kensington Park Road, W11 (020 7221 1150).
Ladbroke Grove tube. **Open** 10am-11pm Mon-Sat; 10am-
10.30pm Sun. **Food served** noon-11.30pm Mon-Sat; noon-
10.30pm Sun. **Credit** AmEx, DC, MC, V.
A corridor of a bar, pleasantly kitted out with green
leatherette banquette seating, stripped wood and bared bricks
enhanced by an open coal effect fire, but with the transient
feeling of an ante-room to an adjoining restaurant – which is
exactly what it is. But neither bar snacks knocked up next
door, nor the bottled beers, cocktails and spirits served in
50ml measures, can completely numb that lingering, anodyne
high-street chain sensation.
Babies and children admitted (restaurant; children's
menu, high chairs). Games (board games). Restaurant.
Specialities: cocktails. Tables outdoors (pavement).
Vegetarian dishes.

Golborne House

36 Golborne Road, W10 (020 8960 6260). Westbourne
Park tube. **Open** noon-11pm Mon- Sat; noon-10.30pm
Sun. **Food served** 12.30-4pm, 6.30-10.15pm Mon-Sat;
12.30-4pm, 6.30-9.45pm Sat, Sun. **Credit** MC, V.
A former corner boozer turned gastropub, Golborne House is
the younger sibling of the hugely successful **Westbourne**
(*see p101*). It has simpler decoration with bared brick and
plain wood consorting with shades of terracotta and khaki
trim. In the last 12 months little has been done to change a
winning formula beyond re-defining the dining area with
bench seating. The chef's taste for experimentation (with
dishes such as beetroot risotto) is hit and miss, but when on
target the results are delicious. The booze situation is less
comprehensive than the Westbourne – there is only one real
ale in the form of London Pride, a basic range of wines and
very limited spirits. Still, this is the best pub at the north end
of Portobello and handy for the busy Golborne Road
Moroccan market outside.
Babies and children admitted. Function room. Satellite
TV. Tables outside (pavement). Vegetarian dishes.

Ground Floor

186 Portobello Road, W11 (020 7243 8701).
Ladbroke Grove tube. **Open** 11am-11pm Mon-Sat;
noon-10.30pm Sun. **Food served** 11am-9pm Mon-Fri;
11am-8pm Sat; 11am-4pm Sun. **Credit** AmEx, DC,
MC, V.
Little by little the Ground Floor cannily updates its image to
keep up with fashion-conscious local clientele. Once closed
down by the police as a heaving den of iniquity, it was reborn as an unpopular Euro bar for tourists. Now it
consolidates its voguish image of distempered colours and
baroque trimmings with standard-issue, beaten-up leather

Bed

WAIKIKI WHEN YOU CAN TRADER VIC'S

Trader Vic's is the legendary cocktail bar and restaurant for tropical-minded urbanites, a mood lagoon tucked away beneath the London Hilton in Park Lane. It is the home of the Mai Tai and sets standards for Island cuisine. It is delicious and exotic in the extreme. Make a reservation for dinner or book our private function room and we are sure you will soon agree, that it's the bee's-knees.

ADVENTURES IN CUISINE

TRADER VIC'S AT THE LONDON HILTON ON PARK LANE
22 PARK LANE, LONDON W1Y 4BE TEL: 020 7208 4113 FAX: 020 7208 4050

chairs. All this helps create the impression of a cool, ambient drinkerie as old as the Hill itself. Although this is palpably untrue, it is a perfectly inoffensive outlet. A corner sighted gold fish bowl, it also has canopies covering seats on the street which make good positions for people watching. Food is reasonable snack versions of dishes from the restaurant upstairs and familiar gastropub fare. Wines are popular varieties and beer is all kegged.
Babies and children admitted (high chairs). Function rooms. Restaurant. Tables outdoors (pavement). Vegetarian dishes.

Ion Bar & Restaurant
161-165 Ladbroke Grove, W10 (020 8960 1702). Ladbroke Grove tube. **Open** 5pm-midnight Mon-Fri; noon-midnight Sat, Sun. **Food served** 6-11pm Mon-Fri; noon-5pm, 6-11pm Sat, Sun. **Credit** AmEx, DC, MC, V.
As black culture in Notting Hill gets eclipsed by public school jet setters, Ion has been adopted by the Afro-Carribean community. Inside it's a strange aesthetic, part swinging sixties, part airport departure lounge. Leatherette benches form obstacles on the stripped wood floor and DJs ensure the decibel level of a Heathrow runway. The bar's previously transient atmosphere has therefore been transformed into a rowdier scene annexing the overhead mezzanine restaurant as a lounge and terrace bar. Variety of drinks and victuals is not a pulling point, but there is a choice of wine and if you can find space to sit, there is standard gastropub food too.
Babies and children admitted (restaurant; high chairs). Disabled: toilet, lift. Games (board games). Music (DJs nightly; live Wed, Fri, Sun). Restaurant. Specialities: cocktails. Tables outdoors (terrace). Vegetarian dishes.

Jac's
48 Lonsdale Road, W11 (020 7792 2838). Ladbroke Grove or Notting Hill Gate tube. **Open** 6-11pm Tue-Sat; 7-10.30pm Sun. **Credit** MC, V.
An underground speakeasy that has expanded piecemeal on the original Scandinavian design – but with some alarming failures of taste. At first glance the false bookshelves, bust upholstery and rugs over concrete floors scattered round an oval central bar with a gurgling fish tank, suggest familiar, scatter-shot Notting Hill bohemianism. However, the platform area to the rear is enveloped by an unsettling fantasy mural of the sort once favoured by '70s metal heads and sci-fi geeks. Style faux pas apart, this is a pretty cool gaff, especially good for larger groups, with occasional DJs operating from a booth under the curious overhead gallery of the function room. There is no food available and the drink selection, like the usually sardonic service, is nothing to write home about.
Function room. Games (backgammon). Music (DJs Thur-Sun). Tables outdoors (pavement).

Market Bar
240A Portobello Road, W11 (020 7229 6472). Ladbroke Grove or Notting Hill Gate tube. **Open** noon-11pm Mon-Fri; noon-midnight Sat; noon-10.30pm Sun. **Credit** MC, V.
The Market Bar distinguishes itself as one of the few remaining watering holes in the area where it is still possible to encounter an increasingly endangered species: the liver spotted Notting Hill louche. They're here because the Market Bar represents one of the area's few undisturbed drinking habitats. The same Indonesian horses have reared over the bar for more than ten years, the cast iron candelabras remain heavy with waxy dreadlocks and the gaff continues to be divided in half by the same thick tasselled curtain – which must now be as full of dust as the bar is full of boozy reprobates. As far as regulars are concerned, it's a winning

formula. Pole Portobello market position and proximity to the club Subterania are further pluses.
Babies and children admitted (until 7pm). Music (DJs Fri, Sat, live jazz Sun). Specialities: cocktails.

Pharmacy
150 Notting Hill Gate, W11 (020 7221 2442/ www.pharmacylondon.com). Notting Hill Gate tube. **Open** noon-3pm, 5.30pm-1am Mon-Thur; noon-3pm, 5.30pm-2am Fri; noon-2am Sat; noon-midnight Sun. **Food served** noon-2.30pm, 6-10.30pm Mon-Sat; noon-2.30pm, 6-10pm Sun. **Credit** AmEx, DC, MC, V.
Pharmacy has now been fully absorbed into the Notting Hill scene. No longer the big fuss about the Damien Hirst-designed display cabinets of hospital drugs, no longer the excitable amazement at the used swabs packed behind the glass urinals and no longer the vast crowd of celebrity spotters. Gone too, however, is the startlingly good value of the house wine (once £9 a bottle, now subject to a 50% rate of inflation at £14). Luckily it's still good quality plonk and the Pharmacy burger and chips still represents one of the best buys in London: quality beef, gherkin and gruyere in a bun with a large number of fries for £6.75. This is just one of the ample bar snacks for under a tenner. But Pharmacy is also one of the best shots and cocktail bars, served under the aegis of 'jabs' and 'prescriptions'. One word of warning: as at hospital A&E departments, long queues can develop late at night.
Babies and children admitted (until 10pm, high chairs). Disabled: toilet. Music (DJs Fri, Sat). Restaurant. Vegetarian dishes.

Portobello Gold
95-97 Portobello Road, W11 (020 7460 4900/ www.portobellogold.com). Notting Hill Gate tube. **Open** 10am-midnight Mon-Sat; 10am-10.30pm Sun; *Buzz Bar* 10am-9pm Mon-Fri; 10am-7pm Sat; noon-7pm Sun. **Food served** 10am-11pm Mon-Sat; 1.15-8pm Sun. **Happy hour** 5.30-7pm daily. **Credit** DC, MC, V.
Traditionally a pub-cum-cocktail bar-cum-restaurant serving the *Lovejoy* community of antique dealers. Upstairs in the so-called Buzz Bar patrons can also surf the net for rare mahogany bureaus while clutching a large G&T with absinthe chaser. Meanwhile, the more free-thinking, Dylan-inspired trustafarian hippy sorts favour Portobello Gold for its apparently non-conformist atmosphere. Nor is there any sense that Portobello Gold fits in with local fashions, mixing its white tiled floors with pea green walls and garish photos for sale. The conservatory restaurant at the back does good deals in seafood, but bar food is also available accompanied by real ales (Directors and Pedigree), a fairly priced wine list and a full set of cocktails.
Babies and children admitted (except bar). Function rooms. Games (backgammon, cards). No-smoking area. Restaurant. Satellite TV. Specialities: organic lager, world beers, wines. Tables outdoors (conservatory, pavement). Vegetarian dishes.

Portobello Star
171 Portobello Road, W11 (020 7229 8016). Ladbroke Grove or Notting Hill Gate tube. **Open/food served** 11am-11pm Mon-Sat; noon-10.30pm Sun. **Credit** MC, V.
Incredible to think that even in Notting Hill, home of the rich, the beautiful (and Peter Mandelson), such a pub as this can still exist. Brightly lit with mock-Tudor white walls and stencilled reliefs, this down-to-earth local is a boozer's sanctuary. Long popular with market traders (that's fruit and veg, not equity and bonds), televised football plays a big part in the pub's atmosphere and although drinks are elementary (no cocktail bar, this) they stock one real ale in the form of Flower's Original – not the best beer brewed but it'll do. Anyone ordering vodka

will be encouraged to drink the cut-price house brand. Several of those and you may find yourself abandoning dignity (as many here do) and dancing to a jukebox packed with old-school gangsta rappers like Frank Sinatra. Marvel also at how they toast their sandwiches in plastic wrappers.
Games (fruit machine, quiz machine). Jukebox. Quiz (8pm every second Thur). Tables outdoors (pavement). TV. Vegetarian dishes.

Woody's
41-43 Woodfield Road, W9 (020 7266 3030/ www.woodysclub.com). Westbourne Park tube.
Open/food served 7pm-2am Mon-Sat. **Admission** £3 after 9pm, £5 after 10pm, £10 after 11pm. **Credit** MC, V.
Woody's major attraction is its late licence, but unless you feature in this month's *Hello!*, you are likely to be greeted with thinly veiled contempt. Once past the meat heads and dolly birds on the door, the ground-floor bar is decorated in brick red and khaki and is fitted with leatherette seating and chrome tables. It's also dominated by a huge photo featuring *Tatler* kids in underwear – echoing the horsily bohemian clientele. Above this there is a swanky restaurant and below a dingy disco. Aside from cocktails, house wines are good but limited. Gastropub food is available, but character of service depends on meteorological conditions: when the wind is in the right direction it can be friendly.
Babies and children admitted (restaurant). Function room. Music (DJs nightly). Restaurant. Vegetarian dishes.

Also in the area...
All Bar One 126-128 Notting Hill, W11 (020 7313 9362).
Café Rouge 31 Kensington Park Road, W11 (020 7221 4449).
Frog & Firkin 96 Ladbroke Grove, W11 (020 7229 5663).
Rat & Parrot 40 Holland Park Avenue, W11 (020 7727 6332).
Ruby in the Dust 299 Portobello Road, W10 (020 8969 4626).

Pimlico

Gallery
1 Lupus Street, SW1 (020 7821 7573). Pimlico tube.
Open 11.30am-11pm Mon-Fri; noon-11pm Sat; noon-9pm Sun. **Food served** 11.30am-2.30pm, 5-9pm Mon-Fri; noon-2.30pm, 5.30-9pm Sat; noon-9pm Sun. **Credit** MC, V.
When this pub was refurbished and renamed some eight years ago it attracted an evening clientele of professionals on their way home to the warren of large flats in surrounding streets. The stage/platform effect was a pleasing novelty, and the comfy bench-seats rather like the sofa at home. These days, statisticians from government offices opposite still lunch on typical pub food, but by night it's now the haunt of a crowd of seedy locals downing IPA, London Pride and Spitfire. Time for another refurb we think. While they're at it, they might hire a more involved bar staff, too, and quit the practice of taking the most expensive wine and calling it 'house'.
Specialities: real ales. Tables outdoors (pavement). Vegetarian dishes.

Jugged Hare
172 Vauxhall Bridge Road, SW1 (020 7828 1543). Pimlico tube. **Open** 11am-11pm Mon-Sat; noon-10.30pm Sun. **Food served** noon-8pm Mon-Thur; noon-3pm Fri-Sun. **Credit** AmEx, DC, MC, V.

Another bank conversion; once a local NatWest, now a Fuller's Ale & Pie House. It's done wonders for the atmosphere. The high banking hall ceiling (adorned with a chandelier) allows space for a mezzanine, where all the gossip and interesting conversation happens. Downstairs, there's a little nook for non-smokers, which has big windows – very nice at lunchtime or on summer nights – and a nook within a nook for private conversations. Walls are covered with historic photos of SW1 and repro Victorian ads. Food is standard Fuller's fare, and there are certainly no complaints about the beer. Staff are helpful, and remember you.
Bar area available for hire. Games (quiz machine). No-smoking area. Vegetarian dishes.

Morpeth Arms
58 Millbank, SW1 (020 7834 6442). Pimlico tube. **Open** 11am-11pm Mon-Sat; noon-10.30pm Sun. **Food served** 11am-6pm Mon-Sat; 11am-3pm Sun. **Credit** MC, V.
A popular four-storey Grade II listed pub sitting regally on the northern bank of the Thames within easy pacing distance of Tate Britain. Go at weekends when MI6 isn't there; Monday to Friday they break step crossing Vauxhall bridge to drink good Young's beer, and now also Bristol's Smiles ales. They favour the bar furthest from the main entrance with its clandestine corners. At weekends the place is the preserve of the soppy dog and cricket brigades over from the Oval, plus of course a stream of refugees from art seeking simpler pleasures. Ask landlord Bernard about his ghost, said to have been a would-be escapee from Millbank Penitentiary who got lost in the labyrinth of passageways beneath the pub. Our one and only gripe is the loss of the wild boar sausages – bring 'em back Bernard.
Babies and children admitted. Function room. Games (fruit machine). No piped music or jukebox. Quiz (occasionally). Tables outdoors (riverside terrace). TV. Vegetarian dishes.

The Page
11 Warwick Way, SW1 (020 7834 3313). Pimlico tube. **Open** 11am-11pm Mon-Sat; noon-10.30pm Sun. **Food served** noon-3pm, 6-10pm Mon-Fri; noon-9pm Sat, Sun. **Credit** AmEx, MC, V.
A welcome reversal of the trend to ensnare London's pub scene with chains, this is a Slug & Lettuce that has been reclaimed as a chic, sleek pub-cum-wine bar. Behind a navy-blue Victorian exterior is soft lighting, modern pine fittings and a comfy lounge area. Unfortunately the well selected list of 13 whites and 15 reds – not to mention the Spitfire and other real ales – is totally wasted on the Beck's-swigging rowdy office crowd that was left behind when the Slug moved on. Staff are friendly and patient and there's a Thai restaurant upstairs too. We just hope the place survives long enough to get the better class of clientele that it deserves.
Babies and children admitted. Restaurant. Satellite TV. Vegetarian dishes.

White Swan
14 Vauxhall Bridge Road, SW1 (020 7821 8568). Pimlico tube. **Open** 11am-11pm Mon-Sat; noon-10.30pm Sun. **Food served** noon-10pm Mon-Sat; noon-9pm Sun. **Credit** AmEx, DC, MC, V.
A great barn of a place (operated by T&J Bernard) that's totally dedicated to serious drinking. Its range of beer is excellent with regular guest ales supplementing the draught Theakston's and Courage range, plus plenty of good stuff in bottles including Bateman's Loxley Liquor. There are bottled wheat beers, too, mostly from Belgium. Food is traditional English pub grub with a selection of six mains such as chicken breast or fish and chips. Even if beer isn't your thing,

the bright, light wood interior and neat bar staff in burgundy aprons are a welcome change from Pimlico's standard dingy drinking holes. As a result the place is heaving most evenings. *Games (fruit machine, quiz machine). No-smoking area. Specialities: cask ales. Tables outdoors (pavement). Vegetarian dishes.*

Also in the area...

Davys at St James Crown Passage, Pall Mall, SW1 (020 7839 8831).

Soho

Admiral Duncan

54 Old Compton Street, W1 (020 7437 5300). Leicester Square or Piccadilly Circus tube. **Open** 11am-11pm Mon-Sat; noon-10.30pm Sun. **Credit** AmEx, DC, MC, V.
Before it was bombed in a homophobic attack in the summer of 1999, this old-fashioned gay pub was home to men of a certain age who, having grown out of wanting to be part of the scene, just needed a quiet place to meet their friends and perhaps sing along to a few show tunes at the end of the night. But since that vicious moment in history, it has taken on something of a martyr status, and has consequently livened up considerably. It still has the same purple and pink façade, narrow underlit interior and cheap (for a gay bar) pints, but more of an all-ages clientele, a higher profile, and most notably given its previously inconspicuous nature, bouncers on the door.
Games (fruit machines). Jukebox. **Map 7/K6**

Alphabet

61-63 Beak Street, W1 (020 7439 2190). Oxford Circus tube. **Open/food served** noon-11pm Mon-Fri; 5-11pm Sat. **Credit** MC, V.
Smart, arty and popular (you may have to queue to get in some evenings), this glass-fronted hangout is beloved of thirtysomething advertising and media types in lounge suits. There's a lengthy cocktail menu (£3.50-£6), wine and a well-chosen small beer collection (including Mexican Negra Modelo, £2.85), and bar food (ambitious snacks at £4.50-£5.50, mains around a tenner). Downstairs in the more laid-back basement, the average age of the punters drops, there's a second bar, a DJ, some interesting 'recycled' furniture and an old-school Space Invaders machine. And they've still got the giant A-Z map of Soho painted on the floor too.
Babies and children admitted (until 5pm). Function room. Games machines. Music (DJs Thur-Sat). Restaurant. Specialities: cocktails. Vegetarian dishes. **Map 7/K6**

Amber

6 Poland Street, W1 (020 7734 3094/www.amberbar.com). Tottenham Court Road tube. **Open** noon-1am Mon-Fri; 4pm-1am Sat. **Food served** noon-3pm, 5pm-midnight Mon-Fri; 4pm-midnight Sat. **Credit** AmEx, MC, V.
Amber is a second effort from the gang behind **Alphabet** (*see above*). Ground floor is a restaurant, the bar is in the basement. Far smarter than its sibling, Amber's bar has beautiful rounded woody booths with odd light fittings that angle in like eavesdroppers, and Gaudiesque floor mosaics. Not that you're likely to notice any of this because already most nights the place is thumping, packed with a raucous after-work crowd. The drinks menu cannily highlights tequilas and rums (rising to £22.30 for a glass of Pyrat Cask), plus cocktails from a list strong on Martinis and classics. The wine list is also excellent. No flies in this amber.
Music (DJs 8pm Thur-Sat; free). Vegetarian dishes. **Map 7/K6**

Argyll Arms

18 Argyll Street, W1 (020 7734 6117). Oxford Circus tube. **Open** 11am-11pm Mon-Sat; noon-9pm Sun. **Food served** 11am-5pm Mon-Sat; noon-4pm Sun. **Credit** AmEx, DC, MC, V.
Stuffed with classy Victorian carved mirrors, snob screens and mahogany, the present Argyll's history goes back to 1866 (although it replaces an earlier pub built in the 1740s). It's been kept in great nick, retaining the original Victorian layout with a corridor leading to the large back saloon and dining area, past three, small, cosy bars that can't have changed in a hundred years. Beers are good (Greene King IPA, Adnam's) and the all-female bar staff do a decent freshly prepared giant sandwich. Given its so-central location (Oxford Circus tube is practically in the cellar) it can get a bit busy and loud, in which case retreat to the quieter upstairs Palladium bar.
Babies and children admitted (restaurant). Dress code (in restaurant). Function room. Games (fruit machines). No-smoking area (until 4pm in restaurant). Restaurant. Satellite TV. Vegetarian dishes. **Map 7/K6**

Bar Chocolate

26-27 D'Arblay Street, W1 (020 7287 2823). Oxford Circus or Tottenham Court Road tube. **Open/food served** 10am-11pm Mon-Sat; noon-10.30pm Sun. **Credit** DC, MC, V.
Last year it was Tactical, this year it's Bar Chocolate, but other than a new 'Bourneville dark' paint job, basically it's the same deal. It's a two-roomed hangout for pseudo-intellectual 21st-century beatniks. There's a checkerboard floor and steel-topped tables with a battered sofa tucked in one corner. Shelves of books offer Burroughs to *Tank*, and all the right kind of magazines are on hand for casual perusing. Beer is bottled (nothing of note) and there are spirits, coffee and a café snack menu.
Babies and children admitted (until 6pm). Music (DJ 5pm every other Sun; free). Tables outdoors (pavement). Vegetarian dishes. **Map 7/K6**

Bar Code

3-4 Archer Street, W1 (020 7734 3342). Piccadilly Circus tube. **Open** 1pm-1am Mon-Sat; 1-10.30pm Sun. **Admission** £3 after 11pm Fri, Sat. **Happy hour** 5-7pm daily. **Credit** MC, V.
Lying at the more rough-edged end of Soho's gay scene, Bar Code is more Tom of Finland than Gary from Boyzone. The crowd is heavy on stubble and tattoos, and the bar is stripped to bare floorboards and minimal furniture to allow maximum room for cruising. But for all that, Bar Code's neither intimidating nor unwelcoming. Moderately busy during the week, the place heaves at weekends (where entrance is free before 11pm) thanks, in no small part, to the equally cruisey basement club-bar that pumps out hip handbag until late.
Comedy (stand up acts 9pm Sun-Tue; free). Games (fruit machine). Karaoke (9pm Wed; free). Music (DJs 9pm Thur-Sun). **Map 7/K7**

Barra

12A Newburgh Street, W1 (020 7287 8488). Oxford Circus tube. **Open** noon-11pm Mon-Fri. **Food served** noon-3pm, 7-10.30pm Mon-Fri. **Credit** AmEx, DC, MC, V.
Quiet cobbled lanes are the preserve of places like Twee-on-Green not Soho, but in Newburgh Street central London's most manic district has its own pretty little thoroughfare of tranquility. And that's where you find Barra, which is essentially a wine bar with a modish, continental and rather expensive menu, but a superb location. Inside it's minimal and tasteful, naturally lit by large picture windows. Staff are

Amber. *See page 73.*

bright and good looking, clientele are well dressed and affluent. They have to be: a glass of the house white costs £4. But that was for a large glass. The wine list is good with most available by the glass.
Babies and children admitted (daytimes). Function room. No-smoking area. Specialities: wines. Tables outdoors (pavement). Vegetarian dishes. **Map 7/K6**

Bar Red & Restaurant
5-6 Kingly Street, W1 (020 7434 3417). Oxford Circus or Piccadilly Circus tube. **Open** noon-midnight Mon-Fri; 6pm-midnight Sat. **Food served** noon-11.30pm Mon-Fri; 6-11.30pm Sat. **Credit** AmEx, MC, V.
'This wouldn't be Bar Red would it?', we asked at the door of the no-name bar with the big red window. 'No,' replied the blonde with clipboard, 'we're Bar Blue but the decorator brought the wrong paint'. Sassy! Then she let us in and it was all downhill from there. Soho bars are a licence to print money, and while some of them *are* good and worth throwing yourself at the mercy of the stormtrooper on the door to get in, others are just taking the piss. Red falls into the latter category. Its concept is limited to red cellophane over the window, and that's about it. The rest of the interior is unfinished concrete with all ducting and wiring exposed; Rogers and Piano can pull this off, here it just looks half-arsed. It makes for a depressing drinking ambience, like squatting a building site. Staff with vision problems didn't help – we felt like Harvey the rabbit, invisible to all but close friends. One plus at the time we visited was that the basement restaurant had first-rate chef Bobby Gutteridge, but he's since left. We'll be surprised if the bar goes the distance.
Babies and children admitted (daytimes). Disabled: toilet. Restaurant (available for hire). Specialities: cocktails. Vegetarian dishes. **Map 7/K6**

Bar Soho
23-25 Old Compton Street, W1 (020 7439 0439). Piccadilly Circus tube. **Open/food served** 4pm-1am Mon-Thur; 4pm-3am Fri, 2pm-3am Sat; 3-10.30pm Sun. **Credit** AmEx, DC, MC, V.
Just to remind you that Soho is a brash haven of hedonistic tourism and after-work abandon, this large, loud, wood-heavy bar is here to cater to the traditional needs of the area's less discerning clientele. It's a place to come to with a crowd of friends prepared to chip in on jugs of Long Island Iced Tea (£9.90) and shout conversation over the (very loud) house music. It's also resolutely straight: the single-sex groups that frequent the place certainly aren't interested in going home with each other. The big windows and high ceilings ensure that it doesn't get too claustrophobic even when packed – which it invariably is. A late licence, dancing, DJs and doormen make this an alternative to going to a club proper. Just beware of drunken businessmen splashing champagne on your jacket.
Dress code. Function room. Satellite TV. Vegetarian dishes. **Map 7/K6**

Bar Sol Ona
17 Old Compton Street, W1 (020 7287 9932). Leicester Square tube. **Open/food served** 5pm-3am Mon-Sat; 5pm-midnight Sun. **Happy hour** 5-10pm Mon-Thur; 5-8pm Fri, Sat; 5-7pm Sun. **Credit** AmEx, DC, MC, V (over £5).
It's easy to miss this basement bar: sandwiched in between the two branches of Café Bohème, it has only a doorway to announce itself and could easily be mistaken for a private club. But head down the narrow corridor decorated with Goya prints, and you'll find a friendly Spanish-style bar that benefits from its clandestine atmosphere. Two low-ceilinged

rooms are packed with large wooden tables and lots of discrete little alcoves, filled on our last visit with couples talking in hushed voices. As the evening progresses the volume rises and the dancefloor gets busy. It's not a bad place to share a large jug of Margarita with friends (£10.80), or even stolen time with someone who you shouldn't strictly be with.
Music (DJs 10pm Mon-Thur; 8pm Fri, Sat; admission £4 Fri, Sat). Tables outside (pavement). TV. Vegetarian dishes. **Map 7/K6**

Blue Posts
28 Rupert Street, W1 (020 7437 1415). Leicester Square or Piccadilly Circus tube. **Open** 11am-11pm Mon-Sat; noon-10.30pm Sun. **Credit** MC, V.
One of Soho's better boozers for beer fans, the Blue Posts always has a decent spread of real ales, including on a recent visit: London Pride, Marston's Pedigree, Flowers and Wadworth 6X. There's next to nowhere to sit – beyond half a dozen stools at the window – so it's one of those places where punters stand in clusters, resulting in plenty of elbow aggravation and jostling as newcomers try and squeeze by to the bar. In fact towards the busy end of the week, it's always unpleasantly packed and is a place to avoid. At other times, however, such as afternoons or early week, the combination of good beer and unpretentious woody surroundings makes for an attractive pint.
Function room. Games (fruit machine). Jukebox. Specialities: real ales, wines. TV. **Map 2/K7**

Blues Bistro & Bar
42-43 Dean Street, W1 (020 7494 1966). Piccadilly Circus or Tottenham Court Road tube. **Open** noon-midnight Mon-Thur; noon-1am Fri, Sat; 5.30pm-midnight Sun. **Food served** noon-11pm Mon-Thur; noon-midnight Fri, Sat; 5.30-11pm Sun. **Credit** AmEx, MC, V.
The blues are usually associated with run-down saloons, no-good women and drained bottles of Jack Daniel's, none of which apply to this smart and diminutive bar at the front of a respected restaurant. It's next door to the Groucho and the punters here seem to be made up of that famous private club's media overspill – well dressed, thirtysomething and verbose. The atmosphere is sophisticated and restrained and it's not a bad place for a generous double or a classy cocktail, especially if you manage to snag one of the two deep sofas. Even so, we can't imagine staying beyond a drink or two, because it's just too small and cramped to be totally comfortable. DJs play rare groove and jazz on Friday and Saturday.
Babies and children admitted. Disabled: toilet. Function room. No-smoking area. Restaurant. Satellite TV. Vegetarian dishes. **Map 7/K6**

Café Bohème
13-17 Old Compton Street, W1 (020 7734 0623). Leicester Square tube. **Open/food served** 8am-3am Mon-Thur; 8am-4am Fri, Sat; 8am-midnight Sun. **Admission** £3 after 10pm, £4 after 11pm Fri, Sat. **Credit** AmEx, DC, MC, V.
During its initial boom in the late '80s, when all any Soho-ite wanted to be was a beret-wearing torch singer in a Left Bank Paris bar, this was the place to come: a bistro hangout that offered its clientele gallic sophistication and a chance to get in touch with their bohemian side. Incredibly, changing fashions have failed to erode the appeal, and Café Bohème has gone from strength to strength. This is perhaps because it has a very good restaurant; friendly, mostly French staff; and a warm, candlelit atmosphere that is neither intimidating nor tacky. Bar snacks are a cut above average too: a proper croque monsieur (£4) for example, or a bowl of moules marinieres (£5.90). The Bohème Kitchen And Bar two doors

down with a starker, more modern feel, was added in 1999, but we still prefer the original.
Babies and children admitted (eating area). Music (jazz 3.30-5pm Tue-Fri, Sun; free). Restaurant. Tables outdoors (pavement). Vegetarian dishes. **Map 7/K6**

Café Lazeez
21 Dean Street, W1 (020 7434 9393/ www.cafelazeez.com). Leicester Square or Tottenham Court Road tube. **Open/food served** 11am-1am Mon-Sat. **Credit** AmEx, DC, MC, V.
Tucked under the new Soho Theatre Building, this is a combination of a lively ground-floor bar and brasserie with a quieter (good) Indian restaurant in the basement. Not unlike the well established **Soho Spice** (*see p85*), it's a stylish affair, although in this case with neutral colours, sloping walls and large open spaces filled with uniform lines of little tables. The bar is anything but an afterthought to the kitchen, and is long and well stocked with a huge list of spirits and cocktails, plus Cobra and Kingfisher beer (£3). There's no pressure to eat, but the brasserie snacks are tempting.
Babies and children admitted. Disabled: lift, toilet. Function room. No-smoking area. Restaurant. Vegetarian dishes. **Map 7/K6**

Candy Bar
23-24 Bateman Street, W1 (020 7437 1977/ www.candybar.easynet.co.uk). Leicester Square or Tottenham Court Road tube. **Open** 5pm-1am Mon, Tue; 5pm-3am Wed,Thur; 5pm-3am Fri; 4pm-3am Sat; 5pm-midnight Sun. **Happy hour** 5-7pm daily. **Credit** MC, V.
London's most successful women-only bar used to occupy a former members club on a tiny Soho sidestreet; now it has come out properly and taken over a bright red corner-bar on one of the area's busiest streets. The clear glass façade and high ceilings of the new place further emphasise that this is no shrinking violet, although the old rules still apply: no men allowed unless accompanied by a woman, and even then there's a good chance that they won't be admitted. Going against the grain of traditional women-only places, the Candy Bar is trendy, design-conscious and raucous: hard house DJs downstairs and a late licence ensure that beer gets spilled, jugs of cocktails are ordered in abundance, and no apologies are made.
Function room. Karaoke (9pm Mon; free). Music (DJs 10pm Wed-Sat, 6.30pm Sun; admission £5/£3 members Fri, Sat). **Map 7/K6**

Circus Restaurant & Bar
1 Upper James Street, W1 (020 7534 4000/ www.circusbar. co.uk). Oxford Circus or Piccadilly Circus tube. **Open** noon-1.30am Mon-Fri; 6pm-1.30am Sat. **Food served** noon-3pm, 5.45pm-1.30am Mon-Fri; 5.45pm-1.30am Sat. **Credit** AmEx, DC, MC, V.
Concealed beneath the sleekly contemporary Circus restaurant, the basement bar claims to be open to all, but we've been turned away in the past with the excuse that it's a private members bar. But if you do get past the door expect a sort of semi-tropical patio look with soft lighting and large leather chairs and footstools, and attentive, roaming white-uniformed bar staff who excel in whisking away barely used ashtrays. Order spirits, or something from the wide array of wines or the dauntingly large selection of whiskies. The night we visited the place was lightly peppered with besuited blokes on the pull but that aside it's flashy and glamorous – there's a great illuminated bamboo garden – and we just wish they'd let us move in here permanently.
Babies and children admitted (restaurant). Music (DJs 10pm Thur-Sat; admission £5 after 11pm, free to restaurant diners). Restaurant. Vegetarian dishes. **Map 7/K6**

Clachan
34 Kingly Street, W1 (020 7494 0834). Oxford Circus or Piccadilly Circus tube. **Open** 11am-11pm Mon-Sat; noon-6pm Sun. **Food served** 11am-4pm, 6-8.30pm Mon-Sat; noon-4pm Sun. **Credit** AmEx, DC, MC, V.
An old-style boozer, complete with well maintained original fixtures and fittings, which, given its just-off Regent Street location, remains remarkably free of either bag-laden shoppers or satchel-wearing tourists. Replete with frosted-glass snob screens, gilt-edged everything, chandeliers, an oak-panelled bar and raised, seated nooks and crannies to the rear, it's favoured by an after-work crowd who often display little regard for the notion of going home.
Babies and children admitted (until 4pm). Function room. Games (fruit machines). Satellite TV. Vegetarian dishes. **Map 7/K6**

Coach & Horses
29 Greek Street, W1 (020 7437 5920). Leicester Square or Tottenham Court Road tube. **Open/food served** 11am-11pm Mon-Sat; noon-10.30pm Sun. **Happy hour** 11am-4pm Sun-Fri. **No credit cards.**
This is what Soho is all about: rickety formica tables, a legendarily rude landlord, last-resort-only sandwiches, and a clientele made up of old soaks, would-be writers, professional bores, has-beens, never-will-be's, art-school students and the odd bewildered tourist – although landlord Norman Balon has been known to turn the latter away at the door. Fame was bestowed on the Coach by regular Jeffrey Bernard, who made a career out of going to seed at his stool by the bar and documenting it for the *Spectator*. Come here in the afternoon (Saturday and Sunday especially) and you'll find the surviving (there are a few less every year) contemporaries of Bernard, but come evening the younger generation move in. Of course, the Coach's other claim to fame is that the editor of this guide worked behind the bar there for all of ten minutes prior to a rapid sacking. But we don't hold grudges.
No piped music or jukebox. **Map 7/K6**

Comptons of Soho
53-57 Old Compton Street, W1 (020 7479 7961/ www.comptons-of-soho.com). Leicester Square or Piccadilly Circus tube. **Open** noon-11pm Mon-Sat; noon-10.30pm Sun. **Happy hour** 7-11pm Mon. **Credit** MC, V.
Ninety-nine per cent male, smoky, beer-soaked and unsubtle. Soho's oldest gay pub is a pick-up joint first and a hangout second: there are plenty of solitary men in suits, beer in hand, who spend about 15 minutes waiting for a companion for the evening before disappearing off with them. Despite a refit that saw the old cubby holes replaced by open spaces, it's still the kind of place where you don't strike up a conversation with a stranger just for the sake of being friendly – and there's not much point anyway, as the loud house and disco keeps talking to a minimum. There's a quieter room upstairs where friends do meet up for a drink, but downstairs it's singles central.
Games (fruit machines, pool table, quiz machines). Music (DJ 5pm Sun; free). Satellite TV. **Map 7/K6**

Couch
97-99 Dean Street, W1 (020 7287 0150). Tottenham Court Road tube. **Open** 9.30am-11pm Mon-Fri; 11am-11pm Sat; noon-10.30pm Sun. **Food served** 11am-10pm Mon-Wed, Sat; 11am-8pm Thur; 11am-7pm Fri; noon-10pm Sun. **Credit** AmEx, DC, MC, V.
Opened in September 2000, Couch occupies the middle ground between proper pub and style bar; it's a bit like the Pitcher & Piano and its ilk, only much less corporate. The same template is there: bare floorboards, big wooden tables, a long

London crawling: Shots on location

The rash of blue plaques across Chelsea boasts that the borough has long been a favourite of artists and writers: Wilde, Thackeray, Turner and George Eliot have all lived here at various times. Less well known is Chelsea's cinematic history; the lost cinemas, the locations, the stars, and above all, the man who invented the flicks.

The **Chelsea Potter** may seem an inauspicious place to start a tour, but its interior was used as a location in the filming of *Monk Dawson*, a 1997 British pic about a defrocked monk's progress along the Via Dolorosa of trendy '70s Cheyne Walk. Grab a place by the window and look over at the opposite side of King's Road. Now just an unexciting row of commercial premises, but at one time, it was home to four cinemas. The Cadogan Electric Palace, Classic and Gaumont Palace are all gone, the Chelsea Cinema is all that remains. Also, on the corner of Sydney Street used to stand the Chelsea Palace Theatre with its stunning terracotta façade, until it was pulled down amid howls of protest in 1960, to make way for the current dreary building.

Walk down King's Road past Habitat and look up for the plaque dedicated to a man called William Friese-Green, who patented a movie camera in 1889 (five years before the Lumière brothers), invented modern movie celluloid, and worked on stereoscopic film techniques. Now, he's all but forgotten.

Carol Reed (best remembered for *The Third Man*) lived at 213 King's Road next door to Peter Ustinov. Manresa Road is where they shot scenes from *The Collector* with Samantha Eggar standing on the steps outside the old library. The basement of LK Bennett (at 239) used to be the '60s lesbian hangout, the Gateways Club, used by Robert Aldrich for *The Killing of Sister George* (1968).

Turn down Old Church Street for the **Front Page**, whose olde worlde interior is film-set genuine. Actors rehearsing at the parish hall down the street use it as their local and audiences from the nearby Cannon cinema drop in for pre- and post-movie pints.

Down on the river, Battersea Bridge was where they shot the last scene from *Lock Stock and Two Smoking Barrels* (1998). The houseboats beyond have been featured in many films, among them *The Naked Truth* (1957) starring Peter Sellers, and the whimsical *The Horse's Mouth* (1958) with Alec Guinness.

Next stop's the **King's Head & Eight Bells**, once the heart of bohemian Chelsea. It's from in front of the pub that they shot Mick Jagger and Marianne Faithfull coming out of their house, No.43, for *The Stones in the Park*. It began life as two small adjacent seamen's pubs on the river bank; the King's Head for officers, the Eight Bells for the crews. The two merged in 1580. No longer on the river since

engineers created the Embankment, it's still a pleasant place with several real ales on tap, Belgian beers and good food served in a busy restaurant at the back. Further along, Albert Bridge has been used in countless films (*Maybe Baby, Sliding Doors, The Man Who Knew Too Little*), but most notably, it was where Alex was beaten up by the tramps in *A Clockwork Orange (1971)*.

Head up Oakley Street to the **Phene**, a perfect example of pub design circa 1960 and which hasn't changed much since the days when Liz Taylor and Ingrid Bergman were among the regulars.

The **Surprise** in Christchurch Street used to be Laurence Olivier's local when he set up home with Vivien Leigh at No.4 in 1940. Walk around Burton's Court to Royal Avenue; No.45 is Richard Rogers' house, Emma Peel's flat in the recent *Avengers* (1998) film, and *The Servant* (1963) was filmed on the other side of the Avenue in No.10.

And finally, back on King's Road, on the spot now occupied by Safeway, was where it all began. It was here that William Friese-Green had his workshop, where he toiled over his cameras, working on ideas that were years ahead of his time. Alas, his efforts were in vain, and he died penniless in 1921.
John O'Donovan

Chelsea Potter (*p26*) 119 King's Road, SW3 (020 7352 9479).
Front Page (*p27*) 35 Old Church Street, SW3 (020 7352 2908).
Kings Head & Eight Bells (*no review*) 50 Cheyne Walk, SW3 (020 7352 1820).
Phene Arms (*p27*) 9 Phene Street, SW3 (020 7352 3294).
Surprise (*p28*) 6 Christchurch Terrace, off Flood Street, SW3 (020 7349 1821).

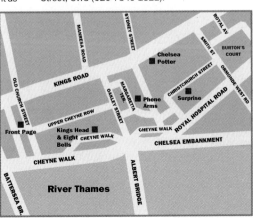

bar staffed by good-looking briskly efficient types, a list of Australian wines chalked up on the blackboard, lagers on tap and a solid brasserie-style menu. It's relaxed, good natured and already an obvious winner – packed on a Monday night when many neighbouring places had customers that could be counted on one hand with three fingers missing. We like it lots as a Friday lunch venue; look out for us, we'll be the people hogging the homely sofas by the front window. *Disabled: toilet. Music (live jazz 2.30-5.30pm Sun; free). Tables outdoors (pavement). TV. Vegetarian dishes.* **Map 7/K6**

Crown & Two Chairmen

31 Dean Street, W1 (020 7437 8192). Tottenham Court Road tube. **Open/food served** noon-11pm Mon-Sat; noon-10.30pm Sun. **Credit** AmEx, DC, MC, V. Despite a recent lick of paint and a refit, this is still something of a spit and sawdust place. It's loud, scruffy and youthful; most of the clientele seem to be students taking a night off from their usual union shenanigans and splashing out on a pint of beer at a normal price. Consequently get-pissed-quick perennials – snakebite and Hooch – are ordered in abundance, and you're likely to hear Travis, Oasis and other indie faves du jour blasting out of the speakers. It doesn't really have much character – it's a blackboard art and chicken-in-a-basket kind of a pub – but it certainly isn't pretentious, and on most nights you can guarantee that there will be a ready-made party of a kind going on. Sometimes that's all you want. *Comedy club (8pm Sat; admission £5). Function room. Games (fruit machines). Music (live jazz band 8pm Wed; free). Satellite TV. Vegetarian dishes.* **Map 7/K6**

Dog & Duck

18 Bateman Street, W1 (020 7494 0697). Piccadilly Circus or Tottenham Court Road tube. **Open** noon-11pm Mon-Fri; 5-11pm Sat; 6-10.30pm Sun. **No credit cards.**

In existence since 1734, this is Soho's oldest pub, and an integral part of its history: it is the site of the one-time home of the Duke of Monmouth, who used to go hare-coursing on the other side of Oxford Street with the rallying cry of 'So-ho', from which came the name we use today. It's tiny, but one of the most beautiful pubs in the area, with an intricate mosaic floor that features a dog chasing a duck, finely etched mirrors on the tiled walls, and a little fireplace at the back that is very cosy on winter nights – if you can manage to get near. It tends to be dominated by middle-aged bitter-drinking men who come here for the regularly changing real ales (London Pride, Adnam's, Tetleys, for example) and warm bonhomie. *Function room. Tables outdoors (pavement).* **Map 7/K6**

Dog House

187 Wardour Street, W1 (020 7434 2116). Tottenham Court Road tube. **Open/food served** 5-11pm Mon-Fri; 6-11pm Sat. **Happy hour** 5-7.30pm Mon-Fri; 6-7.30pm Sat. **Credit** AmEx, DC, MC, V. Easy to miss, this basement bar at the top end of Wardour Street is marked only by an amusing dog-on-its-back sign and chalk board outside. The 'sorry guys, no ties' notice within makes a refreshing change and sets the tone for this small, cartoonish and deliberately idiosyncratic cantina. Decked out in a carnival-like cacophony of primary colours it's unlikely to draw much custom from Soho's trendier set, but it's not without a certain awkward charm. Off the main bar area is a series of smoky, cave-like rooms with bright sofa seating and thick, curving stone walls. There's no draught beer, but plenty of the bottled stuff and, as with many hip bars these days, a penchant for flavoured vodkas. Two lumps of quartz crystal, plonked on top of the bar, soak away all the bad vibes. *Function room. Satellite TV. Vegetarian dishes.* **Map 7/K6**

Intrepid Fox. *See page 80.*

The Edge

11 Soho Square, W1 (020 7439 1313/
www.edgesoho.com). Tottenham Court Road tube.
Open/food served noon-1am Mon-Sat; noon-10.30pm
Sun. **Credit** MC, V.
A four-floored gay bar that's more of a social than a pick-up
joint, The Edge is a relaxed place that attracts a mixed crowd
and a fair few women. The ground-floor bar is the most easy-
going: cream walls, a bright interior and bar snacks (simple
salads £4, chicken supreme with sage, £3.50) give it a
brasserie feel. Journey up the clanging, warehouse-like stairs
and you'll find a more cruisey, industrial space with a large
dancefloor and hard house pumping from the speakers. The
top two floors are more intimate, and often hired out to private
parties. A stalwart on Soho's gay scene, The Edge has long
since passed its place-to-be stage but still manages to pack
them in. In summer the Soho Square location really comes
into its own and the crowds spill on to the street.
Function room. Music (DJs 9pm Mon, Thur-Sun;
live jazz and blues 9pm Tue, Wed; free). Tables outdoors
(pavement). Vegetarian dishes. **Map 7/K6**

Freedom

60-66 Wardour Street, W1 (020 7734 0071). Leicester
Square tube. **Open/food served** 11am-3am Mon-Sat;
noon-midnight Sun. **Admission** £3 after 11pm Mon-Wed;
£6 after 10.30pm Thur-Sat. **Credit** AmEx, MC, V.
Once intimidatingly gay and trendy, Freedom is now
completely mixed and decidedly mediocre. Even so, it remains
hugely busy. It's had another redesign and now leans towards
retro, with purple seating, wooden tables and plastic 'pop art'
lighting. A stereo blasts out disco. Cheap it ain't: a bottle of
Budvar is £3.30, spirits are £4.50-£6, cocktails £6-£7, and
Freedom Spring punch (champagne, vodka and Midori melon
liqueur) is £8.50 – although the latter is seriously excellent.
Presumably prices are justified by the clubby basement

below, except they're not. By day and early evening the place
is fine but security gets progressively picky as the night
wears on, and once inside you're quite likely to wonder why
you ever bothered queueing.
Disabled: toilet. Function room. Music (DJs nightly).
No-smoking area. Vegetarian dishes. **Map 7/K6**

Freedom Brewing Company

14-16 Ganton Street, W1 (020 7287 5267/
www.freedombrew.com). Oxford Circus tube. **Open** noon-
11pm Mon-Sat. **Food served** noon-3pm, 5-10pm Mon-Sat.
Credit AmEx, MC, V.
Fulham's Freedom Brewery Company now has a home in
Soho, just off Carnaby Street. It is virtually a clone of the
original in Covent Garden's Earlham Street (*see p32*). There
is the same kind of basement space with shining steel vats,
beechwood furniture and decent bar food. And, of course,
there's the same five brews; not cheap at £3 a pint but well
worth it. Don't let the small, ground-floor bar deceive you, the
basement is huge.
Bar available for hire. Restaurant. Specialities: organic
beer. TV. Vegetarian dishes. **Map 7/K6**

French House

49 Dean Street, W1 (020 7437 2799). Leicester Square
or Piccadilly Circus. **Open** noon-11pm Mon-Sat;
noon-10.30pm Sun. **Food served** 12.30-3pm, 6.30-10pm
Mon-Sat. **Credit** AmEx, DC, MC, V.
Like the **Coach & Horses** (*see p76*), with which it once
shared a core clientele, the French is a true Soho institution.
It got its name during the war, when it became the meeting
place for the French Resistance in London. For years after it
was run by the famously charming Gaston and was the
watering hole of the most celebrated of '50s bohemia
including Brendan Behan, Dylan Thomas, John Minton and
Francis Bacon. Every inch of wall space is taken up by

theatrical memorabilia, and despite the death of the second Gaston (son of the original), the current landlord keeps the slightly raffish spirit alive and noisy regulars do their best to live up to the bad behaviour of their illustrious forebears. As a resistance to British boorishness, the French still refuses to serve pints (halves only); most people drink wine anyway. The restaurant upstairs is a companion to the highly acclaimed St John in Smithfields and serves excellent modern British food.

No piped music or jukebox. Restaurant. Vegetarian dishes. **Map 7/K6**

Garlic & Shots

14 Frith Street, W1 (020 7734 9505/ www.garlicandshots.com). Leicester Square or Tottenham Court Road tube. **Open** 5pm-midnight Mon-Wed; 6pm-1am Thur-Sat; 5-11.30pm Sun. **Food served** 5-11.15pm Mon-Wed; 6pm-12.15am Thur-Sat; 5-10.45pm Sun. **Credit** MC, V.

London's only garlic restaurant has a basement bar fashioned to resemble Dracula's lair. The black-painted walls, shadowy alcoves and coffin-shaped doors are lit only by candles lodged into wax-encrusted wine bottles. Unsurprisingly it attracts a fair few goths, who come and do their undead schtick while hammering shots from a list of over 100. Most feature Black Death vodka (naturally). How about a Bloodshot – vodka, garlic, tomato juice and tabasco (£2.50)? There are also garlic brandies (£4), garlic vodka coffees (£4) and even garlic beer (£2). If it all gets a bit too smelly, you are allowed to have a normal beer (£2.50). On our last visit, fellow patrons were blonde-haired Swedish tourists clearly enjoying the novelty of the place and being very smiley. Spoilsports.

Babies and children admitted. Function room. Restaurant. Tables outdoors (patio). Vegetarian dishes. **Map 7/K6**

Gold Bar Café

23A Ganton Street, W1 (020 7434 0109). Oxford Circus tube. **Open/food served** 11am-11pm Mon-Sat. **Happy hour** 5-8pm Mon-Sat. **Credit** MC, V.

A bit of a misnomer, as this small West Soho brasserie-bar is now decked out in trendy shades of lime and mustard with red stools giving way to vinyl plastic cushioned seating and magazine racks at the rear. Follow the disco ropes down to a small basement area that's totally OTT in the fab and groovy department. Er, what era are we in again? It's beloved of Soho's muso-trendies, hence the ubiquitous DJs and noticeable decks on entrance.

Babies and children admitted. Function room. Music (DJs nightly). Restaurant. Tables outdoors (pavement). TV. Vegetarian dishes. **Map 7/K6**

Intrepid Fox

99 Wardour Street, W1 (020 7494 0827). Leicester Square, Oxford Circus or Piccadilly Circus tube. **Open** noon-11pm Mon-Sat; 3-10.30pm Sun. **No credit cards.**

From the 'stone' gargoyle over the door to the cobwebs, comedy Halloween masks and carefully accrued layers of grime within, this temple to Rock remains untouched by the vagaries of fashion. It used to be home to London's postcard punks but now it's a predominantly goth and metal crowd. Expect piercings, tattoos, stubble and spilt beer in equal measure. Drink of choice would be snakebite and black (£2.60), while the jukebox, unsurprisingly, contains both rock and roll. For all its rampant, sleeveless black T-shirt machismo, leave any attitude at the door because the Fox is at heart a fun and friendly place.

Function room. Games (fruit machine, pool table, video games). Jukebox. Music (DJs Tue-Sun). TV. **Map 7/K6**

Jazz After Dark

9 Greek Street, W1 (020 7734 0545/ www.jazzafterdark.co.uk). Tottenham Court Road tube. **Open/food served** 5pm-2am Mon-Thur; 5pm-3am Fri, Sat. **Admission** £3 after 8.30pm Mon-Wed; £4 after 8.30pm Thur; £5 after 8.30pm for diners, £8 non-diners. **Credit** AmEx, DC, MC, V.

Despite being around for quite a few years, this place has never really taken off. Perhaps the problem is that it looks dated: its neon signs, chrome tables and chairs, red walls and long, underlit bar have the feel of a slightly tacky singles bar in a market town. But it has the advantage of free live music, with jazz bands playing at the back of the long room. You also usually have a good chance of finding somewhere to sit. Besides, the staff are friendly, cocktails are good value at £5, and there's a decent menu of brasserie faves like steak frites (£9.50) and fillet of salmon (£9.50), so perhaps it deserves a second chance.

Music (live jazz 9pm Mon-Thur; 10.30pm Fri, Sat; admission charges as above). Tables outdoors (pavement). Vegetarian dishes. **Map 7/K6**

Kettners

29 Romilly Street, W1 (020 7734 6112). Leicester Square tube. **Open** 11am-11pm Mon-Sat; noon-10.30pm Sun. **Food served** noon-midnight Mon-Sat; noon-10.30pm Sun. **Credit** AmEx, DC, MC, V.

Most of the proud, white-walled Victorian building, opened in the 1860s by Napoleon III's chef Auguste Kettner, is given over to a pizza restaurant, but turn left off the bright chandeliered lobby and you'll come to a champagne bar that looks like it belongs in a stately home: historic portraits, Regency furnishings and wicker armchairs create a sense of aristocratic splendour. In spite of all this, champagne prices are reasonable: all 32 marques are represented, and a bottle of house bubbly is £27.75 or £6.25 a glass. Punters are expense account businessmen and clients, romantic couples on a treat, and well-heeled ladies. At the back is a brandy bar with a more modern, art deco style, but it lacks the sophistication of the bubbly bar.

Babies and children admitted. Function room. Music (live pianist, nightly). Restaurant. Specialities: champagnes. Vegetarian dishes. **Map 7/K6**

Lab

12 Old Compton Street, W1 (020 7437 7820/ www.lab-bar.com). Leicester Square or Tottenham Court Road tube. **Open** noon-midnight Mon-Fri; 4pm-midnight Sat; 4-10.30pm Sun. **Food served** 5pm-midnight Mon-Sat. **Credit** AmEx, MC, V.

A bar for predominantly straight mid-twentysomethings (on the shrieking pink frontline of Old Compton Street), Lab exploits its lucrative niche with vibrant gusto. It has two bars, ground floor and basement; each room is narrow, low-ceilinged and short on seating. Add to this the gold painted walls, the 'space age bachelor pad' furniture, and the thumping house music (courtesy of the DJ), and you get a loud sweaty crush. The over-stretched bar staff serve excellent cocktails from a long list: try Mimosa Frappe (fresh orange, brown sugar, orange bitter and creole shrub rum over crushed ice, £7.50) or Very Berry (Absolut, lime, blue and black berries, £6.50). Bottled beer is available too and there's also better-than-average bar food, including marinaded chicken skewers at £5.75 and spring rolls at £4.95. Lab was winner of Best Bar in the *Time Out* Eating & Drinking Awards 2000.

Games (board games, Sun). Music (DJs Mon-Sat). Specialities: cocktails. Vegetarian dishes. **Map 7/K6.**

Manto

30 Old Compton Street, W1 (020 7494 2756/
www.mantogroup.com). Leicester Square or Tottenham
Court Road tube. **Open** 3pm-midnight Mon-Thur; noon-
midnight Fri, Sat; noon-10.30pm Sun. **Food served**
6pm-midnight Mon-Thur; noon-midnight Fri, Sat; noon-
10.30pm Sun. **Credit** AmEx, DC, MC, V.
Manto is Old Compton Street's latest gay bar/restaurant (and
the first London venue for the Manchester-based Manto
chain). It's a huge, sleek affair that currently attracts the most
image-conscious of Soho scenesters; a poser's paradise of
worked-out bodies displayed to sickening advantage in tight-
fitting clothes. It takes a certain amount of self-confidence to
drink here. We do love the large mural of Posh and Becks that
greets patrons at the door and the intimate alcove seating –
it's just a pity the same wit and care couldn't have gone into
the food and drink. The menu is easy assembly standards like
burgers and chicken wraps, while drinks are low maintenance
nitrokegs like Boddy's, Stella and Murphy's. But a late licence,
loud music and lots of space ensures a party atmosphere,
which is the real point of the place.
Disabled: toilet. Music (DJs nightly). Restaurant.
Vegetarian dishes. **Map 7/K6**

Mondo

12-13 Greek Street, W1 (020 7734 7157). Piccadilly
Circus tube. **Open/food served** 7pm-3am Mon-Sat.
Admission £5 after 11pm Mon-Sat. **Credit** MC, V.
Soho has its fair share of bars with a surfeit of attitude and
Mondo was once one of the most infuriatingly elitist. Not any
more. There are other far more fashionable bars around and
Mondo can't afford to be so choosy (although it will still turn
away a reviewer in open-toed sandals). It's surprisingly large
inside, and before 11pm it is easy to find an empty alcove on
most evenings, making it a good place to come with a crowd.
The clientele is young and, if not exactly cutting edge, then
certainly label conscious. DJs play on Friday and Saturday
nights, mixing funk, hip-hop and even rock. Drink is bottled
beer (£3-ish) and double measures of spirits (£4.50-£5.50),
and there are bar snacks such as dim sum (£5).
Bar area available for hire. Music (DJs 10.30pm Wed-Sat).
Restaurant. Vegetarian dishes. **Map 7/K6**

O Bar

83 Wardour Street, W1 (020 7437 3490). Leicester
Square or Piccadilly Circus tube. **Open/food served**
5pm-3am Mon-Sat; 4-10.30pm Sun. **Happy hour** 5-8pm
Mon-Sat. **Admission** £3 after 11.30pm Mon-Thur;
£3 after 10pm, £5 after 11pm Fri, Sat. **Credit** MC, V.
Coming on like a gothic castle, complete with wrought iron
candelabra, sweeping staircase, mock stone walls, dark wood
tables and some incongruous leopard-print sofas, the O Bar
continues to straddle the fine line between club and bar. It
draws a boisterous crowd and is not the place for uptown
sophistication: most punters here are fuelled on copious jugs
of cocktails (including O Bar 2000, £15 a jug), and looking to
get off with each other. An opulent book-furnished upstairs
room looks like it belongs in a private club and, as such, is
often closed for private functions – as it was on the night we
last visited.
Function room. Music (DJs 9pm nightly). Specialities:
cocktails. TV. Vegetarian dishes. **Map 7/K6**

Old Coffee House

49 Beak Street, W1 (020 7437 2197). Oxford Circus or
Piccadilly Circus tube. **Open** 11am-11pm Mon-Sat; noon-
3pm, 7-10.30pm Sun. **Food served** noon-3pm Mon-Sat.
Credit MC, V.

Notably lacking in the coffee area but heavy in the dangling-
from-the-ceiling big copper pot department, the Old Coffee
House is a masculine, heavily furnished and dimly lit boozer
that – for all its tatty stuffed wildlife, maritime illustrations
and vaguely erotic portraits of 19th-century strumpets –
retains a rough-hewn charm and welcoming atmosphere. It's
especially popular with nearby Berwick Street market
stallholders, media types straying from Golden Square and,
should the autographed portraits be believed, rough-edged
luminaries as Bob Hoskins, Phil Collins and Frank Bruno.
Function room. Games (fruit machine). Restaurant. TV.
Vegetarian dishes. **Map 7/K6**

Opium

1A Dean Street, W1 (020 7287 9608/
www.thebreakfastgroup.co.uk). Tottenham Court Road
tube. **Open/food served** noon-3am Mon-Fri; 7pm-3.30am
Sat. **Admission** £15 after 10.30pm. **Credit** AmEx, MC, V.
Opium has good pedigree – it's run by the Breakfast Group
also responsible for the popular **Jerusalem** (*see p42*), **Saint**
(*see p56*) and **The Social** (*see p43*), along with several other
successful bars. It's certainly stylish with decor inspired by
no one country in particular, merely 'the Orient': the low
lighting, carved wood and gilded chinoiserie are invitingly
opulent. They're supposed to evoke the feel of a louche
hideaway but really it's much too calculated and sanitised to
be successfully decadent. It's spacious and service is very
smart – you sit down and one of the good-looking, black-clad
staff comes over. But what this place is really all about is
money; a gin and tonic and a Chivas Regal came to £14. A
glass of undistinguished Pinot Grigio is a fiver. There's Dom
Pérignon 64 at £650 a bottle. Food is pretend-Vietnamese
dishes at Soho nightclub prices. So while it's all very pretty,
it's also seriously over-priced and quite soulless – the night
we visited it totally lacked buzz. Definitely not for the masses.
Bar available for hire. Music (cabaret Mon, Tue, Thur;
DJs). Restaurant. Vegetarian dishes. **Map 7/K6**

Phoenix Artist Club

1 Phoenix Street, Charing Cross Road, WC2
(020 7836 1077). Leicester Square or Tottenham Court
Road tube. **Open/food served** 5pm-2.30am Mon-Wed;
1pm-3.30am Thur, Fri; 1pm-3.30am Sat. **Happy hour**
5-8pm Mon-Thur; noon-5pm Sat. **Credit** AmEx, MC, V.
The bar of the Phoenix Theatre keeps its late licence by
operating as a members bar, but come here in the week or
before 8pm Friday or Saturday and you shouldn't have a
problem getting in. It's worth a visit too, for the eccentric
decor: stuffed crocodiles jostle for hanging space with old
canoes in a cavernous room that looks like a Bavarian
drinking hall. A restaurant at the back features ornate little
cubby holes perfect for hiding away with a few friends. But
the service isn't always as charming as the venue: it's not
unknown to be unceremoniously shifted from your table if
the manager decides he needs it for a special party, or to be
served a single malt in a half-pint glass, or to be disappointed
by the unadventurous, meat-and-two-veg menu (char-grilled
chicken and chips, £7.95). Clientele are a mish-mash of St
Martins students, actors and most entertainingly, ageing
goths, whose Dracula Society meets down here once a month.
Babies and children admitted. Function room. Music
(live jazz/easy listening 7pm Mon-Thur; free). No-smoking
area. Restaurant. Theatre. Vegetarian dishes. **Map 7/K6**

Pillars of Hercules

7 Greek Street, W1 (020 7437 1179). Tottenham
Court Road tube. **Open** 11am-11pm Mon-Sat; noon-
10.30pm Sun. **Food served** 11am-10pm Mon-Sat; noon-
10pm Sun. **Credit** AmEx, DC, MC, V.

This must be the woodiest pub in Soho: wood panelling, wood beams, wooden floorboards, and wooden chairs and tables. Spruced up a little bit a few years ago, it remains a very traditional boozer, with Victorian etchings and paintings on the walls, antiquey lamps illuminating the bar and frosted-glass snob screens. It's a real bitter-drinker's home with guest ales each month supplementing the regulars (Marston's Pedigree, Theakston Best). Expect a mixed crowd from groups of businessmen to noisy students to Japanese tourists, plus soccer fans when there's a big game on.
Games (fruit machine). Specialities: real ales. Vegetarian dishes. **Map 7/K6**

Pitcher & Piano
69-70 Dean Street, W1 (020 7434 3585/ www.pitcherandpiano.com). Leicester Square or Tottenham Court Road tube. **Open** noon-11pm Mon-Sat. **Food served** noon-10pm Mon-Fri; noon-9pm Sat. **Credit** AmEx, MC, V.
Flagship branch of the chain that has cornered the *Ally McBeal*-watching market by being a little more sophisticated than its rivals. Knock it if you like, but P&P knows its market and caters to it exceptionally well. This branch captures the chain's ethos perfectly: it looks almost like a members bar from the outside, while inside it's huge but divided into human-scaled areas with large sofas waiting to be occupied by groups of friends meeting after work. The mainstream crowd that pack into the place drink pints at the bar (Marston's Pedigree, Guinness, Kronenburg, Stella and Banks Smooth), order above average but no-nonsense bar snacks (brie and bacon baguette, £6, Cumberland sausage and mash, £7), and are up on their feet shortly before closing time letting go to 'Dancing Queen' and classic disco.
Babies and children admitted (until 5pm). Function room. Vegetarian dishes. **Map 7/K6**

Pop
14 Soho Street, W1 (020 7734 4004/ www.thebreakfastgroup.co.uk). Tottenham Court Road tube. **Open** 5pm-3.30am Mon-Thur; 5pm-4am Fri; 8pm-5am Sat; 6-11.30pm Sun. **Food served** 5pm-midnight Mon-Fri; 8pm-midnight Sat. **Admission** £3 after 9pm Mon-Wed; £5 after 9pm Thur; £10 after 9pm Fri; £10 Sat. **Credit** AmEx, DC, MC, V.
Welcome to pop world, a world of bright oranges and blues, of curves and circles, of plastic and formica, where guitars are twangy and voices chorus in harmony. Hopes were raised by the decor that we might get served by Pan's People, but sadly no, though staff were doing their utmost best to please. They need to work hard because a couple of years after opening, Pop has yet to take off in the big way an enormous place like this needs to. On the nights we've been down it's been uncomfortably quiet. Which is a great shame because there are some unusual '60s-themed club nights here, well worth dropping in on. Prices don't help though with large spirits at £6 and cocktails at £6-£9.
Music (DJs nightly). Specialities: cocktails. Vegetarian dishes. **Map 7/K6**

Rupert Street
50 Rupert Street, W1 (020 7292 7141). Piccadilly Circus tube. **Open** noon-11pm Mon-Sat; 1-10.30pm Sun. **Food served** noon-5pm Mon-Thur; noon-6pm Fri, Sat; 1-6pm Sun. **Credit** MC, V.
What with its massive windows (meant for looking in rather than out) and style-conscious crowd, it's very much scene and be seen at Rupert Street, a small place with a big reputation as London's trendiest gay bar. The surroundings are as stylish as the crowd, all muted mauves

and mustards, with ambient lighting, steel flooring and exposed air ducts. The atmosphere is loud, cruisey and posey. It's extremely popular, especially at weekends. Drinks are expensive with spirits – 50ml measures seem to be mandatory – costing £4.45, although there is bottled beer. Toilets are dead groovy.
Disabled: toilet. Internet access. No-smoking area. Vegetarian dishes. **Map 7/K6**

Sak
49 Greek Street, W1 (020 7439 4159). Leicester Square or Tottenham Court Road tube. **Open/food served** 5.30pm-2am Mon, Tue; 4.30pm-3am Wed-Sat. **Admission** £5 after 10.30pm Fri, Sat. **Credit** AmEx, DC, MC, V.
A couple of years down the line, Sak has lost the aggressively hip attitude it once had and settled for being a class venue for a sophisticated night out. Beyond the frosted glass and burly doorman is a bar that wouldn't look out of place in a *Wallpaper** shoot, yet classic enough not to be in danger of dating any time soon: black leather sofas, modern art on pastel walls, expansive floral arrangements. It's a cocktail kind of place, which are expensive here but very good; try the house cocktail, the Dandy (Courvoisier, white chocolate liqueur and almonds £7). Happy hour offers cocktail jugs at £8, but this is hardly the place to come and get blasted.
Function room. Music (DJs Wed-Sat). Specialities: cocktails. Vegetarian dishes. **Map 7/K6**

Salsa!
96 Charing Cross Road, WC2 (020 7379 3277). Leicester Square or Tottenham Court Road tube. **Open** 5.30pm-2am Mon-Sat. **Food served** 6pm-1.30am Mon-Sat. **Admission** £4 after 9pm Mon-Thur; £2 7-8pm, £4 8-9pm, £8 after 9pm Fri, Sat. **Happy hour** 5.30-7.30pm Mon-Fri. **Credit** AmEx, DC, MC, V.
It seems that Britons still can't get enough of that so-called Latin spirit, the one that those Bacardi Breezer ads are always banging on about; years after opening, this huge bar-cum-dancehall still has them queueing down Charing Cross Road several nights of the week. It's a big hit with office parties, who come along to pelvic thrust in time to Santana and ogle the bona fide Brazilians who groove around with fluid sexy grace. With bands Thursday through Saturday, cheap drink (cocktails at £3.95) and food (chilli ribs, potato wedges, that sort of thing), even the most rhythmically challenged can't fail to make a good night of it.
Dress code. Music (DJs, Latin bands, salsa classes, nightly). Restaurant. Satellite TV. Specialities: cocktails. Vegetarian dishes. **Map 7/K6**

Shampers
4 Kingly Street, W1 (020 7437 1692). Oxford Circus or Piccadilly Circus tube. **Open/food served** 11.30am-11pm Mon-Sat. **Credit** AmEx, DC, MC, V.
Relaxed, cosy and slightly cluttered, with acres of blackboards and wine racks, Shampers is an unreconstructed '80s wine bar that attracts a loyal following (a considerable achievement in the West End). A large wine list is excellently selected with ample choice by the glass; the extensive French section covers all the bases, the choice of Spanish is well developed, and there are even a few very good German wines. It also offers a classic bistro menu. The bar itself is small but there are plenty of stalls and the quiet atmosphere helps you to unwind as much as the wine. Just a pity about the awful braying name.
Babies and children admitted (downstairs). Function room. Restaurant. Satellite TV. Specialities: wines. Vegetarian dishes. **Map 7/K6**

Manto. *See page 81.*

Signor Zilli
40 Dean Street, W1 (020 7734 1853). Tottenham Court Road tube. **Open/food served** noon-midnight Mon-Fri; 5.30-midnight Sat. **Credit** AmEx, DC, MC, V.
Attached to the popular Italian restaurant of the same name, this bar is very much a separate entity and you certainly don't feel out of place just coming here to drink. A recent makeover has given it a classic brasserie style, and the aura of brash sophistication makes it a favourite of young people with money to burn, couples on a night out, and groups of older Italian men. There are bottled Italian beers (Peroni, Dreher) but wine's very much the order of the day, despite some slightly inflated prices (£15 for a bottle of Soave Classico or Montepulciano). Light bar meals include pasta arabiatta (£7.50) and margharita pizza (£8.50). Staff can be rather brusque and businesslike.
Babies and children admitted (daytimes). Specialities: cocktails, wines. Tables outdoors (pavement). Vegetarian dishes. **Map 7/K6**

Six Degrees
56 Frith Street, W1 (020 7734 8300/ www.six-degrees.co.uk). Piccadilly Circus or Tottenham Court Road tube. **Open** noon-11pm Mon-Fri; 6-11pm Sat (ground floor bar). **Food served** 6.30pm-midnight Mon-Sat (restaurant); 6.30pm-midnight Wed-Sat (lounge bar). **Credit** AmEx, DC, MC, V.
A good-looking venue in what used to be Dell'Ugo. Behind a high glass façade the ground floor is kitted out with plush red leather stools, a green glass bar, cream walls, black leather sofas and low tables. Smart and stylish, it's nevertheless big enough that you can find a place to sit most of the time. Bottled beers include Tiger and Sapporo, but cocktails and double measures are more in keeping with the spirit of the place. Bar snacks are vaguely oriental (seafood and vegetable tempura, £5.75, duck spring rolls, £5.95) and there's also a proper restaurant on the first floor. The top floor is a very pleasant lounge bar with lots of deep black leather sofas – but you might have to blag your way in.
Babies and children admitted. Function rooms. Restaurant. Specialities: cocktails. Tables outdoors (pavement). Vegetarian food. **Map 7/K6**

Soho Spice
124-126 Wardour Street, W1 (020 7434 0808/ www.sohospice.co.uk). Oxford Circus or Tottenham Court Road tube. **Food served** 11.30am-midnight Mon-Thur; 11.30am-3.30am Fri, Sat; 12.30-10.30pm Sun. **Happy hour** 5.30-7pm Mon-Sat. **Credit** AmEx, DC, MC, V.
A bright and stylish Indian restaurant valued as much for its downstairs bar as for its food. Decked out in electric shades of saffron and paprika (upstairs and down) – a trippy colour scheme matched by the acid kurtas of the highly efficient staff – the in-your-face vibrancy can't help but raise a smile. And check out the brighter-than-bright tiling toilets. Bench seating is plentiful and a dance-filled jukebox and MTV add to the all-out sensual assault. Drinks to go for are the splendid spiced cocktails, and there's also Kingfisher beer. On a good night (and most nights here are) this place is as unrelenting and exhilarating as Mother India herself.
Disabled: toilet. Function room. Music (DJs Fri, Sat). No-smoking area (restaurant). Restaurant. Satellite TV. Vegetarian dishes. **Map 7/K6**

Spice of Life
37-39 Romilly Street, W1 (020 7437 7013). Leicester Square or Tottenham Court Road tube. **Open/food served** 11am-11pm Mon-Sat; noon-10.30pm Sun. **Credit** AmEx, MC, V.

There was a time when the Spice was a bit edgy. It was a West End meet for an East End sharp haircuts and razor attitude crew, fuelling up for a night at the Wag. But that was then. The boys wouldn't get in now; the monkeys on the door wouldn't let them. A prominent location on Cambridge Circus, rubbing shoulders with *Les Mis*, has seen the place invest in a series of makeovers to present a safer, more hospitable face, one that won't scare off the passing tourist trade. Thankfully, the urge to 'theme' has been resisted and instead the place remains traditional in an undistinguished sort of way. Hertford's independent McMullen brewery supplies the very good real ales. Staff come and go at a rate of knots, possibly because of the foul uniforms they are forced to wear. It's not the nicest of pubs but you no longer risk getting your head kicked in in the toilets.
Function room. Games (fruit machines). Music (live jazz 8pm Mon & Wed). Tables outdoors (pavement). TV. Vegetarian dishes. **Map 7/K6**

Sun & Thirteen Cantons
21 Great Pulteney Street, W1 (020 7734 0934). Oxford Circus or Piccadilly Circus tube. **Open** noon-11pm Mon-Fri; 4-11pm Sat. **Food served** 12.30-3pm Mon-Fri. **Credit** AmEx, DC, MC, V.
A hip but honest-to-god boozer that remains traditional but's also favoured by the club crowd. Most nights the bar area is standing-room only, jammed with young non-suited professionals on draught Staropramen or Hoegaarden, or drinking Budvar by the bottle. You might get lucky and snag a chipped marble-topped table in the wonderful mirror-lined, high-ceilinged back room (which to us always feels a bit Belgian). Bar staff have taste when it comes to music; only fitting given that it's while drinking in this pub that Underworld came up with the sublime 'Born Slippy'. In summer glasses go plastic as punters pile out on to the pavement. This just might be the best pub in Soho.
Function room. Music (DJs Thur, Fri). Vegetarian dishes. **Map 7/K6**

Toucan
19 Carlisle Street, W1 (020 7437 4123). Tottenham Court Road tube. **Open/food served** 11am-11pm Mon-Fri; 1-11pm Sat. **Credit** MC, V.
One of the smallest bars in Soho spent years serving excellent Guinness and fine Irish whiskies to just the select few who knew of it. Then word spread, it got itself a sign, and eventually took over the café upstairs to turn into a bona fide pub. Now on a Friday night you can't get near the place for the crowds on the pavement outside. Come here earlier in the week when you might be able to snag a bar stool or a seat down in the basement and take a gander at the old tin Guinness ads, order superb bar snacks like Irish sausage and champ (£4.95), and appreciate a superb pint of the black stuff. O'Neill's, you bloody fakers.
Satellite TV. Specialities: Irish whiskies. Vegetarian dishes. **Map 7/K6**

Two Floors
3 Kingly Street, W1 (020 7439 1007). Oxford Circus or Piccadilly circus tube. **Open** 11am-11pm Mon-Sat. **Food served** 11am-4pm Mon-Sat. **Credit** MC, V.
Too style conscious to announce itself with something as mundane as a street sign, Two Floors is the place at the southern end of Kingly with the large darkened glass frontage. It was the first bar to put West Soho on the map of cool and it continues to do well through being comfortably hip rather than cutting edge. Dark green walls, parquet flooring scuffed to the colour of burnt cork and candlelight create an easy intimacy, reinforced by simple furniture and

saggy old sofas. The divey and ultra-smoky (on our visit, anyway) deep red basement bar is often hired out for functions but upstairs has a better vibe. Clientele dress according to Henry Ford's dictum. Beers are bottled and disappointing (Heineken, Stella Artois, Red Stripe), but the selection of spirits is good. *Babies and children admitted. Function room. Games (board games).Vegetarian dishes.* **Map 7/K6**

Two Thirty Club
23 Romilly Street, W1 (020 7734 2323). Leicester Square or Piccadilly Circus tube. **Open** 5.30pm-1am Mon-Sat. **Food served** 5.30-11.30pm Mon-Sat. **Credit** AmEx, MC, V.
It's hard to say why this open-to-all basement bar under members-only 23 Romilly Street has such an attractive vibe: it's only a very modestly sized rectangular room after all, with walls panelled by wood veneer, small tables, a few black cushioned stalls and a little bar at the end, but it's just perfect. The crowd are fashionable but friendly, the bar staff efficient but welcoming, the drinks predominantly cocktail staples but extremely well done. The place also benefits from a good location – central Soho but one of its quieter streets. The result is that it feels like a bit of a secret hideaway, marked only by the most discreet of signs, entered via a narrow, unremarkable staircase. Bring a friend here to be complimented on your amazing insider knowledge of the London scene.
Music (DJs Tue-Sat). Specialities: cocktails. Vegetarian dishes. **Map 7/K6**

Village Soho
81 Wardour Street, W1 (020 7434 2124). Piccadilly Circus tube. **Open/food served** 4pm-1am Mon-Sat; 4-10.30pm Sun. **Admission** £2 after 11pm Fri, Sat. **Credit** DC, MC, V.
This friendly, relaxed, bring-your-straight-mates gay bar is a tasteful two-level affair. On the ground floor it's all beiges and browns: brickwork, wooden tables and pews, adorned with ever-so-tasteful B&W erotica and altar-style candles. The latter are strewn with a fine abandon and come in pots, jugs, candelabra and, over the bar, a flickering arrangement enclosed in a Victorian birdcage – it all must save a fortune on the electricity. Upstairs is a smaller, more private affair, with mirror-mosaic tables and bar, Regency-style furniture and views of Old Compton Street.
Function rooms. Music (DJs nightly). Vegetarian dishes. **Map 7/K6**

Yard
57 Rupert Street, W1 (020 7437 2652). Piccadilly Circus tube. **Open** noon-11pm Mon-Sat. **Credit** AmEx, DC, MC, V.
One of Soho's best, most down-to-earth gay bars, the Yard is large enough to feel like a community unto itself. It is indeed built around an open-air courtyard, which is set off the street (beyond the iron gates between the Rupert Street Supermarket and a curry house) and feels something like a hotel patio. The ground-floor bar is upbeat, trendy and loud, while the upstairs bar is more relaxed and sociable. Unlike most of Soho's gay haunts, it's not male-dominated and there is no particular scene: lots of women of both sexual persuasions come here too. Grab a pint of beer (Grolsch and Staropramen, both £2.80) and make some friends; this is a place to sit and have a chat rather than come cruising.
Function room. Tables outdoors (courtyard). **Map 7/K6**

Yo! Below
52 Poland Street, W1 (020 7439 3660/www.yosushi.co.uk). Oxford Circus tube. **Open** noon-midnight Mon, Tue; noon-1am Wed-Sat; 5-10.30pm Sun. **Food served** noon-11pm Mon-Sat; 5-10pm Sun. **Admission** £3 after 11pm Wed-Sat. **Credit** AmEx, DC, MC, V.

It isn't going to be to everyone's taste, but if you are in the mood, this basement addition to the restaurant above (where the bar staff are robots and the food comes on conveyor belts) is a fun break from the norm. It's a large white split-level room with tables and stalls so low that you have to sit cross-legged. Serve yourself beer from the pumps under every table (£1 a glass). Alternatively there are bottled beers (Asahi, Kirin, Sapporro, all £3) a range of sake (£3-£11), and spirits at £2.50 for an oversize measure. Be warned: perky staff periodically jump up and shout 'Yo! Is everything OK?' The atmosphere is rowdy and it's a bit like being part of a MTV video. Oh yes, and there's karaoke.
Music (DJs Wed-Sat, live music Sun). Restaurant. Specialities: cocktails, Japanese beers. Vegetarian dishes. **Map 7/K6**

Also in the area...
All Bar One 36-38 Dean Street, W1 (020 7479 7921).
Café Med 22-25 Dean Street, W1 (020 7287 9007).
Café Rouge 15 Frith Street, W1 (020 7437 4307).
Dôme 57-59 Old Compton Street, W1 (020 7287 0770).
Moon and Sixpence (JD Wetherspoon) 183 Wardour Street, W1 (020 7734 0037).
O'Neill's 34-37 Wardour Street, W1 (020 7479 7941).
Rat & Parrot 77 Wardour Street, W1 (020 7439 1274).
Slug & Lettuce 80-82 Wardour Street, W1 (020 7437 1400).

South Kensington

190 Queensgate
190 Queensgate, SW7 (020 7581 5666). Gloucester Road or South Kensington tube. **Open** 11am-1am Mon-Sat; 11am-midnight Sun. **Credit** AmEx, DC, MC, V.
This townhouse address at the top end of Queensgate, close to the park, houses the smart Gore Hotel, a formal downstairs restaurant, a bistro, and this elegant little bar. By day it serves as a retreat for the local gentry who can while away their afternoons here surrounded by oil paintings and lots of wood panelling. By night, the atmosphere is louche, with low lighting, candles and a younger, hipper crowd boogying in their armchairs to '90s dance music. The attractively back-lit bar is well-stocked and there's an eclectic wine list, with a range of eight wines available in two-glass pichets, accommodatingly priced at £6.
Babies and children admitted (high chairs; restaurant only). Function room. Restaurant. Vegetarian dishes.

Admiral Codrington
17 Mossop Street, SW3 (020 7581 0005). South Kensington tube. **Open** 11.30am-11pm Mon-Sat; noon-10.30pm Sun. **Food served** noon-2.30pm, 7-10.30pm Mon-Fri; noon-3.30pm, 7-10.30pm Sat; noon-3.30pm, 7-10pm Sun. **Credit** AmEx, MC, V.
Its heyday may have been in the '80s when the likes of Lady Diana Spencer were regulars, but the Admiral Codrington still packs 'em in every night of the week. It's now run by Joel Cadbury, of the chocolate family, and his Etonian sensibilities continue to give the place appeal to young beautiful Chelsea and South Ken folk. No longer the standard boozer of old, the place has been transformed into an American-style bar with a large central square serving area. There are a few sofas and low dressing table-type stools around the edges of the room,

but it's really a place to stand at the bar, in groups, everyone raising their voices and vying for attention. Definitely not somewhere to wind down after work, you come to the Admiral Codrington to up the pace.
Babies and children admitted. Games (board games). Restaurant (available for hire). Tables outdoors (garden). Vegetarian dishes.

Blenheim

27 Cale Street, SW3 (020 7349 0056). South Kensington tube. **Open** 11am-11pm Mon-Sat; noon-10.30pm Sun. **Food served** noon-2pm, 6-8pm Mon-Fri. **Credit** AmEx, DC, MC, V.
In this area of high-concept, high-design bars, the Blenheim makes a refreshing change. It's a no-nonsense pub that sells proper pints of beer (Badger, Tanglefoot, Hoffbräu), has a simple comfort-food menu, and a huge screen showing Sky Sports. Its history goes back to 1824 and the back bar was a mortuary at one time. A recent refit (introducing a bit of light wood, bright lighting and uncomfortable seating) hasn't done the place too many favours, but it still remains a boozer of few pretensions, and is highly recommended.
Games (bar billiards, fruit machines). Satellite TV (big screen). Vegetarian dishes.

Cactus Blue

86 Fulham Road, SW3 (020 7823 7858). South Kensington tube. **Open/food served** 5.30pm-midnight Mon-Fri; noon-midnight Sat; noon-11pm Sun. **Happy hour** 5.30-7.30pm Mon-Sat. **Credit** AmEx, DC, MC, V.
A vast atrium of a bar-restaurant with something of a schizophrenic personality: terracotta walls, Navajo-blanket banquettes and massive paintings of buffaloes and Native Americans in a metal and glass building with live jazz three nights a week. Never mind: the vast selection of kickin' tequilas went a good way to making up for the confused ambience, and there are also bottled beers and cocktails. Upbeat music and a laid-back buzz make this a fun place for a bit of Margarita-fuelled mayhem.
Babies and children admitted (restaurant only). Function rooms. Music (live jazz 7pm Tue, Wed, Sun; free). Restaurant. Vegetarian dishes.

The Collection

264 Brompton Road, SW3 (020 7225 1212/ www.the-collection.co.uk). South Kensington tube. **Open** 5-11.30pm Mon-Fri; 11.30am-3.30pm, 5-11.30pm Sat; 11.30am-3.30pm, 6.30-10.30pm Sun. **Food served** 6.30-11.30pm Mon-Fri; 11.30am-3.30pm, 6.30-11.30pm Sat; 11.30am-3.30pm, 6.30-10.30pm Sun. **Credit** AmEx, DC, MC, V.
To reach the intimidating glass catwalk that leads into this bar-restaurant (which is possibly the most dramatic entrance into any London drinking venue) you have to deal with a large doorman and his guest list. Pass the test and you can sashay to the long bar for an excellent Bloody Mary or Hong Kong Fizz. Decorated in a style that can only be described as 'tiki bar meets urban warehouse' – bamboo walls, exposed brick and big leather sofas – the Collection exudes a predatory atmosphere. This is exaggerated by the black-clad waiters who lean over the balcony of the upper-floor restaurant, silently observing customers in the bar below. Cosy booths along the bar do provide some intimacy for those who feel less than relaxed under scrutiny, and the suede chairs are comfortable for a post-work slump. If you're concerned about your finances, stay away.
Babies and children admitted (daytime, Sat, Sun; high chairs). Bar available for hire. Disabled: toilet. Dress code. Music (DJs 8pm nightly). Restaurant. Specialities: cocktails. Vegetarian dishes.

Crescent

99 Fulham Road, SW3 (020 7225 2244). South Kensington tube. **Open/food served** 11am-11pm Mon; 10am-11pm Tue-Sat; 11am-10.30pm Sun. **Happy hour** noon-6pm Mon-Fri. **Credit** AmEx, DC, MC, V.
The Crescent is like an iceberg; it's pretty cool and only a small part is visible at street level. The ground-floor bar seems dauntingly cramped when you enter, but there's a much larger area downstairs – bright, clean-lined and minimalist in look. It's primarily a wine bar and the list, featuring some 200 labels (25 or so by the glass), visits all four corners of the globe, but remains seriously and devoutly Francophile. Each wine (most under £30) has useful notes to help with the job of selecting your tipple. Tutored wine tastings take place one or two Mondays a month. The clientele leans toward post-Brompton Cross shoppers, so expect Prada and Joseph bags strewn around with gay abandon.
Function room. Vegetarian dishes.

Crown

153 Dovehouse Street, SW3 (020 7352 9505). South Kensington tube. **Open** 11am-11pm Mon-Sat; noon-10.30pm Sun. **Food served** noon-3pm, 6-9pm Mon-Fri; noon-4.30pm Sun. **Credit** DC, MC, V.
Situated beside Brompton Hospital, this boozer is a convenient stop-off for nurses, orderlies, medical students and miscellaneous staff tarrying on their way home from work. Recent years have seen a revamp, and from being a solid Victorian pub, it's now modelled more along the lines of a Pitcher & Piano type of place, with two distinct areas: a small over-lit front bar and a carpeted back area that resembles a chintzy tea room. While there's little here to get excited about, there is a welcoming buzz about the place. The Friday we last dropped by, an animated bunch was watching the football on a big screen toward the back of the pub, and there was amiable conversation around the bar. A decent array of beers includes a couple of real ales and there's a gastropub-style food menu.
Babies and children admitted. Tables outdoors (pavement). Vegetarian dishes.

Drayton Arms

153 Old Brompton Road, SW5 (020 7835 2301). Earl's Court or Gloucester Road tube. **Open** noon-11pm Mon-Sat; noon-10.30pm Sun. **Food served** noon-2.45pm, 6.30-9pm Mon-Fri; noon-7.45pm Sat, Sun. **Credit** MC, V.
Occupying a corner site on a busy junction, the Drayton has a marvellously imposing façade, all buff terracotta with art nouveau flourishes. Inside, it's similarly mammoth – in recent times, the Victorian interior partitions and fittings have been stripped out to leave one high-ceilinged airy space with modish bared floorboards and walls painted in flat earthy tones. Furniture is a mishmash of almost-matching dark wood chairs and tables. Light streams in through large windows. There's plenty of floor space, table football in one corner, a cosy sofa area in another. DJ decks stand ready for weekend sessions. Very pukka. If Jamie Oliver did interiors, this would be one of his. On a Tuesday night visit, there was a sociable buzz with groups of South Ken's badder boys and girls lounging artfully with cigs, Guinness and Penguin Classics in coat pockets. We'd come back.
Games (fruit machine, table football). Tables outdoors (pavement). Vegetarian dishes.

Eclipse

113 Walton Street, SW3 (020 7581 0123/ www.bareclipse.com). South Kensington tube. **Open** noon-midnight Sun-Wed; noon-1am Thur-Sat (members only after 7pm). **Food served** noon-4pm daily. **Credit** AmEx, DC, MC, V.

Opium. *See page 81.*

Eclipse is a gem of a bar, concealed behind a glass frontage and only revealed when the gold, fist-shaped door handle is gently pushed. It attracts a young, sociable, in-the-know crowd, plus passing trade from Joseph and the Conran Shop. There's a limited selection of bottled beers, but the focus is firmly on champagne and the fine cocktail list. Decorated in '90s 'good taste' brown-and-cream, it has comfy seats at the back, and enthusiastic young bartenders doing half-decent Tom Cruise impressions at the front. There's a skylight near the back that floods the bar with light during the day and we also like the tricky mirrors in the toilets.
Babies and children admitted (until 6pm). Bar available for hire. Dress code. Specialities: cocktails. Vegetarian dishes.

Latitude

163-165 Draycott Avenue, SW3 (020 7589 8464). South Kensington tube. **Open/food served** noon-11pm Mon-Sat; noon-10pm Sun. **Credit** AmEx, MC, V.
A stylish cocktail venture among the boutiques, Latitude offers nothing radically new but has some nice touches. We like the swimming pool-tile floor and the cigar corner. The array of back-lit bottles ranged along the bar is also highly alluring. We can imagine spending a very happy, alcohol-fuelled evening propped on a high stool working our way through all those that catch our eye. But most punters choose to order from a drinks menu divided into long drinks (all £6.50), shorts (again all £6.50), Martinis and champagne cocktails. There's also a modest wine list of four reds, five whites and one rose, all available by the glass. Expensive they may be, but drinks are a snip compared to the food; a club sandwich is £8, while French fries and mayo is £3.50. How good can chips be to merit that sort of price? We didn't want to encourage them by ordering, so we never found out.
Babies and children admitted (until 7pm). Function room. Games (backgammon). Music (occasional DJs). Vegetarian dishes.

The Oratory

232 Brompton Road, SW3 (020 7584 3493). South Kensington tube. **Open/food served** noon-11pm Mon-Sat; noon-10pm Sun. **Credit** AmEx, MC, V.
Over the road from the Brompton Oratory and mere steps from the South Ken museums, this is a good-value wine bar-cum-brasserie that's well worth knowing about. Its decor is a cross between shabby and grand, with wrought-iron chairs and burgundy velvet banquette seating, walls painted with gold foliage and rather lurid light fittings. Giant terracotta pots of ferns add to its slightly eccentric air. Staff are hugely accommodating and smiley. Food is fairly priced, but it's the wine that comes as the best surprise, with a perfectly decent bottle of house white at just a fiver or a chardonnay for £7.50. Intimate during the day, as the evening wears on the Oratory starts to swing – not surprising with wines at these prices.
Babies and children admitted. Restaurant (available for hire). Tables outdoors (pavement). Vegetarian dishes.

Also in the area...

All Bar One 152 Gloucester Road, SW7 (020 7244 5861).
Bram Stokers Tavern (Eerie) 148 Old Brompton Road, SW5 (020 7373 2818).
Café Flo 25-35 Gloucester Road, SW7 (020 7589 1383).
Rat & Parrot 25 Gloucester Road, SW7 (020 7589 0905).

St James's

Avenue

7-9 St James's Street, SW1 (020 7321 2111). Green Park tube. **Open** noon-11pm Mon-Sat; noon-10pm Sun. **Food served** noon-3pm, 5.45pm-midnight Mon-Thur; noon-3pm, 5.45pm-12.30am Fri, Sat; noon-3.30pm, 7-10pm Sun. **Credit** AmEx, DC, MC, V.
You can tell Avenue is exclusive by the baby grand in its large picture window. Beyond lies a smart back-lit serving area with a marble-tile floor and a dining section with immaculately dressed tables. Customers are seriously well-heeled with a high proportion of suave young men, some in dinner jackets with a pencil-thin beauty worn on one arm. Although we were in, ahem, casual gear the staff were friendly. Despite first appearances, the place is surprisingly relaxed and we felt comfortable even if we didn't have the means to juggle off-shore accounts. Drinks are brought to the table, which is nice. The selection runs to bottled beers, wine and cocktails, all at slightly above average prices.
Babies and children admitted. Disabled: toilet. Music (pianist 8pm Mon-Sat). Restaurant. Specialities: cocktails. Vegetarian dishes. **Map 2/J8**

Buckingham Arms

62 Petty France, SW1 (020 7222 3386). St James's Park tube. **Open** 11am-11pm Mon-Sat; noon-5.30pm Sun. **Food served** noon-2.30pm, 6-9pm Mon-Sat; noon-2.30pm Sun. **Credit** MC, V.
Cosy J-shaped Young's pub favoured by staff from the nearby passport office. Eavesdrop on tales of international paper stamping. Other customers on our visit included non-civil service office workers and blokes in anoraks with thick taped glasses and large beer bellies. Decor is homely with orange flock walls, thick window drapes, shelves of nick-nacks and plenty of old-style woodwork. At the back, past the bar area is a small dining room with nook-like food servery. Expect the likes of 'healthy' baked potatoes, croque monsieur and well stuffed sandwiches, all under £3. The full range of Young's beers is on offer at prices slightly below the norm for the area, plus there's a decent wine list stretching to 18 different bottles, most available by the glass. At the rear there's a bizarre brick corridor where people sit and watch TV.
Games (fruit machine). Satellite TV. Vegetarian dishes.

Critics' choice
toilets

Elbow Rooms (p219)
Two-way mirrors, ladies observe the gents.

Lab (p80)
Toilet seats inset with razor blades – ouch.

Pop (p83)
London's first female urinal.

Public Life (p123)
The bar that was a public toilet.

Princess Louise (p47)
Old fashioned grills – it's a men's thing.

Che

23 St James Street, SW1 (020 7747 9380).
Green Park tube. **Open** 11am-11pm Mon-Fri; 5-11pm Sat.
Food served 11am-3pm, 6-11pm Mon-Fri; 6-11pm Sat.
Credit AmEx, DC, MC, V.
No doubt the eponymous Ernesto de la Serna Guevara is spinning in his mausoleum at having this exclusive St James's bar and restaurant named in his 'honour'. Beyond an intimidating glass and polished steel entrance – designed no doubt to deter stray Argentinian Marxists – escalators connect with an upstairs restaurant. Provided you can get by the discreet but efficient staff inside, you enter a bar that's a cigar lover's paradise. A huge wall-length humidor offers over 70 different types of cigar (Che was a big fan, apparently), provided you've the best part of a tenner or more to burn. The drinks are what you'd expect from a fat cat den like this and range from the obvious (rum, tequila, upmarket cocktails) to 50-odd different wines and even a couple of bottled beers. Just don't mention Marxism or cancer.
Babies and children admitted. Disabled: lift, toilet.
Restaurant. Specialities: cigars, cocktails, rums.
Vegetarian dishes. **Map 2/J8**

Duke's Hotel Bar

Duke's Hotel, 35 St James's Place, SW1 (020 7491 4840/ www.dukeshotel.co.uk). Green Park tube. **Open** noon-11pm Mon-Sat; noon-10.30pm Sun. **Credit** AmEx, DC, MC, V.
This ultra-exclusive bar is reputedly where Di used to meet Dodi all those years ago. The uniformed doorman was friendly enough despite our lack of formal attire (smart casual but tie-less) and we bowled into two small rooms that make up the bar to find a group of well-heeled business people discussing something secret over canapés and cocktails. The pile of the carpet practically tickled our knees, while the furniture is sale room stuff: old dark wood, hand crafted, with leather upholstered sofas. Brimming bowls of roasted almonds and olives adorn every table. No beer here, just champagne, wine and classy cocktails. In a word: expensive.
Dress code. No piped music or jukebox. **Map 2/J8**

Golden Lion

25 King Street, SW1 (020 7925 0007). Green Park or Piccadilly Circus tube. **Open** 11am-11pm Mon-Fri. **Food served** noon-2.30pm Mon-Fri. **Credit** AmEx, MC, V.
One of London's busiest pubs, this five-storey boozer has been around since 1732. It used to be connected to the circle of the fabled St James's Theatre, which once stood next door until in 1959 property vandals demolished it. There's just another office block there now. Nicholson's has done a good job in restoring the place to an image of its former glory. The main bar has wooden floors, plenty of etched glass and partitioned wooden booths. But the real glory is outside, where the Jacobean-style frontage with black marble pillars and extruding windows stands out against the concrete and glass of its neighbours. There's a good selection of real ales, with the Adnam's Best and Pedigree both passing muster and lunchtime pub grub that goes down well with the office workers – many coming from local auction houses – who frequent the place.
Function room. Games (fruit machine). Restaurant. Satellite TV. Tables outdoors (pavement). Vegetarian dishes. **Map 2/J8**

Red Lion

23 Crown Passage, off Pall Mall, SW1 (020 7930 4141). Green Park or St James's Park tube. **Open/food served** 11am-11pm Mon-Sat. **Credit** MC, V.
'London's oldest village inn,' says the sign on the board outside. 'Over 30 malt whiskies,' boasts another. 'Second oldest licence in the West End.' Obviously there's a lot to be said for this quiet, back passage pub, a short march up from St James's Palace. The barman's greeting was the friendliest we received in SW1 and the red carpet and seating were about as welcoming as furnishings can get. Aside from the huge impressive range of malts at pretty reasonable prices, the Adnam's was good, and the small but well chosen wine list seemed to offer enough choice and quality to keep both the spritzer drinker and the connoisseur happy. The sign we'd put up would read: 'A pub lover's paradise in a passage.'
Babies and children admitted (daytime). Function room. No piped music or jukebox. Vegetarian dishes. **Map 2/J8**.

Red Lion

2 Duke of York Street, SW1 (020 7321 0782). Piccadilly Circus tube. **Open** 11.30am-11pm Mon-Sat. **Food served** noon-3pm Mon-Sat. **No credit cards.**
Another of those upmarket boozers that populate this end of town, this Red Lion is virtually a metropolitan version of a posh country pub. We arrived late one Thursday evening to find the place packed and not a seat to be had. The smartly dressed regulars all appeared to know each other and the staff knew most of them by name. Accents were more Chelsea than Charlton and spirits drinkers were in a healthy minority. Here you can ask for a malt and rather than be offered a single propriety brand, you've got a major choice on your hands. Real ales include Adnam's Best and wine drinkers can spend as much as their consciences will allow. The decor is all old wood and engraved glass with a central, framed serving area surrounded by sectioned-off drinking areas.
No piped music or jukebox. Specialities: real ales. **Map 2/J8**.

Two Chairmen

39 Dartmouth Street, SW1 (020 7222 8694). St James's Park tube. **Open/food served** 11am-11pm Mon-Fri. **Credit** AmEx, DC, MC, V.
This stately little pub sits at the bottom end of St Anne's Gate, within a waddle of St James's Park and Methodist Central Hall. It attracts a regular crowd and repels boarders. We arrived mid-evening on a Thursday to find a group of locals sitting on stools that blocked passage to the rear of the pub. The nicest 'pleases' failed to move them and we couldn't get through to the main part of the pub. No help from the bar staff, either. That aside, the Two Chairmen is quite charming. Real ales offered include Bombardier, Courage Best and Directors, while food ranges from the likes of steak kidney and barley wine pie to spicy corn chowder and hot peppered chicken, all at quite reasonable prices.
Function room. No piped music or jukebox. Vegetarian dishes.

Also in the area...

Balls Brothers 20 St James's Street, SW1 (020 7321 0882).
Davys at St James's Crown Passage Vaults, 20 King Street, SW1 (020 7839 8831).
Tapster (Davys) 3 Brewers Green, Buckingham Gate, SW1 (020 7222 0561).

Temple & Aldwych

Columbia Bar

69 Aldwych, WC2 (020 7831 8043). Covent Garden or Holborn tube. **Open** 11am-11pm Mon-Thur; 11am-1am Fri. **Food served** noon-10pm Mon-Fri. **Credit** AmEx, DC, MC, V.

This modern, comfortable bar operates on two floors and is Young's brewery's answer to big and brash All Bar Ones, Fine Lines and what-have-you. The decor leans firmly in the direction of trendy bars, with painted two-tone terracotta and cream walls, blond wood and red carpet, plenty of corners and angles and a tasteful use of concealed lighting and chrome accessories. Handpumps at the bar dispense a couple of real ales as well as the usual stouts and lagers (including Young's Pilsner) and the type of bottled stuff the clientele of youngish office workers go for. The wine list covers 20-odd choices by the glass and bottle, and food is a high point with a constantly changing Modern European menu covering bases from cassoulet to casserole.
Disabled: toilet. Function rooms. Music (DJ, 9pm-1am Fri). No-smoking area (restaurant). Restaurant. TV. Vegetarian dishes. Map 4/M6

George IV
28 Portugal Street, WC2 (020 7831 3221). Holborn or Temple tube. **Open** 11am-11pm Mon-Fri. **Food served** 11am-3pm, 5-9pm Mon-Fri. **Credit** MC, V.
Very much a home from home for students (and the less stuffy staff members) from the surrounding LSE, the George IV is dedicated to giving undergraduates and young local office workers what they want: fun. Its successes are documented on the 'wall of shame', stuck with photos of men and women behaving badly. Despite its dignified setting (it's a fine high-ceilinged Edwardian boozer), the George IV is almost frenetic with loud Capital FM-style music and/or big screen sport practically the whole time. Upstairs there's a games room offering pool, table football, Jenga and Connect 4. Beware of occasional karaoke on Thursdays. Also noted for its choice of three real ales (including Bass and London Pride).
Function room. Games (fruit machines, pool tables, video game). Satellite TV (big screen). Specialities: real ales. Vegetarian dishes. Map 4/M6

Seven Stars
53-54 Carey Street, WC2 (020 7242 8521). Chancery Lane, Holborn or Temple tube. **Open** 11am-11pm Mon-Fri. **Food served** noon-3pm Mon-Fri. **Credit** MC, V.
Built in 1602 and starting life as the Leg and Seven Stars (something to do with Dutch seamen apparently), this small, unspoilt pub at the rear of the Royal Courts of Justice would be a tourists' delight – if they were ever to find it. Its exterior (should you manage to tear yourself away from the window of the Wig Box next door) is two storied, squat and enhanced by colourful hanging baskets and old glass doors engraved 'General Counter' and 'Private Counter'. Inside it's not been 'modernised' for around a century and the cream plaster, emaciated dark wood beams and narrow settles are as real as the beer. Four bitters are on tap (including Courage Directors) and there's a fridge crammed with trendy bottled lager for the kids. More likely are boozy solicitors and other legal types lured by the promise of no piped music, TV or fruit machines.
No piped music or jukebox. Specialities: real ales. Map 4/M6

Ye Olde White Horse
2 St Clements Lane, WC2 (020 7242 5518). Holborn or Temple tube. **Open** 11am-10.30pm Mon-Fri. **Food served** noon-2pm Mon-Fri. **Credit** MC, V.
The handwritten 'No Students' sign in the window drew us into this small, cosy place at the back of the LSE. Although it doesn't look excessively ancient, there is something of the upmarket country pub about the place. Lovers of red are in their element as the ceiling, carpet and walls are coloured in various shades. There are four real ales (including the rarely found Brakspear Bitter and Special) and we were served by a couple straight out of central casting – middle-aged, he big

in a rugger sort of way, she blonde and charming. At the back there's a seated area with comfy banquettes, but most of the apparently well-to-do twentysomething-plus crowd seem to stand or sit on stools in front of the bar.
Games (fruit machine). Specialities: real ales. Map 4/M6

Also in the area...
Shoeless Joe's Temple Place, The Embankment, WC2 (020 7240 7865).

Trafalgar Square & Charing Cross

Gordon's
47 Villiers Street, WC2 (020 7930 1408). Embankment tube/Charing Cross tube/rail. **Open** 11am-11pm Mon-Sat. **Food served** noon-9pm Mon-Sat. **Credit** MC, V.
Forget the tourist trap in Tooley Street, this is the real London dungeon, and just about the only wine bar out of all those we've visited that had genuine dust on its bottles. Allegedly, wine has been sold on this site since 1364, so it seems appropriate that Gordon's has a selection of sherries, ports and Madeiras that it serves straight from the barrel in schooners or beakers. The wine list dips in and out of most wine-producing countries and offers good value for money with many bottles selling for around £12. Ten reds, ten whites and one sparkler are available by the glass. Food includes simple cold platters like rare roast beef salad or poached salmon salad, and a fantastically maintained cheeseboard. Gordon's Gothic surroundings are presided over by Bernadette Giacomazzo, who is seldom without a fag (non-smokers be warned, the air is thick with clouds of exhaled nicotine). The bar gets packed in the evenings, but once the crowds have gone home you wouldn't want to spend the night here alone.
Babies and children admitted (lunchtime). Specialities: wines. Vegetarian dishes. Map 2/L7

Lord Moon of the Mall
16-18 Whitehall, SW1 (020 7839 7701). Embankment tube/Charing Cross tube/rail. **Open** 11am-11pm Mon-Sat; noon-10.30pm Sun. **Food served** 11am-10pm Mon-Sat; noon-9.30pm Sun. **Credit** AmEx, MC, V.
When the JD Wetherspoon chain revolutionised British drinking habits around a decade ago by offering a selection of beers and real ales at non-outrageous, often knock-down, prices, reasonable food, no-smoking areas and pubs free of piped music, this was something of a flagship. Built in 1872 as the headquarters of Cock's & Co (Bankers), and bought from Barclays in 1992, it's a typical high-ceilinged Victorian banking hall, tarted up and made comfortable with lounge furniture and a bar running practically the room's whole, long length. Patrons relieve themselves in what used to be the vaults. But times have changed, the game's been raised by other chains that have followed suit, and while we shouldn't knock good value – not here in London of all places – the Lord Moon does now feel dated and bland.
Disabled: toilet. Games (fruit machine). No piped music or jukebox. No-smoking area. Vegetarian dishes. Map 2/K8

Queen Mary
Victoria Embankment, WC2 (020 7240 9404). Embankment or Temple tube. **Open** noon-11.30pm Mon-Wed; noon-1am Thur; noon-2am Fri, Sat; noon-10.30pm Sun (summer); noon-11.30pm Mon-Thur; noon-2am Fri, Sat; noon-6pm Sun (winter). **Food served** noon-9pm daily (summer); noon-9pm Mon-Sat; noon-6pm Sun (winter). **Admission** £5 after 10pm Thur (summer); £7 after 9pm Fri, Sat. **Credit** AmEx, MC, V.

CUBANA
BAR ★ RESTAURANT
Join the Party!

★ Fresh, juicy tropical fruit cocktails ★ Open late
★ Real Cuban country cooking ★ Fair prices
★ Free-range chicken and pork ★ Live Salsa ★ Salsa lessons

Cubana has become one of the South Bank's most popular bar-restaurants by offering fresh, quality dishes prepared with real Cuban passion at fair prices - and London's best, juiciest tropical fruit cocktails using freshly-squeezed juices. Mojitos and Daquiris made with freshly-squeezed lime and premium spirits, Mango and Strawberry Margaritas and many more - all to juicy Salsa rhythms direct from Cuba.

Cubana has regular live Salsa music and offers free Salsa lessons on Sundays. Our freshly cooked weekday Express Lunch offers two courses for £5.95 and three courses for £7.95 (inc. VAT and excluding service) - and of course we have vegetarian options and only use free-range chicken, eggs and pork.

Now we're open in Paddington too - come and see us!

Check **www.cubana.co.uk** for reservations and opening times or call Cubana at Waterloo on 020 7928 8778 or Cubana at Paddington on 020 7402 7539.

48 Lower Marsh Waterloo London SE1 by Waterloo Station/across from the Old Vic
36 Southwick Street Paddington London W2 between Praed Street and Sussex Gardens

JAZZ IT UP AT DOVER STREET

From your first drink at one of the three newly refurbished bars to last orders at 2.00am from our delicious French/ Mediterranean menu, Dover Street is unique.

With nightly live music & dancing until 3.00am there is no better party atmosphere in town.

Drinking... dancing...fine dining... 22 years and all that jazz at Dover Street

DOVER STREET RESTAURANT & BAR 8-10 DOVER STREET, MAYFAIR, LONDON, W1X 3PJ
TEL: 020 7491 7509   020 7629 9813   FAX: 020 7491 2958   www.doverst.co.uk
Dress code: smart casual, no jeans or trainers

Both the TS Queen Mary and the similar **Tattershall Castle** (King's Reach, Victoria Embankment, SW1 – 020 7839 6548) to be found further up-stream, past Embankment tube station, offer the opportunity for a semi-nautical booze up. That most of the customers seem to be young tourists says plenty, but save the sneers because in summer these floating pubs really come into their own. Watching the river drift by as you doze in the sunshine with a pint is one of the great pleasures of life. Unfortunately neither pub offers anything other than standard keg beers, so take your pick between Caffrey's and Grolsch (QM) and John Smith's Extra Smooth and Fosters (TC). Food is standard pub grub with a leaning towards fish. *Babies and children admitted. Function rooms. Games (fruit machine). Music (DJ Thur – summer; Fri, Sat). Nightclub for hire. Tables outdoors (deck). Vegetarian dishes.* **Map 2/L8**

Sherlock Holmes

10 Northumberland Street, WC2 (020 7930 2644). Embankment tube/Charing Cross tube/rail. **Open** 11am-11pm Mon-Sat; noon-10.30pm Sun. **Food served** noon-10pm daily. **Credit** MC, V.
Hidden away behind Charing Cross station in a part of what was once the Northumberland Hotel, this is a cosy Victorian-style saloon with real ale and Sherlock Holmes memorabilia by the ton. While some may scoff at the authenticity of his 'Monogram on Cigarette Ash' and paw prints of the Hound of the Baskerville, many are convinced. The bar offers three real ales, including a tasty Sherlock Holmes Bitter (which our sleuthing identified as re-badged Adnam's), and plenty of lagers. Measures are a little 'heady', so ask for a top-up. Upstairs there's a mock-up of Holmes's study and a restaurant where typically British grub masquerades under themed names such as Moriaty's mushrooms, Holmes's hamburger and Watson's winkle salad. *Babies and children admitted. Games (fruit machine). No-smoking area (restaurant). Restaurant. Specialities: real ales. Tables outdoors (pavement). Vegetarian dishes.* **Map 2/L8**

Ship & Shovell

1-3 Craven Passage, WC2 (020 7839 1311). Charing Cross tube/rail. **Open** 11am-11pm Mon-Fri; noon-11pm Sat. **Food served** noon-3pm Mon-Fri; noon-4pm Sat. **Credit** AmEx, MC, V.
It's not often you see a pub in two halves, but that's what you've got here. On opposite corners of Craven Passage, both bits have identical signs, polished wood floors, solid mahogany serving areas topped with dried hops and the same food menu offering standard pub grub. Both serve the same range of beers, including rather tasty bitters from Dorset's Hall & Woodhouse, including IPA, Badger Best, Tanglefoot and King and Barnes' Sussex. As the Cask Marque by both doors suggests, it's all kept rather well. The left-hand side (looking towards Villiers Street) is the larger of the two and boasts a wall of fine engraved mirrors. The name comes from Admiral Sir Cloudesley Shovell, who was shipwrecked off the Scilly Isles in the 18th century. *Babies and children admitted (Sat only). Function room. Games (fruit machine, quiz machine). Satellite TV. Specialities: real ales. Vegetarian dishes.* **Map 2/L7**

Two Chairmen

1 Warwick House Street, SW1 (020 7930 1166). Charing Cross tube/rail. **Open** 11am-11pm Mon-Sat. **Food served** noon-2.30pm. **No credit cards.**
We had a real shock on our last visit. We liked the Two Chairmen because despite being on the south side of Trafalgar Square nobody ever seemed to see it. It was a dark,

quiet bolthole for the dedicated boozer. But now it appears as though it's been refitted from Ikea with acres of new light wood panelling – we suppose it'll look all right in a hundred or so years – and matching new furniture. A few real ales are still offered with Courage Best and Directors being the perennial two, plus the usual lagers and spirits. Wine is now being trumpeted as an option and you might pluck up courage to ask the East European barman if they now do cocktails. Remains popular with British Council staff whose offices are round the corner. *Babies and children admitted. Games (quiz machine). Vegetarian dishes.* **Map 2/K7**

Also in the area...

Dôme 8-10 Charing Cross Road, WC2 (020 7240 5556).
Moon Under Water (JD Wetherspoon) 105-107 Charing Cross Road, WC2 (020 7287 6039).
Pitcher & Piano 40-42 William IV Street, WC2 (020 7240 6180).

Victoria

Boisdale

13-15 Eccleston Street, SW1 (020 7730 6922/ www.boisdale.co.uk). Victoria tube/rail. **Open** noon-1am Mon-Fri; 7pm-1am Sat. **Food served** noon-2.30pm, 7-11pm Mon-Sat. **Admission** £10 (£2.95 if already on premises) after 10pm Mon-Sat. **Credit** AmEx, DC, MC, V.
This charming, slightly fogey-ish, whisky bar brings a taste of Scotland – a rather posh Scotland of tartan, grouse shooting and languid malt sipping, mind – to within a caber's toss of Victoria Station. It offers a choice of over 200 whiskies, which glow invitingly from their perch behind the long zinc main counter in the Macdonald Bar. Aside from the dozens of malts and blends, ranging from under £4 a double to well over a tenner a shot, wine of all types is also a feature. Food is available in the neighbouring restaurant or over the bar – how about roast McSween's haggis with mash and neeps? – but it's not cheap. Beware the entry charge, which comes into effect after 10pm. *Function room. Music (live jazz 10pm-midnight Mon-Sat). Restaurant. Specialities: whiskies. Tables outdoors (conservatory). Vegetarian dishes.*

Cardinal

23 Francis Street, SW1 (020 7834 7260). Victoria tube/ rail. **Open** 11.30am-11pm Mon-Sat; noon-10.30pm Sun. **Food served** noon-4pm, 5-9pm Mon-Fri; noon-3pm Sat. **Credit** AmEx, MC, V.
This large and very grand Edwardian pub behind the Roman Catholic Westminster Cathedral looks every inch the traditional (posh) boozer. Yorkshire brewery Samuel Smith has renovated the place with care in regal greens, deep reds and browns, with lots of carved wood and engraved mirrors, plus well chosen portraits of historic cardinals. Just the sort of place His Holiness the Pope is likely to frequent between services whenever he pops over for mass. But picture the scene: His Holiness is just about to take his seat before ordering a pint of foaming ale when he notices – horror of horrors – no real ale! Museum Bitter from the keg, various types of Ayingerbräu lager and keg cider are all there are. His Holiness must try it sharpish. *Babies and children admitted (except Fri). Function room. Games (fruit machine). No-smoking area (dining area). Quiz (Tue). TV (big screen). Vegetarian dishes.*

Tiles

36 Buckingham Palace Road, SW1 (020 7834 7761).
Victoria tube/rail. **Open** 11am-11pm Mon-Fri.
Food served noon-2.30pm, 6-10pm Mon-Fri.
Credit AmEx, DC, MC, V.
From the outside this small wine bar-cum-bistro looks like a
Victorian shop, the sort of place where they serve muffins and
cream teas. They don't. It is run by friendly, welcoming staff
who take their extensive wine list very seriously,
endeavouring to find a suitable alternative if a particular
vintage or producer is unavailable. We counted 16 wines by
the glass (out of a total of 46), including two champagnes. The
balance leans in favour of French wines, but we also found
the elusive and delicious English sparkling Nyetimber 1993
(£23.95). It's a good spot for a light lunch of own-made leek
tart, or perhaps moules marinere, which a neighbouring table
pronounced 'superb'. Prices are all well under a tenner.
Babies and children admitted (lunchtime). Function
room. Restaurant. Tables outdoors (pavement).
Vegetarian dishes.

Zander

45 Buckingham Gate, SW1 (020 7379 9797/
www.bankrestaurants.com). Victoria tube/rail. **Open**
noon-11pm Mon-Sat; noon-10.30pm Sun. **Food served**
6-10am, noon-2.45pm, 5.30-11pm Mon-Thur; 6-10am,
11.30am-3pm, 5.30-11pm Fri, Sat; 6-10am, 11.30am-3pm,
5.30-9.30pm Sun. **Credit** AmEx, DC, MC, V.
Zander's 48m bar is possibly the longest in Europe. As it
happens, we've had a beer in the longest bar in the world,
inside the Mildura Working Men's Club in Australia, and
greatly admired the rough charm of the urinals built into the
bar that cut down on those long walks to the toilets. This is
not that kind of place. The Zander bar is so curve-of-the-earth
long because it's built in a big corridor of a swirly carpet hotel.
Swish, but also fantastically and unbearably loud in the
evenings, and not recommended for those looking for a quiet
night out. (The restaurant out back is a haven of peace by
comparison, with an equally impressive setting.) Further
pluses are friendly, well trained staff, a wine list that's well
thought out, and pretty damn good Martinis (around £6).
Babies and children admitted (daytimes). Bar area
available for hire. Music (DJs Fri,Sat). Restaurant.
Specialities: cocktails. Tables outdoors (restaurant
conservatory). Vegetarian dishes.

Also in the area...

Café Rouge Victoria Place Shopping Centre, 115
Buckingham Palace Road, SW1 (020 7931 9300).
Shoeless Joe's 1 Abbey Orchard Street, SW1
(020 7222 4707).
Wetherspoon's Unit 5, Victoria Station, SW1
(020 7931 0445).

Waterloo

Archduke

Concert Hall Approach, South Bank, SE1 (020 7928
9370). Waterloo tube/rail. **Open** 8.30am-11pm Mon-Fri;
11am-11pm Sat. **Food served** 11am-11pm Mon-Sat.
Credit AmEx, DC, MC, V.
Such has been the regeneration of the South Bank that the
Victorian railway arches housing this wine bar are now a
mega-prime site, while the Archduke itself has become a
popular fuelling point for tourists flooding towards the new
attractions. Its new-look conservatory with terracotta floor
tiles, wooden venetian blinds, rattan chairs, potted palms, fig

trees and hanging ferns, is a lovely place to sit and listen to
the trains clattering overhead. The thoughtful yet
manageable wine list features five wines available by the half-
bottle, including the excellent Le Brun de Neuville Brut non-
vintage champagne (£13). Most geographical bases are
covered and all the table wines cost less than £20. San Miguel
beer is available on draught, but it's hardly cheap at well over
£3 a pint. The Archduke specialises in affordable pre- and
post-theatre eating and drinking, offering two-course dinners
for £10.95 in its upstairs restaurant.
Conservatory for hire. Disabled access. Music (jazz
8.30-11pm Mon-Fri; 9-11pm Sat). No-smoking areas.
Restaurant. Tables outdoors (conservatory, garden,
pavement). Vegetarian dishes.

Auberge

1 Sandell Street, SE1 (020 7633 0610). Waterloo tube/
rail. **Open/food served** 11am-midnight Mon-Fri;
noon-11pm Sat. **Credit** AmEx, DC, MC, V.
A very successful bar (with restaurant upstairs) that's made
its name selling a wide variety of speciality Belgian beers and
some top-notch wines. Curiously, the wine list and bar menu
lean towards France (steak frites, croque monsieur), but the
beers come from Benelux: Hoegaarden and Leffe Blonde on
draught, with the likes of Chimay and Orval in bottles. Expect
to pay between £2 and £2.50 for a half pint, and roughly £4
for the bottled stuff. Customers tend to be upmarket youngish
rail travellers stopping off on the way to Waterloo station,
opposite, although we did encounter a group of very smart
elderly gents who must have been in their eighties.
Babies and children admitted. Function room. No piped
music or jukebox. Restaurant. Specialities: Belgian beers.
Tables outdoors (roof terrace). Vegetarian dishes.

Bar Citrus

36 The Cut, SE1 (020 7633 9144/www.barcitrus.co.uk).
Southwark tube/Waterloo tube/rail. **Open** 11am-11pm
Mon-Sat; noon-10.30pm Sun. **Food served** 11am-11pm
Mon-Sat; noon-9pm Sun. **Credit** AmEx, MC, V.
What was once the Anchor and Hope sits within easy
staggering distance of both Waterloo East and the new
Southwark station, and looks like a cross between a gastropub and a wine bar. The paintwork is a mix of beige and dark
green with rather odd hand-painted signs – 'real ales', 'wines
of the world', etc – dotted around the place. Part of the bar in
the two smallish rooms is taken over by an open kitchen (as
is the trend) with blurry chefs knocking out meals from
breakfast to lunchtime and dinners of good old British grub
(sausage and mash, steak pie, etc) and oriental treats (stir-
frys, the odd Thai curry, etc). Charles Wells' rather fine ales
are on draught (Eagle IPA and Bombardier, plus the
occasional special brew) as well as Kirin and Red Stripe lager
for the globe-trotting drinker.
Babies and children admitted (until 9pm). Bar area
available for hire. No-smoking area. Vegetarian dishes.

Cubana

48 Lower Marsh, South Bank, SE1 (020 7928 8778/
www.cubana.co.uk). Waterloo tube/rail. **Open** noon-
midnight Mon-Sat; 3-8pm Sun. **Food served** noon-3pm,
5.30-11pm Mon-Fri; 6-11pm Sat; 3-8pm Sun. **Admission**
£6 late Sat. **Happy hour** 5-6.30pm daily. **Credit** AmEx,
DC, MC, V.
As with *Che* (*see p90*), the heroes of the Cuban Revolution
incongruously provide the theme for an upmarket theme bar.
The image of Castro is prominent in the front window, just
above a couple of mounted period machine-guns, and the Red
Star flag provides Cubana's logo. The decor is 'cantina' with
plenty of painted bare brick and chunky wood. Even the

Zander

drinks menu is full of tongue-in-cheek cocktail references to the Counter Revolution and suchlike. But don't expect to find too many downtrodden workers here, instead it's a crush of office types – more Young Conservative than Children of the Revolution. Drink includes South American wines and Cuban beers and products by Bacardi – originally a Cuban company but they fled Castro. Food is good and leans towards supposed Cuban favourites such as spicy king prawn with papaya. *Babies and children admitted. Bar area available for hire. Music (Live music Sat; salsa lessons Sun). Restaurant. Tables outdoors (pavement). Vegetarian dishes.*

Fire Station
150 Waterloo Road, SE1 (020 7620 2226). Waterloo tube/rail. **Open** 11am-11pm Mon-Sat; noon-10.30pm Sun. **Food served** noon-11pm Mon-Sat; noon-9.30pm Sun. **Credit** AmEx, DC, MC, V.
Sitting proudly next to the new main entrance to the railway station, the mighty red-fronted Fire Station has become something of a Waterloo institution (although we remember when it really was a fire station). The decor may be looking a little, er, familiar now – those redundant hoses, old signs, pine tables and metal-topped red and white brick bar – but the spirit survives. The original flagstone and tile floor stands up well to the traffic of literally thousands of commuters who pop in every week for a pre-train refresher. Real ales are very much to the fore with four on offer the last time we visited (including Fire Station Bitter) and a very well balanced wine list. The right-hand side of the building is taken up by a restaurant where the likes of pan-fried liver and fillet of cod can be had for around a tenner. *Babies and children admitted (children's menu at weekends, high chairs). Function room. Restaurant. Satellite TV (big screen). Vegetarian dishes.*

King's Arms
25 Roupell Street, SE1 (020 7207 0784). Waterloo tube/rail. **Open** 11am-11pm Mon-Sat; noon-10.30pm Sun. **Food served** noon-3pm Mon-Fri. **Credit** MC, V.
Each weekday evening the side streets leading to Waterloo Station are stampeded by hundreds of workers trotting homeward as fast their legs can carry them. But a good many make a quick stop-off on the way in this ever-popular pub. Its tiny old public bar has been tarted up, as has the slightly larger saloon area – but most patrons head for the back and the 'conservatory', a large brick-walled glass-roofed room packed with tables, chairs and pictures of old Waterloo. You get served in the front bar and carry your pint of Pedigree, Adnam's Best, or whatever through. It's an arrangement that seems to work. A couple of theatrical administrators at the next table were saying what a wonderful pub it was and we would have to agree, but what a pity the wine list isn't longer. *Babies and children admitted (until 6pm Mon-Fri, all day weekends). Function room. Jukebox. Specialities: real ales. TV. Vegetarian dishes.*

Laughing Gravy
154 Blackfriars Road, SE1 (020 7721 7055). Southwark tube/Waterloo tube/rail. **Open** 11am-11pm Mon-Fri; 7pm-midnight Sat. **Food served** noon-11pm Mon-Fri; 7-11pm Sat. **Credit** AmEx, DC, MC, V.
A surprisingly good bar at the 'wrong' (ie Elephant and Castle) end of Blackfriars Road, Laughing Gravy gets its name from a dog in a Laurel and Hardy short. But actually, it's quite a serious affair. It's really a wine bar (what few beers they have are bottled) and champagne is shamelessly plugged. Prices are pretty standard for Blackfriars, so don't expect any under £10 bargains. A more formal restaurant area towards the back serves well thought out and

innovative food: pork chop with anchovy potato gratin, bread and butter pud spiced up with Grand Marnier, wild boar, that kind of thing. *Babies and children admitted (high chairs). Games (board games). Restaurant. Tables outdoors (pavement). Vegetarian dishes.*

Mulberry Bush
89 Upper Ground, SE1 (020 7928 7940). Waterloo tube/rail. **Open** 11am-11pm Mon-Sat. **Food served** noon-3pm, 5-8pm Mon-Fri; noon-4pm Sat. **Credit** AmEx, DC, MC, V.
Wandsworth's Young's brewery is best known for its splendid real ales and for the cosiness of its pubs. The Mulberry Bush is a bit of a departure in that it's a tailor-made development with modern design. It even calls itself a 'Café-Bar'. As well as a standard bar area, there's a small conservatory (dubbed the 'family room') at the rear, and a restaurant described as 'the Bistro bar' on the first floor. Food mixes café/bar-style staples such as three cheese pasta with upmarket pub stuff like a lamb and mint burger. Prices are slightly above average for pub grub, and for a starter, main and pint of 'ordinary' you won't get much change from £15. *Babies and children admitted (conservatory). Bistro available for hire. Disabled: toilet. Games (fruit machine, quiz machine). No-smoking area. Restaurant. Vegetarian dishes.*

Paper Moon
24 Blackfriars Road, SE1 (020 7928 4078). Southwark tube/Blackfriars tube/rail. **Open** 11am-11pm Mon-Sat; noon-10.30pm Sun. **Food served** noon-2.30pm Mon-Fri. **Credit** AmEx, MC, V.
Although it's a proper building, there's the feel of a renovated railway arch about this long rectangular pub. The floor is wood and there are marble-topped round pub tables at the front, with a raised no-smoking seating area at the back. By the entrance is a colourful tile illustration of what could well be William Shakespeare surrounded by dogs and acolytes. A 'regular' told us it was King Richard the Lionheart hearing news of his succession, but as the main characters were all dressed in Elizabethan ruffs, this was clearly bullshit. The drinkers tend to be a jovial lot and a mix of young office workers and older blue collar types who sit at the bar and sip one of the four real ales on offer. They're very keen on their wines here and every table is topped with the short but comprehensive list. *Babies and children admitted (until 6pm). Function room. Games (darts, fruit machine). No-smoking area. Quiz (monthly). Satellite TV. Tables outdoors (pavement). Vegetarian dishes.*

The Ring
72 Blackfriars Road, SE1 (020 7928 2589). Southwark tube. **Open** 11am-11pm Mon-Fri; noon-3pm, 7.30-11pm Sat; noon-3pm, 7.30-10.30pm Sun. **Food served** 11am-2.30pm Mon-Fri; noon-2.30pm Sat, Sun. **No credit cards.**
An old-fashioned boozer given over to the art of boxing; not to everyone's taste maybe, but then there's an All Bar One within easy walking distance. Where Southwark Jubilee line station is now, used to be the Ring – a boxing arena converted in 1910 from the nonconformist Surrey Chapel, and destroyed in raids during World War II. Tradition continues upstairs at the pub where there's a private working gym with a (boxing) ring and zero number of fat-arsed executives running on chrome treadmills. Downstairs the bar walls are practically covered in photographs of old boxing heroes, all of whom would have visited the pub at one time or another. Real ales include Marston's Pedigree and the wine list is brief and to the point. Customers are likely to be male, flat-nosed and

London crawling: Stars in bars

Once upon a time Notting Hill was a Rachman-run slum, a by-word for racial tension, drug dealings and no-go zones. The popular perception has shifted somewhat; W11 drugs are snorted up rolled tenners, and Notting Hill no-go means not being on the guest list at a members-only joint. Sewer rats have been replaced by media rats, scurrying around a warren of private gilded nests. There's a fun evening to be had in tracking down this tragically unendangered species.

Start at **Pharmacy**, the Damien Hirst-designed medical theme bar; Peter Mandelson, Alan Yentob and Giorgio Armani have all been sighted here in recent times. Even without the enticement of name patrons we recommend Pharmacy as a fine place for a kickstart cocktail to set your crawl off at a pace.

Out and round the corner, a few doors before the policemen idling outside Mandelson's multi-million pound home, the **Sun in Splendour** isn't a recognised celeb haunt (although Martin Amis, the self-exiled former literary chronicler of the neighbourhood, still sometimes feeds the fruit machine), but it is an excellent boozer, just reopened after renovations. Next pub up is the **Portobello Gold**, which was paid a surprise visit by president celeb Bill Clinton in December 2000. He downed half a pint of organic Pitfield's lager, and shared prawns, trout, pecan nut paté and a club sandwich with his bodyguards before taking off leaving his tab of £24.70 unpaid.

Continuing up Portobello, crossing Westbourne Grove, celebrity spotters' pulses will be quickened by the scent of Gucci and Calvin Klein as they approach the junction with Colville Terrace; this is the throbbing heart of Notting Hill, and indeed *Notting Hill*, where much of the filming for the Hugh Grant/Julia Roberts movie was perpetrated. Round the corner, on Kensington Park Road, is the wine bar **192**, the epicentre of west London's media culture. Should you manage to get in you're quite likely to find yourself sitting next to a Kate or Robbie, or at the very least someone who's trying very hard to look just like them.

From here, head back to Portobello Road. Don't be tempted to heighten your experience by purchasing drugs off men in hooded jackets; they're likely to be undercover boys in blue. We'd also suggest avoiding the Warwick Castle on the corner with Westbourne

Park Road, a pub favoured by alcohol veterans who have surrendered entire limbs to drink and continue undiscouraged. Instead, take a right at the Warwick passing the formerly blue door (now black) that featured in *Notting Hill* and at the time fronted what was the then home of Richard Curtis, writer of the movie. He's cashed-in on the property boom his scriptwork helped fuel and moved on.

It's worth a diversion south down Ledbury Road to the **Walmer Castle**, a big old Victorian pub where the camera-friendly folk come to fraternise. You want names? Well, a *Time Out* staffer whose recent history involves a bit of moonlighting behind the bar here reckons she flipped bottle tops for the likes of Robert Carlisle, Noel Gallagher, Geri Haliwell and, of course, Robbie and Kate.

Back up to Westbourne Park Road and east toward the twin poles of complacently white well-to-do W11, the **Cow** and the **Westbourne**. The Westbourne usually pulls a decent complement of pretty faces, while over the road in the Cow, even the owner, Tom Conran, is sort of famous – although whether fame by virtue of one's parentage counts is your call. Speaking of inherited fame, Stella McCartney is a Cow person, as well as bona fide self-made celebs such as Anna Chancellor and Madonna.

If your celebrity quotient still hasn't been filled, you could always backtrack to the Great Western Road and head on up to **Woody's**, but get there early or you're probably not going to get in.
Patrick Marmion

192 (*p68*) 192 Kensington Park Road, W11 (020 7229 0482).
Cow (*p99*) 89 Westbourne Park Road, W2 (020 7221 5400).
Pharmacy (*p71*) 150 Notting Hill Gate, W11 (020 7221 2442).
Portobello Gold (*p71*) 95-97 Portobello Road, W11 (020 7460 4900).
Sun in Splendour (*no review*) 7 Portobello Road, W11 (020 7313 9331).
Walmer Castle (*no review*) 58 Ledbury Road, W11 (020 7229 4620).
Westbourne (*p101*) 101 Westbourne Park Villas, W2 (020 7221 1332).
Woody's (*p72*) 41-43 Woodfield Road, W9 (020 7266 3030).

Fire Station.
See page 96.

muscular, although we've noticed a recent influx of groups of young mixed-sex office workers, drawn no doubt by the unique atmosphere and the cheese and pickle sandwiches. *Satellite TV. Tables outdoors (pavement). Vegetarian dishes.*

Studio Six

Gabriel's Wharf, 56 Upper Ground, SE1 (020 7928 6243/www.studiosix.co.uk). Waterloo tube/rail. **Open/food served** noon-11pm Mon-Sat; noon-10.30pm Sun. **Credit** AmEx, DC, MC, V.
Looking not unlike a green-painted wood and glass Swiss mountain chalet or a giant beach hut, Studio Six is part bar, part café. Two rooms are set out for either purpose with wooden dining tables complete with candles. Outside are rows and rows of bench tables for when the weather's hot. Customers tend to be a mixture of young office workers, tourists (enticed by the pedestrianised toy town that is Gabriel's Wharf) and pre- or post-theatre types. The drinks range is good, going on great with a real ale (Old Speckled Hen, when we last sauntered through), a selection of Continental beers (including Hoegaarden) and a 13-strong wine list we heard aptly described as 'most things for most drinkers'. Food is of the mushroom risotto/gigot of lamb and aubergine kind, with most main courses coming in well under a tenner.
Babies and children admitted. Tables outdoors (pavement). Vegetarian dishes.

Waterloo Bar & Kitchen

131 Waterloo Road, SE1 (020 7928 5086). Waterloo tube/rail. **Open** noon-11pm Mon-Fri; 5-11pm Sat. **Food served** noon-2.45pm, 5.30-10pm Mon-Fri; 5.30-10.30pm Sat. **Credit** AmEx, DC, MC, V.
It's hard to fault this stylish and welcoming bar and restaurant tucked away in the lee of the Old Vic. Beers include real ales (Brakspear), wheat beer (Hoegaarden) and Czech lager (Staropramen) and the wine list covers practically every whim at prices that won't raise too many eyebrows. The decor is relaxing with cream walls dotted with exceptionally colourful abstract paintings and candle-lit tables. At the rear on the left of the large seating area is an open kitchen sporting a wood-fired stove from where comes all kinds of goodies, including duck rillette, penne with vegetables and seared tuna. When we were last there a two course dinner could be had for a tenner.
Babies and children admitted. Restaurant. Tables outdoors (pavement). Vegetarian dishes.

Also in the area...

All Bar One 1 Chicheley Street, SE1 (020 7921 9471).

Westbourne Grove

Babushka

41 Tavistock Crescent, W11 (020 7727 9250/www. babushkabars.co.uk). Westbourne Park tube. **Open** 5-11pm Mon-Fri; noon-11pm Sat; noon-10.30pm Sun. **Food served** 6-10pm Mon-Fri; 4-9pm Sat, Sun. **Credit** AmEx, MC, V.
The West London branch of the hip vodka-bar chain with its faintly Middle Eastern interior design, ticks over quietly in this Notting Hill cul de sac. The word 'quiet' is used advisedly because one of the features of this and other Babushkas is noisy DJ nights, especially at the weekend. During the week music is more ambient and there is a better prospect of getting a seat. It's also one of the more agreeably presented branches of Babushka, combining light shades of moulded pine with soothing red ochres – you'd never guess that in its former life

this was the pub used in the 'perfumed ponce' scene in *Withnail and I*. Nor will you be served the same watery beer they served up Grant and McGann; now it's kegged lager, wine and, of course, multiple flavours of vodka.
Babies and children admitted. Barbecues (summer months). Function room. Games (board games). Music (DJs nightly). Specialities: vodkas, cocktails. Tables outdoors (garden). Vegetarian dishes.

Beach Blanket Babylon

45 Ledbury Road, W11 (020 7229 2907). Notting Hill Gate tube. **Open** noon-11pm Mon-Sat; noon-10.30pm Sun. **Happy hour** 4-7pm Mon-Sat. **Food served** noon-3.30pm, 7-10.30pm daily. **Credit** AmEx, DC, MC, V.
No longer quite the cool hangout it once was, it's a strange crowd of monied Euro-types that now favours Beach Blanket Babylon. The decor is still as OTT as ever; a Gaudi-esque design mixing coloured mosaics and a roaring fire set in a gigantic gargoyle maw. The long-running restaurant over a baby drawbridge to the rear is still kept busy too, but recent reports on the Mediterranean cuisine have been mixed. Meanwhile, the bar is unusually expensive, however well mixed its cocktails may be. There's also more than a little sense of being a singles bar for the young and affluent to squander money on garish drinks and so impress the crumpet. During the day the atmosphere is entirely different as it becomes a swish café-bar for Notting Hill arrivistes shopping in local boutiques.
Babies and children admitted. Dress code. Function room. No-smoking area. Restaurant. Tables outdoors (garden/pavement). Vegetarian dishes.

Cow

89 Westbourne Park Road, W2 (020 7221 5400). Royal Oak or Westbourne Park tube. **Open** noon-11pm Mon-Sat; noon-10.30pm Sun. **Food served** 12.30-3pm, 6.30-10.30pm Mon-Fri; 12.30-4pm, 6.30-10.30pm Sat; 12.30-4pm, 6.30-10pm Sun. **Credit** AmEx, MC, V.
The Cow remains one of the best pubs in London. Notionally Irish, Tom Conran's base camp is decorated with thick Celtic lace in the windows, mirrors advertising Guinness and a huge painting of a surreal subterranean Gaelic hunting and fishing fantasy on one wall. Food, drink and service are top of the field. It serves consistently fine real ale (usually London Pride, sometimes the fabulous Smiles Bitter from the West Country) and the wine list is a sensible selection of affordable quality. The main attraction nosh-wise is seafood banked up on an iced counter by the kitchen, while imaginative daily specials supplement the staples such as sausage and mash. The one minus is that the modestly proportioned, bone-shaped room with its poorly ventilated eating area can get rather stuffy.
Babies and children admitted. Function room. Restaurant. Satellite TV. Specialities: whiskies. Vegetarian dishes.

Elbow Room

103 Westbourne Grove, W2 (020 7221 5211/ www.elbow-room.co.uk). Bayswater or Notting Hill Gate tube. **Open/food served** noon-11pm Mon-Sat; noon-10.30pm Sun. **Credit** MC, V.
The Elbow Room has slowly and surely established itself as a top brand in unisex pool halls with a further London outlet in Islington (*see p217*), soon to be followed up by Swiss Cottage. Its formula is based on the simple principle of the opportunity to play pool without sexual harassment for the girls or macho menaces for weedy, sensitive boys. Not to mention genuinely tasty fast food (nachos, satays, sandwiches and burgers) freshly prepared on an open grill. And waitress service means you don't have to interrupt your shot let alone your game. It does get crowded evenings and weekends, but if you can't get

a table the well-stocked bar cues up a good evening out in itself. Tables are bookable by the hour, £6 before 7pm Monday-Friday, or before 5pm Saturday and Sunday, £9 after. *Games (pool tables). Music (DJ, second or third Wed monthly). Vegetarian dishes*

Liquid Lounge
209 Westbourne Park Road, W11 (020 7243 0914). Westbourne Park tube. **Open** 5pm-midnight Mon-Fri; 10am-midnight Sat; 10am-11.30pm Sun. **Food served** 6.30-10.30pm Wed-Fri; 10am-5pm Sat, Sun. **Credit** MC, V.
The combination of cold, all sea-blue design, leatherette bench seating and Roy Lichtenstein-style pop art may be off-putting to conventional tastes. But, for the young faithfuls who keep this joint afloat, the Liquid Lounge is quite a splash. By day it's a fairly cool café-bar serving decent gastropub food and coffee. In the evening it becomes a thronging joint with a late licence. If you're going to eat, eat early before the music gets too loud and the atmosphere too sweaty. There's no real ale but along with the line-up of kegged lagers the wine represents good value.
Babies and children admitted (daytime only). Satellite TV. Tables outdoors (pavement). Vegetarian dishes.

Prince Bonaparte
80 Chepstow Road, W2 (020 7313 9491). Notting Hill Gate or Royal Oak tube/7, 28, 31, 70 bus. **Open** noon-11pm Mon, Wed-Sat; 5-11pm Tue; noon-10.30pm Sun. **Food served** 12.30-3pm, 6.30-10.30pm Mon, Wed-Sat; 6.30-10.30pm Tue; 12.30-3pm, 6.30-10pm Sun. **Credit** MC, V.
One of the least prepossessing of Notting Hill's herd of gastropubs, but none the worse for that. There's a good big spacious interior with a large panelled dining room to the rear set around the open-plan kitchen. Here you can scoff all the usual gastropub suspects (salads, pastas, sausages, lamb shanks) and the cooking is good. At the large, horseshoe shaped bar, real ale is irregularly available, along with an adequate set of wines. Decor is the usual stripped-down, bare boards, plain colours thing, which goes towards creating a relaxed ambience. The clientele here is at the younger, studentier end of the spectrum, but this doesn't make it grungey or gastronomically primitive. *Babies and children admitted (until 9pm). Music (DJ, Fri-Sun). Vegetarian dishes.*

Westbourne
101 Westbourne Park Villas, W2 (020 7221 1332). Royal Oak or Westbourne Park tube. **Open** 5-11pm Mon; noon-11pm Tue-Fri; 11am-11pm Sat; noon-10.30pm Sun. **Food served** 7-10pm Mon; 1-3pm, 7-10pm Tue-Fri; 12.30-3.30pm, 7-10pm Sat; 12.30-3.30pm, 7-9.30pm Sun. **Credit** AmEx, DC, MC, V.
The Westbourne seems to have calmed down in recent months making it an even better pub than it was already. The problem before was not just the listless ranks of brainless poseurs, but also the volumes spilling onto the gas heated terrace and thence onto the pavement and beyond. Bouncers now herd these bright young things back inside the designated pen and perhaps this has contributed to a thinning of the crowds. The Anglo-Med food here is still very good (it has to be with the Cow over the road) and the selection of drink (especially wine at £9 a bottle) excels in both quality and value. The decor is a little overcrowded with posters and mirrors (not to mention the original Francis Bacon) providing a look as varied and visually stimulating as the ranks of fashion victims and pop stars. Sunday lunch in the cheeringly sunny south-facing bar is a particular pleasure, best taken with one of their ass-kicking Bloody Marys.
Babies and children admitted. Games (board games). Tables outdoors (pavement). Vegetarian dishes.

Also in the area...
All Bar One 74-76 Westbourne Grove, W2 (020 7313 9432).
Babushka 41 Tavistock Crescent, W11 (020 7727 9250).

Westminster & Whitehall

Adam & Eve
81 Petty France, SW1 (020 7222 4575). St James's Park tube. **Open/food served** 11am-11pm Mon-Sat; noon-3pm Sun. **Credit** AmEx, DC, MC, V.
Named in a roundabout way after Willi Soukop's Man and Woman statues at the entrance to Petty France, this is one of those T&J Bernard ale houses the Scottish Courage conglomerate are so proud of. Expect plenty of new wood, pillars and cosy drinking alcoves and a range of bog standard real ales (Theakston Best, Courage Best, etc) augmented by a fairly imaginative and ever-changing range of guest beers. Although the beer's a tad pricey, even for the area, wine is good value at well under a tenner a bottle and the food will appeal to those who crave frozen fish and chips and ye olde pies with unfeasibly tall crusts.
Games (fruit machines, video games). Specialities: real ales. TV. Vegetarian dishes.

Albert Tavern
52 Victoria Street, SW1 (020 7222 5577). St James's Park tube/Victoria tube/rail. **Open/food served** 11am-11pm Mon-Sat; noon-10.30pm Sun. **Credit** AmEx, DC, MC, V.
In winter this splendid old Victorian pub can get unbearably hot and stuffy, but it doesn't seem to put off the wide selection of drinkers we've encountered here. We've spotted vicars, priests and MPs, three transvestites drinking Marston's Pedigree bitter, and a group of computer workers down from Doncaster. Most come from the many nearby offices, including New Scotland Yard, a mere frogmarch away. The decor is opulent Victorian inside and out, and the engraved windows (which were taken away for safe keeping during World War II) and showy central staircase should be on every tourist itinerary. The Albert has long-standing political connections and the walls are studded with portraits, cartoons and caricatures. There's a food bar on the ground floor offering the usual pub grub, while in the first-floor carvery you can tuck into large portions of cow, pig and sheep.
Babies and children admitted (weekends only). Function room. Games (fruit machines). Restaurant. Vegetarian dishes.

Clarence
53 Whitehall, SW1 (020 7930 4808). Embankment tube/Charing Cross tube/rail. **Open** 11am-11pm Mon-Sat; noon-10.30pm Sun. **Food served** 11am-9pm Mon-Sat; noon-9pm Sun. **Credit** AmEx, DC, MC, V.
'Famous since 1862' says one sign by the door, 'welcomes all visitors' says another, and this made-over old pub at the top end of Whitehall certainly pulls in the tourists. In summer you can scarcely move for camera-wielding, guidebook-clenching types. You can see the attraction: the bare brick walls, ancient beams, wooden floorboards (said to come from a demolished London pier), framed prints of Victorian London and chunky wooden furniture give the impression that Little Nell has just tripped off to the toilet. There are real ales (Theakston Best, Old Peculiar and a couple more) and food is typical central London pub fare, though overpriced.
Function room. Games (billiards, fruit machine). Jukebox. Tables outdoors (pavement). Vegetarian dishes.

Old Shades

37 Whitehall, SW1 (020 7321 2801). Embankment tube/ Charing Cross tube/rail. **Open** 11am-11pm Mon-Sat; noon-10.30pm Sun. **Food served** noon-8pm Mon-Thur; noon-4pm Fri; noon-7pm Sat, Sun. **Credit** DC, MC, V.
A staging post for tourists and civil servants, this wood-panelled boozer offers the customary prints of old London as well as a nice faux attempt at stained glass. It's a Grade II listed building and the outside, with its neo-Gothic façade, is pretty spectacular. In the not quite as stunning interior – although there's a sweet little cupola over the bar – they serve the usual pie and pudding brand of pub grub and a couple of real ales, including a toothsome draught Bass, as well as the usual lagers, stouts and what-have-you.
Function room. Games (fruit machines). Satellite TV (big screen). Vegetarian dishes.

Page's Bar

75 Page Street, SW1 (020 7834 6791/ www.pagesbar.com). Pimlico or St James's Park tube. **Open** 11am-11pm Mon-Fri; 5-11pm Sat. **Food served** noon-2pm Mon-Fri; 6-10pm Sat. **Credit** AmEx, MC, V.
Eccentric place with a sci-fi theme that attracts a pretty cosmopolitan crowd who aren't all necessarily kooky. We've seen a well-known British boxer slumped in the lounge chairs and a friend once played pool with a TV weather woman here beneath a model of the Starship Enterprise. Sci-fi stuff litters the place: the carpet is patterned with a repeated star fleet logo, there are 3D chess-sets, *Dr Who* miniatures, signed photos of Scully and Mulder, and every Saturday there's a sci-fi theme night with videos of TV classics played to an appreciative crowd, many dressed for the occasion. Drinks carry the theme with Klingon Ale (there's Bass, too, for humans) and cocktails such as Data's Delight. A good fun hangout.
Games (fruit machine, pool table, quiz machine). Music (DJs Sat, karaoke/disco – first and last Fri every month). Satellite TV. Sci-fi night (Sat). Vegetarian dishes.

Paviours Arms

Page Street, SW1 (020 7834 2150). St James's Park tube. **Open** 11am-11pm Mon-Fri. **Food served** noon-2.30pm, 5.30-9.30pm Mon-Fri. **Credit** AmEx, DC, JCB, MC, V.
Lovers of art deco should head down to Page Street sharpish. This modest 1930s pub stands as an unlikely shrine to all things AD. The curves are impressive, the woodwork authentic dark mahogany and the chevron flash-patterned upholstery adds to the experience. Chuck in plenty of chrome, sympathetic black tables and a carpet with a design you'd need a brain tumour to come up with, and it makes for one unique pub. Depending on how the partitioning is set, there are three linked rooms through which the sleek black bar runs in a right-angle shape. Food is dispensed at the rear of the larger room and the usually attentive staff serve up three Fuller's draught beers plus the usual selection of lagers, spirits and wines.
Babies and children admitted (until 7pm, restaurant). Function room. Games (darts, fruit machine, pool table). Restaurant. Satellite TV. Vegetarian dishes.

Red Lion

48 Parliament Street, SW1 (020 7930 5826). Westminster tube. **Open** 11am-11pm Mon-Sat; noon-7pm Sun. **Food served** 11am-3pm Mon-Sat; noon-2.30pm Sun. **Credit** MC, V.
Although rebuilt in 1900, there's been a tavern on this site since 1434. Its Victorian roots are obvious, with plenty of hand-carved mahogany fixtures, etched glasswork and original mirrors. There are also silent TV screens, invariably turned to the BBC Parliamentary Channel, for this is a hub of government, a haunt of MPs and their staff. There are usually three real ales on offer, which might include Benskins Best and Adnam's, as well as a wine list covering a pretty broad range. The cellar bar is small and cosy and attracts a less active crowd. Food in the first-floor restaurant is above average pub grub (just the sort of place where an MP might treat lesser constituents), while the bar menu includes stuff like roast of the day and shepherd's pie.
Babies and children admitted (dining area). Function room. No-smoking area (dining only). Restaurant. Specialities: real ales. Tables outdoors (pavement). TV (parliamentary channels, sport). Vegetarian dishes.

Royal Oak

2 Regency Street, SW1 (020 7834 7046). Pimlico tube/ Victoria tube/rail. **Open** 11am-11pm Mon-Fri; noon-4pm Sun. **Food served** noon-3pm Mon-Fri. **Credit** MC, V.
Comfortable, single-bar Young's pub that's popular with local office workers, especially with bods from the nearby Channel 4 offices. It's smartly decorated with cream walls and the ubiquitous light wood floor. Music tends to be discreet and intelligently chosen and a small TV comes into use when there's a big match on. In the bar a small serving area occupies one corner and is surrounded by a wooden frame upon which are small statues, one of which we think is Laurel and Hardy. There's the usual upmarket Young's pub food at reasonable prices. Nothing exceptional, but pleasant all the same.
Games (quiz machine). No piped music or jukebox. Tables outdoors (pavement).

Sanctuary House

33 Tothill Street, SW1 (020 7799 4044). St James's Park tube. **Open** 11am-11pm Mon-Sat; noon-10.30pm Sun. **Food served** noon-9pm daily. **Credit** AmEx, DC, MC, V.
Looking very stylish from the outside – light coloured all-weather paintwork and enticing lighting – this is one of Fuller's Ale & Pie Houses that's been made up to look old. Well, stylishly old. Maybe it's ironic these days to pile up the wood panelling and sturdy board flooring, add plenty of etched mirrors and (in this case) portraits of religious leaders of old. The Spice Girls soundtrack was possibly meant ironically too, but we have our doubts. On our visit the staff were charming – witty even – and the crowd was a good-natured bunch of mainly young office workers. Beer was up to Fuller's usual high standards, but we were never tempted to try the pies.
Babies and children admitted. Bar available for hire. Disabled: toilet. No-smoking area (restaurant). Restaurant. Satellite TV. Vegetarian dishes.

Westminster Arms

9 Storey's Gate, SW1 (020 7222 8520). St James's Park or Westminster tube. **Open** 11am-11pm Mon-Fri; 11am-8pm Sat; noon-6pm Sun. **Food served** 11am-8pm Mon-Fri; noon-5pm Sat, Sun. **Credit** AmEx, DC, MC, V.
The sort of pub where QCs hobnob with MPs and MMs (maintenance men) consort with MDs, the Westminster Arms is that rare thing: a boozer with class. Upstairs there's a Rules-style restaurant and in the cellars a wine bar that attracts former Speakers of the House of Commons, but it's the small, practically chair-less bar where most of the action is. They offer seven real ales (including a very well kept draught Bass and several ever-changing regional curiosities) plus a large range of wines (some quite pricey) and a cigar selection that would have Michael Grade salivating. The floorboards are bare and original and on closer inspection, the nicotine-coloured walls are actually (our decorating correspondent tells us) scumble wash. So there.
Babies and children admitted (restaurant only). Function room. Games (fruit machine). No-smoking area (wine bar). Restaurant. TV. Tables outdoors (pavement). Vegetarian dishes.

City

Clerkenwell & Farringdon

19:20

19-20 Great Sutton Street, EC1 (020 7253 1920).
Farringdon tube/rail. **Open** noon-11pm Mon-Fri;
6.30-11pm Sat. **Food served** noon-3pm Mon-Fri;
6.30-10pm Mon-Sat. **Credit** AmEx, MC, V.
Everything at this stylish bar/restaurant has been carefully
planned: from the name right through to the phone number.
Looking in from the street through vast picture windows, you
see the upmarket ground floor restaurant (not recommended),
with its light wood flooring and curvaceous beige walls. The
popular bar area is reached down a wide staircase, past a feng
shui-influenced water feature. It's a comfortable, modern
space with sofas, low tables, plenty of reds, oranges and
yellows, and a curved bar that whispers 'class' with an ever-
so-slight Essex accent. Here the besuited and the beautiful
nurse draught nitrokegs or something from an unusual list
of cocktails (well priced at a mere £4.60) and well made by
friendly, efficient bar staff.
Babies and children admitted. Disabled: toilet. Music (DJs,
7pm Thur, Fri). Restaurant. Satellite TV. Tables outdoors
(pavement). Vegetarian dishes. **Map 3/O4**

Abbaye

55 Charterhouse Street, EC1 (020 7253 1612).
Chancery Lane tube/Farringdon tube/rail. **Open/food**
served noon-10.30pm Mon-Fri. **Credit** AmEx, MC, V.
Abbaye offers its version of a typical Belgian bar, all nicotine-
coloured textured walls, blue-and-white decorative plates and
medieval circular metal chandeliers. Operated and run by the
same people behind Café Rouge and Dôme, it took the Belgo-
inspired boom to set them on the bier-wagon. The drinks list
contains a plenty of good Belgian beers, including examples from
Chimay, Leffe and Orval at the going rate (£3-£4), and there's
even draught Stella for idiots. The food is, as you'd expect, based
around mussels, and a kilo costs just under a tenner.
Babies and children admitted. Disabled: toilet. Function
room. No-smoking area. Restaurant. Vegetarian dishes.
Map 3/O5

Al's Bar Café

11-13 Exmouth Market, EC1 (020 7837 4821). Angel
tube/Farringdon or King's Cross tube/rail/19, 38 bus.
Open 8am-midnight Mon; 8am-1am Tue; 8am-2am
Wed-Fri; 10am-2am Sat; 10am-11pm Sun. **Food served**
8am-midnight Mon-Fri; 10am-midnight Sat; 10am-10pm
Sun. **Credit** AmEx, DC, MC, V.
Al's is a busy corner café-bar with tightly packed tables and
a heated outside area, overlooking Mount Pleasant and
Exmouth Market. In summer the floor-to-ceiling windows can
be slid back to allow free movement of air and customers.
Drinks range from beer (including Gambrinus, Leffe and
Hoegaarden) to absinthe, but a good many punters come for
the food alone. There's an impressive selection of breakfasts
(English, Builder's, Rather Big and Super Veggie), excellent
chunky chips and down-to-earth daily specials such as
sausages, beans and mash. Posher dishes, such as fish cakes
and lamb skewers, make an appearance too. The sort of place
which goes down a storm with local journos and wide boys.
Babies and children admitted. Function room. Music
(DJ Fri). Tables outdoors (pavement). TV. Vegetarian
dishes. **Map 3/N4**

Barley Mow

50 Long Lane, EC1 (020 7606 6591). Barbican tube.
Open 11am-11pm Mon-Fri. **Food served** noon-3pm
Mon-Fri. **Credit** MC, V.

A small-to-medium-sized branch of the Hogshead chain with
more soul than most. Service at this long, almost ramshackle
wood and stone boozer is friendly and the contented
atmosphere is nearer that of a suburban local than a typical
City bar. A combination of office workers, nurses and tourists
enjoy a wide range of guest ales (between four to eight, rotated
weekly) and bottled Belgian beers (Leffe Blonde, Leffe Brun
and Hoegaarden). Food's standard pub grub of the steak,
sandwich and soup variety.
Babies and children admitted (restaurant only, lunchtime).
Function room. Games (quiz machine). Jukebox.
Restaurant. TV. Vegetarian dishes. **Map 3/O5**

Bear

2 St John's Square, EC1 (020 7608 2117). Farringdon
tube/rail. **Open** 11am-11pm Mon-Sat. **Food served** noon-
2.30pm, 6-9.30pm Mon-Fri; 11am-4pm Sat. **Credit** MC, V.
A new bar and restaurant from Geronimo Inns – the people
behind Battersea's very good **Duke of Cambridge** (*see*
p152), among others – is an event usually worth supporting.
On the ground floor is the bar, all two-tone and comfy seating,
which already seems popular with a mixture of office casuals,
suits and smartly dressed students. Draught beers are a
disappointing mix of keg concoctions, but there's a much better
wine list, offering around 20 by the glass. Bar snacks include
the likes of potato wedges and salmon goujons, but you can
get bigger and better meals upstairs in the first-floor dining
room. Although a pleasant enough venue, the Bear doesn't
offer anything particulalry new or different in an area that's
already spoilt for choice.
Bar area available for hire. Satellite TV. Tables outdoors
(pavement). Vegetarian dishes. **Map 3/O4**

Bishop's Finger

9-10 West Smithfield, EC1 (020 7248 2341). Farringdon
tube/rail. **Open** 11am-11pm Mon-Fri. **Food served** noon-
2.30pm, 6-9.30pm Mon-Thur; noon-2.30pm Fri. **Credit**
AmEx, MC, V.
Despite the antipodean staff and the Modern European menu,
the Bishop's Finger is the 2001 version of the traditional
British pub. An outpost of Faversham's Shepherd Neame
brewery, it takes its moniker from a beer, itself named after
an old Kentish road sign. Illuminated by large windows, the
ground-floor bar has a solid wood floor, chunky dark wood
furniture and pictures of old Smithfield on green and
mustard walls. Upstairs is a dining room without waitress
service. A small open kitchen occupies half of the bar, and
underneath a blackboard advertising exotic sausages a
white-clad chef knocks out simple but effective pub grub.
Draught beers include Masterbrew, Bishop's Finger and
Spitfire. Well worth a try.
Bar area available for hire. Disabled: toilet. Specialities:
real ales. Tables outdoors (pavement). Vegetarian dishes.
Map 3/O5

Bleeding Heart Tavern

Corner of Bleeding Heart Yard, 19 Greville Street,
EC1 (020 7404 0333). Farringdon tube/rail. **Open**
11.30am-11pm Mon-Fri. **Food served** 11.30am-3.30pm,
5.30-10.30pm Mon-Fri. **Credit** AmEx, DC, MC, V.
The Bleeding Heart Tavern is the restored version of a pub
first built in 1746. Amid the familiar stone wall, chunky
wooden furniture and bare board floor decor, Suffolk's
Adnam's brewery has opted for large picture windows on
which is written (in large red script) a brief history of the
place. Good beers – Adnam's full range, including Best,
Broadside and a seasonal brew – attract a lively mix of suits
plus upmarket associates more likely to be in media than
diamonds, despite Hatton Garden being less than a skip away.

Bear

The menu may be far shorter than the wine list but it's also far above average, mixing bistro-style dishes with traditional British of the 'ale-fed pork from our own farms in Suffolk' sort. Further into the yard is the **Bleeding Heart Bistro**: a brick-walled wine bar/restaurant. Its wine list is so enormous (more than 9,000 bottles) as to verge on intimidating for anyone who's not a complete wine anorak: Bordeaux, Rhône, Burgundy and Champagne regions are all well covered, with prices ranging from £10 to well over £100 per bottle. Pride of place, however, goes to the magnum of Chateau Calon-Segur from 1945, the vintage of the century (a mere £995). *Function room. No piped music or jukebox. Restaurant. Vegetarian dishes.* **Map 3/N5**

Café Kick
43 Exmouth Market, EC1 (020 7837 8077). Angel tube/ Farringdon tube/rail. **Open** noon-11pm Mon-Sat; noon-10.30pm Sun. **Food served** noon-3pm Mon-Fri. **Happy hour** 4-7pm daily. **Credit** MC, V.
Giving a Continental slant on football fandom (ie without the Stanley knives), Café Kick is a shambolic gem of a bar where soccer is king but where you won't find tacky souvenirs, giant Sky sports screens, or replica-shirt-wearing beer monsters. The front section has a garishly painted wooden floor – presumably football colours – upon which sit three table football games (which can be reserved in advance). While first-team players give the machines rough treatment, those on the bench (or here, fold-up wooden chairs) can sip off-the-beaten-track bottled beers (French Jenlain, for example), cocktail standards, chocolate milk or something from the exotic coffee menu. When we visited, the bartender was working overtime even on a wet afternoon, which goes to show that Café Kick's not just a haunt of fair-weather fans. *Games (table football). Tables outdoors (pavement). TV. Vegetarian dishes.* **Map 3/N4**

Cellar Gascon
59 West Smithfield, EC1 (020 7253 5853). Farringdon tube/rail. **Open/food served** noon-midnight Mon-Fri; 5-11pm Sat. **Credit** AmEx, MC, V.
In 1999 Club Gascon was acclaimed as the Best New Restaurant in the *Time Out* Eating & Drinking Awards; a year later they opened this diminutive but well-stocked wine bar next door. The interior (by Fusion Design and Architecture) is simple but appealing, with pod-like seats and map-like designs on the walls. Like the restaurant next door, it specialises in the south-west region of France – featuring feral, farmyardy wines with evocative names such as Irouléguy, Cahors and Jurançon; many of which are rarely available this side of the Channel. Food is limited to pricey regionally inspired snacks, including boudin noir, farmhouse ham from Béarn and foie gras. *Specialities: wines. Vegetarian dishes.* **Map 3/O5**

Cicada
132-136 St John Street, EC1 (020 7608 1550). Farringdon tube/rail. **Open** noon-11pm Mon-Fri; 6-11pm Sat. **Food served** noon-3pm, 6-11pm, Mon-Fri; 6-11pm Sat. **Credit** AmEx, DC, MC, V.
City slickers and Clerkenwell trendsetters share this popular glass-fronted bar-restaurant, an uneasy alliance which on busy nights gives it something of the atmosphere of a stylish frontier town saloon. The ground floor is practically cube-shaped, with beige walls and a dash of leather around the central serving area. Exuberance is fuelled by the steady consumption of a pretty standard range of wines, cocktails, keg lagers and cream-style bitters. There's a raised dining area for chomping pretty decent pan-Asian food, and

downstairs is a suitably laid-back chill-out space, decorated with Chinese lanterns. *Function room. No-smoking area (restaurant). Restaurant. Tables outdoors (piazza). Vegetarian dishes.* **Map 3/O4**

Clerkenwell House
23-27 Hatton Wall, EC1 (020 7404 1113). Chancery Lane tube/Farringdon tube/rail. **Open** noon-11pm Mon-Fri; 5-11pm Sat; 1-10.30pm Sun. **Food served** noon-3pm, 6-10pm Mon-Fri; 6-10pm Sat; 1-5pm Sun. **Credit** DC, MC, V.
A medium-sized bar that attracts a clubby crowd as well as junior media moguls; we overheard a Channel 5 commission being discussed over Hoegaardens. Other draught beers include standards like Murphys, Stella and Heineken, but cocktails seem the preferred choice. The ground floor bar is simply painted in cream, and an assortment of sofas and tables with springy chairs are scattered about – the art being trying to get your backside on one before someone puts their feet up. The L-shaped serving area houses an open kitchen where pasta, char-grilled meat and lamb stew are prepared. Down a spiral staircase is a dingy basement that houses four pool tables. Potentially comfortable but not exceptional. *Downstairs bar for hire. Games (pool tables). Music (DJs Fri-Sun). Restaurant. Vegetarian dishes.* **Map 3/N5**

Crown Tavern
43 Clerkenwell Green, EC1 (020 7253 4973). Farringdon tube/rail. **Open** 11am-11pm Mon-Fri; noon-11pm Sat. **Food served** noon-3pm Mon-Fri; noon-4pm Sat. **Credit** AmEx, DC, MC, V.
This haughty Victorian tavern glowers over Clerkenwell Green like a stern governess watching over her charges. In the good/bad old days the County Sessions were held opposite and the green was a centre for Victorian demonstrations, including spats with the Chartists, Home Rulers and Suffragettes – many of whom found comfort within these walls. Inside it's a typical tarted-up period pub, with plenty of dark wood and comfortable benches and banquettes. Beers include Tetley's and Adnam's, while food is traditional pub grub. A real bonus is that the two main rooms rarely get too crammed to find a seat. On warm days drinkers spill out into the pedestrianised green. *Function room. Games (fruit machine, pool table). Specialities: real ales, Addlestones cider. Tables outdoors (pavement). TV. Vegetarian dishes.* **Map 3/N4**

Dovetail
9 Jerusalem Passage, EC1 (020 7490 7321). Farringdon tube/rail/55 bus. **Open** 11.30am-11pm Mon-Fri; noon-6pm Sun. **Food served** 11.30am-10pm Mon-Fri; noon-6pm Sun. **Credit** MC, V.
Tucked away on a busy rat-run between Clerkenwell and Farringdon, this Belgian-type brasserie – like its Hackney sire, the **Dove Freehouse** (*see p194*) – offers a list of around 100 beers, including exotica such as 8.8 per cent proof McChouffe brown ale (£9 for 75cl) and Mort Subite Gueze, the so-called 'champagne of beers' (£3 for a 25cl glass). There are fruit beers, spicy beers, wheat beers, chocolate beers and Trappist beers, as well as more familiar brands (Stella Artois) on draught. Despite our fears that such excessively alcoholic brews would prove a magnet for boisterous stag parties, the predominantly youthful clientele tends to include a fair proportion of both women and casual suit wearers. Sadly, the food – mussels, Trappist cheeses, venison sausages and mash in Leffe Brun gravy – was, on our visit, pretty uninspiring. *Bar for hire, Sat. Disabled: toilet. No-smoking area. Specialities: Belgian beers. Vegetarian dishes.* **Map 3/O4**

Dust

27 Clerkenwell Road, EC1 (020 7490 5120).
Farringdon tube/rail. **Open** 11am-11pm Mon-Wed;
11am-1am Thur; 11am-2am Fri; 7.30pm-2am Sat; noon-
6pm Sun. **Food served** noon-3pm, 6-10pm Mon-Thur;
noon-3pm Fri. **Credit** AmEx, DC, MC, V.
While other style bars come and go, this turned-on venue
manages to keep Clerkenwell drinkers perennially happy.
Dust's urban earthiness – low comfortable sofas, heavy
square tables and atmospheric lighting – first arrived in the
summer of 1998 amid an avalanche of publicity and since then
it has stuck with its recipe for success. The customers tend
to be what one barman termed 'casual chic with ze attitude',
although groups of office workers in suits don't look too out
of place, especially during the day. There's late-night clubbing
(well, till 2am, anyway) at the weekends and that brings in
its own crowd. Expect interesting beers from Belgium,
cocktails and a Modern European menu.
Disabled: toilet. Music (DJs Thur-Sun). Vegetarian dishes.
Video projections (Fri, Sat). **Map 3/O4**

Eagle

159 Farringdon Road, EC1 (020 7837 1353).
Farringdon tube/rail. **Open** noon-11pm Mon-Sat; noon-
5pm Sun. **Food served** noon-2.30pm, 6.30-10.30pm
Mon-Fri; 12.30-3.30pm, 6.30-10.30pm Sat; 12.30-3.30pm
Sun. **No credit cards.**
The popular and overcrowded Eagle is famous for sparking
off the current fashion in gastropubs. However, since founder
David Eyre has moved on, we have to say culinary standards
have been slipping. Regulars don't seem unduly bothered,
though, and it's still difficult to find a table any evening; on
Fridays it's downright impossible. The kitchen is big and
open plan, taking up around half of the total serving area, and
you can expect the likes of pan-fried guinea fowl, own-made
soups in winter and plenty of grills and pasta. Drinks include
Leffe on draught and there's a good selection of wines. Music
tends towards Latin, jazz and blues and customers are a
mixture of sozzled newspaper journalists – the *Guardian*'s
just round the corner – City couples and groups of office
workers pretending to be wild.
Babies and children admitted. Tables outdoors (pavement).
Vegetarian dishes. **Map 3/N4**

Fluid

40 Charterhouse Street, EC1 (020 7253 3444/
www.fluidbar.com). Barbican tube/Farringdon tube/rail.
Open noon-midnight Tue, Wed; noon-2am Thur, Fri;
7pm-2am Sat; 4-11pm Sun. **Happy hour** 5-7pm Tue-Sat.
Admission after 10pm £3; after 1am £2 Fri, Sat ; all day
Sun £3. **Food served** noon-10.30pm Tue-Fri. **Credit**
AmEx, MC, V.
Things have changed at Fluid in the last year: the Japanese
angle's been reinforced, with oriental script on the walls and
red-tinted windows, and there's more of a clubby feel, with
the decks cleared for action. The bar's to the left as you walk
in, with a small number of low coffee tables and enveloping
leather sofas provided for comfort and ease of noshing your
way through the reasonably priced Japanese menu. Miso soup
is just £1 and you can get an assorted sushi for a tenner.
Expect Japanese beers and Leffe, cocktails and keen if slightly
intense bar staff. Downstairs are rows of booths in an intimate
basement space that's decorated with a back-lit view of
downtown Tokyo. Punters tend to be pre-clubbers for Fabric
and assorted fashionistas.
Babies and children admitted (until 9pm). Function room.
Games (retro video games). Music (DJs Thur-Sun).
Vegetarian dishes. **Map 3/O5**

Fox & Anchor

115 Charterhouse Street, EC1 (020 7253 5075). Barbican
tube/Farringdon tube/rail. **Open** 7am-11pm Mon-Fri.
Food served 7am-3pm Mon-Fri. **Credit** AmEx, MC, V.
Tucked up a side street just off Smithfield and easily missed,
the Fox & Anchor is a gem. It opens at 7am for huge artery-
clogging breakfasts and the kitchen stays busy serving
hearty traditional English lunches (although we've been told
the lunch menu is going to change and become less stodgy
and more international). Most of the day's trade is over by
mid-afternoon, after which it stays fairly quiet; all the better
to appreciate the fine glass and woodwork of the well
preserved Edwardian bar, and the fine facade with tile mural
and gargoyles. At the rear are small, wood-panelled rooms
which can be reserved. Beer includes London Pride and
Adnam's. Staff are absolute winners (*see p121*).
Babies and children admitted (lunchtimes). Function room.
Games (fruit machine). TV. Vegetarian dishes. **Map 3/O5**

Hand & Shears

1 Middle Street, EC1 (020 7600 0257). Barbican tube.
Open 11am-11pm Mon-Fri. **Food served** noon-3pm
Mon-Fri. **Credit** MC, V.
There was an ale house in the precincts of St Bartholomew's
Priory as early as 1123, and this current version – rebuilt as
recently as 1849 – is its successor. Sadly gone is the sign of
the Merchant Taylors' Guild, with which the pub was once
associated, replaced by a more modern rendition of someone
cutting cloth. Inside are two small bars separated by wooden
partitions and the whole place has been carefully restored to
a former wood-dominated glory. The walls are covered with
cartoons and scenes from old Smithfield, regulars include
medics from St Bart's, and the staff are among the friendliest
in the area. Draught beers include Courage Best and
Theakston XB and the usual pub grub fry-ups are available
during lunch hours.
Function room. No piped music or jukebox. TV.
Vegetarian dishes. **Map 3/O5**

Hope

94 Cowcross Street, EC1 (020 7250 1442). Farringdon
tube/rail. **Open** 6-10.30am, 11.30am-9pm Mon-Fri. **Food**
served noon-2pm Mon-Fri. **Credit** AmEx, DC, MC, V.
In the last year there's been a welcome makeover at this small
but welcoming pub on the edge of the Smithfield 'blood zone'.
The walls are still lime green but freshened up, the six
chandeliers have been upgraded, there's floor-to-ceiling
studio-style windows and the original Edwardian tiling has
emerged from a partial shroud of seating. It's now a Young's
house and the usual range of their fine lagers and real ales is
augmented by Webster's bitter, though why is anybody's
guess. 'It's very popular,' the barmaid said when we asked.
You can only assume that retailing animal parts does
something to the taste buds. Lovers of roasted flesh will relish
the upstairs restaurant.
Function room. No-smoking area. Restaurant. Tables
outdoors (patio). Vegetarian dishes. **Map 3/O5**

Jacomos

88 Cowcross Street, EC1 (020 7553 7641). Farringdon
tube/rail. **Open** noon-11pm Mon-Fri. **Food served** noon-
3pm Mon-Fri. **Credit** MC, V.
From its soothing pale green exterior in, Jacomos is about as
laid-back as a bar gets. The decor – light blue walls, neat
wooden tables, bare board floor and occasional scattered
sofas – coupled with the eagerness of staff makes for a
pleasant meeting place. It's primarily a mixed gay bar for the
under-forties, but there doesn't seem to be any rules about

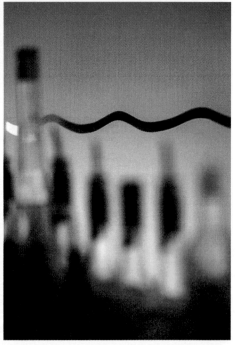

City

Mint

who does or does not get served. Draught beers are standard but there's better in bottles. As we went to press the place was switching ownership so expect possible change. *Bar available for hire. Games (fruit machine, quiz machine). Vegetarian dishes.* **Map 3/O5**

Jerusalem Tavern
55 Britton Street, EC1 (020 7490 4281/ www.stpetersbrewery.co.uk). Farringdon tube/rail. **Open** 11am-11pm Mon-Fri. **Food served** noon-3pm Mon-Fri. **Credit** AmEx, MC, V.
At first glance this small but rather gorgeous former coffee house looks as though the decorators walked out halfway through the job in 1752 and never came back. In fact, the conversion from coffeehouse to pub occured as recently as 1996, but from the ragged Regency-style walls, set off by old white tiles, sturdy mismatched furniture and cosy panelled cubicles, you'd never guess. It's London's sole outpost for Suffolk's St Peter's Brewery – the Ben & Jerry of the beer world – and stocks their full range of excellent and often unusually flavoured beers. Around 20 come in green flask-like bottles and there are half-a-dozen on draught. Look out for Old Style Porter, Lemon and Ginger Spiced Ale and Suffolk Gold. Failing that, Best Bitter's a pint that's always worth a punt. The lunchtime food menu includes well cooked Mediterranean dishes, plus British pie and sausage staples. *No piped music or jukebox. Specialities: real ales. Tables outdoors (pavement). Vegetarian dishes.* **Map 3/O4**

Match
45-47 Clerkenwell Road, EC1 (020 7250 4002/ www.matchbar.com). Farringdon tube/rail. **Open/food served** 11am-midnight Mon-Fri; 6pm-midnight Sat. **Credit** AmEx, MC, V.
In around three years, this former photographic reproduction house has become one of the best known cocktail bars in town (and in the meantime has spawned two similarly successful branches; one in Fitzrovia, *see p43*; one in the Old Street area, *see p132*). You enter from the Clerkenwell hustle to find a seated balcony overlooking the action, with stairs leading down. For decor, think clean, sexy and modern, with louche leather sofas, low lights and more attitude than you'll find at a dozen modelling schools. The bar service is slick and offers a wide range of cocktails prepared without the use of coke-guns and with unusually fresh ingredients. We can vouch for the potency and authenticity of the Martini cocktail. Beers are pretty standard, but the wine list is well worth a browse. Food is upmarket pan-Americana with a Modern European twist. *Babies and children admitted. Bar area for hire. Disabled: toilet. Specialities: cocktails. Tables outdoors (pavement). Vegetarian dishes.* **Map 3/O4**

Mint
182-186 St John Street, EC1 (020 7253 8368/ www.mintbar.co.uk). Farringdon tube/rail. **Open/food served** 11am-midnight Mon-Fri; 5pm-midnight Sat. **Happy hour** 5-7pm Mon-Fri. **Credit** AmEx, DC, MC, V.
Mint's ultra-modern ground floor curvy glass bar is bathed in a blue neon glow, and hidden lighting throws up colourful areas of pink, grey and mauve. Scattered around are white cube tables and recliners, and the smart set eat in the raised dining area. Staff are fanciable, helpful and efficient, knocking up cocktails for the designers and dot.commers who haunt the place. Wines are pushed to the fore and there are regular tastings for those who don't know their Medoc from the mediocre. Fusion food is something of an item here with the likes of sautéed pigeon breast and blue eye cod fillet with mussel and scallop chowder offered at reasonable prices.

Babies and children admitted (daytime). Disabled: toilet. Function room. Music (DJ Wed, Fri). No-smoking area. Specialities: cocktails. Restaurant. Tables outdoors (pavement). Vegetarian dishes. **Map 3/O4**

O'Hanlon's
8 Tysoe Street, EC1 (020 7278 7630). Angel tube/19, 38 bus. **Open** 11am-11pm daily. **Food served** noon-2.30pm Mon-Fri, Sun. **Credit** MC, V.
In these days of style bars and gastropubs it is easy to forget what boozers were invented for. Step forward ale house evangelist John O'Hanlon, who bought a London pub in the mid-'90s, named it after himself, and set up his own modest brewery in Vauxhall railway arch to keep it supplied with decent beer. The kegged Dry Stout is to Guinness what home-baked bread is to Mother's Pride, but not as good as the Port Stout, which is creamy and served from a hand pump. We also relish the malty Blakeley's Best. Furnishings are splendidly erratic, ranging from Pizza Express surplus to Victoriana armchairs, while the back of the pub looks like the storeroom of an antique shop. Food is classic pub grub of the sausage and mash variety, often with a hearty Irish accent. *TV. Vegetarian dishes.* **Map 3/N3**

Peasant
240 St John Street, EC1 (020 7336 7726/ www.thepeasant.co.uk). Angel tube/Farringdon tube/rail. **Open** noon-11pm Mon-Fri; 6-11pm Sat. **Food served** 12.30-3pm, 6.30-11pm Mon-Fri; 6.30-11pm Sat. **Credit** AmEx, DC, MC, V.
These days the former George & Dragon is a gastrobar where predominantly middle-aged local media and business types meet to quaff Chardonnay and guzzle the likes of pan-fried sardines, roasted field mushrooms and Italian sausages with borlotti beans. Eating is very much what it's about here, but the on-the-ball serving staff don't kick up too much of a fuss if you just want to drink. There's no real ale, although bottles of Belgian specialities like Westmalle, Schneide Weiss and La Trappe are available; otherwise it's bog standard lagers and nitrokeg beers on draught, plus wines and spirits. Remnants of the old boozer are limited to the central mahogany serving area, mosaic floor and a fabulous wall-sized tile picture of Saint George slaying the dragon. *Babies and children admitted. Restaurant. Specialities: continental beers. Tables outdoors (conservatory, garden terrace). Vegetarian dishes.* **Map 3/O4**

Critics' choice
cocktails

American Bar (p29)
It has to be a White Lady, invented in-house.

High Holborn (p45)
First-class cocktails in intimate surrounds.

Lab (p80)
Fruity cocktail creations in the heart of Soho.

Mandarin Bar (p51)
Fantastic setting for magical mixology.

Oscar (p41)
Pricey, but certainly worth a little sacrifice.

Potemkin

*144 Clerkenwell Road, EC1 (020 7278 6661/
www.potemkin.co.uk). Farringdon tube/rail.* **Open** noon-
midnight Mon-Fri; 6-11pm Sat. **Food served** noon-3pm,
6-10.30pm Mon-Fri; 6-10.30pm Sat. **Credit** AmEx, DC,
MC, V.

Potemkin is a new Russian bar/restaurant, within a Molotov
cocktail's throw of the *Guardian* offices. The ground floor is
glass-walled with a modern urban feel, small tables and
emaciated chairs that look as if they haven't eaten for a
month. Aside from being Russian-owned, the bartenders, chef
and waiting staff all hail from the land of food queues and the
Kalashnikov. But don't be put off: service and standards are
excellent. Vodka is a speciality, with 30 different types, plus
beer, wine and the usual spirits. Downstairs is a basement
that follows the same simplicity of design, but offers a quieter,
more discreet experience, and this is where the serious eaters
lurk. Zakuski are like Russian tapas (ox tongue, cured
herrings, etc) and the sit-down menu includes hearty peasant
grub like borscht or Siberian pelmeni (dumplings) and caviar.
*Babies and children admitted (restaurant). No-smoking
area (restaurant). Restaurant. Specialities: vodkas.
Vegetarian dishes.* **Map 3/N4**

Rising Sun

*38 Cloth Fair, EC1 (020 7726 6671). Barbican tube/
Farringdon tube/rail.* **Open** 11.30am-11pm Mon-Fri; noon-
11pm Sat; noon-3pm, 7-10.30pm Sun. **Food served** noon-
2pm, 5.30-8pm Mon-Fri; noon-2pm Sat, Sun. **Credit**
AmEx, MC, V.

Cloth Fair was the home of Bartholomew Fair, London's
largest cloth market, from the 12th century until 1855. A
couple of years ago this sturdy corner pub was taken over by
northern brewers Samuel Smith and made over in a bid to
return it to its Victorian splendour. You know the sort of
thing: checkerboard floor, bare boards, chunky wooden
alcoves and furniture you could shelter from an air raid under.
The bar staff when we last popped in were northern, friendly
and incredibly helpful, even going so far as seeking out
somebody who had been looking for someone like us. It was
a false alarm, but a nice thought. Expect the usual Sam
Smith's beers at the typical bargain prices, including a
particularly well kept Old Brewery Bitter from the wood, and
fellow customers who tend towards the younger end of the
office-worker spectrum.
*Function room. Games (fruit machine, quiz machine). Quiz
(Tue). Restaurant. TV. Vegetarian dishes.* **Map 3/O5**

St John

*26 St John Street, EC1 (020 7251 0848/
www.stjohnrestaurant.co.uk). Farringdon tube/rail.*
Open 11am-11pm Mon-Fri; 6-11pm Sat. **Food served**
noon-3pm, 6-11pm Mon-Thur; 6-11pm Fri, Sat. **Credit**
AmEx, MC, V.

'Please turn off your mobile in the dining room' orders the
sign, which in Clerkenwell is akin to asking customers to chop
off their ears. No such luck in the busy bar on the Friday
evening we last called in, as men in shiny Italian-style
numbers were giving directions, arranging meetings or lying
about rail chaos at Fenchurch Street. As the racks above the
bar suggest, this high-walled white-painted building used to
be a meat smokehouse serving nearby Smithfield. These days
it's just lungs and gravy that get the browning, though
efficient air-conditioning doesn't allow too much of that. Beers
include a well-kept pair of real ales, and there's a worthy wine
list. The adjacent restaurant is one of the best places to eat in
Clerkenwell, especially if your palate extends to roast bone
marrow, pig's tongues and trotters.

*Babies and children admitted. Function room. No piped
music or jukebox. Restaurant. Vegetarian dishes.*
Map 3/O5

Sekforde Arms

*34 Sekforde Street, EC1 (020 7253 3251). Farringdon
tube/rail.* **Open** 11am-11pm Mon-Fri; 11am-6pm Sat; noon-
4pm Sun. **Food served** noon-9.30pm Mon-Fri; noon-6pm
Sat; noon-2.30pm Sun. **Credit** MC, V.

It's refreshing to find an old warhorse like this that bucks the
style bar trend. The Sekforde Arms, named after a lawyer
who retired to Clerkenwell, has occupied this corner since the
days when Albert was putting the sparkle into the Queen Vic.
It's a wedge-shaped boozer decorated in trad style, with cream
painted walls and terracotta-coloured ceiling. The beer's
Young's, reasonably priced (Ordinary is under £2 a pint) and
good. The bar staff make a point of knowing the regulars'
names, saying things like 'Hello, Terry. The usual, is it?' and
'Careful how you go, Mary'. Food is a feature here and
although they wouldn't be looking for a Michelin star, it's the
top end of pub grub. Served in the first-floor restaurant,
expect the likes of own-made vegetable soup, cod and chips
and school dinner-style lamb curry.
*Babies and children admitted (dining area only). Digital
TV. Function room. Games (fruit machine). Quiz (football
quiz, Thur, during season). Restaurant. Tables outdoors
(pavement). Vegetarian dishes.* **Map 3/O4**

Smiths of Smithfield

*67-77 Charterhouse Street, EC1 (020 7236 6666/
www.smithsofsmithfield.co.uk). Farringdon tube/rail.*
Open (ground-floor bar/cafe) 7.30am-11pm Mon-Fri;
10.30am-11pm Sat; 10.30am-10.30pm Sun; (first-floor
cocktail bar) 6-11pm Mon-Sat. **Food served** (ground-floor
bar/café) 9am-5pm Mon-Fri; 10.30am-5pm Sat, Sun.
Credit AmEx, DC, MC, V.

A massively scaled bar, brasserie, cocktail bar and restaurant
complex over four floors of a listed building overlooking
Smithfield meat market. The ground floor multi-tasks as a
loungey bar and café and gets very busy indeed. With massive
ducting, bare concrete, industrial light fittings suspended on
chains and drive-through french windows, it's as if the place
has been designed to look like a car mechanic's workshop. The
look may be masculine, but it's softened by some of the '70s-
style squishy brown leather sofas that are standard issue in
these parts. At breakfast the fry-ups are exemplary and
relentlessly blokey, from the sensible big white coffee mugs
to the Formica tables laid with HP sauce. Go up one floor and
you find a plush red cocktail bar. Floor three is the brasserie,
while the fourth is 'fine dining,' overseen by head chef John
Torode, the Aussie chef who appears on GMTV.
*Babies and children admitted (daytime; high chairs).
Disabled: toilet. Function room. Music (DJs 8pm daily).
Restaurant. TV. Vegetarian dishes.* **Map 3/O5**

Spirit

*2-5 Carthusian St, EC1 (020 7253 6009/
www.spiritbar.com). Barbican tube.* **Open/food served**
noon-11pm Mon-Wed; noon-midnight Thur, Fri; 5pm-
midnight Sat; noon-10.30pm Sun. **Credit** AmEx, DC, MC, V.

There are few surprises in store at Spirit, but it's no less nice
a place for that. A long cocktail list, fairly priced, features old
standards, new classics, and some wild 'n' wacky items along
the lines of the Spirit Cooler (Tanqueray gin, Teichenne apple
schnapps, fresh apple juice and ginger beer). The shorter wine
list has some nice bottles and the usual proliferation of
spelling mistakes. The food is familiar bar-material: pasta,
burgers, bangers, steak and such, served at the bar as well as
tables. The interior is light and airy on the ground floor,

darker and moodier (and very inviting) in the basement. DJs are in residence Thursday to Saturday, with a Sunday challenge for all bedroom DJs to come and share their record collections (book yourself in for a slot of up to an hour). A friendly, well-run place. We'd definitely go back.
Babies and children admitted (daytime). Bar area available for hire. Disabled: toilet. Music (DJs Fri, Sat). No-smoking area. Specialities: cocktails. Vegetarian dishes. **Map 3/O5**

Sutton Arms
16 Great Sutton Street, EC1 (020 7253 2462). Barbican tube/Farringdon tube/rail. **Open** 11am-11pm Mon-Fri. **Food served** noon-3pm Mon-Fri. **Credit** DC, MC, V.
They've obviously got nothing to hide at this friendly and (barely) modernised pub: large picture windows run the full length of the single bar, looking out onto a landscape that's changing faster than Pompeii the day lava hit town. The colour scheme is beige, green and brown, with comfortable seating at the front and a small serving area that's invariably surrounded by regular drinkers at the rear. Like most pubs in the area, the Sutton gets busy early on with hordes of after-work suits and suchlike, filtering down to a select few regulars as closing time approaches. There's usually a couple of well-chosen real ales on tap (London Pride and Tiger when we visited) and lunchtime sandwiches (including hot salt beef) are bigger and better than might be imagined.
Disabled: toilet. Function room. Restaurant. Satellite TV. Specialities: real ales. Vegetarian dishes. **Map 3/O4**

Three Kings of Clerkenwell
7 Clerkenwell Close, EC1 (020 7253 0483). Farringdon tube/rail. **Open** noon-11pm Mon-Fri; 7.30-11pm Sat. **Food served** noon-3pm Mon-Fri. **No credit cards.**
A strong contender for best boozer in Clerkenwell, the Three Kings is welcomingly eccentric. The sign outside is made up of what is supposed to look like bits of salvaged scrap, while inside colourful three-dimensional papier-mâché creations hang from the ceiling and off the walls. Some work if you pull a cord or crank a handle, and several are for sale. The staff are friendly, the seats are made for lounging in and the bar offers a good selection of real ales. The clientele has no definite type, although we've spotted students, office wallahs, Internetters, what could have been photographic models and a good selection of Clerkenwell's blue collar clan.
Games (board games). Quiz nights. Satellite TV. Vegetarian dishes. **Map 3/N4**

Vic Naylor
38-42 St John Street, EC1 (020 7608 2181). Barbican tube/Farringdon tube/rail. **Open** noon-midnight Mon-Fri; 5pm-midnight Sat. **Food served** noon-11pm Mon-Fri; 5-11pm Sat. **Credit** AmEx, MC, V.
How times change: just a few years ago, Vic's place was the only bar of interest on this stretch of St John Street. Now, it's surrounded on all sides by eager rivals. Even so, Vic manages to keep up with the pack, and his formula of dark wood, painted brown walls, and white tablecloths has been copied countless times. The bar's to the left as you walk in (look out for the elephant motif that includes models of the Hindu god Ganesh on the bar-back), the restaurant to the right. Here you can dine on high-quality bistro food (smoked haddock, pheasant, steaks, etc), then trot back to the long bar for a drop of the hard stuff. Bottled beers and ciders offer a range of styles and countries of origin: we travelled from Yorkshire to South Africa by way of Belgium. The wine list is good and the prices very reasonable.
Babies and children admitted. Bar available for hire. Music (DJs Fri). Restaurant. Specialities: world beers. Vegetarian dishes. **Map 3/O5**

The Well
180 St John St, EC1 (020 7251 9363/ www.downthewell.com). Farringdon tube/rail. **Open** 11am-11pm Mon-Sat; 11am-10pm Sun. **Food served** noon-3pm, 6-10pm Mon-Wed; noon-3pm, 6-10.30pm Thur, Fri; noon-10.30pm Sat; noon-10pm Sun. **Credit** AmEx, MC, V.
A tiny corner bar on two floors, the Well is a welcome and unpretentious addition to St John Street. With its bare board floor and jutting-out serving area, the ground floor looks uncannily like a traditional wine bar. True to form there's an interesting wine list, with around a dozen Enotria-supplied wines by the 175ml or 250ml glass. Beer lovers are also well catered for with draught versions of Boddington's, Budvar, Guinness, Leffe, Hoegaarden and San Miguel among others. There's also the usual bottled suspects as well as cocktails. A superior menu – don't forget this is the inner-city neighbourhood that reinvented bars serving decent food – offers dishes with a seafood slant, with the likes of bouillabaisse, grilled sea bass and wild boar sausages and mash. Unpretentious and good value.
Babies and children admitted. Bar available for hire. Music (occasional DJs). Specialities: draught beers, wines. Vegetarian dishes. **Map 3/O4**

Also in the area...
All Bar One 93A Charterhouse Street, EC1 (020 7553 9391).
Betjeman's (Jamies) 43-44 Cloth Fair, EC1 (020 7600 7778).
Bierodrome 71 St John Street, EC1 (020 7608 0033).
Burgundy Ben's (Davys) 102-108 Clerkenwell Road, EC1 (020 7251 3783).
Café Med 370 John Street, EC1 (020 7278 1199).
Dôme 57-59 Charterhouse Street, EC1 (020 7336 6484).
Jamies 64-66 West Smithfield, EC1 (020 7600 0700).
Sir John Oldcastle (JD Wetherspoon) 29-35 Farringdon Road, EC1 (020 7242 1013).
Slug & Lettuce 36-42 Clerkenwell Road, EC1 (020 7608 1929).

Chancery Lane & Holborn Viaduct

Castle
26 Furnival Street, EC4 (020 7404 1310). Chancery Lane tube. **Open/food served** 11am-11pm Mon-Fri. **Credit** MC, V.
The Castle is one for those City suits for whom the modern pub world is decidedly unimpressive. An old-fashioned local, replete with pally staff, dim lighting and decent ales, this corner pub hums with conversation in the early evenings, a welcome change from the shouty racket in some of its neighbours. Huge windows provide ample views of an unremarkable stretch of road, but the Castle is not the place where you'd spend time gazing outside; rather it's a place to shoot the breeze over a few pints – just like drinking in your local at home. Additional entertainment comes in the form of two well-kept red pool tables and a dartboard upstairs.
Function room. Games (pool table, quiz machines). Quiz (music, 7pm Mon). Satellite TV. Vegetarian dishes. **Map 4/N6**

Mucky Duck
108 Fetter Lane, EC4 (020 7242 9518). Chancery Lane tube. **Open** 11am-11pm Mon-Fri. **Food served** noon-2.30pm Mon-Fri. **Credit** MC, V.

Potemkin.
See page 110.

Nothing more and nothing less than an entirely pleasant local, in an area profoundly lacking in homely boozers. Don't expect anything spectacular, mind, just a familiar mix of dark woods, cosy upholstery, dim lighting and decent lagers and ales (including on our last visit London Pride and IPA £2.20 each). There is a television, which was tuned to Sky sports but the volume was turned down. No themes, history or gimmicks (unless you count the mounted – ooh er! – saucy postcards on the wall) and all the better for it.
Function room. Satellite TV. Vegetarian dishes. **Map 4/N6**

Ye Old Mitre
1 Ely Court, off Ely Place, EC1 (020 7405 4751). Chancery Lane tube/Farringdon tube/rail. **Open** 11am-11pm Mon-Fri. **Food served** 11am-9.30pm Mon-Fri. **No credit cards**.
London's most ancient pubs have usually survived because of their magnificent locations or grand designs. The Mitre has neither, really, and so is presumably just lucky. A pub was founded here in 1546, its name a reference to the bishops of Ely whose church and prison were around the corner. The present building dates from the 18th century and is an eccentric warren of little rickety rooms, the best of them the first lounge bar you enter. Expect basic food and drink: draughts include Tetley's Cask, Adnam's Best and Pedigree, and there are snacks such as toasted sandwiches. Tourists drop in by day, while evenings are the preserve of local office workers, many of whom are on first name terms with the landlord and his wife – it makes for the kind of convivial atmosphere that drinkers in any century would enjoy.
No piped music or jukebox. Specialities: real ales. Vegetarian dishes. **Map 3/N5**

Terry Neill's Sports Bar & Brasserie
Bath House, 53 Holborn Viaduct, EC1 (020 7329 6653). Chancery Lane tube. **Open** 11am-11pm Mon-Fri. **Food served** noon-3pm Mon-Fri. **Credit** AmEx, DC, MC, V.
Sports bars are normally associated with blaring sound, shiny surfaces and fleecing the customers for all they are worth. Terry Neill's – opened by the ex-Arsenal manager – is more sedate, and aimed at 30- to 50-year-old, unreconstructed males from nearby offices and the local police station. The style is old-fashioned English pub, with added sports memorabilia (framed signed shirts, etc) lining the walls. TV screens at every angle

mean everyone gets a good view. There's a wide range of beers, including Carling of course, and Caffrey's, Bass, Grolsch, Guinness and Staropramen. The sharp Terry Neill's cask ale, however, may not be to everyone's taste. Food ranges from sandwiches and salad in the main bar, scampi-style dishes in the brasserie, to à la carte in the Boardroom restaurant downstairs. Neill's also opens for major sporting events on Saturdays.
Babies and children admitted (daytime). Function room. Games (darts). Restaurant. Satellite TVs. Tables outdoors (patio). Vegetarian dishes. **Map 4/O5**

Tooks Bar & Restaurant
17-18 Tooks Court, Cursitor Street, EC4 (020 7404 1818). Chancery Lane tube. **Open** 11.30am-11pm Mon-Fri. **Food served** noon-8.30pm Mon-Fri. **Credit** AmEx, MC, V.
For location Tooks couldn't have it much worse: tucked away in a tiny side street, which is itself off another tiny side street, around the back of Chancery Lane tube. It's quite a modern place, light woods predominate, and the atmosphere is pleasantly relaxed. Deferential staff serve the likes of draught Bitburger and bottled Adnam's Broadside, and there's a bar menu mostly of sandwiches. A separate, pricier restaurant menu exists for those after a little more formality. Judging by the entertaining conversations we overheard on our visit, the clientele is made up of legal eagles, who perhaps value their own turf. Go and view the people – the smart barrister trying to impress someone opposite us had a ladder in his silk socks.
Babies and children admitted. Disabled: toilet. Function room. Restaurant. Vegetarian dishes. **Map 4/N6**

Also in the area...
Bottlescrue (Davys) 53-60 Holborn Viaduct, EC1 (020 7248 2157).

Fleet Street, Blackfriars & St Paul's

Balls Brothers
6-8 Cheapside, EC2 (020 7248 2708/www.ballsbrothers. co.uk). St Paul's tube. **Open/food served** 11.30am-9.30pm Mon-Fri. **Credit** AmEx, DC, JCB, MC, V.

Balls Brothers has been plying wines to the City of London for five generations, since the partnership was started by Austin and Harry Balls. There are now 16 restaurants and wine bars going under the Balls name. They offer a wise, unflash but not especially cheap range of wines (an oakey white Vernaccia le Colonne will set you back £3.70 for 175 ml), and they don't do beer. This particular branch has been around a good while, although not nearly as long as the pseudo-old notices and signs suggest. It's large, covering two floors, but the time to visit is summer when a circular outdoor sunken terrace is opened with superb views of St Paul's.
No piped music or jukebox. Tables outdoors (sunken garden). Vegetarian dishes. **Map 4/O6**

Black Friar

174 Queen Victoria Street, EC4 (020 7236 5474). Blackfriars tube/rail. **Open** 11.30am-11pm Mon-Fri. **Food served** noon-2.30pm Mon-Fri. **Credit** AmEx, MC, V.
When Black Friar (erected 1875) was refurbished back in 1903, the management got Henry Poole to remodel the exterior and give this cheese wedge-shaped old pub an art nouveau façade; then H Fuller Clarke turned up two years later with extravagant Edwardian marble, mosaics, pillared fireplaces, mirrored alcoves and bas-relief of monks at work and play. The monks are there to remind us that this is the site of the old Blackfriars monastery (1221-1538). Today the marble is beige going on brown, a nicotine-stained shadow of the original incandescent creams, golds and whites, and corners are chipping away. Time for owners Nicholson's to spend a few pounds on restoration, we suggest. The beer's good, with a bunch of real ales at around £2.20 a pint, including Adnam's and Bass. Food is the usual pub stuff, and apart from the odd dewy-eyed art nouveau buff, customers are besuited City workers or staff from Unilever across the road.
Games (fruit machine). Tables outdoors (garden). Vegetarian dishes. **Map 4/O6**

Cartoonist

76 Shoe Lane, EC4 (020 7353 2828). Blackfriars tube/rail. **Open/food served** 11am-11pm Mon-Fri. **Credit** AmEx, DC, MC, V.
About as aptly named as pubs get, the Cartoonist acts as the official HQ for the Cartoonists' Club of Great Britain.

Examples of members' work bedeck the walls to the extent that the place is part pub, part gallery. Unfortunately the super-bright lighting used to illuminate the sketches does little to foster any intimacy or cosiness. On the plus side, downstairs is a bar billiards table, and staff are delightful. Beers include Courage Best and Directors, while food runs to the likes of pork and leek sausages (£4.25).
Function room. Games (fruit machine, pool table). Tables outdoors (terrace). TVs. Vegetarian dishes. **Map 4/N6**

El Vino

47 Fleet Street, EC4 (020 7353 6786/www.elvino.co.uk). Chancery Lane or Temple tube/Blackfriars tube/rail. **Open/food served** 11.30am-9pm Mon-Fri. **Credit** AmEx, MC, V.
El Vino provides incontrovertible evidence (as its largely legal clientele would say) of how a mere wine bar can become 'an establishment'. Regimented stacks of wine racks line the walls and there's a small partitioned dining area towards the back of the premises, with leather upholstered seating and a fireplace. Here you can see portly pinstriped men (there's a jacket and tie rule) in their natural environment, leaning against a wooden bar actually smoking real pipes. As a practising wine merchant, El Vino has a vast and impressive wine list that really goes to town on the claret section, although on our most recent visit, we weren't allowed to scan the list, rather our learned barman said we should choose the Chablis (£4.25 for 125 ml), the house wine of the month. Food, as you might expect, is mainly traditional English with some excellent fish thrown in for good measure. Small carafes of water are put on each table for diluting El Vino's very own Connoisseur's Blend 12-year-old Scotch whiskey (£12 a double).
Dress code. Function room. No piped music or jukebox. Vegetarian dishes. **Map 4/N6**

La Grande Marque

47 Ludgate Hill, EC4 (020 7329 6709). Blackfriars tube/rail. **Open** 11.30am-9.30pm Mon-Fri. **Food served** 11.30am-3pm Mon-Fri. **Credit** AmEx, DC, MC, V.
Grand marque is an obsolete French term for any of the major champagne brands, but can also be applied to anything a bit upmarket. This wine bar in the old City Bank building, just downhill of St Paul's Cathedral, lives up to its name with a

swanky banky posture and some excellent wines. For the look, imagine an incredibly poshed-up Dôme with grand drapery, high ceilings, subdued wallpaper and simple dark wood tables. The wine list is extremely broad ranging and well chosen, with fine wines conveniently segregated from the rest. There's a superb champagne selection ranging from Lay & Wheeler Extra Quality Brut (£30.50 a bottle) all the way up to Louis Roederer Cristal 1993 (£117). Food revolves around posh sandwiches such as crab and lemon mayonnaise. *Function room. Vegetarian dishes.* **Map 4/O6**

Old Bank of England
194 Fleet Street, EC4 (020 7430 2255). Chancery Lane or Temple tube. **Open** 11am-11pm Mon-Fri. **Food served** noon-8pm Mon-Fri. **Credit** AmEx, MC, V.
A Fuller's Ale & Pie house has taken over from what used to be a branch office of the Old Lady of Threadneedle Street, and they've certainly made the most of the space. It's a daunting, marble and brass room that creates a remarkable first impression: ceilings that seem to stretch up forever, a balcony ringing the central bar and massive windows looking out on to the street. It's only after you've been in there a while that the drawbacks begin to become apparent. The fabric of the place is deteriorating (some of the brass fittings have been pilfered); it's extremely noisy (perhaps due in part to the natural echo in a pub of this size); and its popularity among the moneyed moneymen of the area means it can take three minutes short of forever to get served. However, the beer's good (including London Pride, ESB and Chiswick) and it's a great place to impress visiting relatives.
Function rooms. No-smoking area (lunchtimes). Vegetarian dishes. **Map 4/N6**

Old Bell Tavern
95 Fleet Street, EC4 (020 7583 0216). Blackfriars tube/rail. **Open** 11.30am-11pm Mon-Fri; noon-4pm Sat. **Food served** noon-3pm Mon-Fri; noon-4pm Sat. **Credit** AmEx, DC, MC, V.
This cramped yet wonderfully cosy pub, first known as the Swan, was built in 1670 so that Christopher Wren could house workmen rebuilding St Bride's. It's still an old-fashioned spit-and-sawdust type of place with bare wooden floors, little leaded stained glass windows and ancient triangular stools, which look as though they owe their odd shape more to wear than to design. The front part of the pub was originally an off-licence, which must have made the tavern itself very small indeed. There is even now, not a great deal of seating space. It has stiff competition for choosy custom from next door neighbour the Punch Tavern and from the Cheshire Cheese just up the street, but we'd go for the Old Bell every time, for its decent ales (Timothy Taylor Landlord and Brakspear Bitter) and for the way it wears 300 years of history with a studied indifference.
Function room. Games (fruit machine). No piped music or jukebox. Satellite TV. Vegetarian dishes. **Map 4/N6**

Ye Olde Cheshire Cheese
145 Fleet Street, EC4 (020 7353 6170). Blackfriars tube/rail. **Open** 11.30am-11pm Mon-Fri; noon-9.30pm Sat; noon-3pm Sun. **Food served** noon-9pm Mon-Sat; noon-2.30pm Sun. **Credit** AmEx, DC, MC, V.
The Cheese might look closed from Fleet Street, but it probably isn't: its dark frontage conceals the unprepossessing entrance, located down the alley at the side of the pub. You'll be in good company when you finally walk through the door, however: Thackeray used to booze here, Dickens mentioned the Cheese in *A Tale of Two Cities*, and Dr Johnson lived almost next door. In fact over the years many famous customers have signed their names in the large leather-bound books, kept behind the main bar, even if nowadays it's mainly the haunt of the few remaining journos who work in the area.

Just like the 17th-century taverns of popular imagination, it's a warren of narrow corridors and myriad rooms (including three restaurants), all complete with wooden settles, bare boards and sawdust. Pagers are given out to anyone placing an order for sandwiches, nachos, etc; they light up and vibrate when your food's ready at the counter. Booze is Sam Smith's. *Babies and children admitted (restaurant). Disabled: toilet. Function rooms. No piped music or jukebox. Restaurant. Vegetarian dishes.* **Map 4/N6**

Punch Tavern
99 Fleet Street, EC4 (020 7353 6658). Blackfriars tube/rail. **Open** 11am-11pm Mon-Fri. **Food served** 11am-3pm Mon-Fri. **Credit** AmEx, MC, V.
It was here that the famous satirical magazine was founded in 1841, which is why so many of *Punch*'s ancient cartoons line the walls of the impressive main room. Amid the Victorian extravagant-style decor, there's also stacks of Punch and Judy ephemera: a portrait of the unhappy couple hangs in the tiled lobby, there are marionettes, a Mr Punch clock and a great many prints. Split in half after an argument by its two freeholders, the Punch now only consists of what used to be the saloon bar. The refurb has been done brilliantly, though, with rich reds and golds everywhere, plush upholstery and art deco beaded lamps that give out subdued lighting. Even the loos have huge neo-19th century basins. The clientele consists of local office workers supping from a decent beer selection. Lagers come in fridge-frosted glasses (very, very good indeed).
Function room. Satellite TV. Vegetarian dishes. **Map 4/N6**

Rising Sun
61 Carter Lane, EC4 (020 7248 4544). St Paul's tube/Blackfriars tube/rail. **Open** 11am-11pm Mon-Fri. **Food served** noon-3pm, 5.30-10.30pm Mon-Fri. **Credit** AmEx, DC, MC, V.
The windy backstreets tripping down from Ludgate Hill to Blackfriars are an excellent place to drink, liberally sprinkled with convivial little, independently-minded pubs and bars. **Shaw's Booksellers** (*see below*) is the favourite, but the Rising Sun's worth a look too. It's quite trad in a stripped down, stand up sort of way, with little in the way of furniture in a room that's dominated by a large, square central serving area. We're guessing the Guinness must be good here judging by the fact that of the 20 or so blokes propping up the bar last visit, all but one were on the Liffey juice. Real ale alternatives exist in Bombadier and Spitfire. It's loud, boisterous and boozy – perfect if that's what you're in the mood for. How could we not love it when the girls behind the counter sucker-punch us by playing Marvin Gaye's 'What's Goin' On' – the album not the track – and all the way through.
Restaurant. Vegetarian dishes. **Map 4/O6**

Shaw's Booksellers
31-34 St Andrews Hill, EC4 (020 7489 7999). St Paul's tube/Blackfriars tube/rail. **Open** noon-11pm Mon-Fri. **Food served** noon-3pm, 6-9pm Mon-Fri. **Credit** AmEx, MC, V.
This place feels more Islington than City, a big airy room with large picture windows, worn floorboards, a funky red and magnolia colour scheme and a slatted-board ceiling supported by warehouse-style iron columns. Staff are young and stylish, as were most of the punters on our early evening visit, lounging on leather sofas or occupying the mishmatch of wooden tables and chairs. There was trip hop on the tape deck and Hoegaarden, Staropramen and Fuller's ales on draught at the bar. The name comes from a cosmetic makeover the pub underwent for its part in the Helena Bonham-Carter flick *Wings of a Dove* (1997). You're not

Smiths of Smithfield.
See page 110.

likely to encounter any movie stars here nowadays but it's a very decent little den nonetheless.
Disabled: toilet. Vegetarian dishes. **Map 4/O6**

Viaduct Tavern

126 Newgate Street, EC1 (020 7606 8476). St Paul's tube. **Open** 11am-11pm Mon-Sat. **Food served** noon-3pm Mon-Sat. **Credit** AmEx, DC, MC, V.
Some of the fittings in this pub go back to 1870 and it must have been splendidly grand in its heyday. The original wooden bar, the inlay mirrors and mirrored glass are rarely found in pubs which bill themselves as the genuine Victorian article, and there are fascinating bits and pieces and prints of the area to gaze at over your pint of Tetley's. There's also supposed to be the remains of a debtor's prison in the basement, dating back to 1775. During the day, the place is usually full of anxious friends and relatives of the accused on trial at the Old Bailey opposite. If you go in the evening you may find it much emptier, but perhaps with a rather rougher bunch. Maybe they've just been acquitted.
Babies and children admitted. Games (board games, fruit machine). TV. Vegetarian dishes. **Map 4/O6**

Also in the area...

All Bar One 44-46 Ludgate Hill, EC4 (020 7653 9901).
Café Flo 38-40 Ludgate Hill, EC4 (020 7329 3900).
Café Rouge 140 Fetter Lane, EC4 (020 7242 3469); Hillgate House, 2-3 Limeburner Lane, EC4 (020 7329 1234).
City Pipe (Davys) 33 Foster Lane, EC1 (020 7606 2110).
Corney & Barrow 3 Fleet Place, EC4 (020 7329 3141).
Davys 10 Creed Lane, EC4 (020 7236 5317).
Dôme 4 St Paul's Churchyard, EC4 (020 7489 0767).
Jamies 5 Groveland Court, EC4 (020 7248 5551); 34 Ludgate Hill, EC4 (020 7489 1938).
Shoeless Joe's 2 Old Change Court, EC4 (020 7248 2720).

Mansion House, Monument & Bank

1 Lombard Street

1 Lombard Street, EC3 (020 7929 6611/ www.1lombardstreet.com). Bank tube/DLR. **Open** 7.30am-11pm Mon-Fri. **Food served** 7.30-11am, noon-3pm, 6-10pm Mon-Fri. **Credit** AmEx, DC, MC, V.
This spacious bar-restaurant is a converted bank; its impressive circular bar is positioned underneath a dome of glass, which would once have been the main source of light for the clerks and tellers. On our early-evening visit we were surrounded by an efficient people-machine, busily preparing for dining customers. Their working activities, however, did not stop the manager from rebuking staff for what *he* thought was slowness to serve us. You get the impression that the management has a certain clientele in mind and might discourage the impromptu drinker. It means that unless you are really dressed to the nines, like the immaculate *FT* reader who was sipping a coffee, you could feel rather overwhelmed. *Babies and children admitted (restaurant). Disabled: toilet. Function room. Music (live jazz 7pm Wed). Restaurant. Vegetarian dishes.* **Map 6/Q6**

Bar Bourse

67 Queen Street, EC4 (020 7248 2200). Mansion House tube/Cannon Street tube/rail. **Open** 11.30am-11pm Mon-Fri. **Food served** 11.30am-3pm Mon-Fri. **Credit** AmEx, MC, V.

The Rolls-Royce of EC4 bars, if only on account of its cheekily interlinked 'BB' logo. It's a theatrically realised basement bar-restaurant that exudes class in its decor, too: a curved bar with a stunning mix of red-and-gold banquettes and huge tilted mirrors that doubtless give the moneyed punters a buzz as they flash their cash for expensive bottled beers (Staropramen at £3.25, for example), wines (20 white and 21 red) and spirits. We have it on good authority that the place attracts groups who often manage to drink the place out of Krug and Bollinger by 5.30pm. Many stay on to eat at the adjoining restaurant with its excellent stripy inlaid wood floor and catch-all style menu with an Eastern slant.
Babies and children admitted. Disabled: toilet. Restaurant. TVs. Vegetarian dishes. **Map 6/P7**

Bar Under the Clock

74 Queen Victoria Street (entrance on Bow Lane), EC4 (020 7489 9895). Mansion House tube. **Open** 11am-11pm Mon-Fri. **Food served** 11am-3pm, 5.30-9pm Mon-Fri. **Credit** AmEx, DC, MC, V.
This is a Balls Brothers venture (*see p112*), and its modern, funky vibe makes for a welcome change from all the area's surfeit of olde worlde boozers. It's a refreshingly quiet and relaxed place to drink, brightly painted with little candle-like bulbs in the walls. Service is friendly and efficient. There are 11 whites, nine reds and five champagnes on offer, and a glass of Fleurie sets you back £4. There's a heavy rotation of theme evenings and drinks offers every month, plus bottles of international guest beers (Brahma Shopp from Brazil and Lapin Kulta from Lapland on our last visit, both £2.70). They went down a storm with the Clock combo-platter (£6.95).
Babies and children admitted. Vegetarian dishes. **Map 6/P6**

Counting House

50 Cornhill, EC3 (020 7283 7123). Bank tube/DLR. **Open** 11am-11pm Mon-Fri. **Food served** noon-8pm Mon-Fri. **Credit** AmEx, DC, MC, V.
Once the headquarters of NatWest, this Fuller's Ale & Pie house won a City Heritage award for being one of the finest examples of building refurbishment in the City – the first time that this honour has been bestowed upon a pub. It's certainly splendidly ornate with lots of curlicues and flourishes but dare we suggest that it just might be a little over the top? The relationship between the high bar, glass dome and chandeliers is particularly uncomfortable. However, beers are good (a full range of Fuller's including Organic Honey Dew) and the place is large enough that finding some form of free seating (whether bar stools, leather armchairs or a table up on the mezzanine) should rarely pose a problem.
Disabled: toilet. Function rooms. No-smoking area (dining area). Vegetarian dishes. **Map 6/Q6**

Crosse Keys

9 Gracechurch Street, EC3 (020 7623 4824). Monument tube/Bank tube/DLR. **Open** 11am-11pm Mon-Sat. **Food served** 11am-10pm Mon-Sat. **Credit** AmEx, MC, V.
What a coup for JD Wetherspoon to have gained possession of the Grade II listed Hong Kong & Shanghai Bullion bank. The result is a massive monument to liquid lunches and afterwork boozing, a pub the size of a city railway station. With a ceiling supported by trunk-like marble columns, the vast hall must accommodate hundreds if not thousands of drinkers, served by a busy team of around a dozen uniformed staff enclosed within an oval island of a bar. A giant blackboard measuring six foot by seven lists 100 different real ales from around the UK, ranging from Abbot to Zig Zag, with the likes of Old Hooky and Rumpus in between; asterisks denote which are available at any given time. All sell at £1.89 a pint. If you fancy the idea of drinking strange

potent brews in an atmosphere redolent of the concourse at Waterloo, look no further.

Babies and children admitted (Saturdays only in family area). Disabled: toilet. Function rooms. Games (fruit machines, quiz machines). No piped music or jukebox. No-smoking area. Vegetarian dishes. **Map 6/Q7**

Jamaica Wine House

12 St Michael's Alley, EC3 (020 7626 9496). Bank tube/DLR. **Open** 11am-11pm Mon-Fri. **Food served** noon-3pm Mon-Fri. **Credit** AmEx, DC, MC, V.

Tucked down a narrow alley off the south side of Cornhill, the Jamaica originally opened as the first London coffee house way back in 1652. It was destroyed in the Great Fire of London in 1666 but rebuilt on the same site. It became a pub towards the end of the 19th century, which is when the present building dates from. It looks the part too, with bare weathered boards and mahogany partitions, all nicely aged with a patina of nicotine. Despite being called a 'wine house' and the conspicuous wine barrel decor, there are only four whites and four reds (£9.95-£11.95) and most patrons stick with beer, which includes a number of real ales such as St Peter's at a modest £2.30 a pint. Any visiting American would be delighted to be brought here.

Babies and children admitted. Function room. Games (fruit machine). Vegetarian dishes. **Map 6/Q6**

Lamb Tavern

10-12 Grand Avenue, Leadenhall Market, EC3 (020 7626 2454). Monument tube/Bank tube/DLR. **Open** 11am-9pm Mon-Fri. **Food served** noon-2.30pm Mon-Fri. **Credit** AmEx, DC, MC, V.

Of the ever-increasing number of drinking options around Leadenhall Market (each with its own gimmick – one even has a Pizza Hut on the premises) this remains the oldest (built 1880), most basic and the best. Right at the heart of the market it's a 'stand-up', with a ground floor that has been stripped down to the bare boozing minimum of a bar, an easily swabbed flagged floor and a few ledges to perch drinks on. A wrought iron spiral staircase leads up to a small seated mezzanine area and you can go up again to a carpeted top floor no-smoking bar where food is served and there are great views of the market passageways below. It's a Young's pub with their excellent full complement of ales, draught and bottled. Food is standard pub grub but enjoyed nonetheless by lower rank financial types from the likes of Lloyd's next door.

Babies and children admitted. Function rooms. Games (darts, fruit machine). No-smoking room. **Map 6/Q6**

Leadenhall Wine Bar

27 Leadenhall Market, EC3 (020 7623 1818). Monument tube/Bank tube/DLR. **Open** 11.30am-11pm Mon-Fri. **Food served** 11.30am-10pm Mon-Fri. **Credit** AmEx, DC, MC, V.

Tucked away in the centre of Leadenhall market, this small wine and tapas bar provides a welcome retreat from the noisy and often overcrowded pubs that surround it. Climbing up the stairs is a bit of an endurance test, but one that's worth the struggle. The intimate surroundings are perfect for a relaxing drink. Ordering, however, can prove somewhat confusing: a smiling waiter arrives at your table, whereas the wine list invites you to go to the bar. The wine selection is good and varied, and avoids run-of-the-mill Spanish varieties. We enjoyed a glass of Pazo Ribiero from Gallicia (£3.50). There are no draught beers but you can get Peroni, Beck's, Amber and Estrella in bottles.

Babies and children admitted (lunchtimes). Function rooms. Restaurant. Vegetarian dishes. **Map 6/Q7**

Ye Olde Watling

29 Watling Street, EC4 (020 7653 9971). Mansion House tube. **Open** 11am-11pm Mon-Fri. **Food served** 11am-9pm Mon-Fri. **Credit** AmEx, MC, V.

It certainly doesn't look it, neither inside nor out, but the Watling is entirely justified in its 'Ye Olde' prefix, built as it was in 1668. It's current look probably owes more to a refit in 1901. In the main bar area a yellow haze passes for lighting amid the oak columns and flat-arched doorways. It's a 'stand up' pub with just a few stools; if you want to sit you have to go upstairs to the grill restaurant. A back room that used to have seating has been taken over by a pool table. The beer is good (when we visited Ridleys was on guest), which must go some way to explaining why the Society for the Preservation of Ale in the Wood meets here.

Babies and children admitted (restaurant). Function room. Games (darts, fruit machines, pool table). Restaurant. Tables outdoors (courtyard). Vegetarian dishes. **Map 6/P6**

Pacific Oriental

1 Bishopsgate, EC2 (020 7621 9988). Bank tube/DLR/ Liverpool Street tube/rail. **Open** 11.30am-11pm Mon-Fri. **Food served** 11.30am-3pm, 6-9pm Mon-Fri. **Credit** AmEx, DC, MC, V.

Part restaurant, part cocktail bar and part microbrewery: the spacious PO has successfully followed in the wake of fellow bar-brewers Mash and the Freedom Brewing Company. Six shiny copper brewing vessels are the bar's main focal point: visible even from the street outside. We found staff to be very friendly, in spite of being kept busy uncorking champagne (Veuve Cliquot £55) for suits burning bonuses. When, for example, we made some polite enquiries about their brews, they kindly let us sample some. The white beer was not ready, but Pacific Bishop (£2.60, 4.5 per cent abv) was a decent quaffing beer if a little lacking in body, and Pacific Pils (£2.70, 5 per cent abv) had a good sharp, non-metallic taste. Cocktails have an oriental theme – Japanese Slipper (tequila, midori, lime juice and sugar syrup, £6) – and there is a good range of oriental bar snacks (satay beef and chicken, prawn toast, spring rolls and such). The Tokyo branch of CAMRA might consider this bar for their next AGM.

Babies and children admitted (restaurant). Disabled: toilet. Function rooms. No-smoking area (restaurant). Restaurant. Satellite TV. Vegetarian dishes. **Map 6/Q6**

Prism Restaurant & Bar

147 Leadenhall Street, EC3 (020 7256 3888/ www.harveynichols.com). Monument tube/Bank tube/DLR. **Open** noon-11pm Mon-Fri. **Food served** noon-3pm, 6-10pm Mon-Fri. **Credit** AmEx, DC, MC, V.

The airy grand hall of a former bank provides the setting for Prism, a stately, classical, even forbidding arena operated by Harvey Nichols. There's a 130-seat restaurant and bar on the ground floor with mezzanine, and a further bar in the basement. The downstairs bar is a sophisticated, modern twist on a simple 1920s theme, with abundant seating – roulades of suede in a chrome frame – and gentle lighting running the length of a long, rectangular bar. Drinks of choice are cocktails, which are fairly standard with the addition of a mix called an EC3 – Bombay Sapphire, lime and berry juice (£7). Also notable is an extensive whiskey list. Bar staff look disturbingly like department store perfume reps. Food in the restaurant is pricey but worth it, or there's a bar menu with a selection of savouries and a splurge of desserts.

Babies and children admitted (restaurant). Disabled: toilet. Function rooms. No piped music or jukebox (restaurant). Restaurant. Vegetarian dishes. **Map 6/Q6**

Swan Tavern
*Ship Tavern Passage, 77-80 Gracechurch Street,
EC3 (020 7283 7712/www.swanec3.co.uk). Monument
tube/Bank tube/DLR.* **Open** 11am-9pm Mon-Thur;
9am-10pm Fri. **Food served** noon-2.30pm Mon-Fri.
Credit AmEx, MC, V.
Tucked down a narrow alleyway this is a tiny place about the
size of a doubledecker bus but considerably older. Just like the
Routemaster, as you step in the entrance a tight stair spirals
up to the above floor, or push on forward into the squeeze of
the lower bar. Patrons at the bar have to take a deep breath to
allow you to pass. Down here there's a flagged floor, with big
windows on one side matched by a row of mirrors on the other.
Most of the space is taken up by an immaculate old serving
area tended by a consummate professional of a barman, who
expertly draws pints of Fuller's ales, while listening politely
to the rants of half-sodden City suits. The room upstairs is
slightly larger as it extends over the passageway and has
something of the feel of a private club, an impression
reinforced by the 'No jeans or trainers' sign on the door.
*Function room. No piped music or jukebox. Satellite TV.
Vegetarian dishes.* **Map 6/Q7**

Also in the area...
All Bar One 103 Cannon Street, EC1 (020 7220
9031); 16 Byward Street, EC3 (020 7553 0301);
34 Threadneedle Street, EC2 (020 7614 9931).
Balls Brothers 3-6 Budge Row, Cannon Street, EC4
(020 7248 7557); 3 Kings Arms Yard, EC2 (020
7796 3049); 52 Lime Street, EC3 (020 7283 0841);
22 Mark Lane, EC3 (020 7623 2923); 2 St Mary-at-
Hill, EC3 (020 7626 0321).
Bangers Too (Davys) 1 St Mary-at-Hill, EC3
(020 7283 4443).
City Flogger (Davys) Fenn Court, 120 Fenchurch
Street, EC3 (020 7623 3214).
City FOB (Free On Board) (Davys) Lower Thames
Street, EC3 (020 7623 8339).
City Tup 66 Gresham Street, EC2 (020 7606 8176).
Corney & Barrow 44 Cannon Street, EC4 (020 7248
1700); 2B Eastcheap, EC3 (020 7929 3220);
1 Leadenhall Place, EC3 (020 7621 9201);
12-14 Mason's Avenue, EC2 (020 7726 6030);
109 Old Broad Street, EC2 (020 7638 9308);
16 Royal Exchange, EC3 (020 7929 3131).
Fine Line 1 Bow Churchyard, EC4 (020 7248 3262);
1 Monument Street, EC3 (020 7623 5446);
124-127 Minories, EC3 (020 7481 8195).
Heeltap & Bumper (Davys) 2-6 Cannon Street, EC1
(020 7248 3371).
Jamies 54 Gresham Street, EC2 (020 7606 1755);
107-112 Leadenhall Street, EC3 (020 7626 7226);
119-121 The Minories, EC3 (020 7709 9900);
13 Philpot Lane, EC3 (020 7621 9577).
Liberty Bounds (JD Wetherspoon) 15 Trinity Square,
EC3 (020 7481 0513).
London Stone (Eerie) 109 Cannon Street, EC4
(020 7626 8246).
Number 25 (Jamies) 25 Birchin Lane, EC3
(020 7623 2505).
O'Neill's 65 Cannon Street, EC4 (020 7653 9951).
Pitcher & Piano Calico House, 67-69 Watling Street,
EC4 (020 7248 0883); 28-31 Cornhill, EC3
(020 7929 3989).
Russia Court Ale & Port (Davys) 1-6 Milk Street,
EC2 (020 7606 7252).
Slug & Lettuce 25 Bucklersbury, EC4
(020 7329 6222).

Tower Hill & Aldgate

Corney & Barrow
*37A Jewry Street, EC3 (020 7680 8550/
www.corney-barrow.co.uk). Aldgate tube.* **Open** 8am-11pm
Mon-Wed, 8am-midnight Thur, Fri. **Food served**
8am-10.30pm Mon-Fri. **Credit** AmEx, DC, MC, V.
The entrance to the Jewry Street branch of this popular City
chain is more suggestive of a health club than bar, with a
staircase leading down to a foyer furnished with plants and
sofas. The exposed-brick of the cavern-like interior makes a
pleasantly surprising contrast – albeit one that is slightly
sullied by the appearance of '80s-style black and chrome
seating. Wine snobs will appreciate the elegant glasses that
have proper tapering tops to free the bouquet. A fragrant and
lemony Pinot Gris was only £3.50 and a bottle of Veuve
Cliquot a reasonable £39.95. Dishes are Modern British with
a Mediterranean influence – chicken supreme on potato and
tarragon rosti with spinach (£9.75), for instance. Each comes
accompanied by a wine suggestion. Evening snacks such as
sausages and red onion kebabs (£3.25) are a refreshing
change from the tired old nachos and mozzarella.
*Babies and children admitted (daytime). Disabled: toilet.
Function room. Music (DJs 7pm Fri). Restaurant. Satellite
TV. Vegetarian dishes.* **Map 6/R7**

Dickens Inn
*St Katherine's Way, E1 (020 7488 2208). Tower Hill
tube/Tower Gateway DLR.* **Open** 11am-11pm Mon-Sat;
noon-10.30pm Sun. **Food served** noon-4pm Mon-Fri;
noon-6pm Sat, Sun. **Credit** AmEx, DC, MC, V.
Ironically, although named for the famously booze-loving
author this must be about the only old London pub that
doesn't claim he drank on its premises. It can't because at the
time Dickens was alive it was just a warehouse. These days
it's most definitely a pub, a huge one, filling three wooden
storeys with five separate bars and restaurants. It doesn't feel
very old because only the framework is original and all the
fittings were added in the '70s, however its dockside location
makes it a hit with tourists, especially in summer when
customers can flood outdoors to fill sunken drinking areas.
Beers are standard, with a couple of Courage real ales, all at
premium prices. The first-floor pizza parlour and second-floor
Dickens Restaurant (fish) are adequate but nothing more.
*Babies and children admitted (high chairs, nappy changing
facilities). Disabled: toilet. Function room. Games (fruit
machine). Jukebox. No-smoking area (restaurant). Quiz
(Tue). Restaurants. Satellite TV. Tables outdoors
(garden). Vegetarian dishes.*

Hogshead
*1 America Square, EC3 (020 7702 2381). Tower Hill
tube/Tower Gateway DLR.* **Open** 11am-11pm Mon-Fri.
Food served 11am-9pm Mon-Fri. **Credit** AmEx, MC, V.
Disguised behind a gleaming 1990s chrome and glass office
block frontage, this is a low-slung, cavern-like bar occupying
acres of space in a set of converted railway arches. Rumbling
trains from Fenchurch Street and Tower Hill regularly
punctuate the conversation. The overall feel is a bit corporate
(coffee comes courtesy of an on-site branch of Costa) but it
does good ales at fair prices – Brakspear bitter is just £1.49
a pint, and Hopback Red Devil is £2.49. On our visit we
appreciated the wines on a 'try before you buy offer'. Plus we
were impressed by the collection of Belgian and French beers,
including Kriek, Triple and three kinds of Leffe (all at £2.85).
A place for those who value their ales over ambience.
*Disabled: toilet. Function room. Games (fruit machine).
No-smoking area. Vegetarian dishes.* **Map 6/R7**

Hoop & Grapes

47 Aldgate High Street, EC3 (020 7265 5171). Aldgate tube. **Open** 11am-10pm Mon-Wed; 11am-11pm Thur, Fri. **Food served** noon-3pm Mon-Fri. **Credit** AmEx, MC, V.
Somewhat miraculously this pub escaped untouched by the Great Fire of London in 1666. Today it is the only timber-framed building left in the City – give or take some major steel underpinning in the 1980s to stop it from falling down. It was a private house until about 100 years ago and, rather like the Tardis, you enter its narrow doorway and then a bigger than expected space opens out before you. Inside are many features – mysterious bricked-up doorways, charming little Victorian fireplaces, etc – which if not original are certainly old. Situated right at the edge of where the City ends and the East End begins, you'll find as many suits here as students and locals. The staff are very friendly and the standards (Bass, Adnam's, Tetley's and London Pride) are on draught, but we felt it was the delicious steak and ale pie with potatoes (£5.75) that deserved a special mention.
Games (darts, video games). Satellite TV. Vegetarian dishes.

Market Bar & Restaurant

1-2 Crutched Friars, EC3 (020 7480 7550). Aldgate or Tower Hill tube. **Open** 11am-11pm Mon-Fri. **Food served** 11am-9pm daily. **Credit** AmEx, MC, V.
The Market referred to here is not Leadenhall but the stock market, whose operations the bar mimics. The prices of drinks, displayed on screens, go up and down according to demand. The present, highest and lowest prices are displayed so you can decide whether or not to buy. And apparently the computer can simulate French Lorry driver strikes and cause, for example, the price of mineral water to go sky-high. Hoegaarden (£3.80) and house wine (£11) seem to remain static. It is probably a laugh if you work in the field – which presumably most of the punters here do – although the owners are hoping the concept has wider appeal because this is just the flagship in what's intended to be a chain. Soft lighting and big leather pouffes make the place comfortable, the manager's charming, and the restaurant – positioned discreetly behind a glass partition – serves up reasonably priced Mediterranean dishes.
Babies and children admitted. Disabled: toilet. Restaurant. Satellite TV. Vegetarian dishes. **Map 6/R7**

Old Dispensary

19A Leman Street, E1 (020 7702 1406). Aldgate East tube. **Open** 11am-11pm Mon-Fri. **Food served** 11am-3pm Mon-Fri. **Credit** AmEx, DC, MC, V.
This converted dispensary for sick children is a good-looking boozer that resembles a JD Wetherspoon pub with its high ceiling, beige walls and no-smoking area. There's a wooden balcony and a very fetching Victorian marble fireplace for those who like such things, and a giant TV for those who don't. Real ales are well represented with the likes of Adnam's Best and Broadside, among others. Lunchtime food is of the order of mushroom strogonoff, spicy king prawns and calf's liver and spinach, priced mostly around £6. Local salary slaves make up the core of the clientele, but there's more than a smattering of local characters to differentiate this friendly and well-run pub from its neighbours.
Babies and children admitted. Digital TV. Function room. No-smoking area. Restaurant. Specialities: real ales. Vegetarian dishes.

Poet

82 Middlesex Street, E1 (020 7422 0000). Liverpool Street tube/rail. **Open** 11am-11pm Mon-Fri. **Food served** 11am-9pm Mon-Fri. **Credit** AmEx, DC, MC, V.
The purple signs outside with their Nickelodeon lettering have the misleading tagline: 'featuring Adnam's Ales', which the Poet may have done once – and may do again – but didn't on the two occasions we visited. Never mind, the Marston's Pedigree and Shepherd Neame Spitfire made for preferential substitutes. Not that many of the predominantly young drinkers gave a damn which real ales were on offer: they were having far too good a time of it on the bottled stuff and a globe-trotting array of red and white wines (most available by the glass) to worry about brewery politics. The Poet is one of a new chain of chic modern pubs where clean lines and light wood are king. It's a bit like a more canteeny version of a Fine Line or All Bar One. We like the Miro-esque London skyline wall art but otherwise there's little else to distinguish it. Food is taken seriously, and despite the fact that our first three choices were finished for the day (at 2.30pm), we enjoyed our sagey sausage, mash and onion gravy (£6.95), served in an unhealthily generous portion. Eager beaver service was another plus.
Bar area available for hire. Disabled: toilet. Satellite TV. Vegetarian dishes. **Map 6/R6**

Tsunami

1 St Katherine's Way, E1 (020 7488 4791). Tower Hill tube/Tower Gateway DLR. **Open** 11am-11pm Mon-Fri; 6-11pm Sat. **Food served** noon-3pm, 6-10pm Mon-Fri; 6-10pm Sat. **Credit** AmEx, MC, V.
Tsunami is Japanese for the tidal waves caused by underwater earthquakes. It's just a pity that the view from this particular Tsunami is of only the stone wall at the base of Tower Bridge. Still, it's spurred them on to make a special effort with the decor. You walk in past a picture of a tsunami on the wall – it looks good, as does the wave-shaped bar with turquoise and purple uplighting. The black-dressed servers are a very pleasant lot, and they know how to knock up a decent cocktail. The list (consulted on by cocktail know-all Dick Bradsell) runs to 80, including the 'cock-sucking cowboy' ('goes down like you know it should'). There's also an extensive range of flavoured vodkas and schnapps.
Babies and children admitted (lunchtimes). Disabled: toilet. Function room. Restaurant. Specialities: cocktails. Vegetarian dishes.

Also in the area...

Docks & Co (Davys) 66A Royal Mint Street, E1 (020 7488 4144).
Grapeshots (Davys) 2-3 Artillery Passage, E1 (020 7247 8215).
The Habit (Davys) 65 Crutched Friars, Friary Court, EC3 (020 7481 1137).
Half Moon (JD Wetherspoon) 213-233 Mile End Road, E1 (020 7790 6810).
Jamies Aldgate Barrs, Marsh Centre, 10 Whitechapel High Street, E1 (020 7265 1977).
Pitcher & Piano The Arches, 9 Crutched Friars, EC3 (020 7480 6818).
Poet 20 Creechurch Lane, EC3 (020 7623 2020).
Vineyard (Davys) International House, 1 St Katherine's Way, E1 (020 7480 6680).
Water Poet (Slug & Lettuce) 9 Stoney Lane, E1 (020 7626 4994).

Liverpool Street & Moorgate

Bolt Hole Bar

8A Artillery Passage, E1 (020 7247 5056). Liverpool Street tube/rail. **Open** 11am-9pm Mon-Fri. **Food served** 11am-5pm Mon-Fri. **Credit** AmEx, DC, MC, V.

London crawling: Morning brew

'Same again,' says the man to the bartender, handing his glass over the bar. The bartender nods, and slowly pours another pint of Guinness. The man pays, squeezes away from the crowded bar, takes his drink and returns to his friends, who sit drinking, chatting and smoking.

So far, so ordinary. The kind of scene played out in thousands of London pubs every day of the year. So much so, in fact, that we need to look at our watches just to confirm what our sleepy bodies are telling us. Sure enough, we're in the pub. And sure enough, it's 7.15 in the morning.

This isn't the result of a night out gone horribly wrong, either. Rather this is the **Cock Tavern** in Smithfield Market, an area of legendary elasticated boozing hours, where the first pint of the day is served at 5.30am to white-coated, hard-hatted meatpackers and master butchers. There's been a wholesale market on this site since Medieval times, when Smithfield was a convenient place outside the City for buying and slaughtering animals. The modern market kicks off at around 3am. By 7am or 8am, the action's over and the marketeers hit the pub. Deep in the bowels of the market, the Cock Tavern is their 'office watering hole'. Descend the stairs to a utilitarian two-room bunker filled with formica. Around tables with checkered cloths, men in porkpie hats and blood spattered aprons tuck into the 'Full Smithfield' of sausage, egg, bacon, beans, kidneys, black pudding and tomato (all for £5.10), washed down with a pint of Directors. It's not a pretty scene (like something out of a Peter Greenway film) but one every non-vegetarian should experience at least once.

On the south side of Smithfield, the **New Market** is another traders' favourite. It looks a little like an olde English tearoom with bow windows and darkwood tables set with knives and forks, but it's an entirely carnivorous kind of place. Served from 6.30am, it claims the 'Best Breakfast' in London, recognised as such by listeners of London Live.

Over the north side of the market, on Cowcross Street, the **Hope** makes a similar sort of claim to fry-up finesse, backed – or so their signboard says – by the *Sunday Times*. An attractive pub with a big bay frontage, the drinking goes on on the ground floor (with even a few market boozers sat out at pavement tables when we visited, watching commuters hurrying to work) with a dining room above. This was the only place we received a frosty reception; as we walked in the barman flicked his hand at us dismissively and said, 'Upstairs,' as though the option of a drink wasn't on the cards. We did get a pint of Young's Special out of him, but he'd clearly have preferred it if we'd had one of the big breakfasts (£7.50) to go with it.

The myth has always been that the Smithfield pubs have their early licences on agreement that they only serve market workers. That may once, long ago, have

been the case, but no more. Slumped in a seat with our fourth pint of the day (and still only 9.30am) at the charming Edwardian **Fox & Anchor**, arguably the most famous of the Smithfield pubs, we asked the affable manager what sort of percentage of dawn trade was market people and what not. 'Market trade?' he answered, 'You just missed him.' Apparently, there's just one bummaree and occasional colleagues that regularly drink at the Fox & Anchor; instead early morning custom (breakfast from 7am) is almost exclusively business suits and tourists. The pub even has a gay pride flag hanging outside and aims to attract a queer clientele.

Smithfield is a-changing. Push on to the next venue to see the direction in which it's headed. **Smiths of Smithfield** is an excellent new four-storey dining and drinking behemoth occupying a formerly derelict warehouse opposite the market. It doesn't have an early licence but it packs 'em in every morning (from 7am) anyway for great breakfasts, ranging from fry-ups to fruit to pancakes, accompanied by two-hander mugs of milky tea. It's a favourite with more youthful and creative types from the plentiful architects offices roundabout, including lots of women. Its sofas are a great place to slump and snooze if it isn't yet 11am. Once upon that magic hour, the choice is then limitless as Smithfield is home to a rapidly increasing variety of drinking options. How about Japanese beers at **Fluid** (*see p104*) or Trappist ales at **Abbaye** (*see p107*)? Then again, we know it's only midday, but bed might be a far better idea.

Cock Tavern (*no review*) East Poultry Avenue, Central markets, EC1 (020 7248 2918).
Fox & Anchor (*p107*) 115 Charterhouse Street, EC1 (020 7253 5075).
Hope (*p107*) 94 Cowcross Street, EC1 (020 7250 1442).
New Market (*no review*) 26 Smithfield Street, EC1 (020 7248 2464).
Smiths of Smithfield (*p110*) 67-77 Charterhouse Street, EC1 (020 7236 6666).

Hidden away in a characterful alley just off the Liverpool Street/Brick Lane rat-run, this is a classy bar with deep red walls and marble-topped tables visible to the street through a large picture window. There's room for around 25 people and on our midweek visit it had a full complement. Two couples were thirtysomething women executives and their toy boys, others were more evenly age-matched. There's a decent wine list, starting at a tenner a bottle. Beers come bottled, with the exception of a single tap lager. Connoisseurs will appreciate the robust selection of spirits, ports, madeiras and suchlike. Meals are of the soup of the day or Stilton and wild mushroom quiche variety.
Babies and children admitted. Vegetarian dishes.
Map 6/R5

City Limits
16-18 Brushfield Street, E1 (020 7377 9877). Liverpool Street tube/rail. **Open/food served** 11.30am-3pm, 5-11pm Mon-Fri. **Credit** AmEx, DC, MC, V.
Previously a banana wholesaler's within spitting distance of Spitalfields market, City Limits is one of the very few City wine bars that is still independently owned. Despite its belle epoque windows emblazoned with some nifty calligraphy, the small wooden bar and raised perching stools give the impression of a pub selling wine (which is no bad thing). The wine list is both large and lovingly assembled, with a slight leaning towards the French and more than its fair share of cult bottles. Six daily specials (three red and three white) are served by the glass. More affluent drinkers can splash out on more classic vintages. The atmosphere is pleasantly relaxed and there's a downstairs restaurant offering basic bistro fare such as steaks and veal escalope.
Babies and children admitted (restaurant). Function room. Restaurant. Satellite TV. Vegetarian dishes.
Map 5/R5

Dirty Dick's
202 Bishopsgate, EC2 (020 7283 5888). Liverpool Street tube/rail. **Open** 11am-10.30pm Mon-Fri. **Food served** noon-2.30pm Mon-Fri. **Credit** MC, V.
An iron grille drop gate hangs ominously over the entrance to this 19th-century bar with a particularly strange history. 'Dirty Dick' was the nickname of the wealthy ironmonger Nathaniel Bentley, whose fiancée fell ill and died tragically the night before their wedding. He locked up the dining room, wedding breakfast and all, and never washed it or himself again. After Bentley's death, however, a canny entrepreneur bought up his decrepit possessions for display in the newly named Dirty Dick's pub. Today, however, nearly all the grisly trappings have been dismantled, leaving behind little that is unusually maudlin. It's just a welcoming Young's pub with country-style bare brick walls and bare wood floors – oh, and some mummified cats.
Bar for hire. Games (fruit machine). No-smoking area. Restaurant. TV. Vegetarian dishes. **Map 6/R5**

Fleetwood Bar
36 Wilson Street, EC2 (020 7247 2242). Liverpool Street or Moorgate tube/rail. **Open** 11am-11pm Mon-Fri. **Food served** 11.30am-2.30pm, 5.30-9pm Mon-Fri. **Credit** AmEx, DC, MC, V.
A bar that manages to rise above its characterless location (the ground floor of the Broadgate Centre), hiding a funky retro '70s interior behind its drab frontage. Negative impressions are checked at the door by an unusual sunken bar area, subtle lighting and plenty of intimate seating. The place is Fuller's owned, meaning you can rely on their brews and standard fair pricing. It all makes for an appealing combination that draws a mix of students and creatives, rather than just the usual City boys.
Games (fruit machines, quiz machine). Satellite TV. Tables outdoors (pavement). Vegetarian dishes. **Map 5/Q5**

The Well. *See page 111.*

The George

Great Eastern Hotel, 40 Liverpool Street, EC2
(020 7618 7400/www.great-eastern-hotel.co.uk).
Liverpool Street tube/rail. **Open** 11am-11pm Mon-Fri;
noon-11pm Sat; noon-10.30pm Sun. **Food served** noon-
2.30pm, 6-10pm daily. **Credit** AmEx, DC, MC, V.
This Conran twist on the English pub experience is part of
the newly refurbished and extremely smart Great Eastern
Hotel. Consisting of two rooms, the larger is a period piece
with oak panelling from 1879, including an intricately carved
high ceiling. The smaller marigold and beige dining room is
less imposing but serves as a setting for some superb British
cuisine, along the lines of ham hock terrine (£4.50), braised
oxtail and parsnip mash (£8.75) and steamed lemon pudding
with spiced cherries (£4.25). Despite having the grander room,
drinkers get short shrift; choices on draught are a fairly
uninspiring line up of Kronenburg, John Smith's, Becks and
Guinness (the latter two both £2.95 a pint!). Poor show
Terence. The place is popular so it's best to go at lunch (try
and make it by noon if you want to dine) or early evening
since if you don't have a booking you'll be held by the
doormen who operate a 'one out, one in' policy after seven.
Vegetarian dishes. **Map 6/R6**

Hamilton Hall

Unit 32, Liverpool Street Station, EC2 (020 7247 3579).
Liverpool Street tube/rail. **Open** 11am-11pm Mon-Sat;
noon-10.30pm Sun. **Food served** 11am-10pm Mon-Sat;
noon-9.30pm Sun. **Credit** MC, V.
What was once the ballroom of the Great Eastern Hotel has
been turned into the most extravagant station pub in London
– although, unlike **The George** next door (*see above*) and
other parts of the Great Eastern Hotel, it is not Conran owned.
In fact, it's a JD Wetherspoon, and it combines the chain's
value for money ethic with cupids, ornate golden candelabra
and restored gilded stucco-work (although a fair few lovely
architectural features are clumsily covered by giant food and
drink menus). It's nearly always packed – commuters need
some solace during the rail delays – but ideally something
needs to be done to stop the annoying reverb.
Disabled: toilet. Games (card games, fruit machine).
No piped music or jukebox. No-smoking area. Tables
outdoors (pavement).Vegetarian dishes. **Map 6/R5**

Hogge's Bar & Brasserie

East India House, 109-117 Middlesex Street, E1
(020 7247 5050). Liverpool Street tube/rail. **Open**
10am-10pm Mon-Fri. **Food served** 11am-8pm Mon-Fri.
Credit AmEx, DC, MC, V.
This cavernous basement bar and brasserie is supposedly
modelled along Parisian lines. A long bar takes up part of one
wall and there are several separate eating and drinking areas,
some raised, others lurking behind half-walls. The combination
of a decent wine list, smartly laid tables and flickering candles
appeals to those who go out of their way to enjoy fine food and
wine. Pick of the wines are the 'specials' from France, which
range from £3.75 to £8 a glass (£13.95-£33 a bottle), and even
the bottom of the heap Chardonnay Rieu Frais 1996 is
magnificent. We were amused to see 'jerked' chicken on the
menu, but overall the food is bistro-style and good.
Babies and children admitted (until 4pm). Disabled:
lift, toilet. Restaurant. Vegetarian dishes. **Map 6/R5**

Jamies at the Pavilion

Finsbury Circus Gardens, EC2 (020 7628 8224).
Liverpool Street or Moorgate tube/rail. **Open** 11.30am-
10.30pm Mon-Fri. **Food served** noon-3pm, 6-9pm Mon-
Fri. **Credit** AmEx, MC, V.
One of the best-located Jamies bars, this was once a pavilion
for a bowling green, and its large windows still look out onto
the immaculate lawns of Finsbury Circus. Space has been
used to best advantage, with comfortable seating at different
levels, soft lighting and a restaurant squeezed below the
stairs. Staff here are so friendly and well informed that at first
we couldn't believe this was part of a chain. Punters were
noticeably affluent but the atmosphere seemed mellow
regardless. A glass of house white (South Australian
Chardonnay) was a fairly steep £3.30, but we loved the 'wine
flights'; tastings of four 71ml glasses of wines (£9.50), which
are connected by a theme or grape – say, New World
Sauvignon Blanc – after which you can then go for a full bottle
of the one you like best. Bar snacks include very good club
sandwiches or a plate of Neal's Yard incomparable English
and Irish farmhouse cheeses.
No piped music or jukebox. Restaurant. Vegetarian dishes.
Map 6/Q5

One of Two

45 Old Broad Street, EC2 (020 7588 4845/
www.fullers.co.uk). Liverpool Street tube/rail. **Open** 11am-
11pm Mon-Fri. **Food served** noon-10pm Mon-Wed; noon-
9pm Thur, Fri. **Credit** AmEx, DC, MC, V.
One of two visits, because the first time round we found it
impossible to squeeze into this thriving style bar. A full
sound system was playing music straight onto the
pavement and there was a true party atmosphere. The bar
itself is on the first floor of a beautifully designed, modern
little building, and has a galleried floor plus an elegant
outside terrace – lovely in the summer if you can ignore
the choking traffic on London Wall below. Inside the
spotlights are turned down low, there are smoochy corners
and a three-piece suite. Meals include the likes of sausage
and mash (£8.50), rib-eye steak (£10) and pan-fried red
snapper (£10) and beers are good (it's a Fuller's bar), but
sullen staff seem indifferent to your custom and drinks
prices are above average.
Babies and children admitted (daytime, restaurant only).
Function rooms. Restaurant. Tables outdoors (pavement).
Vegetarian dishes. **Map 6/Q6**

Public Life

82A Commercial Street, E1 (020 7375 2425
/www.publiclife.org). Aldgate East tube. **Open/food**
served noon-midnight daily. **Credit** MC, V.
Public Life is a converted underground public toilet right
next to Hawksmoor's Christ Church in Spitalfields, but
there's nothing spooky or dank going on and the running
water's all outside. Some original tiles and the round glass
bricks of the ceiling/pavement look the young architect-
designed part among the newly added concrete and
polypropolene chairs that establish the change of identity
to arty, edgy bunker-cum-bar. During the day Public Life
gets the locals connected if they bring their laptops along;
and there's tapas-style food, coffee, mags and books for
browsing, as well as boozing. By night the baggy trousers
are out and a turntable threatens a louder noise in the
small space later. If you're into the dot.com scene come on
down and you'll be among your own. Just don't expect
exceptional drinks.
Babies and children admitted. Music (DJs most nights).
Vegetarian dishes.

Railway Tavern

15 Liverpool Street, EC2 (020 7283 3598). Liverpool
Street tube/rail. **Open** 9am-11pm Mon-Fri; noon-3pm Sat.
Food served 11am-9pm Mon-Thur; 11am-3pm Fri.
Credit AmEx, DC, MC, V.

Apparently London has 18 Railway Taverns (four of them make it into this book). This one, opposite Liverpool Street Station, is probably one of the few still fully deserving of the name, serving as it does a clientele predominantly made up of people with trains to catch – big picture windows allow anxious commuters a good view of the station clock. It's big and Victorian, perhaps not maintained as well as it might be (the toilets are grim), but characterful with a warm atmosphere and interesting original features like a row of screened booths in the centre of the room. Unusually, what used to be an upstairs seating has been taken over by Pizza Hut – order at the bar and your food will be brought down.
Function rooms. Music (karaoke 7.30pm Fri) Restaurant. Satellite TV (big screen). Tables outdoors (pavement). Vegetarian dishes. Map 6/Q6

Twentyfour/Vertigo 42
Level 24, Tower 42, 25 Old Broad Street, EC2 (020 7877 2424). Bank tube/DLR/Liverpool Street tube/rail. **Open** 9am-11pm Mon-Fri. **Food served** noon-2pm, 6-9pm Mon-Fri. **Credit** AmEx, DC, MC, V.
As well as innumerable offices, Tower 42 (the immense skyscraper formerly known as the NatWest Tower) is home to two bars that complement alcoholic rushes with a thrilling touch of altitude. The imaginatively titled **Twentyfour** (on the 24th floor) is the lower of the two at 342ft. It's a smart but informal venue with comfy suede-covered pouffes and inviting easy chairs, and an extensive wine and cocktail menu that includes a killer Cosmopolitan (£7.50). The exceptional view is, of course, a major selling point – although even at this height the city panorama is not completely unobstructed. For the full Manhattan-style, cinematic experience you'll need to hop back into the lift and zoom up to **Vertigo 42**, the champagne and oyster bar, 600ft up on – where else – the 42nd floor. Vertigo is essentially a viewing platform, with added tables and chairs. Unimaginative, perhaps, but the spectacular view is more than enough to make up for that. Both bars are open to the public, but take note that if you want to have a drink in either you'll need, first, to make a bar reservation in advance and, second, to take a good few quid with you – they're not remotely cheap.
Disabled: toilet. Dress code. Function rooms. Restaurant. Vegetarian dishes. Map 6/Q6

Also in the area...
All Bar One 18-20 Appold Street, EC2 (020 7377 9671); 127 Finsbury Pavement, EC2 (020 7448 9921).
Balls Brothers 11 Blomfield Street, EC2 (020 7588 4643).
Bangers (Davys) 2-12 Wilson Street, EC2 (020 7377 6326).
Bishop of Norwich (Davys) 91-93 Moorgate, EC2 (020 7920 0857).
Bishops Parlour (Davys) upstairs at 91-93 Moorgate, EC2 (020 7588 2581).
Chez Gérard 64 Bishopsgate, EC2 (020 7588 1200).
City Boot (Davys) 7 Moorfields Highwalk, EC2 (020 7588 4766).
Corney & Barrow 19 Broadgate Circle, EC2 (020 7628 1251); 5 Exchange Square, Broadgate, EC2 (020 7628 4367).
Jamies 155 Bishopsgate, EC2 (020 7256 7279).
O'Neill's 31 Houndsditch, EC3 (020 7397 9841); 64 London Wall, EC2 (020 7786 9231).
Orangery (Jamies) Cutlers Gardens, 10 Devonshire Square, EC2 (020 7623 1377).

Pavilion (Jamies) Finsbury Circus Gardens, EC3 (020 7628 8224).
Pitcher & Piano 200 Bishopsgate, EC2 (020 7929 5914).

Shoreditch & Hoxton

Anda da Bridge
42-44 Kingsland Road, E2 (020 7684 1305). Old Street tube/rail. **Open** 11am-11pm Mon-Sat; noon-10.30pm Sun. **Food served** noon-10pm daily. **Credit** AmEx, MC, V.
Anda da Bridge is a great bar with a hint of the Caribbean, located under the bridge (where else?) on Kingsland Road. Its warehouse-like proportions have the familiar exposed beam and brick, but there's also a less usual lighting sculpture of back-lit plastic bottles, an assortment of inviting old sofas and chairs, and a ridiculously uncomfortable sack-cloth banquette. Punters have a broad choice of drinks, highlights being the cocktails and Hoegaarden on tap. The dining area serves Caribbean dishes at night, and tapas-style snacks during the day. From Thursday to Saturday DJs play an eclectic mix of music: reggae, soul, jazz and 'obscure', while on the other nights the music has included such classics as The Bellamy Brothers' 'Let Your Love Flow' and 'Who's Making Love' by Billie Jo Spears.
Disabled: toilet. Tables outdoors (pavement). Vegetarian dishes. Map 5/R3

Artillery Arms
102 Bunhill Row, EC1 (020 7253 4683). Old Street tube/rail. **Open** 11am-11pm Mon-Fri; noon-11pm Sat; noon-10.30pm Sun. **Food served** noon-3pm Mon-Fri. **Happy hour** 5-6pm daily. **Credit** AmEx, MC, V.
This cosy Fuller's pub sits opposite Bunhill Fields cemetery, the last resting place of Daniel Defoe, among others. The friendly bar staff serve a mixed bag of city workers and locals with good cheer and quality beer at reasonable prices: London Pride £2.10, Chiswick £1.70, ESB £2.25. At lunchtime hot and cold food is available, including two daily specials (one vegetarian). If you can play anything more complex than 'Chopsticks' you have the landlord's permission to entertain the punters on the pub piano, otherwise leave it to the CD player behind the bar. The upstairs function room is opened when the bar gets too busy and it can also be hired out for meetings or quiz nights.
Function room. Games (darts, fruit machine). Satellite TV. Tables outdoors (pavement). Vegetarian dishes. Map 5/P4

Barley Mow
127 Curtain Road, EC2 (020 7729 0347). Old Street tube/rail. **Open** 11am-midnight Mon-Sat; 1-10.30pm Sun. **Food served** 1-3pm, 6.30-10.30pm Tue-Sat; 1-5pm Sun. **Credit** MC, V.
The Barley Mow is the pub of choice for those who are tired of wrestling with the throng that now descends on the Bricklayer's Arms nightly. It's smaller and more intimate – carriage lamps provide the muted lighting – with a few wooden tables and chairs and a little dinette-style seating area at the rear. A discreetly trendy crowd of indeterminate age enjoys the good range on tap: Staropramen, Hoegaarden and Scrumpy, with real ales like Landlord, London Pride and Adnam's. Upstairs the restaurant is open in the evenings, though food and service are patchy. Staff really should have removed the strange drunken woman who pestered the pants off diners with unrequested singing and garrulous jokes on the night we were in.
Babies and children admitted (dining area only). Benches outdoors (pavement). Music (DJs occasional Fri, Sat; 6pm Sun.). Vegetarian dishes. Map 5/R4

Liquid Lab. *See page 132.*

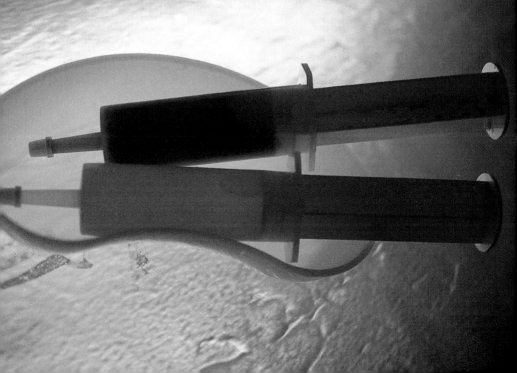

Bluu

1 Hoxton Square, N1 (020 7613 2793/www.bluu.co.uk).
Old Street tube/rail. **Open** 10am-11.30pm daily. **Food
served** 11am-10pm daily. **Credit** AmEx, DC, MC, V.
Bluu is the bar-restaurant that now occupies the sacred
space on the corner of Hoxton Square that was formerly
home to the Blue Note. And while nothing could never
replace BN, Bluu's actually quite good. If, that is, you're
after a '70s trip of a space in brown, burgundy and cream,
with corduroy bucket seating and leather sofas. The long
steel and concrete bar has a good stock of alcoholic drinks
as well as first-class coffee. 'Fuud' is pretty good, if a little
unimaginative, and includes the likes of bangers and mash
with red wine gravy for £6.95. Downstairs is smaller and
slightly dingier (perhaps in an attempt to recreate the
atmosphere of the Blue Note) with DJs playing club music
in the evenings.
*Disabled: toilet. Function room. Music (DJs Fri, Sat).
Vegetarian dishes.* **Map 5/R3**

Bricklayer's Arms

*63 Charlotte Road, EC2 (020 7739 5245). Old Street
tube/rail/26, 48, 55, 242 bus.* **Open** 11am-11pm
Mon-Sat; noon-10.30pm Sun. **Food served** noon-4pm,
6-11.30pm Mon-Fri; noon-11.30pm Sat; noon-9pm Sun.
Credit MC, V.
The Brickies is surely a happy victim of its own success.
Night after night it is standing room only as it packs out with
Hoxton groovers – some of them famous: Jarvis Cocker
dropped in recently for their regular pop quiz (he came in at
a fairly respectable third). The ground floor remains pretty
much shabbily unpretentious: wooden floors, a few
mismatching chairs and tables and a wonderful old mirror
behind the bar. The table football, however, has sadly been
usurped by a couple of decks and a fervent DJ. Upstairs is a
more stylish and sedate affair where a range of food, as well
as drinks, is served. The Thai menu has been replaced by
trendy pub grub: ground floor food includes sausages and
mash (£5), while upstairs there's rib eye steak with chips
(£11). As well as the usual beers and spirits, bitters include
London Pride, Webster's, Directors, Ruddles, John Smith's
and Landlord.
*Games (pinball machine). Jukebox. Music (DJs 8.30pm
Thur-Sun). Quiz (8pm Tue; £1 to play). Restaurant
(available for hire). Vegetarian dishes.* **Map 5/R4**

Cantaloupe

*35-42 Charlotte Road, EC2 (020 7613 4411/
www.cantaloupe.co.uk). Old Street tube/rail.* **Open/
food served** 11am-midnight Mon-Fri; noon-midnight
Sat; noon-11.30pm Sun. **Credit** MC, V.
The first rough-edged former warehouse to inject life into
Shoreditch's bar-restaurant scene still attracts a huge crowd
– an eclectic mix of city suits, locals and designers/graphic
artists who work nearby. There's a huge bar area at the front
with heavy beer-garden tables and benches; a small red-
hued sofa-strewn lounge area beyond; then a back bar with
stools. A screened-off restaurant serves top-quality
Mediterranean food, while tapas (meatballs, tortillas,
mushrooms, big chips with mayo) can be ordered in the bar.
Draught beers are a disappointing line-up of nitrokegs but
there's better in bottles, chalk boards list a decent array of
red and white wines, while cocktails are good and well
priced (£4.50 each). There's also absinthe but only three
shots will be served per person.
*Babies and children admitted (until 8pm, restaurant
only). Disabled: toilet. Music (DJs 8pm Fri, Sat).
Restaurant. Vegetarian dishes.* **Map 5/R4**

Cargo

*Kingsland Viaduct, 83 Rivington Street, EC2
(020 7613 1250/www.cargo-london.com).Old Street
tube/rail.* **Open/food served** noon-1am Mon-Fri;
6pm-1am Sat; noon-midnight Sun. **Admission** £3-£7
(depending on DJ/live act). **Credit** MC, V.
Nominated for the *Time Out* Best Bar Award in 2001,
Cargo is another huge success for the same people who
brought you the revolutonary **Cantaloupe** (*see above*). It's
a vast new venue devoted to 'MDF' (that's Music, Drink,
Food) within three refurbished railway arches. Exposed
brick and a minimalist decor characterise the spacious
lounge-bar, where short films are projected overhead. You
can go through a smaller arch into the club-like area where
top-class DJs, live music and Internet broadcasts keep
things hopping. Besides some great music, there's also a
good drinks list, decent cocktails, an appealing global
tapas menu and a restaurant. Arrive early if you're keen
to avoid queues.
*Disabled: toilet. Film projections. Music (DJs nightly).
Restaurant. Vegetarian dishes.* **Map 5/R4**

Charlie Wright's International Bar

*45 Pitfield Street, N1 (020 7490 8345). Old Street tube/
rail/26, 48, 55, 242 bus.* **Open** noon-1am Mon-Wed;
noon-2am Thur-Sun. **Admission** after 10pm Fri-Sun £3.
Food served noon-3pm, 6.30pm-midnight daily. **Credit**
DC, MC, V (bar only).
Charlie Wright's real name is John, but since he's an ex-power
lifter he can call himself whatever he likes. His bar has become
something of a local institution in that it retains a slightly
seedy image and attracts the old 'up-for-it' Hoxton crowd
looking for a late drink, while also being frequented by the
area's newer residents wishing to avoid all that tiresome
trendiness. The 'International' stems from the worldwide
selection of beers up for grabs: Belgian Leffe and Bangkok
Beer, for example. Food is Thai; staff are friendly; and the DJs
play the sort of irresistible cheese ('Vogue' by Madonna
anyone?) that will make you go for a shuffle on the always-
packed dancefloor, no matter how vertically challenged you're
feeling. Great fun.
*Babies and children admitted (until 7pm).
Games (fruit machine, pinball machine, pool table).
Music (DJs 8.30pm Thur-Sun). Restaurant. Satellite TV
(big screen). Vegetarian dishes.* **Map 5/Q3**

Cocomo

*323 Old Street, EC1 (020 7613 0315). Old Street
tube/rail.* **Open/food served** 10am-6pm Mon; 10am-
11pm Tue-Sun. **No credit cards.**
Since business partners and painters Natasha and Josie
opened the two-floor Cocomo at the end of 1999 it has gone
from strength to strength. In the tradition of Sunday Best,
the DJs follow a Balearic (eclectic) music policy, except on
Mondays when there's a Cuban drumming set. Slightly more
eccentric than some of its Hoxton bedfellows, the café/DJ bar
offers a slice of Moroccan style, juxtaposed with Chesterfield
sofas, '70s wallpaper, an old-school table football and lots
of fairy lights (they also sell lamps and cushions). Food
includes sandwiches, flat-bread pizzas, houmous and olives;
it's also worth having a rummage through the sweetshop at
the back of the bar. Bottled beers include Freedom (organic),
Budvar and Hoegaarden. With two new cocktail waiters
recently employed, they're planning on a smart cocktail
menu too.
*Babies and children admitted (daytime). Games (table
football). Music (DJs 7pm Tue-Sun). Specialities: frozen
cocktails. Vegetarian dishes.* **Map 5/R4**

Dragon

5 Leonard Street, EC2 (020 7490 7110). Old Street tube/rail. **Open** 11am-11pm Mon-Sat; noon-10.30pm Sun. **Credit** MC, V.

This unobtrusive little bar at the City Road end of Leonard Street has a New York loft-feel – albeit a small loft – to it: exposed brickwork, rough wooden floors, a number of battered old Chesterfield sofas and '70s-style leather pouffes. There's a real fireplace, an indoor fig tree and a resident cat called Ruby, who seemed pretty nonplussed hearing tracks by The Who during the day and – not surprisingly – disappears at night. That's when, despite its discreet location, the bar is heaving and the DJs crank the volume up to 11. The only disappointment with this otherwise fine bar was the poor decision to continue the NY-style theme by covering the toilets in graffiti. Anything which appears to support the pathetic rantings of the Sad Poet's Society is to be discouraged.
Babies and children admitted (until 6pm). Comedy (occasional Tue eve). Music (DJs 9pm Wed-Sat; band 8pm Sun). **Map 5/Q4**

Eagle

2 Shepherdess Walk, N1 (020 7553 7681). Old Street tube/rail. **Open** noon-11pm Mon-Fri. **Food served** noon-6pm Mon-Fri. **Happy hour** 7-9pm Fri. **Credit** DC, MC, V.

'Up and down the City Road/In and out the Eagle/That's the way the money goes/Pop goes the weasel': that's the greeting that adorns this attractive pub which was built on the site of a 19th-century music hall at the turn of the century. Weekdays its spacious bar – adorned with historic prints – attracts a mixed local crowd that's in for a quiet Bass (£2.30 for a pint, and a very reasonable £7.50 for four) or London Pride. Food, such as sandwiches and salads, is also available. Friday and Saturday nights, however, are quite a different prospect: the pub tends to get packed to the gills with a pre-clubbing crowd and the noise quotient rises accordingly.
Games (fruit machine, pool table, quiz machine). Tables outdoors (garden, pavement). TV. Vegetarian dishes.

Fox

28 Paul Street, EC2 (020 7729 5708). Old Street tube/rail. **Open/food served** noon-11pm Mon-Fri. **No credit cards.**

This wooden-floored traditional boozer reopened its doors at the end of 2000 and has been lovingly restored, making it a delightful contrast to the clubby bars in surrounding Hoxton. A rich dark-wood island bar forms the centrepiece, surrounded by bar stools and an assortment of wooden tables and chairs, with prints of foxes (among other subjects) adorning the walls. It currently caters to a post-work City crowd, and as such is closed at weekends. Beers include Wadworth 6X and Bombardier (both £2.20 a pint). We had good food on our last visit (bruschetta with minted cucumber and harissa, £5) and that's set to improve further as the upstairs room is going to become a restaurant run by the same team behind Farringdon Road's **Eagle** (*see above*).
Tables outdoors (terrace). Vegetarian dishes. **Map 5/Q4**

Great Eastern Dining Room

54-56 Great Eastern Street, EC2 (020 7613 4545). Old Street tube/rail. **Open/food served** noon-midnight Mon-Fri; 6.30pm-midnight Sat. **Credit** AmEx, DC, MC, V.

This former warehouse houses a bar-restaurant that's proved to be a dynamic force in Shoreditch. Although the title suggests the emphasis is on eating: it's equally (or more) popular as a pre-club hangout, especially as you only need

venture downstairs to find the eclectic short films and serious dance music of Below 54 (7.30pm-1am Thur-Sat). The ground floor bar area is bedecked by crystal chandeliers. There's also a strange glass aquarium with what looks like a mini gas fire inside (is it art?) and plenty of comfortable leather sofas and chairs to lounge in. A wide range of drinks includes draught Hoegaarden and Leffe Blonde (£2.20 a half pint) and a strong cocktail list (around £5). The restaurant area, meanwhile, serves impressive modern Italian cooking at reasonable prices (roasted crispy skin chicken, zucchini, lemon and herb frittelle is £9), albeit in a rather loud environment.
Babies and children admitted (restaurant). Function room. Music (DJs 7.30pm Thur-Sat). Restaurant. Vegetarian dishes. **Map 5/R4**

Griffin

93 Leonard Street, EC2 (020 7739 6719). Old Street tube/rail. **Open** 11am-11pm Mon-Fri. **Food served** noon-3pm Mon-Fri. **No credit cards.**

Though surrounded by some of Hoxton's most studied design bars (both Home and Dragon are a mere stroll away), the tatty and unaffected Griffin has been holding its own against the competition. Possibly the only bar in the area to still have carpet, let alone yellowed net curtains, the Griffin is a truly traditional pub serving cheap bitter (IPA is £1.50 a pint) and hearty pub grub at bargain prices: a roast chicken dinner with vegetables, or sausage toad, costs just £3.90. The crowd is mixed: from young to distinctly grizzled, but all keen on enjoying a relaxing drink or a quiet game of pool without the ubiquitous DJ that has invaded most bars in the area.
Babies and children admitted (until 7pm). Games (darts, fruit machines, pinball machine, pool table, video games). Jukebox. Tables outdoors (pavement). Vegetarian dishes. **Map 5/R4**

Herbal

12-14 Kingsland Road, E2 (020 7613 4462/ www.herbaluk.com). Old Street tube/rail. **Open/food served** 7.30pm-2am Tue-Sun. **Admission** £3-£5, depending on DJs. **No credit cards.**

The only giveaway that this unimposing venue exists is the doorman. Converted from an oak veneer warehouse, it is now a vision in steel and reclaimed wood that benefits from having had an entire floor removed to give the downstairs an airy feel. The dancefloor really 'goes off' at events like Groove Armada and Larger Than Life, while upstairs has a more intimate, lounging vibe, with wooden block seats and a huge wall-to-wall window giving it a distinct air of the East Village. From Thursday to Sunday DJs play a mix of dub, disco, hip hop, Latin flavours, house and electronica on a Turbo Sound system. Draught Leffe and Guinness, bottled Breezers and Scrumpy Jack as well as Source Icelandic vodka keep a relaxed and hip crowd happy.
Disabled: toilet. Music (DJs Tue-Sun). Vegetarian dishes. **Map 5/R3**

Home

100-106 Leonard Street, EC2 (020 7684 8618/ www.homebar.co.uk). Old Street tube/rail. **Open** 5pm-midnight Mon-Fri; 6pm-midnight Sat. **Food served** 12.30-3pm, 7-10pm Mon-Thur; 12.30-3pm, 7-11pm Fri; 7-11pm Sat. **Credit** AmEx, MC, V.

As one of the Shoreditch lounge chic originals, this basement bar may have been replicated throughout London but there's still no place quite like Home. The venue that coined staying in as the new going out bears a suitable resemblance to a lived-in living room. Decor is a mix of post- and pre-war furniture – there's even a sideboard just like granny had. A

DJ Bars

A decade ago DJ bars were pretty much unknown in London. Now there are dozens of them, clustered around Soho and Notting Hill, Sosho and Brixton, and dotted about everywhere else from Ealing to Aldgate East. Whether you call them club bars, dance bars or places where you can't bloody hear yourself think while you drink, DJ bars are where many of us get our nightlife kicks. At their best they combine the sociability and hassle-free culture of bars with the musical and technical standards associated with clubs: great DJs, leftfield grooves, upfront party beats or simply quirky tunes on a decent sound system.

The DJ bar revolution may have first happened three or four years ago, but the evolution is still rapid; Red Star in Camberwell and the White House in Clapham are recent additions. Each aims to combine fine dining with wining and dancing, pushing on a multi-tasking trend already seen at DJ Bars like AKA, the Social, Fluid, the Elbow Room and Monkey Chews. No wonder we like them – you rarely pay admission, and you can eat, drink and be merry to groovy tunes all in one place.

It was only when London boroughs became more liberal with their licences that DJ bars could flourish in the capital. DJ bars vary widely. Some are clubs which open far earlier than usual and don't charge at the start of the night, while others are basically boozers with later licences. Most are free – if not always necessarily easy – to get into. Bar culture has developed rapidly in recent years and the irony is that many West End bars are now far more exclusive than clubs. At certain places (none of which we list here) unless you're fabulously gorgeous and/or in a tabloid-friendly band you can forget it.

Admittedly, you're unlikely to hear Tongy or Julesy down your local DJ bar, but you can hear internationally famous mixers shaking the basslines while you shake your cocktail. No wonder DJ bars are spreading like a rash across the face of the capital: we've listed our 20 favourites below.

AKA (*p18*) 18 West Central Street, WC1 (020 7836 0110).
Bar Code (*p73*) 3-4 Archer Street, W1 (020 7734 3342).
Bar Vinyl (*p202*) 6 Inverness Street, NW1 (020 7681 7898).
Bug Bar (*p164*) The Crypt, St Matthew's Church, Brixton, SW2 (020 7738 3184).
Cocomo (*p128*) 323 Old Street, EC1 (020 7613 0315).

Dogstar (*p164*) 389 Coldharbour Lane, SW9 (020 7733 7515).
Dust (*p107*) 27 Clerkenwell Road, EC1 (020 7490 5120).
Elbow Room (*p219*) 89-91 Chapel Market, N1 (020 7278 3244); (*p99*) 103 Westbourne Grove, W2 (020 7221 5211).
Embassy Bar (*p221*) 119 Essex Road, N1 (020 7359 7882).
Fluid (*p107*) 40 Charterhouse Street, EC1 (020 7253 3444).
Fridge Bar (*p164*) 1 Town Hall Parade, Brixton Hill, SW2 (020 7326 5100).
Funky Munky (*p165*) 25 Camberwell Church Street, SE5 (020 7252 5222).
Herbal (*p128*) 12-14 Kingsland Road, E2 (020 7613 4462).
Medicine Bar (*p222*) 181 Upper Street, N1 (020 7704 9536).
Monkey Chews (*p208*) 2 Queen's Crescent, NW5 (020 7267 6406).
Red Star (*p167*) 319 Camberwell Road, SE5 (020 7703 7779).
Salmon & Compass (*p223*) 58 Penton Street, N1 (020 7837 3891).
The Social (*p43*) 5 Little Portland Street, W1 (020 7636 4992).
Soshomatch (*p132*) 2A Tabernacle Street, EC2 (020 7920 0701).
Vibe Bar (*p200*) The Brewery, 91-95 Brick Lane, E1 (020 7377 2899).

Soshomatch. *See page 132.*

sleek 80-seater dining area on the ground floor has good modern British and world fusion food. Home's fun and friendly atmosphere ensures that it's always busy, and the bar staff are heroic in their aims at keeping the punters happy. DJs play an eclectic musical mix every night. Look out for a revival of the 'Sunday at Home' traditional roast dinner followed by two classic film screenings.
Babies and children admitted. Function room. Music (DJs 10pm Wed-Sun; free). No-smoking area (restaurant). Restaurant. Vegetarian dishes. **Map 5/R4**

Hoxton Square Bar & Kitchen

2-4 Hoxton Square, N1 (020 7613 0709). Old Street tube/ rail/26, 48, 55, 242 bus. **Open** 11am-midnight Mon-Sat; noon-10.30pm Sun. **Food served** 12.30-3pm, 6.30-10.30pm Mon-Sat; 12.30-3pm, 6-9.30pm Sun. **Credit** MC, V.
HSBK looks well used and a tad shabby these days, but maybe that's intentional. The bar next to the Lux cinema and gallery retains its concrete bunker minimalist style, as well as the battered leather sofas covered in lounging artists, photographers and paper-reading locals, but the artworks that once adorned the walls have gone. Beers, wines and cocktails are all available, and good caffè latte is a reasonable £1.50. The bar menu stretches from sandwiches (£5.50) to pan-fried lemon with mash, courgette ribbons and anchovy butter (£8). However, HSBK only really comes into its own in the summer when punters spill out into Hoxton Square.
Babies and children admitted. Disabled: toilet. Tables outdoors (pavement). Vegetarian dishes (on request). **Map 5/R3**

Katabatic

89 Great Eastern Street, EC2 (020 7739 5173/ www.katabatic.co.uk). Old Street tube/rail. **Open** 11am-midnight Mon-Wed; 11am-2am Thur, Fri; 7pm-2am Sat. **Food served** 11am-10pm Mon-Sat. **Admission** after 10pm Fri, Sat £5. **Credit** AmEx, MC, V.
Nothing stays shut for long in Shoreditch, and with the closure of three-year-old Propaganda comes the opening (in the same premises) of Katabatic – apparently the name's a nautical term for 'downward flow of air'. It offers the pleasing, though rather predictable in Shoreditch at least, combination of bar/restaurant/club. The gleaming upstairs bar is fairly run-of-the-mill in a chrome and wooden sort of way, but downstairs the unusual layout, seating and imaginative lighting make a thoroughly appealing basement bar. The venue has a decent-sized capacity of just short of 500 and has hosted a few quality club nights, so we're hoping it will last longer than its predecessor.
Bar area available for hire. Disabled: toilet. Music (DJs Fri, Sat; salsa class Mon). Specialities: cocktails. Vegetarian dishes. **Map 5/Q4**

The Light

233 Shoreditch High Street, E1 (020 7247 8989/ www.thelightE1.com). Liverpool Street tube/rail. **Open/food served** (bar) noon-midnight Mon-Wed; noon-2am Thur, Fri; 6.30pm-2am Sat; noon-10.30pm Sun: (restaurant) noon-3pm, 6.30-11pm Mon-Fri; 6.30-11pm Sat; noon-10.30pm Sun. **Admission** Thur-Sat £2 (upstairs bar). **Credit** AmEx, DC, MC, V.
This former electricity generating station was shortlisted for the 2001 *Time Out* Best Bar Award. 'More Light More Power' is projected above the wall-length bar – playing on the name and former use of the building. The architectural update of the interior is sympathetic, enhancing space and light: exposed Victorian brick with original timberwork and a few bar stools and leather sofas dotted around the walls. An enormous industrial winch hangs from the rafters serving to remind the

mixed crowd of locals and postcode surfers of the venue's humbler origins. The ground floor bar sells bottled beers and the usual lagers – the only surprise being a Belgian lambic beer, the cherry-flavoured Belle-Vue Kriek (£2.60 a half pint) – and a wine list with around 50 bottles from Old World and New. The restaurant offers a short but accomplished menu (the same food can be ordered upstairs) with mouth-watering dishes like stew of beef and olives with bread (£5.50) or salt cod cakes with croutons, parsley and red onion dressing (£5.50). Upstairs there's a 'private' lounge bar: its main attractions being DJs and a small terrace with a view over the city.
Babies and children admitted (restaurant). Disabled: toilet. Music (DJs Thur-Sat). Restaurant. Tables outdoors (courtyard, lawn, roof terrace). Vegetarian dishes. **Map 5/R4**

Lime

1 Curtain Road, EC2 (020 7247 2225/www.limeuk.com). Liverpool Street or Old Street tube/rail. **Open** 11am-11pm Mon-Wed; 11am-1am Thur, Fri. **Food served** noon-11pm Mon-Fri. **Credit** AmEx, MC, V.
If rather like Hitchcock's Marnie you freak at the sight of the colour green, this two-level bar-restaurant is not the place for you. Nearly everything – right down to the transparent loo seats – is neat, minimalist and, of course, lime green. Positioned in the twilight zone between the City and Hoxton and currently surrounded by building works, suits visit by day but scuttle off at night to be replaced by studenty sorts. Cocktails (around £5) are given a greater emphasis than beer (just a few nitrokegs on draught) and we were impressed with our delicious Kir Royale (£6.50). There's a dining area in front of large picture windows and downstairs is a more relaxing space with comfortable chairs and less noise. Both the à la carte and the bar menus are brief, offering bistro-like fare (risotto, langoustine, etc) and snacks (olives with tapas and calamari) respectively.
Babies and children admitted. Disabled: toilet. Function rooms. Satellite TV. Vegetarian dishes. **Map 5/R5**

Liquid Lab

20 City Road, EC1 (020 7920 0372/www.liquidlab.co.uk) Old Street tube/rail. **Open/food served** 11am-11pm Mon-Fri. **Credit** AmEx, MC, V.
Bars don't come much cooler than this new medically-themed arrival at the Hoxton end of City Road. Blue-white cold clinical light shines on stark white paintwork, and the serving area looks remarkably like a shimmering slab of ice. Framed human x-rays pass for decor and there are two dentist's chairs. At the rear, near the ice-bar, a staircase climbs up to a dinky balcony and there's another smaller room downstairs aimed at diners (where tabletop salt and pepper shakers are test tubes). Drinks include a standard range of lagers and even a keg version of London Pride (not nice), but the emphasis is on wine (from £2.50 a glass) and cocktails with names such as Blood Clot, Test Tube Baby and Sperm Bank.
Disabled: toilet. Function room. Specialities: cocktails. Tables outdoors. Vegetarian dishes.

New Foundry

84-86 Great Eastern Street, EC2 (020 7739 6900). Old Street tube/rail. **Open** 4-11pm Tue-Fri; 2-11pm Sat; 4-10.30pm Sun. **No credit cards.**
This ex-bank is filled with battered old sofas, church pews and mismatching tables covered in candles in old wine bottles. Moving security cameras constantly scan the punters, displaying them on TV screens above the doors, while a large gallery space downstairs – in what was once the vaults – showcases contemporary photography and artworks. Most

nights experimental DJs spin their personal play lists, which might include anything from blue grass to electronica to cheese. Service is as quirky as the surroundings, but what the New Foundry lacks in slickness it makes up for with brews like Pitfield Organic on tap and Eco Warrior in bottles, and laid-back charm in spades. How many style bars let you take in your own chips? We bought ours from Franco's over the road. *Art galleries. Babies and children admitted (in separate area). Music (DJs 7pm Thur-Sat; free). Performances (live/art, ring for details). Poetry readings (8.30pm, fortnightly on Sun; free).* **Map 5/Q4**

Pool

104-108 Curtain Road, EC2 (020 7739 9608). Old Street tube/rail. **Open** noon-11pm Mon, Tue; noon-1am Wed, Thur; noon-2am Fri; 5.30pm-2am Sat; noon-10.30pm Sun. **Food served** noon-10.30pm Mon-Fri; 5.30-10.30pm Sat; noon-10pm Sun. **Credit** DC, MC, V.
The Pool is a two-floor romper room for big kids. Suits come out to play early on and louche locals later. Three American pool tables lurk amid the jumbo-sized beanbags that are strewn around the wooden ground floor. Plate glass windows mean you're in full view of the passing commuter traffic – miss an easy pot and you'll have passengers on the 149 laughing all the way to Dalston. Downstairs in the basement bar, where the seating includes strange orange plastic blob-like chairs, well-known DJs turn the place into a complete party. Both bars serve average beers (Hoegaarden is the best on tap) and spirits (including vodka shots and shooters). Decent snacks are available, and there is a tabled area for mains such as ravioli stuffed with squash, ricotta herb butter and toasted walnuts (£6.50).
Babies and children admitted (until 5pm). Bar area available for hire. Games (American pool tables). Music (DJs 8pm Wed-Sat; 2pm Sun). Restaurant. Vegetarian dishes. **Map 5/R4**

Reliance

336 Old Street, EC1 (020 7729 6888). Old Street tube/rail/26, 48, 55, 242 bus. **Open** noon-11pm Mon-Thur; noon-2am Fri; 6pm-2am Sat. **Food served** noon-3pm, 7-10.30pm Mon-Fri. **Admission** after 11pm Fri, Sat £2. **Credit** AmEx, DC, MC, V.
Some of the Reliance's interior features are the product of the creative use of an old barge, while the part-brickwork decor edges towards mock-Tudor. Early evening midweek is a fine time to enjoy its delights with a few of the local residents or nearby workers. Weekends are quite a different matter, as guest DJs crank it up for the pre-club punters and out-of-towners on a Friday and Saturday night. Still, bar staff are friendly and there's a reasonable range of drinks. Upstairs is a very respectable restaurant (which can also be hired out) serving excellent gastro grub. Booking for the restaurant is essential.
Babies and children admitted (restaurant). Function room. Jukebox. Music (DJs 10.30pm Fri, Sat). Restaurant. Tables outdoors (balcony). Vegetarian dishes. **Map 5/R4**

Shoreditch Electricity Showrooms

39A Hoxton Square, N1 (020 7739 6934). Old Street tube/rail/26, 48, 55, 242 bus. **Open** noon-11pm Tue, Wed; noon-midnight Thur; noon-1am Fri, Sat; noon-10.30pm Sun. **Food served** 1-4pm, 7-10.15pm Tue-Sat; 1-5pm Sun. **Credit** MC, V.
At the Leccy Showrooms hip-kitsch (love the giant zebra picture) is proving as popular as ever – whether for coffee and a scan of the Sundays or for a pose and a pre-club drink. We're also impressed that the large plate windows have been

covered in a special red-tinted material that keeps prying eyes away, but still allows punters to look out. Friendly bar staff serve a wide range of drinks including draught Kirin and Anchorsteam (both pricey at £3.10 a pint). There is a short cocktail menu, an extensive wine list (with nine by the glass), and a regularly changing menu (fish pie with baby red chard and caperberries £7.50). DJs play downstairs to a packed house on Fridays and Saturdays.
Babies and children admitted (until 7pm). Disabled: toilet. Film projections. Function room. Music (DJs Fri, Sat). Restaurant. TV. Vegetarian dishes. **Map 5/R3**

Soshomatch

2A Tabernacle Street, EC2 (020 7920 0701/ www.matchbar.com). Old Street tube/rail. **Open** 11.30am-midnight Mon-Wed; 11.30am-2am Thur, Fri; 6pm-2am Sat. **Food served** 11.30am-10.30pm Mon-Wed; 11.30am-11.30pm Thur, Fri; 6-11.30pm Sat. **Admission** after 10pm Fri £5; after 9pm Sat £5. **Credit** AmEx, MC, V.
Soshomatch (Sosho=South of Shoreditch – geddit?) is part of the mini Match chain (shortlisted for the *Time Out* Best Bar award in both 1999 and 2000) and has itself been shortlisted for the 2001 award. Sosho has the same ingredients as its two sister bars: cocktail supervision by Dick Bradsell, good food (fine Mediterranean cuisine like herb roasted sea bass, £12) and reasonable prices. The ground floor is roomy and airy, while downstairs is tiny and cosy. The right names abound: resident DJ Kevin Beadle is joined by such luminaries as Bob Jones or Ross Allen filling the dancefloor with jazzy, Latin and Brazilian tunes; while Antonia Andrasi, one of London's cocktail stars (formerly of Six Degrees), is head bartender. The management is already planning Match 4.
Babies and children admitted. Disabled: toilet. Function room. Music (DJs Wed-Sat). Specialities: cocktails. Vegetarian dishes. **Map 5/Q4**

Wenlock Arms

26 Wenlock Road, N1 (020 7608 3406). Old Street tube/rail. **Open/food served** noon-11pm Mon-Sat; noon-10.30pm Sun. **No credit cards.**
A little off the beaten track, perhaps, but well worth the trek. The Wenlock Arms (established in 1835) was voted north London CAMRA Pub of the Year 2000-2001 and is also the recipient of the Cask Marque 'for excellence in the serving of cask ales'. There are usually eight real ales on at any one time, plus one mild and a cider. You'll nearly always find Adnam's bitter at £1.80, and Crouch Vale Mild for £1.70. The place has a slightly grizzled look (that applies to most of the punters too) but it's certainly friendly and entertaining. Jazz is a weekend feature, while on Tuesdays one of the three resident darts teams plays the Portuguese team from nearby Ponti's sandwich bar, and they are all are treated to pizza slices and turkey rolls (the standard pub grub stretches to the likes of pasties and black-pudding sandwiches).
Function room. Games (darts). Music (jazz 9pm Fri; 3pm Sun; jazz blues 8.30pm Sat). Quiz (9pm Thur; £1 to play). Satellite TV. Vegetarian dishes.

Also in the area...
Colonel Jaspers (Davys) 190 City Road, EC1 (020 7608 0926).
Heeltap & Bumper (Davys) 2 Paul Street, EC2 (020 7375 3203).
Masque Haunt (JD Wetherspoon) 168-172 Old Street, EC1 (020 7251 4195).
Pulpit (Davys) 63 Worship Street, EC2 (020 7377 1574).

West

Barnes & Mortlake

Bull's Head

*373 Lonsdale Road, Barnes, SW13 (020 8876 5241/
www.thebullshead.com). Hammersmith tube/Barnes Bridge
rail/209 bus.* **Open** 11am-11pm daily. **Food served** noon-
2.30pm, 6-10.30pm daily. **Admission** nightly £5-£10.
Credit AmEx, MC, V.

A fixture on the London jazz scene since 1959 (although the
pub dates back to 1845), the Bull's Head is more Humphrey
Lyttleton than Wynton Marsalis. Strictly trad. A large
central bar and high ceiling create a comfortable, if slightly
stark space, with the only relief a back wall covered in
concert posters and pics of past performers. Despite being
next to the river, there's no view to speak of courtesy of an
obstructing concrete parapet. It serves good Young's ales
and has an extensive wine list. Substantial English fare is
offered during the day and the Stable Bistro in the
courtyard out back does Thai food in the evenings. The
clientele leans toward middle-aged jazz fans drawn by the
gigs (held in a back room) that still take place every night
of the week, with a double dose on Sundays, but the place
is rarely crowded.

*Babies and children admitted (until 8pm). Function
room. Music (live jazz, blues nightly). Restaurant.
Tables outdoors (patio). Vegetarian dishes.*

Coach & Horses

*27 Barnes High Street, SW13 (020 8876 2695).
Hammersmith tube/Barnes Bridge rail.* **Open** 11am-11pm
Mon-Sat; noon-10.30pm Sun. **Food served** noon-2.30pm
daily. **Credit** MC, V.

Tucked away off Barnes' high street, the Coach, as the name
would suggest, is an old coaching inn, with a history going
back to the beginning of the 19th century. It has a grand
Victorian serving area with oak casks built into its fascia.
More wooden casks do service as seating, ranged around
the edges of the room. On our last visit we encountered
what seemed to be a Masonic night out – they probably
appreciate the pub's slightly concealed entrance, the
impenetrable leaded windows and the collection of quirky
props that decorate the place. We, on the other hand, like
the well kept Young's. We also love this place in summer
for its narrow, family-friendly courtyard garden with
benches under ivy-trailing hanging baskets and a children's
play area beyond. When the weather permits, excellent
barbecued meals are available.

*Babies and children admitted (family area, outdoor
climbing frame). Function room. No piped music or
jukebox. Satellite TV. Tables outdoors (heated patio
and garden). Vegetarian dishes.*

Ship

Ship Lane, SW14 (020 8876 1439). Mortlake rail. **Open**
11am-11pm Mon-Sat; noon-10.30pm Sun. **Food served**
noon-3pm, 6-9.30pm daily. **Credit** AmEx, DC, MC, V.

Not as well known as riverside pubs in nearby Barnes
(particularly **Ye White Hart**), the Ship gets its trade from
Mortlake residents and weekend strollers along the Thames.
The gleaming, white-fronted Victorian building enlivens
what is actually a dull stretch of water – although it's
somewhat overshadowed by the looming Budweiser brewery
next door. Recent expansion has seen the addition of a
garishly painted conservatory and an enlarged back room
decorated with watery props. Once a year the pub really
comes into its own as the finish line of the annual Oxford-
Cambridge Boat Race. Hordes of semi-interested punters fill
the place to bursting and then stumble out onto the river bank,

plastic pint pot in hand, to see the invariably anticlimactic
climax. At other times of year Sunday roasts and a friendly
family atmosphere offer hearty relief for weekend walkers.
*Babies and children admitted (until 7.30pm). Bar area for
hire. Quiz (9pm every second Tue of month). Satellite TV.
Tables outdoors (garden). Vegetarian dishes.*

Sun Inn

*7 Church Road, SW13 (020 8876 5256). Barnes or Barnes
Bridge rail/209, 283 bus.* **Open** 11am-11pm Mon-Sat; noon-
10.30pm Sun. **Food served** noon-2.45pm, 6-10pm Mon-Sat,
noon-4pm Sun. **Credit** AmEx, DC, MC, V.

Barnes' most lively and welcoming (as long as you're over 21)
pub has a great location on the green. Although a bit ragged
round the edges from wear, it's a pretty Georgian building
with an old-fashioned bowling green round the back where
Elizabeth I was reputedly taught to play bowls. A
labyrinthine, low-ceilinged interior harbours plenty of dark,
private recesses and nooks, but it also amplifies the lager-
fuelled commotion of the students who favour the large back
room. For quiet, venture out onto the front patio overlooking
the duck pond; great for balmy summer evenings, it's also a
fine spot in winter if the management has remembered to turn
the heat lamps on.

*Games (fruit machines). Music (live covers duo 9pm Tue).
No-smoking area. Satellite TV. Tables outdoors (heated
patio). Vegetarian dishes.*

Ye White Hart

*The Terrace, Riverside, Barnes, SW13 (020 8876 5177).
Barnes Bridge rail/209 bus.* **Open** 11am-3pm, 5.30-11pm
Mon-Thur; 11am-11pm Fri, Sat; noon-10.30pm Sun. **Food
served** 12.30-2.30pm, 6.30-10pm daily. **Credit** MC, V.

Right on the river (so close that the outside tables sometimes
get washed by high tides), Ye White Hart is both huge and
hugely popular. A capacious single-room place, its
impressively high ceiling accommodates large windows
overlooking the Thames. The size can mean that it's
sometimes a little lacking in atmosphere (especially on
overcast days) but in summer it comes into its own with prime
seating on the terrace and at those picnic tables on the river
bank. It has an award-winning wine list (Young's wine pub
of the year 1999 and 2000) and excellent Young's ales. It also
offers plenty of decent if unenterprising pub food – Sunday
roasts are especially popular.

*Function room. Games (fruit machine). No piped music
or jukebox. Satellite TV. Tables outdoors (patio, riverside
terrace, towpath). Vegetarian dishes.*

Also in the area...

Café Rouge 248 Upper Richmond Road, SW14
(020 8878 8897).

Chiswick & Kew

Bull's Head

*15 Strand on the Green, W4 (020 8994 1204).
Gunnersbury tube/rail/Kew Bridge rail.* **Open** 11am-11pm
Mon-Sat; noon-10.30pm Sun. **Food served** noon-3.30pm,
6.30-9.30pm daily. **Credit** AmEx, DC, MC, V.

The faded glory of this boozer might be interpreted by some
as endearingly authentic but the reality is that the Bull's
Head is in need of some TLC. It's been battling the damp of
the adjacent Thames for 300 years and are we imagining it
or does the place now have a pronounced lean towards the
river? Of the three riverside pubs in Strand on the Green
this remains our favourite. On our last visit a good part of

the pub's charm for the local bar flies seemed to centre on the girl behind the bar, but we've always liked the place for its mishmash of timber-beamed, butterscotch-painted rooms, and the raised nook at the back – an appealing hideaway with fine Thames views. Beers are well kept and included on our last visit Courage's Directors, Theakston's Best and Wadworth 6X. As with many of the old pubs round here, this one has historical associations: during the Civil War, Oliver Cromwell is said to have escaped Royalist pursuers through a secret tunnel from the pub to Oliver's Island, in midstream.

Babies and children admitted (conservatory). Function room. Games (darts, fruit machines). Satellite TV. Tables outdoors (riverside terrace). Vegetarian dishes.

City Barge
27 Strand on the Green, W4 (020 8994 2148). Gunnersbury tube/rail/Kew Bridge rail. **Open/food served** 11am-11pm Mon-Sat; noon-10.30pm Sun. **Credit** AmEx, DC, MC, V.
Not a barge at all but a riverside boozer, and an old one at that: founded 1484. In the 19th century the Lord Mayor's state barge used to be moored outside for the winter, hence the name. It's divided into two: a spacious reconditioned upper bar replete with river-related props and conservatory, and downstairs the original dark, low-beamed bar with two fireplaces and original warped-pine furniture. Regulars tend to nab the few tables early on and stay put. Entrance from the towpath is through two huge metal doors, a necessity of the area when the tide rises and it is time to batten down the hatches. Oddly, scenes from the Beatles' movie *Help!* were shot here.

Babies and children admitted (restaurant). Games (bar billiards). Music (live jazz 8pm Thur). No-smoking area (conservatory). Restaurant. Tables outdoors (riverside terrace). Vegetarian dishes.

Greyhound
82 Kew Green, Middx (020 8940 0071). Kew Gardens tube/rail. **Open** 11.30am-11pm Mon-Sat; noon-10.30pm Sun. **Food served** 6.30-10pm Thur-Sat (upstairs restaurant), *bar food* noon-3pm, 6.30-9.30pm Mon-Sat; noon-3pm Sun. **Credit** AmEx, DC, MC, V.
Transformed from a soul-sapping old codgers' pub into a bright and airy bar, the Greyhound was greeted as a breath of fresh air by Kewites when it opened a few years ago. The renovators retained the cutesy mock-Tudor front, which looks onto the smaller side of Kew Green and pond, but the interior was completely done over – bar some old wood panelling – with bright colours, new flooring and some voluminous leather sofas. Since then it's been the place that the area's thirtysomethings come to offload a bit of their disposable income on a pretty decent wine list. Of late they've been joined by rogue bitter drinkers (making do with Abbot) in exile from the Coach & Horses across the green, currently closed for renovation. There's an upstairs restaurant (open Thursday to Saturday only) with a weekly changing menu and great views over the Green, and an attractive walled garden, although when we last visited it was in the process of being made over by some sort of 'Ground Force' team.

Babies and children admitted. Function room. Games (backgammon, cribbage). No-smoking area (restaurant). Tables outdoors (garden, pavement). Vegetarian dishes.

Mawson Arms
110 Chiswick Lane South, W4 (020 8994 2936). Turnham Green tube. **Open** 11am-8pm Mon-Fri. **Food served** noon-3pm Mon-Fri. **Credit** MC, V.

Nice pub, shame about the location. It may only be a few hundred yards from the river but it's also miles from the nearest tube or train, right next to the thunderous traffic of the A4. Not a place for a quiet drink then. And note that early closing time. The reason for this pub's existence looms next door in the shape of Fuller's Griffin Brewery. The Mawson acts as a 'tap' for all Fuller's fine brews, and a fresher pint of ESB or Chiswick Bitter you will not find. We were half hoping to see a mass of umbilical shiny copper pipes mainlining beer direct into the pub, but were disappointed to discover the publican changing barrels. Pleasingly though, it does eschew the cod-Victoriana and headache-inducing carpets favoured by Fuller's, and is instead done out with green and cream walls, bare floorboards and leather sofas.

Babies and children admitted. Function room. Games (darts). No-smoking area. Restaurant. Vegetarian dishes.

Also in the area...
All Bar One 197-199 Chiswick High Road, W4 (020 8987 8211).
Café Rouge 227-229 Chiswick High Road, W4 (020 8742 7447); 85 Strand on the Green, W4 (020 8995 6575).
Pitcher & Piano 18-20 Chiswick High Road, W4 (020 8742 7731).
Rat & Parrot 122 Chiswick High Road, W4 (020 8995 4392).

Ealing

Barracuda
8 The Mall, W5 (020 8579 8632). Ealing Broadway tube/rail. **Open/food served** noon-2pm, 6-11pm Mon-Thur; noon-2pm, 6pm-2am Fri, Sat. **Credit** AmEx, DC, MC, V.
Formerly the dingy Bar Rendezvous, since opening in mid-2000 Barracuda has proved itself as one of the more pleasant venues on Ealing Broadway. Bright and modern, it's pleasingly decorated in aqua tones with a mosaic-clad bar, luscious sofas and comfy high-backed chairs. During the day Barracuda operates as a café, but it really comes into its own in the evening when the coffee-drinkers clear the way for patrons possibly looking for a bigger hit than caffeine. Week nights are enjoyably buzzy with friendly service and '70s and '80s sounds, and quite a few non-clubby types dropping in for an after-work pint. Weekends it gets more hardcore and hectic with a crowd dressed for a night out.

Function room. Music (DJs Fri, Sat). Restaurant. Tables outdoors (pavement). Vegetarian dishes.

Baroque
94 Uxbridge Road, W13 (020 8567 7346/ www.baroque-ealing.co.uk). West Ealing rail. **Open** noon-11pm Mon-Sat; noon-10.30pm Sun. **Food served** noon-3pm Mon-Fri; noon-5pm Sat, Sun. **Credit** MC, V.
Don't be put off by an unfortunate location between the Jobcentre and a aged department store, nor by the tacky 'graffiti' sign – Baroque is stylish and fun and an absolute godsend for West Ealing. The place would obviously much rather be in Soho; raspberry pink walls and cream leather-cushioned booths exhibit ambitions towards Dean Street. We like the huge photo-mural of New York hanging on the back wall, too. It's the kind of place where they'd rather you drank spirits and cocktails (the list of the latter is quite good), which is just as well because the range of draught and bottled beers is unexceptional. Food is light bites: interesting soups and salads, wraps, a handful of pastas and

risotto. In contrast to the mellow weeknight-punters, prepare to take on a more dressed-up crowd at the weekend. Even then, it's not so heaving that it's uncomfortable. The chicness of Soho without the squeeze.

Function room. Internet kiosk. Music (jazz band 7pm first Sun of month). Tables outdoors (garden, courtyard). Vegetarian dishes.

Drayton Court
2 The Avenue, W13 (020 8997 1019/www.fullers.co.uk). *West Ealing rail.* **Open** 11am-11pm Mon-Sat; noon-10.30pm Sun. **Food served** noon-3pm, 5.30-9pm Mon-Fri; noon-9pm Sat; noon-6pm Sun. **Credit** MC, V.
Classic Ealing, the Drayton is a vast late-Victorian edifice, all gables and turrets on the outside and a series of congenial spaces within for the clued-up of W13 to relax. The main split-level bar is full of chat and cheap Fuller's ales (Chiswick £1.49 a pint!), while the Coffee Room has an idiosyncratic mix of Pre-Raphaelite prints and a large-screen TV for sports. A pool room also inhabits the ground floor, while downstairs the Court Room is home to fringe theatre. A wrought-iron terrace and large well-landscaped garden provide outdoor seating. There is regular live music in the main bar (the Drayton is also a venue for the annual Ealing Jazz Festival) and internet access is available in the saloon.
Babies and children admitted (family room, playground). Disabled: toilet. Function rooms. Games (board games, fruit machines, pool room). Music (jazz first and last Wed of month). Quiz (8.30pm Sun; £1 to play). Satellite TV (big screen). Tables outdoors (patio, garden). Theatre (Mon-Thur eves & Sun matinee). Vegetarian dishes.

Grange Tavern
Warwick Road, W5 (020 8567 7617). South Ealing tube. **Open/food served** 11am-11pm Mon-Sat; noon-10.30pm Sun. **Credit** AmEx, DC, MC, V.
Traditional locals' local in a quiet residential area overlooking Ealing Common. A large place but split levels, a roaring open fire, comfortable sofas and lots of weathered wood – floors, tables and benches – make for a cosy feel, much appreciated by the several family groups present on our last visit. In the summer, the action moves outside to a small beer garden, where – weather-permitting – staff get the meat sizzling on the barbie each Wednesday evening and Sunday. Other times, the home-cooked food served canteen-style in the back room is excellent.
Babies and children admitted (until 9pm). Function room. Games (board games, darts, fruit machine, table football). Music (live occasionally Sun eve, winter only). Satellite TV. Vegetarian dishes.

Red Lion
13 St Mary's Road, W5 (020 8567 2541). South Ealing tube. **Open** 11am-11pm Mon-Sat; noon-10.30pm Sun. **Food served** noon-2.30pm, 6-9pm daily. **Credit** MC, V.
Its nickname 'Stage Six' (there were five sound stages at the nearby Ealing Studios) derives from when the likes of Jack Warner, Dennis Price and latterly Little and Large inhabited the Red Lion between takes. It hasn't changed much over the years: a small L-shaped single room arranged around a chunky wooden serving area, polished timber floor, green upholstered banquettes, sand-coloured walls studded with pictures of famous (and forgotten) Ealing protagonists. There are no fruit machines, no canned music, and being a Fuller's pub, there are no complaints about the beer, either. The semi-enclosed garden out back has won awards and is well worth a gander.
No piped music or jukebox. Quiz (9pm Mon; £1 to play). Tables outdoors (garden). Vegetarian dishes.

Also in the area...
All Bar One 64-65 The Mall, Ealing Broadway, W5 (020 8280 9611).
Café Rouge 17 The Green, W5 (020 8579 2788).
Edward's 28-30 New Broadway, W5 (020 8567 9438).
Rat & Parrot 23 High Street, W5 (020 8567 3228).

Fulham & Parsons Green

Atlas
16 Seagrave Road, SW6 (020 7385 9129). West Brompton tube. **Open** noon-11pm Mon-Sat; noon-10.30pm Sun. **Food served** 12.30-3pm, 7-10.30pm Mon-Sat; noon-3pm, 7-10pm Sun. **Credit** DC, MC, V.
A first-class foodie pub, where the moment you step through the door you know you've made a good decision. The quality of the wood lining the bar, the real flame fires, the old tiles, the atmospheric black-and-white photographs on the wall, the unobtrusive Latin jazz soundtrack and the friendly welcome offered by the staff – all make for an appealingly comfortable atmosphere. The Mediterranean menu also delivers – we dined on excellent grilled baby mackerel with sautéed potatoes and green beans à la fiorentina. It's perfectly acceptable to drink without eating; there's a wide choice of wines with around ten available by the glass, and Charles Wells' Bombardier and Fuller's London Pride on draught. Come in summer for the added bonus of a lovely garden with outside seating.
Babies and children admitted (until 7pm). Function rooms. Tables outdoors (heated courtyard). Vegetarian dishes.

Bar 246
246 Fulham Road, SW10 (020 7823 3011/ www.bar246.com). Fulham Broadway or South Kensington tube. **Open** noon-11pm Mon-Sat; noon-10.30pm Sun. **Food served** noon-2.30pm, 5-9pm Tue-Fri; noon-5pm Sun. **Happy hour** 5.30-6.30pm daily. **Credit** MC, V.
Sofas, fireplaces and lounge music made us wonder why this bar ever changed its name from Front Room. A well-timed happy hour attracts the well-heeled for cheeky after-work drinks and weekend nights the place can be bustling, but it's never quite as busy as the Fine Line a few doors down. Which is a shame. As well as standard beers, there's a substantial wine list, vegetarian food and even a selection of cigars, but our cocktails were disappointingly amateurish. In truth, despite all the home comforts, 246 doesn't feel quite complete and suffers from a lack of character. All the same, for a few quiet drinks it's got to be an improvement over a chain pub.
TV. Vegetarian dishes.

Bardo
196-198 Fulham Road, SW10 (020 7351 1711). West Kensington tube/14 bus. **Open/food served** 5pm-midnight Mon-Thur; 5pm-1am Fri; noon-1am Sat; 5-11pm Sun. **Credit** AmEx, MC, V.
With a pick 'n' mix smattering of Asian features (Japanese-style pebble dash, a Buddha in an alcove) and a pan-Asian menu (sushi-boxes, spring rolls), Bardo gives a rather muddled nod to the Eastern aesthetic. The minimalist ethic extends to a mean allocation of seating, so come early or stand. If you can snag it, a tiny rear alcove with a welcoming pinky-red glow is ideal for small groups. Champagne dominates the drinks list (cocktails £6, bottles from £29 to £130), most of which is pretty pricey (£6 for a vodka Martini). But with smooth table service and high-quality drinks, Bardo is a cut above. More like a private club than cosy local, this

is a good place to splash out if you have something to celebrate – a pay rise perhaps.
Function room. Games (backgammon). Specialities: cocktails. Vegetarian dishes.

Eclipse Lounge
108-110 New King's Road, SW6 (020 7731 2142/ www.bareclipse.com). Parsons Green tube. **Open** noon-11pm Mon-Sat; noon-10.30pm Sun. **Food served** noon-3pm, 6-9.30pm daily. **Credit** AmEx, MC, V.
Formerly Mixology this venue has now been acquired by the Eclipse chain (who also run **Eclipse** in South Ken, *see p87*). Deep red walls, spotlights and arty photography make for a classy and eye-catching look. It's popular for after-office drinks, when cheerful house acts as a post-work pick up, but the music's not so loud as to preclude conversation. Smartly arranged newspapers and snazzy silver trays hint at exclusivity, but our warm flat mixer was supremely underwhelming. Even so, the place's lively and stylish and we'd go back, if not out of our way.
Satellite TV (big screen). Tables outdoors (pavement). Vegetarian dishes.

Eight Bells
89 Fulham High Street, SW6 (020 7736 6307). Putney Bridge tube. **Open** 11am-11pm Mon-Sat; noon-10.30pm Sun. **Food served** noon-2.30pm, 6-8pm daily. **No credit cards.**
At the quiet end of Fulham High Street on the north side of Putney Bridge this is a small, snug place kitted out with high-backed wooden benches, antiquey furnishings and a multicoloured patterned carpet. It's a pub-lovers pub. Locals watch the footie on two wall-mounted televisions – although on our visit they were straining to catch the commentary over MOR music on the sound system – and all seem to be on first-name terms with the landlord and staff. Draught ales include Shepheard Neame Spitfire, and the kitchen turns out traditional, hearty pub fare of the likes of cottage pie and steak and chips.
Games (fruit machine). Satellite TV. Tables outdoors (pavement). Vegetarian dishes.

Fox & Pheasant
1 Billing Road, SW10 (020 7352 2943). Fulham Broadway tube. **Open** 11am-11pm Mon-Sat; noon-10.30pm Sun. **Food served** noon-2.30pm Mon-Sat. **No credit cards.**
Billing Road is a private lane of pastel coloured cottages, a throwback to the time when Chelsea village meant just that and wasn't the name of a glitzy commercial development. Inside this friendly family-run establishment are two low-ceilinged lounges, separated by a central bar. There's a wall-mounted TV on one side, which will be on if Chelsea is playing. Most of the punters are regulars. Greene King's IPA and Abbot's Ale are on draught. A hand-written note above the bar reads 'No credit cards or cheques, cash only,' but you could probably try bartering with grain.
Games (darts). No piped music or jukebox. Satellite TV. Tables outdoors (garden, pavement). Vegetarian dishes.

Harwood Arms
Walham Grove, SW6 (020 7386 1847). Fulham Broadway tube. **Open** 11am-11pm Mon-Sat; noon-10.30pm Sun. **Food served** noon-2.30pm, 7-9.30pm Mon-Sat; noon-3pm, 7-9.30pm Sun. **Credit** MC, V.
Fulham's always been short on decent pubs, so the acquisition of this backstreet boozer by the owners of Primrose Hill's **Queens** (*see p208*) – a fine pub if ever there was one – was particularly welcome. The place has been tarted up with walls stippled yellow and bare board floors dotted with assorted

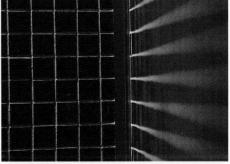

Lunasa. *See page 138.*

sofas and dining furniture. Other aspects are a bit less predictable; there's some pseudo-African art on the walls and the lampshades have the appearance of nuked meringues. The only real ales on offer are Wadworth 6X and Boddington's, a bitter that travels about as well as your average English football fan (and can turn just as nasty). Food is ambitious (brie and cranberry soufflé £4.95, crispy Thai fishcakes £7.95) and not entirely successful, but worth a punt. *Babies and children admitted. Satellite TV. Vegetarian dishes.*

Havana

490 Fulham Road, SW6 (020 7381 5005). Fulham Broadway tube. **Open/food served** 5pm-2am Mon-Thur; noon-2am Fri, Sat; noon-10.30pm Sun. **Admission** £4 after 10pm Wed; £5 after 10pm Thur; £5 after 9pm, £8 after 11pm Fri, Sat. **Happy hour** opening time-7.30pm daily. **Credit** AmEx, DC, MC, V.

A fun, upbeat bar, fabulously ornate on the outside, matched on the inside by clashing leopard and zebra skin patterns, mosaic tables and Latino kitsch. Infectious salsa beats give Havana its bounce. Intimidated novices can warm up with beginners' dance classes. Alternatively, go for cocktails and slammers to loosen stiff English joints. A colourful menu continues the theme (tapas, tortillas, nachos) but the thumping disco background makes it an inappropriate venue for a quiet meal out. Warm beer and prominent sports screens add the (non-Cuban) finishing touches to a package geared far more to havana good time than cultural authenticity. *Music (Latin bands 9pm Fri, Sat; DJ's nightly; salsa classes 7.30pm, 8.30pm Sun; £5 per class). Restaurant. Vegetarian dishes.*

Hollywood Arms

45 Hollywood Road, SW10 (020 7349 9274). Earl's Court or South Kensington tube. **Open** noon-11pm Mon-Sat; 6-10.30pm Sun. **Credit** DC, MC, V.

A traditional Edwardian pub, with a pretty, frosted-window exterior and charming, comfortably tattered insides (although given that the pub is due to undergo a major refit in summer 2001, this may not be the case for too much longer). Friendly staff, down-to-earth regulars and the rambling layout, extending to a pool room and extra bar upstairs (with wide-screen sports), all contribute to its laid-back, unpretentious ambience. There's also an attractive beer garden at the back. The hot-air balloon on the pub sign is a reference to one Jean-Pierre Blanchard who in 1784 took off from a field in front of the pub and became the first person to cross the English Channel by air. Don't be caught out by the 6pm opening time on Sundays. *Function room. Games (fruit machines, pool table). Jukebox. Satellite TV (big screen). Tables outdoors (garden, pavement).*

Ifield

59 Ifield Road, SW10 (020 7351 4900). Earl's Court, Fulham Broadway or West Brompton tube. **Open/food served** 5-11pm Mon-Thur; noon-11pm Fri, Sat; noon-10.30 Sun. **Credit** AmEx, MC, V.

A lively pub-restaurant divided into a bar area at the front and a more formal restaurant behind it. Low leather couches and dark wood tables make for a smart yet informal bar area, where a TV above the door tuned to Sky Sports entertains a young and slightly cliquey crowd. Adnam's Best is on draught and bottled lagers are supplemented by a sizeable wine list, featuring a smattering of Californians alongside European offerings. Food is the big selling point, available both at the bar and in the restaurant. It includes tapas-type offerings as well as a more substantial Modern European

menu. We didn't eat but dishes certainly looked good, if a little pricey (about a tenner for mains). *Babies and children admitted (daytime only). Dress code. Function room. Restaurant. TV. Vegetarian dishes.*

Imperial

577 King's Road, SW6 (020 7736 8549). Fulham Broadway tube. **Open** 11am-11pm Mon-Sat; noon-10.30pm Sun. **Food served** noon-2.30pm, 7-9.30pm Mon-Fri; noon-2.30pm Sat; 12.30-3pm Sun. **Happy hour** 5.30-7pm Mon-Fri (except Chelsea FC home game days). **Credit** AmEx, MC, V.

The majestic name does nothing to prepare you for the awful tackiness of this pub. It has all the trappings of a gaudy theme bar, but without a particular theme. Blue mermaid-like creatures swim across the walls, there are flying-saucer light fittings and a half-baked devil theme promoting 'wickedly wobbly vodka jelly'. Points in its favour, however, are supremely friendly bar staff, lots of space and an animated – occasionally outright rowdy and studenty – atmosphere. Among its real ales, the malty Imperial (£2.40), brewed by the owners at their brewery in Battersea, is the one to go for, although most stick with bottled lagers. There's also a surprisingly decent wine list. A conservatory offers extra seating at the back. *Babies and children admitted (until 3pm). Function rooms. Games (board games). Satellite TV. Tables outdoors (patio/pavement). Vegetarian dishes.*

Legless Ladder

1 Harwood Terrace, SW6 (020 7610 6131). Fulham Broadway tube. **Open** noon-11pm Mon-Sat; noon-10.30pm Sun. **Food served** noon-10pm Mon-Thur; noon-9pm Fri-Sun. **Credit** MC, V.

A spacious airy pub, set back from the New King's Road, just in front of Fulham gas works. Sounds romantic or what? But it's a nice place with light wood flooring and long tables, warmed on our last visit by two real flame gas-powered fireplaces. Best of the draught bunch at the circular bar are Hoegaarden and Shepheard Neame Spitfire and there's a basic wine list. A courtyard at the back provides summer seating, but is partially covered and heated in winter. Along with regular pub grub there are tasty sounding specials available (how about pan-fried chicken in tarragon sauce with garlic mash and french beans £7.25?). Mature diners make up most of the clientele, although on a busy Saturday night the Ladder can fill to bursting with a younger, more vivacious crowd. *Babies and children admitted (until 6pm). Function room. Satellite TV. Tables outdoors (garden, marquee). Vegetarian dishes.*

Lunasa

575 King's Road, SW6 (020 7371 7664/ www.lunasa.co.uk). Parsons Green tube. **Open** 11am-11pm daily. **Food served** noon-4pm, 6-9pm daily. **Credit** AmEx, DC, MC, V.

At the Fulham end of the King's Road, in a pleasant, villagey row, lies Lunasa, which was bought as the fading Adelaide pub by three young friends and given a complete overhaul. They've done a fantastic job, to the extent that Lunasa is exactly the kind of bar we'd like to create too if we had a couple of spare colleagues with all the necessary cash. The front part is a warm, low-lit woody bar with parlour palms. At the back are plenty of comfy armchairs and low tables. Upstairs a spacious function room doubles as a big-screen-action venue. Gorgeous as a spot for a quiet drink, come the end of the week the whole place can also get pretty manic in that Southern Comfort ad kind of way. Armchair and newspaper or party with the beautiful people, Lunasa has got it nailed.

London crawling: Watery pints

London is blessed with innumerable fine riverside pubs, from the gritty boozers of Greenwich in the east to the countryfied watering holes of Richmond and Twickenham in the west; see the **Critics' choice** box (*p145*) for a few favourites. The stretch of the Thames between Chiswick Mall and Hammersmith Bridge is particularly prime, with four pubs right on the river and a fifth little more than an oar's length away. A Hammersmith riverside stroll also has the advantages of artistic and otherwise historical associations that make a stroll by the waterside more than just an excuse for an al fresco piss-up.

Start at Stamford Brook station, head south over Chiswick High Road and across St Peter's Square to Chiswick Mall, a row of sturdy waterfront houses. These have several claims to literary fame, having been home to Edward Johnston (No.3), calligrapher and tutor to artist Eric Gill, printer Sir Emery Walker (No.7) and MP, novelist and Thames-chronicler AP Herbert (Nos.12-13). At the mall's eastern end you'll come to Black Lion Lane where, in 1804, an unfortunate bricklayer by the name of Thomas Millwood was shot dead by one Francis Smith, who mistook him for the 'Hammersmith Ghost'. The cadaver was carried into the nearby **Black Lion**, which had been converted from a piggery into a public house not long before. In more recent history, the pub was famous for its skittle alley, sadly now transformed into a drab dining room.

Moving on past the single brick arcade that's all that remains of the West Middlesex Water Company pumping station, you'll gain your best view of the river, with its tidal flats and moored trawlers. It's a view that can best be admired (ie with drink in hand) from the first floor terrace of the **Old Ship**, another 18th-century pub and your second port of call. It doesn't look particularly old and the nautical theming is a bit naff, but the ales are Fuller's and the atmosphere's breezy.

From the Old Ship, continue along Upper Mall, where you'll come across Kelmscott House, home, in its illustrious history, to poet and novelist George MacDonald (best known for *The Princess and the Goblin*) and poet, designer, craftsman and Socialist writer William Morris. Morris, who rented the house as his London base in 1877 and died there in 1896, named it after his Oxfordshire home Kelmscott Manor. Despite a love of the river, Morris was not entirely happy with his new surroundings, which were evidently less idyllic in his day. In an 1881 lecture he made the following outburst: 'Look you, as I sit at work at home, which is Hammersmith,

close to the river, I often hear go past the window some of that ruffianism of which a great deal has been said in the papers of late.'

It's unlikely, given these sentiments, that Morris would have frequented the **Dove**, Hammersmith's most famous pub, but the literary theme is reprised here nonetheless. In the 18th century, when it was a coffee house, poet James Thomson wrote part of *The Seasons* and possibly also the words to 'Rule Britannia' here. He lodged in an upstairs room, which is also where he died of pneumonia after being caught in a downpour on an open boat. In the 20th century, both Graham Greene and Ernest Hemingway frequented the place, and AP Herbert used the pub as a model for the Pigeons in his novel *The Water Gypsies* (1930). Riverview seating is restricted to a terrace at the rear, but we prefer the tiny bar off to the right as you enter; big enough for four close friends only.

Continue east across the scuffed grass to what's called the Lower Mall, a pedestrianised riverside way. There are two more pubs here, the **Rutland** and the **Blue Anchor**, both rubbing shoulders with the boathouses belonging to various rowing clubs. Although composer Gustav Holst was reputedly inspired to write his 'Hammersmith Suite' while sat at the bow window of the Anchor, the main appeal of both is the plentiful bench tables outside. At this point, in the shadow of knobbly Hammersmith Bridge, you run out of river pubs. Hammersmith tube station is a short walk away. Alternatively, there's always the option of a ride over the bridge on bus No.209 and onward to **Ye White Hart** and other waterside boozers in nearby Barnes.
Rhonda Carrier

Black Lion (*p140*) 2 South Black Lion Lane, W6 (020 8748 2639).
Blue Anchor (*p141*) 13 Lower Mall, W6 (020 8748 5774).
Dove (*p141*) 19 Upper Mall, W6 (020 8748 5405).
Old Ship (*p141*) 25 Upper Mall, W6 (020 8748 2593).
Rutland (*no review*) Lower Mall, W6 (020 8748 5586).
Ye White Hart (*p134*) The Terrace, Barnes, SW13 (020 8876 5177).

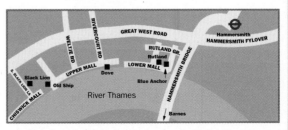

Disabled: toilet. Function room. Music (DJs 8pm Wed-Sat; free). Restaurant. Satellite TVs (big screen). Specialities: Stolnaya Russian vodka. Tables outdoors (pavement). Vegetarian dishes.

La Perla
803 Fulham Road, SW6 (020 7471 4895). Parsons Green tube. **Open** 5-11pm Mon-Fri; noon-11pm Sat; noon-10.30pm Sun. **Food served** 5-10.15pm Mon-Fri; noon-10.30pm Sat; noon-9.45pm Sun. **Happy hour** 5.30-7pm daily. **Credit** AmEx, MC, V.
This Mexican theme bar has a light and airy feel, with ceiling fans, cane chairs and tiled floors. The combination of jokey bar staff and generally relaxed punters makes for a free and easy atmosphere – a rare cocktail indeed in Fulham. Our Pina Coladas (£5) were professionally done, made with the best Cuban rum and served ice-cold, and we doubt you'll find a much better Tequila Sunrise this side of the Border. Tequila binges are facilitated with over 60 different varieties of the stuff. There's a small restaurant that serves up modern Mexican cuisine and generous bar-snacks. Nibble on nachos for a reasonable price but keep Mojitos to hand for those hotter jalapeno moments.
Babies and children admitted (high chairs; restaurant only). Restaurant. Vegetarian dishes.

Salisbury Tavern
21 Sherbrooke Road, SW6 (020 7381 4005). Fulham Broadway tube. **Open** 11.30am-11pm Mon-Sat; noon-10.30pm Sun. **Food served** noon-2.30pm, 7-10.30pm daily. **Credit** AmEx, MC, V.
A large brassy gastropub with separate dining and drinking areas, popular with a maturish pinstripe-and-mobile crowd. The Salisbury's refurb, featuring decorative bookcases, leather sofas and polished wooden floors, reflects assured, affluent, almost Home Counties taste. Claret and cashews mark their territory over lager and crisps (although there are a couple of real ales in the form of Charles Wells' Bombardier and Fuller's London Pride). Bar staff are well mannered and witty and service is quick. The classy circular bar and dimmed lights make for a subdued wine bar feel. Those with a tendency to mourn the disappearance of the traditional pub should steer clear: black cocktail straws, silver tip trays and kettle chips may just push you over the edge.
Babies and children admitted. Disabled: toilet. Restaurant. Satellite TV. Vegetarian dishes.

Shoeless Joe's
555 King's Road, SW6 (020 7610 9346/ www.shoelessjoes.co.uk). Fulham Broadway tube. **Open/food served** noon-midnight Mon-Wed; noon-1am Thur-Sat; noon-5pm Sun. **Admission** (club) £5 after 9pm Fri, Sat. **Happy hour** 5-8pm Mon-Fri. **Credit** AmEx, DC, MC, V.
Shoeless Joe's suffers from the same soullessness that afflicts hotel receptions and airport lounges. Firmly belonging to the light wood-and-chrome school of bar design, office-style plants and a bland colour scheme complete a wholly forgettable look. The hideous swirly upholstery is at least mould breaking. There's a nautical theme of sorts with porthole mirrors and ship-like railings – though this is more cross-Channel ferry than luxury cruise liner. A medium-sized sports screen upstairs and spectacularly wide screens downstairs make this the destination of choice for fans when Chelsea away games are televised. Otherwise, the clientele is made up of mild-mannered youngsters who drink to the sounds of Jennifer Lopez. The place heats up around 11pm with a little help from DJs (Thursday to Saturday).

Babies and children admitted (restaurant only). Disabled: toilet. Function room. Music (club 9.30pm Thur-Sat; admission charges as above). Restaurant. Satellite TV (video wall). Vegetarian dishes.

White Horse
1-3 Parsons Green, SW6 (020 7736 2115/ www.whitehorse@breworld.com). Parsons Green tube. **Open** 11am-11pm Mon-Sat; 11am-10.30pm Sun. **Food served** noon-3pm, 6-10pm Mon-Fri; 11am-10pm Sat, Sun. **Credit** AmEx, MC, V (food only).
It may be known locally as the 'Sloaney Pony' but there's as genuinely mixed a crowd here as anywhere – we spotted a blue rinse and a Hoxton fin on our last visit. Situated at the top end of the green, the front bar has huge windows with Venetian blinds, Chesterfield-style sofas and wooden tables, which make for an ideal environment for hanging out and reading the papers. At the first thawing of spring the action moves to the outside seating in front of the pub. The place is renowned as a haven for real ale buffs; regulars on draught include Harvey's Sussex Best and Rooster's Ranger, brewed especially for this pub (the label on the pump is of a horsey girl wearing pearls). Regular ales are supplemented by special mini festivals. There's over 50 bottled beers, including Belgian Trappist and fruit beers, and an extensive wine list, with some 20 available by the glass. As if that weren't enough, the food is also highly recommended, served in two restaurant areas; it's a good idea to reserve in advance for both.
Babies and children admitted. Function room. No piped music or jukebox. No-smoking area (restaurant). Restaurant. Specialities: real ales, world beers. Tables outdoors (garden). Vegetarian dishes.

Also in the area...
All Bar One 587-591 Fulham Road, SW6 (020 7471 0611); 311-313 Fulham Road, SW10 (020 7349 1751).
Bierodrome 678-680 Fulham Road, SW6 (020 7751 0789).
Café Flo 676 Fulham Road, SW6 (020 7371 9673).
Café Rouge 855 Fulham Road, SW6 (020 7371 7600).
Fine Line 236 Fulham Road, SW10 (020 7376 5827).
Fulham Tup 268 Fulham Road, SW10 (020 7352 1859).
Pitcher & Piano 871-873 Fulham Road, SW6 (020 7736 3910).
Rat & Parrot 704 Fulham Road, SW6 (020 7736 3014).
Ruby in the Dust 53 Fulham Broadway, SW6 (020 7385 9272).
Slug & Lettuce 474-476 Fulham Road, SW6 (020 7385 3209).

Hammersmith, Ravenscourt Park & Stamford Brook

Black Lion
2 South Black Lion Lane, W6 (020 8748 2639). Stamford Brook tube. **Open/food served** noon-11pm Mon-Sat; noon-10.30pm Sun. **Credit** AmEx, DC, MC, V.
The last in a chain of five riverside pubs stretching west from Hammersmith bridge, the Black Lion is the least interesting of the quintet. While it's possessed of 200 years of history, renovations and extensions have destroyed any character and inside it's nondescript and chintzy. More unfortunate still, the pub's set slightly back from the river, separated by a car park and screened by a wall of stone arches. The absence of watery

views means that it's ignored by Sunday strollers and other casual trade. Instead, the place is very much left to the locals, who fail to fill the cavernous interior giving the place a hollow feel. Recommended only as a refugee from the crowds that pack the other river pubs, and for its fine beer garden shaded by a massive chestnut tree that probably pre-dates the pub. *Babies and children admitted. Function room. Games (bar billiards, darts). Quiz (9pm Thur; £1 to play). Tables outdoors (garden). Vegetarian dishes.*

Blue Anchor

13 Lower Mall, W6 (020 8748 5774). Hammersmith tube. **Open** 11am-11pm Mon-Sat; noon-10.30pm Sun. **Food served** noon-2.30pm, 6-8.30pm Mon-Sat; noon-3pm Sun. **Credit** MC, V.

Closest of the riverside pubs to Hammersmith Bridge, the Blue Anchor has been around since 1722. It's a cosy one-room place cluttered with ceiling-hung sculls, oars and assorted rowing paraphernalia (possibly donated by the rowing club next door), old black-and-white photos of the area, and World War I gas masks. It all makes for a slightly studenty feel. A Georgian bow-window looks out on the river but, weather permitting, most customers take seats at the bench tables out on the riverside promenade, supping the likes of Theakston's, Courage Best and IPA Greene King to the accompaniment of cawing seagulls. There's mulled wine (£2.50) in winter, and a fine upstairs dining/function room with balcony. *Function room. Tables outdoors (riverside pavement). TV. Vegetarian dishes.*

Dove

19 Upper Mall, W6 (020 8748 5405). Hammersmith or Ravenscourt Park tube. **Open** 11am-11pm Mon-Sat; noon-10.30pm Sun. **Food served** noon-2pm, 6.30-9pm Mon-Sat; noon-4pm, 6.30-9pm Sun. **Credit** AmEx, DC, MC, V.

Think riverside historic pubs with decent beer and Hammersmith's Dove (with its full range of Fuller's ales) will no doubt be pretty high up a short list. It's 300 years old, steeped in local history, and can count the likes of Graham Greene, Charles II and William Morris (who lived across the way) among its one-time regulars. James Thomson wrote the words of 'Rule Britannia' in an upstairs room. It contains what the *Guinness Book of Records* has decreed is the smallest bar in the UK, measuring just 3.12 square metres, but this is supplemented by a second, larger but still snug bar (warmed by an open fire in winter), a dining area, conservatory and riverside veranda shaded by a thriving vine. A very popular Sunday lunch venue (full roasts £6.95). As signs make abundantly clear, dogs on leads are tolerated but absolutely no children. *No piped music or jukebox. Tables outdoors (riverside terrace). Vegetarian dishes.*

Old Ship

25 Upper Mall, W6 (020 8748 2593). Hammersmith, Ravenscourt Park or Stamford Brook tube. **Open** 10am-11pm Mon-Fri; 9am-11pm Sat; 9am-10.30pm Sun. **Food served** 10am-10.30pm Mon-Fri; 9am-10.30pm Sat; 9am-10pm Sun. **Credit** AmEx, MC, V.

In contrast to the olde worlde atmosphere of the nearby **Dove** (*see above*), the Ship is bright and modern, with a spacious interior decked out in magnolia weatherboarding and filled with blond pine chairs and tables. There's a tacky nautical theme (toilets are designated 'Ableseamen' and 'Ableseawomen') but this in keeping with the loud, brash nature of multiple TVs, high-volume conversations and kids on the loose. Like the Dove, it's a Fuller's pub, but ales are supplemented by an extensive selection of wines by the bottle and glass. The Ship really comes into its own in summer, with acres of outdoor seating, an

upstairs balcony, a ground-floor terrace and neighbouring beer garden, all with superb river views. A family pub par excellence. *Babies and children admitted (children's menu, high chairs, nappy-changing facilities). Disabled: toilet. Function room. Games (fruit machine). Satellite TV. Specialities: flavoured vodkas. Tables outdoors (riverside balcony, terrace). Vegetarian dishes.*

Stonemason's Arms

54 Cambridge Grove, W6 (020 8748 1397). Hammersmith tube. **Open** noon-11pm Mon-Sat; noon-10.30pm Sun. **Food served** 12.30-10pm Mon-Sat; 12.30-4pm, 6-9.30pm Sun. **Credit** AmEx, MC, V.

Looking a little shabby and inconsequential from the outside, this place is actually a bit more unusual than first appearances might suggest. Inside it's a spacious and comfortable pub/bar that serves excellent food with a hint of the southern hemisphere: the burgers are kangaroo and the chips are made from Kumara sweet potato. Or how about wasabi salmon over sautéed pak choi with your Guinness? (Although the menu changes regularly). The large old tables are surrounded by an eclectic selection of chairs, and old church pews are dotted about the light, sparsely decorated room – it's a sort of grungey take on the All Bar One look. Artwork on the wall is constantly changing and for sale. Arrive early if you want a seat as unlike Hammersmith's riverside pubs, this one is busy all year round. *Babies and children admitted. Disabled: toilet. Vegetarian dishes.*

Thatched House

115 Dalling Road, W6 (020 8748 6174). Ravenscourt Park tube. **Open** noon-11pm Mon-Sat; noon-10.30pm Sun. **Food served** noon-3pm Mon-Sat; noon-9.30pm Sun. **Credit** DC, MC, V.

The Thatched House is decorated like an English country living room, with yellow walls, wooden tables and bookshelves – an overly contrived look that's confused by an assortment of 'pop art' paintings. That aside, it's not a bad place at all. Originally a coppers' local, it has outlasted the local nick and now pulls in a wide range of punters angling for the comfy sofas. They come for a casual atmosphere, cheery bar staff, Young's beers, an excellent wine selection and first-class food served in the dining room at the back. *Babies and children admitted (lunchtimes). Function room. No piped music or jukebox. Tables outdoors (courtyard). Vegetarian dishes.*

Also in the area...

Bar 38 1 Blacks Road, W6 (020 8748 3951).
Café Med 320 Goldhawk Road, W6 (020 8741 1994).
Café Rouge 158 Fulham Palace Road, W6 (020 8741 5037).
Edward's 40 Hammersmith Broadway, W6 (020 8748 1043).
Frigate & Firkin 24 Blythe Road, W14 (020 7602 1412).
William Morris (JD Wetherspoon) 2-4 King Street, Swan Island, W6 (020 8741 7175).

Kensal

North Pole

13-15 North Pole Road, W10 (020 8964 9384). Latimer Road or White City tube. **Open** noon-11pm Mon-Sat; noon-10.30pm Sun. **Food served** 12.30-3pm, 7-10pm Mon-Fri; noon-3pm, 7-10pm Sat; noon-4pm, 7-9.30pm Sun. **Credit** AmEx, MC, V.

The North Pole once tried to do too much and be all things to all people, but now this reputable pub serving BBC employees and the fringes of Notting Hill has turned down the heat. DJs only play on occasional nights, the table football has been kicked into touch and the big-screen telly is used much more sparingly. The food is pretty standard gastropub fare and is accompanied by a decent selection of global wine, some well-kept real ales and, on the night of our visit, ambient jazz music easing the digestion. All of this creates a reasonably cool vibe, but the fashionable leather sofas, and church hall-like space with its echoey wooden floors and large plain glass windows can make the atmosphere a little chilly, if not quite polar, on quieter nights of the week.

Babies and children admitted (until 6pm). Games (table football). Music (DJs occasional Thur, Fri; blues band 8pm Sat). Restaurant. Tables outdoors (pavement). TV (big screen). Vegetarian dishes.

Paradise by Way of Kensal Green

19 Kilburn Lane, W10 (020 8969 0098). Kensal Green tube/Kensal Rise rail/52, 302 bus. **Open** 12.30-11pm Mon-Sat; noon-10.30pm Sun. **Food served** 12.30-4pm, 7.30pm-midnight Mon-Sat; noon-4pm, 7.30-11.30pm Sun. **Admission** £7 after 7.30pm Mon. **Credit** DC, MC, V.

Despite taking its name from the Chesterton poem, the title of this W10 gastropub is as much a reference to the bar's ongoing popularity in the fickle world of west London chic. It has struck a formula which, while incorporating a few changes over the course of 10 years, is still as successful as ever. The colour scheme remains a sombre shade of grey and green; the statue of Mercury has been replaced by an ugly cemetery angel in the corner; the front side room has been slightly softened with more characterful antique furnishings; and the main bar enlivened by art college paintings. The spacious restaurant at the rear continues to serve decent, reasonably priced, Eurasian nosh. The result: the place retains its attraction for the local younger bohemian crew and those seeking pub salvation from further afield.

Babies and children admitted (high chairs, menus, nappy-changing facilities). Disabled: toilet. Function rooms. Music (live salsa, DJs, dance class 7.30pm Mon). No-smoking area. Restaurant. Tables outdoors (garden). Vegetarian dishes.

William IV

786 Harrow Road, NW10 (020 8969 5944). Kensal Green tube. **Open** noon-11pm Mon-Thur; noon-midnight Fri, Sat; noon-10.30pm Sun. **Food served** noon-3pm, 6-10.30pm Mon-Wed; noon-3pm, 6-11pm Thur, Fri; noon-4pm, 7-11pm Sat; noon-4pm, 7-10pm Sun. **Credit** MC, V.

Employees of the nearby Virgin records divide their time equally between the **Paradise** (*see above*) and William IV, while other drinkers north of the Harrow Road tend to pledge their allegiance to one or the other. There's not much to choose between them, although William IV has a more classical '30s setting with smart oak panelling, a warren of handsome dining rooms and, crucially, a well-maintained patio garden heated by gas fires. Its bar area seeks to maintain a mellow bohemian scene with battered rugs and '50s box armchairs, but the whole place becomes more rowdy on DJs nights. The menu has a Mediterranean flavour, real ales are well kept and there's a fair collection of wines.

Babies and children admitted (until 7pm). Function room. Music (jazz 8.30pm Mon; DJs 8.30pm Wed-Sat). Restaurant. Satellite TV. Tables outdoors (garden). Vegetarian dishes.

Kingston-upon-Thames

Boaters Inn

Canbury Gardens, Lower Ham Road, Kingston-upon-Thames, Surrey (020 8541 4672). Kingston rail. **Open** Apr-Sept 11am-11pm Mon-Sat; noon-10.30pm Sun; Oct-Mar 11am-3pm, 5.30-11pm Mon-Thur; 11am-11pm Fri, Sat; noon-10.30pm Sun. **Food served** noon-2.30pm, 7-9.30pm daily. **Credit** AmEx, MC, V.

Hardly an inn, the Boaters looks more like a rowing club house – albeit one with plenty of smart green-pine and modern art decorating wall space around an L-shaped bar. Large windows overlook the river and private moorings where patrons can tie up their craft (we wish). Mostly though the clientele is made up from a variety of respectable Kingstonians, both young and old, attracted by the lure of a lazy river view and, in summer, the benefit of a patio that spills into the adjoining park. Regularly changing guest ales (most recently Greene King IPA) are generally ignored by punters in favour of Euro fizz like Stella. Food is unremarkable with a menu of bog standard pub grub. Regular live jazz adds a bit of a buzz to proceedings.

Babies and children admitted (children's menus, nappy-changing facilities). Games (board games, fruit machines, quiz machine). Music (blues band 8.30pm Tue, jazz band 8.30pm Sun). No-smoking area. Quiz (8.30pm Wed; £1 to play). Restaurant. Tables outdoors (riverside patio, front balcony). Vegetarian dishes.

Canbury Arms

49 Canbury Park Road, Kingston-upon-Thames, Surrey (020 8288 1882). Kingston rail. **Open** 11am-11pm Mon-Sat; noon-10.30pm Sun. **No credit cards.**

Bugger your stripped pine, your leather sofas, your orange walls. Bollocks to your white-collar wine drinkers and cocktail flouncing fashionistas. This is a pub about beer and beer-drinking. Concealed down a suburban backstreet you're unlikely to drop by on chance but then this is the sort of place which inspires devotees to travel. They come for the real ales, more than 420 of which have been pulled through the hand-drawn pumps. There are literally hundreds of beer mats decorating the walls to prove it. At any one time five or six guest ales of over five per cent abv will be available, and with names like Titanic Wreckage they probably account for the sedated state of the clientele. Or it could be the absinthe, £3 a shot. Local bands play regularly to try and elicit a bit of dynamism in the punters and draw in a more varied crowd. Do not ask for a Babycham.

Babies and children admitted (separate room). Games (board games, darts, fruit machines). Music (bands 9pm Fri, Sat). Quiz (8.30pm Sun; £1 to play). Satellite TV (big screen). Tables outdoors (forecourt, garden).

Newt & Ferret

46 Fairfield South, Kingston-upon-Thames, Surrey (020 8546 3804). Kingston, Norbiton or Surbiton rail. **Open** 11am-11pm Mon-Sat; noon-10.30pm Sun. **Food served** noon-9.30pm Mon-Sat; 12.30-4pm Sun. **Credit** MC, V.

You can happily get as pissed as the proverbial in this snug boozer on the edge of Fairfield recreation ground, aided by a fine range of Badger ales and Hoffbräu lagers. Active ferrets can rack up a few frames of pool or chance their arm with a game of darts, all played to a constant MTV backtrack. More cerebral visitors can sup pints of Tanglefoot over a game of chess or Scrabble. Generally populated by well-behaved twenty- and thirtysomethings, there's a welcoming burble of activity about the place even on chill midweek mid-winter nights. Rare balmy summer nights are made the most of by the antipodean bar staff who gleefully stoke up the barbie under a marquee in the beer garden out front.

Babies and children admitted (until 6pm). Games (board games, boules, fruit machines, pool table). Jukebox. Quiz (8.30pm Sun; £1 to play). Satellite TV (big screen). Tables outdoors (children's playground, garden).

Norbiton & Dragon

16 Clifton Road, Norbiton, Surrey (020 8546 1951). Norbiton rail. **Open** 11am-11pm Mon-Sat; noon-10.30pm Sun. **Food served** noon-2.30pm, 7-10.30pm Mon-Fri; noon-10.30pm Sat; noon-10pm Sun. **Credit** AmEx, DC, MC, V.

One of the better attempts to combine a Thai restaurant with a standard boozer. The pub part of the package is decidedly less than exotic, a place for pints and pool where the colour of tanned leather prevails – from the suitcases and kettles above the curved bar to the huge deer's head looming over the pool tables. The Dragon is joined to the main bar via a low arch at the back of the pub. Far from beastly it offers quality dishes at reasonable prices, although we do think they ought to do something about enlivening the sub-Harvester decor. Snacks from the restaurant can also be ordered at the bar.

Babies and children admitted (restaurant only; high chairs). Function room. Games (fruit machines, pool table, video game). Restaurant. Satellite TV (big screen). Tables outdoors (garden). Vegetarian dishes.

Park Tavern

19 New Road, Kingston-upon-Thames, Surrey (no phone). Norbiton rail. **Open** 11am-11pm Mon-Sat; noon-10.30pm Sun. **No credit cards**.

In winter when the open fire is roaring, the green upholstered seats and low-ceilinged snugness make this one of the most inviting of pubs, especially if you've been for a bracing constitutional in nearby Richmond Park. The hirsute barman's lot seems a happy one, with devoted locals taking up positions at the bar for a chinwag. With such an easygoing atmosphere complemented by authentic decorations from a bygone era (a 'God Save The King' flag hangs on the wall), you'd be forgiven for lapsing into idle thoughts of a rose-tinted version of England now long gone. In summer there's also the option of taking a seat on the neat front patio.

Games (fruit machine). Jukebox. Satellite TV (big screen). Tables outdoors (garden, patio).

Wych Elm

93 Elm Road, Kingston-upon-Thames, Surrey (020 8546 3271). Kingston rail. **Open** 11am-3pm, 5-11pm Mon-Fri; 11am-11pm Sat; noon-4pm, 7-10.30pm Sun. **Food served** noon-2.30pm Mon-Sat. **No credit cards**.

One for the horticulturalists, or anyone who appreciates a pretty sight. Owners Manuel and Janet Turnes are green-fingered publicans who've covered the front of their pub with a glorious display of hanging baskets and window boxes, a verdancy matched only by the beautifully tended back garden (Fuller's Garden of the Year 1999 and 2000). A vast array of house plants and wall-mounted floral prints also adorn the plushly upholstered lounge bar, where a mix of locals enjoy a quiet pint of well-kept ale (it's a Fuller's house). Darts-playing regulars and a sprinkling of codgers from a nearby old folks' home patronise the far less fancy, lino-floored saloon bar. Food is unremarkable pub grub but it is home cooked and reasonably priced.

Babies and children admitted (dining area only). Games (darts, fruit machine). Tables outdoors (garden). Vegetarian dishes.

Also in the area...

Bar (Puzzle) 1 St James Square, Kingston-upon-Thames, Surrey (020 8549 7366).
Café Rouge 4-8 Kingston Hill, Kingston-upon-Thames, Surrey (020 8547 3229).
Financier & Firkin 43 Market Place, Kingston-upon-Thames, Surrey (020 8974 8223).
Kingston Mill (It's A Scream) 58-62 High Street, Kingston-upon-Thames, Surrey (020 8939 8401).
Kingston Tup 88 London Road, Kingston-upon-Thames, Surrey (020 8546 6471).
O'Neill's 3 Eden Street, Kingston-Upon-Thames, Surrey (020 8481 0131).
Slug & Lettuce Turks Boatyard, Thameside, Kingston-upon-Thames, Surrey (020 8547 2323).

Norbiton & Dragon

Maida Vale

Bridge House
*13 Westbourne Terrace Road, W2 (020 7432 1361).
Warwick Avenue tube.* **Open** noon-11pm Mon-Sat; noon-
10.30pm Sun. **Food served** noon-9.30pm Mon-Sat; noon-
9pm Sun. **Credit** MC, V.
It may be called Maida Vale, but this district ain't made of ale
houses. Happily the Bridge House is one of the few places
around here that's an honest to goodness common man's
boozer. A pub has been here since 1730, serving shepherds
and so on before the industrial revolution, and the manual
working classes since then. Much of the clientele comes from
estates this side of the canal – as well as a smattering of the
middle classes visiting the Canal Café comedy club upstairs.
From the street-side terrace for summer drinking, it's just
possible to view the Grand Union canal – if not the rich folk
in their multimillion pound houses beyond. Lowest common
denominator design means TV sports, fruit machines, simple
pub grub as well as real ales and basic wines.
*Comedy (7.30pm & 9.30pm daily, £6). Function room.
Games (fruit machine, quiz machines). Quiz (8.30pm Tue;
£1 to play). Satellite TV. Tables outdoors (terrace).
Theatre. Vegetarian dishes.*

Warrington Hotel
*93 Warrington Crescent, W9 (020 7286 2929). Maida
Vale tube.* **Open** 11am-11pm Mon-Sat; noon-10.30pm Sun.
Food served noon-2.30pm, 6-10pm daily. **Credit** MC, V.
Pubs don't come much flasher than the Warrington. The
imposing frontage, presiding over a four-road roundabout,
gives it the look of an Eastern European embassy.
Magisterial pillars, wrought-iron lamps and mosaic flooring
at the entrance give an inkling of what's inside. You get
three bars – one huge – with ornate high ceilings, marble
pillars, art nouveau glasswork framed in carved mahogany,
a staircase that'd give Dame Edna a run for her money, plus
a couple of friezes. There is an excellent selection of drinks
and the real ales (including Greene King IPA, Brakspear
and Fuller's London Pride) are well kept and various.
Extremely popular, there is a tendency for the bar to get
vulgar and rowdy. It used to be possible to escape to the
grassy knoll of the roundabout outside, but this has been
planted up – presumably to curb peripatetic lager louts.
Instead, there is other outside seating alongside the listed
red telephone boxes. One more plus: a Thai gentleman
named Ben runs a very popular and fairly priced Thai
restaurant on the first floor.
*Babies and children admitted (restaurant). Games
(darts, fruit machine). No piped music or jukebox.
No-smoking areas. Restaurant. Satellite TV. Tables
outdoors (courtyard, pavement). Vegetarian dishes.*

Warwick Castle
*6 Warwick Place, W9 (020 7432 1331). Warwick Avenue
tube.* **Open** noon-11pm Mon-Sat; noon-10.30pm Sun.
Food served noon-2pm daily. **Credit** MC, V.
A smart pub on the smart side of the canal, this set of simple
four square rooms has enough quiet character to satisfy the
local brotherhood of Euro-yuppies. Each of the spaces has a
serious masculine feel with documentary historical photos
on the walls and decoration stripped back to the existing
moulded original Edwardian features, which include a
separate parlour and doors opening onto the street in
summer. The range of drinks is less than impressive, but
seems to satisfy denizens of surrounding mansion block
appartments who can be identified by chinos and jumpers
worn over the shoulders. There's a limited food menu.

*Babies and children admitted. Games (fruit machine, quiz
machine). No piped music or jukebox. Tables outdoors
(pavement). TV. Vegetarian dishes.*

Also in the area...
Café Rouge 30 Clifton Road, W9 (020 7286 2266).
Slug & Lettuce 47 Hereford Road, W2
(020 7229 1503).

Richmond, Isleworth & Twickenham

Cricketers
*The Green, Richmond, Surrey (020 8940 4372).
Richmond tube/rail.* **Open** 11am-11pm Mon-Sat; noon-
10.30pm Sun. **Food served** noon-8.45pm Mon-Fri;
noon-6.30pm Sat, Sun. **Credit** MC, V.
Rolling Stone Ronnie Wood was rumoured to be interested
in buying this pub a few years back. He didn't – for which
the locals probably heave a sigh of relief – and so having
missed out on an infusion of rock star excesses, it remains a
decidedly MOR sort of place. Unremarkable in all but
location, it sits on the edge of the grand expanse of Richmond
Green, an area that hasn't changed significantly in the last
few hundred years. The local cricket teams that play on the
Green's pitch in summer months uphold the authenticity of
the pub's name, although lackadaisical spectators often seem
more thrilled by the liquid charms of the bar, than the crack
of leather on willow. A spacious rear courtyard and the
proximity of the green make this an ideal spot for lazy hazy
days – you'll just have to look elsewhere for your sex, drugs
and rock 'n' roll.
*Babies and children admitted (restaurant). Function
room. Games (fruit machines). Quiz (music, 9pm Thur;
£1 to play). Restaurant. Satellite TV (big screen). Tables
outdoors (courtyard). Vegetarian dishes.*

Eel Pie
*9 Church Street, Twickenham, Middx (020 8891 1717).
Twickenham rail.* **Open** 11am-11pm Mon-Sat; noon-
10.30pm Sun. **Food served** noon-10.30pm daily. **Credit**
AmEx, MC, V.
The charms of Twickers are few but this place, situated on
an attractive villagey Church Street, we like. The impact of

rugby inevitably looms large: cartoons and pictures fill the walls and on match days the place heaves with pre- and post-game crowds. But otherwise, it's a dimly lit pub with traditional red and cream decor, wooden floors and dried hops hanging here and there. A lively and cheery vibe pervades, due in no small part to a good mix of customers of all ages. Staff are friendly and there's a good selection of Badger beers. On our last visit a group of enthusiastic football fans watching Sky Sport on the back-room TV proved that this isn't just the preserve of rah-rah rugby types.
Babies and children admitted (until 7pm). Games (bar billiards, fruit machines). Quiz (7pm Tue; £1 to play). Satellite TV. Specialities: real ales. Vegetarian dishes.

London Apprentice
62 Church Street, Isleworth, Middx (020 8560 1915). Isleworth rail. **Open** 11am-11pm Mon-Sat; noon-10.30pm Sun. **Food served** 11am-2.30pm, 6-9.30pm Mon-Sat; noon-3.30pm Sun. **Credit** AmEx, DC, MC, V.
Part of Old Isleworth, the Apprentice is a bit out of the way, but its glorious location on a quiet stretch of the river makes it worth the effort. It's best visited in the summer, when from terrace or beer garden seating you can admire both river views and the pub's 17th-century exterior. Inside is less inspiring with unattractive swagged curtains, rugby memorabilia and a cluttering of bog-standard pub bric-a-brac. Only the original beamed ceiling serves to remind of a long history that supposedly takes in visits from Henry VII, Charles I and II, Oliver Cromwell and Dick Turpin. No royals, revolutionaries or highway men these days – instead, customers are more likely to allow themselves be robbed by the *Who Wants to be a Millionaire?* quiz game. Bar food is available in the conservatory and there's an upstairs restaurant with more sophisticated and expensive offerings.
Babies and children admitted (until 9.30pm; dining area only; children's menus). Function room. Games (bar billiards, darts, fruit machine, video games). No-smoking area. Quiz (8.30pm Tue; £1 to play). Tables outdoors (riverside terrace). Vegetarian dishes.

Marlborough
46 Friars Stile Road, Richmond, Surrey (020 8940 0572/www.marlborough-pub.co.uk). Richmond tube/rail. **Open** noon-11pm Mon-Sat; noon-10.30pm Sun. **Food served** noon-3pm daily. **Credit** AmEx, MC, V.
The Marlborough began life in the early 19th century as a temperance hotel, but soon caught on to the profits to be made from alcohol and hasn't looked back since. Behind a verdant frontage is a deceptively large interior; a sizeable front bar with plenty of dark wood, heavy green curtains and two coal fires leads to a long inner seating area and, beyond that, a pool table. It's shabby but homely. Video games, the largest TV in Richmond and regular DJs cater for those who need more stimulation than conversation and beer alone (notably the twentysomethings that crowd the place at weekends). Venture into the walled garden or, better still, take a left out of the pub for a stunning view of Surrey from the top of Richmond Hill. There are summer weekend barbecues in the garden.
Babies and children admitted (until 9pm; garden, play area). Games (fruit machines, pool table, quiz machine, video games). Jukebox. Music (live bands occasional Thur, Fri). No-smoking area. Satellite TV (big screen). Tables outdoors (garden, patio). Vegetarian dishes.

Old Ship
3 King Street, Richmond, Surrey (020 8940 3461). Richmond tube/rail. **Open** 11am-11pm Mon-Sat; noon-10.30pm Sun. **Food served** noon-4pm, 6-9.30pm Mon-Thur; noon-4pm Fri-Sun. **Credit** DC, MC, V.

Situated at the top of the High Street, this is one of Richmond's most popular brown rooms, with its name proudly emblazoned in neon outside. Young's Brewery provides the grog for a rag-tag bunch of fresh-faced young 'uns and gnarled old sea dogs to set themselves fair for the evening. The interior hasn't changed for donkey's years, a comforting fact that helps to maintain the unpretentious atmosphere. Nautical nick-nacks add to the pub's character, with two slightly battered model Clippers appearing to have witnessed some rough nights over the years at the hands of boisterous punters. The location in the heart of Richmond's main shopping drag makes it a regular port of call for weary shoppers as well as those devotees who are content to wait in perpetuity until the next tide before jumping ship.
Babies and children admitted (restaurant only, Sundays). Function room. Games (games machines). No-smoking area (restaurant). Restaurant. Satellite TV. Vegetarian dishes.

Racing Page
2 Duke Street, Richmond, Surrey (020 8940 1257). Richmond tube/rail. **Open** 11am-11pm Mon-Sat; noon-10.30pm Sun. **Food served** noon-3pm, 5.30-10pm Mon-Sat; noon-6pm Sun. **Credit** AmEx, MC, V.
The Page's barn-like interior has been looking a little empty of late. Its regular crowd of lager-loving lads and ladies seem to have removed their affections to nearby Edward's, which has become a late-night honeypot for the suburban button-down shirt brigade. Weekends still remain boisterous with groups of student types happily bellowing across the bar and spilling drinks. An ambitious attempt to woo a new audience has seen the addition of an extensive Laotian and Thai menu. We've yet to taste the dishes but the breadth of choice is impressive. For the moment punters remain unconvinced and are sticking to their shots of flavoured vodka as prelude to a late-night session down the road.
Babies and children admitted. Games (fruit machines). Jukebox. Music (rock bands 8.30pm Sun). Satellite TV (big screen). Vegetarian dishes.

Triple Crown
15 Kew Foot Road, Richmond, Surrey (020 8940 3805). Richmond tube/rail. **Open** 11am-11pm Mon-Sat; noon-10.30pm Sun. **Food served** noon-2pm Mon-Sat. **No credit cards.**
Hidden away behind Richmond Rugby Ground and the A316, the Triple Crown doesn't get much in the way of human traffic. There's usually a couple of regulars chewing the fat with the jolly bar staff and a wandering house cat, but otherwise it's a little lacking in life. (Except of course when there's an international being played up the road at Twickenham, when this and every pub in the area is invaded by rugger buggers.) Shame really as the Crown's endearing shabbiness – leavened by a few homely touches such as fresh flowers – is a pleasing change for anyone tired of identikit bars awash with pine. Beer lovers will appreciate the real ales, four of which are available (including Timothy Taylor's Landlord, Adnam's Best, Marston's Pedigree on our last visit) from a rotating list of about 30.
Babies and children admitted (until 7pm). Function room. Games (fruit machine). Music (jazz 2pm Sun). Quiz (8.30pm Tue; £1 to play). Tables outdoors (balcony). Satellite TV. Vegetarian dishes.

White Cross
Riverside, Richmond, Surrey (020 8940 6844). Richmond tube/rail. **Open** 11am-11pm Mon-Sat; noon-10.30pm Sun. **Food served** noon-3pm, 7-10pm Mon-Sat; noon-4pm Sun. **Credit** MC, V.
Sitting proudly on the riverbank, the grand dame of Richmond pubs remains second to none for summertime

West

White Cross

drinking. The slightest hint of clement weather brings half of Richmond hurrying down to the outside terrace bar for Young's beers and a good selection of wine (food is disappointing; better is available at some of the nearby riverside chain pubs). It's a different prospect in winter, when the Cross goes into semi-hibernation, but the main bar with cosy nooks overlooking the water and two open fireplaces remains an attractive proposition. The tidal reach of the river can catch out unsuspecting punters (cars parked outside have on occasion been submerged), fortunately the loquacious manager is well up on high tide times and knows when to hand out the flippers.
Babies and children admitted (separate room; nappy-changing facilities). No piped music or jukebox. Tables outdoors (garden). Vegetarian dishes.

White Swan

26 Old Palace Lane, Richmond, Surrey (020 8940 0959).
Richmond tube/rail. **Open/food served** 11am-3pm, 5.30-11pm Mon-Fri; 11am-11pm Sat; noon-10.30pm Sun.
Credit MC, V.
There've been major changes since we last visited. Out has gone the stuffy old interior, the clutter and banquettes; instead we now have sturdy, clean-lined aged-pine furniture and a cool grey-green finish on the walls. Upstairs there's an elegant new restaurant run by executive chef Kenny Miller with an enticing Modern European menu. It's a smart makeover, well suited to the 'better' class of customer that frequents this place. On our recent visit there were a fair number of Richmond's *Lovejoy* types (tanned, leather jacket-

wearing 40-plus geezers who should know better) grazing the extensive wine list. They're encouraged by a landlord who we witnessed taking time out from pint-pulling to slip The Who into the sound system before coming over all Roger Daltrey. Very *Stars in their Eyes*.
Babies and children admitted (separate conservatory). Disabled: toilet. No-smoking area (conservatory). Quiz (9pm Mon). Tables outdoors (garden, pavement). Vegetarian dishes.

White Swan

Riverside, Twickenham, Middx (020 8892 2166).
Twickenham rail. **Open** *winter* 11am-3pm, 5.30-11pm Mon-Thur; 11am-11pm Fri, Sat; noon-10.30pm Sun; *summer* 11am-11pm Mon-Sat; noon-10.30pm Sun. **Food served** noon-2.30pm, 7-9pm Mon-Thur; noon-3pm Fri-Sun. **Credit** MC, V.
Characterful riverside pub with over 300 years of history, which attracts pub connoisseurs from miles around. Raised to avoid flooding (don't get stranded in the downstairs toilets), it overlooks Eel Pie Island, the one time '60s rock hangout and still a last refuge for keepers of 'alternative culture'. Inside the pub, rugby memorabilia takes precedence over hippy clippings but even this seems a cut above the usual, with photos of the owner posing with ex-England internationals in pre-professional era 'training'. Echoes of the days when this was one of London's first rock venues persist in occasional live music, usually an acoustic set by locals, interspersing strumming with chatter and drink. A terrace with beer garden overlooking the river is the perfect place to finish a riverside stroll or a visit to Marble Hill Park.
Babies and children admitted. Music (live band 8.30pm every other Wed). Satellite TV. Tables outdoors (balcony, riverside garden). Vegetarian dishes.

Also in the area...

All Bar One 11 Hill Street, Richmond, Surrey (020 8332 7141).
Café Flo 149 Kew Road, Richmond, Surrey (020 8940 8298).
Dôme 26 Hill Street, Richmond, Surrey (020 8332 2525).
Edward's 1 Kew Road, Richmond, Surrey (020 8940 5768).
Flicker & Firkin 1 Duke's Yard, Duke's Street, Richmond, Surrey (020 8940 6423).
Moon Under Water (JD Wetherspoon) 53-57 London Road, Twickenham, Middx (020 8744 0080).
Pitcher & Piano 11 Bridge Street, Richmond, Surrey (020 8332 2524).
Slug & Lettuce Riverside House, Water Lane, Richmond, Surrey (020 8948 7733).
Twickenham Tup 13 Richmond Road, Twickenham, Middx (020 8891 1863).

Shepherd's Bush W12

Albertine

1 Wood Lane, W12 (020 8743 9593). *Shepherd's Bush tube.* **Open** 11am-11pm Mon-Fri; 6.30-11pm Sat. **Food served** noon-10.45pm Mon-Fri; 6.30-10.45pm Sat. **Credit** MC, V.
Owned by actor Jonny Lee Miller's family, Albertine is a tiny unpretentious wine bar on a corner of Shepherd's Bush Green. Mismatched wooden chairs and pews and candlelit tables give it a laid-back almost studenty feel, yet the terrific wine list is obviously compiled by folk who know their

Barsac from their Elba. It offers hundreds of wines from a three-page list, more than 50 of them by the glass. Many are under a tenner but if money's no object ask to look at the separate fine wine list. Cheese makes the perfect accompaniment; otherwise mains range from salads to wild boar sausages and mash and are really quite good. Grumpy BBC staff from nearby Television Centre who complain about being stuck out in White City should count themselves lucky to have such a place.
Function room. Vegetarian dishes.

Anglesea Arms
35 Wingate Road, W6 (020 8749 1291). Goldhawk Road or Ravenscourt Park tube. **Open** 11am-11pm Mon-Sat; noon-10.30pm Sun. **Food served** 12.30-2.45pm, 7.30-10.45pm Mon-Sat; 1-3.30pm, 7.30-10.15pm Sun. **Credit** DC, MC, V.
The hinterland between Shepherd's Bush and Ravenscourt Park seems to have become 'Brackenbury Village'. It's a place unknown to the *A to Z*, but a term popular with estate agents. They probably love the Anglesea because its presence in the 'village' can't help but add value to surrounding properties. It is one of the best pubs in London, drawing punters in from far and wide. Boozers are catered for by well-kept ales (Marston's Pedigree and Old Speckled Hen) served with charm in a dimly-lit setting of wood panelling and leather settees, and if the 'real' fire is actually gas, well it does the trick anyway. Most are here for the food. The menu, which changes daily, is chalked on a blackboard. On our last visit it included char-grilled chump of lamb and breast of Gascony duck with broad beans and sweet and sour cherries. We ate it and it was superb. Good value too with both dishes under a tenner. There's also a decent selection of wines.
Babies and children admitted. No piped music or jukebox. Restaurant. Tables outdoors (patio). Vegetarian dishes.

Bush Bar & Grill
45A Goldhawk Road, W12 (020 8746 2111). Goldhawk Road tube. **Open** 11am-11pm Mon-Sat; 11am-10.30pm Sun. **Food served** noon-3.30pm, 7-11pm Mon-Sat; noon-4pm, 7-11pm Sun. **Credit** DC, MC, V.
So exciting is the appearance of this stylish venue in an otherwise forlorn corner of west London that a bouncer is employed at the narrow mews entrance – even at lunchtime – to prevent undesirables pressing their noses against the glass walls. A fine restaurant with an ace bar attached, Bush has been set up by the people behind the Groucho Club and 192 in collaboration with the team behind Woody's Bar. Why Shepherd's Bush? Who cares. Just enjoy the Tchaik Chassay-designed, well lit, airy and modern space, with lovely leather banquettes in the bar area. No beers but a great drinks menu of excellent cocktails and wines from wine merchant John Amrit, one of the Bush team. Bar space is limited so arrive early or you may not get in.
Babies and children admitted. Disabled: toilet. Function room. Specialities: cocktails.

Havelock Tavern
57 Masbro Road, W14 (020 7603 5374). Hammersmith or Shepherd's Bush tube/Kensington (Olympia) tube/rail. **Open** 11am-11pm Mon-Sat; noon-10.30pm Sun. **Food served** noon-2.30pm, 7-10pm Mon-Sat; noon-3pm, 7-9.30pm Sun. **No credit cards.**
Imagine everything you'd expect from a popular gastropub, from the stripped wood floorboards to the huge plate-glass windows, put it in a spacious corner location, add some extra panache, and that's the Havelock Tavern. It wouldn't look out of place in Primrose Hill. Staff are friendly, and it

has the feel of a real local, partly because the obscure location (between Olympia and Shepherd's Bush) eliminates passing trade, but more because of its lively and intimate atmosphere. Moneyed-but-hip clientele munch on scoops of pistachios or olives, before invariably going on to richer, generously proportioned fare from a largely carnivorous menu (roast loin of pork, roasted partridge, etc). Get there early if you want a seat, especially on Sunday when people queue for tables.
Babies and children admitted (high chairs). Games (board games). No piped music or jukebox. Tables outdoors (garden, pavement). Vegetarian dishes.

Vesbar
15-19 Goldhawk Road, W12 (020 8762 0215). Goldhawk Road or Shepherd's Bush tube. **Open/food served** 11am-11pm Mon-Fri; 10am-11pm Sat, Sun. **Credit** AmEx, DC, MC, V.
Smart, sleek and modern with floor-to-ceiling plate glass windows and a beech-finish interior: if Muji designed bars then this is what they'd look like. It's the only bar of character right on the Green – all the rest belong to chains. Staff play it cool, wear black (what else?), spike their hair and can tell you if anything on the menu contains nuts. Newspapers are provided. Depending on the time of day, patrons are just as likely to order a large cappuccino (so big you'd be wise to order it decaf) as a beer, but avoid the house wine (awful) and cocktails (so packed with ice they need to be gulped down before becoming too watery). Dinner options tend towards the over-ambitious, but that doesn't stop Vesbar from being the perfect venue for an indulgent brunch of a smoked-salmon bagel or a restorative DIY Sunday detox of a freshly made smoothie.
Disabled: toilet. Vegetarian dishes.

West 12
74 Askew Rd, W12 (020 8746 7799). Shepherd's Bush tube. **Open** noon-11pm Mon-Sat; noon-10.30pm Sun. **Food served** noon-2.30pm, 6-11pm Mon-Fri; noon-11pm Sat; noon-10.30pm Sun. **Credit** MC, V.
Looking for a nice cocktail bar in the Shepherd's Bush area, but can't face the exclusive luvvieness of the Bush Bar & Grill? Try West 12. It looks dark and vaguely gothic with its blood red walls and gilded light fittings, but both music and cocktail list are achingly oh-so-now. Cocktails (all at £6) – Wibbles, Brambles, Mojitos and the like – were carefully made. The bar menu's pretty good too – pan-fried skate body with green beans, or a rare and tender rib-eye steak, each costing around a tenner. The wine list could be better and the draught beers are the usual nitrokegs, but for a neighbourhood bar it's still pretty impressive.
Babies and children admitted (lunchtimes Mon-Fri). Disabled: toilet. Function room. Specialities: cocktails. Vegetarian dishes.

Also in the area...
Café Med 320 Goldhawk Road, W6 (020 8741 1994). **Café Rouge** 98-100 Shepherd's Bush Road, W6 (020 7602 7732). **Edward's** 170 Uxbridge Road, W12 (020 8743 3010). **Frigate & Firkin** 24 Blythe Road, W14 (020 7602 1412). **O'Neill's** 2 Goldhawk Road, W12 (020 8746 1288). **Slug & Lettuce** 96-98 Uxbridge Road, W12 (020 8749 1987). **Walkabout Inn** 58 Shepherd's Bush Green, W12 (020 8740 4339).

South

Balham

Balham Tup

21 Chestnut Grove, SW12 (020 8772 0546). Balham tube/rail. **Open** noon-11pm Mon-Sat; noon-10.30pm Sun. **Food served** noon-3pm, 6-10pm Mon-Fri; noon-6pm Sat, Sun. **Credit** MC, V.

Known locally as the fuc ('fuc-tup', ya' see), this is a big, brash, beered-up saloon with bar snacks advertised on blackboards, football on the big screen and insufficient furniture to draw attention away from its cavernous dimensions. It relies principally on locals for its business (although its proximity to the station ensures there is always a certain amount of passing trade) and on weekends it's a particularly popular venue, where a boisterous crowd sups pints (and a glass of white wine for the lady) and plucks choice MOR tunes from the jukebox. On such nights, however, be warned: it can tip over into full-on lager boy territory. Not a Balham favourite, but if you like your beer fizzy, your wood blond and your windows big, you'll get on just fine.

Babies and children admitted (until 6.30pm). Disabled: toilet. Satellite TV. Tables outdoors (garden). Vegetarian dishes.

Bar Interlude

100 Balham High Road, SW12 (020 8772 9021). Balham tube/rail. **Open** noon-11pm Mon-Fri; 11am-11pm Sat; 11am-10.30pm Sun. **Food served** noon-10pm Mon-Thur; 10am-9pm Fri, Sat; 10am-10pm Sun. **Credit** AmEx, MC, V.

A couple of years ago this brand of smartly decorated, brightly lit, stripped pine and sofas bar was all but unheard of in earthy Balham; and even now, as young professionals encroach and house prices creep up, it's still quite an unexpected find. Its open layout, low tables, suede-covered pouffes and moody photographs are complemented by a wide range of draught and bottled beers, including Hoegaarden on tap, a limited but palatable palette of wine, and above-average bar food. The recent addition of two American pool tables (£5 for 30min) is welcome.

Disabled: toilet. Games (pool tables). Music (DJs 8pm Fri, Sat). Tables outdoors (patio). Vegetarian dishes.

Bedford

77 Bedford Hill, SW12 (020 8673 1756/ www.thebedford.co.uk). Balham tube/rail. **Open** 11am-11pm Mon-Wed; 11am-midnight Thur; 11am-2am Fri, Sat; noon-10.30pm Sun. **Food served** noon-2.45pm, 7-10pm Mon-Fri; noon-3.30pm, 7-10pm Sat; noon-3.45pm, 7-9.45pm Sun. **Credit** MC, V.

It was never less than reliable, but after a major refurbishment in 2000, the Bedford has become one of Balham's finest boozers. The spacious saloon is centred around a huge stone fireplace, with an elaborate flue to the ceiling (decorated with the Bedford arms) and a deep leather Chesterfield opposite. The smaller public bar was also smartened up a good deal during the refit, but retains a dartboard, footy on the TV and even a row of chain-smoking oldies (so perfect they could almost have been imported specially to add that authentic touch). Behind the bar is a standard selection of beers and wines, plus (more unusually) a large open grill, upon which there's generally a couple of chicken fillets sizzling. Another big plus is that the Bedford's host to the Banana Cabaret comedy club, home to the *Mark Thomas Product* and a whole host of other comics and cabaret.

Babies and children admitted (until 6pm). Banana Cabaret (7.30pm Fri, £10; 7pm Sat, £12). Comedy (new acts 8pm Tue; £3). Disabled: toilet. Function rooms. Games (darts, fruit machines). Line dancing (7.30pm Mon; £5). Magician (lunchtime Sun). Quiz (9pm Wed; £2). Salsa classes (7pm Wed; £5). Satellite TV (big screen). Swing dance classes (8pm Tue; £5). Tables outside (pavement). Vegetarian dishes.

Duke of Devonshire

39 Balham High Road, SW12 (020 8673 1363). Balham tube/rail. **Open** 11am-midnight Mon-Thur; 11am-2am Fri, Sat; noon-midnight Sun. **Food served** 11am-10pm Mon-Sat; noon-10pm Sun. **Credit** MC, V.

A gargantuan Young's boozing palace of the ornate Victorian variety, the Duke is popular with all-comers, from Clapham North trendies to after-work drinkers and mumbling old regulars. The interior looks like it probably hasn't changed in the last 80 years: there's still a typically long horseshoe bar backed by ranks of optics, a panoply of patterned glass and flock wallpaper. The cosy back bar, with its exposed floorboards and walls full of olde prints, is a perfect place for spiralling into inebriation whatever time you visit. Beyond that, the large beer garden is an attractive, spilt-level terrace with pretty trellises and a kid-engrossing playground. Add to this a 2am licence on Friday and Saturday and you know you're on to a winner.

Babies and children admitted (until 7pm; separate room; children's play area in garden). Games (darts, fruit machines, pinball machine, table football). Satellite TV. Tables outdoors (garden, open May-Sept). Vegetarian dishes.

Exhibit

Balham Station Road, SW12 (020 8772 6556/ www.theexhibit.uk.com). Balham tube/rail. **Open** 5-11pm Mon-Fri; 11am-11pm Sat, Sun. **Food served** 6.30-10.45pm Mon-Thur; 7-10.45pm Fri; 12.30-3.30pm, 7-10.45pm Sat; 12.30-4pm, 7-10.45pm Sun. **Credit** MC, V.

Although it looks more like the science annex of an adult education centre from outside, the Exhibit is actually the latest in a string of new bars to hit Balham, and one of the better ones at that. Inside is like a physical facsimile of a *Wallpaper** photoshoot: low leather sofas, shin-high tables (a potential hazard when you're carrying drinks) and a space-age, sunken fireplace imbue the bar with the naff-cool of a '70s Scandinavian chalet (there's even wood-chip on the toilet walls). However, the most striking feature is an ever so slightly incongruous tropical aquarium that runs the entire length of one wall. The vibe is cool and reserved but not exclusive. Exhibit's separate upstairs restaurant offers dishes from an eclectic Modern European menu in equally hip surroundings.

Babies and children admitted (until 7pm). Disabled: toilet. Restaurant. Specialities: cocktails. Tables outdoors (beer garden, pavement). Vegetarian dishes.

Lounge

76 Bedford Hill, SW12 (020 8673 8787). Balham tube/rail. **Open** 5-11pm Mon-Fri; 11am-11pm Sat, Sun. **Food served** 6-10.30pm Mon-Fri; 11am-5pm Sat, Sun. **Credit** MC, V.

Despite the name this Balham newcomer is hardly the height of louche luxury. There is one deep sofa for the more lax of posture but most of the furniture requires a straighter back: sturdy stripped pine chairs with tables and flooring to match. That's not to say that the Lounge isn't cosy – a row of low-hanging lamps above the bar and the broadly striped, warmly coloured walls make for a homely charm. Background music is relaxed and unobtrusive and the mix of young locals and suited commuters creates a good buzz. It's very much the sort of place where you could easily end up spending a whole evening, when you only intended nipping in for a half.

Babies and children admitted. Disabled: toilet. Function room. Games (board games). Music (DJs occasional Sun). TV. Vegetarian dishes.

Point
16-18 Ritherdon Road, SW17 (020 8767 2660).
Tooting Bec tube/Balham tube/rail. **Open** 10am-11pm
Mon-Sat; 10am-10.30pm Sun. **Food served** 10am-10pm
daily. **Credit** MC, V.
With its big picture windows, light wood tables and comfy
sofas, Point could pass for a posh member of the Slug &
Lettuce chain. Common as this sort of venue might be in other
parts of the capital, until now such a thing has been curiously
lacking in the no-man's-land (for nightlife, at least) that exists
between Balham and Tooting Bec. So it is that during the day
Point is patronised by happily lunching locals, while at night
it fills up rather nicely with a youngish sort of crowd who
have the look of newly-weds and first-time mortgagees.
Babies and children admitted (restaurant; children's
menu, high chairs). Disabled: toilet. Restaurant (available
for hire). Satellite TV. Vegetarian dishes.

Also in the area...
Moon Under Water (JD Wetherspoon) 194 Balham
High Street, SW12 (020 8673 0535).

Battersea

All Bar One
32-38 Northcote Road, SW11 (020 7801 9951).
Clapham Junction rail. **Open** noon-11pm Mon-Sat;
noon-10.30pm Sun. **Food served** noon-10pm Mon-Sat;
noon-9pm Sun. **Credit** AmEx, MC, V.
As far as drinking dens go, Londoners are spoilt for choice,
from warm-hearted boozers serving the community, to ethnic
bars giving a genuine taste of the world's cultures. It's curious
that with this embarrassment of riches, the spread of the
identikit All Bar One brand continues unchecked across the
capital (39 branches and counting). This is yet another cream-
walled, pine-tabled barn with sensible lighting, sensible chairs
and a sensible length bar with a passable range of beer and
wine. There's a centrally produced menu of standard rocket 'n'
shoelace fries fare; heaven forbid that a chef should be allowed
to rise or fall according to his own creativity. Evenings see the
place full of conservative-looking late twentysomethings who
are all having a conservatively good time. It says something
that they're always so popular. The question is: what?
Disabled: toilet. Games (board games). Vegetarian dishes.

Artesian Well
693 Wandsworth Road, SW8 (020 7627 3353/
www.artesianwell.co.uk). Clapham Common tube.
Open noon-11pm Mon-Thur; noon-2am Fri, Sat; noon-
10.30pm Sun. **Food served** noon-3pm, 7-11pm Mon-Sat;
noon-8.30pm Sun. **Admission** after 9.30pm Fri, Sat £5
(club only). **Credit** AmEx, MC, V.
The people who brought us the **Cross Keys** (*see p26*) in
Chelsea and Notting Hill's **Beach Blanket Babylon** (*see*
p99) took 17 months to renovate Battersea's old Nag's Head
and the result is every bit as overblown as you'd expect. From
the figure of Poseidon fixed to the front of the building, the
decor tramples all over the line between fantastical exuberance
and kitsch. Signs of the zodiac feature heavily and the bar is a
feast of twisted metal and coloured glass. Mosaics of broken
mirror adorn pilasters that sprout wrought iron tentacles.
Fossils and geodes are built into the bare brick and in the
restaurant one of the walls is an imposing leonine mask. With
so many Pierre et Gilles touches, it should really be a delicious
St Sebastian serving behind the bar, or at least a fragile
androgyne in Jean-Paul Gaultier haute couture. It deflates just
a little to find it's only hearty Bob in his regulation issue polo
shirt, and is it absurdly churlish to grumble that the chairs in
the bar are uncomfortable? A stunning place to be seen in.
Babies and children admitted (children's menus).
Function rooms. Music (live Mon, Wed, Sat, Sun;
DJs 9.30pm Fri, Sat). Restaurant. Tables outdoors
(pavement). Vegetarian dishes.

Babel
3-7 Northcote Road, SW11 (020 7801 0043/
www.faucetinn.com). Clapham Junction rail. **Open** 11am-
11pm Mon-Sat; noon-10.30pm Sun. **Food served** noon-
10pm daily. **Credit** AmEx, MC, V.
It's a funny thing when retro turns to passé, but the props at
Babel are passing their sell-by date for a second time. The
wooden veneer covering one wall is as classy as the
dashboard of a Mark I Ford Capri, while the light fittings and
tan pouffes might have walked from *Abigail's Party*. On
Friday and Saturday nights when the music thumps and the
joint jumps with a young and happy crowd, this is fine. At
quiet times, however, it just looks a bit, well, tired. The bar
itself, however, is a striking steel and neon number, and the
late-night queues and bouncers attest to its pulling power.
The lively and enthusiastic staff serve up a fair selection of

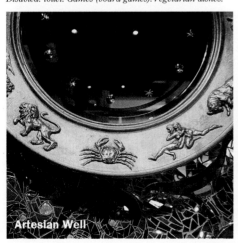

Artesian Well

wines (including four by the glass), but Babel's emphasis is on lager, cocktails and hormone-fuelled nights of fun. *Babies and children admitted (until 6pm). Disabled: toilet. Games (Dreamcast consoles). Music (DJs 8pm Fri, 7pm Sat). Tables outdoors (patio). TV. Vegetarian dishes.*

Base Bar Grill

1 Battersea Rise, SW11 (020 7228 6026). Clapham Common tube/rail then 35 or 37 bus/Clapham Junction rail. **Open/food served** 11am-11pm Mon-Sat; noon-10.30pm Sun. **Credit** DC, MC, V.

Base revels in its split personality. When Dr Jekyll's on duty, it's a swanky, somewhat restrained bar-restaurant with smooth jazz playing on Sunday afternoons. Medicinal Bloody Marys and restorative brunches are dispensed at the weekend: kedgeree (£6.95), muesli with fresh fruit and Greek yoghurt (£4.95) and big fry-ups (£6.95). However, when Mr Hyde takes over on Friday and Saturday nights, the music is turned up to 11 and the place throngs with a flirty, chatty crowd drinking Leffe and Budvar. The large area for diners at the back seems to remain full throughout, and there's a small people-watching terrace at the front. The halves-only policy is, we were told, to 'keep the riffraff out'. So, not to disguise some fairly audacious pricing, then? *Babies and children admitted (high chairs). Music (live jazz 2-4.30pm Sun; soul/funk band 8-10pm Sun). Restaurant. Tables outdoors (terrace). Vegetarian dishes.*

Beehive

197 St John's Hill, SW11 (020 7207 1273). Clapham Junction rail. **Open** 11am-11pm Mon-Sat; noon-10.30pm Sun. **Food served** noon-3pm Mon-Sat. **No credit cards.**

It would be nice to think that all London pubs used to be like this; a focus for the community where locals pop in for a pint and a chat with whoever's in. Now, of course, it seems as dated as a friendly bobby on his beat. It looks very quaint from the outside, but inside it's rather more ordinary; standard fixtures and fittings from a few years back and a well-used pub carpet. They serve pub grub at lunchtime, Fuller's beers (Pride, Chiswick Bitter and ESB) and Guinness, Caffrey's, Scrumpy Jack and Grolsch. It's been around for far longer than all the parvenu drinking warehouses hereabouts and one suspects its heart will still be beating long after they've gone. *Babies and children admitted (lunchtimes). Games (fruit machine). Satellite TV. Tables outdoors (pavement). Vegetarian dishes.*

Castle

115 Battersea High Street, SW11 (020 7228 8181/ www.thecastlebattersea.co.uk). Clapham Junction rail/14, 239, 344, 345 bus. **Open** noon-11pm Mon-Sat; noon-10.30pm Sun. **Food served** noon-3pm, 7-9.45pm Mon-Sat; noon-9.30pm Sun. **Credit** MC, V.

Shame, really, that the outside of the Castle is so uninspiring. It's been around since the 17th century, but a rebuild in the mid-'60s was in a rather joyless council estate style. The impression is one of Watney's Red Barrel and congealing pies, but nothing could be further from the truth. In these times of pubs serving food at near restaurant rates, the Castle manages to produce an excellent daily menu at keen prices; bacon-wrapped chicken breast stuffed with brie, spring onion and avocado, and haddock fillet stuffed with basil and peppers and wrapped with parma ham, were both £8.50, both excellent. The atmosphere is warm and local, with an over-30s emphasis; City types rub shoulders with cabbies and enjoy a full range of Young's ales and a fine selection of wines. The large garden is well used in warmer weather and there's a conservatory and sofas too.

Babies and children admitted (until 7.30pm). Function room. Games (board games). Tables outdoors (courtyard, garden). Vegetarian dishes.

Drawing Room & Sofa Bar

103 Lavender Hill, SW11 (020 7350 2564). Clapham Junction rail/77, 77A, 345 bus. **Open/food served** 6pm-midnight Mon-Fri; 11am-midnight Sat, Sun. **Credit** MC, V.

Visiting this shabbily eccentric joint is like stepping into the drawing room of an artistic but impecunious grande dame. There's an unusual collection of gilt sunburst wall-clocks which conspire with the fraying tapestries and the tatty velvet to lend an air of fading bohemian grandeur. Time runs at a slower pace here. Anyone would feel comfortable whiling away an evening alone, curled up on one of the sofas with a drink and a book. It comes into its own at night, when low lamps and candles add warmth to the terracotta walls and sky blue ceiling. It's hard to believe such an evocative place exists on this nondescript stretch of road. It serves either wine or a regrettably slim range of bottled beers, and the adjoining restaurant serves good food, including some interesting vegetarian options. The 21st-century pricing may come as a bit of a shock. *Babies and children admitted (toys). Function room. Restaurant. Tables outdoors (pavement). Vegetarian dishes.*

Duke of Cambridge

228 Battersea Bridge Road, SW11 (020 7223 5662). Battersea Park or Clapham Junction rail/19, 49, 344, 345 bus. **Open** 11am-11pm Mon-Sat; noon-10.30pm Sun. **Food served** noon-2.30pm, 7-9.45pm Mon-Sat; noon-2.45pm, 7.30-9.30pm Sun. **Credit** MC, V.

There's a good choice of gastropubs round here and it's a testament to the quality of the old Duke that he's still going strong. This particular *rus in urbe* look, especially the hops over the windows, may be looking a tad dated, but it's none the worse for that; comfortable with itself rather than slavishly following minimalist fashion. Newspapers are on the front table and there are sofas around the open fire. The heated outside terrace offers covered drinking. Many of the braying voices seem to have decamped to the **Settle Inn** (*see p155*) down the road, leaving a less frantic atmosphere that's even more redolent of a brasserie. It's a Young's pub with a good selection of wines to go with the decent food – snapper with lime, tomato and coriander mussels, and roast duck breast with bacon, mushroom and chestnut risotto, both £10.95. *Babies and children admitted (dining area). Disabled: toilet. Function room. Satellite TV. Tables outdoors (garden). Vegetarian dishes.*

Eagle

104 Chatham Road, SW11 (020 7228 2328). Clapham Junction or Wandsworth Common rail. **Open** 11am-11pm Mon-Sat; noon-10.30pm Sun. **Credit** MC, V.

A great CAMRA-supported local from the days before this area was taken over by gentrifying breeders. As well as the usual beers, it sells Hoegaarden and about four guest ales a week. Regular favourites are Flowers, London Pride, Timothy Taylor's and Adnam's but in the last four years about 1,500 different types have passed through the taps. Big sporting events feature heavily, especially rugby internationals when the big TV screen comes down. Midweek, however, it's board games and banter between regulars, whose every birth, marriage and anniversary is recorded with decorated champagne bottles on the shelves. There's a large beer garden at the back, free to hire, which is covered and heated during the cold months. The Eagle has everything a friendly local should have: a well-kept cellar, two open fires, comfy sofas and Alfie the handsome pub dog who scrounges your crisps. *Games (board games, quiz machine). Jukebox. Satellite TVs (big screen). Specialities: real ales. Tables outdoors (garden, marquee).*

Fox and Hounds

66 Latchmere Road, SW11 (020 7924 5483). Clapham Junction rail. **Open** noon-2.30pm, 5-11pm Mon-Fri; noon-11pm Sat; noon-10.30pm Sun. **Food served** noon-2.30pm, 7-10.30pm Mon-Fri; 12.30-3pm, 7-10.30pm Sat; 12.30-3pm, 7-10pm Sun. **Credit** MC, V.

The stolid Victorian exterior belies an airy, stripped back interior, recently made over but still retaining the old serving area. The decor (stripped boards, dark heavy furniture) attracts the area's new arrivals and yet it's relaxed enough to keep the old-timers happy. It's better when there are plenty of people in to soak up some of the space; agoraphobics should head for the leather sofas in a more intimate side room. It's owned by the same brothers who have the **Atlas** (*see p136*) in Fulham and the standard of the Spanish/Italian rustic cooking is as high. The menu changes daily, but on our visit a Moroccan lamb tagine (£9.50) was excellent, as was the Spanish oxtail casserole (£10). The ribeye steak (£11.50) was succulently tender and perfectly cooked, although accompanying veg were a little oily. The bar serves London Pride, Adnam's and Bass and there's an extensive reasonably priced wine list. Well worth the trek from Clapham Junction. *Babies and children admitted (daytime). Disabled: toilet. Specialities: wines. Tables outdoors (garden). TV. Vegetarian dishes.*

GII

339 Battersea Park Road, SW11 (020 7622 2112). Battersea Park rail. **Open** 11am-11pm Mon-Sat (occasional late licence Fri, Sat to 1am); 11am-10.30pm Sun. **Food served** noon-3pm, 6-10pm Mon-Fri; noon-9pm Sat, Sun. **Credit** MC, V.

The former Legless Ladder has moved up a few modernising rungs to become the George II (GII to its friends). Even before it was the Legless Ladder, this place started life as the Prince of Wales and quite why they've renamed this sleek reincarnation after an irascible Hanoverian monarch is anybody's guess. Apart from the old tiles on the wall bearing drinking songs through the ages (allegedly a listed feature), it's completely changed inside, and now boasts a stylish central bar, abstract art on the walls and very slick lighting throughout. There's an interesting menu (pork fillet with curried risotto and parmesan crackling at £7.95) and a limited but select wine list. The large back room, complete with open fire and leather sofas, is available for hire and there's a beer garden at the back. Midweek can be a bit dead, but DJs on Friday and Saturday nights pull in a young and hip crowd. *Babies and children admitted (Sun lunchtimes). Digital TV. Function room. Music (DJs Fri, Sat 7pm). Restaurant. Tables outdoors (garden). Vegetarian dishes.*

Holy Drinker

59 Northcote Road, SW11 (020 7801 0544/ www.holydrinker.com). Clapham Junction rail/35, 37 bus. **Open** 4.30-11pm Mon-Fri; noon-11pm Sat; 1-10.30pm Sun. **Credit** MC, V.

Individuality on Northcote Road has been stifled by a blanket of branded drinking malls. Some revolutionaries are even thinking of cordoning off the whole street with signs saying 'Independent drinkers enter at your peril.' But keep your head down, hurry past the usual suspects and head for this split-level gem, where the lighting's never more than low and the funky music's never less than loud. Early in the evening it's

the place to curl up on a sofa in front of the fire and flick through the glossies or read the Joseph Roth novel from which the bar takes its name. They only serve Guinness on tap, but the range of bottled beers is very impressive – Everard's Tiger, Fuller's Honey Dew, Schneider Weisse and Golden Promise are just a few – and there's an extensive range of wines, with eight available by the glass (including a summer rosé). A DJ plays an eclectically mellow selection at weekends. *Babies and children admitted (Sun daytime only). Music (DJs 6pm occasional Sun). Tables outdoors (pavement). TV.*

Latchmere

503 Battersea Park Road, SW11 (020 7223 3549). Battersea Park or Clapham Junction rail/44, 49, 344, 345 bus. **Open** noon-11pm Mon-Sat; noon-10.30pm Sun. **Food served** noon-9pm Mon-Fri; noon-8pm Sat; noon-6pm Sun. **Credit** AmEx, MC, V.

Despite yet another change of ownership and further attempts at repackaging and rebranding (it's now a 'Smith & Jones' pub, whoever they might be), the Latchmere still has heaps more character than most done-up pubs. It could be because they've kept the dark Victorian bar, complete with decorative mirrors and pillars. Or maybe it's the down-to-earth theatre upstairs that doesn't let this pub get ideas above its station. Anyway, it's a fine local stalwart that's popular with all types. There's a large garden at the back away from the traffic and several TV screens for sporting action. The food is reasonably priced (mains around a fiver) if unadventurous, and they serve the usual beers as well as Adnam's and Greene King IPA. *Babies and children admitted (until 8pm). Function room. Games (fruit machine). Quiz (9pm Tue; £1 to play). Satellite TV (big screen). Tables outdoors (garden). Theatre (7.30pm Tue-Sat, 4pm Sun; £6-£9). Vegetarian dishes.*

Lavender

171 Lavender Hill, SW11 (020 7978 5242). Clapham Junction rail/77, 77A, 345 bus. **Open** noon-11pm Mon-Fri; 11am-11pm Sat; 11am-10.30pm Sun. **Food served** noon-3pm, 7-11pm Mon-Fri; 11am-4pm, 7-11pm Sat; 11am-4pm, 7-10.30pm Sun. **Credit** AmEx, MC, V.

During the winter months this is very much a brasserie with just a handful of locals propping up the bar. When the weather is warmer, however, the outside terrace fills with youngish professionals laughing off the smog and knocking back bottles of Chardonnay and jugs of Sea Breeze or 'Lavender Tea' (similar to Long Island Iced Tea). Year round it's a cheerful place with painted brick walls, wooden floors and school chairs. The imaginative menu changes daily, and well-prepared dishes made with quality ingredients rarely exceed a tenner. On our visit, the leek and cheese tartlet was rather functional, though the home-made piccalilli was a good idea (£4.50). The lamb shank (£10.50) was tender and fell off the bone, and the accompanying mint and clove jus was well judged. Only bottled beers are available, but there's a good selection of wines. *Babies and children admitted (high chairs). Tables outdoors (pavement). Vegetarian dishes.*

Le Bar des Magis

5-9 Battersea Rise, SW11 (020 7738 0307). Clapham Common tube/Clapham Junction rail/35, 37 bus. **Open** 10am-11pm Mon-Sat; 10am-10.30pm Sun. **Food served** noon-11pm Mon-Sat; noon-10.30pm Sun. **Credit** AmEx, MC, V.

It's not just the name, there's hardly a Gallic twist missed off the list at Le Bar des Magis: copies of the freebie French mag *Ici Londres* by the door, ceiling fans, croques monsieur, filled baguettes, and even, goddammit, a waiter who looked like Tintin and whose English was even worse than our French.

Had it not been for the smattering of suits around the bar we could almost have been a Eurostar away from south London. Punters drink a lot of wine in keeping with the surroundings, but there's also an interesting range of Belgian and French bottled beers including Leffe, Brunne, Pelforth Blonde, Jenlain, Duvel and Chimay, as well as Kronenburg 1664 on tap. Grab a table and prepare to try them all. But, mes enfants, just remember pastis only tastes nice in France. Don't try it at home.
Babies and children admitted (children's menu; crèche 1-3pm Sat, Sun; high chairs). Function room. Satellite TV. Tables outdoors (pavement). Vegetarian dishes.

Mason's Arms
169 Battersea Park Road, SW8 (020 7622 2007). Battersea Park rail/44, 137, 344 bus. **Open** noon-11pm Mon-Sat; noon-10.30pm Sun. **Food served** noon-4pm, 6-9.30pm daily. **Credit** AmEx, MC, V.
When quiet, the inside of the Mason's Arms seems cavernous and rather spartan; there are a couple of sofas huddling like frightened sheep round the fire at the back, but apart from this, it's a fleet of mismatched tables on a sanded floorboard sea, with an open-plan kitchen to the right of the bar. However, when the place is jumping (which is pretty much every evening) it comes into its welcoming own as a place for solid young professionals to relax and enjoy the top quality comfort food (club sandwiches, posh bangers and mash, osso bucco with saffron risotto). There's an impressively catholic selection of beers (including Brakspears, 6X, Leffe, Hoegaarden and Freedom Organic on tap) and a good selection of wines.
Babies and children admitted. Disabled: toilet. Music (DJs 9pm Sat). Tables outdoors (pavement). Vegetarian dishes.

raven oneforty
140 Westbridge Road, Battersea Square, SW11 (020 7801 0140). Clapham Junction rail. **Open** 5-11pm Mon-Sat; 5-10.30pm Sun. **Credit** MC, V.
Bodies under the floorboards; the ghost of a murdered scullery maid; smugglers' tunnels running from the cellar to the river; Dick Turpin as a regular: over the last 400 years the Raven has been a hotbed of illicit goings on. All of this leaves the new owners with something of a dilemma; they would like to turn this into a slick bar in the style of its sister, 126, on St John's Hill, but nothing in this listed building can be altered, not even the name – hence the awkward compromise of 'raven oneforty'. The low wooden window frames suggest swirly carpets and velour banquettes, but passers-by bending to

Critics' choice
kids

Bread & Roses (p169)
Toys, play area and kiddies' food.

Duke of Devonshire (p150)
Engrossing playground in large Balham garden.

Freemason's Arms (p214)
Run around the garden or the Heath.

Leather Bottle (p186)
Summer barbecue in Wimbledon garden.

Coach & Horses (p134)
Family-friendly courtyard garden with play area.

squint through the panes are rewarded by a bare, brightly lit and boldly painted bar, complete with table football, uplit bottles of cocktail staples and all the trimmings of your fashionable Battersea drinking hole. Staff are friendly and enthusiastic, and you want it to succeed, you really do, but in its latest incarnation it is going to have to work hard to establish an identity before it starts pulling the punters in.
Bar available for hire. Games (table football). Music (DJs Sat). Satellite TV (big screen).

S Bar
37 Battersea Bridge Road, SW11 (020 7223 3322). South Kensington tube/Clapham Junction rail/19, 49, 219, 345 bus. **Open** noon-11pm Mon-Wed; noon-midnight Thur-Sat; noon-10.30pm Sun. **Food served** noon-3pm, 6-9pm daily. **Credit** AmEx, MC, V.
Recently done up in a mature lounge/café style with big comfy sofas, potted ferns and newspapers on hand, it's a reinvention that may be a little too pre-planned for some. But the students from the Royal College of Art sculpture school across the road still pile in for their pints. It would be nice to think that the prints of classical sculpture on the walls were put there to inspire them (and the pre-Raphaelite paintings on the ceiling continue the good work when said students are flat on their backs after a few too many). The outside awnings always seem to be down which adds to the intimacy within.
Babies and children admitted (until 6pm). Disabled: toilet. Function room. Games (fruit machine). Music (live salsa band 8pm Thur; DJs 8pm Fri, Sat; live jazz 8pm Sun). Satellite TV. Tables outdoors (pavement). Vegetarian dishes.

Settle Inn
186 Battersea Bridge Road, SW11 (020 7228 0395/ www.thesettleinns.co.uk). Clapham Junction rail. **Open** noon-11pm Mon-Sat; noon-10.30pm Sun. **Food served** noon-3pm, 6-10pm Mon-Fri; noon-9.30pm Sat, Sun. **Credit** AmEx, MC, V.
When we first saw the sign Settle Inn we charitably allowed the possibility that it's an old name, one that predates the arrival of awful, toe-curling puns. Unfortunately, no; until recently this was the Rising Sun, and the new name truly is the pub equivalent of the hairdressers' 'His 'n' Hairs'. The temptation is to stay well away in protest, but then you'd be missing out on what isn't such a bad pub. It has a stylish if unoriginal interior of bare floorboards, chunky pale wood tables, sofas and biscuit-coloured walls, but daily newspapers and flowers in the ladies' loo are nice touches. A menu offers both decent pub grub (home-made burgers for £7) as well as more adventurous dishes such as white onion and rosemary soup (£4.50), or chicken breast wrapped in pancetta and stuffed with roast peppers with a porcini jus (£9). The chef used to be at Bah Humbug and although the diners here are certainly a far more conservative bunch, they still come in droves, especially for Sunday lunch. There's a good selection of wine and Bombardier, 6X, Courage Best supplement the usual draughts. Early summer 2001 should see the large garden at the side finished; the plans are for decking, a canopy and heaters.
Babies and children admitted. Games (board games). Satellite TV (big screen). Tables outdoors (garden). Vegetarian dishes.

South Circular
89 Battersea Rise, SW11 (020 7207 0170). Clapham Common tube, then 35 or 37 bus/Clapham Junction rail. **Open** 5.30-11pm Mon-Sat; 5.30-10.30pm Sun. **Happy hour** 5.30-8pm daily. **Credit** MC, V.
A welcome antidote to the bad dream of bleached pine and cream walls that is the Battersea bar scene, South Circular

(named for the road it's on) is way out on its own. Back-lit panels throw shades of galaxy blue, astral orange and silver over the metallic grey walls. Buck Rogers would finally feel at home here, leaning against the curvilinear pod bar sipping a cocktail or lounging on the banquette in the frosted window. The smaller back room is very relaxed; chilled-out space hoppers take it easy on neo-'70s furniture while bathed in mellow diffused lighting. The friendly Brazilian guys in command serve mostly bottled beers (including Freedom) or cocktails (the most popular are half price between 5.30 and 8pm). It is all too rare that an independent bar like this comes along and bravely sets its own style. Effortlessly cool.
Function room. Games (board games). Music (DJs Fri, Sat). Specialities: cocktails.

Tea Room des Artistes

697 Wandsworth Road, SW8 (020 7652 6526/ www.sanctum.org). Clapham Common tube/Wandsworth Town rail/77, 77A, 137 or 345 bus. **Open** 5.30pm-1am Fri-Sun. **Food served** 5.30pm-12.30am Fri-Sun. **Credit** MC, V (in restaurant only).
Thankfully it seems the wild excesses of the **Artesian Well** (*see p151*) next door have failed to seduce many of the Tea Room's loyal following, and it remains as busy as ever – on the three nights of the week that it's open. Fifteen years ago, this was the wild place, complete with fairy lights, chandeliers, salvage yard chairs with leopard skin cushions, and trippy projections on the ceiling. Now, however, there's something reassuring about it; like a safe haven from the changing tides of fashion. The food is good value, too: puy lentil red curry with spiced broccoli, coconut rice and banana and pineapple chutney for £6.95 and artichoke and parmesan risotto balls deep-fried and served on rocket at £7.25. Never really a place to just drop in on, it remains a favourite for birthday parties and big nights out.
Babies and children admitted (until 9pm). Function room. Games (table football). Music (DJs 10pm Fri, Sat; 8pm Sun). Restaurant. Tables outdoors (garden). Vegetarian dishes.

Woodman

60 Battersea High Street, SW11 (020 7228 2968). Clapham Junction rail/239 bus. **Open** 11am-11pm Mon-Sat; noon-10.30pm Sun. **Food served** noon-10pm Mon-Sat; noon-9.30pm Sun. **Credit** MC, V.
A few doors away is the Original Woodman (the background to the conflict is lost in the mists of time) but we prefer this boozer, the usurper. Its front room is delightfully cosy with a horseshoe-shaped bar selling excellent beers from Hall & Woodhouse (Badger, Tanglefoot and King & Barnes Old Ale), as well as interesting pilsners on tap. The standard pub grub probably won't bring foodies flocking, but with panelling on the walls, an open fire and convivial atmosphere, it's always popular. The large beamed room at the back is a more recent addition and what it lacks in character it attempts to make up for with table football, pool, board games and big-screen TV. A garden at the rear is equipped with heaters to combat chilly Battersea nights.
Babies and children admitted (until 4pm). Games (fruit machine, pool table, table football, video games). Music (bands 8pm Tue). Quiz (8.30pm Wed; £1 to play). Satellite TV (big screen). Tables outdoors (garden). Vegetarian dishes.

Also in the area...

All Bar One 7-9 Battersea Square, SW11 (020 7326 9831).
B@1 85 Battersea Rise, SW11 (020 7978 6595).
Bar Coast 281 Lavender Hill, SW11 (020 7924 8020).

Bar Risa 49 Lavender Gardens, SW11 (020 7228 3744).
Bar Room Bar 441 Battersea Park Road, SW8 (020 7223 7721).
Café Rouge 39-49 Parkgate Road, SW11 (020 7924 3565).
O'Neill's 66A-66C Battersea Rise, SW11 (020 7350 0349).
Falcon (JD Wetherspoon) 1-13 Falcon Road, SW11 (020 7801 0048).
Fine Line 31-37 Northcote Road, SW11 (020 7924 7387).
Pitcher & Piano 94 Northcote Road, SW11 (020 7738 9781).
Puzzle 47-49 Lavender Hill, SW11 (020 7978 7682).
Slug & Lettuce 4 St John's Hill, SW11 (020 7924 1322).

Bermondsey & Rotherhithe

Blacksmith's Arms

257 Rotherhithe Street, SE16 (020 7237 1349). Canada Water or Rotherhithe tube. **Open** noon-11pm Mon-Sat; noon-10.30pm Sun. **Food served** 6.30-9.30pm Tue-Sat; noon-6pm Sun. **Credit** (restaurant only) AmEx, MC, V.
This is a good old-fashioned Fuller's boozer (with saloon bar, public bar and games room out back) in a riverside of corporate bars and heritage pubs. Signed pictures of Joanna Lumley and Chris Tarrant are prominent; look harder, behind bar menus and a golf trophy, and you'll also find Cilla and Beadle. Bar food is available and there's a restaurant upstairs with more substantial fare such as mussels in cream and cider sauce. Punters tend to be a mix of new- ('Pint of Pride, please') and old-style ('Gissus a Black Label, Tone') Rotherhithe locals, augmented by American tourists from the adjacent Holiday Inn.
Babies and children admitted. Games (darts, fruit machines, pool table). Restaurant. Tables outdoors (garden). TV. Vegetarian dishes.

Famous Angel

101 Bermondsey Wall East, SE16 (020 7237 3608/ www.famousangel.co.uk). Bermondsey tube. **Open** 11.30am-11pm Mon-Sat; noon-10.30pm Sun. **Food served** noon-2.30pm, 7-9.30pm Mon-Sat; noon-2pm Sun. **Credit** AmEx, DC, MC, V.
The former Angel, officially renamed the Famous Angel (does Gabriel know about this?), has been a feature on the river since the 15th century. Originally a home from home for dockers and seamen, it's seen custom from the likes of Samuel Pepys, who mentioned it in his diary, Judge Jefferies, who used to watch pirates being drowned at Execution Dock opposite, and the ubiquitous Charles Dickens. These days it's a haunt of groups of cigar-chomping executives drawn by the upmarket upstairs restaurant (more reasonably priced bar food includes spinach and ricotta tortellini, soup of the day, and the like) and tourists, no doubt drawn by the word 'famous' in the new title. The fact that it was once made up of five bars explains the curious octagonal shape, but not the striped Regency-style wallpaper.
Function room. Games (fruit machine, quiz machine). Music (jazz duo 7.30pm Sun). Restaurant. Tables outdoors (riverside patio). Vegetarian dishes.

Mayflower

117 Rotherhithe Street, SE16 (020 7237 4088). Canada Water or Rotherhithe tube. **Open** noon-11pm Mon-Sat; noon-10.30pm Sun. **Food served** 6.30-9pm Tue-Sat; noon-4pm Sun. **Credit** AmEx, DC, MC, V.

South

London crawling: London pride

Tate Modern has been a sensation, undoing most of the damaging publicity that the Dome unleashed upon the capital and, more importantly, reminding Londoners what a terrific city they live in. Taking in this and other architectural adventures old and new – the grand Assembly Building, the amusingly troubled Millennium Bridge and the historic Globe theatre – a South Bank stroll will do much to (re)kindle your lust for London. So too will the fine riverside pub pickings.

Blackfriars is a good bridge (a minute from the tube station) to kick off from; though when the Millennium Bridge reopens for business, you can use that and back-track to the **Founder's Arms**. Phenomenally ugly in itself, it features large picture windows and a riverside terrace that gets tediously busy in the summer. Backpacking tourists from all over the world flock here to crouch on the floor and share glasses of Coca Cola. The beer's good, and the view is even better – especially at night when the wonky bridge, and St Paul's and the City opposite are lit up brighter than a Californian Christmas tree.

Moving on past Tate Bankside and Shakespeare's Globe theatre (stop-offs optional), we eventually hit the **Anchor Bankside**, an historic old pub named after a long-gone local brewery, that's been here in one guise or another since before the Normans conquered. Don't expect a traditional pub welcome – it's too much of a tourist trap to have time for such niceties – and although the creaking staircases and various wood timbered rooms have a unique atmosphere, we can only bear it when drinkers are thin on the ground.

The nearby **Old Thameside Inn** is about as old as your Tweenies CD, but it's in a reconstructed spice warehouse and some of the beams and stonework are original. Its waterside terrace is one of the best on this stretch of the river.

Taking a detour away from the Thames, we head down to the **Market Porter**, one of London's most beer-friendly hostelries, where you'll find at least eight real ales and drinkers predominantly drawn from the wholesale fruit and veg market opposite. This is especially true when the pub opens at 6am. If you find the Market Porter a little upmarket, especially after the recent refit, try the **Wheatsheaf**, a few doors down. There's a similar dedication to real ale, although the range is smaller.

Heading away from the river, down Borough High Street, you'll find the **George Inn**, the last of London's galleried coaching inns. Built in 1676, and set behind a large courtyard, have fun traipsing through the many corridors and small rooms (most do) and check out the half-a-dozen cask-conditioned ales on offer. Their own-brand Restoration Ale is usually worth a slurp.

As we're so close to one of London's best pubs, it would be a shame to pass the **Royal Oak** by without a visit. The only London outpost for Lewes' superb Harveys brewery, it's a sympathetically refurbished Victorian boozer that's won awards for its decor as well as its beer. We tend to run through the card of beers, starting with the Mild and progressing through Pale, Sussex and Old. On walks like this it's best to make do with halves. Sadly.

Assuming we're still steady on our feet, we head back towards the river, stopping off to sample a pint of locally brewed Andy Bishop's Bitter at the **Shipwrights Arms**, a large free house nestling in the shadow of London Bridge station. Then it's a fairly long but pleasant stroll along the riverside path, past Ken's office-to-be, the headlamp-like Assembly Building, to **Bridge House**. This is a relatively new bar decked out in bistro-style decor that offers Adnam's bitters and a fine view of the City across the water that at night is almost Manhattenish.

From there walk across Tower Bridge and feel like a million (inebriated) dollars, high on the sight of age-old Tower-side Thames to your left and, to your right, the thrusting 21st-century glass-and-steel arrogance of Canary Wharf and Docklands. Intoxicating. Now go home, and drink plenty of water before you go to bed. *Jim Driver*

Anchor Bankside (*p159*) 34 Park Street SE1 (020 7407 1577).
Bridge House (*p160*) 218 Tower Bridge Road, SE1 (020 7407 5818).
Founder's Arms (*p161*) 52 Hopton Street, SE1 (020 7928 1899).
George Inn (*p161*) 77 Borough High Street, SE1 (020 7407 2056).
Market Porter (*p161*) 9 Stoney Street, SE1 (020 7407 2495).
Old Thameside Inn (*p161*) Pickford's Wharf, Clink Street SE1 (020 7403 4243).
Royal Oak (*p161*) 44 Tabard Street, SE1 (020 7357 7173).
Shipwrights Arms (*no review*) 88 Tooley Street, SE1 (020 7378 1486).
Wheatsheaf (*p162*) 6 Stoney Street, SE1 (020 7407 1514).

Cave Austin

You've got to wonder where the gangs of students and inordinate numbers of young northerners who pack this place out most evenings come from and why. At first glance you wouldn't think that this historic seafaring inn would be their cup of tea with its rackety wooden floors, small wood-partitioned areas and narrow settles. Do they know that the timbers here are reputed to come from the Mayflower ship that moored alongside on its return from the Americas? Would they care? Maybe it's the Greene King bitters and short but fairly interesting wine list that draws them. In winter you get roaring fires, in summer oodles of roaring tourists appreciating the view down the Thames.
Babies and children admitted (restaurant). Games (fruit machine). Music (bands 8pm occasional Mon, Tue). Quiz (9pm Thur; £1 to play). Restaurant. Tables outdoors (riverside terrace). Vegetarian dishes.

Spice Island
163 Rotherhithe Street, SE16 (020 7394 7108). Rotherhithe tube. **Open** 11am-11pm Mon-Sat; noon-10.30pm Sun. **Food served** noon-10pm Mon-Sat; noon-9pm Sun. **Credit** AmEx, MC, V.

If you were designing old spice warehouses on the Thames, it's unlikely that you'd construct such an intricate roofing pattern as they have here. Nevertheless, this building is converted from a genuine riverside structure and is very popular with footballers from the nearby sports fields and their adoring paramours. Tourists seem bemused by the place and tend to hang round the entrance in groups, although there's enough room for a Japanese army and the American Sixth fleet. Spice Island is a two-tiered wooden structure with a restaurant upstairs and seating areas running around a central serving area below. The music is a little louder than necessary. Out back a large heated riverside veranda has an enviable view of the City opposite.
Babies and children admitted (until 8pm; children's menu, high chairs). Disabled: lift, toilet. Games (fruit machine, pool table, quiz machine). Music (DJs 8pm Fri). No-smoking area (restaurant). Restaurant. Satellite TV. Tables outdoors (riverside terrace). Vegetarian dishes.

Also in the area...
Surrey Docks (JD Wetherspoon) 185 Lower Road, SE16 (020 7394 2832).

Blackheath

Cave Austin
7-9 Montpelier Vale, SE3 (020 8852 0492). Blackheath rail.
Open 11am-midnight Mon-Wed, Fri, Sat; 11am-2am Thur;
11am-10.30pm Sun. **Food served** noon-10.30pm Mon-Fri;
11am-10.30pm Sat; 11am-9.30pm Sun. **Credit** MC, V.
Cave Austin's sandy-beige paintwork, internal windows and
clever subdued lighting effects vie with Zero Degrees for the
title of Blackheath's best designed hangout. One of the
incredibly good-looking serving staff behind the metal bar
will probably be fiddling with the cappuccino machine or
struggling with the lid of a cocktail shaker – it's all part of
the Austin experience. To your right there's the restaurant (a
mixed menu features a fair amount of fishy mains, with prices
around the £11 mark) and downstairs a beige basement with
the power to impress anyone who goes for sleekly understated
surroundings. Alternatively, you can enjoy the tranquillity of
Cave Austin's back garden, complete with waterfall and
colourful fish.
Babies and children admitted (restaurant, until 6pm).
Function rooms. Music (DJs 9pm Thur, £2; live music
8.30pm Sun). Restaurant. Tables outdoors (garden).
Vegetarian dishes.

Crown
49 Tranquil Vale, SE3 (020 8852 0326). Blackheath rail.
Open/food served 11am-11pm Mon-Sat; noon-10.30pm
Sun. **Credit** AmEx, DC, MC, V.
The plaque outside states that this is one of Blackheath's
oldest buildings, dating back to 1740 with a proud place in
history as a staging post for the horse-drawn omnibus. In
winter there's a roaring fire, in summer there's the provision
of enough bench tables outside to keep even the Pickwick
Club content. As with most Blackheath boozers, the
customers have a tendency to be young and sturdy (rugger
buggers and their consorts), with a smattering of older gents
sporting cravats, as well as assorted blue collar drinkers. Real
ale freaks are well catered for (Old Peculiar, Speckled Hen and
Courage, plus two guest ales rotated weekly), as are lovers of
keenly priced traditional pub grub of the bubble and squeak,
chicken and bacon pie variety.
Games (fruit machine, video game). Tables outdoors
(pavement). Vegetarian dishes.

Hare & Billet
1A Hare & Billet Road, SE3 (020 8852 2352). Blackheath
rail. **Open** 11am-11pm Mon-Sat; noon-10.30pm Sun.
Food served noon-7pm daily. **Credit** MC, V.
A fair trot from the station, this very pleasant outpost from
Hogshead is a cut above the average chain pub. The wood
floors are possibly authentic, the split-level seating areas and
half panelling show an individual design, and modern art dots
the walls. Expect to find slightly older examples of
Blackheath bar life, with an average age of 30, many of them
drawn by the range of real ales that Hogsheads were set up
to provide. There are standards (like Courage and
Theakston's), cheap pints (Flowers £2, Boddingtons £1.90)
and often some interesting regional bitters. Effort has been
put into food, but don't expect Michel Roux to pop out of the
kitchen, this is pie and pasta territory.
Babies and children admitted (dining area). Games (quiz
machine). No-smoking area (noon-9pm). Vegetarian dishes.

Princess of Wales
1A Montpelier Row, SE3 (020 8297 5911). Blackheath
rail. **Open** noon-11pm Mon-Sat; noon-10.30pm Sun.
Food served noon-9pm daily. **Credit** MC, V.

Unlike most other pubs of the same name, this good-looking
Georgian boozer was not renamed following the untimely
death of Princess Di, but takes its moniker from Caroline of
Brunswick, George IV's missus. It's a big pub, with two large
cream-painted bars, comfy sofas and a striking curtain-
topped dome to the conservatory. The first-ever Rugby Union
international (played in Edinburgh in 1871) was organised
here, and thanks to the prominence of Blackheath RFC, there's
still a strong link. Aside from the young rugby crowd,
customers cover most age groups and types, though under
30s are in the majority. It can get busy, and on summer
weekends you may prefer to drink out on the heath: just ask
for a plastic glass and bring your own designer shades.
Disabled: toilet. Games (fruit machine, quiz machine). Satellite
TV. Tables outdoors (garden, patio). Vegetarian dishes.

Zero Degrees
29-31 Montpelier Vale, SE3 (020 8852 5619/
www.zerodegrees-microbrewery.co.uk) Blackheath rail.
Open/food served noon-midnight Mon-Sat; noon-
11.30pm Sun. **Credit** AmEx, DC, MC, V.
Just off the edge of the heath, looking a bit like an upmarket tin
shack, Zero Degrees attracts a cross-section of local life from
bright young things to gnarled old codgers. The decor's
industrial in style – exposed stonework, pipes and ducting, and
a wrought-iron balcony. The in-house brewery at the heart of
the operation takes up a major chunk of the ground floor. There
are usually five 'hand-crafted' beers on tap: pilsner, pale ale,
brown ale, wheat ale and a 'special' that's usually a stout or
porter. Strictly speaking these aren't 'real ales' as gas is used to
dispense them, but they are close cousins. The wine list is short
but sweet, and the slightly smoky atmosphere comes from the
open kitchen's wood-fired pizza oven. A small menu revolves
around superb thin-crust pizzas and kilo pots of mussels.
Babies and children admitted (high chairs). Restaurant.
Satellite TV (big screen). Specialities: own-brewed beers.
Vegetarian dishes.

Also in the area...
Café Rouge 16-18 Montpelier Vale, SE3
(020 8297 2727).
O'Neill's 52 Tranquil Vale, SE3 (020 8297 5901).

Borough & Southwark

Anchor Bankside
34 Park Street, SE1 (020 7407 1577). London Bridge
tube/rail. **Open** 11am-11pm Mon-Sat; noon-10.30pm Sun.
Food served noon-2.30pm, 6-9.30pm daily; bar snacks
noon-5pm Sat, Sun. **Credit** AmEx, DC, MC, V.
Although there's been a pub on this Thames-side site for a
millennium or more, the current version is relatively modern,
constructed in 1775 over the ruins of what was the Castell on
the Hoop and partially rebuilt after a fire in 1876. In times
gone by, Bankside was a notorious den of prostitutes and
bear-baiters and there's an unconsecrated graveyard for
brothel workers nearby. Pick of the pub's numerous bars and
crannies is the Johnson Room, where the great man actually
stayed and wrote parts of his dictionary. These days there's
quite a bit of patronage from the staff of the nearby *Financial*
Times, and hoards of tourists in raptures over the exposed
stone, historic oak beams and rattling staircases. Tom Cruise
and Ving Rhames were also filmed drinking here for the final
scene of the *Mission Impossible* movie. Real ales include
Marston's Pedigree, Courage Directors and Wadworth 6X.
Food (typically lamb cutlets and grilled salmon) comes at
slightly inflated prices but is said to be good.

Zero Degrees.
See page 159.

Babies and children admitted. Function room. Games (fruit machine). Restaurant. Tables outdoors (riverside terrace). Vegetarian dishes.

Anchor Tap

20A Horsleydown Lane, SE1 (020 7403 4637). Tower Hill tube/ London Bridge tube/rail/Tower Gateway DLR. **Open** 11am-11pm Mon-Sat; noon-10.30pm Sun. **Food served** noon-9pm Mon-Sat; noon-5pm Sun. **Credit** MC, V.
This good-looking riverside pub with its 'olde worlde' half-panelled walls and exposed stonework is operated by Yorkshire's Samuel Smith brewery, so at least you can expect decent beer at knock-down prices (Ayingerbräu lager is just £1.90 a pint, for example). Being right by Tower Bridge there's a chalk board in the front bar telling of imminent 'raisings', which is useful for eager visitors and late sailors. There's a bar for almost every mood, ranging from a small games room by the main entrance to a family room, garden and an upstairs lounge. We found the staff friendly and on the ball on the Wednesday night we crossed the threshold.
Babies and children admitted (high chairs). Function room. Games (darts, fruit machine, games machine, pool table). No-smoking area (restaurant). Quiz (8pm Thur). Restaurant. Tables outdoors (garden). TV. Vegetarian dishes.

Belushi's

161 Borough High Street, SE1 (020 7939 9700/ www.st-christophers.co.uk). London Bridge tube/rail. **Open** 11am-11pm Mon-Wed; 11am-midnight Thur, Sat; 11am-12.30am Fri; 11.30am-10.30pm Sun. **Food served** 11am-3pm, 6-10pm Mon-Wed; 11am-3pm, 6-11pm Thur; 11am-3pm, 6-11.30pm Fri; 11am-midnight Sat; 11am-10.30pm Sun. **Happy hour** 5-8pm Mon-Fri. **Credit** MC, V (over £10).
From the split-level aluminium and wood flooring to the pop and movie posters plastered all over the walls and the blasting MTV, Belushi's screams 'PARTY!' On the midweek evening we visited, a dozen or so from the nearby St Christopher Inn – 'the hostel with attitude', we kid you not – were certainly doing their best to have a good time. Excluding, that is, the four who were earnestly speaking into their mobile phones by the diner-style entrance. The beers are pretty standard – John Smith's Smooth, Guinness, etc – and nothing was

remotely cask-conditioned, but the punters we stumbled upon were happy caning bottled beers and wine.
Function room. Games (fruit machine, golf machine). Karaoke (8pm Thur). Music (DJs 8pm Fri, Sat; live bands 8pm Thur, Sat; £3/£2 concs). Quiz (8pm Wed). Vegetarian dishes

Blue Eyed Maid

173 Borough High Street, SE1 (020 7378 8259) Borough tube. **Open** 11am-11pm Mon-Fri. **Food served** 11am-10pm Mon-Fri. **Credit** MC, V.
A gentrified bistro-style pub, the Blue Eyed Maid has floor-to-ceiling wooden shelving behind its long bar and windows shaded by venetian blinds. There's a large selection of wines, and although their single real ale (Greene King IPA the last few times we've been) is usually well kept and rather tasty, it's quite often 'off'. The menu is very keen to compliment itself on freshness and the lack of GM ingredients, although the tendency is towards standard dishes like pasta and fish and chips. We usually find young men in suits drinking here, plus groups of after-work women and once a gang of middle-aged Americans who claimed to be a penitentiary golfing society. As if…
Function room. Games (fruit machine). Tables outdoors (pavement). Vegetarian dishes.

Bridge House

218 Tower Bridge Road, SE1 (020 7407 5818). Tower Hill tube/Tower Gateway DLR. **Open** noon-11pm Mon-Sat; noon-10.30pm Sun. **Food served** noon-3pm daily. **Credit** MC, V.
Whatever next, a destination bar practically on Tower Bridge. The large picture windows offer an impressive view of the river and the Tower (and of Tower Bridge, if you crane your head round sufficiently), even if a new block does suddenly obscure the view of St Paul's. Plenty of seating is available in the spacious, beige and terracotta-painted ground floor bar and there's also a quiet wine bar-type cellar, but the smart drinkers head for the stools by the window shelf. Service was friendly and efficient and the Adnam's bitters on tap were well looked after, if maybe a tad too cool for traditional tastes. There's a comprehensive wine list and a restaurant upstairs opens for the tourist season.
Babies and children admitted (restaurant). Disabled: toilet. Function room. Games (fruit machine). Restaurant. Tables outdoors (pavement). TV. Vegetarian dishes.

Cantina Vinopolis
*1 Bank End, SE1 (020 7940 8333). London Bridge
tube/rail.* **Open/food served** noon-3pm, 6-10.30pm
Mon- Sat; noon-4pm Sun. **Credit** AmEx, MC, V.
This cavernous converted railway arch houses a small drinking
area at the front, with a couple of rows of large wooden dining
tables (full of young execs talking animatedly about football, sex
and parking when we visited) and a group of brick-vaulted
dining rooms with soaring ceilings beyond. Food is restricted to
formal meals, so no bar snacks. Service is spot-on, however, and
the menu excellent: modern Italian and French, with New World
influences and good prices. There's also an encyclopaedic,
reasonably priced wine list – around 400 bins, all available by
the glass – and you can visit Vinopolis (the permanent exhibition
of wines from around the world, £11.50/£10.50 concs) in the
same complex. A great place to sink a couple of decent bottles.
*Babies and children admitted. Function room. No piped
music or jukebox. Restaurant. Vegetarian dishes.*

Cynthia's Robotic Bar & Restaurant
*4 Tooley Street, SE1 (020 7403 6777/www.cynbar.co.uk).
London Bridge tube/rail.* **Open** noon-1am Mon-Wed;
noon-3am Thur-Sat; noon-midnight Sun. **Food served**
noon-3pm, 5-10pm Mon-Sat. **Admission** after 9pm
Thur-Sat £3-£10. **Credit** AmEx, MC, V.
Enter under London Bridge and you stumble upon a future
world of mirrored caverns that could have been envisioned
in the 1980s: do we really expect red and blue LED bar
decorations in the hereafter? Sadly, this bar-diner is more
tacky than fantastically witty and kitsch. During the day it's
open 'for humans of all ages', but after dark it's strictly adults
only. Family food includes kids' favourites like joy sticks (fish
fingers), plus stir fries, burgers and pasta for bigger people.
Cocktails like Space Benders or Full Thrust are dispensed by
pressing buttons on the consoles of robots Cynthia and Rasta,
and Leffe Blonde and Brun are also available. At weekends
we're assured you can't move for the crush of clubbers, but
on the mid-evening Tuesday we visited, it was just two
Japanese students, a table of pissed-up office workers and us.
*Babies and children admitted (children's menu, high
chairs, toys). Disabled: toilet. Function room. Music (DJs
most nights, club nights 9pm Thur-Sat). No-smoking area.
Restaurant. Vegetarian dishes.*

Founder's Arms
*52 Hopton Street, SE1 (020 7928 1899). Blackfriars
tube/rail.* **Open** 11am-11pm Mon-Sat; 11am-10.30pm Sun.
Food served noon-8.30pm Mon-Sat; noon-7pm Sun.
Credit AmEx, MC, V.
The large plate glass windows of this modern riverside pub
offer truly awesome views, especially at night when the City is
lit up. St Paul's is practically opposite and the Millennium
Bridge a mere swing away. The story Young's tells is that
although the pub was completed in 1979, it had to wait a year
for the roads and paths of the Bankside development to be
finished so that beer and customers could get here. Now summer
sees the riverside terrace awash with tourists, and there's never
much room inside. It's a decent pub with food that's a cut above
the usual, veering towards Modern European. Beer comes from
Young's so it's good and the wine list well worth a look.
*Games (fruit machines). No-smoking area. Tables
outdoors (riverside patio). Vegetarian dishes.*

George Inn
*77 Borough High Street, SE1 (020 7407 2056). Borough
tube/London Bridge tube/rail.* **Open** 11am-11pm Mon-Sat;
noon-10.30pm Sun. **Food served** noon-3pm Mon-Fri;
noon-4pm Sat, Sun. **Credit** MC, V.

The National Trust doesn't own many pubs, and this is its
flagship, currently leased to Whitbread. Built in 1676, it is
London's only surviving galleried coaching inn and still has
the myriad of small bars that was the fashion in the 17th
century. Looking almost like a parody of an old pub – old stone
walls, weathered timber and exposed beams – it's not
surprising that this has become a haunt of tourists and
language school students. The array of real ales is impressive,
including an 'own label' Restoration Ale that was brewed by
Crouch Vale when last we heard. The picnic-tabled courtyard
(with its own little bar and toilets) gets unbelievably busy in
summer and pub food with pretension is served all year round.
*Babies and children admitted (high chairs). Function
rooms. Games (quiz machine). Music (live folk bands
8.30pm first Mon in month). No piped music or jukebox.
No-smoking room (afternoons only). Restaurant. Tables
outdoors (courtyard). Vegetarian dishes.*

Market Porter
*9 Stoney Street, SE1 (020 7407 2495). London Bridge
tube/rail.* **Open** 6-8.30am, 11am-11pm Mon-Sat; noon-
10.30pm Sun. **Food served** noon-2.30pm daily.
Credit AmEx, DC, MC, V.
Purists will be appalled to learn that there's been a shake-up
at this highly regarded cornerstone of the Borough Market
scene. The management might be pleased with its tarted-up
new venue, but some of us aren't quite so happy. There's still
the wooden beams and plenty of etched glass, but gone are the
peculiar little fenced-off areas, and in has come corporate toilet
advertising and more efficient lighting. Yet despite our Luddite
tendencies, we still consider this one of London's finest boozers,
offering a wide and imaginative selection of real ales – we
counted eight the last time we swanned along – and an
atmosphere most pub companies would love to bottle.
Customers come from all walks of life, from arts students to
the market's spud salesmen to Middle Eastern journalists. It'll
be even better when the shine wears off the new paint…
*Function room. Games (darts, fruit machines).
Restaurant. Satellite TV. Vegetarian dishes.*

Old Thameside Inn
*Pickfords Wharf, 1 Clink Street, SE1 (020 7403 4243).
London Bridge tube/rail.* **Open** 11am-11pm Mon-Fri;
11am-11pm Sat; noon-6pm Sun. **Food served** noon-3pm
daily. **Credit** AmEx, MC, V.
The views from the rows of bench tables on the riverside
terrace save this otherwise unremarkable pub (bare brick
walls, low beams and dark wood) from obscurity. A
reconstructed Thameside warehouse, the 'Old' part of the
name is tempered by the flashing lights on the fruit machines
and by the ubiquity of Nicholson's (whose pub this is) logo.
Customers are an uneasy mix of local office wallahs, backpacking tourists and slumming media workers. The real ale
choice isn't bad (London Pride, Adnam's Best and Tetley's)
and there's certainly enough lager to float the nearby *Golden
Hinde* – which is also a replica.
*Babies and children admitted (restaurant). Disabled: toilet.
Function room. Games (fruit machine, pool table, quiz
machine, video games). No-smoking area. Restaurant.
Tables outdoors (riverside terrace). Vegetarian dishes.*

Royal Oak
*44 Tabard Street, SE1 (020 7357 7173). Borough tube/
London Bridge tube/rail.* **Open** 11am-11pm Mon-Fri. **Food
served** noon-2.30pm, 6-9.15pm daily. **Credit** MC, V.
A strong candidate for London's best pub, this is Harvey of
Lewes' only boozer in the Big Smoke. It was recently restored
to Victorian splendour and although the carefully carved
mahogany and sparkling etched glass may seem a little too

new, as the landlord reminds people, that's exactly what it looked like when it was first built. There are two bars, separated by a central serving area, with decent traditional pub food. The full range of Harvey's cask-conditioned canon is on offer, from Mild to Old, including seasonal brews. Service is friendly and knowledgeable and although it's not the easiest pub to find, the walk is well worth the trouble. *Disabled: toilet. Function room. Quiz (8.30pm Tue). Vegetarian dishes.*

Wheatsheaf

6 Stoney Street, SE1 (no phone). London Bridge tube/rail. **Open** 11am-11pm Mon-Sat; noon-4pm first Sun in month. **Food served** noon-2.30pm Mon-Sat. **No credit cards**. This rough diamond of a boozer is the preferred choice for most of the vegetable wholesalers from Borough Market. And if you want an intelligent conversation about cheese, this is the place to come. It's a small, scruffy, two-bar pub that usually has five proper beers on, many of them rarities that the landlord has winkled out from Britain's most obscure breweries. Competitive darts is played on a regular basis and our last visit coincided with an off-board dispute that became pretty animated. Customers are the type who wouldn't be seen dead in an O'Neill's or Rat & Parrot. Not a pub for everyone, but a great find for traditionalists. *Babies and children admitted. Games (darts, fruit machine). Music (Irish folk band first Sun in month). Satellite TV. Vegetarian dishes.*

Wine Wharf

Stoney Street, SE1 (020 7940 8335). London Bridge tube/rail. **Open** 11am-11pm Mon-Sat; noon-10pm Sun. **Food served** noon-10pm Mon-Fri; noon-6pm Sat, Sun. **Credit** AmEx, DC, MC, V. It's just a few minutes walk from London Bridge station but we've never failed to find a seat yet at this latest of Vinopolis wine bars (*see p160*). It's a spacious stone and wood place with lovely big leather sofas – although stupidly low tables that not even pipe-cleaner people could sit at. There's a very good selection of wines by the glass, or better still are the wine flights, five small measures on a theme, such as South American or 'winter warmers', which is five fruity, full-bodied reds; prices range from £7.25 to £14.40. There are superb Spanish tapas platters (£4.25 a plate) to nibble with the wines, and the cheeses (£3.25 a plate) are top quality too, supplied by Neal's Yard Dairy and Brindisa. Highly recommended. *Babies and children admitted (lunch). Bar area available for hire. Disabled: toilet. Vegetarian dishes.*

Also in the area...

All Bar One Fieldon House, 26-30 London Bridge Street, SE1 (020 7940 9981); 34 Shad Thames. **Café Rouge** Hays Galleria, Tooley Street, SE1 (020 7378 0097). **Elephant & Castle (JD Wetherspoon)** Metro Centre, Metro Central Heights, Newington Causeway, SE1 (020 7940 0890). **Goose & Firkin** 47 Borough Road, SE1 (020 7403 3590). **Heeltap & Bumper (Davys)** Chaucer House, White Hart Yard, Borough High Street, SE1 (020 7357 7454). **Mug House (Davys)** 1-3 Tooley Street, SE1 (020 7403 8344). **Pommeler's Rest (JD Wetherspoon)** 196-198 Tower Bridge Road, SE1 (020 7378 1399). **Skinkers (Davys)** 42 Tooley Street, SE1 (020 7407 7720). **Slug & Lettuce** 32 Borough High Street, SE1 (020 7378 9999).

Brixton & Streatham

Bar Lorca

261 Brixton Road, SW9 (020 7274 5537/ www.barlorca.com). Brixton tube/rail. **Open** 5pm-2am Mon-Thur; noon-3am Fri, Sat; noon-midnight Sun. **Food served** 5-11pm Mon-Thur; noon-11pm Fri-Sun. **Happy hour** 5-9pm Mon-Fri. **Admission** £5 after 10pm Fri, Sat. **Credit** AmEx, DC, MC, V. It's fast becoming a rather tiresomely tried and tested formula but Brixton's Bar Lorca, like its Stoke Newington counterpart (*see p229*), does the tapas and salsa thing pretty well. The wide and varied finger-pickin' menu is bolstered at weekends by paella and Spanish-style casseroles. On the drinks front there's a good selection of bottled Iberian beers supplemented by a decent wine list and the excellent Pacharan liqueur. The decor holds few surprises: two spacious connecting rooms are liberally scattered with uniform light wood furniture and painted in Mediterranean white and beige, with a few low-hanging blue table lights to add a welcome dash of stylish individuality. Salsa and world music bands play most weekends and there are the inevitable dance lessons. *Babies and children admitted (children's menus, high chairs, nappy-changing facilities, toys). Dance classes £5/hour, £7 two hours Mon, Tue; £6/hour, £7 two hours Fri, Sat; times vary). Disabled: toilet. Function room. Games (table football). Music (DJs most nights; live world music every other Sun). No-smoking area. Restaurant. Satellite TV (big screen). Tables outdoors (terrace yard). Vegetarian dishes.*

Baze 2 Baze

10-12 Tunstall Road, SW9 (020 7737 4797). Brixton tube/rail. **Open/food served** 8.30am-midnight daily. **Happy hour** 4-8pm daily. **Credit** MC, V. It's hard to imagine a worse name, but don't let that put you off – Baze 2 Baze is actually quite a sophisticated little watering hole. From its Arne Jacobson-style chairs, to the discreet corner bar, modern art prints and some pleasant decorative touches such as the large, steel-framed mirror on the back wall, the whole place is nicely understated. The interior is laid out more like a restaurant than a bar, and along with the usual bottled beers and cocktails, there's a classy Creole-influenced menu. The clientele appears, on the whole, to be a pretty discerning bunch, with a cool cut in clothes, although the place is often strangely quiet during the week, especially odd given a prime location, almost directly opposite the chaos of Brixton tube. *Babies and children admitted (daytime Mon-Fri). Function room. Tables outdoors (terrace). Vegetarian dishes.*

Brixtonian Havana Club

11 Beehive Place, SW9 (020 7924 9262/ www.brixtonian.co.uk). Brixton tube/rail. **Open** noon-1am Tue, Wed; noon-2am Thur-Sat. **Food served** 7-10.30pm Tue-Sat. **Happy hour** 5.30-7.30pm Mon-Fri. **Credit** MC, V. Tucked away on a narrow L-shaped street near the market, the Brixtonian is a good deal easier to locate on summer evenings, when its small courtyard becomes awash with loud music and lively punters. Come on a chilly night, though, and you'll have little to guide you but a small sandwich board sign (usually knocked over). Once you find it, you'll be glad you did. Inside, a short staircase leads up to the spacious attic loft space, where colourful perspex sheeting decorates the bar and cool junk-sculptures hint at the Cuban provenance. The Caribbean flavour is further enhanced by the staggering choice of rum (over 300

Wheatsheaf

varieties) displayed on sagging shelves behind the bar. There's also some fine Caribbean food, served in an increasingly formal dining area to the left of the bar. Cocktails are a strong point, usually delivered with the full bottle slinging, glass spinning performance. *Dance classes (7pm Mon; £4). Function room. Music (live jamming 8pm Tue; Brazilian music Wed; soca/Latin Fri; Latin/salsa Thur, Sat; jazz Sun). Restaurant. Specialities: cocktails, rums. Tables outdoors (paved area). Vegetarian dishes.*

Bug Bar
The Crypt, St Matthew's Church, Brixton Hill, SW2 (020 7738 3184/www.bugbar.co.uk). Brixton tube/rail. **Open** 7pm-1am Wed, Thur; 7pm-3am Fri, Sat; 7pm-2am Sun. **Food served** 5pm-3am Fri, Sat; 7pm-2am Sun. **Credit** MC, V.
Weeknights at the Bug Bar are generally a low-slung, laid-back affair, with Brixton's hipsters relaxed on comfy sofas slugging back bottled beer in the midst of fading semi-ecclesiastical murals (BB resides in the crypt of St Matthew's church). Visit on a weekend, however, and you'll find the same sofas are standing space only, providing underfoot spring for a buoyant up-for-it crowd, present in such numbers that the peaceful wall paintings you remember from Monday night will be barely visible behind the sea of bodies. Regular DJs spin an edgy mix of beats, breaks and house, and recent months have seen some genuinely big names at the decks, including Basement Jaxx and David Holmes. *Babies and children admitted (restaurant). Disabled: toilet. Music (DJs 9pm Wed-Sun; admission £3 9-11pm, £5 after 11pm Fri, Sat; live band twice monthly 8pm Wed; £2 admission). Restaurant. Specialities: organic wines and beers. Tables outdoors (garden). Vegetarian dishes.*

Dogstar
389 Coldharbour Lane, SW9 (020 7733 7515/ www.dogstarbar.co.uk). Brixton tube/rail. **Open** noon-2.30am Mon-Thur; noon-4am Fri, Sat; noon-2am Sun. **Food served** noon-5pm Sun. **Admission** £3 9-10pm, £4 10-11pm, £5 11pm-4am Fri; £4 9-10pm, £5 10-11pm, £7 11pm-4am Sat; £3 after 10.30pm Sun. **Credit** AmEx, DC, MC, V.
This whacking great corner pub is a true Brixton stalwart, with drinking and dancing seven nights a week. Its comfortably ageing interior – all big, battered tables and peeling paintwork – belies its booming reputation and the unpretentious punters make a refreshing change from the preeners in certain nearby venues. Fridays and Saturdays are loud and boisterous and generally involve queueing if you don't arrive early enough. In our experience, though, the bar really comes into its own on a Sunday evening when, as the weekend is winding down elsewhere, the Dogstar keeps the beer flowing and cranks up the sound an extra notch. It's worth dropping by during the day, too, when a veggie lunch can be enjoyed in a more mild-mannered environment. *Babies and children admitted (until 6pm). Disabled: toilet. Function rooms. Games (fruit machine, pinball machine, pool table). Music (DJs 9pm nightly; admission charges Fri, Sat; see above). Satellite TV (big screen). Tables outdoors (garden). Vegetarian dishes.*

Duke of Edinburgh
204 Ferndale Road, SW9 (020 7924 0509). Clapham North tube/Brixton tube/rail. **Open/food served** noon-11pm Mon-Sat; noon-10.30pm Sun. **Credit** MC, V.
The archetypal local, the Duke of E's traditional corner-pub façade gives way to a compact public bar, behind which is a larger, louder saloon, with a massive roaring fire. Decor-wise it's wood panelling and thinning carpets throughout with a good selection of games – including pool and darts – livening up the front bar. The mix of long-time regulars and younger, newer-to-the-area types makes for a surprisingly upbeat crowd, even on midweek evenings. Congenial bar staff also do their bit to ensure punters succumb to the 'alright, just another one then' syndrome. *Babies and children admitted (until 7pm). Games (fruit machine, pool table, table football). Jukebox. Music (DJs, 8pm most weekends; free). Satellite TV (big screens). Tables outdoors (garden).*

Fridge Bar
1 Town Hall Parade, Brixton Hill, SW2 (020 7326 5100/ www.fridge.co.uk). Brixton tube/rail. **Open** *main bar* 9pm-2am Mon-Wed; 7pm-2am Thur; 7pm-4am Fri; 8pm-4am Sat; 8pm-3am Sun; *chill-out bar* 6am-noon Sat, Sun. **Admission** *main bar* £5 until 11pm Fri-Sun; £8 after; *chill-out bar* £3 Sat; £5 Sun. **Credit** AmEx, DC, MC, V.
Narrow, noisy and typically packed to the rafters, the Fridge Bar is popular both as pre-club preparation for the hedonistic shenanigans of the neighbouring Fridge Club, and for chill-out sessions afterwards. In fact, its late, late licence and cellar dancefloor have made it an increasingly popular venue in its own right. There's nothing spectacular about the drinks menu, although a while back the Fridge did make a bit of a name for itself as the first London bar to revive the consumption of absinthe (and it's still sold here). Neither is the decor anything much to write about, but then, you won't find too many present who've come to admire the surroundings. *Dress code (weekends). Music (DJs nightly). Specialities: large range of absinthe. Tables outdoors (pavement).*

Hope & Anchor
123 Acre Lane, SW2 (020 7274 1787). Clapham North tube/Brixton tube/rail. **Open** 11am-11pm Mon-Sat; noon-10.30pm Sun. **Food served** noon-2.30pm, 6-9pm Mon-Fri; noon-4pm Sat, Sun. **Credit** MC, V.
A reliable, if largely unremarkable pub on drab Acre Lane, the Hope continues to garner a steady crowd of drinkers from the surrounding residential areas. There's generally a gentle buzz about the place as chatty, youngish groups gather around the central bar or slouch at the tables that hug the walls. Wooden partitions make some attempt to break up the space and counter what can (especially on quiet nights) be a slightly warehouse-like atmosphere. Notable plus points are that it's a Young's pub, so you can count on decent beers, and the huge garden, complete with shrubberies and water features, which makes for a cracking summer retreat. *Babies and children admitted (lunchtimes only). Disabled: toilet. Function room. Games (fruit machines, video golf). Satellite TV (big screen). Tables outdoors (garden). Vegetarian dishes.*

Junction
242 Coldharbour Lane, SW9 (020 7738 4000). Loughborough Junction rail/P4, 35, 45, 345 bus. **Open** 4pm-midnight Mon; 4-11pm Tue, Wed; 4pm-2am Thur, Fri; noon-2am Sat; noon-midnight Sun. **Admission** after 11pm Fri, Sat £3. **Happy hour** 4pm-midnight Mon; 4-8pm Tue-Sun. **Credit** AmEx, MC, V.
It's been a couple of years now, but this atmospheric bar is still remembered as the place where dance duo Basement Jaxx hosted now legendary parties. Since then, the pair have moved on to bigger and better things, and the same could be said, to a certain extent, of the Junction. It certainly hasn't

looked this good for a few years; a few thick coats of shiny red and black paint and some moody low lighting have helped to transform the interior of what was a rather shabby old boozer into a decadent, laid-back opium den of a venue. Drinks include a wide selection of bottled beers and some good stuff on tap. Entertainment is still a strong point with regular DJs playing underground house four nights a week, and even find the odd poetry and arts event on the bill. *Babies and children admitted (daytime only). Disabled: toilet. Function room. Games (board games, table football). Music (DJs Thur-Sun).*

Living Room Bar & Grill

443 Coldharbour Lane, SW9 (020 7326 4040). Brixton tube/rail. **Open** 5pm-2am Mon-Thur; 5pm-4am Fri; noon-4am Sat; noon-2am Sun. **Credit** AmEx, MC, V.
Attracting an über-cool crowd this recent addition to Brixton's nightlife scene seems slightly out of place in the shabby, shady environs of Coldharbour Lane. But turn up on a Saturday night and you'll find yourself wedged four-deep at the bar – and that's only if you manage to get in at all. The secret of its success isn't especially complicated: the Living Room is a real hoot, self-consciously retro, with broad strips of hideous '70s-style wallpaper and some sparse, faux-functionalist bits and bobs of furniture. Sophisticated chat takes place over pints of Kirin lager, accompanied by muted Manga films on the big screen. Weekends are particularly fine as the funky upstairs bar plays host to DJs spinning cheesy pop and disco choons and the whole first floor undergoes a transformation into a makeshift dancefloor.
Film screenings. Games (pool tables, table football, video games). Music (DJs nightly).

Satay Bar

447-450 Coldharbour Lane, SW9 (020 7326 5001/ www.sataybar.co.uk). Brixton tube/rail. **Open** noon-11pm Mon-Thur; noon-2am Fri, Sat; noon-10pm Sun. **Food served** noon-3pm, 6-11pm Mon-Fri; noon-2am Sat; noon-10pm Sun. **Happy hour** 5-7pm daily. **Credit** AmEx, DC, MC, V.
Despite a prime location just behind Brixton's Ritzy Cinema, judging by our last few visits, the popularity of the Satay Bar appears to be on the wane. Maybe we've just hit it at a bad time, but the once bustling, occasionally full to bursting, venue has seemed rather empty and soulless of late. One possible explanation is that, compared to finger-on-the-pulse new bars such as the Living Room, the Satay is beginning to look a little bit dated. The regimented rows of tables have always had a hint of the works canteen about them, but the dark wood tables and chairs have a few more scratches on them now and some of the ethnic art and artefacts dotted around the bar also look like they've seen better days. Don't get us wrong, on a good night the Satay Bar can still dish up a fine mix of drink and dining (the Indonesian food is still a winner), but we can't help thinking that its salad days may have passed.
Babies and children admitted (until 6pm). Disabled: toilet. Restaurant. Tables outdoors (pavement). Vegetarian dishes.

SW9

11 Dorrell Place, SW9 (020 7738 3116). Brixton tube/rail. **Open** 9am-11pm Mon-Thur; 9am-1am Fri; 10.30am-1am Sat; 11am-11pm Sun. **Food served** 9am-10pm Mon-Thur; 10am-10pm Fri; 10.30am-10pm Sat; 11am-10pm Sun. **Happy hour** 5-8pm Mon-Fri. **Credit** MC, V.
Flanked by railway arches of breakers-yards and noisy car mechanics, SW9 may not be blessed with the most salubrious of locations, but once inside you couldn't wish for a cosier, venue. Perhaps it's the teashop layout that's so conducive to a few absent-minded pints or the pleasingly diverse clientele.

There's quite a strong gay presence here (and the music can sometimes veer towards camp, hi-NRG) although it's by no means a gay bar, it's simply inclusive. Good soups and more substantial daily specials mean that the place is a popular lunchtime stop-off.
Babies and children admitted. Tables outdoors (patio). Vegetarian dishes.

Trinity Arms

45 Trinity Gardens, SW9 (020 7274 4544). Brixton tube/rail. **Open** 11am-11pm Mon-Sat; noon-10.30pm Sun. **Food served** noon-3pm Mon-Fri. **No credit cards.**
Some disparagingly refer to the Trinity as an old man's pub, but while it is definitely trad – plenty of dark wood panelling and furniture – and does good Young's ales (with guest ales on tap), we like the place for its welcoming atmosphere. The clientele comprises a genuine cross-section of the local community – oldsters, suits and young 'uns in need of a break from pill poppin' in the dance bars – and the bar staff are charming. Beers are supplemented by a good range of wines. In summer, punters can usually be found supping in the crumbling square out front, although plans are afoot to add a proper beer garden.
Games (fruit machine). Satellite TV. Tables outdoors (garden).

Also in the area...

Babushka 40 St Matthews Road, SW2 (020 7274 3618).
Beehive (JD Wetherspoon) 407-409 Brixton Road, SW9 (020 7738 3643).
Crown & Sceptre (JD Wetherspoon) 2 Streatham Hill, SW2 (020 8671 0843).
O'Neill's 78A Streatham High Road, SW16 (020 8696 5941).

Camberwell

Funky Munky

25 Camberwell Church Street, SE5 (020 7252 5222). Denmark Hill rail/12, 36 bus. **Open** noon-midnight Mon-Wed; noon-1am Thur; noon-2am Fri, Sat; noon-10.30pm Sun. **Food served** noon-3pm, 6-10pm Mon-Fri; noon-5pm Sat, Sun. **Credit** MC, V.
Funky Munky was one of the first bars in the mini-revival that's hit Camberwell in the last two or three years, and it remains one of the best. Anyone who's enjoyed a night out in Brixton in the last ten years or so will be familiar with the look; a single, high-ceilinged room, with large picture windows on two sides, terracotta walls and the ubiquitous wooden flooring; but Funky Munky is not just a facsimile, it has an easy, laid-back vibe all its own – supplied mainly by local Camberwell Arts students. The drinks menu offers a basic selection (John Smith's bitter, Kronenbourg and the like) but the food is good value, hearty fare, especially the doorsteps of Welsh rarebit for around £4. DJs are wheeled in at weekends and proceedings get that little bit more drunken, noisy and animated, and all the more fun for it.
Babies and children admitted (daytime only). Games (board games, Sun eve). Music (DJs Thur-Sun). Tables outdoors (pavement). Vegetarian dishes.

Grove House Tavern

26 Camberwell Grove, SE5 (020 7703 4553). Bus 12, 36, 68, 68A, 171, 176, 185, 345. **Open** 11am-11pm Mon-Sat; noon-11pm Sun. **Food served** noon-8pm daily. **No credit cards.**

The approach along gorgeous Georgian Camberwell Grove leads you to expect great things of the Grove House Tavern. Pity, then, that once inside you're confronted with a pub that has clearly seen some better days. A few architectural flourishes survive – the ornate Victorian bar, some pretty coving and an impressive fan-window above the rear door – but far more noticeable are the lumpy, torn seating, the nicotine stained walls and the cig-burned carpet. It's not all bad: the bar staff are friendly, and the large beer garden to the rear, and cobbled terrace to the front are both pleasant in the summer. With a lick of paint and some new upholstery this could be a great boozer, but until then, it's distinctly mediocre.
Games (fruit machine, quiz machine). Jukebox. Quiz (8pm Tue; £1 to play). Satellite TV (big screen). Tables outdoors (garden, pavement). Vegetarian dishes.

Hermit's Cave
28 Camberwell Church Street, SE5 (020 7703 3188). Denmark Hill rail/12, 36, 171, 185 bus. **Open** 11am-11pm Mon-Sat; noon-10.30pm Sun. **Food served** noon-3pm daily. **No credit cards.**
You'd be hard pressed to think of a more appropriate name for this compact, comfy, hideaway of a corner pub. The trad decor, all heavy dark wooden furniture and grubby cream wallpaper, and congenial mix of punters combine to create about as archetypal a local pub atmosphere as you could hope to find. Add to this a heady supply of real ales, including Speckled Hen, Batcombe Bitter and regular guests, and fans of good, honest, no-frills pubs have got themselves a perfect little bolthole in which to duck the worries of the world.
Babies and children admitted. Games (fruit machine). No piped music or jukebox. Satellite TV (big screen). Tables outdoors (pavement). Vegetarian dishes.

Red Star
319 Camberwell Road, SE5 (020 7703 7779/ www.redstarbar.co.uk). Denmark Hill rail. **Open** 5pm-2am Mon-Thur; noon-4am Fri, Sat; noon-2am Sun. **Food served** 1-6pm Sun. **Happy hour** 5-8pm daily. **Admission** after 10pm Fri, Sat £4; after 11pm Sat £6. **Credit** MC, V.
Located at the top end of Coldharbour Lane on Camberwell Green, Red Star at first feels a bit like the responsible older brother to the delinquent **Dogstar** *(see p164)*. While there's none of the Brixton venue's peeling paint and battered banqueting tables here (instead punters are treated to low tables, comfy armchairs, tall plants, soft lighting; and giant video screens showing shorts and music promos), you can still see the family resemblance. The crowd's young and hip, there are nightly DJs, and a fine array of cocktails and bottled beers, all keeping energy levels higher than a barrel of Red Bulls. There are even a couple of pool tables for anyone missing their fix of shooting stick. It's the sort of place Dogstar might be when it grows up.
Disabled: toilet. Function room. Games (space invaders, table football). Music (DJs nightly). Satellite TVs (big screen). Tables outdoors (pavement). Vegetarian dishes.

Sun & Doves
61-63 Coldharbour Lane, SE5 (020 7733 1525/ www.sundoves.com). Oval tube/Brixton tube/rail/35, 45 bus. **Open** 11am-11pm Mon-Fri; noon-11pm Sat; noon-10.30pm Sun. **Food served** noon-11pm Mon-Sat; noon-9pm Sun. **Credit** AmEx, DC, MC, V.
A bastion of all that's middle class, liberal and polished at the less fashionable (Camberwell) end of Coldharbour Lane, the Sun & Doves gives the impression of having been waiting all

Red Star

these years for gentrification to catch up and envelop its environs. Its combination of comfortably battered, school-style furniture, bare boards and modern art on monochrome walls, has always drawn in a fair crowd, but recent upmarket trends seem to have signaled boom time. It now gets packed even on weekday afternoons. Pluses include an extensive wine list of over 30 bottles (five by the glass), and an imaginative food menu featuring things like grilled Mediterranean vegetable skewers and seasonal spiced fish (both around £10). The pleasant patio garden (with fine totem pole) is as welcome on a summer day as the Sun's renowned hot toddies are on a winter's one.
Babies and children admitted (lunchtimes, restaurant only). No-smoking area (restaurant). Restaurant. Tables outdoors (garden). Vegetarian dishes.

Also in the area...
Fox on the Hill (JD Wetherspoon) 149 Denmark Hill, SE5 (020 7738 4756).

Catford

Catford Ram
9 Winslade Way, SE6 (020 8690 6206). Catford or Catford Bridge rail. **Open** 11am-11pm Mon-Sat; noon-10.30pm Sun. **Food served** 11am-3pm, 7-10.30pm Mon-Sat. **No credit cards.**
Catford Shopping Centre might not be London's most salubrious area but this well-appointed Young's pub rises above its surroundings and offers an inviting bolt-hole in times of shopping stress. Overcoming the lack of windows – just one at the front – by using mirrors and framed prints,

this is a large and cream-painted boozer with a raised area strewn with neat furniture. It's a popular destination for workers from the nearby Lewisham Town Hall, library and theatre, and as such the clientele is a more urbane than might be first supposed. The beer's Young's so no problem here, with a decent selection of wines by the glass and bottle. Food is very popular, offering huge portions of dishes like very cheesy cauliflower cheese or steak and kidney pudding for under a fiver.
Disabled: toilet. Games (darts, fruit machine, pinball machine). Vegetarian dishes.

Rutland Arms
55 Perry Hill, SE6 (020 8291 9426). Catford Bridge rail/ 54, 185 bus. **Open** 11am-11pm Mon-Sat; noon-10.30pm Sun. **Food served** noon-2.30pm daily. **No credit cards.**
Although the current landlord was born here 60-odd years ago, this large '20s-style pub became an '80s disco pulling joint, before it returned to the family fold at the beginning of the '90s. These days you'll find jazz nights, and the guv'nor himself even tickles the ivories in Fats Waller fashion from time to time. The L-shaped boozer is decorated in an old-fashioned style with a large wooden-backed serving area, rows of dark wood furniture and a piano at one end. The other side is almost a pub in itself, with groups of young men watching a couple of TVs tuned to Sky Sports. There are six beautifully kept and well chosen real ales on offer as well as the usual lager suspects. Excluding sports fans, customers are a mixture of jazzers and real ale buffs, aged from 18 upwards.
Function room. Games (fruit machines). Music (trad jazz 8.30pm Mon, Sat; modern jazz 8.30pm Tue, 1pm Sun lunch; R&B 9pm Thur; pianist 8.30pm Wed, Fri, 8pm Sun). Quiz (first Sun in month; £1 to play). Satellite TV. Tables outdoors (pavement). Vegetarian dishes.

Clapham

2 Brewers
114 Clapham High Street, SW4 (020 7498 4971). Clapham Common or Clapham North tube/Clapham High Street rail. **Open** 4pm-2am Mon-Thur; 4pm-3am Fri; 2pm-3am Sat; noon-midnight Sun. **Admission** after 11pm Tue-Thur £2; 9.30-11pm Fri, Sat £3, after 11pm Fri, Sat £4. **Happy hour** 4-9pm Tue-Sat; noon-7pm Sun. **Credit** MC, V.
A gay pub'n'club of impressive proportions, the 'Two Sewers', as it's affectionately known, manages to stuff hundreds of meaty men into its party pants, compressing them in the pulsing full-on disco at the back or in the more sociable pub-like area at the front. This is lit brightly enough to get a pre-check-out look at your intended, and is regularly filled with camp entertainment from drag queens and karaoke nights to salsa classes. Equally diverting is the accelerating level of cruisiness as each night gets older and the clientele gets hungrier. It's the kind of place you'd go for a pre-club drink, and then realise that you might as well stay and dance. Actually it's the kind of place you'd go for a pre-club drink, and then realise that you've already gone home with someone.
Cabaret (11pm nightly). Disabled: toilet. Games (fruit machines). Music (DJs 10pm nightly).

100 Pub
100 Clapham Park Road, SW4 (020 7720 8902/ www.100pub.com). Clapham Common tube. **Open** 5-11pm Mon-Fri; noon-11pm Sat, Sun. **Food served** noon-7pm Sun. **Credit** MC, V.

No one could accuse the 100 Pub of being dull – it has a colour scheme to put a Goa hippie bus to shame, scratchy Magritte clouds drift across its upper frontage while a rainbow wraps round its lower half, and a neon sign shouts '100'. It's a relief when you enter and see that the standard Edwardian pub interior is fairly muted save for a lick of yellow, and that the bulk of the inhabitants are wearing regulation young-graduate-professional black and olive. It's a boisterous place with a competitive table football corner and the outbreak of loud pre-club behaviour never far away. There's a busy but relaxing brunch atmosphere at weekends and a DJ on Saturday. The menu has moved up in the world and a pub that used to feed itself on cheap toasties now prefers to digest eggs Benedict and swank £7 pizzas. There are 100 seats in the rear courtyard (which is space-heated, as is the one out front at roadside).
Babies and children admitted (until 7pm). Function room. Games (table football). Satellite TV (big screen). Tables outdoors (garden, patio). Vegetarian dishes.

Alexandra
14 Clapham Common Southside, SW4 (020 7627 5102). Clapham Common tube. **Open** 11am-11pm Mon-Sat; noon-10.30pm Sun. **Food served** noon-5pm Mon-Sat; noon-4pm Sun. **No credit cards.**
Imagine a windowless bare-board wild west saloon – stone floors and no end of shadowy booths and nooks – filled with the horse collars and hop shovels of an agricultural implements museum and then finished off with hundreds of enigmatic enamel signs ('Wingarniss – gives increased vigour in cases of brain fag'). An interesting space to drink in, and much credit for fighting the trend for pubs lit like supermarkets. That's the ground floor. Up the stairs at the back you'll find a grand old room with windows over the common and big-screen footie. The atmosphere depends on who's in (and how many there are of them), but most nights you'll find a settled over-25 bunch with a sprinkling of students, Euro and otherwise. Good solid grub includes excellent Sunday roasts and there are always chalk-board drinks specials to lure you back from the bus stop outside.
Function room. Games (fruit machine, pinball machine). Jukebox. Satellite TV (big screen).

Arch 635
15-16 Lendal Terrace, SW4 (020 7720 7343). Clapham North tube/Clapham High Street rail. **Open/food served** 5pm-11pm Mon-Fri; noon-midnight Sat; noon-10.30pm Sun. **Happy hour** 5-8.30pm Mon-Fri; 6-8.30pm Sat; noon-6pm Sun. **No credit cards.**
Full marks go to this laid-back railway arch conversion for its amiable coolness. Quality music from live DJs (jazzy/funky/housey, with volume sensitively matching the needs of the crowd) washes over a friendly set of local youngsters, including a visible club/music biz tendency who wear their record bags with pride. There's a good racial mix, which in itself distinguishes the place from most of Clapham's youthful drinkeries. It veers toward Hoxton-style trendiness but rather than emerging fully formed from some architecture student's degree project, the relaxed decor has actually evolved over two or three incarnations, so it has a very homely vibe. There's table football, a small purple pool table and sofa areas front and rear, with the latter enjoying the star-lit cover of a new glass-roofed extension. Another recent addition is a second bar in illuminated glass bricks, serving an area that on busy nights twitches and shuffles itself into a dancefloor.
Games (chess, pool table, table football). Music (DJs 8.30pm Thur-Sun). Satellite TV (big screen). Vegetarian dishes.

Belle Vue

1 Clapham Common Southside, SW4 (020 7498 9473).
Clapham Common tube. **Open** 5-11pm Mon-Fri; 10am-
11pm Sat, Sun. **Food served** 6.30-10.30pm Mon-Fri;
12.30-4.30pm, 6.30-10pm Sat; 12.30-4pm, 6.30-10pm Sun.
No credit cards.
This blue-hued corner house is a leather sofa sort of place,
with library panelling, Sunday supplements and thoughtful
twentysomethings meeting for an open-ended catch-up. So
it's a shame that demand for the overstuffed Chesterfields
greatly outstrips supply. You could hover by the lounge area
and hope someone gets up, but chances are you'll be sitting
elsewhere on a scrubbed pine chair, eating your tasty bistro
grub off one of the tightly packed tables. Food carries more
weight than do drinks, so the bar is little wider than a Toulouse
sausage (with mash and onion gravy). However, an energetic
continental waitress will serve liquids at your table to make
up for this, and the thrift-store-style paintings on display are
conversation pieces from any seat.
Vegetarian dishes.

Bierodrome

44-48 Clapham High Street, SW4 (020 7720 1118/
www.belgo-restaurants.co.uk). Clapham Common
or Clapham North tube. **Open/food served** noon-
midnight Mon-Wed; noon-1am Thur; noon-2am Fri, Sat;
noon-10.30pm Sun. **Credit** AmEx, DC, MC, V.
The queues for late-night drinking outside certain Clapham
High Street restaurants have diminished noticeably since this
lively Belgo's offshoot opened its doors and wangled a 2am
weekend licence. It looks like a drinking sauna, with Ikea
graphics, a grand arch of blond wood, sodium uplighters and
a high tech open fire. Big secluded booths at the back
encourage big secluded boisterousness from the lifestyle-
living clientele, while the bar squeezes together blonde bobs
and sleeveless T-shirts, and the restaurant area chows down
on mussels and sausages. There are literally hundreds of
beers to choose from: Belgian wheat beers, bottle-conditioned
Trappist ales, lambic and fruit ales, complemented by around
100 types of Belgian schnapps. Our tip? Try the devilishly
good Lucifer. Staff are happy to offer tasters of anything on
tap, but faced with such an enticing choice, the free-thinking
crowd downs Hoegaarden by the bucket.
Babies and children admitted (until 9pm, restaurant;
children's menus, high chairs, nappy-changing facilities).
Disabled: toilet. Jukebox. Restaurant. Tables outdoors
(pavement). Vegetarian dishes.

Bread & Roses

68 Clapham Manor Street, SW4 (020 7498 1779).
Clapham Common or Clapham North tube. **Open** 11am-
11pm Mon-Sat; noon-10.30pm Sun. **Admission** every
other Thur comedy £5/£3 concs. **Food served** noon-3pm,
7-9.30pm Mon-Fri; noon-4pm, 6-9.30pm Sat, Sun (African
buffet 1-4pm). **Credit** MC, V.
An excellent and spacious award-winning hostelry, whose
starkly minimalist interior somehow preserves a traditional
pub atmosphere, replete with the ghosts of Edwardian
costermongers' knees-ups. Permanent home to famed festival
booze-tenters the Workers' Beer Company, it lifts its name
from the 1912 cry of some down-trodden New York textile
workers: 'Hearts starve as well as bodies, give us bread, but
give us roses'. The pub does its bit to elevate the proletariat
by paying its bar staff above the going rate, by serving a solid
selection of real ales (including its own brand), and by
providing a fine conservatory and garden for the youth wing
of the party (it is child friendly to a fault, especially at
weekends). The customers are far from down-trodden, more

a phalanx of New Labour young marrieds, with the odd
militant throwback waging eternal revolution in the corner.
Music, poetry and comedy events plus weekend African
buffets add to the Internationalist flavour.
Babies and children admitted (until 9pm; colouring books,
games, high chairs, nappy-changing facilities, toys).
Comedy (8pm every other Thur). Disabled: toilet. Function
room. Games (board games, Jenga). Music (live African
band 1-5pm Sun, occasional folk band 8.30pm Sun).
No-smoking area (until 6pm). Quiz (8.30pm 3rd Mon in
month; £1 to play). Tables outdoors (conservatory,
garden, patio). Vegetarian dishes.

Falcon

33 Bedford Road, SW4 (020 7274 2428). Clapham North
tube/Clapham High Street rail. **Open** noon-11pm Mon-Sat;
noon-10.30pm Sun. **Food served** noon-3pm, 6-10pm Mon-
Fri; noon-10pm Sat, Sun. **Credit** MC, V.
The sign for this fun and unpretentious pub has been
graphicked into a puzzlingly fascistic red and blue symbol.
Only when you realise that it's a stylised 'F' do you stop
worrying that some nasty corporate takeover has happened
and discover with relief that the Falcon is still the same
spacious, friendly and gregarious watering hole it always
was. The much-used pool table has been shunted out, leaving
room for more big pine tables, and as ever, it's enjoyed mostly
by groups of four and up, aged roughly 25-35. The gaggles
get even bigger when the summer terraces of the back garden
are opened up, enjoying day-long beer banquets facilitated
by an outside bar and regular cook-outs. Good Thai food is
served year-round.
Tables outdoors (garden, patio). Vegetarian dishes.

Frog & Forget-Me-Not

32 The Pavement, SW4 (020 7622 5230). Clapham
Common tube. **Open** 4-11pm Mon-Fri; noon-11pm Sat; noon-
10.30pm Sun. **Food served** 1-4pm Sun. **Credit** MC, V.
Squash down on one of the flagging flea-market sofas and it
becomes the coffee shop from *Friends*, except that the decor
(especially those lamps, my god!) looks like a particularly
unpleasant 'before' shot on *Changing Rooms* or an ageing
South coast rooming house. The big room fills up fast with
young, loud and well turned-out lads and laddesses, and in
summer the clientele races up to the sunny roof terrace. Dim
but fanciable barstaff serve lager and vodka Red Bulls, and
everyone checks everyone out with lascivious intent as people
meander through the sea of tables to visit the loos. Popular
and flirtatious with a buzz in the air, a bar billiards table in
the corner and a marmalade cat asleep among the cacophony.
Babies and children admitted (until 6pm). Games (bar
billiards, fruit machine). Quiz (8pm Tue). Satellite TV (big
screen). Tables outdoors (roof terrace). Vegetarian dishes.

Kazbar

50 Clapham High Street, SW4 (020 7622 0070/
www.the kudosgroup.com). Clapham North tube/Clapham
High Street rail. **Open/food served** 4pm-midnight Mon-
Fri; noon-midnight Sat, Sun. **Happy hour** 4-8pm Mon-Fri;
noon-8pm Sat, Sun. **Credit** AmEx, DC, MC, V.
The customer who looked like Captain Mainwaring doing
Cher was a bit of a fright, all poodle-curl wig and patent
leather drainpipes, but be assured he's an anomaly among
the cute men to be found in this friendly homo hostelry. So
sedate by day that you could forget you're in a gay bar – isn't
that a potted palm lurking in the upstairs lounge area – by
night Kazbar becomes quintessentially queer and zips along
to the hum of mirror-balls, neon chase lights, non-stop TV
Europop and garrulous gayness. Slightly less cruisey than
its neighbour the 2 Brewers, but that's like saying slightly

younger than the Queen Mother. Drinks specials, club vouchers and free buses to the Fridge complete the picture.
Games (fruit machine). Music (video DJs 7pm nightly). Tables outdoors (pavement). TV (video screen). Vegetarian dishes.

Landor
70 Landor Road, SW9 (020 7274 4386). Clapham North tube/Clapham High Street rail. **Open** noon-11pm Mon-Sat; noon-10.30pm Sun. **Food served** 5.30-9pm Tue-Sat; 1-6pm Sun. **Credit** AmEx, DC, MC, V.
You have no idea what the codger with the Guinness is trying to tell you. You have no idea what goes on in the mysterious theatre upstairs, you have no idea who wins all those darts trophies in the cabinet, and you really don't know whether you can see straight enough for another game of pool. Welcome to a night at the Landor. A flashback to a lost age of real pubs (with the real ales to match), the Landor wears the best kind of scuffed, lived-in ambience, and its bizarre nautical makeover of a couple of years ago is already wearing an amiably dusty patina. On the Clapham/Stockwell/Brixton frontier, this large bar room fills with local locals next to young professionals who bought at the right time. Afternoons that become evenings, quick pints that become nights out, animated anecdotes, weird conversations with interesting strangers. It's that kind of place.
Games (fruit machine, pool tables, quiz machine). Quiz (8pm 2nd Sun of month; £2 to play). Satellite TV (big screen). Tables outdoors (garden). Theatre. Vegetarian dishes.

Loaffers
102-104 Clapham High Street, SW4 (020 7720 9596). Clapham Common or Clapham North tube/Clapham High Street rail. **Open** 4.30-11pm Mon-Fri; noon-11pm Sat; noon-10.30pm Sun. **Food served** 6-10pm Mon-Fri; noon-10.30pm Sat, Sun. **Happy hour** 4.30-7.30pm, 10-11pm Mon-Thur; 4.30-7.30pm Fri. **Credit** MC, V.
We all love to loaf, and the well-heeled thirtysomething drinkers here have an air of successfully decadent relaxation about them as they down cocktails, bottled beers and the house speciality, Loaffers' punch. They drape themselves against buttoned red-leather padded walls, their feet propped on cubic suede stools. Music and brightness levels are usually more lively than loaf-ful, so even when the bar's sparsely populated the atmosphere is more animated than the name might suggest. There's a decent restaurant tucked in the back, serving cuisine of Clapham (Modern European). Giant blue on blue cherubs decorate the outside walls, giving Loaffers maximum stand-out, even on this bar-heavy stretch of pavement.
Babies and children admitted. Restaurant. Vegetarian dishes.

Mistress P's
29 North Street, SW4 (020 7622 5342). Clapham Common tube. **Open** 11am-11pm Mon-Sat; noon-10.30pm Sun. **Food served** noon-3pm, 7-10pm Mon-Sat; noon-10pm Sun. **No credit cards.**
Quirky and genuine, this is a proper local that makes a proper – albeit slightly unhinged – effort: proper decorations (year-round fairy lights; Parisian murals in the loos); a proper pub quiz (free microwaved sausage rolls and plenty of questions unanswerable by the under-forties); and proper regulars (old dears by the roaring fire talking to their dog and younger Claphamites who need neither a napkin under their drink nor their change on a tin plate). A capricious empress of a landlady rules with an iron voice over a good-time jukebox and enough satellite tellies for a place twice the size. The sticky worn carpet is even trod by the occasional live band. Clapham has plenty of forgotten pubs

in between its sleek style bars but this is a rare gem truly worthy of the name 'boozer'.
Games (fruit machine). Jukebox. Quiz (8.30pm Thur). Tables outdoors (pavement). TVs (satellite & digital). Vegetarian dishes.

Oblivion
7-8 Cavendish Parade, Clapham Common Southside, SW4 (020 8772 0303). Clapham South tube. **Open** noon-11pm daily. **Happy hour** 5-7pm daily. **Food served** noon-8pm Mon-Fri; noon-9pm Sat, Sun. **Credit** AmEx, MC, V.
Oblivion would be a really cool designer bar, but only in somewhere like Minsk. It tries ever so hard with its decor and gets it all horribly, innocently, amusingly wrong. Bizarre wrought iron, mutant medusa sculptures, broken mirror mosaics and a colour scheme worthy of a train company – it's a bit like drinking in a wacky student union. Still, there are plenty of takers for its rather gauche attempts at decadence and since there are few alternatives roundabouts, the place is filled to bursting with the young hormones of north Balham and South Clapham. DJ nights add to the fun, as does a common-facing front terrace which positively bursts its banks come summertime.
Music (DJs 8pm nightly). Satellite TV (big screen). Tables outdoors (terrace). Vegetarian dishes.

Pentagon
64 Clapham High Street, SW4 (020 7498 8822) Clapham Common tube. **Open** 5pm-2am Mon-Sat; 5pm-1am Sun. **Food served** 5-9pm daily. **Credit** AmEx, MC, V.
Since it's on Clapham High Street, this address is forced to be either a pretentious bar or a charity shop. Fierce competition from Arthritis Research means Pentagon chose the easy option and called up the interior designers. There are huge canvases in primary colours with sexy slashes in them. The bar has a lot of curves in it. There is a condom machine knowingly placed in public view. The bogs have comic-book murals of techno dominatrices and superhero gunmen. The stools are twinned like giant bongo drums. And there is no earthly reason for any of this. Pentagon is a concept bar in search of a concept – it ends up as bland as it is contrived. Nevertheless, it's open late, it serves drinks, it fills to bursting at weekends and it attracts a slightly more up-for-it crowd than most of the strip's yup-centric hangouts.
Music (DJs Fri, Sat). Tables outdoors (pavement). Vegetarian dishes.

Polygon Bar & Grill
4 The Polygon, SW4 (020 7622 1199/ www.thepolygon.co.uk). Clapham Common tube. **Open/food served** noon-3pm, 6-11pm Mon-Fri; 11am-4.30pm, 6-11pm Sat; 11am-4.30pm, 6-10.30pm Sun. **Happy hour** 6-7.30pm daily. **Credit** AmEx, MC, V.
Hidden behind a little cottage (actually a very rustic ex-public toilet) on the church corner of the Common, Polygon set the standard for classy Clapham and despite incursions by, for example Sequel, it's holding its own as the most elegant place roundabout to indulge in a cocktail. We love an excuse not to have to venture all the way into Soho and this restrained and stylish joint is it. Knowledgeable and perky mixologists cater to liquid requirements with a regularly updated menu of enticing intoxicants, while a restaurant deals with solids c/o a varied modern European menu and good value brunches.
Babies and children admitted (restaurant; high chairs). Disabled: toilet. Restaurant. Vegetarian dishes.

Prince of Wales
38 Old Town, SW4 (020 7622 3530). Clapham Common tube. **Open** 5-11pm Mon-Fri; 1-11pm Sat; 1-10.30pm Sun. **No credit cards.**

South

White House.
See page 172.

Just off the common and a few steps away from reality, the POW could be *Steptoe and Son*'s cupboard under the stairs or the annexe to some strange lost local junk shop. Among its rosy underlit shadows, customers weave their pints through a peerless collection of nutty and captivating clutter. You won't see the Edwardian food mixer shaped like a pear, the stuffed armadillo playing cards has been sent for cleaning and the photo of WG Grace wearing a wedding dress has strangely disappeared, but you will see plenty of equally strange objects perched on the roof, hanging from the ceiling or squeezed in between the cosy tables. A camp and dignified refuge for a sedate pint that can turn into a very festive place given half an excuse.
Babies and children admitted (until 7pm). Benches outdoors (pavement). TV.

Railway
18 Clapham High Street, SW4 (020 7622 4077). Clapham North tube/Clapham High Street rail. **Open** 11am-11pm Mon-Sat; noon-10.30pm Sun. **Food served** noon-3pm, 6-10.30pm Mon-Fri; noon-10.30pm Sat, Sun. **Credit** AmEx, MC, V.
It used to look like a surfboard designer had been let loose on the premises with a head bursting with hallucinogens. Now, as the large and loyal bunch of regulars reach the end of their twenties and delve into their forties and beyond, the day-glo decor has been reworked to a more sober pastel yellow, with even the name board enjoying a more utilitarian lettering style. Inside, you don't really notice how pleasantly scruffy it all is, because there's always a full complement of drinkers to hide the cracks. A low central bar and acres of big curving windows make for great people-watching (both passers-by and your fellow customers). Like it's partners in crime, the Sun and the Falcon, there's good Thai food and plenty of high-octane chat. If you sprint, you can sup up and make it to the station when you see your train come over the bridge.
Babies and children admitted (until 7pm). Function room. Tables outdoors (pavement). Vegetarian dishes.

Sand
156 Clapham Park Road, SW4 (020 7622 3022/ www.sandbarrestaurant.co.uk). Clapham Common tube/ Brixton tube/rail, then 35 or 37 bus. **Open/food served** 5pm-2am Mon-Sat; 5pm-1am Sun. **Admission** after 9.30pm Fri, Sat £5. **Credit** MC, V.
As the forces of twisty Levi's gentrification push the boundaries of Clapham and Brixton's style-zones ever closer together, and with the mini-Hampstead of Abbeville Road within walking distance, this area is starting to look like prime bar real estate. Sand proves the fact, turning a scruffy old pub in the dead zone at the wrong end of Acre Lane into a rectilinear haven of *Wallpaper** modernism, complete with a *GQ* bouncer and a pouting blonde with a clipboard. There are comfy sofa areas and a fairly intimate dining section, and the overall decor is vaguely North African. Movies on miniature screens add to the distractions as the place fills up with confident designer-clad young things.
Disabled: toilet. Music (DJs 10.30pm Thur-Sun). Vegetarian dishes.

Sequel
75 Venn Street, SW4 (020 7622 4222). Clapham Common tube. **Open** 5-11pm Mon-Fri; 11am-11pm Sat; noon-10.30pm Sun. **Food served** 5-11pm Mon-Fri; 11am-4pm, 5.30-11pm Sat; noon-5.30pm, 6-10.30pm Sun. **Credit** AmEx, DC, MC, V.
The eggs Benedict here has decided the location for Sunday brunch many times, although the wait-staff usually give off the idea that they were up partying all night and you're

starting to annoy them. It's essentially a classy restaurant, (serving a global trot of dishes), but it mixes up a fine cocktail and is very conducive to a soirée à deux after a movie at the Picture House next door. Interesting music adds to the atmosphere, as does a big TV over the bar showing (silently) a movie which is usually *Live and Let Die* or *The King and I*. Oh, and it was here that news of little Leo Blair was first announced to the world.
Babies and children admitted. Disabled: toilet. Restaurant. Vegetarian dishes. Video screen.

SO.UK
165 Clapham High Street, SW4 (020 7622 4004). Clapham Common tube. **Open** 4pm-midnight Mon-Thur; 11am-midnight Fri, Sat; 11am-11.30pm Sun. **Food served** 4-11.30pm Mon-Thur; noon-11.30pm Fri, Sat; noon-11pm Sun. **Credit** AmEx, MC, V.
Should we give a fcuk about SO.UK? Well, if you like the idea of laid-back communal eating and drinking amongst minimally Moorish surroundings, it's an interesting addition to Clapham's bar scene (though, as it takes over from a specialist decorators' shop, another nail in the coffin of its retail high street). 'Global warming where tastes collide,' proclaims the poetry on the menu. (It also says, squirmingly, 'There are no rules – just enjoy'.) The elegant interior has low-lit sand-textured walls with a subtle Moroccan relief, plus cushioned banquettes, low brass tables and elongated windows. There's a secluded area at the back and some very classy loos. Waitress service means you can lounge to your heart's content, though at weekends there are plenty of folk standing around the bar area too. The young professionals who come here tuck into the very good food, a global mix with its heart in North Africa. On our visit the portions weren't as large as the wait.
Babies and children admitted. Disabled: toilet. Music (DJ Tue-Sat). Vegetarian dishes.

Sun
47 Old Town, SW4 (020 7622 4980). Clapham Common tube. **Open** 11am-11pm Mon-Sat; noon-10.30pm Sun. **Food served** noon-10.30pm Mon-Sat; 12.30-10pm Sun. **Credit** MC, V.
With such a capacious garden (especially when it spills out three lanes into the road), it's no wonder that the Sun was one of the first pubs in the country to invest in those now-ubiquitous convection space heaters. In summer climes this is as close to the beach that Clapham gets, with underdressed young pretties and rugger-shirted blades connecting over pints. Inside there's a big square ground-floor bar plus upstairs room and balcony where much the same socialising happens year round. Like its sisters the Falcon and Railway, it's friendly, unpretentious and brightly decorated, with poppy R&B music and a strong and reasonably priced Thai menu.
Babies and children admitted (until 7pm). Function room. Tables outdoors (garden). Vegetarian dishes.

White House
65 Clapham Park Road, SW4 (020 7498 3388/ www.thewhitehouselondon.co.uk) Clapham Common tube. **Open** 5pm-midnight Mon, Tue; 5pm-1am Wed; 5pm-2am Thur, Fri; noon-2am Sat; noon-midnight Sun. **Food served** 5-11.30pm Mon, Tue; 5pm-12.30am Wed; 5pm-1.30am Thur, Fri; noon-1.30am Sat; noon-11.30pm Sun. **Admission** after 10pm Fri, Sat £5. **Credit** AmEx, DC, MC, V.
With a name like the White House we were expecting a club-bar-restaurant complex the size of the US President's home. But Clapham's White House is merely a small but attractive bar, already popular with groups of young and well groomed

good-lookers who were lapping up the Thievery Corporation CD on our visit. The White House is halfway between Clapham's SO.UK bar and the Sand Bar in both location and approach. The cocktails are okay, but the wine list is dull. The bar food snacks are tapas-sized portions, and vary from superb ('Yorkshire puddings' £6) to so-what (quesadilla £4.50). The 'Private Members' Bar' is two gorgeous small rooms on the first floor, but there's already a long waiting list – and the criteria and membership cost are still undecided.
Disabled: toilet. Function rooms. Games (board games). Music (DJs Wed-Sun). Tables outdoors (pavement). TV (special events). Vegetarian dishes

Windmill on the Common
Clapham Common Southside, SW4 (020 8673 4578). Clapham Common tube. **Open** 11am-11pm Mon-Sat; noon-10.30pm Sun. **Food served** noon-2.30pm, 7-10pm Mon-Fri; noon-9pm Sat, Sun. **Credit** AmEx, DC, MC, V.
When on a summer's day the dusk finally arrives, the Windmill can look proudly on the pyramids of plastic glasses left on the grass of Clapham Common by the daily encampments of its happy drinkers. On the warmest days it can be virtually empty inside, just a beer outlet with busy toilets. When winter comes the place becomes an elegant, unremarkable Young's pub, never too crowded, and rarely noisy, but with a fair few regulars keeping the bar warm. Occasional poetry and comedy events testify to the older, more sedate nature of the clientele. Solid pub food and, should you find yourself on Clapham Common needing one, a hotel.
Babies and children admitted (separate area; children's menu, high chairs). Disabled: toilet. Function room. Restaurant. Tables outdoors (garden). Vegetarian dishes.

Also in the area...
Boom Bar (Po Na Na) 165-167 St John's Hill, SW11 (020 7924 3449).
Café Rouge 40 Abbeville Road, SW4 (020 7373 3399).
Fine Line 182-184 Clapham High Street, SW4 (020 7622 4436).

Pitcher & Piano 8 Balham Hill, SW12 (020 8673 1107).
Slug & Lettuce 4 St John's Hill, SW11 (020 7924 1322).

Deptford
Dog & Bell
116 Prince Street, SE8 (020 8692 5664). New Cross tube/rail/Deptford rail. **Open** noon-11pm Mon-Sat; noon-10.30pm Sun. **Food served** noon-2.30pm, 6-9pm Mon-Fri. **No credit cards.**
The name comes from the days when this part of the riverside was marshland: hunters would ring a bell to scare wild fowl into the air, then once they'd been 'sorted' (as they say in these parts) their dogs would paddle out and retrieve the carcasses. Don't be put off by the graffiti outside reading 'Millwall rules OK': this green-paint and brick-fronted pub is one of London's best. Built in 1849, it's a genuine freehold and landlord Charlie keeps his range of real ales (based around Fuller's London Pride and ESB, with three guests always on hand pump) superbly, with most priced at well under £2. Similarly, the food is simple but good. Regulars include builders, musicians, actors, students and lecturers from nearby Greenwich University, writers and market traders. There's a shove ha'penny board and a bar billiards table at the back.
Games (bar billiards). Quiz (9pm Sun; 50p to play). Tables outdoors (garden). TV. Vegetarian dishes.

Dulwich
Crystal Palace Tavern
193 Crystal Palace Road, SE22 (020 8693 4968). East Dulwich or North Dulwich rail/40, 176, 185 bus. **Open** noon-11pm Mon-Sat; noon-10.30pm Sun. **No credit cards.**
A century or more after it was a well known staging post between London and the coast, this magnificent Victorian pub still stands proud. At the front is a spartan public bar, behind

Ashburnham Arms

which the comfortable saloon bar comes in two parts – both with a roaring fire in winter, red velvet banquettes and a brown-painted ceiling hung with period chandeliers. The delicately carved period serving area offers a variety of real ales, as well as the usual lagers, stout and what-have-you. Customers are a mixed bunch, reflecting the area. We've spotted builders, students, elderly and middle-aged couples as well as a group of what looked like bouncers on a pub crawl. The pub's namesake, which was re-erected in nearby Sydenham, gets plenty of attention in framed pictures and newspaper clippings.
Babies and children admitted (daytime). Games (darts, fruit machine). Quiz (9pm Wed). Satellite TV. Tables outdoors (pavement).

Crown & Greyhound

73 Dulwich Village, SE21 (020 8299 4976). North Dulwich rail. **Open** 11am-11pm Mon-Sat; noon-10.30pm Sun. **Food served** noon-2.30pm, 5.30-10pm Mon-Sat; noon-3pm Sun. **Credit** MC, V.
A huge, well maintained Victorian pub that's one of south London's best known boozers. The name refers to the days when two pubs – the Crown and the Greyhound – stood on either side of what was then the High Road. The Greyhound was the meeting place of the fashionable Dulwich Club, of which Charles Dickens was a regular, and as Mr Pickwick retired here, the road that replaced the pub was named Pickwick Road. The current boozer is a good example of Victorian opulence: high ceilings, four large bars decorated with vast mirrors, etched glass and plenty of solid mahogany. Out back there's a garden you could get lost in and a conservatory you couldn't. The range of real ales (four when we last called by) is pretty decent and food – especially Sunday roasts – is a cut above, ensuring that the pub has a strong local weekend following.
Babies and children admitted (children's menu, high chairs, nappy-changing facilities). Disabled: toilet. Function rooms. Games (fruit machine). No piped music or jukebox. No-smoking area (restaurant). Restaurant. Satellite TV (big screen). Tables outdoors (garden). Vegetarian dishes.

Also in the area...

Café Rouge 84 Park Hall Road, SE21 (020 8768 0070).

Forest Hill

Railway Telegraph

112 Stanstead Road, SE23 (020 8699 6644). Forest Hill rail/122 or 185 bus. **Open** 11am-11pm Mon-Sat; noon-10.30pm Sun. **Food served** noon-2pm Mon-Fri. **Credit** MC, V.
This large Shepherd Neame pub has been knocked through into a single bar with the large-screen TV occupying almost a whole (small) wall. It's hard to escape the sport when a game's on – speakers by the bar relay every thrilling second – but that aside, this is a good local pub with bar pretensions. It sells at least a couple of Shep's rather fine ales, plus Oranjeboom and Hürlimann lager. The decor is light and airy: yellow, beige, gold and cream are the central colours on to which framed art nouveau prints are displayed. Service is pleasant and the punters tend to be male, around thirtyish, with the odd group of young women on the razz.
Babies and children admitted (until 7pm). Games (darts, fruit machine, quiz machine). Jukebox. Satellite TV (big screen). Tables outdoors (garden, pavement). Vegetarian dishes.

Greenwich

Ashburnham Arms
25 Ashburnham Grove, SE10 (020 8692 2007).
Greenwich rail/DLR. **Open** noon-3.30pm, 6-11pm Mon-Sat; noon-3.30pm, 7-10.30pm Sun. **Food served** noon-2.30pm, 6-8.30pm Tue-Fri; noon-2.30pm Sat, Sun. **Credit** (food only) MC, V.
This small but immaculate backstreet boozer is one of London's best locals' pubs. A Shepherd Neame house, it's run by a couple who know pretty much all there is to know about pub hospitality and keeping beer. The real ales cover the Kent brewery's range and come in perfect condition; plus a trusted pub regular we know insists that the lager (Hürlimann is the top choice) is 'the best in Greenwich and Deptford'. The brown patterned carpet handles anything SE10 can throw at it, the dark walls are painted red and green. There's a little conservatory at the rear, a brilliant little garden and a bar billiards table in its own small room leading to the toilets. Food is limited to tasty home-cooked pasta dishes served lunchtimes and most weekday evenings.
Babies and children admitted (conservatory only; children's menu). Games (bar billiards). Quiz (9pm Tue). Tables outdoors (garden, patio). Vegetarian dishes.

Cutty Sark Tavern
Ballast Quay, off Lassell Street, SE10 (020 8858 3146).
Greenwich rail/DLR/Maze Hill rail. **Open** 11am-11pm Mon-Sat; noon-10.30pm Sun. **Food served** noon-9pm Mon-Sat; noon-7pm Sun. **Credit** MC, V.
If it weren't for the fact that this is run by a big brewery almost entirely for the tourists, the former Union Tavern – once a place to catch seamen – wouldn't be a bad boozer. The decor is old world distress: beams are exposed, walls are bare brick and the floor is bare board. A timber gallery provides further seating and opportunities for a discreet rendezvous. In winter, when tourists are thin on the ground, Greenwich's young drinkers take advantage of the thoughtfully stocked CD jukebox, otherwise it's wall to wall visitors who trek up the tow-path from Greenwich to sit on upturned barrels or crowd on to the riverside terrace and gaze across the Thames.
Babies and children admitted (children's menu). Function room. Games (fruit machine). Jukebox. Restaurant. Tables outdoors (riverside terrace). Vegetarian dishes.

Gipsy Moth
60 Greenwich Church Street, SE10 (020 8858 0786).
Greenwich rail/DLR. **Open** 11am-11pm Mon-Sat; noon-10.30pm Sun. **Food served** noon-5pm, 6-9.30pm Mon-Fri; noon-6pm Sat, Sun. **Credit** (food only) MC, V.
Until 1973 this busy pub was called the Wheatsheaf, but Sir Francis Chichester went and sailed around the globe and his boat came to rest in a dry dock close by. Were Sir Francis still alive, however, it's unlikely he'd want to sail in this particular Gipsy Moth. The front bar is a wooden affair given over largely to big screen sport, which might pass sailing time quite agreeably, were it not for the groups of young men who turn up to drink lager and cheer on their teams. There's a carpeted larger back area, with a raised seating section that's surrounded by a sturdy wooden fence. There are normally a couple of real ales on tap and food of the fish and chips and Thai green curry variety. In summer it's packed with tourists, in winter local youth congregate to discuss sailing, seamanship and suchlike.
Babies and children admitted (before 7pm; high chairs, nappy-changing facilities). Disabled: toilet. Games (fruit machine, quiz machine). Satellite TV (big screen). Tables outdoors (garden). Vegetarian dishes.

North Pole
131 Greenwich High Road, SE10 (020 8853 3020).
Greenwich rail/DLR. **Open** 5.30-11pm Mon; noon-11pm Tue-Sat; 9.30am-10.30pm Sun. **Food served** noon-3pm Tue-Sat; 9.30am-4pm, 6.30-10pm Sun. **Credit** AmEx, DC, MC, V.
We've never felt particularly welcome at this vast gastro-bar, and rather get the impression that the North Pole is overly fond of giving out a frosty reception. The ground floor bar has low sofas and red walls, offers reasonably priced bottled beer and Hoegaarden (no real ales) and plays a soundtrack that's loud and clubby. Upstairs the restaurant serves up the likes of pheasant, pan-fried cod and roast lamb chump. Prices are quite high (£12 and up) given the food's adequate but largely unspectacular nature. The clientele tends to be young and we had two people squinting at us through dark glasses the last time we popped along: it was February and dark.
Babies and children admitted (high chairs). Function room. Music (DJs 7.30pm Thur-Sun; live jazz 7.30pm Thur). Restaurant. Tables outdoors (pavement). TV. Vegetarian dishes.

Richard I
52-54 Royal Hill, SE10 (020 8692 2996). Greenwich rail/DLR. **Open** 11am-11pm Mon-Sat; noon-10.30pm Sun. **Food served** noon-2pm, 6-10pm Mon-Sat; noon-2pm, 6-9.30pm Sun. **No credit cards.**
Situated in the old part of Greenwich, between the park and the main tourist drag, this is a cosy two bar pub with a firm local following and a light, airy feel to it. Both the tiny 'public' side and the larger 'saloon' have bowed windows, with correspondingly curved settles inside, and low, maroon-painted wooden ceilings. You're as likely to find a resting Shakespearean actor here as a painter or plasterer, though the nearby town hall and police and fire stations both provide a fair share of customers. The beer comes from Wandsworth's Young's brewery, so no room for complaint there, and food tends to be simple but tasty such as gammon, steaks or 'pie of the day'. A large beer garden at the rear is popular when the sun shines.
No piped music or jukebox. Tables outdoors (garden, pavement). Vegetarian dishes.

Time
7A College Approach, SE10 (020 8305 9767). Greenwich Maritime DLR. **Open** noon-11pm Mon-Thur; noon-11.30pm Fri, Sat; noon-10.30pm Sun. **Food served** 7-10.30pm Tue-Sat; noon-3pm, 7-10.30pm Sun. **Credit** MC, V.
Once a Victorian music hall, the funky Time now manages an odd combination-look that mixes original features such as stone walls and steps, with comfortable sofas, weekend DJs and ever-changing contemporary art on the walls. The main bar is on the first floor, with the restaurant perched in a glass encased balcony above. There's no real ale – just standard draught lagers and stout – but bottles offer Continental delights, cocktails are popular and the wine list is medium-sized but wide-ranging. Solidly Modern European food is good not stunning, but the likes of char-grilled monkfish with creamy mash still outshine most of Greenwich's usual offerings.
Babies and children admitted (high chairs). Dress code (weekends). Function room. Music (DJs 8.30pm Fri, Sat; live jazz 9pm Sun). Restaurant. Vegetarian dishes.

Trafalgar Tavern
Park Row, SE10 (020 8858 2437/www.gmt2000.co.uk).
Cutty Sark Gardens DLR/Maze Hill rail. **Open** 11.30am-11pm Mon-Sat; noon-10.30pm Sun. **Food served** noon-3pm Mon; noon-10pm Tue-Sat; noon-5pm Sun. **Credit** MC, V.

Time. *See page 175.*

This historic pub occupies the site of the Old George Inn and was built in 1837 as a tribute to naval hero Horatio Nelson, whose body passed by on its last voyage home. Between then and 1915 it was a famous tavern, welcoming the likes of Charles Dickens, Doctor Crippen and Gladstone, who joined Cabinet ministers at regular 'Whitebait Dinners'. The pub closed, became a home for seamen, a working men's club and finally lay derelict. It was rescued in 1965 and refurbished to its current high standard. There are three main rooms on the ground floor, choc-a-bloc with mahogany panelling, stone fireplaces and the like, finished with green paint. The riverside terrace offers views of the Millennium Dome and, if you crane your neck past the University buildings, the nearby Cutty Sark. Beers come from Courage and upmarket food includes a modern version of the whitebait dinner for little more than a fiver.
Babies and children admitted (children's menu, high chairs). Function rooms. Music (live jazz band 9pm Sat). Restaurant. Tables outdoors (riverside terrace). Vegetarian dishes.

Also in the area...
Auctioneer (It's A Scream) 217-219 Greenwich High Road, SE10 (020 8269 1410).
Café Rouge Hotel Ibis, SE10 (020 8293 6660).
Davys Wine Cellars 161 Greenwich High Street, SE10 (020 8858 6014).

Kennington, Lambeth & Oval

Beehive
60 Carter Street, SE17 (020 7703 4992). Kennington tube/12, 68, 68A, 171, 176 bus. **Open** 11am-11pm Mon-Sat; noon-10.30pm Sun. **Food served** noon-3pm, 5.30-10pm Mon-Fri; noon-10pm Sat, Sun. **Credit** MC, V (minimum £15).
Walworth pubs sure ain't what they used to be. Time was you knew what to expect when walking into a backstreet boozer like this: threadbare furnishings, fuggy air and a scattering of old lags sucking on pipe cleaner-tight rollies at the bar. Well, no more. Shuffling geezers pushing open this particular door are confronted with cream paint, bare boards,

exposed ducting, book-lined walls and staff in white aprons and dicky-bows. The Beehive's a modern bistro-style bar, with its real ales (Fuller's Pride, Courage Best and Directors) supplemented by wines and a fine selection of malt whiskies. Food is served in a cosy, candlelit area with railway carriage-like benches – surprisingly pleasant surroundings for what is little more than American diner fare of burgers, potato skins, steaks and such. Punters are young Walworth: well-heeled and up-and-coming.
Babies and children admitted. Satellite TV. Specialities: malt whiskies. Tables outdoors (patio). Vegetarian dishes.

Dog House
293 Kennington Road, SE11 (020 7820 9310). Kennington or Oval tube. **Open** noon-11pm Mon-Fri; 6-11pm Sat; noon-10.30pm Sun. **Food served** noon-3pm Mon, Tue; noon-3pm, 7-10pm Wed, Thur; noon-3pm Sun. **Credit** MC, V.
On our several visits here we've found the service so casual it bordered on the non-existent, but colleagues tell us we've just been unlucky. It's certainly a laid-back kind of place, attracting the kind of fashionable newcomers that have earned this area the local nickname 'Islington-by-Oval'. The chic bohemian interior features distressed paintwork and gilded mirrors, and a central wooden bar surrounded by candle-topped tables. Drinks are a pretty standard range (no real ale), while food is East meets West, light snacks and hearty meals: toasted sarnies and stuffed ciabatta to Thai and Moroccan mains or steak sandwiches and various platters, for example.
Babies and children admitted. Function room. Games (board games). Tables outdoors (pavement). Vegetarian dishes.

Greyhound
336 Kennington Park Road, SE11 (020 7735 2594). Oval tube. **Open** 11am-11pm Mon-Sat; noon-10.30pm Sun. **Food served** noon-4pm daily. **Credit** MC, V.
Well used by sportsmen from the nearby Kennington Park playing fields, as well as by spectators from the Oval just around the corner, the Greyhound is predominantly a locals' pub proud of its sporting connections. It's a long, thin boozer of the old school with leather-padded settles and

South

plenty of knick-knacks. Add in friendly bar staff, a core of Irish and 'Kennington cockney' regulars and you've got one of the area's more welcoming pubs. Beer comes from Scottish Courage, so expect the likes of Courage Best and Directors, and more lagers than the average football team can sink in a month.

Babies and children admitted (lunchtimes). Games (fruit machine). Jukebox. Satellite TV (big screen). Vegetarian dishes.

Prince of Wales
48 Cleaver Square, SE11 (020 7735 9916). Kennington tube. **Open** noon-3pm, 5-11pm Mon-Wed; noon-11pm Thur, Fri; 5-11pm Sat; noon-10pm Sun. **Food served** noon-2pm, 5.30-8.30pm Mon-Fri. **Credit** MC, V.
This used to be the only posh pub in Kennington and a haunt of the Richardson gang. Since its acquisition by Faversham's Shepherd Neame brewery and subsequent makeover, however, it's slipped downmarket somewhat – doubly unfortunate because its decline coincides with a general gentrification of the area. It's not a big pub; there's a square-shaped room with the bar at the front and a smaller room at the back. Decor is nautical blue with cartoons of Victorian politicians, while customers seemed to include a fair number of young professional types.
Tables outdoors (pavement). Vegetarian dishes.

Three Stags
67-69 Kennington Road, SE1 (020 7928 5974). Lambeth North tube. **Open** noon-11pm Mon-Sat; noon-10.30pm Sun. **Food served** noon-8.30pm daily. **Credit** AmEx, MC, V.
Known for a time as Brendan O'Grady's, the Three Stags has reverted to its more sensible name now that much of south London's Irish population has returned to the booming Eurozone that's modern Eire. Being a Greene King pub, the beer's good (IPA, Abbot), plus there's decent English food (salmon fishcakes, Cumberland sausage, Yorkshire puddings), designed to appeal to the tourists who drop in thanks to the pub's links with Charlie Chaplin, who lived nearby and who's dad is reputed to have drunk himself to death within these walls. The Imperial War Museum's also just round the corner.
Babies and children admitted (until 5pm). Disabled: toilet. Games (fruit machine). No-smoking area. Tables outdoors (pavement). TV. Vegetarian dishes.

White Bear
138 Kennington Park Road, SE11 (020 7735 8664). Kennington or Oval tube. **Open/food served** 11am-midnight Mon-Sat; 11am-11pm Sun. **No credit cards.**
This flamboyant purple and blue-painted pub is home to the White Bear Theatre (at the rear), as the framed posters of past productions proudly trumpet. As such it attracts theatre-goers, along with a cross-section of local life with a preponderance of large, stubbley-chinned men downing pints of Greene King IPA and Grolsch. Last visit we spied a couple of ruddy-faced middle-aged women sipping bottled Guinness who might have stepped straight out of a Dickens' novel. Maybe they're all RADA-trained extras? The bar staff are friendly, efficient and have been known to be wickedly cheeky to regulars.
Babies and children admitted (until 7pm). Games (fruit machines). Jukebox. Quiz (10pm Mon; £1 to play). Satellite TV (big screen). Tables outdoors (courtyard, garden). Theatre. Vegetarian dishes.

Also in the area...
Bar Room Bar 111 Kennington Road, SE11 (020 7820 3682).

Dog House

Lee

Crown
117 Burnt Ash Hill, SE12 (020 8857 6607). Lee rail. **Open** 11am-11pm Mon-Sat; noon-10.30pm Sun. **Food served** noon-2.30pm, 7-9pm Mon-Sat; noon-3pm, 7-9pm Sun. **Credit** MC, V.
Given its lousy location just off the South Circular, there can't be much (any?) passing trade, but nevertheless this large Young's pub always seems reasonably busy. A large bar is scattered with chunky wooden dining tables, grandad chairs and the odd armchair. There's also a cosy snug at the rear, referred to by staff as the 'cuckold's corner'. Otherwise, punters are a complete cross-section of Lee life, from spotty young men downing lager and lime to middle-aged and older types perched on stools at the bar, sipping superb Young's Special. The percentage of women is surprisingly high, and although children are not allowed inside, there's a functional family drinking area outside with the usual bench tables where much food (mostly with chips) is consumed.
Function room. Games (fruit machine). Quiz (Sun). Tables outdoors (garden). TV. Vegetarian dishes.

Also in the area...
Edmund Halley (JD Wetherspoon) 25-27 Lee Gale Centre, SE12 (020 8318 7475).

Lewisham

Hogshead
354 Lewisham High Street, SE13 (020 8690 2054). Ladywell rail. **Open** 11am-11pm Mon-Sat; noon-10.30pm Sun. **Food served** noon-6pm daily. **Credit** AmEx, MC, V.

Situated near Lewisham Hospital, this smaller than average outpost of the Hogshead chain is popular with medical staff, as well as with residents of nearby housing estates. Being a Hogshead, you can expect plenty of real ales as well as usually hard to find – especially in SE13 – country wines and bottled Belgian beers. The place is dumb-bell shaped, with two small drinking areas crammed with solid timber furniture, connected by a wooden serving area and decorated with pictures of old Lewisham. Out back there's a small drinking area with regimented rows of bench tables that are popular in summer.
Babies and children admitted (summer only; beer garden). Games (fruit machine, quiz machine). Satellite TV. Tables outdoors (garden). Vegetarian dishes.

Quaggy Duck
139-141 Lewisham High Street, SE13 (020 8297 8645). Lewisham rail/DLR. **Open** 11am-11pm Mon-Sat; noon-10.30pm Sun. **Food served** 11am-3pm, 6-9pm Mon-Thur; 11am-5pm Fri; 11am-6pm Sat; noon-5pm Sun. **Credit** MC, V.
The Quaggy is a once mighty local river reduced to a trickle, and the Duck is a purpose-built pub in the pedestrian precinct in Lewisham Centre. There's a high ceiling, a High Noon-style wooden balcony and large-screen TVs that will invariably be celebrating some aspect of Britain's football fixation. Light coloured walls are decked out with all manner of duck pictures and the long wooden bar offers the likes of Hancock's HB (rarely found in London) and their own Quaggy Bitter, which we suspect is rebadged Worthington BB. The Capital Radio-style music appeals to the majority of the drinkers who are young and lively, while the old codgers lured by regular cheap deals on the beer grin and bear it.
Disabled: toilet. Games (fruit machines). Music (DJs 8pm Fri, Sat). No-smoking area. Satellite TV. Tables outdoors (pavement). Vegetarian dishes.

Also in the area...
Fox & Firkin 316 Lewisham High Street, SE13 (020 8690 8925).
Watch House (JD Wetherspoon) 198-204 Lewisham High Street, SE13 (020 8318 3136).

New Cross

Hobgoblin
272 New Cross Road, SE14 (020 8692 3193). New Cross Gate tube/rail/36, 89, 136, 171, 177 bus. **Open** 11am-11pm Mon-Sat; noon-10.30pm Sun. **Happy hour** 2-8pm Mon-Fri (student ID). **Food served** noon-5pm Mon-Sat; noon-4pm Sun. **No credit cards.**
It's not often a barman compliments you on your choice of drink and then proceeds to tell you about it, but that's just what happened when we ordered a pint of Wychwood's seasonal bitter at this busy New Cross pub. Before Wychwood rescued it, this was a local's hangout called the Rose; fresh air was at a premium and on a Friday night you could have smoked kippers. It's a much airier space now, with a square central bar and – during term time, at least – students and younger staff from nearby Goldsmith's College. Non-academics are welcome and there's a smattering of locals drawn by the fine Wychwood real ales, Pedigree and others. The large enclosed beer garden out the back gets very busy in summer months and bar food is Thai.
Babies and children admitted (garden). Disabled: toilet. Games (fruit machines, quiz machines). Jukebox. Satellite TV. Specialities: real ales. Tables outdoors (conservatory, garden). Vegetarian dishes.

Peckham

Clock House
196A Peckham Rye, SE22 (020 8693 2901). East Dulwich or Peckham Rye rail/12, 37, 63, 176, 185, 312 bus. **Open** 11am-11pm Mon-Fri; 10am-11pm Sat; 10am-10.30pm Sun. **Food served** 12.30-9pm Mon-Fri; 10am-9pm Sat, Sun. **Credit** MC, V.
Before the recent refurbishment, clocks played a major part in the decor of this knockout Young's boozer. These days they've been curtailed to three large timepieces (only one of which seems to work) in the small, timber-floored front bar, as well as a couple of giant hour glasses. Pride of place now goes to a wall painting of the pub, in which bluebirds are prominent. More beautiful, perhaps, is the olive tree in the centre of the large back saloon bar. Indeed, greenery is a bit of a passion here and the terraced garden at the front has been the recipient of more than one award. Food is basic (pies, salads, quiche, etc) and – should anyone be looking to get hitched – the place is also a licensed venue for weddings.
Disabled: toilet. Games (pianist 8.30pm Wed). Quiz (8.30pm Tue; £1 to play). Tables outdoors (patio). Vegetarian dishes.

Wishing Well Inn
77 Choumert Road, SE15 (020 7639 5052). Peckham Rye rail. **Open** 11am-11pm Mon-Sat; noon-10.30pm Sun. **Food served** 11am-2.30pm Mon-Fri; 1-5pm Sun. **Happy hour** 11am-6pm Mon-Fri; noon-1pm Sun. **No credit cards.**
Vandalism or an onset of taste on the part of the management has seen the removal of the wishing well that used to sit in the concreted front garden. Once the Victoria Hotel, it can still boast an ornate Edwardian wooden ceiling and bar-back, and a tasteful patterned green wallpaper enhances the ambience. At the back there's a small games room dominated by pool tables. Being Irish-owned there's usually a contingent of middle-aged men gazing into the middle distance over pints of the 'black stuff', but you can also expect to find as cosmopolitan a mix of punters as Peckham has to offer. Food is cheap and cheerful pub grub, and the £3.95 Sunday roast has many admirers.
Babies and children admitted (until 7.30pm). Function room. Games (fruit machine, pool tables, quiz machine). Jukebox. No-smoking area (dining area). Quiz (9.30pm Thur). Satellite TVs (big screen). Tables outdoors (pavement).

Also in the area...
Kentish Drovers (JD Wetherspoon) 71-79 High Street, SE15 (020 7277 4283).

Putney

Bier Rex
22 Putney High Street, SW15 (020 8394 5901). Putney Bridge tube. **Open** 5-11pm Mon-Thur; 3-11pm Fri; 1-11pm Sat; 1-10.30pm Sun. **Food served** 5-10pm Mon-Thur; 3-10pm Fri; 1-10pm Sat; 1-9pm Sun. **Credit** MC, V.
A dark, narrow tunnel, lined with sexy young things hunched at low-lying tables, opens out into an even darker back room, where a fashionable south London crowd sprawls over sofas and arranges itself around a pool table to a background of DJ-driven sounds. The sounds are louder at weekends (with added flashing lights) and muted during the day, when the clientele thins out and addresses itself to the short bar menu. The neon-tinged, efficiently operated bar occupies the space

between the tunnel and the back room, from which a cheerful staff dispenses a selection of lagers.
Bar area available for hire. Disabled: toilet. Games (fruit machine, pool table). Music (DJs 8pm Thur-Sat). Satellite TV. Tables outdoors (pavement). Vegetarian dishes.

Coast

50-54 High Street, SW15 (020 8780 8931). Putney Bridge tube. **Open** noon-midnight Mon-Thur; noon-1am Fri, Sat; noon-10.30pm Sun. **Food served** noon-7pm daily. **Happy hour** 5-8pm daily. **Credit** MC, V.
By day, Coast provides a sleek if somewhat formulaic refuge for the tired shoppers of Putney. It sits on a corner site, handsomely enhanced with high windows, its uncluttered space dominated by a back-lit, bottle-rich bar, itself decorated with a selection of plastic gizmos. Sofas and chairs occupy one end, the rest is left relatively clear. Coffee and snacks are available. By night (and this is particularly true of Fridays and Saturdays), the place metamorphoses into a dark-blue den of post-teen partying, sticky with lager, hair gel and pheromones. Bizarrely (for this is Putney), there are also queues. And bouncers. And, silhouetted in the huge windows, a shifting parade of necking couples.
Babies and children admitted (until 5pm). Bar available for hire. Disabled: toilet. Games (fruit machine). Vegetarian dishes.

Coat & Badge

8 Lacy Road, SW15 (020 8788 4900). Putney Bridge tube/Putney rail/14 bus. **Open** 11am-11pm Mon-Sat; noon-10.30pm Sun. **Food served** noon-2.30pm, 7-9.30pm Mon-Fri; noon-3pm, 7-9.30pm Sat, Sun. **Credit** MC, V.
A very popular pub, set back from the High Street, which manages to combine the idiosyncrasies of an independent with the efficiencies of a chain. The close-packed, L-shaped room is littered with wooden tables, oars, old books, paintings, masks and clutter of all kinds; just as it's filled, most days, with a jovial bunch of young(ish) locals, fuelling up on Young's ales and possibly even one of the fine malts. Most nights, the music's good and a shouty crowd creates a jovial atmosphere. If that's all a bit too much, then head for the front courtyard, where a number of tables are covered by vast white umbrellas, thoughtfully (if not blisteringly) heated in the winter months. The food is particularly good, in a posh pub sort of way.
Babies and children admitted (until 7pm). Function room. Games (board games). Tables outdoors (terrace). Vegetarian dishes.

Duke's Head

8 Lower Richmond Road, SW15 (020 8788 2552). Putney Bridge tube/265 bus. **Open** 11am-11pm Mon-Sat; noon-10.30pm Sun. **Food served** noon-2.30pm, 6-10pm Mon-Sat; noon-3pm Sun. **Credit** MC, V.
A large Victorian riverside pub, still fresh from a recent revamp, which manages to attract one of Putney's more mixed crowds, mainly because it divides neatly into three distinct parts. Nearest to the road is the lad's bar, with a welter of sports prints on the walls, table football and two screens for sensurround sports viewing. In the middle is where a boisterous crowd of both sexes makes merry by the bar; while at the back, overlooking the river, is the third, quieter bar, with tightly packed tables, sofas, a real fire, whirring fans and a bunch of people who look like they might be vaguely interested in combining their alcohol intake with something off the brief but thoughtful menu. The club sandwich isn't at all bad (£5.85). Make for the riverside patio in fine weather.

Games (table football). No piped music or jukebox. Tables outdoors (riverside patio). Satellite TV. Vegetarian dishes.

Green Man

Wildcroft Road, Putney Heath, SW15 (020 8788 8096). East Putney tube/Putney rail/14, 39, 85, 93, 170 bus. **Open** 11am-11pm Mon-Sat; noon-10.30pm Sun. **Food served** noon-2.30pm daily. **Credit** MC, V.
If it's possible for a London pub to feel like it's in the depths of the countryside, then this is the place. Wild woodland blooms on three sides, on the other (bringing a dash of urban grit) is a bus turning point and the rumbling source of the A3. Inside – with its close-huddled locals, its chipped, butterscotch walls and cheap striped curtains, its fruit machines, peanuts and pies – you can also feel like you're in deep country. But this is no Slaughtered Lamb; the regulars and staff are friendly, a TV usually burbles away in the background, and the two small bars and twisting alcoves give a great sense of secluded space. Outside are two small courtyards, which are eagerly filled in summer.
Games (board games, darts, fruit machine). No piped music or jukebox. Quiz (Tue). Tables outdoors (children's play area, garden, patio). TV. Vegetarian dishes.

Half Moon

93 Lower Richmond Road, SW15 (020 8780 9383/ www.halfmoon.co.uk). Putney Bridge tube/Putney rail. **Open** noon-11pm Mon-Sat; noon-10.30pm Sun. **Happy hour** 8.30-11pm Mon. **Credit** MC, V.
Music remains central to the Half Moon's appeal. Bands of all standards and styles continue to appear in the back room (they've had the Stones in the pub, you know, and not that long ago either) and on Sunday there's a popular lunchtime trad jazz session. But it's also a great place to while away an evening. The large bar splits the big, blowsy room in two: pool tables down one end; sofas, crocked wooden tables and chairs, and fruit machines down the other. The more sedate part of the Half Moon's clientele makes for the sofa end, while a louder crowd oversees the intense pool sessions and loiters in the central aisle (where they can get up close to the Young's ales). Naturally enough, there's a swinging jukebox and an appropriately louche vibe.
Disabled: toilet. Games (fruit machines, pool tables). Jukebox. Music (bands nightly, 8.30pm, from £2; live jazz 2-5pm Sun). Tables outdoors (garden). TV (big screen).

Parisa Café Bar

146-148 Putney High Street, SW15 (020 8785 3131/ www.parisa.com). East Putney tube/Putney Bridge rail. **Open/food served** 8am-11pm Mon-Sat; 10am-10.30pm Sun. **Credit** AmEx, MC, V.
The upper slopes of Putney High Street are hardly blessed with decent venues, so the unassuming Parisa is a welcome fixture. What impresses is its relaxed blend of fresh, generous food and serious drinking: you can dine all day here, on bacon for breakfast, via a handsome brunch and steak for lunch, through to club wraps and Caesar salads for dinner. Not forgetting several rounds of tea and toast. You can also drink deep from the weighty, global wine list (try a bottle from Lebanon) or put your trust in any number of beers, including Parisa's very own silver ale (which despite the brewery trappings at the bar is not made on site). A dark interior of wooden floors and tables, a side of caged champagne bottles and pinkish walls covered with 'amusing' quotes complete an appealing picture.
Babies and children admitted (high chairs). Disabled: toilet. No-smoking area. Specialities: cocktails, wines. Vegetarian dishes.

Putney Bridge

Embankment, 2 Lower Richmond Road, SW15 (020 8780 1811/www.putneybridgerestaurant.com). Putney Bridge tube. **Open** noon-midnight Mon-Thur; noon-1am Fri, Sat; noon-10.30pm Sun. **Food served** noon-2.30pm, 7-10.30pm Tue-Sat; 12.30-3pm Sun. **Credit** AmEx, DC, MC, V.
Putney's most self-consciously civilised venue is only really worth visiting if a) you're off to the impressive restaurant upstairs or b) you have a penchant for a posh cocktail. The bar occupies the entire ground floor of an architect's wet dream of a building (and winner of a clutch of awards), that to our jaded eye is now looking a little dated. The narrow entrance is impressive, as are the sensuous curve of the blue-lit bar and the wonderful Frink statues, but the brown banquette seating – which is set too low for what should be a great view of the river – is a let-down. Still, the drinks list is a winner: every kind of cocktail (from £5.85), many malts and even more fine wines. Just three beers, though, which presumably won't trouble the smooth-talking smattering of management consultants, smoothly accepting their complimentary nuts from the bar's black-clad beauties.
Babies and children admitted (lunch Sat, Sun; restaurant only). Disabled: toilet. Restaurant. Specialities: cocktails, wines. Tables outdoors (riverside terrace). Vegetarian dishes.

Also in the area...

Café Rouge 200-204 Putney Bridge Road, SW15 (020 8788 4257).
Fez (Po Na Na) 200B Upper Richmond Road, SW15 (020 8780 0123).
Railway (JD Wetherspoon) 202 Upper Richmond Road, SW15 (020 8788 8190).
Rat & Parrot 160 Putney High Street, SW15 (020 8780 1282).
Slug & Lettuce 14 Putney High Street, SW15 (020 8785 3081).

South Norwood SE25

Alliance

91 High Street, SE25 (020 8653 3604). Norwood Junction rail. **Open** 11am-11pm Mon-Sat; noon-10.30pm Sun. **Food served** noon-2pm Mon-Fri. **No credit cards.**
Standing corner-proud opposite Norwood Clocktower and within a dash of Norwood Junction station, this is an atmospheric two-bar locals' pub. Green patterned upholstery and matching carpet, brass knick-knacks dangling from the ceiling and framed Victorian photographs, however, might not be to everybody's taste. No matter when prices here are such a steal. Practically everything on the food menu is a virtual giveaway: £3 or less for the likes of scampi, coleslaw and chips, or grilled gammon, egg, pineapple, chips and peas. Drinks are cheap, too. There are four real ales, none over £1.80, and five wines are just £1.60 a glass. Recently we've noticed how homeward bound commuters have started to catch on, piling in from 6pm onwards.
Games (fruit machines). Jukebox. TV. Vegetarian dishes.

Goat House

2 Penge Road, SE25 (020 8778 5752). Norwood Junction rail. **Open** 11am-11pm Mon-Sat; noon-10.30pm Sun. **Food served** noon-3.30pm, 5.30-9.30pm Mon-Fri; noon-9.30pm Sat; noon-6pm Sun. **Credit** AmEx, DC, MC, V.
It seems to be the kids who flock to the large open-plan Goat House, surrounded by its own car park and generous drinking terrace. The goat motif, however, is largely absent, except

above the bare brick and steel fireplace; elsewhere it's tame green and cream paintwork and less staid framed pictures of cavorting couples. A pool table is elevated on a wooden stage by the main entrance and an elongated U-shaped serving area connects two large rooms, each divided up by wooden partitions. Food is the typical pie and pasta stuff, but portion sizes are semi-legendary. Plus it's a Fuller's, so beers are well worth trying.
Babies and children admitted (until 7pm). Disabled: toilet. Games (darts, fruit machines, pool table). Satellite TV (big screen). Tables outdoors (patio). Vegetarian dishes.

Stockwell

Bar Estrela

111-115 South Lambeth Road, SW8 (020 7793 1051). Stockwell tube/Vauxhall tube/rail. **Open/food served** 8am-midnight Mon-Sat; 11am-9pm Sun. **Credit** AmEx, MC, V.
The flag of Portugal sails high over this slice of the South Lambeth Road – a gabbling, gambling refuge for ex-pat Lusitanians who prefer the Bar Estrela over neighbouring Grelha D'Ouro and the Almonda. The decor is a little too prim and proper to be authentically Portuguese – particularly the star-clad ceiling – but at the counter an authentic weight of assorted slabs of pork, cake and cheese bow the lower snack shelves and at bar level is a suitably solitary tap of Sagres beer. The picture is completed by bowls of butter beans regularly served by waistcoated waiters against the lulling tones of the latest news from Lisbon. A chalked menu of espada (cuttlefish), sopa feijao (bean soup) and filetes pescada (hake fillets) may be better passed over in favour of the restaurant that shares the same name and management next door.
Babies and children admitted (children's menu; high chairs). Games (pool table). No-smoking area. Restaurant. Satellite TV. Tables outdoors (pavement). Vegetarian dishes.

Circle

348 Clapham Road, SW9 (020 7622 3683). Stockwell or Clapham North tube. **Open** noon-11pm Mon-Sat; noon-10.30pm Sun. **Food served** noon-3pm, 7.30-10pm Mon-Thur; noon-3pm Fri, Sat; noon-9pm Sun. **Credit** MC, V.
The Circle is a sum of contradictory gimmicks that don't quite add up to a whole – but its loyal clientele seem to have a royally fine time nonetheless. The outside screams gastropub but punters are just as likely to be there for the cool music, not least on weekend DJ nights. Food is featured – the smells of cooking permeate half the bar – doled out in huge portions to thin young things who don't touch half of it. The back restaurant area is done out in US diner style, but with continental bar football as added distraction. Sky Sports presentations are screened on to a delicate Japanese blind. Meanwhile the bar counter is classic Parisian zinc, and the tables are of sturdy pub stock. Jugs of cocktails at £12 to £14 encourage the general confusion. To record this incongruous mix disposable Circle cameras are sold at bar.
Function room. Games (board games, fruit machine, table football). Music (DJs 8pm Thur-Sat). Satellite TV (big screen). Tables outdoors (garden). Vegetarian dishes.

Plug

90 Stockwell Road, SW9 (020 7274 3879). Stockwell tube/Brixton tube/rail. **Open** noon-midnight Mon-Wed, Sun; noon-2am Thur; noon-3am Fri, Sat. **Admission** after 10pm Fri, Sat £5. **Credit** DC, MC, V.

The Plug is what Brixton used to be before Toby and Tricia moved in. This is a place to sink liquor fast and dance in the same fashion, aided by Plug special drinks of ludicrous strength, DJs who know their onions and enough dancefloor space to swing an angry puma. Atmosphere is reluctantly provided by candles, a mirror ball and a curly-wurly patterned bar counter. Subtle it ain't. Then again what can you do with a head full of Plug Buster (vodka, tequila, absinthe and Red Bull, all for £6.50, no time wasters) but sidle around a sliding dancefloor and let those demons lull you into a false sense of shag on. Action on quieter weekday nights (of which Wednesday is not one, thanks to a 'happy hour' that lasts all day) shifts to the large pool table at the back. Tawdry but delicious.
Babies and children admitted (until 9pm). Disabled: toilet. Function room. Games (fruit machine, pool table, table football). Music (DJs 9pm Thur-Sun). Satellite TV (big screen).

Priory Arms
83 Lansdowne Way, SW8 (020 7622 1884). Stockwell tube. **Open** 11am-11pm Mon-Sat; noon-10.30pm Sun. **Food served** noon-3pm Mon-Sat; 1-3.30pm Sun. **No credit cards.**
The Priory is a collectors' item, the kind of warm local hive that attracts a loyal, discerning clientele who would otherwise be pressing butterflies or delicately unhinging misplaced postage stamps. Instead, they have a constantly changing collection of microbrewery ales to choose from, as proclaimed by the plethora of beer mats swarming the bar. This is the kind of place that gives CAMRA a good name. The Priory has even won its London Pub of the Year award four times since 1992, stressing the point by offering mead, cowslip, sloe and damson wines from the extensive Adnam's range, any number of cask beers and even Kölsch, a slight, summery shandy-type beer that no German outside Cologne would dream of touching. The whole affair – intimate and amiable as it may be – smacks of a local preservation society's informal monthly get-together. Framed quiz-winning certificates hang behind the bar. Golf and cricket club membership optional.
Babies and children admitted (until 8pm). Function room. Games (fruit machine). Quiz (9pm Sun). Satellite TV. Tables outdoors (garden). Vegetarian dishes.

Surprise
16 Southville, SW8 (020 7622 4623). Stockwell tube/ Vauxhall tube/rail. **Open** 11am-11pm Mon-Sat; noon-10.30pm Sun. **Food served** noon-2.30pm daily. **Credit** MC, V.
Believed to have been here since 1839, a Young's pub since the 1920s, the Surprise developed from a quiet working-class backstreet boozer to a party-zoned fleshy summer hangout due to the neighbouring expansion of Larkhill Park in the 1970s. Now the pub will happily organise your summer do, even throw in regular evening games of boules and a barbie in the back garden. In winter it's a cosy hideaway from the busy Wandsworth Road, with three distinct bar areas. The back one is for pub regulars whose framed and full-bellied caricatures on the walls prove a healthy interest in the wide range of beers in stock. South Bank University students break up the monotony of a mainly male clientele, forever on the re-bond over quality bitters and *Monty Python* repeated repeats.
Babies and children admitted (until 8pm, dining area). Games (board games, boules pitch, fruit machine, pinball machine). Satellite TV. Tables outdoors (patio). Vegetarian dishes.

Swan
215 Clapham Road, SW9 (020 7978 9778/ www.theswanstockwell.com). Stockwell tube. **Open** 5-11pm Mon-Wed; 5pm-2am Thur; 5pm-3am Fri; 7pm-3am Sat; 7pm-2am Sun. **Admission** £2 after 11pm Thur; £2.50 before 9pm, £5 after 9pm Fri; £3 before 9pm, £7 after 9pm Sat; £4 after 9pm Sun. **Credit** AmEx, DC, MC, V.
This is where tanked-up custom from Stockwell's many Irish bars lets good, bad and indifferent times roll way past closing time. Slap opposite Stockwell tube station, the Swan puts indifferent live music first and pub banter be damned. From the bouncers on the door (regular faces or preferably members only Thursdays and Sundays) to the friendly Eastern European girls serving behind the huge, long bar, the Swan somehow smacks of a money-making operation appealing to undiscerning Celts or Aussies happy to rock heads along to U2 cover bands.
Babies and children admitted (until 7pm weekdays). Dress code (weekends). Games (fruit machine). Internet kiosk. Music (DJs 9pm Thur-Sun; live bands 9pm nightly). Satellite TV.

Sydenham

Dulwich Wood House
39 Sydenham Hill, SE26 (020 8693 5666). Sydenham Hill rail/63, 202 bus. **Open** 11am-11pm Mon-Sat; noon-10.30pm Sun. **Food served** *winter* noon-2.30pm Mon-Fri; noon-3pm Sat, Sun; *summer* noon-3pm, 6-9pm Mon-Fri; 11am-11pm Sat; noon-10.30pm Sun. **Credit** MC, V.
You encounter a variety of customers at this busy Young's pub, not least because it's in an area split between large and expensive detached houses and acres of council estate. Indeed there can't be many boozers boasting their own golf society and a much-used dartboard. There's a snug public bar at the back and a large front bar with dark wood panelling that's studded with items of local interest, mostly concerning the nearby Crystal Palace. Being a Young's boozer, the beer's above reproach and 13 wines are available by the bottle (12 by the glass). Food is better-class pub grub (lamb chops, bangers and mash) and worth a go.
Games (fruit machines, quiz machine). No piped music or jukebox. Quiz (7.30pm last Wed in month; £1 to play). Satellite TV. Tables outdoors (garden). Vegetarian dishes.

Two Half's
42 Sydenham Road, SE26 (020 8778 4629). Sydenham rail. **Open** 11am-11pm Mon-Sat; noon-10.30pm Sun. **Credit** AmEx, DC, MC, V.
By day youthful customers give the draught lager and real ales (Greene King IPA a very consumer-friendly £1.70 a pint) a hammering to a comforting soundtrack of Sheryl Crow and Hendrix. Here they can relax in mismatched sofas outside the comfort of their own homes. By night the Two Half's (why the apostrophe?) becomes Sydenham's number one style hangout. The dark teak and brass decor remains in situ, but tables and chairs in the club-lit back room get pushed against the wall and the sound system is cranked up to 11. The minimally dressed female of the species encourages enough male predators to warrant two doormen at weekends.
Babies and children admitted (until 8pm). Disabled: toilet. No-smoking area. Quiz (8pm Thur; £1 to play). Restaurant. Satellite TV. Tables outdoors (pavement). Vegetarian dishes.

Tooting

Freedom & Firkin
*196 Tooting High Street, SW17 (020 8767 6582).
Tooting Broadway tube.* **Open** noon-11pm Mon-Sat;
noon-10.30pm Sun. **Food served** noon-8.30pm daily.
Credit AmEx, MC, V.
Freedom for Tooting! The *Citizen Smith* theme is an
unusually appropriate one for this particular pub; not so much
because it's based on Tooting High Street, but more
particularly, because, like Wolfi (the lone communist crusader
in the BBC sitcom) the Freedom continues to plough its own
unmistakable furrow despite the fact that the rest of its kind
has all but died out. The once mighty Firkin chain has almost
disappeared in recent years, but fans of its trademark barrel-
based tables, tacky memorabilia (Ken's uniform from *Citizen
Smith* is exhibited here) and endless Firkin puns will be
pleased to hear you can still enjoy them all at the Freedom.
Of course Firkin's own brews have long gone, but there's still
a decent array of ales and lager on draught, plus a good-value,
though corporate-looking, menu.
*Disabled: toilet. Games (fruit machine, pool table, quiz
machine, video games). Jukebox. Satellite TV (big screen).
Tables outdoors (garden, patio). Vegetarian dishes.*

Spirit
*94 Tooting High Street, SW17 (020 8767 3311).
Tooting Broadway tube.* **Open** 11.30am-11pm Mon-Sat;
noon-10.30pm Sun. **Food served** noon-10.30pm Mon-
Thur, Sun; noon-6pm Fri, Sat. **Credit** AmEx, MC, V.
While nearby Balham's profile continues to rise in the
nightlife stakes, poor old Tooting is generally stuck with the
same sleepy old pubs. No surprise then that this lively little
establishment has all but cornered the local youth market. It's
not that Spirit is particularly trendy, or particularly smart,
but it is bright, noisy and, perhaps most valuable of all in
these parts, friendly. The decor is, on the whole, pretty basic,
with functional furniture and bar, although strips of tinsel
and glittered walls in the back room add a little sparkle. The
sound system cranks up a notch towards the end of the week
to create the biggest buzz there is down here off Broadway
(Tooting, that is).
*Babies and children admitted (children's menu, high
chairs). Function room. Music (DJs Thur-Sat). Satellite
TV. Tables outdoors (pavement). Vegetarian dishes.*

Also in the area...
JJ Moons (JD Wetherspoon) 56A High Street, SW17
(020 8672 4726).
Tramshed (It's A Scream) 48A Mitcham Road, SW17
(020 8682 7181).

Wandsworth

Alma Tavern
*499 Old York Road, SW18 (020 8870 2537/
www.thealma.co.uk). Wandsworth Town rail.* **Open**
noon-11pm Mon-Sat; noon-10.30pm Sun. **Food served**
12.30-10.30pm Mon-Sat; noon-4pm Sun. **Credit** AmEx,
DC, MC, V.
'Popular beyond belief' is how Queen Victoria once
described the success of the Crimean campaign. The phrase
could also describe this memorial flagship, built post-war in
the name of the famous Russian retreat. Now a post-work
retreat for locals pouring out of Wandsworth Town station
opposite, the Alma boasts a grand serving area in the middle
of the main saloon, a handsome art deco fireplace and
delicately decorated glass panels. It's most relaxed at
lunchtimes, with slightly Frenchified set meals (£8.45/
£11.45 for two/three courses) served in the fine back
restaurant under a Victorian frieze (revealed during a 1980s
renovation). Recently under the same Charles Gotto yoke as
the nearby **Ship** (*see p184*), and a Young's pub since
Victoria's day, the Alma offers the expected cask ales and
bottled beers, double chocolate stout, waggle dance honey
beer and Acclaim passion fruit beer at £2.90 a half-litre, and
Stella at £2.80 a pint.
*Babies and children admitted. Function room. Games
(pinball machine). No piped music or jukebox. Restaurant.
Satellite TV (big screen). Vegetarian dishes.*

B@1
*350 Old York Road, SW18 (020 8870 5491/
www.beatone.co.uk). Wandsworth Town rail.* **Open**
5-11pm Mon-Sat; 5-10.30pm Sun. **Happy hour** 6-8pm
Mon-Fri; 7-8pm Sat. **Credit** AmEx, MC, V.
The third in a chain of B@1 bars (Battersea and Richmond
are the other two) instigated by a trio of award-winning TGI
Friday barmen. Cocktails are the order of the day, chosen
from a drinks directory featuring two pages of vodka
variations, mixed by friendly and outgoing staff. Beer
options are limited to San Miguel at £2.70 a bottle. Regulars
have their photos framed in the candlelit back room, a cosy
alternative to the buzz at the front of house, where the dance
sounds create the kind of clubby atmosphere the founding
fathers were looking for. B@1 is definitely at its best after
happy hour kicks in, when Cookie the barman is busy mixing
the drinks and the music, and blowing the hell out of all the
neighbouring competition.
Specialities: cocktails. Tables outdoors (pavement).

ditto
*55-57 East Hill, SW18 (020 8877 0110). Wandsworth
Town rail.* **Open** 11am-11pm Mon-Fri; noon-11pm Sat;
noon-10.30pm Sun. **Food served** noon-3pm, 7-11pm
Mon-Sat; noon-4pm, 6-9pm Sun. **Credit** MC, V.
A swish modern restaurant with a low-key, long bar that
has acquired a life of its own. Discerning clientele from the
Putney/Barnes overspill gather to sip aperitifs while
reclining on comfy cushions, pouffes and sofas, waited on
by efficient Polish staff. On the upper walls, photos of East
Hill and sailing shots deflect from the branded ashtrays and
matchboxes displayed elsewhere. Inevitably there's live jazz

and TV rugby according to occasion. As well as a promising selection of vodkas, Erdinger Weissbrau beer is £2.95 a pint, cocktails £5, and champagne around £6 a glass. For a tenner you can fine dine on bar fare such as thyme-flavoured polenta, duck breast and braised red cabbage, woodland mushrooms or a Sunday roast; weekend morning breakfasts cost a fiver.

Babies and children admitted (restaurant only). Function room. Games (backgammon). Restaurant. Satellite TV. Specialities: cocktails. Vegetarian dishes.

Ship

41 Jew's Row, SW18 (020 8870 9667/www.theship.co.uk). Wandsworth Town rail. **Open/food served** 11am-11pm Mon-Sat; noon-10.30pm Sun. **Credit** AmEx, DC, MC, V.
Honourably mentioned in any number of guides and pub awards – as indicated by the stickers of varying years and denominations on the front door – the Ship in the shadow of Wandsworth Bridge stands at the helm of Charles and Linda Gotto's fleet (the couple also runs the nearby **Alma Tavern**, *see p183*). The riverside barbecue, the Doolali conservatory bar overlooking it, and the cherished interior – with its creams and browns of a post-war childhood, old toys, trinkets and trophies – have all been lovingly selected. Unfortunately, the recent completion of the neighbouring Riverside West development means that the Ship is now less of a secret oasis and more like other Young's pubs: the usual good beers and popular enough to sink under the weight of its crew.

Babies and children admitted (high chairs). Function room. No piped music or jukebox. Restaurant. Tables outdoors (riverside garden). Vegetarian dishes.

Tír Na Nóg

107 Garratt Lane, SW18 (020 8877 3622). Earlsfield rail. **Open** 11am-11pm Mon-Sat; noon-10.30pm Sun. **Credit** MC, V.
Standing on its own in some godforsaken dog leg of Garratt Lane, its outside all lit up like a Christmas tree, its interior like a candlelit walk around a car boot sale in deepest Kilkenny, Tir Na Nóg is what Irish pubs were like before there was any money in them. As such, it's almost charming in its authenticity, with its notices for charity horse races to sponsor, rooms to let or traditional music on a Saturday night. It would be the perfect venue for a four-day wake – albeit one at which the regular rattle of the 44 bus shakes the scuffed-up floorboards. Expect the usual rounds of drinks (Guinness, Holsten, Foster's), and children seem almost obligatory.

Babies and children admitted. Games (arcade game, darts, fruit machine, table football). Music (Irish bands Sat; DJ Sun). Satellite TV (big screen). Tables outdoors (garden).

Tonsley Tup

1 Ballantine Street, SW18 (020 8877 3766/ www.massivepubs.com). Wandsworth Town rail. **Open** 3-11pm Mon-Fri; noon-11pm Sat; noon-10.30pm Sun. **Credit** AmEx, DC, MC, V.
Sitting five years ago in the **Chelsea Ram** (*see p26*), that sporting fellow Hugh Corbett of Slug & Lettuce fame suddenly had a wizard wheeze. 'I say,' he said, 'how about a chain of Tups, what?' So now a dozen rugger-loving landlords preside over part-half, part-traditional, ram-themed pubs called Tups and sold into the Massive chain in 1999. The new Wandsworth branch, opened in November 2000, still has the spruce of fresh pine. A corner pub with a wine bar feel, and a small brown lounge area at the end, the Tonsley Tup features well mannered professionals of either sex dressed in

rugby shirts with their collars turned up, sipping unwooded Chardonnay from Curico, Chile, at £3 a glass. Draught beers are Kronenbourg, IPA, Bombadier and Guinness, all at reasonable prices. The gimmick is no menu but takeaway food phoned in from the bar. All good, if Hugh's your name and rugby's your game.

Bar available for hire. Disabled: toilet. Games (backgammon, chess). Music (occasional live bands). Satellite TVs.

Also in the area...

All Bar One 527-529 Old York Road, SW18 (020 8875 7941).
Grid Inn (JD Wetherspoon) 22 Replingham Road, SW18 (020 8874 8460).
Pitcher & Piano 11 Bellevue Road, SW17 (020 8767 6982).
Puzzle 332 Garratt Lane, SW18 (020 8874 4209).
Rose & Crown (JD Wetherspoon) 134 Putney Bridge Road, SW18 (020 8871 4497).

Wimbledon

Alexandra

33 Wimbledon Hill Road, SW19 (020 8947 7691). Wimbledon tube/rail. **Open** 11am-11pm Mon-Sat; noon-10.30pm Sun. **Food served** noon-3pm, 6-9.30pm daily. **Admission** after 9.30pm Fri, Sat £5 (wine bar). **Credit** AmEx, DC, MC, V.
The Alex, or 'Smart Alex' as emblazoned in traffic-light red on the black staff uniforms, is a mix of Victorian entrepreneurial design and modern-day multi-purpose exigency. With as many rooms as a Cluedo board, it tries to provide all bars to all men: traditional lounge for the post-work pint; no smoking for that swiftie sans cigarette; big-screen sports variety; restaurant, wine bar and terrace. Trouble is, being right by Wimbledon station, the Alex fills with town centre hoi polloi larging it on lager, leaving the spacious and attractive wine bar woefully under-used. The terrace roof is a boon, albeit one offering panoramic views of Wimbledon through barbecue smoke. Built by Young's in 1876, there's the usual range of beers, plus pub grub like chicken, steaks and panini.

Disabled: toilet (wine bar). Dress code (weekends, wine bar). Games (fruit machine, quiz machine). Music (live band Fri, Sat). No-smoking area. Tables outdoors (garden, pavement). TV (big screen). Vegetarian dishes.

Bar 366

366 Garratt Lane, SW18 (020 8944 9591). Earlsfield rail. **Open** 5-11pm Mon-Fri; 1-11pm Sat; 1-10.30pm Sun. **Happy hour** 5-7pm Mon-Fri. **Food served** 5-9.30pm Mon-Thur; 5-8pm Fri, Sat; 7-9pm Sun. **Credit** MC, V.
Diagonally opposite Earlsfield station, the 366 is a popular victory for plain, simple, sensible presentation. Under 35-year-old commuters mingle in a fairly small space, made narrow by the bright, open mirror-backed bar in the middle. Rothko prints decorate the back wall; the attention out front is drawn to two unobtrusive sports screens and a large window on to Garratt Lane. Conversation masses uncritically thanks to funky music at perfectly palatable pitch, while attentive bar staff serve food and drink at reasonable prices: Budvar bottled beer is £2, Hoegaarden £3.50 a pint; cocktails £2.50-£4.50; chicken wings, burgers and salads around £5 or £6. Altogether pleasantly but not pretentiously minimal.

Games (board games). Satellite TV. Tables outdoors (garden). Vegetarian dishes.

Cavern

100 Coombe Lane, SW20 (020 8946 7911). Raynes Park rail. **Open** 11am-11pm Mon-Sat; noon-10.30pm Sun. **Food served** noon-2.30pm Mon-Fri. **Credit** AmEx, DC, MC, V.

Named after the Fab Four's first venue, this rock-themed pub is a mecca for the Raynes Park baseball-capped fraternity. Tucked into a row of shops, the place even seems as unassuming as the boys' house in *A Hard Day's Night*. Once inside, Macca and the lads dominate proceedings, in rare framed black-and-white print, Ludwig drumkit, poster and album cover form. Gig tickets adorn the tables, shots of the Stones, The Who – some autographed – and a red telephone kiosk complete the picture. The outside promise of 'The Best Rock 'n' Roll Jukebox in London' is not kept; inside it's a CD one with hardly any rock 'n' roll at all (Phil Collins!) – and the live music has stopped since management moved into the Cartoon pub venue in Croydon. But in essence the Cavern is nothing but a friendly boozer, attracting pot-bellied ex-long-hairs who practise and preach the religion of chewing gum. There's London Pride on draught and food's the order of luncheon meat sarnies.
Games (fruit machines). Jukebox. No-smoking area. Satellite TV (big screen). Tables outdoors (pavement). Vegetarian dishes.

Eclipse

57 High Street, SW19 (020 8944 7722/ www.bareclipse.com). Wimbledon tube/rail/93 bus. **Open/food served** noon-midnight Mon-Wed; noon-1am Thur-Sat; noon-10.30pm Sun. **Credit** AmEx, MC, V.
Eclipse is the Wimbledon version of its forerunning Chelsea counterpart (*see p137*), knocking out the below-average Volleys bar that was previously seeded here. Its Japanese theme is underplayed, although the low furniture and tiny lights do make you feel like taking your shoes off. Attention to detail is the key, whether it's the delicate spoons or sushi at £6/£12 per half/dozen set. Blini, yakitori and sashimi also feature, with a Combi selection for four at £30. The walls are done out in mirror, maroon and white; the bar has no beer pumps but there's a blaze of cocktail ingredients in clear glass behind it. The stylish menus indicate a fine selection of champagnes (£30-£200 a bottle), cocktails, short and long drinks, shots and two kinds of beer: Lapin Kulka from deepest Lapland and Freedom from Fulham (both £3.25 a bottle).
Babies and children admitted (daytime). Bar available for hire. Satellite TV (big screen). Specialities: cocktails. Tables outdoors (pavement). Vegetarian dishes.

Fog

2 Groton Road, SW18 (020 8874 2715). Earlsfield rail. **Open** 11am-11pm Mon-Sat; noon-10.30pm Sun. **Food served** noon-2.30pm daily. **Credit** MC, V.
Remember pubs? Before big windows, minimal decor, web designers, Moscow Mules, polenta and the Euro, pubs were dank, dark, dingy dives where scaffolders, roofers and welders hunkered over cottage pie and Courage Best to frap the fruit machine and slap the pool table. Such is the Fog, formerly the Country House, changed in name since September 2000 but not, shall we say, in style. A dictionary is kept behind the bar in case you need assistance with the *Mirror* crossword; trashy hardbacks litter the window sills in the saloon bar; and the dartboard thuds to occasional grunts of glee. One day there will be pub-theme pubs and the Fog will be the model.
Games (darts, fruit machine, pool table). Jukebox. Satellite TV. Vegetarian dishes.

Fox & Grapes

9 Camp Road, SW19 (020 8946 5599). Wimbledon tube/ rail. **Open/food served** 11am-11pm Mon-Sat; noon-10.30pm Sun. **Credit** AmEx, DC, MC, V.
A stately public house that dates from the 18th century, the Fox & Grapes features a delightfully relaxing main room of rafters, beams, roaring fire and classy bar counter. Stained glass windows, several pre-war caricature doodles and the clip-clop of horses from neighbouring stables disturbing the obligatory labrador complete the picture, if somewhat tarnished by garish foreign bodies, such as the wine maps of New Zealand and the plastic rugby balls on display. Caesar's Bar alongside is thoughtfully reserved for non smokers, children or charitable private functions. The Kiwi manager, called Buzz, has exercised a positive effect on the fine selection of wines and antipodean touches to the fish, meat and roasts on the menu.
Babies and children admitted. Function room. No-smoking area. Satellite TV (big screen). Vegetarian dishes.

Hand in Hand

6 Crooked Billet, SW19 (020 8946 5720). Wimbledon tube/rail. **Open** 11am-11pm Mon-Sat; noon-10.30pm Sun. **Food served** noon-2.30pm, 7-10pm Mon-Sat; noon-2.30pm, 7-9pm Sun. **Credit** MC, V.
Wimbledon Village green is where the June hordes swarm in scantily dressed droves after the men's and women's singles, often popping into this packed Young's pub for some much-needed refreshment. A former bakehouse then beerhouse, it comprises a hexagonal bar circled by cosy, oak-lined alcoves that are tastefully decorated with old maps or prints of Dutch masters. There's also the usual Young's pics of Charles and the Queen Mum pulling pints, plus the usual Young's range of good beers. Parents are directed to take kids into the no-smoking room left of the main entrance. Tuesday quiz nights go a long way towards helping with slack winter trade, which is otherwise barely encouraged by a decidedly unimaginative selection of jacket potatoes and ploughman's lunches.
Babies and children admitted (separate area; children's menu). Games (darts, pinball machine). No piped music or jukebox. Quiz (8.30pm Tue; £1 to play). Tables outdoors (courtyard). Vegetarian dishes.

Hartfield's Wine Bar

27 Hartfield Road, SW19 (020 8543 9788/ www.hartfields.com). Wimbledon tube/rail. **Open** noon-11pm Mon-Fri; 6-11pm Sat. **Food served** noon-2.30pm, 6-10pm Mon-Fri; 6-10pm Sat. **Credit** AmEx, DC, MC, V.
Hidden from Hartfield Road, a brief bustle away from the busy commuter/consumer crossroads of central Wimbledon, Hartfield's is a corner wine bar splashed out in fierce Mediterranean reds and yellows. Mañana doesn't wash here, however. Apart from the swift service, the management has poured much work into developing the place since its opening in 1994. The enticing wine list caters for both connoisseur and casual alike, down to the simplest Sauvignon at £2.50 a glass; while the menu can offer smoked haddock topped with Welsh rarebit served with Dauphinoise potatotes and a medley of vegetables (£9.75) among a dozen other mains – plus some lively starters, and a two-course deal at under £12. Beers are bottled Beck's, San Miguel and Fosters Ice (£2.50 each). Live music – duos, jazz guitar, flamenco – every Saturday and wine delivered to your door overnight, or so they boast.
Babies and children admitted. Disabled: toilet. Music (acoustic guitarist/jazz 8pm Sat). No-smoking area. Quiz (7.30pm last Mon of month). Vegetarian dishes.

Hogshead

25-27 Wimbledon Hill Road, SW19 (020 8947 9391). Wimbledon tube/rail. **Open** 11am-11pm Mon-Sat; noon-10.30pm Sun. **Food served** noon-9pm Mon-Thur; noon-8pm Fri-Sun. **Credit** AmEx, DC, MC, V.

Hogshead are high-street pubs of character, comfort and cask ale, where independent breweries receive rare spotlights along a lovingly prepared bar counter. Wimbledon's branch consists of one large bar room, with scattered sofas and a skylight clarifying an attractive raised area to the rear. Chalked up on the blackboard are lists of guest ales and beers of the month, studiously depicted by ABV degrees, some given the award of an exclamation mark afterwards. Breweries honoured with regular beertap presence include Nethergate, Shepherd Neame, Ridley's and Robinson's. Infidels can choose from standard draught lagers or wines listed by small/large glass or bottle. You can double up on jacket potatoes, pies or pasties with a two-for-one meal deal after 2pm.

Disabled: toilet; low bar accessible for wheelchair-users. Games (fruit machines, quiz machine). No-smoking area. Vegetarian dishes.

Leather Bottle

538 Garratt Lane, SW17 (020 8946 2309). Earlsfield rail. **Open** 11am-11pm Mon-Sat; noon-10.30pm Sun. **Food served** noon-3pm daily. **Credit** MC, V.

Summer uncorks the Leather Bottle, opening up its garden, kiddies' play area and barbecue, transforming it from a disgruntled male hostelry to all-in family holiday camp. For the rest of the year, this is another rustic Young's pub, halfway between Earlsfield and Tooting, where locals see out the winter on ale and stock pub grub, gazed down on by stuffed pheasants and foxes. Plus points include a wide selection of wines, Young's bitter at under £2 a pint, and a cosy raised chat-room area accessible by a small staircase hidden behind the main bar counter. Laudable smiling service is given to diehard regulars by continental bar staff.

Babies and children admitted (garden play area only). Satellite TV. Tables outdoors (garden). Vegetarian dishes.

Old Garage

20 Replingham Road, SW18 (020 8874 9370). Southfields tube. **Open** noon-11pm Mon-Sat; noon-10.30pm Sun. **Food served** noon-9pm daily. **Credit** AmEx, DC, MC, V.

When Bass was looking for large, lively bars to introduce its new superchilled draught lager, Arc, they could barely overlook the Old Garage. A short walk from Southfields tube, this 'Ale Café' attracts a young crowd – and at weekends we mean crowd – drawn by its starting salary economics. The cheapest draught lager is Carling at £2.20 a pint; Beck's is £2.25 a bottle; indeterminate wines cost £1.85/£2.40 a glass; plus there's any number of four-pint pitcher and doubles deals; and a £6 midweek lunchtime two-course meal. Nor is it a bad-looking place: old lanterns and light fittings, bare floor and tables lend a saloon-type feel. Go on a Thursday for professional comedy, or brave listening to local open mike amateur variety on Sundays.

Comedy nights (8pm Thur, £3.50; 7.30pm Sun, free). Games (fruit machines). TV. Vegetarian dishes.

Rose & Crown

55 High Street, SW19 (020 8947 4713). Wimbledon tube/rail/93 bus. **Open** 11am-11pm Mon-Sat; noon-10.30pm Sun. **Food served** noon-2.30pm, 6-9.30pm Mon-Sat; noon-3pm Sun. **Credit** MC, V

One of London's oldest surviving pubs, the Rose was first established here in 1659, gaining its 'Crown' a century later.

It became a literary watering hole, frequented by the poet Swinburne during its time as a Victorian fophouse. Horrified when his custom was remarked upon in the *Pall Mall Gazette*, Swinburne would then sneak in by a side-door. Today there's a labyrinth of hideaways: the main bar has discreet alcoves and at least three fireplaces, before leading down to the conservatory, restaurant and beer garden. The best seats, however, are little perches under the front windows: either facing into the pub interior and its rare 18th-century prints of London or out onto the high street. Tuck into standard lunch specials at under £6, the typical range of Young's ales and a reasonable selection of wine.

No-smoking area. Tables outdoors (garden). Vegetarian dishes.

Sultan

78 Norman Road, SW19 (020 8542 4532). Colliers Wood or South Wimbledon tube/Wimbledon tube/rail. **Open** noon-11pm Mon-Sat; noon-10.30pm Sun. **No credit cards.**

Awards are heaped on this innocuous little boozer, timidly perched on a quiet suburban crossroads the wrong side of a ten-minute walk from South Wimbledon tube. It does enjoy prime position, however, as Hopback Brewery's sole representative in London. This explains the wall brimming with certificates from CAMRA's south-west London branch (there's now Pub of the Year 2000 to mount alongside the others) and the prodigal fanbase supping on Salisbury's finest Summer Lightning, Thunder Storm, GFB and Entire Stout at silly prices. There are two bars – one of which is only open in the evenings – with scrubbed pine tables and fireplaces, trophy cabinets and dartboard, plus a fabulously nosey cat just dying to get her paws on the London Pub Pussy of the Year award for 2001.

Babies and children admitted (till 7pm). Disabled: toilet. Games (fruit machine). Quiz (8.30pm Tue; £1 to play). Tables outdoors (patio).

Willie Gunn Wine Bar

422 Garratt Lane, SW18 (020 8946 7773). Earlsfield rail. **Open/food served** 11am-11pm Mon-Sat; 11am-10.30pm Sun. **Credit** MC, V.

The young professionals of Earlsfield tend to speak in hushed tones in this stylish corner bar/restaurant, whose dining and drinking areas are divided by a green-tiled raised bar counter. Candles, plants and large mirrors soak up the whispers and cast their atmosphere around the bar. Here wines from £10.50 a bottle are the order of the day, with more than 50 to choose from, a dozen by the glass. The beer is San Miguel, either £1.75 a half-pint glass, or £6.95 for a two-pint jug. The varied food menu entices imbibers with garlic and rosemary grated mackerel (£10.50), Thai green chicken curry (£8.75) or even a full English breakfast served right up until 1pm (£5.95).

Babies and children admitted (high chairs). Restaurant. Satellite TV (big screen). Vegetarian dishes.

Also in the area...

All Bar One 37-39 Wimbledon Hill Road, SW19 (020 8971 9871).
Café Rouge 26 High Street, SW19 (020 8944 5131).
Dôme 91 High Street, SW19 (020 8947 9558).
O'Neill's 66 The Broadway, SW19 (020 8545 9931).
Pitcher & Piano 4-5 High Street, SW19 (020 8879 7020).
Po Na Na 82 The Broadway, SW18 (020 8540 1616).
Wibbas Down Inn (JD Wetherspoon) 6-12 Gladstone Road, SW18 (020 8540 6788).

East

Bethnal Green

Approach Tavern

47 Approach Road, E2 (020 8980 2321). Bethnal Green tube/rail. **Open** 5-11pm Mon; noon-11pm Tue-Sat; noon-10.30pm Sun. **Food served** 1-3pm, 6-10pm Tue-Sat; 1-4pm Sun. **Credit** DC, MC, V.
An art gallery upstairs showcases local artists and defines the style at this busy two-bar pub. Drinks are a cut above those at neighbouring boozers: five real ales were on tap (including Timothy Taylor Landlord) on the Saturday night we visited. All right, so beige-painted walls have become an industry standard, the tiles in the gents were in need of a wipe, and the food menu, once intrepid, has taken a downward step to the breaded plaice and spicy spiral fries – but there's still a long way to go before terminal decline overtakes this loveable nest of East End bohemia. The outside patio is a good spot to be when the sun shines, and the cosy bar at the rear of the pub is just the place to take someone you want to impress – be it a romantic possibility or the head of Channel 4 drama.
Art gallery (noon-6pm Thur-Sun). Babies & children admitted. Jukebox. Quiz (8.30pm Tue; £1 to play). Satellite TV. Tables outdoors (pavement). Vegetarian dishes.

Cock & Comfort

359 Bethnal Green Road, E2 (020 7729 1476). Bethnal Green tube/rail/8 bus. **Open** 4-11pm Mon-Thur; 2pm-2am Fri; 1pm-2am Sat; noon-midnight Sun. **Food served** noon-4pm Sun. **Credit** MC, V.
Ultra-macho Befnal Green Road seems an unlikely place for a brightly coloured, windowless gay pub, as the ironic whistles of the two young women who saw us enter, go to show. Leaving the world of fried chicken shops and pawnbrokers behind, you pass through double doors into a land where orange and blue gloss paint is queen, and where the music is loud and thrusting. There's usually a single real ale on, but it had fallen off the perch the last time we sauntered in and only standard lagers were available. Most men we encountered (not a woman in the whole place) were clutching bottled beers or knocking back less flamboyant cocktails. The tiny black stage framed in pink neon hosts solo drag artistes like Paula Pure at weekends. There aren't many seats, and standing at the bar or against the walls is the thing to do.
Cabaret (11pm Fri, Sat). Games (fruit machine, pool table, quiz machine). Vegetarian dishes.

Royal Oak

73 Columbia Road, E2 (020 7739 8204). Bethnal Green tube/Old Street tube/rail/26, 48, 55 bus. **Open** 1pm-2am Mon-Sat; 8am-10.30pm Sun. **Food served** 8am-2pm Sun. **No credit cards.**
This small, unspoilt single-room pub is supposed to be a gay bar, but as the barman said: 'We don't usually turn anybody away.' The original '60s look of wood panelled walls, glass tile ceiling and etched glass has seen more than its fair share of TV and film exposure, not least in *Goodnight, Sweetheart* and as the scene of Victor Meldrew's last drink. Last Christmas *Blue Peter* decorated the place. Peak drinking hours are on Sundays from 8am, when a mixture of returning clubbers, Columbia Road Flower Market stallholders and punters keep the staff busy all day. The beers are a slightly disappointing mixture of standard lagers and cream flow nitro-keg bitter, while upstairs is the Crazy Maracas Tex-Mex café-bar, where you can find bargain-price cocktails, Mexican beer and Southwestern/Mexish nosh.
Babies and children admitted (until 6pm; high chairs, menus). Function room. Games (fruit machine, pool table). Jukebox. Quiz (Thur). Tables outdoors (pavement; yard). TV (big screen). Vegetarian dishes.

Sebright Arms

34 Coate Street, E2 (020 7729 0937). Bethnal Green tube/rail/Cambridge Heath rail. **Open** 11.30am-11pm Mon, Tue; 11.30am-midnight Wed-Sat; noon-10.30pm Sun. **Food served** 12.30-2pm Mon-Sat; 1-3pm Sun. **No credit cards.**
Down a little passageway off the Hackney Road is an old East End boozer, with a remarkable Thursday night twist. That's when Dockyard Doris (or Colin Devereaux) gives a variety show in old-fashioned music hall style and brings the house down. Drawing in a mixed crowd of grannies, trannies and glammies, the atmosphere is rich in fun and good humour and it's usually standing room only. In the break, the pub's hosts provide free sandwiches. Other entertainments include karaoke on Fridays; Helen Keating's Jazz Band on Saturdays (which usually encourages a number of would-be Sinatras to give their lungs an airing), and a monthly music quiz. Sunday roast lunches are good value at £7 including dessert.
Babies and children admitted (restaurant). Function room. Games (darts, fruit machine, pool table). Music (music hall 9pm Thur; karaoke 9pm Fri; jazz 9pm Sat). Quiz. Restaurant. Tables outdoors (courtyard). Vegetarian dishes.

Also in the area...

Camdens Head (JD Wetherspoon) 456 Bethnal Green Road, E2 (020 7613 4263).
Hayfield (It's A Scream) 156-158 Mile End Road, E1 (020 7780 0011).

Bow

Bow Bells

116 Bow Road, E3 (020 8981 7317). Bow Road tube/Bow Church tube/DLR/25, D8 bus. **Open** 11am-11pm Mon-Sat; noon-10.30pm Sun. **Food served** 11.30am-2.45pm Mon-Fri; noon-4pm Sun. **No credit cards.**
Just along from Bow Church DLR – and a useful place to pass those long waits between trains – this is a modernised Victorian pub where we've always found a friendly cross-section of Bow life. The ground floor bar's U-shaped around a solid wood servery, with a games area – dominated by a pool table that's played non stop – at the rear, and chunky wood furniture elsewhere. There are usually two or three real ales, of which we preferred Adnam's Best. Blackboards announce daily specials that tend to be good-value dishes along the lines of Quorn and vegetable pie, Thai chicken curry and burgers.
Babies and children admitted (until 7pm). Function room. Games (darts, fruit machines, pool table). Jukebox. Music (DJs 8.30pm Fri, Sat). Quiz (8.30pm Wed). Satellite TV (big screen). Tables outdoors (pavement). Vegetarian dishes.

Coborn Arms

8 Coborn Road, E3 (020 8980 3793). Bow Road or Mile End tube. **Open** 11am-11pm Mon-Sat; 11.30am-10.30pm Sun. **Food served** noon-2.30pm, 6-10pm Mon-Fri; 1-9pm Sat, Sun. **Credit** MC, V.
A large Young's boozer where the comfortable main room's walls glow in cream and yellow, and a hundred tassled lampshades shimmer as you pass. Two adjuncts house separate dartboards. Darts is big in Bow. Aside from a pair of chain-smoking students – complete with black-rimmed glasses and striped jerseys – and a group of large men who looked as if they could show Guy Ritchie a good time, the place was packed with alternating nests of senior citizens and thirtysomething couples. A good number of them were eating. The menu lists variations on the theme of standard Young's pub grub – from beef and sausage casserole to

Crown

T-bone steak – with at least four vegetarian options. What is the East End coming to?
Disabled: toilet. Games (darts). Satellite TV (big screen). Tables outdoors (patio). Vegetarian dishes.

Crown
223 Grove Road, E3 (020 8981 9998). Mile End tube then 277 bus. **Open** 5-10.30pm Mon; 10.30am-10.30pm Tue-Sat; 10.30am-9pm Sun. **Food served** 6.30-10pm Mon; 10.30am-3.30pm, 6.30-10pm Tue-Sat; 10.30am-9pm Sun. **Credit** AmEx, DC, MC, V.

An elegant new sister to Islington's award-winning **Duke of Cambridge** (*see p219*) and just as organic – even down to the tampons in the ladies' loo. Esther Boulton and Geetie Singh, the eco-warriors who own both businesses, strictly apply the rule that every product and every ingredient has to be organic and, as far as possible, fair trade. The Crown's huge corner site has a light and airy ground floor with massive windows overlooking the Crown Gate of Victoria Park. Two quiet no-smoking rooms upstairs (where you can reserve a table) offer an even better park view. Furniture is a mix of old sofas and armchairs (some maybe a little too old) with upright wooden dining tables and chairs. Organic Modern European food (pan-fried wild salmon £11 or a tart of spinach and butternut squash £7, for example) tends to be simply prepared, low on sauces and high on accompanying greenery – offering what's available at market. Organic draught beers, including Pitfield's excellent Eco Warrior (and if you're lucky, Shoreditch Stout) as well as the Singhboulton house bitter, are quite costly at £2.70-£3 pint. The organic wine list (detailing which are vegetarian or vegan) is cheaper by comparison, starting at £2.75 a glass or £11 for a bottle of the house bianco.
Babies and children admitted. Disabled: toilet. Function room. No piped music or jukebox. No-smoking area. Restaurant. Tables outdoors (pavement). Vegetarian dishes.

New Globe
359 Mile End Road, E3 (no phone). Mile End tube. **Open** noon-midnight Mon-Wed; noon-2am Thur-Sat; noon-10.30pm Sun. **Food served** noon-3pm Mon-Fri. **Admission** after 11pm Thur-Sat, £2. **Credit** MC, V.

During term time, students and younger staff from the adjacent Queen Mary College make up a good proportion of the drinkers at this pleasantly modernised pub. Aside from a tone-lowering wall-sized advert for Stella Ice, the walls and ceiling are painted bright blue, and there's enough exposed wood around to give a lumberjack the hots. The food is angled at student tastes and includes not so much 'a vegetarian option' as omnivore options on a vegetarian menu, with the likes of veggie sausage and mash and veggie chilli to the fore for £3 upwards. The couple of real ales (of which London Pride seems the best bet) didn't get much action the midweek evening we called in, as most of the young academics went for lager and wine. In warm weather the canalside tables provide a pleasant urban setting.
Disabled: toilet. Games (fruit machine, pool table, quiz machine). Jukebox. Music (DJs Thur-Sat). Tables outdoors (canalside). Vegetarian dishes.

Also in the area...
Bar Risa 221 Grove Road, E3 (020 8980 7874).

Clapton

Anchor & Hope
15 High Hill Ferry, E5 (020 8806 1730). Clapton rail/653 bus. **Open** 11am-3pm, 5.30-11pm Mon-Sat; noon-10.30pm Sun. **No credit cards**.

If a combination of good beer and trad neighbourhood boozer (locals of all ages, as many women as men) takes your fancy – think *EastEnders'* Queen Vic – then the Anchor & Hope is for you. Looking across the Lea towards the water filtration plant and the electrified rail line from the riverside terrace is one of

London crawling: Office drinks

When it comes to after-work or celebratory drinking, Docklands is London's rising star. Covent Garden may have more choice, Clerkenwell more style, but E14 has purpose-built bars for every mood, all within easy staggering distance of each other. A sound tip is to forget the DLR for journeys of less than three or four stops. The Isle of Dogs is smaller than you think: as the crow flies (which it occasionally does), Island Gardens in the south is less than 2.5km from West India Quay in the north, a trip of seven stops.

The neon glow of **Via Fossa** is clearly visible from West India Quay DLR. This stylish three-storey bar is a good starting point for any pub crawl, especially as its bizarre gothic decor and labyrinthine layout are best viewed sober. Think medieval by way of *Gormenghast* and you'll get the general idea. The building it stands in is a converted coffee warehouse, built by Napoleonic prisoners in 1802 and renovated beyond recognition half a decade ago. The ground floor is where you'll find most of the action, with loud sub-club pop, a busy bar and groups of young local workers letting their collective hair down. They sometimes let it down so far, you're in danger of tripping over it. Gangs of attractive young women tend to congregate in the basement bar, with its comfortable armchairs and less frenetic atmosphere, while the more middle-aged risk coronary attack and pull themselves upstairs to the first floor.

Next door sits **Bar 38**, which we suspect is run by the same people. The drinks list is almost identical, so unless you're a fan of coloured lights, Foster's and Kronenbourg, you won't need to stay long.

Exiting Bar 38, you cross the lit footbridge towards Canary Wharf and find yourself on Fisherman's Walk. This waterside footpath isn't shown on most maps, but it's home to a long line of purpose-built bars. Real ale drinkers will be relieved to see the **Cat & Canary**. This and the **Fine Line** (next door) are both owned by Chiswick's Fuller's brewery, although only the Cat stocks the full range of bitters. Groups of men in suits come to drink London Pride and Stella and pretend they're in an old waterside inn. The Cat has been around for less than a decade, despite the impression of age conveyed by woodwork nicked from an old Essex church. The Fine Line is similarly youthful and looks it: polished pine and peach walls with splashes of primary colour. This is where self-assured thirtysomethings come to slurp Chardonnay and nosh tagliatelle.

Further on is **Davys at Canary Wharf**, probably the walk's best bet for decent wines and simple, tasty food. This is where bosses and people who think they should be bosses come to ponder over the extensive wine list and impress their underlings.

Heading south, through the Canary Wharf centre, brings us to an almost identical bar-lined waterside walkway, this time christened Mackenzie Walk. The **All Bar One** and **Slug & Lettuce** tend to attract a similar younger crowd, and being next door to each other means that a change of scenery doesn't require much leg work. While ABO is typically constructed from the best part of a forest, Slug favours bright green walls. The food is very similar (think big plates, platters and hot sandwiches), and the outside drinking areas are interchangeable. Both these bars – and most of the others on the walkway – will be heaving with office workers, so unless you're a fan of corporate 'style' bars, continue south.

It's a bit of a trek to Docklands standards – a little under half a mile if you cut through Admirals Way – but it's worth the hike to Millwall Dock. The **Tollesbury Wine Bar** is a converted East Coast grain barge and the only Thames sailing barge to have returned from Dunkirk in 1940. Nowadays it's a quiet bolt hole from Docklands scurry that seldom gets crowded, and sells Adnam's Best and/or Harvey's Sussex (seldom both at once) straight from the cask and a couple of draught lagers. Despite the name, it's not a great wine drinking centre. The old guy who runs the place can get a little grouchy and will close early (or not open at all) as the mood moves him. Dissenters may return to Mackenzie Walk.
Jim Driver

Map key:
1. All Bar One
2. Bar 38
3. Cat & Canary
4. Davys
5. Fine Line
6. Slug & Lettuce
7. Tollesbury Wine Bar
8. Via Fossa

All Bar One (*no review*) 42 Mackenzie Walk, Canary Wharf, E14 (020 7513 0911).
Bar 38 (*no review*) West India Quay, Canary Wharf, E14 (020 7515 8361).
Cat & Canary (*p191*) 1-24 Fisherman's Walk, Canary Wharf, E14 (020 7512 9187).
Davys at Canary Wharf (*p191*) 31-35 Fisherman's Walk, Canary Wharf, E14 (020 7363 6633).
Fine Line (*no review*) 29-30 Fisherman's Walk, Canary Wharf, E14 (020 7513 0255).
Slug & Lettuce (*no review*) 30 South Colonnade, Canary Wharf, E14 (020 7519 1612).
Tollesbury Wine Bar (*p193*) Millwall Inner Dock, Marsh Wall, E14 (020 7363 1183).
Via Fossa (*p193*) West India Quay, Canary Wharf, E14 (020 7515 8549).

East

Clapton's great views. Inside it's tiny: the 'main' bar is pretty small, but the room housing the dartboard is even smaller. There's a red lino floor, and framed mementos and coronation plates on two-tone paintwork. The landlord is approaching his 50th year in the boozer and it looks as if most of the furniture was past its best when he took over. The beer is Fuller's and the London Pride and ESB are among the tastiest we've had. *Games (darts, fruit machine). Tables outdoors (riverside). TV.*

Docklands

Cat & Canary

1-24 Fisherman's Walk, Canary Wharf, E14 (020 7512 9187). Canary Wharf tube/DLR. **Open** 11am-11pm Mon-Fri. **Food served** noon-2.30pm Mon-Fri. **Credit** AmEx, DC, MC, V.
Built in 1992, but mixing old-style fittings with a twist of modernity, this big Fuller's house attracts a complete cross-section of Canary Wharf life. Occupying a pair of waterside units next to Fine Line (Fuller's other Docklands enterprise), this seems the busier of the two: every table on the large raised seating area was taken on the early evening we last strolled along. Much of the dark woodwork inside is rumoured to have come from a Victorian church in Hornchurch; the phone kiosk was apparently fashioned out of the pulpit. The full range of Fuller's ales is on tap, bar staff are knowledgeable and – though rushed off their feet – generally fit in the occasional smile. *Babies and children admitted. Disabled: toilet. Function room. Games (darts, fruit machine). No-smoking area. Satellite TV (big screen). Tables outdoors (dockside terrace). Vegetarian dishes.*

City Pride

15 Westferry Road, E14 (020 7987 3516). Canary Wharf tube/DLR/Heron Quays DLR. **Open** noon-11pm Mon-Sat; noon-10.30pm Sun. **Food served** noon-9.30pm daily. **Credit** AmEx, MC, V.
Barrels and bare brick decor are used to evoke the era of working docks at this large '50s-built corporate pub. Even the island serving area is constructed from red brick and barrel staves, with dark green paintwork and hanging bunches of dehydrated hops topping the whole thing off. There's been a pub called the City Pride on this site since 1823, and up until a decade or so ago it catered mainly to dock workers and those brought to Westferry Road on business. Nowadays it's a haunt of local office workers who flock here to drink lager, cask ales (including Tetley's bitter) or shooters, and indulge in drunken after-work office politics. Food maybe tries a little too hard to be cosmopolitan, in a corporate kind of way, offering paella, Mediterranean risotto, Hungarian stroganoff and hamburgers. Expect to pay £6-£7 per dish for the world tour. *Function room. Games (fruit machines, pool tables, quiz machines). Tables outdoors (garden). Vegetarian dishes.*

Davys at Canary Wharf

31-35 Fisherman's Walk, Canary Wharf, E14 (020 7363 6633/www.davy.co.uk). Canary Wharf tube/DLR. **Open** 11am-11pm Mon-Fri. **Food served** 11am-9pm Mon-Fri. **Credit** AmEx, DC, MC, V.
This large Canary Wharf branch of the wine bar chain is typically Davys: flagstone floors, chunky wooden furniture, and exposed brickwork dotted with ancient metalwork implements. You know it's all fake, but it looks alright anyway. Serving staff are friendly and customers seem more relaxed here than at other Canary Wharf bars. We've heard rumours that Davys Old Wallop draught bitter is rebadged Courage Directors, but whatever, it seems to go down well

with the thirty-plus men who generally sup it. Everyone else – a pretty evenly matched array of upmarket after-workers – was on wine. House red and white are just over a tenner a bottle, though you can spend plenty more if you want. The simple and effective menu offers starters like dill marinated Scottish herring fillets, with cold mains such as a plate of finest ham or hot dishes like grilled salmon supreme. *Babies and children admitted (restaurant). Disabled: toilet. Function rooms. Tables outside (riverside pavement). Restaurant. Satellite TV (big screen). Vegetarian dishes.*

Gun

27 Cold Harbour, E14 (020 7987 1692). Blackwall DLR. **Open** 11am-11pm Mon-Sat; noon-10.30pm Sun. **Food served** noon-2.30pm Mon-Fri; 1-4pm Sun. **Credit** DC, MC, V.
In Nelson's time this was where England's naval guns were cast and an old foundry called Gun Yard lent its name to this imposing riverside pub. In turn it gave the street its Cold Harbour appellation by serving only cold food to lodging sailors. It's always been a nautical boozer: in days gone by smugglers kept an eye out for passing excise men through a spy hole overlooking Blackwall Reach, and it's said Emma Hamilton secretly met Lord Nelson in a room upstairs – now called the Lady Hamilton Room. Seamen still come here and their signed flags are pinned to the slatted-wood bar ceiling. Though the riverside terrace offers great views, Gun's location on the 'wrong end' of Docklands means you get only discerning tourists and a few office workers venturing along from Canary Wharf. The Marston's Pedigree and own-label Nelson's Bitter are well looked after and both worth a try. *Babies and children admitted (until 9pm; children's menus). Function rooms. Games (darts, fruit machine, pool table, quiz machine). Music (live bands 9.30pm Fri, Sat; 4pm Sun). Satellite TV (big screen). Tables outdoors (riverside balcony). Vegetarian dishes.*

Harry's Bar

21 Pepper Street, E14 (020 7308 0171). Crossharbour DLR. **Open** 11am-11pm Mon-Fri; noon-5pm Sun. **Food served** noon-3pm, 5.30-10pm Mon-Fri; noon-3pm Sun. **Credit** AmEx, DC, MC, V.
Aiming for a more sophisticated crowd than the opposition, Harry's Bar makes the most of its dockside location. Sliding french windows give a superb view down Millwall Dock; there's a terrace outside and a balcony upstairs. Decor is elegantly modern, almost like a smart urban hotel, with lots of space between tables, tan woodwork, cream paint, black details and strikingly angular furniture. Champagne's a feature, together with non-sparkling wines and cocktails. We found relatively sedate after-work drinkers, maybe a few rungs further up the career ladder than the lads and grrrls who frequent **Via Fossa** (*see p193*). The menu encompasses Modern European fare that comes at a price: expect to pay £9-£16 for mains such as pasta, or well put together pizzas. *Babies and children admitted (high chairs, nappy-changing facilities). Disabled: toilet. Function room. Tables outdoors (riverside terrace, balcony). Restaurant. Satellite TV. Vegetarian dishes.*

Henry Addington

22-28 Mackenzie Walk, Canary Wharf, E14 (020 7513 0921). Canary Wharf tube/DLR. **Open** 12.30-11pm Mon-Sat; 12.30-5pm Sun. **Food served** 12.30-9.30pm Tue-Fri; 12.30-4pm Sat-Mon. **Credit** AmEx, DC, MC, V.
You can tell that this large dockside bar is aiming posh by its somewhat pricey light-bite menu: six Pacific oysters £7.95, ploughmans £7.25, and sandwiches starting at £4.25 for honey roast ham. But what, we wonder, do any upmarket

Truly Original

TimeOut

**LONDON'S
LIVING GUIDE**
EVERY WEEK

timeout.com

PHOTO: JONATHON FOSTER WILSON

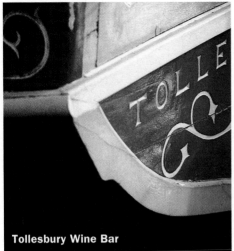

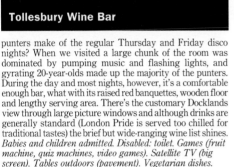

Tollesbury Wine Bar

punters make of the regular Thursday and Friday disco nights? When we visited a large chunk of the room was dominated by pumping music and flashing lights, and gyrating 20-year-olds made up the majority of the punters. During the day and most nights, however, it's a comfortable enough bar, what with its raised red banquettes, wooden floor and lengthy serving area. There's the customary Docklands view through large picture windows and although drinks are generally standard (London Pride is served too chilled for traditional tastes) the brief but wide-ranging wine list shines. *Babies and children admitted. Disabled: toilet. Games (fruit machine, quiz machines, video games). Satellite TV (big screen). Tables outdoors (pavement). Vegetarian dishes.*

Rogue Traders
25 Westferry Road, E14 (020 7987 3439). Canary Wharf tube/South Quay DLR/D3 or D7 bus. **Open** 11am-11pm Mon-Sat; noon-10.30pm Sun. **Food served** noon-3pm daily. **Credit** AmEx, DC, MC, V.
What was until recently the Blacksmith's Arms, one of the area's last unspoilt old-style boozers, has been transformed into Rogue Traders, a cross between the traditional pub it was and the style bar the owners were hoping for. The saving grace is that it's still a pub at heart, with a couple of real ales (including one regularly rotating guest) and an atmosphere that only real locals have. The main room's way too brightly lit (a teething pain, hopefully), not helped by the acres of white paint in the front bar. A smaller room at the back is more like it, with orange ragged walls and smart light wood furniture. When we visited a table of smartly dressed casual types were discussing the 'thrust' of their web campaign over bottled lagers, an indication that the makeover could be working. *Games (fruit machine). Vegetarian dishes.*

Tollesbury Wine Bar
Millwall Inner Dock, Marsh Wall, E14 (020 7363 1183). South Quay DLR. **Open/food served** 11.30am-11pm Mon-Fri. **No credit cards.**
Forget the wine bar tag, we've only ever seen two people drinking vino on all the occasions we've visited this well hidden but atmospheric old barge moored at the top end of Millwall Inner Dock. It was once used for hauling goods up and down the Thames, and in 1940 the Tollesbury saw action bringing

soldiers back from Dunkirk. Today you enter across a gangplank, down a tight staircase and into the barely lit wooden bowels of the barge. It's small and not very tall, so mind your head. It must be a bit of a comedown for this historic old girl to end up as a smoky drinking den for the young office workers who sit at large wooden tables and usually drink Stella Artois, Harvey's or Adnam's bitter straight from the cask. Snacks are limited to the likes of baked potatoes and sarnies. *Babies and children admitted (daytimes). Tables outdoors (quayside). Vegetarian dishes.*

Via Fossa
West India Quay (opposite footbridge), Canary Wharf, E14 (020 7515 8549). West India Quay DLR. **Open/food served** noon-11pm Mon-Sat; noon-10.30pm Sun. **Credit** AmEx, DC, MC, V.
Occupying three floors of an old warehouse, Via Fossa is the Docklands branch of a small chain. There's another in West Kensington, and others in Manchester and Nottingham have been adopted by the gay fraternity. Here it seems to draw the raciest of local twentysomethings, roughly half of them women. Walls are orange ragged, with wrought iron medieval decoration and solid wood beams: it looks as if it was decorated by the Spanish Inquisition on acid. There's a maze of drinking areas, dedicated dining sections and a bar on every floor. Real ale is sold but the emphasis is firmly on shooters, draught and bottled lagers and wine. Global cooking is a little above the average pub grub: sample stir-fried noodles, Moroccan lamb kebab or juniper duck, priced between £6.45 and £12. *Disabled: lift, toilet. Function room. Restaurant. Tables outdoors (pavement). No-smoking area. Vegetarian dishes.*

Also in the area...
All Bar One 42 Mackenzie Walk, South Colonnade, Canary Wharf, E14 (020 7513 0911).
Café Rouge 29-35 Mackenzie Walk, 10 Cabot Square, Canary Wharf, E14 (020 7537 9696).
Corney & Barrow 9 Cabot Square, Canary Wharf, E14 (020 7512 0397).
Fine Line 10 Cabot Square, Canary Wharf, E14 (020 7513 0255).
Slug & Lettuce 30 South Colonnade, Canary Wharf, E14 (020 7519 1612).

East

Via Fossa. *See page 193.*

East

Hackney

291

291 Hackney Road, E2 (020 7613 5676). Bus 26, 48, 55.
Open/food served 7pm-midnight Tue-Thur; 7pm-2am
Fri, Sat; noon-5pm Sun. **Admission** £3 after 10pm Fri,
Sat. **Credit** MC, V.
A remarkable conversion from a neo-Gothic church (Saint
Augustine's by name) with a tall, spacious art gallery in what
was once the nave, a thin bar and a small Modern European
restaurant upstairs (starters are around £5, mains £10). The
stylish bar – check out the painted altar and font – packs out
at weekends, when DJs and musicians (mainly jazz) appear.
During the week it's quieter, with plentiful seating available
in the row of tables and chairs that runs down the wall
opposite the serving area. Hoegaarden is £4 a pint, other
draught beers being standard lager and nitro-keg swill. Most
of the predominantly young crowd we encountered – many
in the roll neck/thick-rimmed specs uniform much admired
by a certain breed of arty Hackneyite – seemed to go for
bottled beers, but there's also a good selection of spirits.
*Art gallery. Babies and children admitted (high chairs).
Disabled: toilet. Function rooms. Music (DJs Fri, Sat;
occasional live music). Restaurant. Tables outdoors
(garden). Vegetarian dishes.*

Dove Freehouse

24-28 Broadway Market, E8 (020 7275 7617). Bus 55.
Open noon-11pm Mon-Thur; noon-midnight Fri, Sat;
noon-10.30pm Sun. **Food served** noon-3pm,
6-10pm Mon-Thur; noon-3pm, 6-10.30pm Fri; noon-
10.30pm Sat; noon-10pm Sun. **Credit** MC, V.

From the outside the Dove looks like a cross between Walt Disney's idea of a London tavern and a Swiss mountain chalet; inside the Hollywood theme continues with small framed portraits of early movie stars. It's with speciality Belgian beers, however, that the Dove's heart and soul lies: expect to pay around £2.15-£2.25 for a half of draught De Koninck, Leffe Blonde or Mort Subite Gueuze, or £2.50 for a pint of Stella Artois (well, it is from Belgium). The freehouse is also making an effort elsewhere: three real ales were on last time we called round, including Flowers IPA and Marston's Pedigree. Plus we overheard a couple praising the selection of wines ('covers every base') with 20 available by the bottle and six by the glass, starting at £11.99/£2.99. Expect plenty of sausages, mussels and meats cooked in beer from the Flemish-influenced menu, served at chunky candlelit tables in the bar or in the flag-stoned restaurant adjacent.
Babies and children admitted (restaurant; high chairs; toys). Games (board games). No-smoking area. Restaurant. Specialities: Belgian beers. Tables outdoors (pavement). Vegetarian dishes.

Maddigans
225 Mare Street, E8 (020 8985 7391). Hackney Central rail/38 bus. **Open** 11am-11pm Mon-Thur; 11am-midnight Fri, Sat; noon-10.30pm Sun. **Food served** noon-3pm, 6-9pm Mon-Fri; 6-9pm Sat, Sun. **Credit** MC, V.
Being sited almost directly opposite the new Ocean concert venue can't hurt this recently renovated pub's chances of a successful relaunch. It seems aimed at the area's more cosmopolitan residents, the sort that appreciates organic chicken, real ales and bottled Belgian beers. Drinkers are predominantly under 30 – though older people do occasionally slip in – and include a few glassy-eyed regulars who sit on stools around the horseshoe-shaped bar. We surveyed our surroundings from a raised platform in one corner, drank our draught Bass and generally let the world pass us by. We were impressed by the pair of magnificent brass art nouveau 'spirit'-style lamps that greet you as you arrive, and by the clean, uncluttered decor. Less splendid are the drinking slogans painted on to the beige walls: 'candy's dandy, but liquor's quicker' and suchlike. Out back a heated garden provides al fresco opportunities in warmer months.
Babies and children admitted. Games (fruit machine). Music (occasional live). Satellite TV. Tables outdoors (garden). Vegetarian dishes.

Prince George
40 Parkholme Road, E8 (020 7254 6060). Bus 38, 242, 277. **Open** noon-2.30pm, 5-11pm Mon-Fri; noon-11pm Sat; noon-10.30pm Sun. **Food served** noon-3pm Sun. **Credit** AmEx, DC, MC, V.
These days the accents in this cheery backstreet boozer tend to be more courtly than 'cor blimey', and the conversations we overheard centred on why your mobile needs a scart socket and the complexities of academic pay structures. It's a friendly pub with three cosy drinking areas inside a neo-Georgian exterior. In winter the tiny beige-painted room at the rear offers a roaring fire in a brown tiled fireplace; there are bench tables outside for al fresco drinking when summer arrives. A small games room, dominated by a much-used pool table, sits behind the oblong front bar, where the diminishing number of locals sip their lager and bitter. There were four real ales on tap when we visited, including Brakspear's Special, London Pride and Adnam's Best, with the former in peak condition. Food centres around snacks and Sunday roast.
Babies and children admitted (until 8.30pm). Games (pool table). Jukebox. Quiz (Mon). Satellite TV. Specialities: real ales. Tables outdoors (forecourt). Vegetarian dishes (Sun).

Critics' choice
real ale pubs

Anchor & Hope (p189)
Best kept London Pride east of Edgware Road.

Crown (p189)
Fully organic range includes the mighty Shoreditch Stout.

Canbury Arms (p143)
They've served over 420 guest ales you know.

Royal Oak SE1 (p161)
Beers by Harvey's of Lewes, one of the country's finest family brewers.

Wenlock Arms (p132)
One of the few London pubs that always stocks a mild ale.

Railway Tavern
339 Mare Street, E8 (020 8985 4184). Hackney Central rail. **Open** 11am-11pm Mon-Sat; noon-10.30pm Sun. **Food served** noon-3pm Mon-Sat; noon-4pm Sun. **No credit cards.**
Not one of Hackney's gentrified boozers, this is a solid corner pub opposite Hackney Central rail station that defiantly sticks to its old-fashioned style and latter-day Irish roots. Some find its mix of stained-glass windows, elegant pillars, Vegas-type bar stools and tables divided by wooden fretwork over-the-top and kitsch, others regard it as a classic of pub decor. The convivial atmosphere is down to the mix of local blue collar workers and middle-aged Irish couples. Bar staff tend to be of the old school and friendly, and usually there's a single real ale on offer. We were treated to Charles Wells' special Valentine's brew, though in our experience you're more likely to find Eagle IPA. There are few signs of the times other than the pizza menu and a blackboard wine list.
Babies and children admitted (until 7pm). Digital TVs. Games (fruit machines). Jukebox. Vegetarian dishes.

Royal Inn on the Park
111 Lauriston Road, E9 (020 8985 3321). Mile End tube then 277 bus. **Open** noon-11pm Mon-Wed; noon-midnight Thur-Sat; noon-10.30pm Sun. **Food served** noon-2.30pm, 6-9.30pm Mon-Fri; noon-9.30pm Sat; noon-4pm Sun. **Credit** MC, V.
Although the sign in the window promises six real ales, there were only four on the day we wandered in – but they were good (including Timothy Taylor Landlord, Abbot and Adnam's Best). The L-shaped ground-floor bar is wooden floored, with large windows and a fetching gilt-edged mirror sitting on a white marble fireplace. Blackboards give notice of rib of lamb, steaks and suchlike – available in the small restaurant next door – all under a tenner. Evening customers tend to be young Hackneyites, drawn by the imposing soundtrack that veers between trip hop and Cuban jazz of the *Buena Vista Social Club* type. During the day it's more sedate, with a smattering of chess players and middle-aged eccentrics. A garden on the edge of the park provides picnic tables for those who like to drink in E9's version of the countryside.
Babies and children admitted (nappy-changing facilities). Disabled: toilet. Function rooms. Jukebox. Life-drawing classes

(7.30pm Mon, Wed; book in advance). Music (DJ 2pm Sun). No-smoking area (restaurant). Quiz (Tue). Restaurant. Specialities: Belgian & Czech beers, real ales. Tables outdoors (garden). TV. Vegetarian dishes.

Also in the area...
Falcon & Firkin 360 Victoria Park Road, E9 (020 8985 0693).

Leyton & Leytonstone

Birkbeck Tavern
45 Langthorne Road, E11 (020 8539 2584). Leyton tube. **Open** 11am-11pm Mon-Sat; noon-10.30pm Sun. **Food** served noon-3pm Mon-Sat. **Credit** MC, V.
This calmly understated late Victorian boozer is one of London's most revered real ale pubs. Ignore the Courage Best in favour of own-label Rita's (named after the landlady and something of a bargain at £1.60 a pint), plus up to two more guest ales and a 'real' cider. The two bars – simply decked out in brown and cream – are separated by a mahogany serving area and partition. An original Arts and Crafts fireplace takes pride of place in the 'posh' side, which used to be the hotel lobby. Rather than serve up dodgy pre-cooked dishes the management has sensibly stuck to its regime of lunchtime sandwiches, served at ridiculously low prices. Students and older real ale fans make up most of the drinkers. *Function room. Games (darts, fruit machine, pool table). Jukebox. Quiz (8.30pm Sun; £4 to play). Satellite TV. Tables outdoors (garden).*

North Star
24 Browning Road, E11 (020 8532 2421). Leytonstone tube. **Open** noon-11.30pm Mon-Sat; noon-10.30pm Sun. **Food served** noon-3pm, 6-9pm Mon-Fri; noon-5pm Sat, Sun. **Credit** MC, V.
The orange stippled walls of this worthy backstreet local are dotted with framed pictures of steam trains (the North Star was a railway engine) and brewery posters. There are three rooms: a long, thin comfortable saloon; a small public bar with barely enough space for a dartboard and players; and a dining area with crossed lacrosse sticks over the bar hatch. Regulars are predominantly twenty- and thirtysomething men, and occasionally their partners. The choice of real ales is a tricky one between Bass and Adnam's Best, with quite a few locals going for lager. Being a chain pub, 'sizzling steaks' (from £3.45 for an 8oz rump with chips) are the order of the day, but being a locals' pub as well, there's the noticeboard tacked with letters of thanks from children's charities. *Games (fruit machine). Tables outdoors (garden, pavement). TV (satellite & digital). Vegetarian dishes.*

Sir Alfred Hitchcock Hotel
147 Whipps Cross Road, E11 (020 8530 3724/ www.hitchcock.clara.net). Leytonstone tube/Walthamstow Central tube/rail. **Open** 11am-11pm Mon-Sat; noon-10.30pm Sun. **Food served** noon-7.30pm daily. **Credit** MC, V.
The tall, ivy-covered façade of this majestic edifice on the edge of Epping Forest has been unfairly compared to the Bates Motel. We, however, prefer to think of its late-Edwardian splendour as the perfect setting for an Agatha Christie murder mystery. The main bar has a circle of settle-lined cubby holes arranged around a central island bar that offers up to four real ales, all under £2 a pint, and the usual lagers. Sir Alf makes guest appearances in framed prints on the walls, plus there are scenes from his various movies. The adjacent restaurant is a branch of the local Star of India, and

reasonable formula curries are available at typical high-street prices. Being near Whipps Cross Hospital, a good proportion of the customers are young medical staff, with older locals making up the rest. *Babies and children admitted. Bar area for hire. Games (fruit machine). Quiz (8pm Tue; £1 to play). Restaurant. Satellite TV (big screen). Tables outdoors (garden).Vegetarian dishes.*

William the Fourth
816 Leyton High Road, E10 (020 8556 2460). Leyton tube/Walthamstow Central tube/rail. **Open** 11am-11pm Mon-Sat; noon-10.30pm Sun. **Food served** noon-3pm, 5.30-8.30pm Mon-Sat; 12.30-5pm Sun. **No credit cards.**
For non-locals this can be a tricky pub to reach, but we think it's worth the journey. Despite the 'wine bar' signs that dominate the front windows, this is a traditionally decorated Victorian boozer dedicated to real ale. We found six of them on offer including regulars such as Fuller's London Pride and ESB, and specials from Sweet William Brewery, including East London Mild and Just William. The two large bars have masses of framed pictures, and enough clocks, pub mirrors and brass instruments to stock a Portobello antiques stall for a year. Escape the big-screen action in the front bar to the quieter rear room with its chunky wood tables, fine domed skylight and well chosen musical soundtrack (Van Morrison, and John Lee Hooker on our last visit). Customers tend to be more white collar than blue. *Babies and children admitted (until 7pm). Games (fruit machines, quiz machine). Quiz (8.30pm Sun; £1 to play). Satellite TV (big screen). Tables outdoors (paved area). Vegetarian dishes.*

Also in the area...
Drum (JD Wetherspoon) 557-559 Lea Bridge Road, E10 (020 8539 6577).
George (JD Wetherspoon) Wanstead High Street, E11 (020 8989 2921).
O'Neill's 762 High Road, E11 (020 8532 2411).
Walnut Tree (JD Wetherspoon) 857-861 High Street, E11 (020 8539 2526).

Limehouse

Barley Mow
44 Narrow Street, E14 (020 7265 8931). Limehouse DLR. **Open** noon-11pm Mon-Sat; noon-10.30pm Sun. **Food served** noon-2pm, 6.30-9.30pm Mon-Thur; noon-2pm, 6.30-10pm Fri; noon-3pm, 6.30-10pm Sat; noon-3pm, 6.30-9pm Sun. **Credit** AmEx, MC, V.
This graceful red brick Edwardian building was converted into a pub in 1989, and it's probably London's only boozer entered down stone steps. It used to be the house of the dockmaster of the Limehouse Basin, and is named after a nearby brewery operated nearby by Taylor Walker from 1730 until 1960. The panorama from the canopied veranda takes in the Thames as well as the slightly less grand Limehouse Marina. Drinkers are a mix of tourists, office workers and a strange breed of nautically minded gents in blue blazers who seem to come with the marina. Real ales include well-kept Burton Ale, Marston's Pedigree and Tetley's Bitter. A separate restaurant serves better-than-average pub fare, including plenty of pasta and fish mains for around a fiver. *Babies and children admitted. Disabled: toilet. Games (fruit machine, quiz machine). Music (live jazz fortnightly). Restaurant. Tables outdoors (riverside terrace). TV. Vegetarian dishes.*

East

London crawling: EastEndings

The best place to start any walk through Whitechapel or Spitalfields is the **Pride of Spitalfields**. Not because the former Romford Arms has any particular claim to notoriety, it's just that it's one of the few pubs in E1 that serves a decent pint. As you sip your Crouch Vale IPA you can reflect that you're in the heart of what ghouls and tour guides refer to as the 'Ripper's East End'. Between 31 August and 9 November 1888 five women were brutally slaughtered within a mile's radius of this pub by the man (or woman) dubbed 'Jack the Ripper'.

When you leave the Pride, turn left, and left again for Spelman Street and a corner pub called the **Alma**. If you can find it open (hours are erratic and it was up for sale as we went to press), ask the landlord to show you the back room, where you'll find portraits of the principal suspects and victims.

Next, follow the road round to the left until it becomes Hanbury Street and head west. About ten metres on from the junction with Brick Lane, you pass all that's left of 29 Hanbury Street, demolished in 1970 to build a warehouse for the now defunct Truman's Black Eagle Brewery. This was the scene of the second Ripper murder, that of Annie Chapman. If stylish bars in former breweries are your thing, then drop into the **Vibe Bar** for a cocktail or a bottle of Bud. Otherwise continue to Commercial Street and the **Ten Bells**, a 'regular' for all the Ripper's victims and venue of final victim Mary Kelly's last noggin. As we write it's closed and up for sale, so it's anyone's guess how it will end up. **Ye Olde Axe** is another 'Ripper' pub, reached by walking up Commercial Street, turning right into Shoreditch High Street and right again into Hackney Road. Today presenting strippers from noon to midnight, it nonetheless retains aspects of its Victorian splendour. Where booths now face the bar used to be an alleyway up which a Ripper suspect fled, closely followed by an angry mob. (NB: it's good form to put £1 in the stripper's jug, 50p at the very least. No coppers.)

More recent and marginally less ghoulish are the exploits of the Krays – twins Ronnie and Reggie – who made something of an impact as protection racketeers in the East and West Ends from 1954 until their arrest in May, 1968. Cut through Columbia Road, Swanfield Street and Brick Lane to the **Carpenters Arms**, very much a local pub for the boys. They usually serve a decent pint of London Pride, but last time we called in it was 'off'. We didn't make a fuss.

Head east past Repton Boys Club (where the brothers boxed) to Vallance Road. Just to the left are the flats that replaced Charles and Violet Kray's terraced house at number 178. The plaque that states that Prince Charles laid the foundation stone marks the precise site of 'Fortress Kray'.

If the fancy takes you, you can cut down through Dunbridge Street to the **Lion** in Tapp Street, the pub where Ronnie was drinking when he heard that rival hard man George Cornell was guzzling light ales in the Blind Beggar. Ronnie was driven to Whitechapel Road, but we hoof it down Vallance Road, turning right at the end. We hurry past the **Grave Maurice**, the pub where the Twins chose to meet 'business' contacts and – despite a recent makeover – still something of a shrine to the '60s.

When Ronnie entered the **Blind Beggar**'s public bar (using the door into what is now one big bar), Cornell looked up and said, 'Well, look who's here.' Kray pulled a pistol out of his pocket and shot Cornell in the forehead. What Kray remembered most was the sneer on Cornell's face as he fell, and that the needle on the juke box got stuck and kept on repeating the words 'The sun ain't gonna shine anymore... anymore... anymore...' He calmly walked out of the pub and was driven back to the Lion, where the drinking continued. The Blind Beggar has been spruced up a lot since 9 March 1966, and they now sell a pretty decent pint of draught Bass.
Jim Driver

Alma (*no review*) 41 Spelman Street, E1 (020 7247 5604).
Blind Beggar (*p199*) 337 Whitechapel Road, E1 (020 7512 9187).
Carpenter's Arms (*no review*) Cheshire Street, E1 (no phone).
Grave Maurice (*no review*) 269 Whitechapel Road, E1 (020 7247 0960).
Lion (*no review*) 8 Tapp Street, E1 (020 7247 0960).
Pride of Spitalfields (*p200*) 3 Heneage Street, E1 (020 7247 8933).
Ten Bells (*no review*) 84 Commercial Street, E1 (020 73677 2145).
Vibe Bar (*p200*) The Brewery, 91-95 Brick lane, E1 (020 7377 2899).
Ye Olde Axe (*no review*) 69 Hackney Road, E2 (020 7729 5137).

Booty's Riverside Bar

92A Narrow Street, E14 (020 7987 8343). Westferry DLR. **Open** 11am-11pm Mon-Sat; noon-10.30pm Sun. **Food served** 11am-9.30pm Mon-Sat; noon-9.30pm Sun. **Credit** AmEx, DC, MC, V.

Once a store for 18th-century barge builders Sparks, then the Waterman's Arms, Booty's is a cosy local that came about in 1979. Its single ground-floor drinking area has a traditional wooden bar, internal pebble-dashed walls and ceiling, and a neatly arranged dining area with dinky gingham-clothed tables overlooking the Thames. When it floods (as it regularly does) these end up afloat. There are two well kept real ales – including an excellent pint of draught Bass – yet this is still a pub that aspires to be a bar, even resorting to pinning maps of French wine regions on the ceiling. Some two dozen predominantly French vinos start at under a tenner a bottle, £2.50 a glass. Customers tend to be a mix of canny tourists and ebullient locals. *Babies and children admitted. Games (fruit machine, quiz machine). Specialities: wines. Tables outdoors (pavement). TV. Vegetarian dishes.*

Grapes

76 Narrow Street, E14 (020 7987 4396). Westferry DLR. **Open** noon-3pm, 5.30-11.30pm Mon-Fri; 7-11.30pm Sat; noon-3pm, 7-10.30pm Sun. **Food served** 7-9pm Mon-Sat; noon-3pm Sun. **Credit** AmEx, DC, MC, V.

If you visited all the pubs in London that claim a Dickens connection, you'd end up with a pretty sore head. The Grapes is said to be the Six Jolly Fellowship Porters as described in *Our Mutual Friend*, though it's only fair to point out that Wapping's **Prospect of Whitby** (*see p199*) holds an identical claim. Built in 1583, this is a long, multi-levelled pub with wooden floors and panelling, chunky furniture and a staircase leading up to a well-regarded fish restaurant. The bar menu offers simple food, so expect fish and chips, bangers and the like for £5-£6. It was overly smoky the night we called in, with tables packed with men in suits and women in pressed jeans debating the finer points of TV soaps and football. Bitters include Adnam's Best and Burton Ale and the wooden riverside terrace is one of east London's best. *Games (board games). Restaurant (available for hire). Tables outdoors (riverside balcony). Vegetarian dishes.*

House Bar & Restaurant

27 Ropemaker's Fields, E14 (020 7538 3818). Limehouse or Westferry DLR/15, 277, D6, D7 bus. **Open** 11am-11pm Mon-Sat; noon-10.30pm Sun. **Food served** noon-2.30pm, 6.30-10pm Mon-Sat; noon-4pm Sun. **Credit** MC, V.

Formerly the House They Left Behind (it's all that's left of a demolished terrace), the renamed House Bar reflects the changes that have taken Limehouse from a haunt of seamen and cut-throats to a place of rampaging estate agents. The journey from traditional pub to its current status as upmarket watering hole for the loft dwellers of E14 has taken barely a decade. It may be the same thin ground-floor room of old, but these days the walls are pastel painted, the bar is marble topped and clever lighting effects cast some additional colour. Draught beers are standard (nothing cask conditioned), but the large wine list is refreshingly diverse and friendly staff seem eager to please. A smart dining area at the rear offers well-cooked Modern European/British nosh like panfried skate wing and sautéed lambs kidneys. *Function room (conservatory). Restaurant. Specialities: vodkas. Tables outdoors (boules pitch). Vegetarian dishes.*

Queen's Head

8 Flamborough Street (020 7791 2504). Limehouse DLR. **Open** 11am-11pm Mon-Sat; noon-10.30pm Sun. **Food served** 11.30am-3pm Mon-Fri. **No credit cards.**

There's been a refit at this characterful Young's boozer, but thankfully it was more of a tidy up than a complete transformation. Gone are the green velvet curtains and banquettes in the saloon, replaced by checked curtains and dinky wooden tables and chairs. The public bar, however, is still very much as we remember, with its London Fives dartboard and rare Queen's Head Sports & Social Club scoring device. Being a Young's pub, it's the beer that dominates – the 'ordinary' bitter and Special were both delicious. More surprisingly, a blackboard offers a wide variety of wines and house champagne (£21.95 a bottle), and we spied one couple downing a bottle of Rioja. Customers are a Stepney mix of cabbies and carpenters, with a smattering of middle-class execs muscling in as the area becomes more gentrified. *Games (darts).*

Also in the area...

Bar 38 Unit C, 16 Hertsmere Road, West India Quay, E14 (020 7515 8361).
Slug & Lettuce 30 South Colonnade, Canary Wharf, E14 (020 7519 1612).

Plaistow

Black Lion

59-61 High Street, E13 (020 8472 2351). Plaistow tube. **Open** 11am-3.30pm, 5-11pm Mon-Thur; 11am-11pm Fri, Sat; noon-10.30pm Sun. **Food served** noon-2.15pm, 5.30-7pm Mon-Fri. **Credit** MC, V.

This grand former coaching inn has been here since the 16th century and is still something of a haven for the weary traveller, even if you've only come from Plaistow tube. It hasn't been too gentrified, so expect plenty of bare brick and boards and just the odd nick-nack. The larger split-level front bar attracts a stalwart crowd of local drinkers, all of whom seem to be on nodding terms, with most of them tapping along to the sounds of Roy Orbison when we popped in. At the rear is a little saloon bar where solitary newspaper readers tend to congregate, and an outside courtyard with tables. Three real ales are always on tap, including a tasty Brakspear's Special the last time we went. Food is simple and inexpensive, offering pies, baked potatoes and the like. *Babies and children admitted (until 7pm, restaurant only). Function room. Games (fruit machine). Restaurant. Tables outdoors (garden). TV. Vegetarian dishes.*

Stratford

Golden Grove

146-148 The Grove, E15 (020 8519 0750). Stratford tube/DLR/rail. **Open/food served** 11am-11pm Mon-Sat; noon-10.30pm Sun. **Credit** AmEx, MC, V.

Named after a line in a poem by local lad Gerard Manley Hopkins, this is a thriving JD Wetherspoon's that's become an E15 institution. We settled down with a hugely enjoyable guest pint of Ridleys Witchfinder Porter (a bargain at only £1.49) in the large no-smoking area and admired the interior. Green ceiling, floral carpet and beige patterned walls may not be an obvious first choice, but the decor certainly helps turn a split-level warehouse (they used to sell jeans here) into a comfortable boozer. Its location on the edge of the shopping centre, near the Theatre Royal and within staggering distance of the station, makes for a mixed clientele. There's a reasonably comfortable concrete terrace garden outside, though relaxing on such a busy road junction does require a Jeremy Clarkson-like enthusiasm for motor vehicles.

East

Disabled: toilet. Games (fruit machines). No piped music or jukebox. No-smoking area. Specialities: changing guest ales. Tables outdoors (two gardens). Vegetarian dishes.

King Edward VII
47 Broadway, E15 (020 8221 9841). Stratford tube/rail/ DLR. **Open** noon-11.30pm Mon-Sat; noon-10.30pm Sun. **Food served** noon-7pm Mon-Fri; noon-6pm Sat, Sun. **Credit** MC, V.
This large, three-roomed boozer by the old West Ham town hall used to be called the Prussia, a name that's stuck with the older locals who frequent it. Basically it's an old tavern that's not been much messed with: textured plaster walls, dark ceilings and the sort of framed pictures you used to see in junk shops before Wayne Hemingway put them in a book and they became collectable. The two front bars (saloon and lounge) are small and comfortable, with a larger dining room up the steps behind. Draught Bass and London Pride are usually available, as well as a couple of guest ales that might come from Badger, Shepherd Neame or Timothy Taylor. Modest pub food, such as spicy Mississippi chicken or burgers, is served until early evening. *Games (arcade game, fruit machines, quiz machine). Restaurant. Tables oudoors (yard). TVs (big screen; satellite & digital). Vegetarian dishes.*

Also in the area...
Golden Grove (JD Wetherspoon) 146-148 The Grove, E15 (020 8519 0750).
Hudson Bay (JD Wetherspoon) 1-5 Upton Lane, E7 (020 8471 7702).
Pigeons (It's A Scream) 120 Romford Road, E15 (020 8522 7101).

Walthamstow

Goose & Granite
264 Hoe Street, E17 (020 8223 9951). Walthamstow Central tube/rail. **Open** 11am-11pm Mon-Sat; noon-10.30pm Sun. **Food served** noon-3pm daily. **Credit** MC, V.
Walthamstow's biggest and brashest boozer is a haunt of lively young drinkers, of which there appears to be plenty. On a Thursday evening the only seats to be had were in the small and nearly empty no-smoking section. It's a recently refurbished pub with nicotine-coloured walls, heavily timbered drinking sections and marble-topped tables. A couple of real ales are available (draught Bass, Adnam's Best), but when we visited it was the lager, wines and Breezers that were taking a hammering. The food (hot sandwiches, burgers and suchlike) has its admirers and the gentle aroma of deep-frying beats even the air-conditioning. *Disabled: toilet. Games (fruit machines, golf machine). Music (DJs 6pm-close Fri, Sat). No-smoking area. Vegetarian dishes.*

Wapping

Prospect of Whitby
57 Wapping Wall, E1 (020 7481 1095). Wapping tube. **Open** 11.30am-3pm, 5.30-11pm Mon-Fri; 11.30am-11pm Sat; noon-10.30pm Sun. **Food served** noon-2.30pm, 6-9pm Mon-Sat; noon-3pm, 6-9pm Sun. **Credit** AmEx, DC, MC, V.
Built in 1520 and last remodelled in 1777, this historic pub has aged gracefully while seeing some action. The first fuchsia to enter this country in 1780 was sold by a sailor here for a noggin of rum, and in 1953 a robber called Scarface (Robert Harrington-Saunders to his mum) led an armed raid on a party held upstairs – he was hanged after murdering one of his pursuers. Charles Dickens, Samuel Pepys, Dr Johnson and Judge Jeffries (the 'hanging judge') are all recorded as having drunk here. No wonder it's become a tourist attraction. The pewter-topped counter resting on wooden casks, stone-flagged floors, low ceilings, giant timbers, fireplaces and pebbled windows are all miraculously preserved, while the river views from the terrace and balcony are well worth a look. Draught beers include Courage Best, Directors, Marston's Pedigree and the occasional guest ale. Pricey fish-based dishes (halibut steak £14.25, fish and chips £9.95, pork Grand Marnier £14.95) are served in the restaurant upstairs. Alternatively, it's a good place for a Sunday roast dinner (£6.95).
Babies and children admitted (dining area). Function room. Games (fruit machine, video games). No-smoking area. Restaurant. Tables outdoors (beer garden, riverside terrace). Vegetarian dishes.

Town of Ramsgate
62 Wapping High Street, E1 (020 7264 0001). Wapping tube/100 bus. **Open** noon-11pm Mon-Sat; noon-10.30pm Sun. **Food served** noon-2.30pm, 5.30-8.30pm Mon-Fri; noon-4pm Sat, Sun. **Credit** MC, V.
Fishermen from Ramsgate used to offload their catches for market via the adjacent Wapping Old Stairs, hence the name. It's a pleasant old boozer with a tiny garden offering a view across the Pool of London to downtown Bermondsey, and – though it doesn't care to shout too loudly about it – it's packed with history. Captain Bligh and Fletcher Christian had a farewell noggin here before setting off on the Bounty; Captain Kidd shivered his timbers nearby; and prisoners were once locked in the cellars before being transported to Australia. Inside it's long and thin, dark and atmospheric, with plenty of old wood planking, mahogany and glass-partitioned drinking areas, and floral-patterned banquettes. It's invariably packed with young locals out for a good time and visitors soaking up the ambience. London Pride's usually the only real ale on offer, while unexciting but cheap food includes fish and chips, pizzas and pies.
Games (fruit machine, golf machine). Quiz (9.30pm Mon; £1 to play). Satellite TV. Tables outdoors (riverside courtyard). Vegetarian dishes.

Also in the area...
Babe Ruth's 172-176 The Highway, E1 (020 7481 8181).
Docks 66 Royal Mint Street, E1 (020 7488 4144).
Grapeshots 2/3 Artillery Passage, E1 (020 7247 8291).

Whitechapel

Blind Beggar
337 Whitechapel Road, E1 (020 7247 6195). Whitechapel tube. **Open** 11am-11pm Mon-Sat; noon-10.30pm Sun. **Food served** noon-3pm daily. **Credit** MC, V.
Some idiot told us that the warm red glow generated by the traditional shaded wall lights and deep red carpets, curtains and furnishings in this East End pub, is supposed to represent the litres of 'claret' that leaked out of George Cornell on the night (9 March 1966) when Ronnie Kray shot him. Nowadays you get the idea that the management would rather people forgot about the murder. Certainly we'd never be brave enough to broach the subject, just in case one of the large gentlemen slurping draught Bass or Marston's Pedigree at this large family pub turned out to be a descendent of either party. In summer many of the punters (who include plenty of local students) desert the sofas in the two bars in favour of the large heated conservatory and the roomy garden, which has to be one of the East End's best outdoor drinking areas.

Prospect of Whitby.
See page 190.

*Babies and children admitted (conservatory only). Games
(fruit machine, video game). Restaurant. Satellite TV.
Tables outdoors (garden). Vegetarian dishes.*

Half Moon

*213-223 Mile End Road, E1 (020 7790 6810). Stepney
Green tube.* **Open** 11am-11pm Mon-Sat; noon-10.30pm
Sun. **Food served** 11am-10pm Mon-Sat; 11am-9.30pm
Sun. **Credit** MC, V.

From time to time JD Wetherspoon accomplishes a spectacular
conversion, and this impressive L-shaped building could be its
best yet. Home to the Half Moon Theatre Company from 1979
to the late '90s, and long before that a Welsh Calvinist chapel,
this high-ceilinged pub won Best Conversion in the Camra 2000
Pub Design Awards. The main room has a gallery overlooking
the serving area (six real ales include regulars Spitfire and
Theakston's Best) and rows of wooden alcoves along one wall.
On the wet Tuesday we called in there wasn't a seat to be had
in the place. Most drinkers were students, including a noisy
group on the quiz machine who lost a fortune. A pleasant
terrace with bench tables gets packed when the sun shines.
*Babies and children admitted (until 9pm). Disabled: toilet.
No piped music or jukebox. No-smoking area. Tables
outdoors (garden). Vegetarian dishes.*

Pride of Spitalfields

*3 Heneage Street, E1 (020 7247 8933). Aldgate East
tube.* **Open** 11am-11pm Mon-Sat; noon-10.30pm Sun.
Food served noon-3pm Mon-Fri. **No credit cards.**

Those who spurn the sterile habitat of All Bar Ones and all
that's chain-like, in favour of eccentric, old-fashioned pubs are
especially well served in Whitechapel, and this small and
genial family-run pub just off Brick Lane is top of the list. The
clientele is a microcosm of the area: arty types from nearby
studios rub shoulders with Asian businessmen, medical
students, builders and slack-jowelled pensioners. The beer's
good and well under £2 a pint, with Crouch Vale Woodham
IPA and London Pride our particular favourites. Decor is a
mix of red velvet and dark wood furniture, with the walls and
ceiling covered in old photos of Victorian enterprise – it's not
going to win any design awards, but it's comfortable. Basic
and cheap home-cooked lunches like ham, egg and chips, roast
beef and Yorkshire pudding are served from Mary's Kitchen.
*Babies and children admitted (separate area; children's
menus). Satellite TV (big screen). Vegetarian dishes.*

Urban Bar (LHT)

*176 Whitechapel Road, E1 (020 7247 8978). Whitechapel
or Aldgate East tube/25 bus.* **Open/food served** 11am-
11pm Mon-Wed; 11.30am-1am Thur-Sat; noon-10.30pm
Sun. **Credit** MC, V.

The former London Hospital Tavern has undergone an extreme
pub conversion. Once a stately Victorian boozer, it's now been
painted with orange and black zebra-stripes on the outside and
more orange within. 'Why?' you might well ask. Fortunately for
us the sign on the window explains all: 'Cause this city is a
jungle, baby'. Fair enough. Inside the columns that presumably
hold up the ceiling are glass cases containing 'Pete the plated
desert lizard' and 'Annie the yellow anaconda'. Annie, however,
is either exceptionally good at camouflage or she wasn't in
residence on the night we visited. The drinkers are pretty much
the same bunch of students – medical and otherwise – as before
the refurb, some drinking real ale (London Pride, Bass, Adnam's
Best), others preferring lager or wine.
*Function room. Games (fruit machine). Internet access.
Jukebox. Music (live Tue, Sun). Vegetarian dishes.*

Vibe Bar

*The Brewery, 91-95 Brick Lane, E1 (020 7377 2899/
www.vibe-bar.co.uk). Aldgate or Aldgate East tube.* **Open**
11am-11.30pm Mon-Thur; 11am-1am Fri, Sat; 11am-10.30pm
Sun. **Food served** noon-7pm daily. **Credit** MC, V.

Among the first of many style bars to hit the area – we're within
ambling distance of Shoreditch, don't forget – Vibe has
managed to retain its loyal following. In summer, the bench
tables in the courtyard of what was once Truman & Co's Black
Eagle Brewery, swarm with young drinkers, practically all of
whom are under 25. Inside we've spotted many a juvenile music
mogul lounging in Vibe's almost too-comfy sofas. The space
is large and square, with a bar in the corner that shifts the usual
selection of bottled and draught lagers (Grolsch, Staropramen,
and such), although the serious-looking bar staff give the
impression they'd rather be making cocktails (not that they're
particularly good at it). A graffiti-style mural haunts one wall,
and a couple of computer consoles and PlayStations are laid
on for those who don't feel particularly sociable. Music is
generally cutting-edge dance and loud, with DJs some nights.
There's no food, but then this is Brick Lane, so go grab a great
Indian takeout on the way home.
*Function rooms. Music (DJs 7pm Tue-Sun). PlayStation.
Satellite TV. Tables outdoors (heated courtyard).*

East

North

Camden Town, Chalk Farm & Primrose Hill

Adelaide

143 Adelaide Road, NW3 (020 7722 3777). Belsize Park or Chalk Farm tube. **Open** noon-11pm Mon-Sat; noon-10.30pm Sun. **Food served** noon-3pm, 6-10.30pm Mon-Fri; noon-10.30pm Sat; noon-10pm Sun. **Credit** MC, V.
A bit off the beaten track but well worth seeking out – just look for the big blue 'A' sign – the Adelaide has a high-ceilinged bar warmed by terracotta walls, large round mosaic tables and intricate Moroccan-style metal lanterns. It's an appealing, not to say popular, mix – so much so that most nights there's stiff competition for seating. We've never visited in summer but we imagine it's then that the pub really comes into its own courtesy of a large beer garden with a children's play area. Thai food is a speciality, and a mild yellow curry (£4.95) was one of the best we'd ever eaten.
Babies and children admitted (until 6pm; outdoor play area). Function room. No-smoking area. Tables outdoors (garden, patio). Vegetarian dishes.

Bar Gansa

2 Inverness Street, NW1 (020 7267 8909). Camden Town tube. **Open** 10am-midnight Mon, Tue; 10am-1am Wed-Sat; 10am-11pm Sun. **Food served** 10am-11.30pm Mon, Tue; 10am-12.30am Wed-Sat; 10am-10.30pm Sun. **Credit** MC, V.
Perenially popular, since coming under new management in mid-2000, this tapas bar and restaurant seems to have got even busier. The Sunday lunchtime we visited it was like rush hour on the Northern line – except people seemed to be enjoying themselves. The fiery painted walls remain, as do the red roses and potted plants, to which have been added all manner of props Espanol. Favoured drink here has always been Spanish red wine, sloshed around in copious amounts, and now there are also Spanish brandies and schnapps, Mexican beer and 'Bar Gansa' draught lager. Unfortunately, it was so heaving on our visit we couldn't get a table and so missed out on eating, but on past, less crowded occasions, we've enjoyed classic tapas (£2.50-£4) and good value wake-up breakfasts. Fun and friendly, but get there early for a seat.
Babies and children admitted. Specialities: own premium draft Bar Gansa lager. Tables outdoors (pavement). Vegetarian dishes.

Bar Risa

11 East Yard, Camden Lock, NW1 (020 7428 5929). Camden Town or Chalk Farm tube. **Open** 11am-11pm Mon-Sat; noon-10.30pm Sun. **Happy hour** 4-7pm Mon-Fri. **Food served** noon-9pm daily. **Credit** AmEx, MC, V.
A large barn of a bar in the middle of Camden Market, with a spacious balcony area, acres of exposed brick and a wooden roof. It's just a shame that operators Jongleurs chose to daub everything with gaudy paint and enormous – and enormously irritating – slogans ('eat', 'drink', 'laugh'). We do, however, like the Smarties-hued armchairs upstairs, which are indulgently comfortable. Last time we visited we were met with a mellow ambience and music that remained pleasingly background, but as early-evening custom increased bar staff cranked up the volume and the place rapidly metamorphosed into a full-on party joint. Securely seated and enjoying the buzz, we were even thinking that perhaps the golden sculptures over the bar weren't so naff after all. At which point we caught ourselves, downed our beers and legged it out of there fast.
Babies and children admitted (until 9pm). Games (fruit machine). Tables outdoors (roof terrace). Vegetarian dishes.

Bartok

78-79 Chalk Farm Road, NW1 (020 7916 0595/ www.meanfiddler.co.uk). Camden Town or Chalk Farm tube. **Open/food served** 5pm-midnight Mon-Thur; 5pm-1am Fri; noon-1am Sat; noon-midnight Sun. **Happy hour** £3 most cocktails; 5-8pm Mon-Thur. **Credit** MC, V.
Get pissed to Puccini; blotto to Bach; hammered to Holst – what a fine idea. Get classical music out of prissy concert halls and into the boozer. Be downing an eighth vodka Red Bull while Beethoven's on his Fifth. Except this is not that sort of place. Bartok is a bar, but it's terribly well behaved; a place of lilting sonatas and strains of concertos. Despite some ultra-modern design, it has an almost homely feel with Habitat-style furniture and comfy sofas. As night falls it becomes a little more sultry – lighting is low, ultraviolet strips glow and the walls and curtains are an opulent red, causing passers-by to press their noses against the windows. Saturday night, things loosen up a little with more contemporary, upbeat music. Added interest during the week comes from regular live sessions and DJs. It can be hard to find a seat later in the evening, particularly before and after shows at the Roundhouse opposite.
Babies and children admitted (until 7pm). Music (DJ Tue, Fri; live music Wed, Thur; string quartet Sun). Vegetarian dishes.

Bar Vinyl

6 Inverness Street, NW1 (020 7681 7898). Camden Town tube. **Open/food served** 11am-11pm Mon-Sat; noon-10.30pm Sun. **No credit cards.**
The most Camdenesque of Camden bars, this was reputedly one of the first places to hit upon the idea of setting up decks in the corner. Fronted by no-frills aluminium-framed windows, it's a long, sparse box of a room, with a slow curve of a bar along one wall and limited seating towards the back. Decoration is non-existent, just some slap-dash art on the walls. Additional colour comes courtesy of piles and racks of event, dance and gig flyers. It's all very studiedly casual. Punters are similarly carefully unkempt, dressed baggy and loaded with combat chic. Along with the low-fi ambience are serious hi-fi sounds, with the bass so heavy it rattles the fillings in your teeth. That's just the sound system behind the bar; later on in the evening thumping house, breakbeat, funk or 'ironic 80s' (their term) is spun by a roster of DJs. Food is served from a counter at the back, but it's low grade fare of the order of potato wedges and toasted sandwiches.
Babies and children admitted. (DJs nightly; daytime Sat, Sun). Vegetarian dishes.

Bistroteque

4 Inverness Street, NW1 (020 7428 0546). Camden Town tube. **Open/food served** 9am-midnight daily. **Happy hour** 5-7.30pm Mon-Fri. **Credit** MC, V.
Blissfully attitude-free bar-cum-café that's Camden's version of *Friends'* Central Perk, where staff are often found sitting with friends rather than behind the bar. Punters are a hotch-potch of rollie-smoking Camden Marketeers, mates of the Serbian manager, and anyone looking for a decent bite to eat. Food is reasonably priced bistro basics, ranging from ciabattas and a simple veggie pancake to Thai smoked fish cakes and Jamaican jerk chicken. We like the invitingly squidgy sofa on a raised platform at the entrance but most people head on, past the cluttered bar to the main room at the back. Whatever, it's a fine place to sit and stew. On Fridays and Saturdays the beats get harder, when the manager's brother sets up his decks for a bit of house and techno.
Babies and children admitted (high chairs). Music (DJs Fri-Sun). Satellite TV (big screen). Tables outdoors (pavement). Vegetarian dishes.

Bartok

Blakes

31 Jamestown Road, NW1 (020 7482 2959). Camden Town tube. **Open** 11am-11pm Mon-Sat; noon-10.30pm Sun. **Food served** noon-3pm, 7-10.30pm daily. **Credit** AmEx, DC, MC, V.
Never judge a book by its covers or a bar by its doors. Those at Blakes are ceiling-high, heavy and wooden, with clanking metal handles – straight out of the catalogue at Dungeons 'R' Us. Another ghastly pub in the Eerie Chain then? Absolutely not. While there is the odd bit of gothickry inside (rough-hewn rafters, rustic bare floors), what strikes more are the warm red walls, spiky flower arrangements and the incredibly good-looking crowd of cool folk. This is a rather good modern gastropub, bustling and frenetic during our midweek visit. It was a scrum to get to the ground floor, unlike the deserted upstairs dining area, which by contrast was candlelit, subdued and relaxed. A wide-ranging menu lives up to its ambitions; in the past we've enjoyed excellent tempura prawns, delicate honey cod with sun-dried tomato, and a tasty ravoli of duck and a green Thai sauce. Beers are less exceptional and a bit on the pricey side with Hoegaarden at £4.40 a pint, a good 50p dearer than we'd paid in Soho the night before.
Babies and children admitted (Sun lunch). Restaurant. Specialities: cocktail bar. Tables outdoors (pavement). Vegetarian dishes.

Café Corfu

7-9 Pratt Street, NW1 (020 7424 0203). Camden Town or Mornington Crescent tube. **Open/food served** noon-12.30am Mon-Sat; noon-10.30pm Sun. **Credit** MC, V.
An immensely popular Greek bar-restaurant that forgoes the usual plate smashing and bouzouki bollocks in favour of modish elegance. Check out the devastatingly simple but striking back-lit bottle display in the large, paprika-red cube-shaped back room. On the night we visited it was quiet, but the brother-sister team who run the place were chatty and kept

us from feeling lonely. They assured us it gets very busy most nights. Signature Corfu cocktails take pride of place on the drinks menu (Zorba the Freak, Greece'd Lightning, Ionian Seabreeze, all at £4.50), and there's also a wide selection of Greek beers, wine, retsina and ouzo. Food is Greek-based and includes good meze, marinated octopus (£3.50), grilled swordfish (£9.50) and garlic pork chop with Greek oregano (£8.95). As well as the regular crowd of Camden office types and thirtysomething locals, the odd celeb has been known to drop by – Uri Geller bent one of the spoons here recently.
Babies and children admitted (high chairs). Dance shows (9pm Thur-Sat). Function room. Jukebox. No-smoking area. Restaurant. Satellite TV. Specialities: cocktails, Greek wines. Tables outdoors (patio). Vegetarian dishes.

Camden Brewing Co

1 Randolph Street, NW1 (020 7267 9829). Camden Town tube/Camden Road rail. **Open** noon-11pm Sun-Thur; noon-midnight Fri, Sat. **Food served** noon-3pm Mon-Fri; 2-5pm Sat; 4-8pm Sun. **Credit** MC, V.
Ten minutes' walk from the high street, and consequently unknown to many, this place gets our vote as Camden's best pub. It strikes a perfect balance between living room comfort and sleek design. The bar resembles a particularly stylish lounge with beach-hut blue walls set off by cool yellow and spicy red splashes. The compact horseshoe bar looks like a tugboat. Thoughtful touches abound such as big buckets of lilies above the fireplace and fairy lights twisted through the ornate winding staircase. Even in mid-winter, the airy room has a warm, summery feel (and there's an outdoor terrace for when it genuinely is summer), with real heat courtesy of two open fires, around which are several comfy sofas. The Thai food is good and fairly priced, and Adnam's ales and Hoegaarden are on tap. Best of all, when we walked in here for the first time several of the customers actually turned and smiled at us – surely a London first. We feel so guilty now,

telling everybody else about this place and ruining the regulars' little secret. Sorry, guys.
Disabled: toilet. Satellite TV. Specialities: real ales, Hoegaarden, vodkas. Tables outdoors (pavement). Vegetarian dishes.

Crown & Goose
100 Arlington Road, NW1 (020 7485 8008). Camden Town tube. **Open** 11am-11pm Mon-Sat; noon-10.30pm Sun. **Food served** 11am-3pm, 6-10pm Mon-Sat; noon-9pm Sun. **No credit cards.**
Although one of London's original gastropubs, the Crown & Goose was devoid of anyone eating on our recent visit (and it was dinner time). But it is still a very agreeable place. Bare board flooring, lime green rag-washed walls and wooden shutters make for a café-like atmosphere. We remember years ago when it all seemed very smart, now it's slightly worn and tatty we like it better. The clientele fits perfectly, an idiosyncratic bunch, as trendily scruffy as their surroundings. Reassuringly, it's still a pints pub and hasn't gone the way of the bottle like so many Camden establishments. For those who do fancy eating, specials change daily and on this occasion included a chicken liver and hazelnut pate (£3.75), lemon sole stuffed with garlic prawns (£8.25) and a rocket and spinach pie (£6.15).
Babies and children admitted. Disabled: toilet. Function room. Restaurant. Tables outdoors (pavement). Vegetarian dishes.

Dublin Castle
94 Parkway, NW1 (020 7485 1773). Camden Town tube. **Open** 11am-midnight daily. **No credit cards.**
When it's busy, there are few pubs more unpleasant than the Dublin Castle: hot, sweaty and cramped, it can also be a nightmare to get served. But that, of course, is exactly how the indie kids like it because the point of the place is the music. And any gig from which you fail to emerge sticky, shaken and stirred just isn't a gig worth going to. Although three bands on average play every night in the big back room, the music at the Dub has seen better days and it gets by on past rep. Apart from the gigs, the pub doesn't have much to recommend. It's a shabby old Victorian building with mock-Tudor trimmings, bathed in depressingly low red light. Don't make our mistake and arrive around 7.30pm – screaming over the sounds of a rehearsing band is not the best way to kick off an evening.
Games (fruit machine). Jukebox. Music (indie/rock bands nightly). Satellite TV.

Edinboro Castle
57 Mornington Terrace, NW1 (020 7255 9651). Camden Town or Mornington Crescent tube. **Open** noon-11pm Mon-Sat; noon-10.30pm Sun. **Food served** noon-3pm, 6-9pm Mon-Fri; noon-9pm Sat; noon-6pm Sun. **Credit** MC, V.
Come 8pm on any moderately temperate summer's evening, 300 to 400 drinkers will descend on the Edinboro Castle. Many will have spent the day in nearby Regent's Park and they flock here to pack out the spacious beer garden and partake in Pimms on tap. During the winter months, the action switches to the large open-plan interior. A tri-colour paint scheme of red, orange and green helps break down and humanise the enormous space, while tables are snugly separated by high bench backs made of wood and stained glass. A raised section at one end of the pub is decked out with comfortable armchairs and a pool table. Clientele is mixed, ranging from media types on shorts to loud, beery students, and the atmosphere is nothing if not friendly.
Disabled: toilet. Games (fruit machine). Music (DJs every second Friday). Satellite TV (big screen). Specialities: bottled Belgian beers. Tables outdoors (garden). Vegetarian dishes.

Engineer
65 Gloucester Avenue, NW1 (020 7722 0950). Camden Town or Chalk Farm tube/C2 bus. **Open** 9am-11pm Mon-Sat; 9am-10.30pm Sun. **Food served** 9-11.30am, 12.30-3pm, 7-10.30pm Mon-Sat; 9-11.30am, 12.30-3.30pm, 7-10pm Sun. **Credit** MC, V.
The Engineer is definitely at the posher, more refined end of London's range of gastropubs. It has an unpretentious, countrified look, with a monotony of stripped blond wood relieved by edgings of bright tiling. A triangular main room leads to a rabbit warren of a restaurant, painted orange and red and panelled with mirrors. A bit of an Engineer obsession, mirrors – we counted 56 in total. Food is excellent. In the past we've enjoyed baby squid pan-fried and free-range chicken breast marinated in yoghurt and spices; we didn't eat this time but were sorely tempted by the likes of butternut squash ravioli (£12.10) and braised venison (£14.50). Service is pleasantly informal and due to a choice location it has no trouble filling its tables, so book ahead. If you just fancy dropping in for a pint, there's Fuller's London Pride and Grolsch on tap.
Children admitted. Function rooms. Tables outdoors (garden). Vegetarian dishes.

Good Mixer
30 Inverness Street, NW1 (020 7916 7929). Camden Town tube. **Open/food served** 11am-11pm Mon-Sat; noon-10.30pm Sun. **No credit cards.**
Listen, if Tom Cruise and Nicole Kidman were nude jell-o wrestling on the pool table for custody rights, you still couldn't get us interested in a drink at the Good Mixer. So if a few musos of the moment (and that moment was the mid-'90s) on occasion played some pool here (but did their drinking in the **Spread Eagle**; *see p209*), so what? The pub is one of those purpose-built 1950s efforts with a horseshoe-shaped serving area between two bar rooms littered around the edges with low settees, stools and tables. Mustard-coloured curtains hang limply over the windows. The ambience is bottom of a student wash bag when the Zanussi has been out of order for weeks and a visit to the launderette is critical. Action focuses on the two pool tables until 9pm when the covers go on and it's down to serious drinking. Most nights the place is chocka with greasy lads and grungey girls with brave haircuts, and a number of trampish-looking old boys. Two things in the Mixer's favour: the jukebox is still good and it serves Staropramen on tap.
Games (fruit machine, pool table). Jukebox. Satellite TV.

North

Bar Vinyl. *See page 202.*

Hawley Arms
2 Castlehaven Road, NW1 (020 7428 5979). Camden Town tube. **Open** 11am-11pm Mon-Sat; noon-10.30pm Sun. **Food served** 11am-9pm Mon-Sat; noon-9pm Sun. **No credit cards.**
What was formerly the sultry and exotic Bar Hawley has been reborn as the Hawley Arms, made over in a simple but effective back-to-basics style. Walls that were formerly red and yellow are now a soothing cream colour; combine that with a high ceiling and big windows, and you've got a pub you can actually take great gulping breaths of air in. Exposed stonework, a potted tree with fairy lights and flickering candles add ambience, and nostrils are set pleasantly twitching by the smell of cooking (a chalk board lists dishes, which included good things like pork and apple pie, and moules and frites the Sunday we dropped by). Quiet during the early half of the week, the Hawley fills up towards the weekend with Camden Market tourists and a youngish local crowd. Besides decent real ales, it lays claim to the best range of spirits in Camden (displayed impressively on high altar-like shelving behind the bar), and the staff are engagingly good humoured. Stuck for company some night, you could do a lot worse than taking a seat at the bar here.
Babies and children admitted (daytime). Music (acoustic duo every other Sat). Specialities: spirits. Tables outdoors (patio). Vegetarian dishes.

JD Young Sports Bar
2 Lidlington Place, NW1 (020 7387 1495). Mornington Crescent tube. **Open** 11am-11pm Mon-Sat; noon-10.30pm Sun. **Food served** noon-2pm Mon-Fri. **Credit** MC, V.
Nothing to do with Young's the brewery (drinks are predominantly lagers, not ales), but 'sports' and 'bar' pretty much tells the rest of the story. When we strolled in, the few punters in the main bar were transfixed by the footie on the huge screen in front of them – one of two such screens, supplemented by five televisions. Some conversation had been going on around a pool table, but our appearance brought it to a halt as the mob of lads instead took to eyeing us with suspicion. Other possible distractions include a dartboard, arcade games, neon Americana and sports paraphernalia. In fact, the sports theme has been stretched to the limit, with boxing-ring ropes for banisters and mini-footballs stencilled onto bright yellow pillars. Probably a great place to watch a big game, but if testosterone's not your thing, steer clear.
Babies and children admitted (until 7pm). Function room. Games (fruit machines, pool tables). Satellite TVs (big screen). Tables outdoors (garden). Vegetarian dishes.

Julono
73 Haverstock Hill, NW3 (020 7722 0909/www.julono.com). Chalk Farm tube. **Open** 6pm-midnight Mon-Sat; 6-11pm Sun. **Happy hour** 6-7.30pm Mon-Sat. **Food served** 6-11pm Mon-Thur; 6-11.30pm Fri, Sat. **Credit** MC, V.
Ambitious Moorish-themed late-licence bar and restaurant that oozes money and North London chic. Hardly the place for a quick post-work pint, Julono only starts to get busy from 9pm on, when the well-heeled strut in for a candlelit dinner or seriously pricey cocktails at the thin front bar, done up in glowing terracotta and lined with mosaic Moroccan tables. Further back is the intimate split-level dining room painted in rag-washed sky blue. Downstairs, the Maghrebi vogue really comes into its own with a seductively lit, softly furnished room with low tables and wicker stools, huge squidgy leather sofas and kilim-covered benches backed by perfectly plumped cushions. If you're fond of name-dropping,

Julono is a must: Jonathan Ross, Lennox Lewis and Lisa from Steps are all regulars, apparently.
Babies and children admitted. Function room. Music (occasional live latin jazz/world music bands 8pm Mon, Wed, Fri). Restaurant. Specialities: Casablanca, imported Moroccan beer. Tables outdoors (terrace). Vegetarian dishes.

Lansdowne
90 Gloucester Avenue, NW1 (020 7483 0409). Chalk Farm tube/31, 168 bus. **Open** 7-11pm Mon; noon-11pm Tue-Sat; noon-4pm, 7-10.30pm Sun. **Food served** 7-10pm Mon-Sat; 1-2.30pm, 7-10pm Sun. **Credit** MC, V.
Simply but strikingly decorated in black and white, the Lansdowne is enormously popular with all those Primrose Hill types who not only look famous, but in some cases actually are. Every inch of space has been used in an interior crammed with sturdy tables like some sort of candlelit school dining hall. Well worn sofas are slotted into any gaps. Nine huge blackboards detail an impressive array of drinks such as non-alcoholic elderflower presse and organic pear juice (stand-out beers include Staropramen and Fuller's London Pride), and a salivatingly fine selection of food, which when we dropped by included butternut squash soup (£4), winter greens gratin (£6.50) and monkfish with poivrade sauce (£11). There's no music, but all the same the Lansdowne has an animated and relaxed atmosphere, enhanced by the vague allure of vicarious glamour.
Babies and children admitted (high chairs, nappy changing facilities). Disabled: toilet. Function room. No piped music or jukebox. Restaurant. Tables outdoors (pavement). Vegetarian dishes.

Liberty's
100 Camden High Street, NW1 (020 7485 4019). Camden Town tube. **Open/food served** noon-11pm Mon-Sat; noon-10.30pm Sun. **Credit** MC, V.
The first time we visited Liberty's it was a Sunday night and the place was practically empty. Nice pub (large windows, bare floorboards, chunky furniture) but all the atmosphere of an IKEA showroom. So we left. But we did come back the following Saturday and were glad we did. We found people, plenty of them, creating a happy burble of conversation. Candles and fresh flowers were pleasing touches. When we asked for Kettle Chips they were served to us in bowls, which we also liked. And if the music was just a little too loud we enjoyed dancing along to the two screens of pop videos. Probably not a place to go out of your way to visit, but if it was in your neighbourhood you'd be well pleased.
Satellite TV. Specialities: real ales. Tables outdoors (pavement). Vegetarian dishes.

Lord Stanley
51 Camden Park Road, NW1 (020 7428 9488). Camden Town tube/Camden Road rail, then 29, 253 bus. **Open** 6-11pm Mon; noon-11pm Tue-Sat; noon-10.30pm Sun. **Food served** 7-10pm Mon; noon-3pm, 7-10pm Tue-Sun. **Credit** AmEx, DC, MC, V.
A friendly and easy-going local, with its mixed clientele matched by its variety of chairs, the Lord Stanley also straddles genres; on the one hand it's a regular street pub with a smoky atmosphere, an old piano in one corner and the odd dog sleeping on the floor. On the other, it has gastropub ambitions, with bare wood tables adorned by fresh flowers, bottle-green ceiling and an open kitchen behind the bar. On the menu when we last visited were lentil dahl (£6.50) and roast baby chicken (£8); we didn't eat this time but we have in the past and the food was good. The fact the pub occupies an interstice between neighbourhoods seems not to have affected its popularity at all. Appealingly ramshackle and

relaxing all round, it is definitely worth going the extra mile for and challenging Bobby the resident cat for possession of the huge battered sofa.

Babies and children admitted. Music (jazz band occasional Mon). Tables outdoors (garden, pavement). Vegetarian dishes.

Mac Bar

102-104 Camden Road, NW1 (020 7485 4530). Camden Town tube/Camden Road rail. **Open** noon-11pm Mon-Sat; noon-10.30pm Sun. **Food served** noon-3pm, 6-9pm Mon-Fri; noon-9pm Sat, Sun. **Credit** MC, V.

Occupying the premises of the former Camden Falcon – grotty but essential indie music venue – new management has sent in the steam cleaners, wall-strippers and refit crew and got itself a self-consciously hip venue (red light, pop art, low-slung furniture) with a few quirky gimmicks up its sleeve. The indie kids are gone, replaced by preening blokes in tight T-shirts and girls in kitten heels and strappy tops who lounge artfully on the funky red leather sofas provided. Instead of the pints of cider favoured of old, current customers are more likely to go for concoctions in ultramarine or lavender – selections from a list of 55 cocktails. The one thing that hasn't changed is the volume: LOUD. Best gimmick is the food 'sticks' – a selection of dishes carried in on a plank of wood that slides into a groove on the table. The idea is that a group orders a stick (£14.95) to share; choose from 'meze stick', 'Thai stick' or 'miscellaneous world stick'.

Music (acoustic duos Wed; occasional DJs). Specialities: cocktails, wines. Tables outdoors (pavement). Vegetarian dishes.

Monarch

49 Chalk Farm Road, NW1 (020 7916 1049). Camden Town or Chalk Farm tube. **Open** 8pm-midnight Mon-Thur; 8pm-2am Fri, Sat. **Admission** £5. **No credit cards**.

A favoured drinking hole for an indie crowd who come for a Hoegaarden and game of table football, and for the gigs upstairs at the Barfly club. The place has a rough and ready feel with wires snaking across the ceiling, music posters of past performers (Coldplay, Badly Drawn Boy, Muse) pasted up on raw burgundy-coloured walls and well-scuffed floorboards. The '60s-style round-edge benches and curving stools are comfortable and a welcome break from North London's overload of chunky tables and leather sofas. The feel is vital and vibrant. The bar also hosts regular indie-based club nights.

Cash-point machine. Music (DJs, live bands nightly).

Monkey Chews

2 Queen's Crescent, NW5 (020 7267 6406). Chalk Farm tube. **Open** 3-11pm Mon-Fri; noon-11pm Sat; noon-10.30pm Sun. **Food served** 5-11pm Mon-Fri; noon-11pm Sat; noon-10.30pm Sun. **Credit** AmEx, MC, V.

On a rainy Sunday afternoon we found Monkey Chews highly soporific. The seductive lighting was to blame: red bauble lamps hanging from the ceiling and rows of Jack Daniel's bottles back-lit and glowing amber. We felt ourselves in some far-flung opium den. Heavenly. Only a sign on the door requesting punters to 'respect the neighbourhood' when leaving gave any hint of the rowdy crowd that usually packs the place at evenings and weekends. By contrast, a back room restaurant is practically laid bare to the elements by a giant skylight. It combines the seemingly unlikely match of a rotisserie specialising in spit-roast chicken ('the wall of flame') and an upmarket shellfish selection artfully displayed to rival the show at Harrods' foodhall. For those needing such things, it would be worth noting that Monkey Chews has a portable oyster bar available for hire.

Function room. Music (DJs Thur-Sun). Restaurant. Satellite TV. Tables outdoors (pavement). Vegetarian dishes.

Oh! Bar

111-113 Camden High Street, NW1 (020 7383 0330). Camden Town or Mornington Crescent tube. **Open** noon-11pm Mon-Sat; noon-10.30pm Sun. **Food served** noon-10pm daily. **Credit** AmEx, MC, V.

Oh! Bar? Oh dear. 'Our policy is to have an excellent time in a unique and safe environment: So chill out, have fun and keep on coming back!' If you, like us, are set gagging by mission statements like this one, prominently writ huge across one lime-green wall of the bar, then steer clear. Bar staff don't wear little tags proclaiming 'Hi I'm Terry, what can I get you?' but it's only a short step away. Not that most of the party-crowd custom cares, as long as the jugs of cocktails (£9.95) keep coming. Since we last visited the place has secured a late licence and has started putting on DJs so it's liable to become even more popular.

Dress code (smart/casual). Function room. Games (fruit machine, quiz machine). Tables outdoors (pavement). Vegetarian dishes.

Queens

49 Regent's Park Road, NW1 (020 7586 0408). Chalk Farm tube/31, 168 bus. **Open** 11am-11pm Mon-Sat; noon-10.30pm Sun. **Food served** noon-2.30pm, 7-9.45pm Mon-Sat; 12.30-4pm, 6-8pm Sun. **Credit** MC, V.

This neo-Georgian Young's pub is purportedly haunted by the ghost of Lillie Langtry who once lived next door; the current manager told us he hates being in the cellar alone because of the strange goings on – gas taps turning themselves on and off and the like. This doesn't put off the punters, generally local media types and dog walkers. Thanks to a ludicrously thin corridor of a bar area, getting a drink can be a squeeze, but once you've emerged from the bottleneck choose between chunky farmhouse tables at one end of the room or the slightly raised area with sofa at the other. Upstairs is a dining room with good views of Primrose Hill and the house where Friedrich Engels once lived. We can only imagine what Engels would have thought of the concept of the gastropub – the middle classes elbowing the working class out of their own playground – but at least the menu here is fairly unpretentious. Real ales include the excellent West Country Smiles. Gents should check out the 'Kings' toilets, lined with floor-to-ceiling black-and-white tiles and looking like something out of *Alice in Wonderland*. On leaving the pub, cross the road and climb the hill for one of the best views of London.

Babies and children admitted. Restaurant. Tables outdoors (balcony). Vegetarian dishes.

Quinns

65 Kentish Town Road, NW1 (020 7267 8240). Camden Town tube. **Open/food served** 11am-midnight Mon-Thur; 11am-1am Fri, Sat; noon-10.30pm Sun. **Credit** MC, V.

Halfway between Kentish Town and Camden, Quinns is a conservative, Irish-owned pub with a predictable bias towards the colour green – leaf-patterned alcoved bench seating and a bright green speckled floor that's actually painful on the eyes. The other distinguishing feature is that Quinns is one of the best places in Camden for Belgian and continental beers. On our last visit some 25 different varieties were offered, listed on scrappy pieces of paper stuck to the bar. Complementing these are five real ales (usually including Greene King Abbot and Greene King IPA). Food is home-cooked and centred on unadventurous staples (chilli con carne, shepherd's pie). As a comfortable, if uninspiring, place to drink good beer, then this'll do admirably. Just don't annoy the bar staff – on our visit they were decidedly hostile.

Babies and children admitted. Satellite TV. Tables outdoors (patio garden). Vegetarian dishes.

Sir Richard Steele

97 Haverstock Hill, NW3 (020 7483 1261). Belsize Park or Chalk Farm tube. **Open** 11am-11pm Mon-Sat; noon-10.30pm Sun. **Happy hour** Mon all day. **No credit cards.**

Named after a Victorian philanthropist playwright, Steele's (to use the local terminology) is made up of one main bar and a couple of cosy side-rooms. Walls and ceilings of the main bar resemble a white elephant stall, groaning with tin signs, quirky paintings, posters and branches. Sir Richard appears twice, portrayed in a painting and adorning a large stained-glass window. Best of all is the frescoed ceiling depicting Judgement Day, and starring diehard regulars, bar staff and an old cleaner. It all makes for a highly appealing Bacchanalian air that draws in punters from miles around including, last time we were there, a certain mono-browed brother from Manchester. Flower's Original and Hoegaarden on tap, along with regular live music help fuel the occasional descent into anarchy.

Function room. Games (fruit machine). Music (rock duos Sun lunch, trad Irish Sun; trad jazz Mon; flamenco jazz guitarist or blues duo Wed). Satellite TV (big screen). Tables outdoors (patio).

Spread Eagle

141 Albert Street, NW1 (020 7267 1410). Camden Town tube. **Open/food served** 11am-11pm Mon-Sat; noon-10.30pm Sun. **Credit** MC, V.

This is where Bruce Robinson and the spacers he immortalised in *Withnail and I* sank their double gins, cider (ice in the cider) and pork pies in the sleazy late '60s. These days they've been replaced by booksellers and computer gurus drinking damn-near-perfect pints of Young's. Other customers include representatives of Camden's music scene (who, when the weather's right, monopolise the outside bench tables). If the Spread Eagle (a Roman sign signifying nobility) looks like several houses knocked into one, that's because it is. The core of the boozer was built in 1858 when Albert Street was Gloucester Street and Parkway was Park Street. The Parkway entrance arrived in 1963. The decor gives a nod to the pub's Victorian roots, with cream-painted walls, wood panelling, framed prints and picture windows that look out onto a Camden that's gentrified but still trying desperately to appear streetwise. Food is better than average, offering the likes of smoked haddock mornay and beef bourguignon for just under six quid.

Games (fruit machines). Satellite TV. Tables outdoors (pavement). Vegetarian dishes.

WKD

18 Kentish Town Road, NW1 (020 7267 1869). Camden Town tube/Camden Road rail. **Open** noon-2am Mon-Thur; noon-3am Fri, Sat; noon-1am Sun. **Admission** £1-£7. **Happy hour** 4-8pm Mon-Fri; 1-9pm Sat, Sun. **Food served** noon-9pm daily. **Credit** MC, V.

A cool oasis tacked onto the stark glass and steel of the Sainsbury's building next door, WKD ('Wisdom, Knowledge, Destiny') is colourful, characterful and warm. There's a balmy lightness to the place by day, and a pleasantly lazy feel underscored by a gently chugging soul-jazz-hip hop soundtrack. All of which is quietly enjoyed by the laid-back, racially mixed punters. By night the joint hots up, and there's a mini stage for jams, plus a range of club nights. Cocktails are fairly priced (£4.95 or £21.50 for a jug), and the usual beers are sold (including Kirin by the bottle). Food ranges from Thai cuisine to Cajun chicken with rice and peas.

Babies and children admitted (till 8pm). Disabled: toilet. Function room. Music (bands Sun; DJs nightly). Tables outdoors (pavement). Vegetarian dishes.

World's End

174 Camden High Street, NW1 (020 7482 1932/ www.theworldsend.co.uk). Camden Town tube. **Open** 11am-11pm Mon-Sat; noon-10.30pm Sun. **Food served** 11am-3pm, 6.30-10.30pm Mon-Fri; 6.30-10.30pm Sat, Sun. **Admission** (club only) £4-£8. **No credit cards.**

Claiming (somewhat unoriginally) to be 'probably the largest pub in the world' and, more possibly, to sell more pints per year (over a million is the claim) than any other pub in the country, the World's End is a beer-serving monster. Never arrange to meet anyone here at the weekend because you'll have no chance of finding them in the heaving mass that fills the huge, partially glass-roofed main bar and the three smaller ones off it. Revisiting at a quieter hour for the purposes of this review it was a revelation to see that the main bar is themed to look like a Victorian street with a paved floor, fake bay windows and the old sign from the pub's days as 'Mother Red Caps'. All this is rendered invisible most of the time by the massed boozers, a complete mix, from well coiffed trendies and tourists to dreadlocked crusties, many waiting on the opening of Underworld, the live music venue down below. Bar staff are admirably tolerant and quick on their feet. Food is served but tables take up valuable space so there are hardly any and you may end up eating on your feet.

Disabled: toilet. Games (fruit machine, pinball machine). Music (in club: bands most nights). Satellite TV. Vegetarian dishes.

Also in the area...

Belgo Noord 72 Chalk Farm Road, NW1 (020 7267 0718).
Café Rouge 18 Chalk Farm Road, NW1 (020 7428 0998).
Camden Tup 2-3 Greenland Place, NW1 (020 7482 0399).
Dôme 58-62 Heath Street, NW1 (020 7431 0399).
Edward's 1 Camden High St, NW1 (020 7387 2749).
Man in the Moon (JD Wetherspoon) 40-42 Chalk Farm Road, NW1 (020 7482 2054).
Rat & Parrot 25 Parkway, NW1 (020 7482 2309).
Ruby in the Dust 102 Camden High Street, NW1 (020 7485 2744).

Crouch End

Banners

21 Park Road, N8 (020 8348 2930). Archway tube/ Finsbury Park tube/rail/Crouch Hill rail. **Open/food served** 9am-11.30pm Mon-Thur; 9am-midnight Fri; 10am-midnight Sat; 10am-11pm Sun. **Credit** MC, V.

Afternoons at the ever-popular Banners can be a bit like a Crouch End boho parents' club, but evenings see the drinkers arrive. With its multicoloured paintwork, Cuban flag, creaky wooden tables, little cloth lampshades, global music and easygoing, friendly staff, Banners resembles a mellow welcome-all-comers bar somewhere hot and bright. The globe-trotting menu has enjoyable, flavoursome things from jerk chicken and fried plantains to English breakfasts, omelettes, pasta and salads. Likewise, the drink menu is exceptionally wide-ranging. Unusual beers (Mexican Negra Modelo, Carib from Trinidad and small-brewery Belgian brews) and Breton cider are worth exploring, as are the rums, tequilas and vodkas. For cold nights there are specials like mulled wine, while warmer times call for iced coffees, fruit teas and ice-cream floats.

Babies and children admitted (crayons, high chairs, toys). Music (world music played). Satellite TV. Vegetarian dishes.

Bar Rocca

159A Tottenham Lane, N8 (020 8340 0101). Hornsey rail. **Open** 10.30am-midnight daily. **Food served** noon-11pm daily. **Credit** MC, V.

Devotees of the Hornsey Snooker Club were devastated when their favourite den, in an old Victorian chapel, was taken from them at the end of 2000. Now it's reopened as something a bit like an All Bar One – blond wood, metal rails, big ventilation pipes dangling from the ceiling – but with more personality. The old chapel is a roomy, airy space, with sofas as well as tables and lots of mingling room around the bar. There's a big food range, from sandwiches and soup of the day via burgers to daily specials and grilled sea bass. Cocktails are fairly standard and the wine list is hardly worth the bother (supermarket labels like E & J Gallo and Jacob's Creek), but there's a decent beer selection including Hoegaarden and Boddington's on draught.
Babies and children admitted (daytimes). Disabled: toilet. Music (live jazz Sun). Vegetarian dishes.

Florian's

4 Topsfield Parade, Middle Lane, N8 (020 8348 8348). Highgate tube/Finsbury Park tube/rail. **Open/food served** noon-11pm Mon-Fri; 11am-11pm Sat; 11am-10.30pm Sun. **Credit** MC, V.

Florian's Italian bar-restaurant has kept up its high standards and stayed consistently popular with local professionals over several years now. The bar is fairly noisy and a bit smoky, but it's still easy to settle in for a comfortable evening amid the artworks and old posters displaying images of Italy. There are only a few beers (Beck's, Italian lagers), but the all-Italian wine list is carefully selected, with decent house bottles and some superior wines such as a crisp Vernaccia di San Gimignano, available by the glass (£9.70) or bottle (£16.30). The good value bar menu mainly features simpler versions of the modern Italian dishes served in the relaxed restaurant at the rear: spiedini of calamari and prawns, char-grilled mixed vegetables, for example (starters £3.50, mains £6.50).
Babies and children admitted (high chairs). Restaurant. Tables outdoors (courtyard). TV. Vegetarian dishes.

Harringay Arms

153 Crouch Hill, N8 (020 8340 4243). Finsbury Park tube/rail, then W3, W7 bus/Crouch Hill rail. **Open** noon-11pm Mon-Sat; noon-10.30pm Sun. **Food served** noon-3.30pm daily. **No credit cards**.

The Irish landlord and his family preside over the well run Harringay Arms like folk born to the trade. It's a long and narrow space, running back from pebble-glass windows to the dartboard beyond the bar. The wood panelling lined with a curious collection of porcelain, posters and photos of old Crouch End can make it seem a slightly grizzled boozer. Yet the red plush seating is still an excellent retreat for sitting calmly over a pint. The beer range is straightforward – Courage Best (just £1.70), Directors, John Smith's, Guinness and mainstream lagers – but well kept and cheaply priced. There's not much food (just a few sandwiches), no music of any kind and a small TV for watching sports. Such peaceful charms draw in a varied cast of regulars, from fruity-voiced bohemians to a younger arty crowd.
Games (fruit machine). No piped music or jukebox. Quiz (Tue; £1 to play). Satellite TV. Tables outdoors (garden).

ice

18-20 Park Road, N8 (020 8341 3280). Crouch Hill or Hornsey rail. **Open/food served** 5-11pm daily. **Credit** AmEx, MC, V.

This dimly lit cutting-edge of cool (with a sibling in Islington; *see p221*) mixes minimalist and vaguely '60s decor in muted colours. Sleek stools are poised around the bar, while elsewhere there's soft black leather sofas and pouffes that push your knees up towards your chest in a fashionably louche manner. ice's main selling point appears to be its promise of spirit-induced oblivion. A huge cocktail list includes mind-blowing options like Liquid Cocaine (champagne, vodka, Red Bull), and all spirit measures are 35ml (40 per cent bigger than the norm). Sadly the choice of beers (bottled only) and wines is limited and quite expensive, from £2.70 for a Beck's. Frequent weekend party nights with DJs are reputedly worth turning up for.
Bar available for hire (weekdays). Disabled: toilet. Music (DJs Thur-Sun). Specialities: absinthe, cocktails.

King's Head

2 Crouch End Hill, N8 (020 8340 1028). Finsbury Park tube/rail/Crouch Hill rail. **Open** *ground floor bar* 11am-11pm Mon-Sat; noon-10.30pm Sun; *cellar bar/comedy club* noon-midnight Mon-Thur; noon-1am Fri, Sat; noon-10.30pm Sun. **Food served** noon-9pm Mon-Fri; noon-6pm Sat; noon-5pm Sun. **No credit cards**.

It may not be much to look at – after each refurb it ends up with more fake-Victorian wood-veneer fittings – but the King's Head is perhaps the most appreciated pub hereabouts. The 'Downstairs' cellar is one of north London's top comedy venues, covering everything from established names like Ed Byrne or Otiz Cannelloni to try-out nights for tyro comics. It also squeezes in an ever-enterprising range of entertainment: live dance music and comedy extravaganza at Club Senseless; Freestyle-Funky Nation club nights; salsa; live jazz; poetry sessions; record fairs; and the occasional but irreplaceable Kalamazoo acoustic club, which seems to specialise in finding guitar greats of the '60s and '70s. Upstairs the bar is young and buzzy with an unfussy atmosphere and friendly prices. London Pride features among the beers, while the pub nosh runs from snacks and moreish hot baguettes (about £2.50) up to Sunday roasts.
Comedy club (7.30pm Thur, Sat, Sun; £5-£6). Function room. Games (fruit machines, pool table). Music (bands 8.30pm Wed-Fri, £6; live jazz noon-5pm Sun, £3). Salsa club (7.30pm-midnight Mon; £5). Satellite TV. Vegetarian dishes.

Also in the area...

All Bar One 2-4 The Broadway, N8 (020 8342 7871).
Café Rouge 66-68 Crouch End Hill, N8 (020 8340 2121).
Tollgate (JD Wetherspoon) 26-30 Turnpike Lane, N8 (020 8889 9085).

Finchley

Catcher in the Rye

317 Regent's Park Road, N3 (020 8343 4369/ www.catcherintherye.co.uk). Finchley Central tube. **Open** 11am-11pm Mon-Sat; noon-10.30pm Sun. **Food served** noon-2.30pm, 6-9pm Mon-Sat; noon-9pm Sun. **Credit** AmEx, DC, MC, V.

In new hands since December 2000, the Catcher remains a good local pub with a loyal following. The new manager confessed that the faintly ludicrous name was inexplicable – this is hardly the kind of place where Holden Caulfield would be likely to pitch up – but then maybe that's the joke. No plans for change are afoot, which is probably just as well: Friday nights the pub's several different areas are usually packed, while the comedy and quiz nights (with a £100 prize) are as popular as ever. The range of beers is nothing exceptional, the menu straightforward low-priced Tex Mex and the coffee

London crawling: Heath haze

The beloved English tradition of a cold, wet walk in the country followed by a pint requires two kinds of pub: the one you start from and the one you end up in. If you're lucky, there may be a few more in between. These elements – wet, cold and boozers — can be found in and around Hampstead Heath through most of the year. The heath being where lots of Londoners pretend to be in the country, many walkers look for a pub that somehow reflects the nature of their achievement in tackling steepness of hill and depth of mud. Something faintly rural perhaps, preferably with open fires and lots of wood-panelling. Also, somewhere that the dog can flop or the pram be parked. In those few weeks (days?) of summer when the mud turns to dust and sunbathers and picnickers emerge from under layers of clothing, priorities change and beer gardens become vital.

On the eastern side, two pubs stand out: the **Bull & Last** near Gospel Oak and the **Flask** in Highgate village. The former, with open fires, bare floorboards and big windows, combines a gastropub vibe with a certain muddy shabbiness, perfect for the trendy lurcher-walker or the thirtysomething pram-pusher. No beer garden, alas, just a couple of tables out on the pavement that get quickly filled in summer. The Flask, nestling in an achingly pretty Georgian enclave, with low ceilings and yards of polished mahogany, is a more august experience altogether with the added bonus of many more tables out front. Less muddy, more villagey and very respectable, it is perhaps better as a starting point for a crawl rather than an end, as dirty footwear might not be tolerated.

There being, unfortunately, no pub in the centre of the Heath, we are forced to skirt its northern side until we reach **Spaniards Inn**. Picture postcard sweet on the outside, unpretentious inside, creaking with history and blessed with an idyllic beer garden, the Spaniards is in many ways the ideal Heath watering hole. Further on, the eccentric clapper-board vastness of **Jack Straw's Castle** seems positively insane, though strangely endearing. Due to overcrowding, regular Heath walkers tend to avoid both these inns on sunny weekends, preferring them empty in winter.

Both places, though excellent fuelling stops, are essentially half-way houses. The destination pubs for those hiking – or rather now stumbling — westwards are more likely to be the **Freemason's Arms** or the **Wells Tavern** in Hampstead proper. The Freemason's, though a welcome sight after a summery frolic in the greenery, lacks charm in spite of a large and verdant beer garden where hordes get loud and hammered. Inside, the atmosphere is chintzy-corporate and, though child-friendly, not well-suited, we felt, to mud and dogs; a definite drawback for those seeking country make-believe. This is a shame since the location – Hampstead ponds on one side and

Downshire Hill, one of London's prettiest streets, on the other – is irresistible. The Wells, much smaller and more relaxed, is a straightforward boozer and all the better for it. We once saw what looked like a bearded collie supping a pint here, which seemed to hit the right note amid the dartboards and old geezers.

Once in Hampstead, it's worthwhile pushing on a little further into the village, to **Ye Olde White Bear** for cluttered Victorian snugness and then to the **Hollybush** for the full wood-panel, open-fire, Keats-woz-'ere trip. Both are mainly interior pubs and cosy beyond belief, better suited for the winter rambler in need of warming than the fair-weather thirst quencher. But be warned: the Hollybush, perched on the very top of Hampstead, is best reached from Heath Street by a steep set of stairs which could prove the coup de grace to any who drink their way round this route.
Yves Baigneres

Bull & Last (*p224*) 168 Highgate Road, NW5 (020 7267 3641).
Flask (*p216*) 77 Highgate West Hill, N6 (020 8348 7346).
Freemason's Arms (*p214*) 32 Downshire Hill, NW3 (020 7433 6811).
Hollybush (*p214*) 22 Holly Mount, NW3 (020 7435 2892).
Jack Straw's Castle (*p214*) North End Way, NW3 (020 7435 8885).
Ye Olde White Bear (*p215*) New End, NW3 (020 7435 3758).
Spaniards Inn (*p215*) Spaniards Road, NW3 (020 8731 6571).
Wells Tavern (*p214*) 30 Well Walk, NW3 (020 7794 2806).

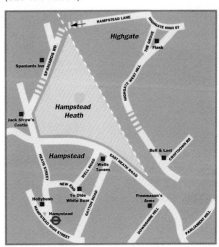

King's Head.
See page 210.

North

mediocre, but the genial hum of conversation, around the guesthouse suites by the windows out front and in the darkened TV room up at the back, suggest that that is exactly how the good people of Finchley are happy to keep it. *Comedy club (9pm Sun). Games (fruit machine, quiz machine). No-smoking area (11am-3pm). Quiz (9pm Tue; £1 to play). Satellite TV. Tables outdoors (patio). Vegetarian dishes.*

Also in the area...
Café Rouge Leisure Way, N12 (020 8446 4777). **Tally Ho (JD Wetherspoon)** 749 High Road, N12 (020 8445 4390).

Finsbury Park & Stroud Green

Old Dairy
1-3 Crouch Hill, N4 (020 7263 3337). Finsbury Park tube/rail/Crouch Hill rail. **Open** 11am-11pm Mon-Sat; noon-10.30pm Sun. **Food served** 11am-9pm daily. **Credit** AmEx, DC, MC, V.
The friezes around the outside of this elaborate 1889 building show life in a Victorian dairy, and were painted when the building was surrounded by fields. It's Stroud Green's most prominent landmark. A few years ago it was made over into a big bar-café, still with a fairly simple, slightly rustic interior. It seemed to be doing pretty well, but in the past year it's been revamped again with a more youth-oriented look: bigger spaces, brighter lights and lighter colours. The main bar is noisy and hopping, while one room has been made into a more mellow retreat with artwork on the walls. Party-on drinks include cheap jugs of vodka Red Bull (£10) but there are also real ales (including Adnam's and Abbot). Food has been comprehensively overhauled, and now offers a cheap and chic array running from French onion soup, panini sandwiches and savoury quiches via porcini ravioli and red snapper with couscous to Thai fish cakes (no dish over £8). *Babies and children admitted (until 8pm, high chairs). Disabled: toilet. Function rooms. Games (board games, quiz machines, table football). Music (acoustic guitar Thur; DJs Fri, Sat) No-smoking areas. Quiz (9pm Tue,Thur; £1 to play). Restaurant. Satellite TV. Vegetarian dishes.*

Triangle
1 Ferme Park Road, N4 (020 8292 0516). Finsbury Park tube/rail, then W3 bus/Crouch Hill rail. **Open/food served** noon-midnight Tue-Fri; 11am-midnight Sat, Sun. **Credit** MC, V.
Advertising itself on the street with bright, hard-to-miss colours, inside the Triangle – low lighting, orange tones, intricate metalwork, odd paintings and Moroccan lamps – resembles a hippy's dream of Marakesh. Its main trade is as a restaurant, with a French and North African-leaning menu that includes the likes of Mediterranean fish cakes or chicken with couscous, plus smaller tapas-like snacks. Triangle, however, is not just about dining; it also has intimate corners with low tables, sofas and kilims – ideal places to chill out and sample the cocktails (well priced at £4.95), bottled beers (not so good, £3), a decent wine selection or varied teas and coffees. Music is global, with the likes of raï and eastern European gypsy bands, and staff are similarly multinational and friendly. *Babies and children admitted (high chairs; nappy-changing facilities). Disabled: toilet. Music (jazz 7pm Sun). Specialities: cocktails, world beers. Tables outdoors (garden, pavement). Vegetarian dishes.*

White Lion of Mortimer
125 Stroud Green Road, N4 (020 7561 8880). Finsbury Park tube/rail/Crouch Hill rail. **Open** 11am-11pm Mon-Sat; noon-10.30pm Sun. **Food served** 11am-10pm Mon-Sat; noon-9.30pm Sun. **Credit** AmEx, DC, MC, V.
Until late 2000 the White Lion was one of the more old-fashioned parts of the JD Wetherspoon chain, which still had plush seats, dim lighting, a dark wood Victorian-style bar and a large number of older regulars who seemed to stay there all day long. Then, it too was given the cream paint and blond wood treatment. Unusually for a corporate revamp the White Lion seems to have kept its regular codgers (even though the seats aren't nearly as comfy) and succeeded in drawing in a new, younger crowd that gets the place buzzing on weekends. It has Wetherspoon's spectacularly low beer prices (£1.29 a pint for most bitters, £1.49 for Foster's, £1.79 for Stella), and a fairly enterprising range of well-kept ales, including an interesting roster of guest ales. Food follows Wetherspoon's standard extensive menu, priced mostly under £5. *Games (fruit machines). No-smoking area. No piped music or jukebox. Vegetarian dishes.*

World's End
21-23 Stroud Green Road, N4 (020 7281 8679). Finsbury Park tube/rail. **Open** noon-midnight Mon-Thur; noon-12.30am Fri, Sat; noon-10.30pm Sun. **No credit cards**.
Finsbury Park's grunge temple seems to have smartened its act up a tad of late: gone are the offers of jugs of lager at knock-down prices – perhaps because they were a bit too much of an incitement to wild behaviour – although there are still shooters with names like Springbok Blowjob (£2.55) and loads of fruit schnapps flavours (£1). It's still a big, battered, dimly lit, smoky old place that draws in students of all nationalities, punkish locals, wandering antipodeans and well-worn old geezers looking for a dark spot to sit. One attraction is the cheap-ish beers: Heineken and Boddingtons, for example, are £1.50 a pint from noon-7pm Mon-Fri. Another draw is the live pub rock programme presented in a big black space next to the bar. Lately blues seems to have become a bit of a speciality, but all sorts of tyro bands have appeared at this low rung on the musical ladder. *Babies and children admitted (till 6pm). Games (fruit machine, pinball, quiz machine, video games). Music (bands 9.30pm nightly). Satellite TV. Tables outdoors (pavement).*

Also in the area...
Old Suffolk Punch (JD Wetherspoon) 10-11 Grand Parade, N4 (020 8800 5912).

Hampstead

Bar Room Bar
48 Rosslyn Hill, NW3 (020 7435 0808). Hampstead tube/Hampstead Heath rail. **Open** 11am-11pm Mon-Sat; 11am-10.30pm Sun. **Food served** noon-11pm Mon-Sat; noon-10.30pm Sun. **Credit** MC, V.
A cut above the run-of-the-mill chains, the Bar Room Bars make a good stab at providing everything you could reasonably want in a pub. By day this particular branch operates as a quiet bar/café, complete with coffee, snacks (big on pizza) and newspapers, offered in a handsome, large-windowed locale. Walls serve as sales space for neighbourhood artists. As the sun sets, Hampstead turns up to play and the place is transformed into a thumping cruising joint for the young and not-so-young. A DJ helps the party along three nights of the week, as do early-evening happy

hours. If the volume gets too much there's a pleasant (heated in winter) covered yard to escape to at the rear. However, despite all the whistles and bells, there is one failing – the lack of any decent beer.
Babies and children admitted (until 6pm). Music (DJs Thur, Sat, Sun). Tables outdoors (garden). Vegetarian dishes.

Duke of Hamilton
23-25 New End, NW3 (020 7794 0258). Hampstead tube. **Open** 11am-11pm Mon-Sat; noon-10.30pm Sun. **Food served** noon-2.30pm Mon-Sat (bar snacks only). **No credit cards.**
An imposing regency pile set high above the road next to the New End Theatre, the Duke of Hamilton is ideal for a quiet pint when better known haunts such as the Flask and Spaniard's Inn are heaving with tourists, celeb spotters and stalkers. It's a free house with a central grandiose oak bar that dominates the room. If there's a theme, it's sport, and the walls are peppered with signed cricket bats, rugby shirts and a photo of pre-war miler Sydney Wooderson, the landlord's uncle. Other than the half hour before curtain-up next door and a post-show rush it's rarely busy and the resident old geezers give new arrivals the once over.
Disabled: toilet. Function room. Games (darts). No piped music or jukebox. Tables outdoors (terrace). TV.

Flask
14 Flask Walk, NW3 (020 7435 4580). Hampstead tube. **Open** 11am-11pm Mon-Sat; noon-10.30pm Sun. **Food served** noon-3pm Mon; noon-3pm, 6-8.30pm Tue-Sat; noon-4pm Sun. **Credit** DC, MC, V.
Not to be confused with the similarly named boozer across the heath, this high-ceilinged Young's pub is at the bottom of a pretty pedestrianised lane just off the high street. It has two bars, public and saloon, separated by a noteworthy Victorian carved oak screen plus, at the rear, a restaurant (chips and salad with everything) and conservatory where occasional 'events' take place. It remains an attractive place, and deservedly popular, but in recent times it does seem to have lost much of the slightly anarchic and seedy atmosphere that we used to value it for.
Babies and children admitted (until 7pm). Disabled: toilet. Function room (conservatory). Games (fruit machine, quiz machine). Music (jazz occasional Tue). No piped music or jukebox. No-smoking area. Quiz (8.30pm Thur; £1 to play). Restaurant. Satellite TV (big screen). Tables outdoors (pavement, terrace). Vegetarian dishes.

Freemasons Arms
32 Downshire Hill, NW3 (020 7433 6811/ www.vintage-inns.co.uk). Belsize Park or Hampstead tube/Hampstead Heath rail. **Open** noon-11pm Mon-Sat; noon-10.30pm Sun. **Food served** noon-10pm Mon-Sat; noon-9pm Sun. **Credit** MC, V.
A prime location beside the heath means the Freemasons Arms is a magnet for large thirsty crowds in the summer. This may explain the plethora of blackboards throughout the cavernous interior chalked up with repeated demands to fold pushchairs, explaining how and where to order food, and presenting idiotic pearls of wisdom such as 'wine is bottled poetry'. Otherwise it's a frenzy of scrubbed wood, thick pelmets and olde prints, to the extent that it's in danger of passing beyond being merely a Hampstead pub and becoming a parody of a Hampstead pub. There is, however, a large and pleasant beer garden and if you take a seat facing the greenery it's possible to forget the gaucheness behind you.
Babies and children admitted (dining area). Disabled: toilet. Games (fruit machine). No-smoking area. Tables outdoors (garden, patio). Vegetarian dishes.

Hollybush
22 Holly Mount, NW3 (020 7435 2892). Hampstead tube/Hampstead Heath rail. **Open** noon-11pm Mon-Sat; noon-10.30pm Sun. **Food served** 1-3.30pm, 6.30-10.30pm Mon-Sat; noon-4pm, 6.30-10pm Sun. **Credit** MC, V.
A pub since the early 1800s, and before that part of the painter George Romney's substantial Hampstead property, the Hollybush is one of the oldest and most picturesque drinkers' haunts in the area. It's also well hidden, tucked up a tiny backstreet, or reached up a long flight of steps from Heath Road. It has four bars, low ceilings, wood and plaster walls, ancient furniture and a real coal fire. At the time of writing, the back room, which occasionally used to host acoustic music, was being transformed into a dining area and we can only hope the owners don't ruin the pub's unstudied cosiness in the process.
Babies and children admitted. Benches outdoors (pavement). No piped music or jukebox. Vegetarian dishes.

Jack Straw's Castle
North End Way, NW3 (020 7435 8885). Golders Green or Hampstead tube. **Open** 11am-11pm Mon-Sat; noon-10.30pm Sun. **Food served** noon-9pm daily. **Credit** MC, V.
A huge crenellated, clapper-board structure on the north-west side of the heath that resembles a gigantic beach hut as built by Randolph Hearst. It dates from the 1960s but there's been a coaching inn on this site since way back when it provided a bolt hole for the eponymous Mr Straw, a leader of the 1381 Peasant Revolt. Located at the junction of several main roads and surrounded by greenery, in winter it feels more like a spookily isolated hotel on the Borders than a London local. At present, the place is up for sale, so while the large L-shaped ground floor bar is functioning, all the upstairs areas are closed and the impression of an abandoned folly is even greater. Come summer, it's bound to be business as usual and the beer garden will be crammed with hordes of heath visitors and coach loads of tourists.
Babies and children admitted (children's menu). Function rooms. Games (fruit machine, pool table). No-smoking area. Tables outdoors (pavement, terrace). Vegetarian dishes.

King William IV
77 Hampstead High Street, NW3 (020 7435 5747). Hampstead tube. **Open** noon-11pm Mon-Sat; noon-10.30pm Sun. **Food served** noon-6pm Mon-Sat; noon-4pm Sun. **Credit** AmEx, DC, MC, V.
Hampstead's only gay pub is more Hampstead than gay. The decor is Sussex cottage, with open fire, books, crockery and thick curtains, plus a fruit machine. Only the smallest of mirrorballs hangs almost forgotten from the ceiling as a tribute to a less straight-laced lifestyle. Not to say it doesn't get busy here, because it does, particularly in the summer when the smell of aftershave inside can get a little overpowering. Staff are never less than efficient, and polite, and sport smart green T-shirts emblazoned with the logo KW4, adding a strangely corporate touch to the mix. After the food finishes at 5pm excellent crêpes can be had from a trailer outside.
Function room. Games (fruit machine). Music (DJ Fri). No-smoking area (noon-6pm only). Quiz (9pm Wed; £2 to play). Tables outdoors (garden). Vegetarian dishes.

Magdala
2A South Hill Park, NW3 (020 7435 2503). Hampstead Heath rail/24, 168 bus. **Open** 11am-11pm Mon-Sat; noon-10.30pm Sun. **Food served** noon-3pm, 6.30-10pm Mon-Fri; noon-10pm Sat; noon-9.30pm Sun. **Credit** MC, V.

A couple of years back a makeover transformed this place from a seedy boozer to a wannabe hip bar/restaurant. Sadly, we can't say that it's been an unqualified success. There are two rooms: one for dining, with cacti in pots, candles on tables and an open-plan kitchen; the other for drinkers, all light wood and the feel of a soulless hotel bar off the A1. The clientele in the former was youthful and cheerfully dipping bread into olive oil, while in the latter a couple of old soaks sat staring into pints of bitter, perhaps wondering what on earth had happened to their local. A framed newspaper cutting and three small round holes in the cream tiled frontage are reminders that this is the pub where Ruth Ellis shot her lover, for which she was subsequently hanged.
Babies and children admitted. Function rooms. Restaurant. Tables outdoors (patio). Vegetarian dishes.

Spaniards Inn

Spaniards Road, NW3 (020 8731 6571). Hampstead tube/210 bus. **Open** 11am-11pm Mon-Sat; noon-10.30pm Sun. **Food served** noon-10pm daily. **Credit** MC, V.
The Spanish ambassador to the court of James I is said to have lived here, in refuge from plague ravaging the city. Dick Turpin supposedly stabled his horse Black Bess in the little blockhouse across the road (now creates a dangerous bottleneck). Goldsmith, Keats, Reynolds and Byron were all some time customers, and the pub gets mention in Dickens' *The Pickwick Papers* and in *Dracula*. The place positively shrieks history. Thankfully, management has resisted the urge to indulge in an orgy of ye oldieness, and beyond the flintlocks above the bar and a 'Dick Turpin' room (a snug upstairs bar), the interior is a restrained low-ceilinged, wood-panelled, country-style pub complete with fruit machine and piped music. Weather-permitting, do visit the lovely flag-stoned beer garden at the back, with pergola and a small aviary full of budgies. A reasonably ambitious gastro menu is served in the evening.
Babies and children admitted (children's menu). Function room. Games (board games, fruit machine, quiz machine). Tables and purpose-built bar outdoors (garden). Vegetarian dishes.

toast

First Floor, 50 Hampstead High Street, NW3 (020 7431 2244). Hampstead tube. **Open/food served** 6pm-midnight Mon; noon-midnight Tue-Sat; 11am-11pm Sun. **Credit** AmEx, MC, V.
Note that irritating lower case; it's a fair warning of what's to come. Climb a stair beside Hampstead tube and enter a hideaway of subdued lighting, smoked glass, a kinky leather-padded wall and voguishly good-looking staff dressed in black. Drinks of choice are surprisingly decent cocktails (£6 each, 'shooters' £5), while food is served from three different menus (bar/brasserie/'fine dining'). After 11pm there's a members-only policy imposed. Come back then, said our waiter with a wink, and the place will be heaving with 'talent'. Sexy as an ankle chain and just as classy.
Babies and children admitted (high chairs). Music (DJs 10pm Mon, Thur). Vegetarian dishes.

Washington Hotel & Bar

50 England's Lane, NW3 (020 7722 8842). Belsize Park or Chalk Farm tube. **Open/food served** 10am-11pm Mon-Fri; 11am-11pm Sat; noon-10.30pm Sun. **Credit** MC, V.
Imposing from the outside, the Washington also boasts a fantastically lush Victorian interior – all thick carpet, etched glass and dark polished-oak partitions. Padded banquettes are snug and the ideal place from which to admire the impressive carved horseshoe bar and fine plasterwork ceiling, painted an intriguing combination of vanilla and dark navy. The display cabinet containing various dusty bits relating to

the Washington Cricket Club we understand, but next to it is a collection of Americana (pictures of Washington, Bogart, a native Indian Chief) for which we can't figure a link. Other distractions include fruit machines, video games, board games, darts and TV sport, while the cellar bar hosts the Hampstead Comedy Club. Beers are good (real ales include Adnam's, London Pride and Greene King) and British and Thai dishes are served until 10pm.
Comedy (8pm Sat; £6/£5 concs). Function room. Games (board games, darts, fruit machines, video games). Jukebox. Quiz (9.30pm Tue; £1 to play). Satellite TV (big screen). Tables outdoors (pavement). Vegetarian dishes.

Wells Tavern

30 Well Walk, NW3 (020 7794 2806). Hampstead tube/ Hampstead Heath rail. **Open** 11am-11pm Mon-Sat; noon-10.30pm Sun. **Food served** noon-3pm daily. **Credit** MC, V.
Behind an attractive exterior on one of Hampstead's beautiful residential streets, this is a genuinely unpretentious and relaxed local often full of muddy-booted walkers, dogs and kids. Compared with other pubs in the area, the lack of either tweeness or grot is notably refreshing. Sport is taken seriously; off to one side as you enter is a vast television screen, while on the other is a shrine-like alcove for darts. The place can be packed on big match days. During summer, it's mobbed most weekends as it makes a perfect destination if you're coming over from Highgate. Standard bar food and Sunday roasts are available.
Babies and children admitted (daytimes). Games (darts, fruit machine, quiz machine). Jukebox. Quiz. Satellite TV (big screen). Tables outdoors (garden, terrace). Vegetarian dishes.

White Horse

154 Fleet Road, NW3 (020 7485 2112). Belsize Park tube. **Open** 11am-11pm Mon-Sat; noon-10.30pm Sun. **Food served** noon-3pm, 5-8pm Mon-Fri; noon-5pm Sat, Sun. **Credit** AmEx, DC, MC, V.
A large triangular building on a corner near the Royal Free, the White Horse is primely positioned for hospital visitors and heath walkers alike. It seems a little sombre from the outside, but management has made a stab at brightening up the interior, resulting in a not entirely harmonious mix of Victorian dark oak and aquamarine and yellow walls, topped off by a strange and wonderful tiled ceiling. At the back, beyond the fruit machines, there's a hint of the gastropub with pleasantly candlelit tables but a thoroughly unremarkable menu. Beyond is a small beer garden-cum-yard. A comedy club downstairs and quiz nights on Wednesdays and Saturdays are further indications of a once dingy establishment doing its best to move with the times.
Comedy (8pm Sat; £6). Function room. Games (fruit machine, quiz machine). No-smoking area (11am-6pm only). Tables outdoors (garden). TV. Vegetarian dishes.

Ye Olde White Bear

New End, NW3 (020 7435 3758). Hampstead tube. **Open** 11am-11pm Mon-Sat; noon-10.30pm Sun. **Food served** noon-10pm daily. **Credit** DC, MC, V.
Despite the cloying prefix, the White Bear easily steers the right side of tweeness. It is picturesque – a white-shuttered house draped with flowers, occupying one of the prettiest corners in Hampstead – but inside it's also pure unreconstructed pub. On one side of the central bar is a quiet drinking area with a mishmash of furniture and dusty prints and photographs around a beautiful carved wood fireplace; on the other, more of the same without a fire but with a very discreet TV. The night we visited a few people were vaguely watching football with the sound turned down. An imaginative selection of food is served until 10pm amid the charming, cluttered tattiness.

Babies and children admitted. Quiz (9pm Thur; £1 to play). Satellite TV. Tables outdoors (courtyard, pavement). Vegetarian dishes.

Also in the area...
All Bar One 79-81 Heath Street, NW3 (020 7433 0491).
Café Rouge 38-39 High Street, NW3 (020 7435 4240).
Rat & Parrot 250 Haverstock Hill, NW3 (020 7431 0889).
Three Horseshoes (JD Wetherspoon) 28 Heath Street, NW3 (020 7431 7206).

Highgate

Flask
77 Highgate West Hill, N6 (020 8348 7346). Archway or Highgate tube/143, 210, 214, 271 bus. **Open** 11am-11pm Mon-Sat; noon-10.30pm Sun. **Food served** noon-3pm, 6-9pm Mon-Sat; noon-4pm Sun. **Credit** AmEx, MC, V.
A classic inn from the days when Highgate Village was exactly that and John Keats walked over from Hampstead making notes. In front is a triangular yard with plenty of tables that get packed to overflowing with tourists and locals each summer. Inside is a charming up-and-down labyrinth of low-ceilinged rooms and dark-timbered corners; nice, but the lighting could be dimmer. The excellent beer range includes common real ales like Adnam's and London Pride, less usual brews like Harveys from Sussex (a reasonable £2.10) and Staropramen lager on draught, and there's a decent wine selection. Lately the range of bar food has been much improved. A while ago it was run-of-the-mill pub grub, now it includes papardelle pasta with herby tomato sauce, wild mushrooms and parmesan (£5.90), Caesar salad (£6.95), generously-sized steaks (£9.50) and enjoyable multi-layered sandwiches from around £4.50.
Babies and children admitted. Games (fruit machine). Tables outdoors (garden). Vegetarian dishes.

Also in the area...
All Bar One 1-3 Hampstead Lane, N6 (020 8342 7861).
Café Rouge 6-7 South Grove, N6 (020 8342 9797).
Gatehouse (JD Wetherspoon) 1 North Road, N6 (020 8340 8054).

Holloway

Coronet
338-346 Holloway Road, N7 (020 7609 5014). Holloway Road tube. **Open** 11am-11pm Mon-Sat; noon-10.30pm Sun. **Food served** 11am-10pm Mon-Sat; noon-9.30pm Sun. **Credit** AmEx, DC, MC, V.
London has its style bars, and, right at the opposite end of the chic-scale, places like the Coronet. Originally a 1930s cinema (the art deco exterior is a listed monument), it has been transformed by JD Wetherspoon into a giant mega-pub with one long bar, loads of booths and tables of different sizes, a raised no-smoking area and banks of games machines. It's so big it's always easy to find a seat, and despite the acres of space it has a surprisingly cosy atmosphere. A great attraction is JDW's bargain prices (£1.29 a pint for real ales like Abbot, 6X, Spitfire and guest ales, £1.29-£1.79 for lagers like Carling or Stella), which are as much appreciated by the old characters who spend all day here, as by the younger, mixed crowd later on. Wetherspoon's varied pub-grub menu (everything under a fiver) also adds to the budget appeal.

Disabled: lift, toilet. Games (fruit machine). No piped music or jukebox. No-smoking area. Specialities: guest real ales. Vegetarian dishes.

Landseer
37 Landseer Road, N19 (020 7263 4658). Archway tube/43, 217 bus. **Open** 5-11pm Mon-Fri; noon-11pm Sat; noon-10.30pm Sun. **Food served** 6.30-10pm Mon-Fri; 12.30-3.30pm, 6.30-10.30pm Sat; 1-5pm, 6-9.30pm Sun. **Credit** MC, V.
An old pub a short walk from the Holloway Road that was given a gastropub makeover a few years ago with light-painted walls, chunky wooden tables, bookshelves and ample leather sofas. Its windows are big and uncurtained, so it really comes into its own when the weather's sunny and the evenings long. Regular beers on tap include a good choice of real ales (Marston's Pedigree, Young's Special, Greene King, £2-£2.25) and the usual lagers (Stella, Heineken), and the global wine selection is above pub average for variety, quality and price, with several good labels at £9-£12. The chalked-up food menu follows the usual gastro lines, with mains like venison and red wine sausages with herb mash, or monkfish and vegetable kebabs on basmati rice (all priced around £6-£10). A whole assortment of board games can be asked for at the bar.
Babies and children admitted. Function room. Games (board games). Satellite TV. Tables outdoors (pavement). Vegetarian dishes.

Shillibeer's
Carpenters Mews, North Road, N7 (020 7700 1858). Caledonian Road tube. **Open** noon-midnight Mon-Thur; noon-2am Fri; 6pm-2am Sat. **Happy hour** times vary; Mon-Thur. **Food served** noon-3pm, 6-10pm Mon-Sat. **Credit** AmEx, DC, MC, V.
Location isn't exactly an asset at this curious 'bar-brasserie and venue'. It's in the Carpenters' Mews development, home to colleges, workshop units and the Pleasance Theatre, surrounded by industrial units and flats on the gaunt North Road. Shillibeer's, though, is a big, smart space, divided between the bar, a raised dining area and an upper gallery, with stripped-wood floors, potted plants and lofty windows. Its relative isolation means that the main clientele are local workers, students and theatre-goers. Entertainment nights draw in additional trade, and the whole venue is regularly booked out for parties and events. German Warsteiner lager is the only beer on tap, but there's an extensive choice of bottled beers and cocktails. Food is enjoyable though perhaps a little expensive, with fashionably eclectic offerings such as goat's cheese salad, Thai chicken with five-spice rice and sea bass with bok choi and aubergine mash (bar dishes around £4.50-£6.50, restaurant mains £7-£10).
Babies and children admitted (dining only; children's menus, high chairs). Disabled: toilet. Function room. Music (DJs Sat). Restaurant. Specialities: cocktails. Tables outdoors (courtyard). Vegetarian dishes.

Also in the area...
O'Neill's 456 Holloway Road, N7 (020 7700 8941).

Islington

25 Canonbury Lane
25 Canonbury Lane, N1 (020 7226 0955/ www.25canonburylane.com). Highbury & Islington tube/rail. **Open** 5-11pm Mon-Fri; noon-11pm Sat, Sun. **Food served** 6-10pm Mon-Thur; 6-8pm Fri; 12.30-3.30pm, 6-8pm Sat; 12.30-3.30pm Sun. **Credit** DC, MC, V.

North

The notes on the back of the menu confidently state that 25 has 'redefined Islington bar culture', but thankfully the charm of this tiny unflashy bar just off Upper Street lies in its straightforward exposition of the simple pleasures of social drinking. Its mish-mash of dark wood floor, red, duck-egg blue and gold colour scheme, antique fittings and frescoes that belong in the singers' bar at a Viennese opera house is successful at creating a warm and homely atmosphere. Music is kept low, and drinks centre on cocktails (£6) and an extensive wine list (£10.95-£15.95). As a result patrons are encouraged to engage in the forgotten art of conversation rather than bellow over pints. Refreshing.
Babies and children admitted (daytimes). Bar areas available for hire. Tables outdoors (garden). Vegetarian dishes.

Albion

10 Thornhill Road, N1 (020 7607 7450). Angel tube/ Highbury & Islington tube/rail. **Open/food served** 11am-11pm Mon-Sat; noon-10.30pm Sun. **Credit** AmEx, DC, MC, V.
The ivy-clad, flower bedecked Albion brings a bit of rustic charm to N1. Although the hunting/fishing interior comes across as contrived, the place is genuine late Georgian. When it was built it probably stood in countryside. Come summer the beer garden at the back with vine-covered pergolas and roses remains as close as it gets to the Cotswolds without crossing the North Circular. Inside, the grand front bar attracts Barnsbury's fortysomethings popping in for a pint while the au pair puts the kids to bed. There's no jukebox, and the TV remains lodged on BBC1. Served throughout the pub, food largely reminds of Sunday at granny's (shepherd's pie, sausage and mash, £5.45), with a few concessions to the demanding grandchild (Singapore noodles £6.45). House ale is Theakston's; house adjective: charming.
Babies and children admitted (dining only; children's menus). Disabled: toilet. Games (fruit machine, quiz machine). No-smoking area. Tables outdoors (garden). Vegetarian dishes.

Bar Latino

144 Upper Street, N1 (020 7704 6868). Angel tube. **Open/food served** 8pm-2am Mon-Thur; 6pm-2am Fri, Sat. **Happy hour** 8-9.30pm Mon-Thur; 6-8.30pm Fri, Sat. **Admission** £6 after 10pm Fri, Sat. **Credit** AmEx, MC, V.
With its host of regular DJs, frequent bands and late licence, Bar Latino doesn't bother over much with seating (a few bar stools only); raging crowds here are expected to be up on the feet inflicting additional damage on the chipped floorboarding. Assembled arse-wigglers range from trend-setters to office boys working up a sweat with their ties around their heads – in fact, pretty much anyone who's having a good night on Upper Street and doesn't want to go home come pub chuck-out time. For a quieter Margarita or Caipirinha (cachaça, fresh lime and sugar over crushed ice, £5) turn up well before the post-pub surge.
Dress code. Function room. Music (DJs/live bands 9pm nightly). Tables outdoors (pavement). Vegetarian dishes on request.

Camden Head

2 Camden Walk, N1 (020 7359 0851). Angel tube/19, 38 bus. **Open/food served** 11am-11pm Mon-Sat; noon-10.30pm Sun. **Credit** AmEx, DC, MC, V.
A bastion of traditional pubdom among the designer bar onslaught and, appropriately enough, the local for the stallholders of Camden Passage antiques market. It's been around since 1899 and – thanks to uncommonly sensitive renovation in the 1960s – many of the original features remain, such as a ridiculously ornate island bar, plenty of woodwork with acid-etched glass and a benevolent spook named George. Trivia machines and a guitar-classic heavy jukebox are among the few concessions to modernity. There's a brick-walled beer garden for summer use.
Comedy club (8.30pm Thur-Sat and every other Mon; £3-£5). Function room. Games (fruit machines, quiz machines). Jukebox. Quiz night (8.30pm Tue; £1 to play). Satellite TV (big screen). Tables outdoors (terrace). Vegetarian dishes.

Centuria

100 St Paul's Road, N1 (020 7704 2345). Highbury & Islington tube/rail/30, 277 bus. **Open** 5-11pm Mon-Fri; noon-11pm Sat; noon-10.30pm Sun. **Happy hour** 5-8pm Mon-Thur (occasional). **Food served** 6-10.45pm Mon-Thur; 12.30-4pm, 6-10.30pm Fri, Sat; 12.30-10.30pm Sun. **Credit** MC, V.
With its huge windows and whitewashed walls, this superior gastropub brings a touch of Upper Street chic to one of Islington's quieter areas. One part of a large and beautifully lit room is given over to dining (with a kitchen open to view), while a separate area serves as a bar, complete with predictable sofas and candles. Diners probably appreciate the relative hush, barely intruded on by trip hop played low, but for a drinking venue it left something of a vacuum where the atmosphere should be. Apparently it does get more boisterous at weekends. Bring a close personal friend and get quiet together over the likes of cinnamon and honey roasted poussin (£9.95) and a good bottle of plonk.
Babies and children admitted. Dining room. Tables outdoors (patio, pavement). TV. Vegetarian dishes.

Chapel

29A Penton Street, N1 (020 7833 4090/ www.chapel.co.uk). Angel tube. **Open** 5-11pm Mon-Wed; noon-midnight Thur; noon-1am Fri, Sat; 5-10.30pm Sun. **Food served** noon-9pm Tue-Sat. **Credit** MC, V.
As the name suggests, this Irish boozer is fashioned along distinctly ecclesiastical lines. Huge arches separate the two rooms whilst the bar itself looks like Notre Dame's little sister. Other touches, however, are more high-chic than high-church: lights like stalactites hang from the ceiling, ridiculously capacious sofas abound, and the frosted urinals in the gents are plumbing's answer to Norman Foster. The booze is also très moderne, with an extensive range of cocktails and sophisticated alcopops (beers are bog-standard Stella, Boddingtons and Guinness). During the week there's a pleasant womb-like ambience, but weekends are rampant as the music is turned up and the cocktails are knocked back.
Function room. Music (live jazz 9pm Thur; DJs 10pm Fri, Sat). Restaurant. Tables outdoors (terrace). Vegetarian dishes.

Compton Arms

4 Compton Avenue, N1 (020 7359 6883). Highbury & Islington tube/rail. **Open** 11am-11pm Mon-Sat; noon-10.30pm Sun. **Food served** noon-3pm, 6-9pm Mon, Wed-Sun; noon-3pm Tue. **Credit** MC, V.
Low beamed ceilings, old wood benches and an ivy-covered beer garden conspire to keep the 21st-century city at bay and place customers firmly in a cosy countryfied setting. It almost works. But that constant shaking of the floor is, alas, not a randy bull escaped from the local farm, but a Victoria line train braking into Highbury and Islington. Never mind, as long as you're seated at the bar supping the likes of Greene King IPA and Abbot, without a vodka Red Bull or focaccia (it's meat and two veg on the menu here) in sight, you can remain contentedly in the world of Ambridge.
Babies and children admitted (separate area). No piped music or jukebox. Satellite TV (big screen). Tables outdoors (garden). Vegetarian dishes.

North

TheTriangle

This cosy corner en route to Crouch End was taken over in 1999 by ex-'Vine' chef Aziz Begdouri and his brother Youssef. A simple homely entrance cons you into thinking that you might only have one drink here and then move on. But once you've been in one of this bar/restaurant's many corners, it's easy to lose track of time and suddenly realise that you should have been somewhere else hours ago.

The idiosyncratic interior is a quiet combination of Mediterranean and Moroccan, full of sculptures and quirky charms. Fall into one of the deep brown leather sofas, or maybe relax on a low Arabic-Influenced bank scattered with cushions in the alcove.

In summer the back doors slide open into a cute and colourful garden. It's the perfect place for an intimate rendezvous, and there is plenty of scope for scandal among the candles.

For cocktails there are the usual suspects but staff are happy to mix your own recipes for a customised tipple. True to form the food (served until 11.45pm) is an eclectic mix and the desserts like Bailey's cheesecake are well worth a try.

What makes this one of the most comfortable spots to waste time in is the effortless, friendly service and the fact that unlike a bad blind date, no one seems to mind what your name is or where you come from.

Don't be ☐ go to the ◺ and get lost.

The Triangle, 1 Ferme Park Road, N4 4DS   Closest ⊖ ≿ Finsbury Park   tel: 020 8292 0516
Drinks and food served: noon to late Tuesday to Thursday, 10am to late Friday to Sunday, closed Mondays

Crown

116 Cloudesley Road, N1 (020 7837 7107). Angel tube.
Open noon-11pm Mon-Sat; noon-10.30pm Sun. **Food
served** noon-3pm, 6-10pm Mon-Sat; noon-3.30pm Sun.
Credit AmEx, MC, V.
If there's one thing that Islington is not short of, it's
gastropubs. Maybe that's why even at 1.30pm on a Friday
lunchtime we could still pick and choose where to sit at the
Crown, either in the wooden Victorian bar room, with some
fantastically low-slung armchairs, or in the smaller area
reserved for diners, which benefits from a skylight. You order
from the bar, where you can run a tab, provided you hand
over a credit card. The open kitchen at the rear serves up
quality modern British and continental cuisine which, last
time we ate here, was remarkably good. There's a decent wine
list, and Hoegaarden and London Pride on draught. Service
is painstaking and friendly, and the atmosphere refined
without being at all stuffy.
*Babies and children admitted. Function room. Tables
outdoors (patio). Vegetarian dishes.*

Cuba Libre

72 Upper Street, N1 (020 7354 9998). Angel tube.
Open 11am-11pm Mon-Thur; 11am-2am Fri, Sat;
11am-10.30pm Sun. **Happy hour** 5-8pm Mon-Fri;
noon-8pm Sat; noon-10.30pm Sun. **Food served**
11am-10.30pm Mon-Thur; 11am-midnight Fri, Sat;
11am-10pm Sun. **Credit** MC, V.
Concealed beyond the diners at the back of Upper Street's
answer to a Copacabana beach restaurant, is this spirited,
good-time bar. Walls are adorned with logos of exotic-looking
Latin American spirits, while cheap and cheerful furniture
gives the place a sunny outlook even on the coldest of winter's
evenings. It's at its loudest and liveliest late Friday and
Saturday when the music and booze keeps on well after
midnight for samba fun and self-inflicted cocktail abuse.
*Babies and children admitted (restaurant). Restaurant.
Specialities: Cuban beers, cocktails. Tables outdoors
(pavement). Vegetarian dishes.*

Dove Regent

65 Graham Street, N1 (020 7608 2656). Angel tube.
Open 11am-11pm Mon-Wed; 11am-midnight Thur-Sat;
11am-10.30pm Sun. **Food served** 11am-10pm Mon-Wed,
Sun; 11am-10.30pm Thur-Sat. **Credit** DC, MC, V.
Tucked away in a quiet backstreet behind the Angel, the Dove
is a former gay bar that after undergoing a change of
management now attracts a mixed – but gay-friendly – and
exuberant crowd most nights of the week. Beers are excellent,
with a solid array of continental brews, especially Belgian
(Leffe and Hoegaarden, £2 a half), and the bar is happy to
arrange tasting sessions accompanied by Trappist cheese. If
you're feeling friendly or Flemish, it's a great place to be.
*Comedy (8.30pm Thur-Sat; £5-£6). Disabled: toilet.
Function rooms. Games (board games, table football).
Music (live jazz, Sun lunchtime). No-smoking area.
Specialities: Belgian beers. Tables outdoors (pavement).
Vegetarian dishes.*

Duke of Cambridge

30 St Peter's Street, N1 (020 7359 3066/
www.singhboulton.co.uk). Angel tube. **Open** 5-11pm Mon;
noon-11pm Tue-Sat; noon-10.30pm Sun. **Food served**
6.30-10.30pm Mon; 12.30-3pm, 6.30-10.30pm Tue-Fri;
12.30-3.30pm, 6.30-10.30pm Sat; 12.30-3.30pm, 7-10pm
Sun. **Credit** AmEx, MC, V.
Award-winning organic gastroboozer that's quintessentially
Islington. Pristine pine fills two airy rooms – main bar room

and smaller dining area – waited on by rather sullen staff,
soft lighting, no music, and even the beer is supposed to be
good for you (we had pints of Pitfield Eco Warrior, brewed
down the road in Hoxton). The wine list is excellent if you're
prepared to pay. Food is ambitious and mains start at over
the tenner mark. Eavesdrop on North London's finest, the self-
assured tones of trustafarians mingling, on our last visit, with
exchanges of section editors deciding what we might be
reading in some coming Sunday broadsheet. It's broccoli chic;
not cheap but it looks appealing and tastes even better.
*Babies and children admitted (high chairs, organic baby
food). Function room. No piped music or jukebox. No-
smoking areas. Restaurant. Specialities: all-organic beers
and food. Tables outdoors (conservatory, courtyard).
Vegetarian dishes.*

Elbow Room

89-91 Chapel Market, N1 (020 7278 3244/
www.elbow-room.co.uk). Angel tube. **Open/food served**
6pm-2am Mon; noon-2am Tue-Thur; noon-3am Fri, Sat;
noon-11pm Sun. **Admission** £2 9-10pm, £5 after 10pm
Fri, Sat. **Credit** MC, V.
Off the chaotic raggle-taggle of Chapel Market lies this huge,
purple-fronted, neon-signed aircraft hangar of a pool hall,
with bar attached. Despite its size, it retains the panache and
attention to detail of its smaller sister branch in Westbourne
Grove (*see p89*), wrapping a faint hint of sleazy glamour
around modern, efficient and comfortable surroundings. The
purple baize pool tables are hired out by the hour (up to £9
depending on the time of day/week). A gender-balanced mix
of students, office workers and hipsters hangs out here; the
mood is bustling rather than hustling. The bar has the usual
draught and bottled beers, and serves snack food (the potato
skins are recommended). The place is turning into a quality
music venue in its own right, with name DJs like Ross Allen
guesting in recent months. It's also becoming a victim of its
own success, however, and you might be wise to become a
member if you want to chalk your cue here on a regular basis.
Alternatively, a new four-level branch is due to open on the
Finchley Road in Swiss Cottage.
*Disabled: toilet. Games (American pool tables; noon-7pm
£6/hour, after 7pm £9/hour). Music (DJs nightly). TVs
(plasma screens & satellite; big screens). Vegetarian
dishes. V.I.P. room.*

Embassy Bar

119 Essex Road, N1 (020 7359 7882/
www.embassybar.co.uk). Angel tube/Highbury & Islington
tube/rail/38, 56, 73, 341 bus. **Open/food served**
5-11pm Mon-Thur; 5pm-1am Fri; 4pm-1am Sat; 5-10.30pm
Sun. **Credit** AmEx, DC, MC, V.
With its smoked glass windows and black frontage, from the
outside the Embassy puts us in mind of a celebrity limousine
(or possibly an undertakers). But like all those long white
stretches you see cruising the West End on a Saturday night,
inside it's just a bunch of leery youths dressed down for a big
night out. Except the Embassy's a bit cooler-than-thou, with
fuggy low-lighting and kitsch posters, a look it carries off with
a bit more panache than many of its art-bar rivals. Check out,
for example, the cheekily named 'corporate hospitality'
cocktail (£4.20), which affords a level of intoxication and a
degree of moral superiority that the trusty company AmEx
simply cannot match – or a ride in a stretch limo, for that
matter. Beware, however, for a place so popular and crammed
with trip hop trendsters, the Embassy is inexplicably cursed
with the world's smallest toilet.
*Bar area available for hire. Music (DJs 8pm Thur-Sun).
Vegetarian dishes.*

Elbow Room.
See page 219.

Filthy McNasty's
68 Amwell Street, EC1 (020 7837 6067). Angel tube/ Farringdon tube/rail/19, 38, 341 bus. **Open** noon-11pm Mon-Sat; noon-10.30pm Sun. **Food served** noon-3pm, 6-9pm Mon-Fri; noon-7pm Sat, Sun. **Credit** MC, V.
The name, the decrepit 'Whiskey Bar' sign above the entrance, and the memorabilia on the walls (Pogues silver discs and photos of ruddy types drinking at Galway races) all point to a seedy celebration of dipsomania on the Emerald isle. But with regular book and poetry readings (see *Time Out* magazine for listings) and quality live music in the tiny back bar, this place is more sophisticated than it lets on. Knackered sofas and the dingy corners make it the ideal haunt for the contemplative drinker rather than the wreckless alcoholic. Real ale fans and lager boys beware, however, the booze is unapologetically Celtic and if you're not a fan of the black stuff or happy with a dram, then you're likely to be on the lime and sodas for the night.
Babies and children admitted (daytime). Digital TV. Disabled: toilet. Function room. Literary readings (8.30pm Wed, Thur). Music (band 2-6pm, 9-10.30pm Sun). Songwriters night (9pm Tue). Specialities: whiskies. Quiz (8.30pm Mon). Tables outdoors (pavement). Vegetarian dishes.

Hen & Chickens Theatre Bar
109 St Paul's Road, N1 (020 7704 7621/ www.henandchickens.com). Highbury & Islington tube/rail. **Open/food served** noon-midnight Mon-Wed, Sun; noon-1am Thur-Sat. **Admission** £3 after 11pm Fri, Sat. **Credit** MC, V.
A rival to the **Hope and Anchor** (*see below*) for the Liam Gallagher award for shaggiest haircuts, this is a pared down, spruced up, no frills, single room boozer on the corner of St Paul's and Canonbury roads. Big windows keep the place bright during the day. At night they fill with a blur of passing traffic; perfect for bus spotters. Inside, the minimal amount of tables and chairs leaves maximum space for standing punters. Even at 6.30pm on a wet Monday evening it was busy, with the whistling friction of wet puffa jackets at the bar almost drowning out the barmaid's choice of Air on the tape deck. Draught options include Fuller's ales and Staropramen. Upstairs is a 60-seat theatre that plays host to fringe productions (see *Time Out* magazine for what's on), as well as weekly comedy nights, DJs and live music.
Games (fruit machine, quiz machine). Music (DJs 10pm Wed; live music 11pm Thur-Sat, 10pm Sun). Theatre (comedy Mon, Sun; fringe theatre eves Tues-Sat, matinees Sun; box office 020 7704 2001). TV. Vegetarian dishes.

Hemingford Arms
158 Hemingford Road, N1 (020 7607 3303). Caledonian Road tube. **Open** 11am-11pm Mon-Sat; noon-10.30pm Sun. **Food served** 12.30-2.30pm, 6.30-10.30pm Mon-Fri; 6.30-10.30pm Sat, Sun. **Credit** MC, V.
Hidden under all the jokey bric-a-brac, suspended from the ceiling and obscuring the walls, is quite a splendid boozer. The *Beezer* on the bookshelves, stuffed badgers, a mannequin astride a broomstick marking the gents, a huge sign over the bar reading 'Methodist Chapel' – all of this makes for pleasant distraction, but what we really appreciate is the distinctly catholic selection of beers (including Courage Director's, 6X) and the oddball mix of clientele that congregates among the clutter and candlelight. Fans of the Hemingford range from City professionals to old hippies, and we get the impression that those who drink here, drink here a lot. Another plus is the Thai food, ordered at the bar, which is cheap and excellent (most dishes £4.50).

Babies and children admitted (until 8pm). Function room. Games (fruit machine, poker machine). Music (bands 9pm Mon-Wed, Fri-Sun). Quiz (9pm Thur; £1 to play). Satellite TV. Tables outdoors (pavement). Vegetarian dishes.

Hope & Anchor
207 Upper Street, N1 (020 7354 1312). Highbury & Islington tube/rail. **Open** ground floor noon-11pm Mon-Sat; noon-10.30pm Sun; basement 8.30pm-1am Mon-Sat; 7pm-midnight Sun. **Food served** noon-3pm, 5-7pm Mon-Fri; noon-5pm Sat. **Credit** AmEx, DC, MC, V.
Its heyday was in the 1970s and '80s when the Clash, the Stranglers and the Pistols ripped the place up, U2 made their London debuts here, and Frankie Goes to Hollywood filmed the videos for *Relax* and *Two Tribes* in the basement. Now it's 'London's most famous music venue'™, filled most nights with Justine Frischman lookalikes and aspirational Thom Yorkes. Far from becoming some indie Rock Circus, the Hope & Anchor still hosts young hopefuls every night of the week. If the thundering from below gets too much in the appropriately named 'rattle and hum' bar (Greene King Abbot on tap) on the ground floor, retreat to the wonderfully decrepit pool room upstairs.
Disabled: toilet. Games (fruit machines, pool tables, video games). Music (bands nightly 8.30pm; £5). Vegetarian dishes.

ice
142 Essex Road, N1 (020 7359 2661). Angel tube/ Highbury & Islington tube/rail/Essex Road rail. **Open** 5pm-midnight Mon-Thur, Sun; 5pm-2am Fri; noon-2am Sat. **Food served** 5-11pm daily. **Credit** AmEx, MC, V.
The Essex Road crawl has for some time been more rewarding than cruising on Upper Street, and its cool drinking status is further enhanced by the addition of ice. Behind a tea room-style frontage a former barbers has been converted into a long, narrow chill-out zone aimed squarely at the clubbing fraternity. Front of the house is plasticky bench seating, while to the rear is a long bar and, opposite, a row of dinky, wall-mounted laptop-sized tables each with its own kitschy orange or blue lamp. Very Wayne Hemingway. The area between bar and tables serves as a cramped dance space for weekend DJ sessions. Bar staff are accomplished cocktail shakers eager to prepare from a long list (average price £4.50) or there's DeKoninck (£2.75) on tap (correctly served in a bollecke), plus standard bottled beers. A late licence has been applied for.
Bar available for hire (weekdays). Disabled: toilet. Music (DJs Thur-Sun). Specialities: absinthe, cocktails. Vegetarian dishes.

Island Queen
87 Noel Road, N1 (020 7704 7631). Angel tube. **Open** noon-11pm Mon-Sat; noon-10.30pm Sun. **Food served** noon-3pm daily. **Credit** MC, V.
One of London's best-looking historic boozers, the Island Queen has a great curving wood-and-etched glass frontage that puts us in mind of the stern of an Elizabethan man-o-war. This is entirely appropriate given that the place is named after a ship. The nautical theme used to feature heavily with mannequins of pirates and rigging stretched across the ceiling, but last year that all went leaving just a smattering of maritime prints and a large, weathered wooden figurehead from a ship's prow at the rear of the pub. Also back there are some wonderful, huge mirrors etched with palms that give the place the feel of a conservatory. The impressive, dark wood central bar has Bass, London Pride and Staropramen on tap. There's also a decent juke box and a pool room.
Function room. Games (pool table). Tables outdoors (pavement). Vegetarian dishes.

King's Head

*115 Upper Street, N1 (020 7226 0364). Angel tube/
Highbury & Islington tube/rail.* **Open** 11am-midnight
Mon; 11am-1am Tue-Thur; 11am-2am Fri, Sat; noon-1am
Sun. **Food served** noon-3.30pm Tue-Sat; noon-9pm Sun.
Pre-booked theatre dinner available Tue-Sat only; three-
course with coffee £9.50. **No credit cards**.

Technically a theatre bar, though equally a late-night pub and
music venue, the King's Head has survived Upper Street's
transition into bistro centrale and remains one of London's
most eccentric boozers. The bar, built 'in the round', is
splendidly scruffy, while much of the seating was scavenged
from the old Scala theatre. Old playbills and autographed
posters are plastered across the walls. Nightly theatrical and
live music performances, combined with the obvious
advantages of a 2am licence, ensure a wonderfully eclectic
crowd. On our visit a multitude of thesps, students, rastas
and rock types made for an atmosphere that was more
Camden c.1968 than Blairite Islington. Fans of *Withnail and
I* look no further.
*Babies and children admitted (until 7pm). Disabled: toilet
(bar and theatre). Music (live music 10pm nightly).
Theatre. Vegetarian dishes.*

Marquess Tavern

*32 Canonbury Street, N1 (020 7354 2975). Highbury &
Islington tube/rail/Essex Road rail.* **Open** 11am-11pm
Mon-Sat; noon-10.30pm Sun. **Food served** 11am-9.30pm
Mon-Sat. **No credit cards.**

As we clattered through the door here one recent weekday
night, voices raised in youthful exuberance, we felt like we'd
broken the silence of a thousand years. There was an old
codger in the corner with dog and the dregs of a pint, and a
few scattered punters, fags in hand, silently scanning their
papers. The grotesque ornate chandeliers and embossed
wallpaper looked like they'd seen a world war or two, and
there was a CAMRA poster on the walls denouncing the
chancellor's beer tax, lending an Old Tory feel to this most
New Labour of neighbourhoods. Close to the canal on a quiet
street, this is the Islington of your grandparents' days; you
may not appreciate it now, but you'll miss it when it's gone.
*Function room. Games (board games, darts, fruit
machine). No piped music or jukebox. Quiz (8pm first
Mon of month). Satellite TV. Tables outdoors (patio).
Vegetarian dishes.*

Matt & Matt Bar

112 Upper Street, N1 (020 7226 6035). Angel tube.
Open/food served 6pm-midnight Tue-Thur; 6pm-2am
Fri; 7pm-2am Sat. **Happy hour** 6-8pm Tue-Fri.
Credit MC, V.

As a nouveaux pub, this has much to recommend it: cosy
premises, a host of quality DJs, and service a lot less snooty
than many of Upper Street's more 'cutting edge' venues.
There's even a concession to traditional pub pursuits in the
form of a pool table. During the week this is a great place to
relax to hyper-chilled music and work through a hefty jug or
two of cocktail. Alas, such blissful lethargy is hard to find of
a weekend, and M&M has fallen victim to that scourge of the
free-drinking individual: a members-only policy.
Games (pool table). Music (DJs 9pm Thur-Sat).

Medicine Bar

*181 Upper Street, N1 (020 7704 9536/
www.liquid-life.com). Angel tube/Highbury & Islington
tube/rail.* **Open** 5pm-midnight Mon-Thur; 3pm-2am Fri;
noon-2am Sat; noon-10.30pm Sun. **Admission** £3 (non-
members) after 10pm Fri, Sat. **Credit** MC, V.

Islington bar culture epitomised, this is a sleek minimalist
nightspot for the nonchalantly cool devotee of *i-D* and *Dazed
& Confused*. It oozes dressed-down stylishness, from the
daylight-bathed tables by the shop-front window to the dim
red light and fug of cigarette smoke at the large, dark tables
and vast, buttoned leather sofas in the evening. This popular
hangout also benefits from its recently opened upstairs space
(available for hire), which is divided into two dark, cosy rooms
full of comfortable leather sofas and chairs. If you can bear
feeling like Worzel Gummidge at a beauty convention, this is
a great place to chill to a global music soundtrack. Be warned,
however, such effortless chic is in demand, and at weekends
a strictly members-only policy leaves mere mortals dreaming
on Upper Street.
*Games (board games). Music (DJs 9pm Fri, Sat). Tables
outdoors (mews). Upstairs bar/back lounge for hire.*

Narrow Boat

119 St Peter Street, N1 (020 7288 9821). Angel tube.
Open noon-11pm Mon-Sat; noon-10.30pm Sun. **Food
served** noon-3pm daily. **Credit** MC, V.

Under threat from an explosion in property prices aside the
Grand Union Canal, this unique little pub is worth visiting
while you still can. It occupies a couple of former Victorian
workers' cottages overlooking the moorings at Wenlock
Basin. For the most part the interior retains a cottagey
atmosphere with a blend of pastel paintwork, stripped floor
boards and an amount of period bric-a-brac. It gets a little
more gimmicky in the dining extension, which is done out to
resemble the inside of a barge with sloping wood-panelled
walls and a slightly claustrophobic feel. Favourite spot in the
summer is a tiny deck-style balcony with a wrought-iron
spiral staircase leading down to the tow path. The effusive
barman here has just been offered a contract to go and
prospect for gold in New Zealand but he's staying put; he
knows a good pub when he sees it.
*Babies and children admitted (until 7pm). Games (fruit
machine, quiz machine). Tables outdoors (balcony,
towpath). Vegetarian dishes.*

nubar

*196 Essex Road, N1 (020 7354 8886) Angel tube/
Highbury & Islington tube/rail/Essex Road rail.* **Open**
4-11pm Mon-Thur; noon-11pm Fri; 11am-11pm Sat; noon-
10.30pm Sun. **Happy hour** changing monthly promotions.
Credit MC, V.

If you're going to revitalise a flagging and aged boozer, this
is certainly a decent way to breathe life back into the poor old
soul. Despite the rather painful attempts to teach an old dog
new tricks (see self-consciously quirky car door on rear wall),
plenty of original features remain (engraved glass and ornate
Victorian bar) making for an engaging mix. Our weekday
visit saw a steady trickle of locals pop in for a quiet ale on the
sofa, but judging by the DJ's crow's nest over the bar, we
imagine the place a little louder at weekends.
*Babies and children admitted (until 6pm). Games (quiz
machine). Music (occasional live showcases, DJs from
7.30pm nightly).*

Old Queen's Head

44 Essex Road, N1 (020 7354 9273). Angel tube. **Open**
noon-11pm Mon-Sat; noon-10.30pm Sun. **No credit cards**.

Just up Essex Road from the green, this is a great reinvention
of an old pub. It's been stripped out so that it's one big
uncluttered room, painted up in red and purple (nursery
gothic) and furnished with an assortment of rough wooden
benches, chairs and tables that encourage group gatherings.
A magnificently ornate fireplace remains dominating one
corner and apart from that the only other decoration is a large

North

black-and-white close-up of a stylus on a record. Apart from a shaggy pub dog there are no soft surfaces, which means that even when nearly empty the place sounds full. Our only quibble with the place is the beers – a disappointing line-up of nitrokeg standards. The bottled selection is hardly any better. If they would get something better on draught then you'd see us here most nights of the week.
Babies and children admitted (until 9pm). Function room. Games (table football). Satellite TV. Tables outdoors (pavement).

Old Red Lion
418 St John Street, EC1 (020 7837 7816). Angel tube.
Open/food served 11am-11pm Mon-Fri; 11am-3pm, 7-11pm Sat; noon-3pm, 7-10.30pm Sun. **Credit** MC, V.
On a recent visit a northern companion commented that this place felt exactly like the kind of boozers he used to frequent at home, where he'd down a few pints of snakebite, arm wrestle the barmaid, eye the birds, face off with their boyfriends, then grab a bag of chips and savloy to eat on the bus back. But at the Old Red Lion, despite gruesome lighting and walls the colour of the inside of a two-packs-a-day coal miner's lungs, the punters are definite N1 rather than far flung M1. The proximity of Sadler's Wells, not to mention the theatre upstairs, means that many, in fact, are luvvie types – witness the queues at the bar pre- and post-performance – with even, if rumours are to be believed, the odd celebrity.
Babies and children admitted (daytimes). Games (fruit machines, pool table). Satellite TV. Tables outdoors (patio). Theatre. Vegetarian dishes.

Purple Turtle
108 Essex Road, N1 (020 7704 9020). Angel tube/38, 56, 73, 341 bus. **Open** noon-11pm Mon-Sat; noon-10.30pm Sun. **Happy hour** noon-7pm daily. **No credit cards.**
Clearly decorated after a clearance sale at the HMV poster counter, the Turtle is a self-consciously divey celebration of the student lifestyle. From the porno in the gents to the retro arcade games, the goth-stocked jukebox and the terrible, graffiti-art rock star mural, this is definitely more NUS card than AmEx. The management seems to have overlooked one small point, however: Islington is not exactly crawling with students. Consequently on our midweek visit we were the only customers at the bar (where we were kept happy with Hoegaarden). We were assured, though, by the girl behind the bar that come weekend the place does fill up – we hope so, because this is not a place to be seen drinking alone.
Comedy (8pm Mon). Games (fruit machine, pinball machine, video game). Jukebox.

Rosemary Branch
2 Shepperton Road, N1 (020 7704 2730/ www.rosemarybranch.co.uk). Angel tube/Old Street tube/rail. **Open** noon-11.30pm Mon-Thur; noon-midnight Fri, Sat; noon-10.30pm Sun. **Food served** noon-3.30pm, 7-9.30pm Mon-Sat; noon-5pm Sun. **Credit** MC, V.
Punters here reflect the changing status of the area as the influence of the Hoxton rennaissance spreads ever further. While there's still the odd old boy at the bar, he's likely to be spluttering into his pale ale at the sight of all the artfully styled-types moving in on the territory. Walls are covered with artwork that tends toward abstract doodlings, and if the examples here are by the area's feted local bohos, we fear for the future of British art. But, if you want a night out and the chance to meet the next Damien Hirst, this is a great place to come: there's a good selection of beers, and a good modern British and Mediterranean menu.

Babies and children admitted (until 8pm). Function room. Jukebox. No-smoking area. Quiz (Wed, music quiz Mon). Satellite TV. Tables outdoors (pavement). Theatre. Vegetarian dishes.

Ruby in the Dust
70 Upper Street, N1 (020 7359 1710). Angel tube.
Open 8pm-2am Fri, Sat. **Admission** £3 after 9pm. **No credit cards.**
You wonder why, with so many late licences in this neck of the woods, people continue to queue to cram into the sort of clammy underground pit that gives World War II air raid shelters a bad name. It could be the forced intimacy of so many people squeezed into such a tight space, thumping music providing the excuse to get sweaty and close with total strangers. So what if the volume precludes getting to know each other better, with so much unavoidable body contact who needs words? It's all a bit school disco-ish but then who wouldn't relish the chance to be transported back to the best bits of school days with the added attraction of alcohol. Plenty do, especially at weekends when if you don't get there early enough you don't get in at all.
Music (DJs Fri, Sat).

Salmon & Compass
58 Penton Street, N1 (020 7837 3891). Angel tube.
Open 5pm-midnight Mon-Wed; 5pm-2am Thur; 4pm-2am Fri, Sat; 4-10.30pm Sun. **Admission** £3 after 9pm Fri, Sat. **Credit** MC, V.
Don't be misled by the name, which suggests an idyll of seafaring types slugging rum and mistreating parrots. No, this place should really be called the Up For It Arms or the Largin' It Tavern or even just the Red Bull, after the customers' drink of choice. It's a place for boozing and partying to a DJ'd soundtrack. There is the odd table or sofa but it's a place to keep on your feet – how do you expect to pull otherwise? Likely lads line up for a turn at the pool table and a chance to impress the girls with displays of bad-ass, hustling ghetto-pimp style. You've got to be in the mood but if you are (and most people here are) then it's a fine place to kick-start a big night.
Games (pool table). Music (DJs Thur-Sun).

York
82 Islington High Street, N1 (020 7713 1835). Angel tube. **Open** 11am-11pm Mon-Sat; noon-10.30pm Sun. **Food served** noon-3pm daily. **Credit** MC, V.
Archetypal 'swift half' pub, situated right outside Angel tube station at the business end of Upper Street. Most trade here appears to be transient: suits and tradesmen popping in for a quick one at lunchtime, or folk lubricating their gullets before heading off on a night out. It also seems the logical terminus for an arduous pub crawl that might start in Highbury and work its way down Upper Street. In fact, the York is a very ordinary pub with little identity, a severe lack of local custom, and nothing to shout about other than its location. But it's certainly there if you need it.
Games (fruit machines). Satellite TV (big screen). Tables outdoors (patio, pavement). Vegetarian dishes.

Also in the area...
All Bar One 1 Liverpool Road, N1 (020 7843 0021); 131-132 Upper Street, N1 (020 7354 9535).
Babushka 125 Caledonian Road, N1 (020 7837 1924).
Bierodrome 173 Upper Street, N1 (020 7226 5835).
Café Flo 334 Upper Street, N1 (020 7226 7916).
Dôme 341 Upper Street, N1 (020 7226 3414).
Islington Tup 80 Liverpool Road, N1 (020 7354 4440).
Mitre (It's A Scream) 129-130 Upper Street, N1 (020 7704 7641).

O'Neill's 59 Upper Street, N1 (020 7704 7691).
Pitcher & Piano 68 Upper Street, N1
(020 7704 9974).
Slug & Lettuce 1A Islington Green, N1
(020 7226 3864).
Walkabout Inn 56 Upper Street, N1 (020 7359 2097).
White Swan (JD Wetherspoon) 225-226 Upper
Street, N1 (020 7288 9050).

Kentish Town & Gospel Oak

Auntie Annie's
*180 Kentish Town Road, NW5 (020 7485 3237). Kentish
Town tube/rail.* **Open** 11am-11pm Mon-Sat; noon-10.30pm
Sun. **Credit** MC, V.
Don't be misled by the banana yellow exterior, Auntie Annie's
is actually quite trad and dark inside. In fact the heavy
wooden interior is so dark it's almost black, but the effect is
soothing rather than gloomy, with low lighting casting little
cocoons of warmth over the tables. Although the AA isn't an
Irish pub, it lays claim to Europe's biggest range of Irish
whiskies (around 35 in all). It rarely gets overly busy, and
even on a Friday night it's usually possible to snag a table.
The manager occasionally books a guitar-playing musician
who occasionally succeeds in getting the laid-back crowd
singing along to some classic old covers.
Satellite TVs (big screen). Tables outdoors (pavement).

Bull & Last
*168 Highgate Road, NW5 (020 7267 3641). Kentish
Town tube/rail, then C2, 214 bus.* **Open** 11am-11pm
Mon-Sat; noon-10.30pm Sun. **Food served** noon-10.30pm
Mon-Sat; noon-10pm Sun. **Credit** MC, V (over £10).
Another of North London's original gastropubs, the Bull &
Last has a distinctive mix of chunky wooden furniture and
bare board floors, deep, buttoned-leather armchairs and
chintzy lamps in its old pub bar – kind of gentleman's club-
cum-ski chalet. Simultaneously snug, warm and stylish, this
makes it an inviting place to settle into and helps draw a
regular stream of trendy, affluent punters. Bar snacks are
available all day, and a more extensive menu is offered for
lunch and in the evening in the bar as well as in the large
upstairs dining room. Food has a Mediterranean-slant and
includes things like pasta carpaccio bresaola with watercress
and spicy pecorino (£5.50) and pan-fried sirloin steak (£12).
Wash down with grappas (£2). The pub's location opposite
Hampstead Heath makes it an ideal pre- or post-walk venue.
*Babies and children admitted (until 8.30pm). Function room.
Restaurant. Tables outdoors (pavement). Vegetarian dishes.*

Pineapple
*51 Leverton Street, NW5 (020 7485 6422).
Kentish Town tube/rail.* **Open** 3-11pm Mon-Fri;
noon-11pm Sat; noon-10.30pm Sun. **No credit cards.**
The boozers of Kentish Town have always been great value
in terms of local characters, the Pineapple most of all. We were
treated to the pissed-up businessman on the mobile to wifey,
stage-shushing his mistress very audibly, and a group of art
lovers getting excited about stoneware. Add in a conversation
about enemas for enjoyment and who needs a TV? Even
making an entrance has a stagey feel to it: a lavish red velvet
curtain confronts you as you step in. Swish past and you'll
bump into a dark wood, Edwardian-style bar, with the room
wrapped around it on either side in an elongated horseshoe
shape. The wallpaper is vintage Laura Ashley, plus there are
roaring fires and impressive vases of fresh flowers. They don't
do food, but beers include Brakspear Special and a particularly

toothsome drop of Marston's Pedigree. One word of warning:
the pub can get very smoky in the evenings and during footie
matches, when you'll be hard pushed to find somewhere to sit.
*Babies and children admitted. Disabled: toilet. Games (darts
room). Quiz. Satellite TV. Tables outdoors (pavement).*

Platinum Bar
*15A Swains Lane, NW5 (020 7485 2435). Gospel
Oak rail/C2, C11, 214 bus.* **Open** noon-midnight Mon-
Sat; noon-10.30pm Sun. **Happy hour** 6-8pm Mon-Fri.
Food served noon-8pm daily. **Credit** MC, V.
There seems to be no end to the number of makeovers going
on with Kentish Town's pubs. This used to be the dingy Duke
of St Albans, but a refurb of a year or so back has seen it
reborn with a fresh, almost summery feel with plenty of
white-painted wood, rusty red walls, bottle green sofas and
large sprouting pot plants. Punters are still predominantly
local although they're younger in age, and many seem to be
mates with the manager. Warm and informal.
*Babies and children admitted (until 6pm). Games (fruit
machine). Music (covers bands 8.30pm occasional Sat).
Specialities: cocktails. Tables outdoors (courtyard).
Vegetarian dishes.*

Vine
*86 Highgate Road, NW5 (020 7209 0038). Tufnell Park
tube/Kentish Town tube/rail.* **Open** 11am-11pm Mon-Sat;
noon-10.30pm Sun. **Food served** noon-2.30pm, 7-10pm
Mon-Sat; noon-3.30pm, 5.30-9.30pm Sun. **Credit** AmEx,
MC, V.
A top-end outfit, Vine remains the style leader in North
London's gastropub club, with one of the hipper versions of the
de rigueur rustic wood decor and a sophisticated, regularly
changing, globe-trotting menu. There's a clear split between
daytime and evening offerings, but both menus display
imagination and great attention to detail. Service is outstanding.
Success as a restaurant has tended to eclipse its role as a bar,
but that might change with the recent addition of two new
boozing-only rooms upstairs. Beers take a back seat (just a
couple on tap and a few bottled varieties) to a big line in cocktails
and the same carefully selected wine list as in the dining area.
For brighter days, there's an ivy-clad canopied, paved garden
at the back and a slightly less attractive seated forecourt.
*Babies and children admitted. Restaurant. Specialities:
cocktails, flavoured vodkas. Tables outdoors (conservatory,
paved garden). Vegetarian dishes.*

Kilburn

Black Lion
*274 Kilburn High Road, NW6 (020 7624 1520). Kilburn
tube/Brondesbury rail.* **Open** 11am-11pm Mon-Sat; noon-
10.30pm Sun. **No credit cards.**
Opposite the Tricycle cinema and the Zd bar, the Black Lion
is a grand old Victorian drinking palace blessed with an
extraordinary gold and red decorative ceiling, etched glass
and beaten copper wall reliefs of 18th-century gentry at play.
The bright lighting displays these interesting features, and
also shows up the shabby carpet and some of the hard
drinking going on at the vast bar that divides the saloon and
public areas. A dancefloor to one side is usually deserted.
Ample space, constant TV, busy fruit machines and
inexpensive booze encourage studied indifference to the
sumptuous decor from the regulars.
*Babies and children admitted. Function room. Games
(darts, fruit machine). Satellite TV (big screen). Tables
outdoors (garden).*

Power's

332 Kilburn High Road, NW6 (020 7624 6026). Kilburn tube/Brondesbury rail. **Open** noon-11pm Mon-Sat; noon-10.30pm Sun. **No credit cards.**
Easily one of the most crowded bars on the Kilburn High Road of a cold Saturday night, Power's is scruffy, fairly loud and very convivial. Long, narrow and dark (almost Gothic), pushing through to the front bar from the small back rooms can be quite a challenge, but then the good humoured atmosphere doesn't encourage restlessness. Irish ales and lager are the drinks of choice, while the jukebox pumps out the kind of music that has made owner Vince Power's Mean Fiddler organisation famous. The Sunday evening ceilidhs are something of a local institution.
Babies and children admitted (Sun afternoons only). Jukebox. Music (Irish band, 4-6pm Sun). Tables outdoors (pavement). TV.

Salusbury

50-52 Salusbury Road, NW6 (020 7328 3286). Queens Park tube. **Open** noon-11pm Mon-Sat; noon-10.30pm Sun. **Food served** 12.30-3.30pm, 7-10.30pm Mon-Sat; noon-4pm, 7-10pm Sun. **Credit** MC, V.
Very much a pub of two halves, the Salusbury's odd pine-cabin exterior belies a happening bar-restaurant that has found firm favour with Queens Park upmarket twenty- and thirtysomethings. Battered furniture, assorted table sizes and dark-red walls make for an arty bar venue where poses can be struck. At the back of the bar, past the open kitchen, the restaurant room is more mature and cerebral – a good setting to enjoy a menu with serious pretensions and prices: lobster and seafood brodetto (£15), swiss chard and pumpkin risotto (£6.50/£9) or roast rabbit with rosemary and red wine (£11.50). The wine list is excellent too.
Restaurant. Specialities: Freedom organic beer, EB Polish beer. Vegetarian dishes.

Zd Bar

289 Kilburn High Road, NW6 (020 7372 2544). Kilburn tube/Brondesbury rail . **Open/food served** 5pm-1am Mon-Thur; 5pm-2am Fri, Sat; noon-11pm Sun. **Admission** £2 10pm-11pm, £4 after 11pm Fri, Sat. **No credit cards.**
The slightly tatty-looking Zd bar has clearly seen better days; the style bar decor – metal wall, blond wood floor, mock-leather seating – is all looking a little worn, and early on in the evening the place has a faintly neglected air. But once the loud music kicks in no one really cares. This is still Kilburn High Road's most popular late-night drink and dance venue, which fills up late most nights with a dressed-to-impress crowd. The small, sunken dance floor with built-in DJ's crow's nest is rammed at weekends, overlooked by a gallery area at the back where drinkers hang out. Expect lager on tap and bottled beers, plus basic food.
Disabled: toilet. Music (DJs nightly). Satellite TV. Vegetarian dishes.

Muswell Hill & Alexandra Palace

Ha! Ha! Bar & Canteen

390 Muswell Hill Broadway, N10 (020 8444 4722/ www.hahaonline.co.uk). Highgate tube/43, 134, W7 bus. **Open/food served** 11am-11pm Mon-Sat; 10am-10.30pm Sun. **Credit** AmEx, MC, V.
The Ha! Ha!s might have the silliest name of all the modern bar and food groups, but this small chain is also one of those that keeps up the best standards, especially for food. The look is a predictable mix of blond wood and steel fittings, plus comfy chairs for reading the papers or chatting over a coffee. Draught beers are standard lagers (Stella, Heineken), with Boddingtons as a token bitter, but there's a big choice of bottles and a compact but enjoyably varied global wine selection. The Muswell Hill branch gets very busy with evening drinkers, but it's worth checking out the above-average menu: dishes like chicken stuffed with taleggio cheese and wrapped in parma ham with spinach and pasta (£9) or rocket salad with grilled halloumi and pistachios (£6) are made with quality ingredients and put together with imagination. An enjoyable place for brunch.
Disabled: toilet. No-smoking area. Vegetarian dishes.

O'Neill's

87 Muswell Hill Broadway, N10 (020 8883 7382). East Finchley or Highgate tube/43, 134 bus. **Open** noon-11pm Mon-Sat; noon-10.30pm Sun. **Food served** noon-7pm daily. **Credit** MC, V.
Ownership of this popular N10 pub is a licence to print money, because of the Muswell Hill effect (once you've got to the top of the hill, it's a pain to go anywhere else). A giant old Victorian church with three floors, two bars and a soaring panelled wood roof that magnifies the boom of the music, it's young Muswell Hill's drinking hole of choice. It was a Firkin brew pub, but has now passed to the O'Neill's chain with its brand of off-the-peg Irishry. The formula is pretty pared-down, really, with none of those pesky individual choices that complicate the company's distribution network: you can have any bitter so long as it's Caffreys or Guinness, either that or go with the standard range of lagers (Grolsch, Stella, a few others). The food list has Emerald Isle-y stuff – lamb shank or sausages with colcannon, heavy puddings – alongside offerings such as cajun chicken or steak sandwiches. Prices are average to high, with beers from £2.30 a pint. Even so, it still seems to pull in the crowds.
Digital TVs (big screen). Disabled: toilet. Games (fruit machine, giant Connect 4 & Jenga, quiz machine). Music (occasional bands). No-smoking area. Vegetarian dishes.

Phoenix

Alexandra Palace Way, N22 (020 8365 2121). Wood Green or Turnpike Lane tube/Alexandra Palace rail/W3 bus. **Open/food served** 11am-11pm Mon-Sat; noon-10.30pm Sun. **Credit** MC, V.
The Phoenix, aka the pub in Alexandra Palace, is a half-hidden, unassuming treasure of a bar. With its high ceilings, columns, sofas, potted plants and conservatory windows it looks like it could be on the seafront in Torquay, especially when there are some elderly ladies up for a weekend antiques fair. Instead, from inside the bar or the big terrace outside you get wonderful views southwards over the whole of the urban jungle from north London's highest point. It's most popular in summer, but in winter it's also an atmospheric, tranquil place to spend an afternoon. To eat there's fairly standard pub-grub, with several pastas and salads, but the beer range is more enterprising, with the excellent products of the local Crouch Vale brewery such as Transmitter and Snowdrop (around £2.40 a pint) as well as Adnam's, Tetley's and a big choice of bottled and draft lagers.
Babies and children admitted (nappy-changing facilities). Disabled: toilet. Function room. Satellite TV. Tables outdoors (patio, terrace). Vegetarian dishes.

Also in the area...

Ruby in the Dust 256 Muswell Hill Broadway, N10 (020 8444 4041).

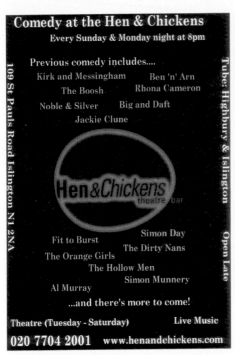

Palmers Green

Fox
*413 Green Lanes, N13 (020 8886 9674). Southgate
or Wood Green tube/Palmers Green rail/329, W2 bus.*
Open/food served 11am-11pm Mon-Sat; 11am-10.30pm
Sun. **Credit** MC, V.
A large and unreconstructed north London Edwardian
boozer, the Fox is famous for its big and little name Friday
comedy night 'Bound and Gagged'. Otherwise it's a fairly
standard local. Old men sit alone at tables nursing very cheap
big-brand beer – from Sunday to Thursday pints of
Kronenbourg or Guinness are £1.69, Fosters £1.59 – and the
youth patrol the green baize on the two pool tables at the back
or watch footie on the big screen. Food is hearty, basic and
good value: 'biggest breakfast' being three sausages, three
rashers of bacon, two eggs, tomato and baked beans for £3.99,
or jacket potato with two toppings £1.99.
*Comedy (8pm-1am Fri: £6, £2 membership/year).
Disabled: toilet. Disco (8.30pm Sat). Function room.
Games (pool tables). Jukebox. Music (karaoke 8.30pm
Tue,Thur). Quiz (9pm Sun; £1 to play). Satellite TVs
(big screen). Tables outdoors (garden). Vegetarian dishes.*

Woodman
*128 Bourne Hill, N13 (020 8882 0294). Southgate
tube/W9 bus.* **Open** 11am-11pm Mon-Sat; noon-10.30pm
Sun. **Food served** noon-3pm, 6-9pm Mon-Sat; noon-
3pm Sun. **Credit** AmEx, MC, V.
A dinky old country pub on the edge of Grovelands Park, the
Woodman has clearly been around for years. The tiny and
cosy front bar is still popular with locals, while in the summer
the kids' playground and beer garden come into their own. A
modern extension at the back houses another bar, and a
conservatory extension to one side provides a no-smoking,
no-mobile setting for the likes of sweet and sour chicken with
rice (£6.25) or the house speciality 'a whale of a cod', a one-
pounder in beer batter with fries and peas (£8.95). Strangely
enough, the menu also suggests diners should 'step back in
time' with a set meal of prawn cocktail, steak and chips, and
black forest gateaux (£14.95).
*Babies and children admitted (high chairs, climbing frame
in garden). Games (fruit machine). Music (guitarist,
occasional Sun). Quiz (occasional Sun). Restaurant.
Tables outdoors (gardens, patio). Vegetarian dishes.*

St John's Wood

Clifton
*96 Clifton Hill, NW8 (020 7372 3427). Maida Vale or
St John's Wood tube.* **Open** 11am-11pm Mon-Sat; noon-
10.30pm Sun. **Food served** noon-3.30pm, 6.30-10pm
Mon-Sat; noon-10pm Sun. **Credit** AmEx, MC, V.
Blending in perfectly with the surrounding houses and
marked out only by a discreet temporary sign, the Clifton
can be difficult to spot (except in the summer when outside
tables are packed to overflowing). Contrast this with an
interior that's a lovingly maintained riot of carved wood; the
bar resembles a mini Gothic cathedral, an impression
enhanced by the intricate altar rails that divide drinking
areas. Ornate open fireplaces, low ceilings and thickly
curtained quiet corners make for a snug atmosphere, ideal
for seducing the vicar's daughter (or son for that matter). The
Prince of Wales (later Edward VII) apparently used to
rendezvous here with mistress Lily Langtry. There's a
modern conservatory at the rear that operates as a
restaurant, and tables in the garden.

*Babies and children admitted (conservatory). Games (fruit
machine). Satellite TV. Tables outdoors (garden, patio).
Vegetarian dishes.*

Crocker's Folly
*24 Aberdeen Place, NW8 (020 7286 6608). Edgware
Road or Warwick Avenue tube.* **Open** 11am-11pm Mon-
Sat; noon-10.30pm Sun. **Food served** noon-3pm, 6-9pm
Mon-Fri; noon-3pm, 6-8pm Sat; noon-8pm Sun.
Credit AmEx, MC, V.
In 1898, Frank Crocker sank his fortune into building this
hotel hoping to catch the railway trade. Unfortunately, the
railway went to Marylebone instead and the poor man
threw himself out of an upstairs window in despair. His
folly's our gain, however, since his palatial building and its
interior are a glorious tribute to Victorian plastic arts. A
central room is dominated on one side by a battleship of a
mahogany bar and on the other by a monumental marble
fireplace. Two rooms flanking, though less outré, are
equally vast; one is reserved for dining (Sunday lunches are
reputedly excellent), the other is given over to sport (table
football, chess, watching Sky). Given the proximity to
Lords, expect crowds in the cricket season, kept happy no
doubt supping from a decent variety of real ales (Adnam's,
Greene King and Hancock's).
*Babies and children admitted (restaurant only). Disabled:
toilet. Games (darts, fruit machines, table football). Music
(live band 9pm Sat, jazz 8pm Sun). Quiz (9pm Thur).
Restaurant. Satellite TV (big screen). Tables outdoors
(pavement). Vegetarian dishes.*

Duke of York
*2A St Anne's Terrace, NW8 (020 7722 1933). St John's
Wood tube.* **Open** 11am-11pm Mon-Sat; 11am-10.30pm
Sun. **Food served** noon-11pm Mon-Sat; noon-10.30pm
Sun. **Credit** MC, V.
With its brass lamps, mosaic tables and delicate screens, this
gastropub at the end of St John's Wood High Street is more
Sheikh of Araby than grand old duke. The bar area is small
but appealing with the atmosphere of a café rather than a pub.
The North African theme extends to the food (babaghanoug,
Moroccan meat stews etc), which is quite reasonably priced.
Drinks are a limited list of wines – the token Moroccan bottle
is to be avoided – standard nitrokegs such as Stella, Caffrey's
or Guinness, and a small selection of cocktails. Exotic,
charming and eccentric even, it's certainly worth a look if
you're in the area.
*Babies and children admitted (daytimes). Music (live
jazz Tue, Thur). Restaurant. Tables outdoors (pavement).
Vegetarian dishes.*

Lord's Tavern
*Grace Gates, St John's Wood Road, NW8 (020 7266
5980). St John's Wood tube.* **Open/food served** 11am-
11pm Mon-Fri; 10am-11pm Sat; 10am-10.30pm Sun.
Credit AmEx, MC, V.
An ugly concrete box next to the cricket ground that's
surprisingly pleasant and salubrious once inside. It's roomy
and light, with a vaulted brick ceiling, large pine tables and
a cosier corner harbouring a clutch of Chesterfield-type sofas.
Obviously the theme is cricket, with prints of famous players
and such, but restraint has been shown and the sport isn't
rammed down your throat. It is the HQ of the Barmy Army
during summer, but the rest of the year it's a fairly laid-back
pub catering largely to a pint-after-work crowd. A dining area
off to one side serves decent if unimaginative food.
*Babies and children admitted (until 7pm). Restaurant.
Satellite TV. Tables outdoors (terrace). Vegetarian dishes.*

Salt House

63 Abbey Road, NW8 (020 7328 6626). St John's Wood tube. **Open** noon-11pm Mon-Sat; noon-10.30pm Sun. **Food served** 12.30-3pm, 6.30-10.30pm Mon-Fri; noon-4pm, 7-10.30pm Sat, Sun. **Credit** AmEx, MC, V.

Just up from the famous zebra crossing, the Salt House is gastropub swank at its finest. The exterior is a clean white; the airy interior all pastel mauves and scrubbed floorboards. A comfortable naturally lit bar filled with blue sofas occupies the front with a restaurant area to the rear. What with the big windows, the piped jazz and the sunny sound of money being spent on high quality, GM-free product, the vibe is faintly and pleasantly Californian. Staff are young and smile a lot. Blackboards are chalked up with an extensive wine list (ranging up to around £40 a bottle) but it would be a shame to come here just for a drink and not sample the superb food. *Babies and children admitted (children's room; high chairs). Function room. Restaurant. Tables outdoors (pavement). Vegetarian dishes.*

Star

38 St John's Wood Terrace, NW8 (020 7722 1051). St John's Wood tube. **Open** 11am-11pm Mon-Sat; noon-10.30pm Sun. **No credit cards.**

An old-fashioned snug stashed away among the classy stucco and Porsches, the Star seems to cater largely to the painters and plasterers who are kept in constant employment round these parts revamping the local mansions. Expect pints of Bass and conversations centred on the Premier League (fixtures shown on a big-screen TV). On our visit we were blessed with sun shining through dusty stained-glass and a glowing open fire. Diamond.
Games (fruit machine). Tables outdoors (garden). TV.

Also in the area...

All Bar One 60 St John's Wood High Street, NW8 (020 7483 9931).
Café Med 21 Loudoun Road, NW8 (020 7625 1222).
Café Rouge 120 High Street, NW8 (020 7722 8366).

Stoke Newington

Bar Lorca

175 Stoke Newington High Street, N16 (020 7275 8659/ www.barlorca.com). Bus 73. **Open** noon-1am Mon-Thur; noon-2am Fri, Sat; noon-midnight Sun. **Food served** noon-11pm Mon-Thur; noon-midnight Fri, Sat; noon-10pm Sun. **Admission** £4 after 10pm Fri, Sat. **Happy hour** 6-9pm Mon-Fri. **Credit** AmEx, MC, V.

Salt House

Decorated in the red and gold of the Spanish flag, this Iberian-themed bar is large enough to accommodate three areas, each with a distinctive atmosphere. At one end a youthful crowd eyes each other up in the ultra-violet glow, occasionally strutting to loud, sometimes live, music. At the other couples quietly dine on tapas among the palms and pretty Mediterranean pottery. Separating these two worlds is a drinking area dominated by a high mosaic bar, where a lively, often Spanish, crowd slugs bottles of Estrela or sips Mojitos. Weekend nights are definitely for partying and possibly not for the faint-hearted, but during the day the Continental tradition of welcoming children holds, with clowns distracting the bambinos while dad watches Spanish league footie on the box.
Babies and children admitted (until 8pm; clowns, high chairs, toys). Dance classes (7-9pm Mon, Fri; £5). Disabled: toilet. Games (pinball machine). Music (Latin bands 9.30pm Tue, Wed, Sun; DJs 9pm Mon, Thur-Sat). Restaurant. Satellite TV. Specialities: Mexican & Spanish beers. Vegetarian dishes.

Coach & Horses
178 Stoke Newington High Street, N16 (020 7254 6697). Stoke Newington rail/67, 73, 106 bus. **Open** 11am-11pm Mon-Sat; noon-10.30pm Sun. **Food served** noon-10pm Tue-Sat; 1-9pm Sun. **No credit cards.**
Embracing the success of its venture into South-east Asian cuisine, the management of this one-time Irish boozer has taken the next logical step: the Coach & Horses' decor has been Thai-fied. Buddhas, shadow puppets and Eastern prints adorn walls recently painted tan, while large ceiling fans rotate indolently (and slightly superfluously) above. Most of the clientele, including a smattering of Thais, are here for the food and no wonder, the traditional curries and pad thai are fresh and aromatic and there are a few unusual Eastern salads on the menu. The effect is slightly let down by the beers (Guinness and Old Speckled Hen) but they are served with quiet oriental-style courtesy by a trio of female bar staff.
Babies and children admitted (until 7pm). Games (fruit machines). Internet access (£1/10 min). Quiz (8pm Mon, £1 to play). Satellite TV. Vegetarian dishes.

Fox Reformed
176 Stoke Newington Church Street, N16 (020 7254 5975/www.fox-reformed.co.uk). Bus 73. **Open/food served** 5-11pm Mon-Fri; noon-11pm Sat, Sun, bank holidays. **Credit** AmEx, MC, V.
The Fox Reformed may be decorated in hunting pink, but Stoke Newington's only wine bar is much more relaxed than the smart exterior initially suggests. Local artists hold exhibitions in the smallish front drinking area (very much a hit-and-miss affair), but the landlord manning the bar looks so distinguished he could have stepped straight out of an Old Master. The small gap between the tables is admirably convenient for players in the Monday night backgammon drive; it also means eavesdropping is a doddle for all those aspiring N16 writers. Drinks include a choice of nearly 30 wines (six sold by the glass), complemented by a small selection of mainly Belgian beers, as well as Stella on tap.
Babies and children admitted (high chairs). Games (board games). Tables outdoors (heated garden). Theme nights (backgammon Mon; book club monthly, Tue; investment club first Sun monthly; wine tasting club every other Thur; all £30 per year). Vegetarian dishes.

Oak Bar
79 Green Lanes, N16 (020 7354 2791/www.oakbar.co.uk). Manor House tube/73, 141 bus. **Open** 5pm-midnight Mon-Thur; 5pm-2am Fri, Sat; 1pm-midnight Sun. **Food**

served 1-7pm Sun. **Happy hour** 5-7pm Mon-Thur. **Admission** £3-£5 (depending on club night) Fri, Sat. **No credit cards.**
Friday is still women-only night at the Oak Bar and while during the rest of the week it becomes more a mixed gay local, most of the atmosphere is generated by groups of twentysomething disco dykes. Painted purple and lit only by green lamps and reflections from a mirror ball, the interior is more club than pub, but luckily this doesn't extend to the bar prices. It's also mainly hard seating so those taking full advantage of regular tequila promotions have to fight for possession of one of the two soft armchairs. Sunday night karaoke shows exhibit a remarkably (and consistently) high standard.
Disabled: toilet. Games (pinball machine, pool table). Karaoke (Sun). Music (DJs Fri, Sat; live music Tue). Satellite TV (big screen). Vegetarian dishes.

Rose & Crown
199 Stoke Newington Church Street, N16 (020 7254 7497). Bus 73. **Open** 11.30am-11pm Mon-Sat; noon-10.30pm Sun. **Food served** noon-2.30pm Mon-Fri; noon-4pm Sun. **No credit cards.**
Having long attracted born and bred Stokies, the charms of this well preserved suburban boozer have started to become apparent to recently arrived Islington migrants, arguably making the Rose & Crown the most popular pub on Church Street. With the original wood panelling and art deco windows still intact, a real fire blazing in the grate and a choice of Adnam's, Pedigree or Ruddles at the bar, it's no wonder it packs in the punters. The seats in the large bay window are the most popular, possibly because they afford a trackside view on a particularly accident prone mini-roundabout, while more conventional entertainment includes Sky sports on the box and a very popular fortnightly quiz.
Games (fruit machine). No piped music or jukebox. Quiz (8.30pm first Tue monthly; £1 to play). Satellite TV. Tables outdoors (pavement). Vegetarian dishes.

Shakespeare
57 Allen Road, N16 (020 7254 4190). Bus 73. **Open** noon-2pm Mon, Wed-Fri; 5-11.30pm Mon-Fri; noon-11.30pm Sat; noon-10.30pm Sun. **No credit cards.**
The Shakespeare, once regarded as N16's best pub, suffered a slump in form but now seems set back on its old winning ways. Most importantly, the beer has improved of late, which is a good thing as punters here take their drink seriously (and seriously like a drink). Four real ales are always on tap. In addition, there's a sizeable wine and malt whiskey list. A large wooden bar dominates the place and a lot of the seating is made from old church pews. Large pre-war, French drinks posters provide a welcome splash of colour. Best of all is the jukebox that ranges from Mingus to Madchester, and contains no chart fodder – just the way the roll-up smoking clientele likes it.
Babies and children admitted. Jukebox. Quiz (8.45pm Mon; £1 to play). Satellite TV. Tables outdoors (garden).

Vortex
139 Stoke Newington Church Street, N16 (020 7254 6516/www.palay.ndirect.co.uk/vortex.jazz). Stoke Newington rail/73 bus. **Open** 10am-midnight daily. **Admission** £2-£10 after 9pm. **Food served** 11am-10pm daily. **Credit** MC, V.
With the recent announcement that the Vortex is not moving to Hackney but staying on Church Street, jazz fans throughout the capital will be scrabbling to retrieve their discarded No.73 timetables. The modest dimensions of this first floor venue along with the attentiveness of the audience make this a great place to catch quality small groups, while

being so close to the stage ensures big bands almost literally blow you away. The hard furnishings can be tough on the buttocks during particularly long drum solos, but candles and all-year-round fairy lights keep the atmosphere pleasantly intimate. The bar stocks the usual selection of bottled beers, so most punters choose from the more imaginative wine list. During the day the Vortex is more of a café and as the mainly veggie menu is popular with Stokie parents, you're likely to encounter more papooses than on an Indian reservation. *Cabaret (8.30pm first Mon of month; £6/£5). Karaoke (first Sun of month). Music (jazz/indie rock 8.30pm Mon-Sat; DJs 8pm Sun). Vegetarian dishes.*

Also in the area...
Rochester Castle (JD Wetherspoon) 145 High Street, N16 (020 7249 6016).

Swiss Cottage

Babe Ruth's
02 Centre, 255 Finchley Road, NW3 (020 7433 3388/www.baberuths.com). Finchley Road tube. **Open/ food served** 5-11pm Mon-Fri; noon-11pm Sat; noon-10.30pm Sun. **Credit** AmEx, MC, V.
Located in a monolithic US-style shopping mall, complete with supermarket, cinema multiplex and giant fish tanks, Babe Ruth's is just one of numerous theme-restaurants within. It's vast and brightly coloured, filled with garish murals, and has countless TV sets hanging from the ceiling screening major sporting events. There's a smallish bar off to one side where you can take a stool and order draught Miller, bottled lagers, or select from a fairly comprehensive list of cocktails which, at £4.50 each, are decent enough for the price. Food is oriental and American favourites – bland but served in generous proportions. Perfect for a lads' night out after catching the latest with Nicolas Cage. *Babies and children admitted (children's menu, high chairs, nappy-changing facilities). Cinema deal (from 5pm Mon; ticket to Warner Village cinema on selected films, main course meal and drink; £9.99). Disabled: toilet. Function room. Games (sports video games, basketball court in restaurant). No-smoking area. Restaurant. Satellite TV (big screen). Vegetarian dishes.*

Zuccato
02 Centre, 255 Finchley Road, NW3 (020 7431 1799). Finchley Road tube. **Open/food served** 10.30am-midnight Mon-Sat; 10am-11pm Sun. **Credit** AmEx, DC, MC, V.
The lack of decent watering holes around the Swiss Cottage area drove us to try this café/bar/restaurant. Why food and drink in this part of North London can only be sold on the back of a theme (see **Babe Ruth's**, above) is a mystery, but at least unlike other outlets nearby, this place was heaving. Maybe the boys and girls know enough to associate Italy (the theme) with fine food and drink. Maybe it's just that cheap and cheerful pasta and pizza is a safe bet. Or that the coffee's good (which it is). Besides the food, a small bar offers a standard selection of cocktails, augmented by a few Italian beers. It's about as close to the Piazza Navonna as Iceland frozen lasagne but the multinational youth present certainly seemed to like it. *Babies and children admitted (restaurant; high chairs). Disabled: toilet. No-smoking area. Restaurant. Vegetarian dishes.*

Also in the area...
Café Flo 205 Haverstock Hill, NW3 (020 7435 6744).

Tufnell Park & Archway

Dartmouth Arms
35 York Rise, NW5 (020 7485 3267). Tufnell Park tube. **Open** 11am-11pm Mon-Fri; 10am-11pm Sat; 10am-10.30pm Sun. **Food served** 11am-10pm Mon-Fri; 10am-10pm Sat; 10am-10pm Sun. **Credit** MC, V.
With its real wood fire, mustard yellow ceiling, pale green walls and semi-panelled pine pillars, the Dartmouth Arms already feels like a local institution. In fact it's a foodie pub that pays considerable attention to detail. The cappuccinos come in Illy cups, the ketchup is Heinz and the sauce HP, accompaniments to some fairly pricey but satisfying 'Brunch around the world' options on Sunday mornings. We tried Paris Eggy Bread (£3.50), two slices with a tomato, and London Full English breakfast (£6.95) – both were fine. The full money-back guarantee on all the food and real ales didn't seem in the least bit necessary. Good value Sunday lunches (£7.95) are also served in the light, wood-panelled back room. A bookshop shelf for browsing or buying completes the picture of a thoroughly civilised destination pub. *Babies and children admitted (until 8pm, highchairs). Bookshop. Function room. Games (board games). Quiz (8pm every other Tue; £1 to play). Satellite TV. Vegetarian dishes.*

Grand Banks
156-158 Fortess Road, NW5 (020 7419 9499). Tufnell Park tube. **Open** 5-11pm Mon-Thur; 5pm-midnight Fri, Sat; noon-10.30pm Sun. **Food served** 6-10pm Mon-Fri; noon-10pm Sat, Sun. **Credit** MC, V.
One of the hipper bars in Tufnell Park, the Grand Banks is wedged between Brecknock and Fortess roads on the busy junction right opposite the tube. It may once have been a bank, but the telling counters have given way to some seriously comfy leatherette office sofas and chairs, photo art on the walls, a happening music policy and offbeat designer touches like the sylvan scene surrounding the tiny hearth in the quieter back room. A full variety of cocktails are all £4.95, while food includes pizzas for £5.95 or peri peri chicken wings for £4.75. All in all a good-value and very laid-back venue for Tufnell Park's bright young things (though over-21s only). *Babies and children admitted (high chairs). Exhibitions (art, photography). Music (live jazz Mon, Tue; DJs 8pm Wed-Sat). Restaurant. Specialities: cocktails, Freedom organic lager. Vegetarian dishes.*

Lord Palmerston
33 Dartmouth Park Hill, NW5 (020 7485 1578). Tufnell Park tube. **Open** noon-11pm Mon-Sat; noon-10.30pm Sun. **Food served** 12.30-3pm, 7.30-10pm Mon; 12.30-3pm, 7-10pm Tue-Sat; 1-4pm, 7-9pm Sun. **Credit** MC, V.
For some time now the Lord P has been a favourite rendezvous for Tufnell Park's chattering classes, young and old. Its bare boards, duck-egg blue and brown paint job and wobbly wooden chairs aren't cosy or comfortable, but then most people are here for the fine fresh food and wine. A gastropub that takes pared-back simplicity to new heights, it divides up into three areas: the old front bar, with two large lamps suspended above and wine racks behind; a square room on the right; and beyond it the brightly sun- or atmospherically candlelit conservatory. Dishes such as roast duck breast with honey and ginger (£10.95), or moules mariniere and chips (£9.95) can be enjoyed anywhere here with an excellent selection of wines by the glass or bottle.

Babies and children admitted. Function room. No piped music or jukebox. Tables outdoors (garden, pavement). Vegetarian dishes.

The Saint
St George's Theatre, 49 Tufnell Park Road, N7 (020 7609 9046). Tufnell Park tube. **Open** 6-11pm Mon-Fri; 11am-11pm Sat; 11am-10.30pm Sun. **Food served** 6-10pm Mon-Fri; 11am-11pm Sat; 11am-10.30pm Sun. **Credit** MC, V.

An oasis on the lower residential reaches of Tufnell Park Road, the Saint is a jazzy bar-restaurant front of house at St George's Theatre. The place is an unusual Victorian imitation of a fifth-century Byzantine church, and although the foyer looks unimpressive from the outside, inside it's a different story. Centrally heated pews line the red walls beneath an ochre ceiling sloping down to little windows. Uneven floorboards, wheelback chairs and a bar that looks as if it's been adapted from an organ-screen complete the impression of an attractive north London apotheosis of village hall chic. It's a warm and unhurried place, occasionally livened up by recitals and theatre events and their audiences young and old, but otherwise already popular with quietly glamorous locals tucking into the likes of deep-fried goat's cheese and couscous (£7.20), sausages and mash (£6.95) or chicken stuffed with mushrooms and spinach (£8.45).

Babies and children admitted. Bar available for hire. Disabled: toilet. Vegetarian dishes.

St John's
91 Junction Road, N19 (020 7272 1587). Archway or Tufnell Park tube. **Open/food served** 11am-11pm Mon-Sat; noon-10.30pm Sun. **Credit** MC, V.

Formerly a large box of an Irish boozer on the now up-and-coming Junction Road, St John's has been converted into an exceptionally successful gastropub. Comfortable armchairs and wooden tables wrap around the large front bar, while the big dining room out back with its open fire and artwork on the walls gives a convincing impression of a bustling Parisian

Lord Palmerston

North

The Saint. *See page 231.*

bistro. The menu – chalked up in an almost indecipherable scrawl on blackboards – includes starters such as parmesan, spinach, roast tomato and olive tart (£5) and accomplished mains: roast monkfish, saffron, pea and mussel risotto (£13) or roast sirloin of beef (£11), for example. Booking has become essential for the dining room towards the end of the week, while front of house the locals mix congenially enough with visitors from further afield.
Babies and children admitted. Games (board games).

West Hampstead

Cane
283-285 West End Lane, NW6 (020 7794 7817). West Hampstead tube/rail. **Open** noon-11.30pm Mon-Sat; noon-10.30pm Sun. **Food served** noon-7pm daily. **Happy hour** 5.30-8pm Mon, Tue, Thur, Fri; 5.30-11.30pm Wed. **Credit** MC, V.
On a prominent corner site in West End Lane formerly occupied by Scruffy Murphy's comes Cane, bringing a bit of funkin' style to West Hampstead. Out go the bicycles hanging on the ceiling and all that Oirish palaver, and instead you get stone flooring, modishly cool blue/sandy-coloured textured walls, cubish blond wood tables and leather pouffes. DJs take on the crowds on Thursday nights and Sunday afternoons, and other times there's a thumping jukebox. Beers are largely of the bottled kind (just Kirin and Stella on tap), and there's a menu of inexpensive classic cocktails (£4 for a Sea Breeze or Singapore Sling), or if you're feeling more adventurous, flavoured sakes (Lemon Tsuzi £3.50). All in all, a welcome hard-drinking and shaking arrival in an otherwise fairly buttoned-up strip.

Disabled: toilet. Function room. Games (arcade game). Jukebox. Music (DJs Thur, Sun). Specialities: cocktails. Tables outdoors (terrace). Vegetarian dishes.

No 77 Wine Bar
77 Mill Lane, NW6 (020 7435 7787). West Hampstead tube/rail/C11, 28, 139 bus. **Open** noon-11pm Mon, Tue; noon-midnight Wed-Fri; 1pm-midnight Sat; 1pm-10.30pm Sun. **Food served** noon-2.30pm, 7-10.30pm Mon, Tue; noon-2.30pm, 7-11.30pm Wed-Fri; 1-3.30pm, 7-10pm Sat, Sun. **Credit** MC, V.
This unreconstructed '80s wine bar has been keeping its regulars well fed and watered since 1982. Typical of the genre, a small warren of rooms spreads back from the main candle-lit dining area, festooned with rugby team photos, wine memorabilia and potted plants. Thoroughly unpretentious, it's a provincial formula that clearly still goes down well in West Hampstead, a contented hum filling the place on the Saturday night we visited. Although the food is nothing out of the ordinary (the former 'posh' menu has been dropped in favour of simpler fare like pasta, '77 burgers', steaks), it's reasonably priced and the service is charming. No 77 may not be a prime destination, but it's a place definitely worth knowing about.
Babies and children admitted. Function room. Music (jazz 1.30pm Sun). Restaurant. Satellite TV. Specialities: guest wines monthly. Tables outdoors (pavement). Vegetarian dishes.

Also in the area...
Café Rouge 203 West End Lane, NW6 (020 7372 8177).
Rat & Parrot 100 West End Lane, NW6 (020 7624 7611).

Advertisers' index

Please refer to relevant sections for addresses/telephone numbers

Covers

Perrier	**IFC**
Charlie Wright International	**IBC**
Perrier	**OBC**

Early

Absolut Vodka	**4**
Elbow Room	**10**
Sebor Absinth	**8**

Central

Bank	**58**
Bar Atlantis	**58**
Barcode	**100**
Bar Logic	**46**
Bar Monaco	**46**
Collection	**100**
Cubana	**92**
Dover Street	**92**
Farringdon Bars	**46**
Flutes	**58**
Gordon's	**82**
Henry J Bean's	**100**
JD Wetherspoon	**34**
Jamies Bar	**82**
Late Night London	**21**
Lunasa	**15**
Nadine's	**100**
Porterhouse Brewing Company	**82**
Trader Vic's	**70**

City

Café Kick	**126**
City Limits	**126**
Fluid	**126**
Sitar	**114**

West

Emporium	**142**
Garlic & Shots	**142**
Q Bar	**142**

South

Bah Humbug	**166**
Bar du Musee	**180**
Boom	**180**
Brixtonian Havana Club	**154**
Castilla	**154**
Ditto	**154**
Dog House	**166**
Entertaining London	**180**
Sequel	**180**
Swan	**166**

North

Bar Gansa	**206**
Bar M	**226**
Bar Solo	**206**
Café Corfu	**206**
Crown & Goose	**218**
Hen & Chickens	**226**
Triangle	**218**

Where to go for...

Critics' choice
index

Index

COCKTAILS

Index

Index

Index

index

Index

Index

A-Z index

Index

Index

Index

Index

Index

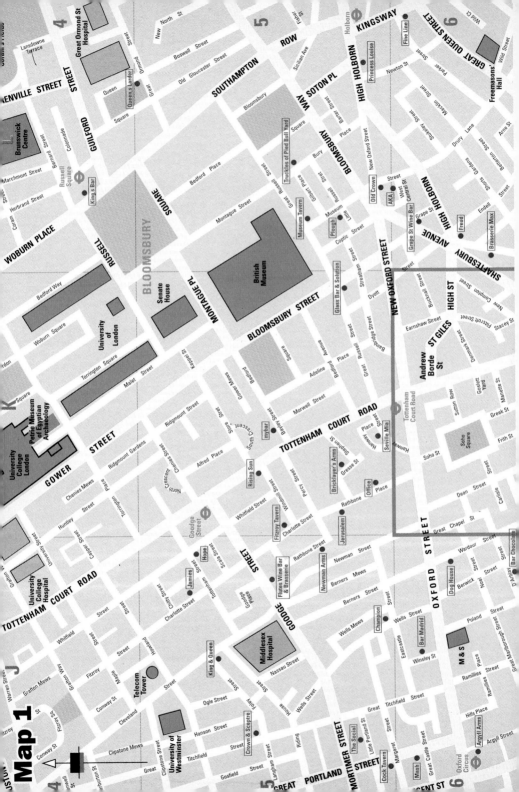

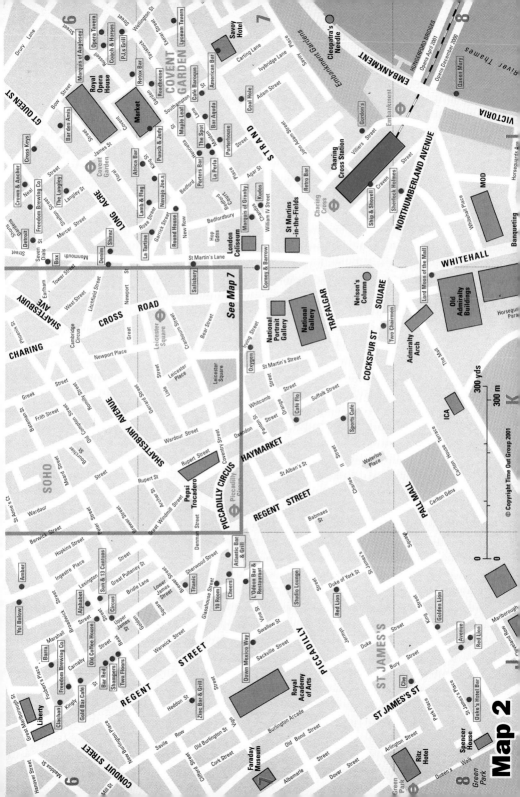

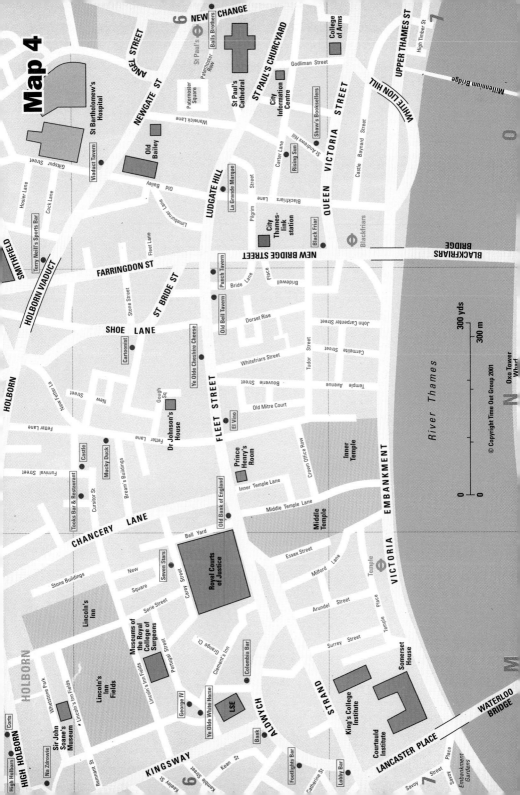

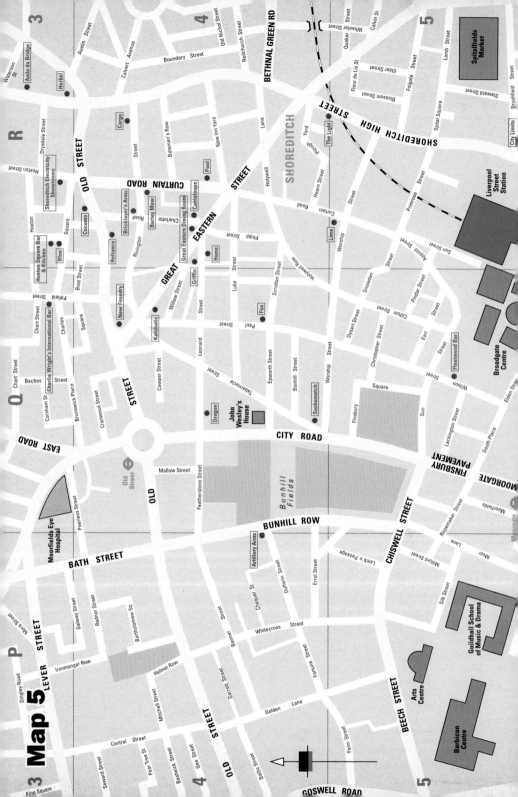

Map 7

Tottenham Court Road

NEW OXFORD STREET

Point 101

OXFORD STREET K

ANDREW BORDE ST

First Out

ST GILES

Vespa Lounge

HIGH STREET

Pop

Taylors Of Soho

The Edge

Soho Street

Sutton Row

Angel

Couch

Opium

Great Chapel Street

Dean Street

Soho Square

Goslett Yard

CHARING

Denmark Street

Filcroft Street

New Compton Street

Toucan

Carlisle Street

Greek Street

Manette Street

CROSS

Wardour Street

6

St Anne's Court

SOHO

Café Lazeez

Six Degrees

Frith Street

Pillars of Hercules

Jazz After Dark

ROAD

Phoenix Artist Club

Stacey Street

SHAFTESBURY AVENUE

Soho Spice

Candy Bar

Mondo

Phoenix Street

Earlham

Dog & Duck

Sak

Lab

Salsa!

Crown & Two Chairmen

Bateman Street

Soho Soho

Wardour Street

Pitcher & Piano

Garlic & Shots

Frith Street

Signor Zilli

Café Boheme

Greek Street

Spice of Life

Tower Stre

Meard Street

Blues Bistro & Bar

Street

Bar Sol Ona

Coach & Horses

West Street

Intrepid Fox

Manto

Bar Soho

Romilly St

Cambridge Circus

Litchfield Street

Berwick Street

Compton

Kettner's

Newport Pl

79 CXR

Peter Street

Freedom

Admiral Duncan

Old

Two Thirty Club

French House

Ku Bar

O Bar

Comptons of Soho

De Hems

Great

Saint

Village Soho

Newport St

Brewer Street

Yard

Rupert Street

SHAFTESBURY

Dive Bar

AVENUE

Gerrard Street

West Central

Great

CHARING

Archer St

Bar Code

Lisle Street

Leicester Square

LONG ACRE

Great Windmill Street

Rupert St

Leicester Place

CROSS

Blue Posts

Wardour Street

Imperial

Cranbourn Street

Cork & Bottle

ROAD

7

Denman St

Pepsi Trocadero

Rupert Street

Sound

Bear Street

OnAnon

Leicester Square

PICCADILLY CIRCUS

Coventry St

Oxendon

Dôme

Piccadilly Circus

0   150 yds

0   150 m

REGENT ST

HAYMARKET

Street

© Copyright Time Out Group 2001

Oxygen

Irving Street

Time Out 2001/2002 Pubs & Bars Guide
Please let us know what you think

Your feedback is invaluable to us! Please take a few minutes to let us know what you think of London's pubs & bars and of this guide – you could win £100 worth of Time Out guides and merchandise. Just send in this card by 30 November 2001, and if yours is the first out of the hat in our prize draw, you'll get the goodies.

1. How often, on average, do you visit pubs & bars?
Four or more times per week ☐
Two to three times per week ☐
Once a week ☐
Once/twice a month ☐
Less than once/twice monthly ☐

2. Which of the following do you most often drink when visiting pubs & bars? (please tick only one box)
Wine ☐
Spirits ☐
Draught lager ☐
Bottled lager ☐
Canned lager ☐
Draught ale ☐
Bottled ale ☐
Canned ale ☐
Cocktails ☐
Alcopops ☐
Mineral water ☐
Soft drinks ☐

3. How many people use your copy of the Time Out _Pubs & Bars Guide_?
Just me ☐
One other ☐
Two others ☐
Three others ☐
Four others ☐
More than five others ☐

4. Have you ever bought/used Time Out magazine?
Yes ☐   No ☐

5. Have you ever bought any Time Out City Guides?
Yes ☐   No ☐

If yes, which ones?
....
....
....

6. Have you ever bought/used other Time Out publications?
Yes ☐   No ☐
If yes, which ones?
....
....

7. Have you ever used timeout.com?
Yes ☐   No ☐

8. Are you?
Single ☐
Living with a partner ☐

9. Are you?
Employed full-time ☐
Employed part-time ☐
Self-employed ☐
Unemployed ☐
Student ☐
Home-maker ☐

(BLOCK CAPITALS PLEASE)
10. Title (Mr, Mrs, Ms etc).......................
First name...
Surname..
Address..
....
Postcode...
Email address..
Daytime telephone..................................

11. Year of birth.......................................

12. Sex...

13. At the moment do you earn?
Under £10,000 ☐
Over £10,000 and up to £14,999 ☐
Over £15,000 up to £19,999 ☐
Over £20,000 up to £24,999 ☐
Over £25,000 up to £39,999 ☐
Over £40,000 up to £49,999 ☐
Over £50,000 up to £59,999 ☐
Over £60,000 ☐

14. Where did you first hear of/see this guide?
Advertising in _Time Out_ magazine ☐
Other press advertising ☐
Advertising on London Underground ☐
Bookshop/newsagent ☐
timeout.com ☐
Other (write in) ☐
....

15. Your recommendations
I wish to recommend the following pub/bar for future inclusion ☐
Recommend the following pub/bar for non-inclusion ☐

Name of pub/bar
....
Address of pub/bar
....
....
....
Phone no. of pub/bar
....

Comments
....
....
....
....
....
....

Please tick here if you do not wish to receive information about other Time Out products. ☐

Please tick here if you do not wish to receive information from third parties. ☐

Now fold your completed report and questionnaire in half, tape together (no staples please) and return to us FREEPOST. Thanks very much.

**Time Out Magazine
Freepost 20 (WC3187)
LONDON
W1E 0DQ**

Fold here and tape together